I0105344

ASIAN DEVELOPMENT
OUTLOOK 2017

TRANSCENDING THE MIDDLE-INCOME CHALLENGE

50 YEARS

ADB

ASIAN DEVELOPMENT BANK

Creative Commons Attribution 3.0 IGO license (CC BY 3.0 IGO)

© 2017 Asian Development Bank
6 ADB Avenue, Mandaluyong City, 1550 Metro Manila, Philippines
Tel +63 2 632 4444; Fax +63 2 636 2444
www.adb.org

Some rights reserved. Published in 2017.
Printed in the Philippines.

ISBN 978-92-9257-787-2 (Print), 978-92-9257-788-9 (e-ISBN)
ISSN 0117-0481
Publication Stock No. FLS178632-3
DOI: http://dx.doi.org/10.22617/FLS178632-3

Cataloging-In-Publication Data

Asian Development Bank.
        Asian development outlook 2017. Transcending the middle-income challenge.
Mandaluyong City, Philippines: Asian Development Bank, 2017.

1. Economics.   2. Finance.   3. Asia.   I. Asian Development Bank.

The views expressed in this publication are those of the authors and do not necessarily reflect the views and policies of the Asian Development Bank (ADB) or its Board of Governors or the governments they represent.

ADB does not guarantee the accuracy of the data included in this publication and accepts no responsibility for any consequence of their use. The mention of specific companies or products of manufacturers does not imply that they are endorsed or recommended by ADB in preference to others of a similar nature that are not mentioned.

By making any designation of or reference to a particular territory or geographic area, or by using the term "country" in this document, ADB does not intend to make any judgments as to the legal or other status of any territory or area.

This work is available under the Creative Commons Attribution 3.0 IGO license (CC BY 3.0 IGO) https://creativecommons.org/licenses/by/3.0/igo/. By using the content of this publication, you agree to be bound by the terms of this license.

This CC license does not apply to non-ADB copyright materials in this publication. If the material is attributed to another source, please contact the copyright owner or publisher of that source for permission to reproduce it. ADB cannot be held liable for any claims that arise as a result of your use of the material.

Attribution—In acknowledging ADB as the source, please be sure to include all of the following information:
    Author. Year of publication. Title of the material. © Asian Development Bank [and/or Publisher].
URL. Available under a CC BY 3.0 IGO license.

Translations—Any translations you create should carry the following disclaimer:
    Originally published by the Asian Development Bank in English under the title [title] © [Year of publication] Asian Development Bank. All rights reserved. The quality of this translation and its coherence with the original text is the sole responsibility of the [translator]. The English original of this work is the only official version.

Adaptations—Any adaptations you create should carry the following disclaimer:
    This is an adaptation of an original Work © Asian Development Bank [Year]. The views expressed here are those of the authors and do not necessarily reflect the views and policies of ADB or its Board of Governors or the governments they represent. ADB does not endorse this work or guarantee the accuracy of the data included in this publication and accepts no responsibility for any consequence of their use.

Please contact publications@adb.org if you have questions or comments with respect to content, or if you wish to obtain copyright permission for your intended use that does not fall within these terms, or for permission to use the ADB logo.

Notes:
In this publication, "$" refers to US dollars.
Corrigenda to ADB publications may be found at: http://www.adb.org/publications/corrigenda
ADB recognizes "China" by the name People's Republic of China.

Contents

Foreword

Developing Asia is set to grow steadily, and it is well positioned to handle any risks that might stem from policy uncertainty abroad. *Asian Development Outlook 2017* forecasts gross domestic product in the region expanding by 5.7% in 2017 and 2018, near the 5.8% pace in 2016. Higher external demand, rebounding global commodity prices, and domestic reform support widespread acceleration, with growth picking up in two-thirds of the region's 45 economies. Developing Asia will continue to be the largest regional contributor to global growth, even with growth moderation in the People's Republic of China (PRC), its largest economy.

Consumption expenditure last year drove growth at 6.7% in the PRC, where the authorities are rebalancing the economy to rely more on domestic demand than exports. This is expected to temper growth further to 6.5% in 2017 and 6.2% in 2018, with the government prioritizing financial and fiscal stability. While the forecast is for slower growth in East Asia, all other subregions will see growth accelerate in the near term.

In South Asia, India moderated to 7.1% growth in 2016 as fixed investment stalled and the demonetization of large banknotes temporarily stymied cash-reliant commerce. As reform gains momentum, it is spurring investor confidence, and the economy is expected to rebound to higher growth at 7.4% in 2017 and 7.6% in 2018.

An expected recovery in global fuel and food prices will benefit commodity producers in Southeast Asia, Central Asia, and the Pacific. Yet rises for commodities will be too modest to endanger price stability. While regional inflation is projected to accelerate to 3.0% in 2017 and 3.2% in 2018, these rates remain well below the region's 10-year average of 3.9%.

Prospects for developing Asia are supported by improving fortunes for the major industrial economies in the United States, the euro area, and Japan. Yet uncertain policy direction in these economies, including the pace of interest rate normalization in the US, poses risks to the region's outlook. While short-term risks are manageable, policy makers need to monitor developments closely and intervene decisively if warranted.

When the Asian Development Bank opened its doors in 1966, most of the region's citizens lived in low-income economies. Since then, cumulative national development efforts have transformed the region. Today, with most economies having successfully climbed the income ladder—including the most populous economies in the PRC, India, and Indonesia—roughly 95% of the population lives in a middle-income economy. The development challenge now is to climb one more rung to high income.

History has shown this last rung to be a reach. The key is to move from a basic development model that drives growth by applying more factors of production—land, labor, and capital—toward a more sophisticated model that emphasizes catalyzing the productivity of all factors. The *Asian Development Outlook 2017* special chapter points to the nexus of innovation, human capital, and infrastructure to boost productivity. Innovation enables the development of a diverse and sophisticated product mix. Investment in human capital helps workers meet emerging workplace needs, and investment in infrastructure facilitates structural change.

We at the Asian Development Bank take pride in our role supporting the region's transformation over the past 50 years. But we cannot be complacent. Several challenges remain and new challenges have emerged in Asia. As governments adapt their development paradigms to sustain growth and eliminate the poverty that remains along the path to high income, we will adapt to help our clients meet their new challenges.

TAKEHIKO NAKAO
President
Asian Development Bank

Acknowledgments

Asian Development Outlook 2017 was prepared by staff of the Asian Development Bank (ADB) in the Central and West Asia Department, East Asia Department, Pacific Department, South Asia Department, Southeast Asia Department, and Economic Research and Regional Cooperation Department, as well as in ADB resident missions. Representatives of these departments constituted the Regional Economic Outlook Task Force, which met regularly to coordinate and develop consistent forecasts for the region.

The authors who contributed the sections are bylined in each chapter. The subregional coordinators were Dominik Peschel and Fatima Catacutan for Central Asia, Akiko Terada-Hagiwara for East Asia, Masato Nakane for South Asia, Jin Cyhn and Dulce Zara for Southeast Asia, and Rommel Rabanal and Maria Carina Tinio for the Pacific.

A team of economists in the Economic Research and Regional Cooperation Department, led by Joseph E. Zveglich, Jr., director of the Macroeconomics Research Division, coordinated the production of the publication, assisted by Edith Laviña. Technical and research support was provided by Shiela Camingue-Romance, Cindy Castillejos-Petalcorin, Gemma Esther Estrada, Marthe Hinojales, Nedelyn Magtibay-Ramos, Pilipinas Quising, Aleli Rosario, Dennis Sorino, Lea Sumulong, and Mai Lin Villaruel. Additional research support was provided by Emmanuel Alano, Zemma Ardaniel, Raymond Gaspar, and Andrea Loren Sy. The economic editorial advisors Robert Boumphrey, Joshua Greene, Srinivasa Madhur, Richard Niebuhr, and Reza Vaez-Zadeh made substantive contributions to the country chapters and regional outlook.

The theme chapter benefited from the insightful comments of discussants and other participants at the workshop held at the London School of Economics on 16–17 November 2016 as well as two workshops held at ADB headquarters on 22 November 2016 and 25 January 2017. The valuable support and guidance of Yasuyuki Sawada, Juzhong Zhuang, and Joseph E. Zveglich, Jr. throughout the production process is gratefully acknowledged. Margarita Debuque-Gonzales provided editorial advice on the theme chapter.

Peter Fredenburg advised on ADB style and English usage. Alvin Tubio handled typesetting and graphics generation, in which he was assisted by Heili Ann Bravo, Elenita Pura, and Azaleah Tiongson. Art direction for the cover design was by Anthony Victoria, with artwork from Design Muscle. Critical support for the printing and publishing of the report was provided by the Printing Services Unit of the ADB Office of Administrative Services and by the Publishing and Dissemination Unit of the ADB Department of External Relations. Fermirelyn Cruz and Rhia Bautista-Piamonte provided administrative and secretarial support. The Department of External Relations, led by Satinder Bindra, Omana Nair, and Erik Churchill, planned and coordinated the dissemination of *Asian Development Outlook 2017.*

Definitions

The economies discussed in *Asian Development Outlook 2017* are classified by major analytic or geographic group. For the purposes of this publication, the following apply:

- **Association of Southeast Asian Nations** comprises Brunei Darussalam, Cambodia, Indonesia, the Lao People's Democratic Republic, Malaysia, Myanmar, the Philippines, Singapore, Thailand, and Viet Nam.
- **Developing Asia** comprises the 45 members of the Asian Development Bank listed below.
- **Newly industrialized economies** comprises the Republic of Korea, Singapore, Taipei,China, and Hong Kong, China.
- **Central Asia** comprises Armenia, Azerbaijan, Georgia, Kazakhstan, the Kyrgyz Republic, Tajikistan, Turkmenistan, and Uzbekistan.
- **East Asia** comprises the People's Republic of China, the Republic of Korea, Mongolia, Taipei,China, and Hong Kong, China.
- **South Asia** comprises Afghanistan, Bangladesh, Bhutan, India, the Maldives, Nepal, Pakistan, and Sri Lanka.
- **Southeast Asia** comprises Brunei Darussalam, Cambodia, Indonesia, the Lao People's Democratic Republic, Malaysia, Myanmar, the Philippines, Singapore, Thailand, and Viet Nam.
- **The Pacific** comprises the Cook Islands, Fiji, Kiribati, the Marshall Islands, the Federated States of Micronesia, Nauru, Papua New Guinea, Palau, Samoa, Solomon Islands, Timor-Leste, Tonga, Tuvalu, and Vanuatu.

Unless otherwise specified, the symbol "$" and the word "dollar" refer to US dollars. *Asian Development Outlook 2017* is generally based on data available up to **3 March 2017**.

Abbreviations

ADB	Asian Development Bank
ADO	Asian Development Outlook
ASEAN	Association of Southeast Asian Nations
CPEC	economic corridor linking Pakistan with the PRC
EEU	Eurasian Economic Union
FDI	foreign direct investment
FSM	Federated States of Micronesia
FY	fiscal year
GDP	gross domestic product
ICT	information and communication technology
IMF	International Monetary Fund
JCS	job creator share
KORUS FTA	free trade agreement between the US and the ROK
Lao PDR	Lao People's Democratic Republic
LNG	liquefied natural gas
M1	money that includes cash and checking accounts
M2	broad money that adds highly liquid accounts to M1
M3	broad money that adds time accounts to M2
mbd	million barrels per day
MAS	Monetary Authority of Singapore
NIE	newly industrialized economy
NPL	nonperforming loan
NTA	National Transfer Accounts
OECD	Organisation for Economic Co-operation and Development
OPEC	Organization of the Petroleum Exporting Countries
PNG	Papua New Guinea
PPP	public–private partnership, purchasing power parity
PRC	People's Republic of China
PWT	Penn World Tables
R&D	research and development
RCA	revealed comparative advantage
RMI	Republic of the Marshall Islands
ROK	Republic of Korea
saar	seasonally adjusted annualized rate
SMEs	small and medium-sized enterprises
SOE	state-owned enterprise
TFP	total factor productivity
US	United States
VAT	value-added tax

ADO 2017—Highlights

Developing Asia continued to perform well even as recovery in the major industrial economies remained weak. The region is forecast to expand by 5.7% in 2017 and 2018, nearly the 5.8% growth achieved in 2016, as moderation in the People's Republic of China is balanced by a healthy pickup in most other economies in the region.

Inflation revived to 2.5% in 2016 on the back of strong consumer demand and rebounding global commodity prices. The pace will accelerate further to 3.0% in 2017 and 3.2% in 2018, still below the average rate for the past 10 years.

The region faces risks from uncertain policy direction in the advanced economies, including the pace of interest rate normalization in the United States. While short-term risks seem manageable, regional policy makers should remain vigilant to respond to possible spillover through capital flows and exchange rate movements.

Decades of rapid growth transformed developing Asia from a low-income region to middle income. Sustaining growth to power the transition into high income will depend on much greater improvement to productivity. Innovation, human capital, and infrastructure are the three pillars of productivity growth. Supportive institutions and policies, underpinned by macroeconomic stability, can strengthen all three pillars. Asia's dynamic track record suggests that the journey to high income, while challenging, is achievable.

Yasuyuki Sawada
Chief Economist
Asian Development Bank

Solid growth despite policy uncertainty

Asia tacks to shifting headwinds

■ **Continued expansion helps developing Asia deliver more than 60% of global growth.** Gross domestic product (GDP) for the region as a whole is expected to grow by 5.7% in 2017 and 2018, a tick down from the 2016 outcome of 5.8% as the controlled moderation of growth in the People's Republic of China (PRC) is balanced by expected healthy growth elsewhere. Excluding the high-income newly industrialized economies— the Republic of Korea, Singapore, Taipei,China, and Hong Kong, China—regional growth is expected to reach 6.3% in 2017 and 6.2% in 2018. Growth is picking up in 30 of the 45 economies in developing Asia, supported by higher external demand and rebounding global commodity prices.

　　» **The industrial economies are gathering some growth momentum.** After slowing in the first half of 2016, the euro area, Japan, and the United States are forecast to grow collectively by 1.9% in both 2017 and 2018. Recovery in the US is solid as unemployment has declined to 4.7%, and as consumer and business confidence soar, but confidence depends on the policy directions under the new administration. In the euro area as well, recovery is evident but more fragile in light of the uncertain future of the economic union. In Japan, the recovery will continue but may lose some steam unless export growth maintains its new momentum.

　　» **The PRC continues to rebalance, depending more on consumption to drive growth.** A further shift of economic activity from industry to services shows rebalancing progressing as planned. Growth in the PRC now relies more on internal demand and less on exports. Moderate deceleration of growth to 6.5% is expected in 2017, within the government's target range, and further to 6.2% in 2018. The authorities are likely to emphasize the maintenance of financial and fiscal stability and accept the cost of marginally lower growth.

　　» **India's expansion will bounce back from a temporary liquidity squeeze.** The decision to demonetize high-denomination banknotes in November 2016 quelled cash-intensive economic activity, but the impact is expected to be short lived. Government deregulation and reform of taxes on goods and services, among other areas, should improve confidence and thus business investment and growth prospects. Growth is expected to edge up to 7.4% in 2017 and 7.6% in 2018.

　　» **Growth in Southeast Asia is forecast to accelerate further.** After rising 0.1 percentage points to 4.7% in 2016, growth will continue to improve to 4.8% in 2017 and 5.0% in 2018, with nearly all Southeast Asian economies showing an upward trend. Recovery for global food and fuel prices and in agricultural output will help commodity producers such as Indonesia, Malaysia, and Viet Nam. Indonesia, the largest economy in the subregion, should see fiscal and structural reforms boost domestic demand.

　　» **Prospects for Central Asia and the Pacific rise along with commodity prices.** Higher oil prices will support fiscal spending in Azerbaijan and Kazakhstan, and one-off currency depreciation in these economies has already improved net exports. Growth in Central Asia is projected to accelerate to 3.1% in 2017 and 3.5% in 2018, though individual economies are growing at significantly different rates. In the Pacific, rising commodity prices are taking some pressure off a fiscal crunch in Papua New Guinea. With Fiji and Vanuatu recovering from natural disasters suffered in 2015, the Pacific subregion as a whole will grow by 2.9% in 2017 and 3.3% in 2018.

■ **Strong consumer demand and rising global commodity prices will boost inflation.** After rising 0.3 percentage points to 2.5% in 2016, regional inflation is projected to accelerate further to 3.0% in 2017 and 3.2% in 2018. The pickup also reflects the temporary effects of the large devaluations in some Central Asian economies. Overall, price rises are still reasonable, below the 10-year average of 3.9%, and unlikely to alter Asian expectations of relatively stable prices.

■ **The region's current account surplus will narrow even as exports recover.** As a share of world GDP, developing Asia's current account surplus is forecast to narrow from 0.7% in 2016 to less than 0.5% in both 2017 and 2018. Recent data suggest improved exports from many Asian economies, particularly traditional exporters of manufactured goods, yet the recovery in imports is even stronger. At the same time, though, rebalancing is progressing in the PRC as it relies more on private consumption for growth.

■ **Uncertain policy directions abroad could undermine the regional outlook.** While baseline assumptions have factored in gradual increases in US interest rates, sharper-than-expected US monetary tightening could have further consequences for developing Asia. Economies in the region with high corporate or household debt would be particularly vulnerable to financial shock. Possible shifts in trade and tax policies, especially policy changes being discussed in the US, could create uncertainty for business investment and export growth in developing Asia. While a potential boon to the region's oil importers, weaker-than-expected oil price trends could delay recovery in oil and gas exporters in Central Asia and the Pacific.

Risk of sharper US interest rate hikes

■ **The US Federal Reserve is unlikely to raise interest rates sharply.** As Asia braces for higher US interest rates, the question is how much higher? A recent surge in US inflation may accelerate the tightening cycle for interest rates that is now under way. However, interest rate increases sharper than the expected gradual rise would have to be accompanied by more acceleration in US economic growth than is currently forecast. Such a scenario could be envisaged under a possible fiscal stimulus later in 2017, but even then, any pickup in US growth would take time to materialize.

■ **The consequences would differ across Asia depending on exchange rate regime.** US monetary tightening would put pressure on Asian currencies to depreciate against the dollar, but the impact would depend on how the exchange rate is managed. Absent monetary policy response from regional authorities, economies with more open capital accounts would tend to experience deeper currency depreciation. Economies where the authorities intervene to maintain a stable currency would tend to forfeit export price competitiveness to those with more flexible exchange rate regimes. However, inflation could intensify under flexible arrangements, imperiling domestic macroeconomic stability. In this case, the authorities might find it necessary to tighten domestic liquidity to contain pressures on exchange rates and consumer prices.

Capital flows and financial risks

■ **Economies in emerging Asia are already experiencing net capital outflows.**
The PRC drives the overall direction of flows in the region, and outflows from its banking
activities and portfolio investments generated net outflows of $35 billion beginning in
the second quarter of 2014 that expanded to exceed $130 billion in the third quarter
of 2016. Even foreign direct investment has turned to net outflow since the second half
of 2015 as PRC investment abroad has risen and inflows declined. Despite the negative
trend in net flows overall, some variation persists, with India, Indonesia, and Viet Nam
notable among those still capitalizing on net inflows of foreign direct investment.

■ **Net outflow from economies in emerging Asia is expected to continue next year.**
As the global economy starts to pick up, uncertainty will become a key theme for
investors in 2017. Continuing US economic improvement, as marked by normalization of
its monetary policy, will be a pull factor for capital to flow out of the region. Other major
risks to financial markets in emerging Asia are policy and political uncertainty in the US
and the euro area, as well as possible further currency depreciation in the PRC.

■ **Global liquidity conditions mitigate the risk of destabilizing capital outflows.**
Although US monetary policy normalization raises the prospect of outflows from
developing Asia, the continuation of accommodative monetary policies in other
advanced economies limits the tightening of overall global liquidity. Since this eases the
pressure on central banks to raise interest rates to manage capital movements, they still
retain some scope for supporting the region's growth momentum.

■ **One risk is mounting household debt in some Asian economies.** The ratio of debt to
GDP has surged in several economies, notably rising in the Republic of Korea from 74%
in late 2008 to nearly 91% in the third quarter of 2016, and to about 71% in Malaysia
and Thailand. So far the risk from high household leverage in the region is contained
by favorable growth and employment conditions, fairly stable asset prices, and well
capitalized banking sectors with low nonperforming loan ratios. However, there is scope
to further bolster macroprudential policy, such as tightening ratios of debt to income and
of loans to asset values. Policy makers may also have to stress-test their banking sectors
regularly to track bank exposure and identify needs for special reserves. They may have
to intervene more decisively in housing markets as well to cool speculative demand and
head off asset bubbles.

Outlook by subregion

- **Average growth in developing Asia slows, upstaging higher projections for most economies.** Growth is forecast to accelerate in two-thirds of the region's economies and in all of the subregions except East Asia. The external environment generally supports growth. A projected mild rise in commodity prices will help oil and gas exporters but not at the expense of importers. Demand for the region's exports in general will benefit from an expected pickup in the major industrial economies and the Russian Federation. However, country-specific factors still generate considerable diversity in expected growth and inflation across the region.

- **East Asia's growth slowdown reflects continued moderation in the PRC.** Subregional growth dipped by 0.1 percentage points to 6.0% in 2016. The PRC slowed to 6.7% despite fiscal and monetary support as private investment weakened. Growth also dipped in Mongolia as construction faltered and in Hong Kong, China as tourist arrivals dropped. The rate is projected to moderate further in the PRC to 6.5% this year and 6.2% next as structural reform continues and the authorities emphasize financial stability. This will push the subregional average down to 5.8% in 2017 and 5.6% in 2018. Yet large government outlays will lift growth in Taipei,China and Hong Kong, China this year and the next. Mining investment will buoy growth in Mongolia, and the return of political stability in the Republic of Korea should pay a mild growth dividend in 2018. Inflation accelerated in East Asia last year but slowed in Mongolia on lower meat prices. Subregional inflation is expected to pick up modestly from 1.9% in 2016 to 2.3% in 2017 and 2.6% in 2018.

- **South Asia resumes faster growth after a brief pause.** Subregional growth dropped by 0.5 percentage points to 6.7% in 2016 on account of slowing growth in India. Despite stronger government consumption and external demand, growth faltered in India to 7.1% from 7.9% in 2015 as fixed investment languished and demonetization temporarily stymied commerce. Growth in South Asia is forecast to rebound to 7.0% in 2017 and pick up further to 7.2% in 2018. India will see growth reaccelerate to 7.4% in fiscal 2017 and 7.6% in 2018 despite drag caused by excessive corporate investment in the past and bank lending currently constrained by a heavy load of stressed assets. Elsewhere, growth will be lifted by spending on earthquake reconstruction in Nepal, hydropower investment and output in Bhutan, and economic corridor investment from the PRC in Pakistan. Inflation in South Asia has trended lower in recent years, easing to 4.6% in 2016 as buyers benefited from low prices for oil and other commodities. With these prices turning upward over the forecast period, inflation is projected to revive to 5.2% in 2017 and 5.4% in 2018.

- **Southeast Asian prospects brighten with buoyant growth across the subregion.** Economic expansion accelerated by 4.7% in 2016, up by 0.1 percentage points from the previous year, as growth edged higher in several larger economies: Indonesia, the Philippines, Singapore, and Thailand. With normal weather supporting agriculture and steady recovery in the major industrial economies boosting exports, growth will pick up in nearly all of the economies in the subregion, nudging average growth to 4.8% in 2017 and 5.0% in 2018. The only exception is the Philippines, where growth will moderate from its record 6.8% in 2016 to a pace approximating 6.5% this year and next. While higher infrastructure investment will provide an additional impetus to growth in Brunei Darussalam, Indonesia, the Lao People's Democratic Republic, the Philippines, and Thailand, record foreign direct investment will be a key factor supporting growth in Viet Nam. Strengthening growth and rising international oil prices will mean higher inflation and a narrower current account surplus for the subregion. Average inflation is forecast to rise from 2.1% in 2016 to 3.3% this year, edging up further to 3.5% next year.

■ **Central Asia looks forward to a modest growth rebound.** Continued low oil prices, recession in the Russian Federation, and weakness in other trading partners cut growth in Central Asia to 2.1% in 2016 from 3.1% a year earlier. Declining oil revenues hit Azerbaijan and Kazakhstan particularly hard, with the former falling into recession. Anticipated recovery for international oil prices and for growth in the Russian Federation are projected to boost expansion in the subregion to 3.1% in 2017. Growth will accelerate further to 3.5% in 2018 as every economy except Kazakhstan improves its performance. The lagged effects of currency depreciation in Azerbaijan and Kazakhstan, and to a lesser extent in Tajikistan, stoked inflation by almost 5 percentage points to 11.1% in 2016, even as inflation slowed in Georgia, the Kyrgyz Republic, Turkmenistan, and Uzbekistan and sank into deflation in Armenia. As the effects from currency depreciation abate, inflation is projected to decelerate to 7.8% in 2017 and 7.3% in 2018.

■ **The Pacific will see growth revive on developments in Papua New Guinea.** Growth slowed substantially to 2.6% in 2016 as contraction hit the oil and gas sector in Papua New Guinea, slashing the growth rate in the subregion's predominant economy by 10.0 percentage points to 2.0%. Elsewhere, growth picked up in 2016 in most Pacific economies—by more than 4 percentage points in Nauru, Samoa, and Vanuatu. Increased mining and agriculture output is forecast to spur a mild recovery in Papua New Guinea, which will translate into a modest rebound for the subregion to 2.9% growth this year and 3.3% next. Steady or slower growth is expected in most other economies, with declines in public expenditure inducing relatively sharp slowdowns in Nauru, Samoa, and Timor-Leste. Although inflation eased in most economies in 2016, the aggregate inflation rate rose by 0.6 percentage points to 4.6%, driven by rising consumer prices in Papua New Guinea. Rising oil and food prices will push inflation higher in most of the economies this year. Subregional inflation is expected to be 5.2% in 2017 and 5.4% in 2018.

Transcending the middle-income challenge

Sustaining growth at middle income

■ **Rapid growth has lifted most economies in developing Asia to middle income.**
The rise of Asia's newly industrialized economies in the 1970s and 1980s was well
documented. Less publicized was that more than 90% of the people in the region still
lived in low-income economies in 1991, half again the global average of less than 60%.
By 2015, the story had changed. Propelled by the rising fortunes of the most populous
Asian economies—the PRC, India, and Indonesia—more than 95% of the population
lived in middle-income economies. The question now is how a largely middle-income
region can build on its past success.

■ **Global experience suggests that the jump to high income can be difficult.** The rapid
transition of the Republic of Korea and Taipei,China, which moved from middle income
to high in barely a quarter of a century, raised hopes for the region's current middle-
income cohort. However, the experience of most developing economies globally
threatens to put these hopes on hold. Brazil and Colombia, for example, have been
middle income for more than half a century. Middle-income economies face a difficult
task in sustaining growth sufficiently to clear the hurdle to high income.

■ **As economies evolve from low to middle income, so do their growth drivers.**
While accumulating physical and human capital remains important for growth in middle-
income economies, these economies have already significantly expanded their stocks
of both. The median number of years of schooling for middle-income economies is 6.1,
more than double the 2.5 years for low-income economies. Similarly, middle-income
economies have more capital per worker and better-developed financial systems than do
low-income economies. Total factor productivity improvement, or growth in production
not derived from higher use of inputs, plays a bigger role in growth for middle-income
economies, particularly those successfully reaching high income.

■ **The successful middle-income growth model emphasizes productivity.** Innovation
becomes more important when economies already reap the benefits of efficiently using
existing resources. Even as they accumulate more physical and human capital, the focus
shifts to areas with more positive productivity spillover, like advanced infrastructure and
higher education. Finally, the whole process must be underpinned by a supportive policy
environment and a stable macroeconomic environment.

Innovation for diversifying and upgrading production

■ **Innovation matters more as economies approach the technological frontier.**
A more central role in productivity growth falls to innovation with the decline of other
sources, such as labor's migration from agriculture to manufacturing. Middle-income
economies that have graduated to high income have more than 2.5 times the research
and development stock per worker as other middle-income economies. Risk-taking
entrepreneurs take the lead in fostering innovation, and these individuals respond
to incentives that are either strengthened or weakened by economic policies and
institutions. Governments can promote innovative entrepreneurship through stronger
intellectual property protection and rule of law, better access to finance, and effective
competition policies.

- **Entrepreneurship turns new ideas or technology into innovation-based growth.**
  As economies become more sophisticated, opportunity-driven entrepreneurship, which is often built on new ideas or technology, increasingly outweighs necessity-driven entrepreneurship, which responds to existing market needs. The ratio of opportunity-driven to necessity-driven entrepreneurship is 1.6 times higher in high-income economies than in middle-income ones. Therefore, to reach high income, middle-income economies should encourage and nurture new business entries that pursue new business opportunities and provide products or services novel to the market.

- **Graduation to high income requires a diverse and sophisticated product mix.**
  In addition to producing a wider range of goods, middle-income economies must aim to produce more complex goods, such as sophisticated machinery and modern chemicals and alloys, that support higher productivity and better wages. Noteworthy is the experience of the PRC, which ranked for product complexity at only 48 in the mid-1990s but at 19 in 2014. Enhanced human capital is the foundation for a transition to a more diverse and complex product mix.

Human capital for emerging marketplace needs

- **Human capital accumulation can promote both growth and equity.** Estimates indicate that a 20% increase in human capital spending per capita can raise labor productivity by up to 3.1% and narrow labor income inequality by up to 4.5%. The bonus in income growth is more salient among poorer families, which may explain the income-equalizing effect. Public education in particular enhances equity, yet some regional economies spend less per child than other economies at the same income. Evidence shows that higher public spending on education need not harm public finances. Augmented labor incomes expand the tax base and hence tax revenues. Finally, as regional populations age, enhancing worker quality can help compensate for the shrinking share of the working-age population.

- **The emphasis needs to be on ramping up the quality of education.** Increasing the average years of schooling a young person receives can boost growth but less so than improving the quality of education and enhancing cognitive skills like math and science. Economies with relatively high cognitive skills benefit from having a critical mass of students likely to become innovators. Research indicates that, as economies move closer to the technological frontier, the returns on research-oriented innovation pick up tangibly. Consequently, middle-income Asia needs to strengthen its research-oriented education while sustaining its achievements in basic education.

- **Middle-income economies need to close education gaps with high-income economies.** While differences in educational attainment remain substantial, especially in tertiary education, gaps in the quality of education offered by different education systems are spectacular. In globally standardized math and science tests, the proportion of top-performing 15-year-old students in the advanced economies is on average 4–5 times the proportion in middle-income economies, while the share of low performers in middle-income economies is more than 2 times the advanced average. An exception like Viet Nam, which ranks at 8 among the 72 economies covered, appears to demonstrate that the gap can be closed with sound education policies.

Infrastructure investment for facilitating structural change

■ **Economies prioritize different types of infrastructure as they develop.**
ADB reported this year that developing Asia has large investment needs across all
types of infrastructure—from water supply and sanitation to transport, power, and
telecommunications. But infrastructure needs shift as an economy becomes more
complex and sophisticated. Low-income economies focus first on such basic needs
as water supply, sanitation, and a transportation network to get goods and people to
market. As basic needs are met and economic structures evolve, more importance is
attached to electricity supply and advanced infrastructure such as information and
communication technology.

■ **Advanced infrastructure can help sustain growth in middle-income economies.**
The fastest-growing middle-income economies differ from their slower-growing peers in
a couple of important ways. They invest more in infrastructure and tend to have more of
certain types of infrastructure. Mobile telephone and broadband networks, for example,
are vital tools for creating and disseminating knowledge. Middle-income economies
that graduate to high income have 18 more internet users and 31 more mobile phone
subscriptions per 100 people than their peers. Investment in advanced infrastructure can
boost growth by promoting both innovation and human capital. The nexus of advanced
infrastructure, highly developed skills, and innovation can help sustain growth enough to
ensure a successful transition to high income.

■ **Investment in infrastructure boosts output, not least in middle-income economies.**
Analysis using a sample of developing economies shows that a one-time increase in
public infrastructure investment that equals 1.0% of GDP immediately lifts output
by 0.3% of GDP and by nearly 1.2% after 7 years. Notably, this significantly positive
effect, both in the short term and over the long run, is still robust when the sample is
narrowed to middle-income economies. This underscores the potential benefits of an
infrastructure push.

Reaching toward high income

■ **Sound policies and institutions are vital to transformative growth.** The role of
government necessarily evolves as an economy progresses, becoming more nuanced
as the private sector develops. Government must shape an environment conducive to
innovative entrepreneurship by promoting investment in education and infrastructure.
As shown by Thailand's successful experience with industry–government coordination
in the automobile industry, direct government intervention can, if selective and well
targeted, foster an output mix that is more diverse and sophisticated. The case for
intervention is stronger when a government has adequate institutional capacity.

■ **An environment conducive to growth needs macroeconomic stability.** Empirical
estimates show that when a country reaches middle income, its growth rate is more
vulnerable to indicators affecting macroeconomic stability—such as whether the country
faces a banking or currency crisis, the extent of capital inflows other than foreign
investment, and government debt as a share of GDP. The region should continue to
protect macroeconomic stability, as it has done very well in the past.

- **Sustaining rapid growth is not easy but is within reach for middle-income Asia.** Many norms that served the region well at low income, such as macroeconomic stability and high investment, still serve it well at middle income. At the same time, the pattern of growth will have to evolve if Asia is to sustain rapid growth and eventually reach high income. In particular, education, innovation, and infrastructure all have vital roles to play. The region's dynamic track record encourages optimism that governments can adapt their growth models to meet the middle-income challenge.

GDP growth rate and inflation, % per year

	Growth rate of GDP					Inflation				
	2014	2015	2016	2017	2018	2014	2015	2016	2017	2018
Central Asia	**5.2**	**3.1**	**2.1**	**3.1**	**3.5**	**5.9**	**6.3**	**11.1**	**7.8**	**7.3**
Armenia	3.6	3.0	0.2	2.2	2.5	3.0	3.7	−1.4	1.2	1.8
Azerbaijan	2.8	1.1	−3.8	−1.1	1.2	1.4	4.0	12.4	9.0	8.0
Georgia	4.6	2.9	2.7	3.8	4.5	3.1	4.0	2.1	4.2	4.5
Kazakhstan	4.2	1.2	1.0	2.4	2.2	6.7	6.6	14.6	8.0	7.0
Kyrgyz Republic	4.0	3.9	3.8	3.0	3.5	7.5	6.5	0.4	5.0	4.0
Tajikistan	6.7	6.0	6.9	4.8	5.5	6.1	5.1	6.1	8.0	7.0
Turkmenistan	10.3	6.5	6.2	6.5	7.0	6.0	6.4	6.0	6.0	6.0
Uzbekistan	8.1	8.0	7.8	7.0	7.3	9.1	8.5	8.4	9.5	10.0
East Asia	**6.6**	**6.1**	**6.0**	**5.8**	**5.6**	**1.9**	**1.3**	**1.9**	**2.3**	**2.6**
China, People's Rep. of	7.3	6.9	6.7	6.5	6.2	2.0	1.4	2.0	2.4	2.8
Hong Kong, China	2.8	2.4	1.9	2.0	2.1	4.4	3.0	2.4	2.0	2.1
Korea, Rep. of	3.3	2.6	2.7	2.5	2.7	1.3	0.7	1.0	1.7	1.8
Mongolia	7.9	2.4	1.0	2.5	2.0	12.8	6.6	1.1	3.5	3.9
Taipei,China	4.0	0.7	1.5	1.8	2.2	1.2	−0.3	1.4	1.3	1.2
South Asia	**6.7**	**7.2**	**6.7**	**7.0**	**7.2**	**6.3**	**4.9**	**4.6**	**5.2**	**5.4**
Afghanistan	1.3	0.8	2.0	2.5	3.0	4.7	−1.5	4.5	5.5	5.8
Bangladesh	6.1	6.6	7.1	6.9	6.9	7.3	6.4	5.9	6.1	6.3
Bhutan	4.0	6.1	6.4	8.2	9.9	9.6	6.6	3.3	4.9	5.4
India	7.2	7.9	7.1	7.4	7.6	6.0	4.9	4.7	5.2	5.4
Maldives	6.0	2.8	3.4	3.8	4.1	2.1	1.0	0.5	2.1	2.3
Nepal	5.7	2.3	0.8	5.6	5.4	9.1	7.2	9.9	6.0	6.5
Pakistan	4.1	4.0	4.7	5.2	5.5	8.6	4.5	2.9	4.0	4.8
Sri Lanka	5.0	4.8	4.4	5.0	5.0	3.3	3.8	4.0	6.0	6.0
Southeast Asia	**4.6**	**4.6**	**4.7**	**4.8**	**5.0**	**4.1**	**2.8**	**2.1**	**3.3**	**3.5**
Brunei Darussalam	−2.5	−0.4	−2.5	1.0	2.5	−0.2	−0.4	−0.7	0.1	0.1
Cambodia	7.1	7.0	7.0	7.1	7.1	3.9	1.2	3.0	3.4	3.5
Indonesia	5.0	4.9	5.0	5.1	5.3	6.4	6.4	3.5	4.3	4.5
Lao People's Dem. Rep.	7.5	6.7	6.8	6.9	7.0	4.2	1.3	1.6	2.5	3.0
Malaysia	6.0	5.0	4.2	4.4	4.6	3.1	2.1	2.1	3.3	2.7
Myanmar	8.0	7.3	6.4	7.7	8.0	5.9	11.4	6.5	7.0	7.5
Philippines	6.2	5.9	6.8	6.4	6.6	4.1	1.4	1.8	3.5	3.7
Singapore	3.6	1.9	2.0	2.2	2.3	1.0	−0.5	−0.5	1.0	1.5
Thailand	0.9	2.9	3.2	3.5	3.6	1.9	−0.9	0.2	1.8	2.0
Viet Nam	6.0	6.7	6.2	6.5	6.7	4.1	0.6	2.7	4.0	5.0
The Pacific	**9.6**	**8.3**	**2.6**	**2.9**	**3.3**	**3.5**	**4.0**	**4.6**	**5.2**	**5.4**
Cook Islands	4.5	4.8	5.5	5.0	5.0	1.6	3.0	−0.1	0.5	1.2
Fiji	5.6	3.6	2.0	3.5	4.0	0.6	1.4	3.9	2.5	2.5
Kiribati	2.4	3.5	1.8	2.0	1.5	2.1	0.6	0.7	2.0	2.0
Marshall Islands	−0.9	0.6	1.5	4.0	2.5	1.1	−2.2	−1.3	1.5	1.5
Micronesia, Fed. States of	−2.4	3.7	3.0	2.5	2.5	0.7	−0.2	−0.3	1.5	2.0
Nauru	36.5	2.8	7.2	4.3	−4.5	3.0	11.4	7.2	5.7	1.8
Palau	4.8	11.6	2.2	3.0	5.5	4.0	2.2	−1.3	1.5	2.0
Papua New Guinea	13.3	12.0	2.0	2.5	2.8	5.2	6.0	7.0	7.5	7.5
Samoa	1.2	1.6	6.6	2.0	1.5	−1.3	1.9	0.1	2.0	2.0
Solomon Islands	2.0	2.9	3.2	3.0	2.8	5.2	−0.5	1.1	1.8	2.2
Timor-Leste	5.9	3.5	5.4	4.0	6.0	0.7	0.6	−1.4	1.2	3.0
Tonga	2.0	3.7	3.1	2.6	2.6	2.5	−1.0	2.0	2.5	2.5
Tuvalu	2.2	2.6	3.0	3.0	3.0	1.1	3.2	2.0	2.0	2.0
Vanuatu	2.3	−1.0	3.8	4.3	3.8	1.0	2.5	0.9	2.4	2.6
Developing Asia	**6.3**	**6.0**	**5.8**	**5.7**	**5.7**	**3.0**	**2.2**	**2.5**	**3.0**	**3.2**
Developing Asia excluding the NIEs	**6.8**	**6.6**	**6.3**	**6.3**	**6.2**	**3.2**	**2.4**	**2.7**	**3.2**	**3.5**

Note: The newly industrialized economies (NIEs) are the Republic of Korea, Singapore, Taipei,China, and Hong Kong, China.

1

SOLID GROWTH DESPITE POLICY UNCERTAINTY

Solid growth despite policy uncertainty

Growth in Asia moderated in 2016 despite improving trends in the second half. The main reasons for the nascent turnaround were the bottoming out of oil prices, higher external demand from the United States and the European Union, and fiscal stimulus and a slight easing of financial conditions in some economies (Figure 1.0.1). This occurred against the backdrop of looming structural change in the People's Republic of China (PRC) and other East Asian economies that, coupled with a need for corporate debt restructuring, could undermine growth. Some fast-growing economies in South and Southeast Asia will need to pick up the slack. The PRC is now the world's second-largest economy and larger than the rest of developing Asia and the Pacific combined (Figure 1.0.2). The next largest economies, India and Indonesia, are implementing important structural reforms that should improve their medium-term growth prospects, and the benefits are already coming into view in the turnaround in regional growth.

Inflation rose in 2016, and the forecast for 2017 and 2018 is for more increases across the board except in Central Asia, where inflation will moderate because of a high base in 2016 following currency devaluation the year before. Asia's external current account maintained its surplus with the rest of the world in 2016, but it is likely to narrow in 2017 and 2018.

Asia's near-term outlook is solid. Growth in the PRC will continue to moderate but do so manageably as long as financial flows remain stable. The outlook assumes that, as the United States economy normalizes in 2017 and 2018, the Fed funds rate will rise. However, if US rates rise too quickly, central banks in Asia may need to follow suit. Possible changes in US tax and trade policies may dampen business sentiment for globally oriented companies investing in Asia. In general, developing Asia's outlook would be undercut if trade became less open, but real impact from any policy changes is unlikely to materialize until the second half of 2018.

1.0.1 World growth and forecasts

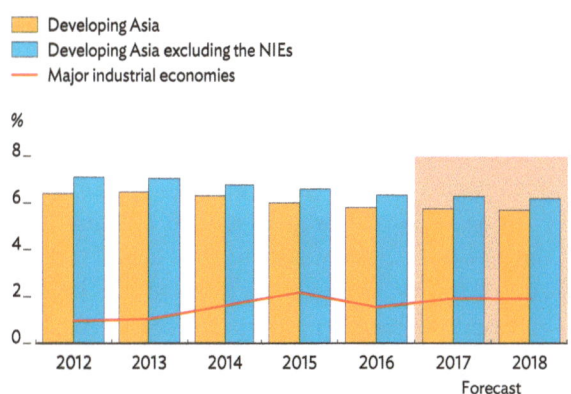

Notes: The major industrial economies are the euro area, Japan, and the United States. The newly industrialized economies (NIEs) are the Republic of Korea, Singapore, Taipei,China, and Hong Kong, China.
Sources: US Department of Commerce, Bureau of Economic Analysis, http://www.bea.gov; Eurostat, http://epp.eurostat.ec.europa.eu; Economic and Social Research Institute of Japan, http://www.esri.cao.go.jp; Consensus Forecasts; Asian Development Outlook database; ADB estimates.

1.0.2 Global shares of income, 2015

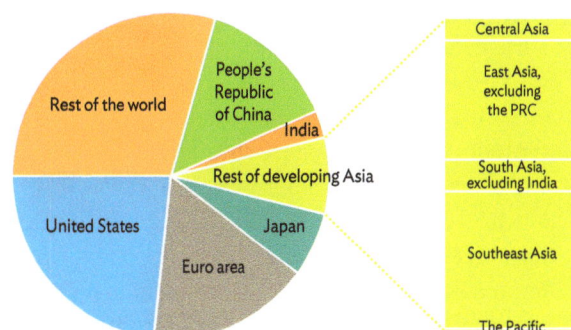

Note: Weights are based on gross national income in current US dollars, Atlas method.
Source: ADB estimates using data from World Development Indicators online database.

This chapter was written by Valerie Mercer-Blackman, Arief Ramayandi, Benno Ferrarini, Madhavi Pundit, Shiela Camingue-Romance, Cindy Castillejos-Petalcorin, Marthe Hinojales, Nedelyn Magtibay-Ramos, Pilipinas Quising, and Dennis Sorino of the Economic Research and Regional Cooperation Department, ADB, Manila.

Asia tacks to shifting headwinds

Developing Asia is forecast to maintain stable growth this year and the next. Aggregate gross domestic product (GDP) in the region will expand by 5.7% in 2017 and 2018, down slightly from 5.8% in 2016 (Figure 1.1.1). The slower expansion reflects moderating growth in the PRC that more than offsets faster expansion elsewhere. The PRC continues its shift toward less dependence on investment and manufacturing. In 2017, growth in the region will remain steady as solid growth in India and a pickup in other larger economies, notably in Southeast Asia, offset continued slowing of growth in the PRC. Average inflation in the region will rise from 2.5% in 2016 to 3.0% in 2017 on strengthening domestic demand and recovery in global commodity prices, and further to 3.2% in 2018 with a further rise in oil prices (Figure 1.1.2).

The region's aggregate current account surplus will narrow from 2.3% in 2016 to 1.9% in 2017 and further to 1.7% in 2018 as export growth is likely to be outpaced in most economies by import growth to support domestic economic activity (Figure 1.1.3). Further, the recovery in the industrial economies remains modest (Box 1.1.1).

Slower growth in 2016

Growth in developing Asia slowed in 2016 for a third consecutive year, mirroring continued growth moderation in the PRC and the modest outturn in most economies last year. The growth slowdown was widespread, affecting most economies in the region, particularly in East and Central Asia. Average growth slipped from 6.0% in 2015 to 5.8% in 2016.

Growth in East Asia edged down to 6.0% in 2016 from 6.1% in 2015 as private consumption slowed and exports withered. Moderating growth in the PRC continued to weigh on the region's performance, reducing growth for a third straight year. In Mongolia, growth dropped by 1.4 percentage points, and in Hong Kong, China by 0.5 points, because of lackluster consumer spending. Growth improved by less than a percentage point in the Republic of Korea (ROK), and by 0.8 percentage points in Taipei,China, as strong investment—propelled by higher construction in the ROK and by strong demand for machinery and transport equipment in Taipei,China—countered feeble exports.

In Central Asia, growth weakened to 2.1% from 3.1% in 2015 as seven of the eight economies, excepting only Tajikistan, posted slower growth on account of weaker global oil prices, higher prices for nonfood imports resulting from currency depreciation, and recession in the Russian Federation, a key trade partner and source of remittances, which quelled

1.1.1 Growth in developing Asia and subregional contributions

■ Central Asia
■ East Asia
■ South Asia
■ Southeast Asia
■ The Pacific
● Developing Asia

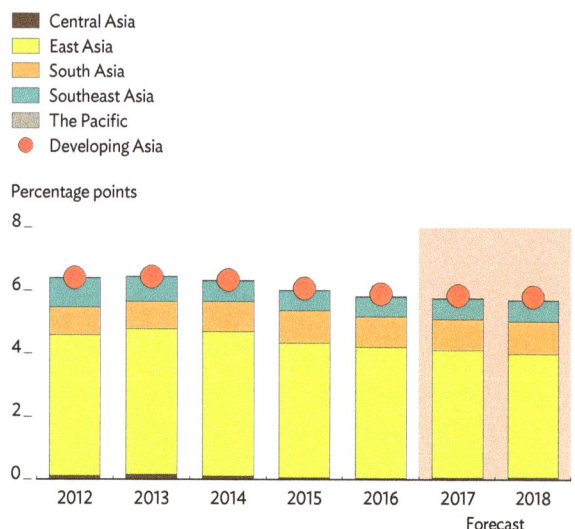

Source: Asian Development Outlook database.

1.1.2 Inflation in developing Asia

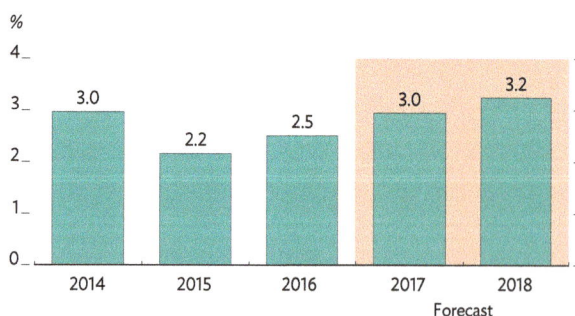

Source: Asian Development Outlook database.

1.1.1 Clear but fragile recovery in 2016

Combined growth in the major industrial economies—the US, the euro area, and Japan—was stronger in 2016 and the first quarter of 2017 than forecast. On that basis, the baseline outlook is stable to positive.

GDP growth in the major industrial economies (%)

Area	2015	2016	2017	2018
	Actual		ADO projection	
Major industrial economies	2.2	1.6	1.9	1.9
United States	2.6	1.6	2.4	2.4
Euro area	1.9	1.7	1.6	1.6
Japan	1.2	1.0	1.0	0.9

ADO = Asian Development Outlook.

Notes: Average growth rates are weighted by gross national income, Atlas method. More details in Table A1.1 on page 32.

Sources: US Department of Commerce, Bureau of Economic Analysis, http://www.bea.gov; Eurostat, http://ec.europa.eu/eurostat; Economic and Social Research Institute of Japan, http://www.esri.cao.go.jp; Consensus Forecasts; Bloomberg; CEIC Data Company; Haver; World Bank, Global Commodity Markets, http://www.worldbank.org; ADB estimates.

After a weak start in the first half of 2016, US economic activity strengthened significantly in the second half, particularly in the third quarter. Consumption continues to grow, with consumer confidence rebounding quite strongly in February 2017 to reach its highest monthly level since July 2001. Manufacturing is gradually recovering, while industrial production and purchasing managers' indexes show moderate expansion in February 2017, suggesting continuing production recovery. Meanwhile, a positive trend in the labor market continued as the unemployment rate fell further in February 2017 to 4.7%.

With signs that the output gap may have closed, the Federal Reserve is expected to tighten monetary policy in 2017. Headline inflation is on a rising trend since 2015. The trend continued in 2017 with inflation climbing to 2.5% in January. The Fed raised the target range for the federal funds rate by 25 basis points in December 2016 and by another 25 basis points in March 2017. Continuing gradual increases are expected during the next 2 years, bringing the rate to about 1.4% by the end of 2017 and 2.4% at the end of 2018. This expectation of rate hikes have been incorporated into the baseline projections. Higher interest rates will likely strengthen the US dollar further, as it continues to appreciate against most major currencies. GDP will grow at 2.4% in both 2017 and 2018 as growth continues.

Growth momentum in the euro area strengthened in the past year. After a blip in the second quarter of 2016, which coincided with the United Kingdom's Brexit referendum in June, recovery in the euro area continued to accelerate in the second half, bringing GDP growth to 1.7% for the whole of 2016. Domestic demand was supported by accommodative policies and improving labor markets.

The recovery in exports remains fragile. The unemployment rate improved to 9.6% in December, its lowest since April 2009. Consumer confidence remains upbeat while the composite purchasing managers' index has risen to its highest since April 2011, suggesting that corporate activity is picking up. In February, economic sentiment climbed to its highest point in 6 years. The United Kingdom's decision to leave the European Union seems thus far to have slowed regional growth less than expected, and economic sentiment appears to be positive, however fragile.

Despite emerging price pressures, the European Central Bank kept its interest rates unchanged at its March 2017 meeting. Earlier in December, it decided to extend its quantitative easing program by 9 months to the end of 2017. In February, inflation accelerated further to 2.0% with a sharper jump in energy prices. The euro remains somewhat weak, but this may help net exports recover.

The baseline projection assumes GDP growth will hold steady at 1.6% in 2017 and 2018. While negotiations on the United Kingdom's separation from the European Union have been triggered, they are unlikely to drag significantly on growth until perhaps late 2018, when the shape of Brexit may be clearer. Meanwhile, concerns about Greek debt have resurfaced and could dampen business confidence as elections loom in France, Germany, and possibly Italy. The baseline forecast assumes an improving outlook for global growth and trade, as well as some recovery in investment.

Japan's economy grew by 1.0%, less than in 2015. Growth in 2016 came from strong expansion in the first half of the year, first an uptick in consumption and net exports, and then in private investment. Exports contributed to growth, particularly in the fourth quarter, when they rose by 8.9%. As recent monthly indicators suggest that domestic demand remains sluggish, the recovery may lose steam. For example, manufacturing growth turned positive in the third quarter of 2016 but improved only slightly thereafter. Other data suggest that business sentiment remains cautious, though the purchasing managers' index is above the threshold of 50, indicating expansion in manufacturing. Consumer confidence, which in September hit its highest point in 3 years, declined in the following months owing to weak wage growth. With government stimulus, the Bank of Japan projects that public investment will rise through FY2017 (ends 31 March 2018). With inflation stirring to only 0.5% in January 2017, the short-term policy interest rate was kept at –0.1 percent and the target yield for 10-year Japanese government bonds continues to be zero.

The Japanese economy is expected to continue expanding at a modest pace, with growth forecast at 1.0% for 2017. The recovery is precariously balanced. While a weak yen and an uptick in global demand have boosted exports recently, confidence has yet to show a very robust response.

demand. Azerbaijan fell into recession with the decline in domestic demand on top of the adverse impact of weaker oil production and exports. Oil-dependent Kazakhstan and Turkmenistan also slowed, but less than in 2015 as declining oil export earnings were countered by higher government spending in Kazakhstan and increased investment in Turkmenistan. In Tajikistan, growth improved by 0.9 percentage points thanks to timely and robust expansion in public investment, and despite lower remittances. Weak exports slowed growth marginally in the Kyrgyz Republic and Uzbekistan.

Growth in South Asia eased to 6.7% in 2016 from 7.2% in 2015 even as five of the eight economies posted higher growth. The deceleration was largely attributed to India, where growth decelerated to 7.1% in 2016 from 7.9% in 2015 on account of weak expansion in private investment, a halt to the slide in international oil prices, and the government's demonetization of high-denomination banknotes in November 2016, which temporarily stymied many transactions in this cash-intensive economy. Growth in Nepal also slowed, hurt by delayed reconstruction following an earthquake in April 2015 and by trade and supply disruptions in early 2016. In Sri Lanka, growth moderated as adverse weather weakened agricultural production. Steady growth in the rest of the South Asian economies reflected higher consumption and investment and a rebound in high-end tourism.

In the Pacific, aggregate growth in 2016 eased to just a third of the subregion's remarkable 8.3% expansion in 2015 as growth slowed in the larger island economies. Low commodity prices and soft global demand sharply weakened growth in the subregion's largest economy, Papua New Guinea. In Fiji, growth eased due to damage and losses from Cyclone Winston, while in Timor-Leste growth improved as higher infrastructure investment offset slack petroleum exports and revenues.

In contrast with slower growth elsewhere, aggregate growth in Southeast Asia improved slightly to 4.7% in 2016 from 4.6% in 2015, even as growth slowed in 4 of the 10 economies and recession deepened in Brunei Darussalam. This largely reflected a higher weighting for Indonesia, where growth accelerated last year on higher fixed investment and consumption after slowing for 4 straight years. In Malaysia, growth dipped for a second year in a row, weighed down by declining fixed investment, weaker government spending, and lower exports. In Thailand, growth improved marginally from last year on higher consumption, aided by a tax rebate for shopping and dining, higher rural incomes, and recovery in net exports. Growth in Viet Nam slowed as weaker agriculture and mining production offset robust expansion in manufacturing and construction. Adverse weather hurt agricultural production in the Philippines and Viet Nam. In the Philippines, though, huge improvements in public infrastructure kicked in, lifting growth to a rate on par with the Lao People's Democratic Republic and behind only Cambodia.

External demand slowed growth in several large economies. In 7 of the 11 regional economies with data on contributions to growth, net exports trimmed growth in 2016 (Figure 1.1.4).

1.1.3 Current account balance in developing Asia

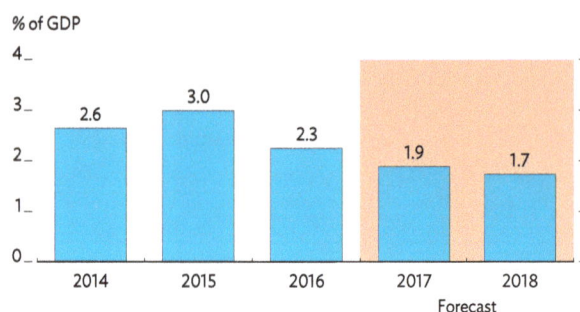

Source: Asian Development Outlook database.

Consumption remained the dominant source of expansion last year, with over half of growth in most of these economies fueled mainly by private spending, even as consumer confidence was mostly bleak (Figure 1.1.5).

Consumer confidence started low in 2016 in most of the large economies examined but rose gradually in four of the seven in the second half of the year. In the PRC, consumer confidence was strong throughout 2016 and translated into higher spending on a wide range of goods and services. In Hong Kong, China, consumer confidence fluctuated as more cautious views took hold about the economic outlook, job prospects, and spending plans. After slipping in mid-2016 because of declines in tourist arrivals, particularly from the PRC, consumer confidence in Hong Kong, China recovered in the second half on better expectations about jobs and stock market movements. Consumer confidence in Indonesia also swung, soaring to a 21-month high in October 2016 on public approval for government reform programs, including tax amnesty, before falling slowly toward the end of last year due to a modest change in outlook for jobs and incomes. In the Philippines, the better outlook for business activity, jobs, and incomes improved consumer sentiment.

Faced with a sluggish economic outlook and critical domestic issues, the ROK, Thailand, and Taipei,China saw consumer sentiment slump and remain negative for most of 2016. In the ROK, consumer sentiment fell to its lowest in more than 7.5 years in December, as residents anticipated a weaker economy because of the crisis surrounding the President and resulting turbulent financial markets. In Taipei,China, consumer confidence weakened from January to June in line with economic contraction in the first quarter and fragile recovery in the second. Slight improvement occurred in the second half, but confidence remains low, reflecting uncertainty over the economic outlook.

1.1.4 Demand-side contributions to growth, selected economies

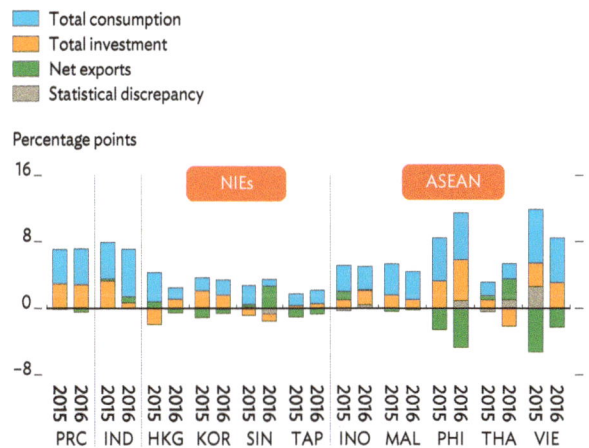

ASEAN = Association of Southeast Asian Nations, HKG = Hong Kong, China, IND = India, INO = Indonesia, KOR = Republic of Korea, MAL = Malaysia, NIEs = newly industrialized economies, PHI = Philippines, PRC = People's Republic of China, SIN = Singapore, TAP = Taipei,China, THA = Thailand, VIE = Viet Nam.
Sources: Haver Analytics; CEIC Data Company (both accessed 1 March 2017); ADB estimates.

1.1.5 Consumer confidence and expectations, selected developing Asia

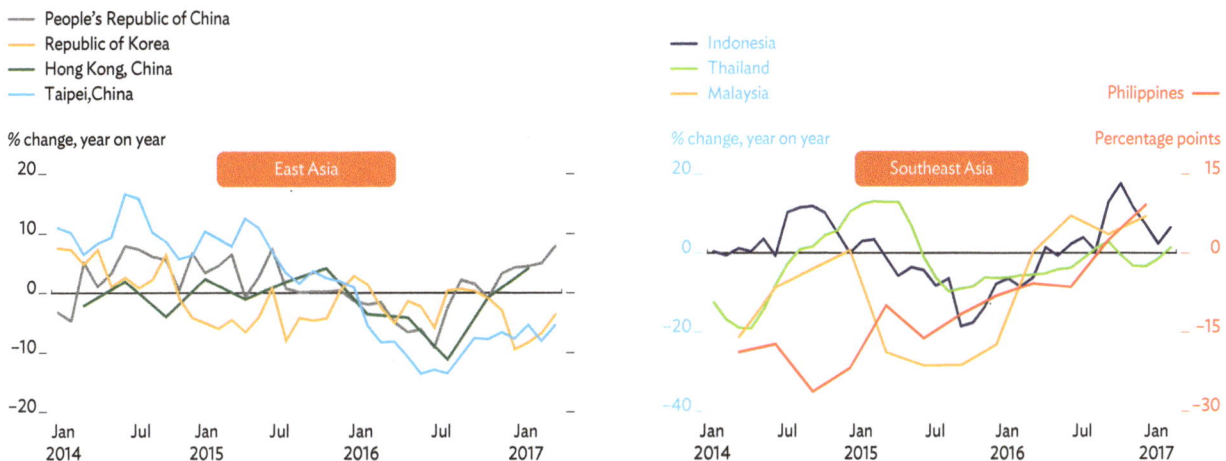

Note: Data for Malaysia, the Philippines, and Hong Kong, China are quarterly. Data for the Philippines refer to the percentage of households that were optimistic less the percentage that were pessimistic. A positive percentage point change indicates a favorable view, negative unfavorable.
Sources: Haver Analytics; CEIC Data Company (both accessed 23 March 2017).

1.1.6 Retail sales, selected developing Asia

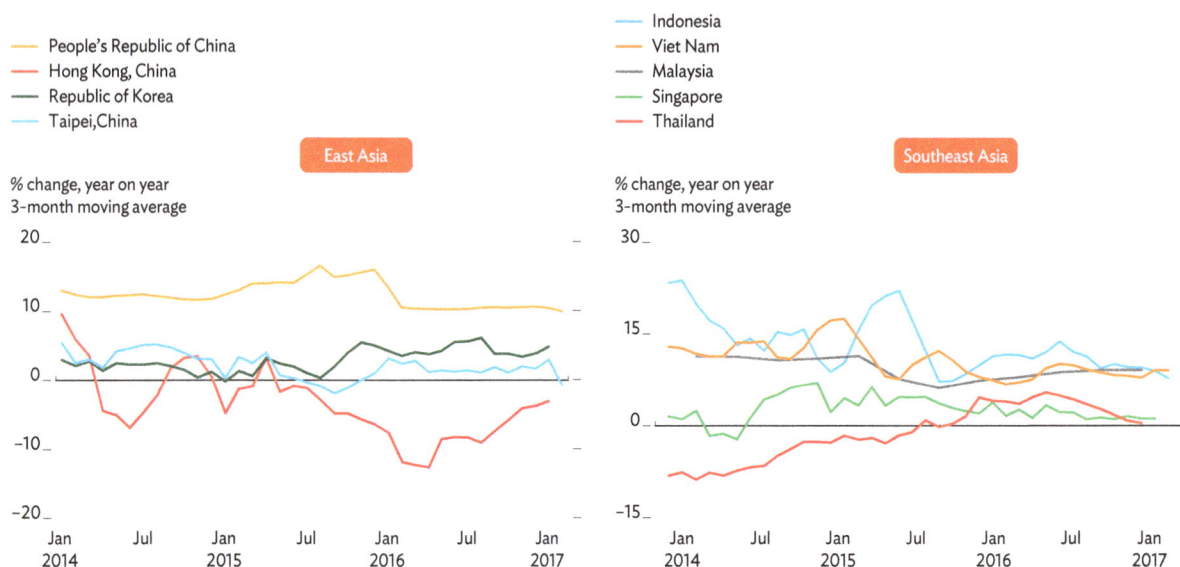

People's Republic of China
Hong Kong, China
Republic of Korea
Taipei,China

Indonesia
Viet Nam
Malaysia
Singapore
Thailand

East Asia

Southeast Asia

% change, year on year
3-month moving average

% change, year on year
3-month moving average

Note: Data for Malaysia refer to year-on-year quarterly percent change.
Source: Haver Analytics (accessed 23 March 2017).

In contrast, consumer confidence in Malaysia improved in 2016 as consumers remained hopeful despite worries about the economic outlook and job security.

Retailers in most economies saw better growth in 2016 with the fragile recovery in consumer sentiment (Figure 1.1.6). Retail sales in Hong Kong, China dropped year on year during most of 2016, reflecting lower tourist spending and, to some extent, volatility in equity markets. Spending in February, usually a better month because of the Lunar New Year, was particularly weak in Hong Kong, China compared with other economies in East Asia. February retail sales were lower as well in the PRC than in the previous year, but sales held up well toward the end of the year. On average, consumption improved in line with rising consumer sentiment for the medium term. The ROK and Taipei,China, by comparison, enjoyed higher sales during February and saw this trend continue to December.

In Thailand, retail sales recovered after contracting during most of 2015. Retail sales continued to rise year on year in Malaysia and Viet Nam, sustained by rising incomes, but they fell in Singapore as spending on recreational goods, clothing and furniture, and other consumer goods slowed. In Indonesia, better macroeconomic and banking conditions, supported by relatively stable electricity rates and moderate gas and oil prices, helped boost retail sales.

Trends in industrial production reflect modest economic expansion in export-oriented economies. In East Asia, industrial production in 2016 rose by 6.0% in the PRC, 2.9% in the ROK, and 1.5% in Taipei,China, while it contracted by 0.4% in Hong Kong, China (Figure 1.1.7). Industrial expansion in Taipei,China came as a wide array of manufacturing industries such as electronics, electrical machinery, manufactured goods, and base and fabricated metals grew, fueled by

1.1.7 Industrial production index

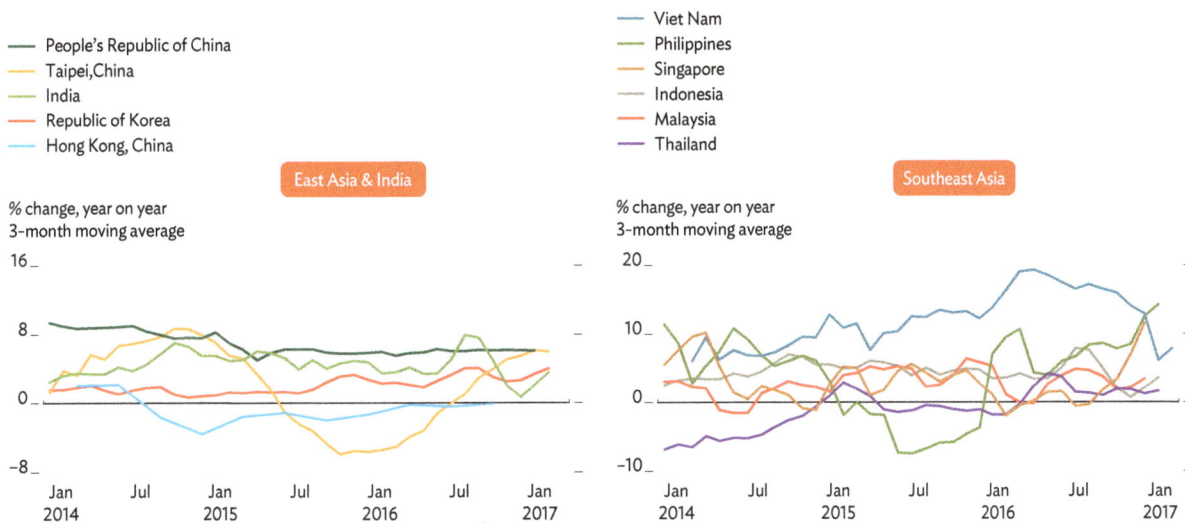

Legend (left):
People's Republic of China
Taipei,China
India
Republic of Korea
Hong Kong, China

Legend (right):
Viet Nam
Philippines
Singapore
Indonesia
Malaysia
Thailand

East Asia & India

% change, year on year
3-month moving average

Southeast Asia

% change, year on year
3-month moving average

Note: Data for Hong Kong, China refer to year-on-year quarterly percent change.
Sources: Haver Analytics; CEIC Data Company (both accessed 10 March 2017).

expansionary fiscal policies. Industrial production fluctuated in the ROK, rising toward the second quarter of 2016 and then falling in the third with a slump in the production of automobiles and mobile devices, but it remained generally positive. Lower car sales with the expiration of the government's excise tax cuts on passenger cars prompted car manufacturers to cut production—and strikes in some plants did the same. Meanwhile, the worldwide production halt and massive recall of a newly released Samsung phone caused output of mobile devices to fall. Industrial production held steady in the PRC thanks largely to a strong high-tech industry.

In Southeast Asia, industrial production was volatile, except in Viet Nam, where it fell steadily after February because of a steep decline in mining. Countering this decline were strong gains in processing and manufacturing that lifted overall production by 16.5%, up from 12.3% growth in 2015. Recovery in the Philippines and Thailand followed a contraction in 2015, while expansion in Singapore remained at 3.6% because of double-digit increases in electronic and pharmaceutical output in the last 2 months of the year. After posting solid gains in 2015, growth in Indonesian industrial production moderated to 4.0% in 2016 as performance varied across subsectors and spending by goods producers turned cautious. In Malaysia, production gains halved in 2016 from 4.5% in the previous year as mining output shrank and production fell for electrical and electronics products and for transport equipment.

Cautious spending by the private sector and uncertainty in both the domestic and the external environment weakened investment in most of the larger economies. Gross investment declined in India, the ROK, Malaysia, Singapore, and Thailand in 2016. Investment expansion in Indonesia, the Philippines, Viet Nam, Taipei,China, and Hong Kong, China came mainly from increased private sector investment, spurred by higher outlays for industrial machinery and equipment, construction, and inventories in anticipation of higher domestic activity later in the year (Figure 1.1.8). Investment growth in the PRC declined only slightly in 2016, reflecting the offsetting effects of lower industrial investment, rising infrastructure and real estate investment, and large outlays by emerging high-value technology firms.

Reform in India and the PRC to consolidate growth

India's economy continued to recover strongly. Its high dependence on oil imports meant it benefited from a large improvement in its terms of trade. Further, effective policy actions over the past year brought a new bankruptcy code, formalized an inflation-targeting framework, enacted constitutional changes to allow the implementation of a goods and services tax, and gradually lifted fuel subsidies. For the past 4 years or so, the economy has experienced a gradual cyclical recovery and is estimated to have grown by 7.1% in 2016. Favorable agricultural output aided by well-timed monsoon rains also supported growth. Stronger consumer demand even under gradual fiscal consolidation helped boost consumer sentiment.

India decided in November 2016 to withdrawal from circulation, or demonetize, Rs500 and Rs1,000 banknotes—about 86% of the currency in circulation by value—and replace them with new Rs500 and Rs2,000 notes. The decision was designed to trip up corruption, counterfeiting, and the funding of terrorism in the near term while, over the medium term, improving tax compliance and increasing the amount of savings channeled through the formal financial system. This initiative caused temporary disruption in sectors heavily dependent on cash. These disruptions, along with a continued slowdown in private investment and stabilization in oil prices, decelerated GDP growth from 7.9% in 2015 to 7.1%. The economy is expected to fully recover from demonetization in 2017 and grow at 7.4%. Over the medium term, structural policies already implemented should help maintain long-term GDP growth well above 7.0%.

Investment was sluggish in much of 2016 as private investment was weighed down by low capacity utilization and slow progress in deleveraging. Demonetization may have temporarily stalled investment plans in some sectors. Nonetheless, net foreign direct investment inflows in FY2016 rose by about 15%, reflecting steps to augment investment by simplifying guidelines and allowing foreign direct investment in sectors such as real estate, airport and air transport services, and e-commerce. Better business conditions going forward should improve investment prospects in general.

India's current account deficit has declined sharply in recent years with lower commodity prices, in particular for oil and gold, which together accounted for 27.3% of imports in 2016.

1.1.8 Contributions to investment growth in developing Asia

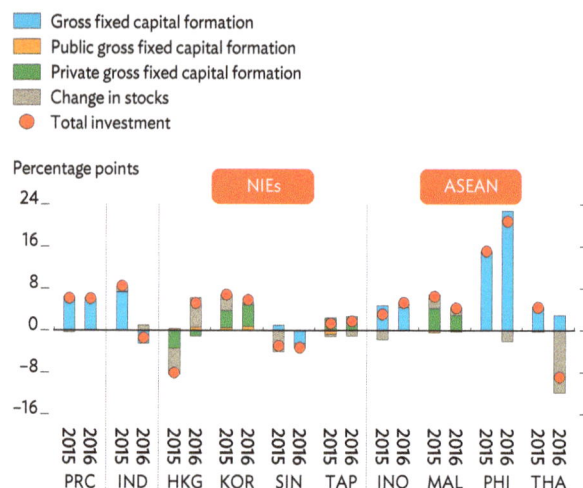

- Gross fixed capital formation
- Public gross fixed capital formation
- Private gross fixed capital formation
- Change in stocks
- Total investment

ASEAN = Association of Southeast Asian Nations, HKG = Hong Kong, China, INO = Indonesia, KOR = Republic of Korea, MAL = Malaysia, NIEs = newly industrialized economies, PHI = Philippines, PRC = People's Republic of China, SIN = Singapore, TAP = Taipei,China, THA = Thailand.
Sources: Haver Analytics; CEIC Data Company (both accessed 10 March 2017); ADB estimates.

External vulnerabilities are in check, while international reserves provide an adequate buffer, standing at $360 billion in late December 2016 and providing 8 months of import cover. Nonetheless, as commodity prices rebound, import demand strengthens, and foreign demand continues to decline, especially from the Gulf, the deficit is projected to expand a bit in the next 2 years. The current account deficit is expected to be comfortably financed by stable capital inflows.

Rebalancing in the PRC further moderated growth last year, and expansion in 2017 will likely slow a bit more with continuing structural reform. Growth has been decelerating steadily since 2010, slowing from 6.9% in 2015 to 6.7% as Asia's largest economy changes its development paradigm. On the supply side, services remained the main growth driver, with strong growth across many service industries. Real estate investment grew from a low base but was buoyed by the lowering of mortgage interest payments and down-payment requirements. The balance of payments weakened slightly in 2016 as exports of goods fell by 7.2% year on year, more steeply than the 4.5% drop in 2015. As exports are measured in US dollars, some of this drop reflects renminbi appreciation against the dollar in 2016.

More recent monthly data show industrial production growing steadily by 6% throughout 2016 as manufacturing expanded on spillover from an invigorated real estate market, a jump in car production, robust construction, and continued high electricity generation.

In India, industrial production shook off its malaise to expand in mid-2016, though industry expansion at 1% was well below the 6% recorded in the PRC in the fourth quarter (Figure 1.1.9). Merchandise export growth in India turned positive toward the end of 2016, and the purchasing managers' index turned positive for both the PRC and India in 2016, indicating renewed economic activity (Figure 1.1.10). The two major economies together account for almost 70% of regional GDP.

Growth is expected to remain strong in the near term in the PRC, helped by fiscal stimulus from infrastructure spending, robust credit growth, and strong real estate investment. However, slower progress with reining in credit and reforming state enterprises is a risk to medium-term growth. As the government is concerned about maintaining stability in financial and labor markets, it will not push for faster growth. Likewise, India's economy is expected to continue to record strong and broad growth, aided in part by favorable external demand. In both economies, momentum from strong growth in major export markets, the mild rebound of commodity prices, and robust public investment in particular present upside risks to the growth forecast.

1.1.9 Production indicators

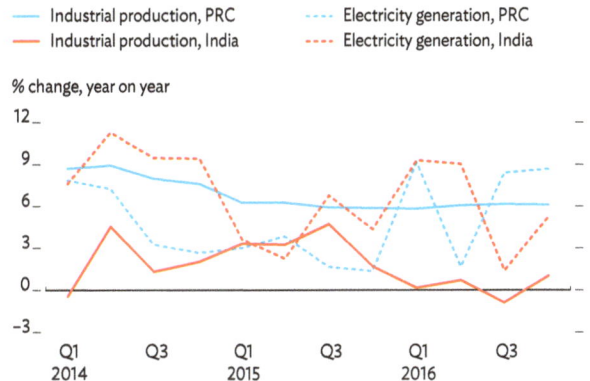

Industrial production, PRC
Industrial production, India
Electricity generation, PRC
Electricity generation, India

PRC = People's Republic of China, Q = quarter.
Source: CEIC Data Company (both accessed 13 March 2017).

1.1.10 Merchandise exports and purchasing managers' index

Exports growth, PRC
Exports growth, India
Purchasing managers' index, PRC
Purchasing managers' index, India

PRC = People's Republic of China.
Notes: For the purchasing managers' index, a value above 50 means expansion while below 50 is contraction.
Sources: Bloomberg; CEIC Data Company (both accessed 23 March 2017).

Inflation inches back up

Inflation was generally higher in 2016 than in 2015. However, many of the factors that kept inflation low in 2016, notably lackluster demand in the region and falling international prices for oil and other commodities, reversed in the second half of the year. The highest inflation rates occurred in Central Asia, particularly in Azerbaijan and Kazakhstan, where producer prices shot up in 2016 as a lagged result of currency depreciation by roughly half in 2015 and, toward the end of the year, as recovery in demand stabilized oil and food prices. Elsewhere, especially in Southeast Asia and in some newly industrialized economies, notably the ROK and Taipei,China, fiscal stimulus is helping to revive domestic demand. However, inflation is expected to remain generally low in East Asia and, to a lesser extent, in Southeast Asia. With inflation in single digits throughout these subregions in 2017, consumer and business expectations are for stable inflation.

Producer price indexes have been low to negative in some economies (Figure 1.1.11). However, monthly data suggest that producer price inflation, having lagged the consumer price index, began to creep up toward the end of 2016.

Substantial differences in inflation remain across the subregions. Inflation is still lowest in East Asia, in line with substantial moderation in growth over the past few years (Figure 1.1.12). Inflation rose in most subregions in 2016, the exceptions being Southeast Asia, where it slowed from 2.8% in 2015 to 2.1% mainly because inflation halved in Indonesia, and South Asia, where a very small decline largely reflected lower inflation in India. In South Asia and the Pacific, inflation was broadly steady below 5%. The biggest jump occurred in Central Asia, as sharp increases in Azerbaijan and Kazakhstan offset deceleration in most other economies.

Exports return to growth

After falling dramatically in 2015, merchandise exports have begun to recover, except in East Asia, where exports shrunk anew, most notably in the PRC, and in the Pacific, because of poor export performance by Papua New Guinea. Export earnings in Central Asia fell mainly because of the drop in commodity prices, but lower demand from trade partners had a role in the slow recovery in earnings for South Asia and Southeast Asia (Figure 1.1.13). With demand recovering in major trading partners, exports are expected to recover gradually in 2017 and 2018. It is still early days, but monthly merchandise exports have risen noticeably since the end of 2016 (Figure 1.1.14), reversing the trend of the past 2 years, particularly in the newly industrialized economies, the larger economies in Southeast Asia, and, as discussed above, the PRC and India. Moderating growth in the PRC has been partly responsible for the decline in exports over

1.1.11 Consumer and producer prices, 2016

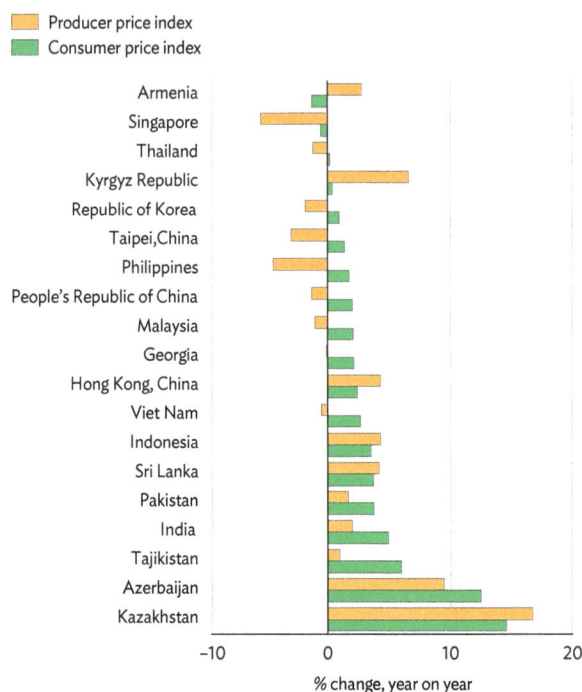

Note: India shows the wholesale price index, not the producer price index.
Sources: Haver Analytics; CEIC Data Company (both accessed 15 March 2017).

1.1.12 Subregional inflation

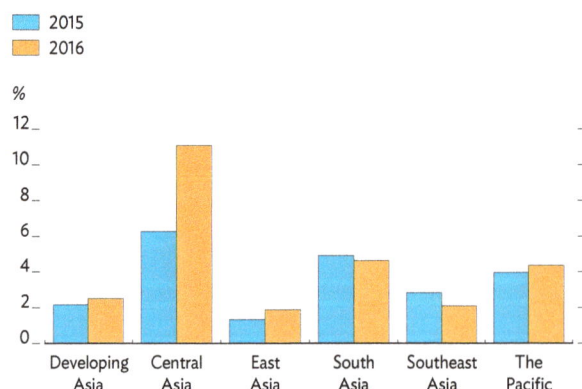

Source: Asian Development Outlook database.

the past 2 years, particularly from Singapore, the ROK, and Taipei,China (Figure 1.1.15), but the larger slowdown was in demand from other trading partners, mainly the major industrial economies.

Merchandise imports in 2016 were mixed by subregion (Figure 1.1.16). In Central Asia, a steep drop in imports resulted from slower growth and the lagged impact of large currency devaluation in Azerbaijan and Kazakhstan. Imports in East Asia also fell, mostly in the PRC, but less so than in 2015. In the other subregions, import growth resumed on recovering domestic demand after fairly steep declines in 2015 that partly reflected falling US dollar costs for commodity imports. The forecast for 2017 and 2018 is for import growth to accelerate as expansion in major trading partners outside of Asia remains steady and commodity prices inch up. Nonetheless, as discussed in more detail below in the section on risks, substantial uncertainty bedevils this forecast. That said, because many of the risk scenarios stem from possible policy changes in the European Union, PRC, and US, their impact is likely to be muted in 2017 but possibly affect trade flows in 2018.

The region's current account surplus narrowed to 2.3% in 2016, with East and Southeast Asia still showing significant surpluses (Figure 1.1.17). A narrower surplus for the PRC in 2017 and a slightly wider deficit in South Asia as imports to India rise will likely trim the region's surplus to the equivalent of 1.9% of GDP.

Asia and the Pacific continue to have a current account surplus vis-à-vis the rest of the world (Figure 1.1.18). In particular, the combined surpluses of the PRC and Japan roughly match the US deficit, with the rest of the world showing a combined surplus equal to 0.36% of world GDP in 2016. The surplus in developing Asia is expected to narrow somewhat, from 0.7% of global GDP in 2016 to less than 0.5% in 2017 and 2018. This will reflect lower net exports for the PRC as it progressively replaces outward-oriented growth with growth led by domestic consumption. Rebalancing towards smaller surpluses and deficits is a welcome trend for global financial stability.

Stable growth outlook continues

Growth in developing Asia will likely slow slightly this year and in 2018 as controlled deceleration in PRC growth continues, slightly offsetting robust growth elsewhere—a strong effect as GDP in the PRC accounts for 58% of regional GDP (Figure 1.1.19).

Despite growth moderation since 2010, developing Asia will still be the world's fastest-growing region and greatest contributor to global growth (Figure 1.1.20). Early in 2016, global economic uncertainty and meager expansion in the major industrial economies hampered export growth in economies with strong trade and financial links with

1.1.13 Export growth by subregion

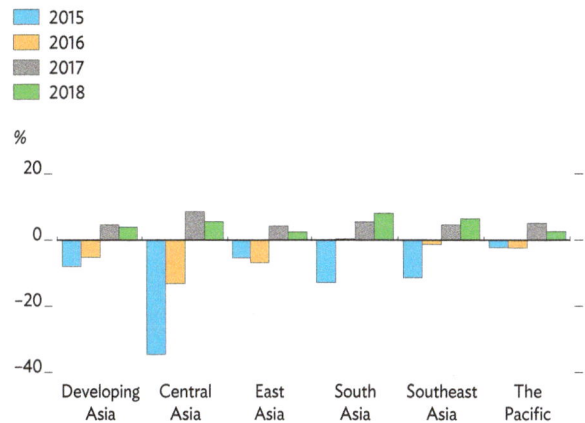

Source: Asian Development Outlook database.

1.1.14 Export growth, selected economies

ASEAN-5 = Indonesia, Malaysia, the Philippines, Thailand, and Viet Nam, NIEs = Republic of Korea, Singapore; Taipei,China, and Hong Kong, China.
Source: Asian Development Outlook database.

the West, but this trend is reversing. Higher exports will help the newly industrialized economies, which have grown more slowly than the rest of developing Asia because of their advanced stage of development (Box 1.1.2). Economies in the region can attain higher growth trajectories in the future through continued structural reform to boost productivity, support for domestic demand, and, particularly in South Asia, a better investment climate.

East Asian growth is expected to slow to 5.8% in 2017 and further to 5.6% in 2018, mirroring growth moderation in the PRC. The PRC is likely to grow by 6.5% in 2017 and 6.2% in 2018. Recent monthly data show infrastructure and real estate investment still strong. The desire to keep the medium-term growth strategy on track will require stable financial markets and employment, so the government will strive to avoid deviating from a smooth minor deceleration.

Though on a lower trajectory, growth in the PRC will reflect strong domestic consumption, solid wage growth, urban job creation, and public infrastructure investment. Downward pressure on PRC growth will continue to come from a declining working-age population, the ongoing shift toward consumption and services and away from investment and industry, and convergence with slower-growing high-income economies. However, structural reform to help ease growth in corporate and household debt can help offset these pressures, as discussed below. Despite continued monetary and fiscal support, growth in 2018 is expected to moderate to 6.2%.

South Asia's expansion is forecast at 7.0% in 2017 with faster recovery expected in India, and growth is forecast to rise further to 7.2% in 2018 as expansion in the rest of the region also accelerates. In India, government reform and ongoing deleveraging by private corporations will support recovery in investment, and the slight rise in growth prospects for the advanced economies will boost exports this year and next. Growth in 2018 is expected to accelerate slightly to 7.6%. As India's GDP is 80% of South Asian aggregate GDP, India's improved outlook dominates the subregional forecast, masking some uncertainty in Afghanistan and Pakistan.

In Southeast Asia, growth is forecast at 4.8% in 2017 and 5.0% in 2017, with Malaysia and Viet Nam recovering from slow growth in agricultural output and, in particular, a surge in public and private investment. Thailand is pursuing structural reform and will continue its public spending to boost productivity, which promises to lift growth slightly to 3.5% in 2017 and 3.6% in 2018. The Philippines is the only economy in Southeast Asia projected to see lower growth in 2017, as smaller remittances from the Gulf states and lower demand from trading partners offsets a healthy rise in domestic consumption and investment.

1.1.15 Change in exports to the People's Republic of China and others

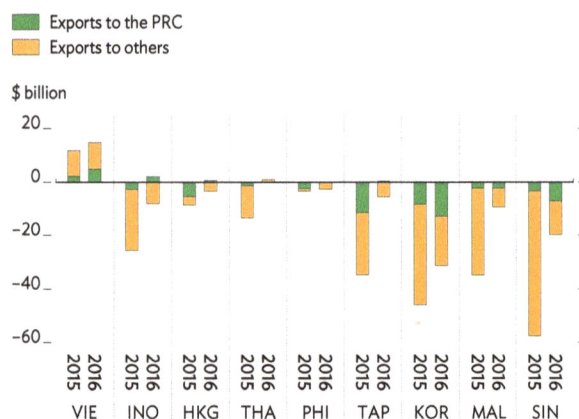

HKG = Hong Kong, China, INO = Indonesia, KOR = Republic of Korea, MAL = Malaysia, PHI = Philippines, PRC = People's Republic of China, SIN = Singapore, TAP = Taipei,China, THA = Thailand, VIE = Viet Nam.
Source: CEIC Data Company (accessed 13 March 2017).

1.1.16 Import growth by subregion

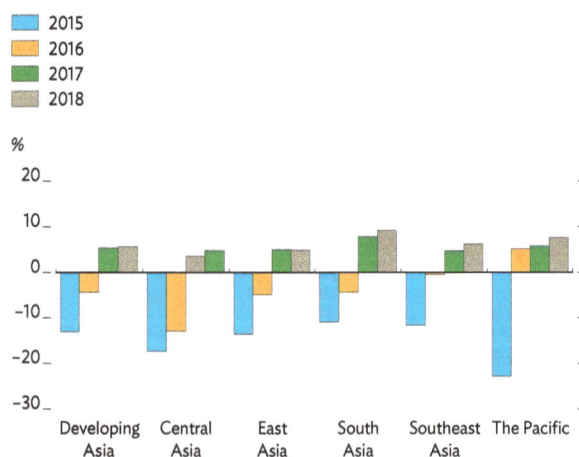

Source: Asian Development Outlook database.

1.1.2 Has high-income Asia converged?

Convergence occurs when poorer economies grow faster than richer ones, closing the income gap between them. As their incomes rise and the gap with the richest economies narrows, growth tends to slow. This is the case for the newly industrialized economies (NIEs) in Asia—the ROK, Singapore, Taipei,China, and Hong Kong, China—which experienced rapid growth in the 1960s and 1970s. Now, with average 2015 population-weighted per capita income at $28,824—which is 6.8 times greater than the $4,239 average in the rest of developing Asia—slower growth is the norm. Yet even at the slower growth pace, these economies continue to converge with the major industrial economies. The NIEs grew in the decade ending in 2016 at an average annual rate of 3.4%, which is 4 times growth in the major industrialized economies, but much less than the 7.8% average in the rest of developing Asia (box figure 1).

1 Average growth and per capita income, the newly industrialized economies versus the rest of developing Asia

10-year average GDP growth, %

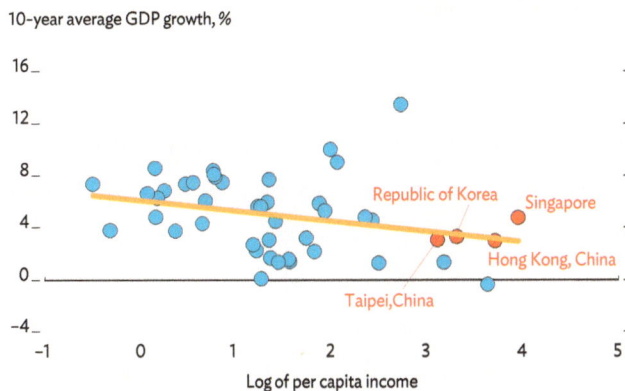

Sources: World Bank. World Development Indicators online database; Haver Analytics (both accessed 27 March 2017); *Asian Development Outlook* database.

Despite the different growth rates, spillover from the slowdown in external demand from the PRC and the major industrial economies affected the NIEs as much as it did the rest of developing Asia because of their high dependence on exports. The NIEs were well equipped to weather these shocks, however, with their healthy fiscal positions and well-regulated financial systems. Indeed, all the NIEs provided fiscal stimulus to some extent in 2015 and 2016 as growth slowed (box figure 2).

Going forward, lower potential growth rates in the NIEs relative to the rest of developing Asia will reflect reduced labor supply because of changing demographic factors such as aging populations and higher dependency ratios, and their response by shifting production toward high technology. The NIEs are expected to grow by 2.3% in 2017

2 Growth in the newly industrialized economies

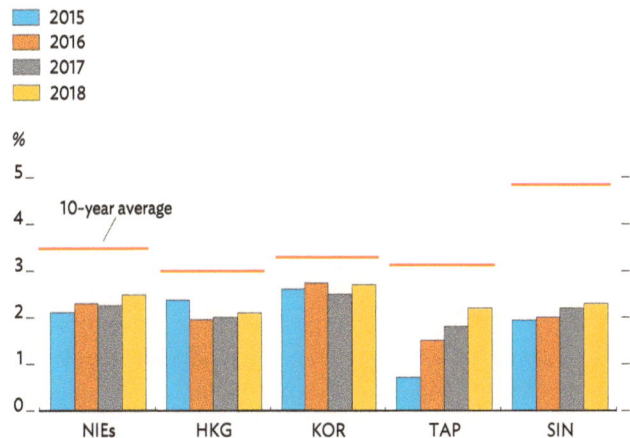

HKG = Hong Kong, China, KOR = Republic of Korea, NIEs = newly industrialized economies, SIN = Singapore, TAP = Taipei,China.
Source: Asian Development Outlook database.

and 2.5% in 2018 as the rest of developing Asia grows by 6.3% and then 6.2%.

Hong Kong, China depends heavily on services in its role as a trading and financial hub. This makes it vulnerable to volatility in global financial markets, unexpected changes in demand from the PRC, and US interest rate hikes that are higher than expected, especially as it would have to raise its own interest rates to avoid putting too much stress on its exchange rate link to the US dollar.

The ROK has seen growth weakened considerably over the past 3 years by lower external demand, as exports make up more than half of GDP. Uncertainty brought on by political troubles dampened consumer demand in 2016 and will do the same in the first part of 2017. The ROK faces a number of structural challenges, including an impending decline in its working–age population, a limited social safety net for its stage of development, a need for corporate restructuring, and high household debt.

Singapore's average growth in the past 3 years has slowed partly from structural factors such as restrictions on foreign worker inflows but also slow trade growth and soft manufacturing as low oil prices hit its refining industry. Economic support is expected from increased fiscal outlays to improve public services and investment incentives for high-tech manufacturing.

Taipei,China has also struggled with lower trade growth and shifting demographics. The authorities have expanded infrastructure spending through an ambitious new industrial strategy. The plan is to develop a program of investment in high technology.

In sum, with inflation below 2.5%, the short-term outlook for the NIEs is robust.

Central Asia will reverse its growth slowdown and accelerate expansion in the next 2 years with recovering oil prices and higher export demand following currency depreciation in 2015 in Azerbaijan and Kazakhstan. Growth is expected to quicken to 3.1% in 2017 and 3.5% in 2018.

The Pacific is seen improving its aggregate growth rate to 2.9% in 2017 and further to 3.3% in 2018, mostly on account of the economic recovery in Papua New Guinea, the subregion's largest economy. Fiji and Vanuatu are recovering from natural disasters in 2015.

Growth in the NIEs will slow marginally in line with deceleration in the PRC, to 2.2% in 2017 and then rising to 2.5% in 2018. Growth is expected to rise in particular in Singapore and Taipei,China as government investment in infrastructure and higher growth in manufacturing and electronics boosts these economies. However, growth in Hong Kong, China will be a modest 2.0% in 2017 as services are not expected to recover quickly and the economy is very susceptible to changes in monetary policy and the value of the US dollar—and, for that matter, to any financial developments in the US. In the ROK, the political uncertainty that suppressed domestic demand in 2016 is expected to dispel somewhat by mid-2017, and export-led growth should resume in 2018.

Regional inflation is projected to accelerate from 2.5% last year to 3.0% this year and 3.2% in 2018 because of rising global commodity prices and consumer demand. In the PRC, strong credit and household income growth will, along with the fiscal stimulus from infrastructure spending, underpin growth in domestic demand. Inflation in the PRC will thus accelerate at a similar pace, from 2.0% last year to 2.4% this year and 2.8% in 2018. South Asia in particular will see demand prod inflation from 4.6% last year to 5.2% this year, rising a bit further to 5.4% in 2018. A few commodity exporters in Central Asia will continue to experience inflation approaching 10% as the effects of earlier currency depreciation pass through from imports to consumer prices. A rise in the Pacific will be led by higher inflation in Papua New Guinea, resulting from higher growth and the expected return of gold and copper mines to full production capacity.

Risks to the outlook

Risks to the outlook seem to come from all directions yet not really from anywhere. An eventful 2016 brought a US presidential election fraught with potential policy change, the historic Brexit referendum, and sudden demonetization in India. Yet these events seem so far to have had only minor short-term effects on consumer and business confidence. The resumption of growth in the advanced economies and in developing Asia, and the corresponding rise in exports indicated in very recent data, suggest that the output gap in the US has closed,

1.1.17 Current account balance by subregion

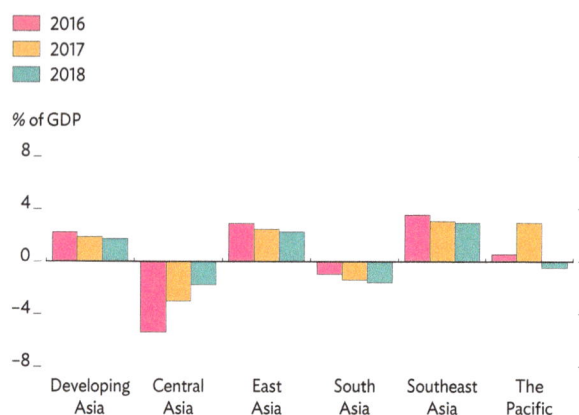

Source: *Asian Development Outlook* database.

1.1.18 World current account balance

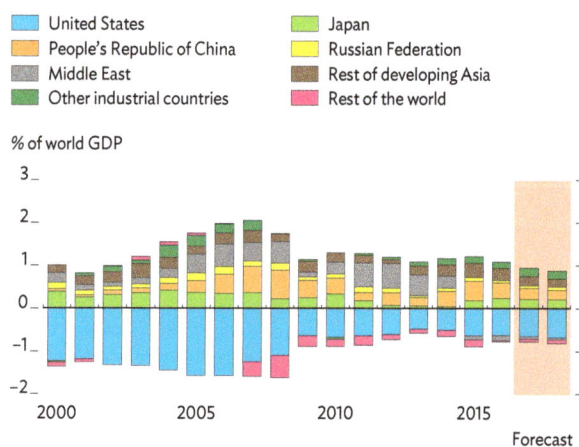

Sources: International Monetary Fund. 2016. *World Economic Outlook* database. October. www.imf.org; Haver Analytics (both accessed 14 March 2017).

making future interest rate hikes there more certain. Markets have already factored in this apparent inevitability, and the baseline forecast assumes a modest rise in interest rates.

The forecast faces four main risks that could undermine developing Asia's growth trajectory, but the region as a whole can easily manage them over the short term. The first involves monetary tightening in the US and an ensuing response from Asian central banks to avoid capital outflows. The second risk is that abrupt changes in financial flows could imperil highly indebted corporations and households. The impact of higher interest rates in the US on the region's economies, and on rapidly rising household debt, are analyzed in the following section. The third risk is sudden shifts in trade and tax policies in the major industrial economies. The final risk—a less likely one—is oil price recovery that is weaker than expected.

The first risk to the forecast comes from higher-than-expected real interest rates in the US and further slight appreciation of the dollar against many Asian currencies. This could cause asset prices to plunge and private capital to flow out of emerging Asia in search of higher returns elsewhere. A sudden shift would be destabilizing and possibly erode consumer confidence. If, on the other hand, rate changes come gradually, central banks in the region will have sufficient time to respond by tightening monetary policy without undermining balanced growth.

A second risk, related to the first, comes from unexpectedly sharp interest rate hikes in the US and Europe, which could affect highly leveraged corporations and governments in the region. Such corporations in large economies are vulnerable to sudden shifts in asset prices that could undermine their ability to service debt. Moreover, economies in the region with growing household debt may see households spend less in response to higher debt servicing obligations, undermining heretofore strong growth in consumer demand.

A third uncertainty comes from possible shifts in US tax and trade policy. The new administration withdrew from the Trans-Pacific Partnership, has called for the renegotiation of the North American Free Trade Agreement, and has raised the possibility of stiff tariff increases. If stiff taxes and tariffs are implemented, however, they would likely take effect in mid-2018 at the earliest. The immediate risk is that rising rhetoric could encourage beggar-thy-neighbor tendencies outside of developing Asia that squelch international trade to the benefit of large domestic conglomerates, particularly in South and Southeast Asia. No one can say how great the impact will be or where it will be felt, especially as most manufactures and traded services are produced by global value chains present in different parts of the world. Thus, policy-induced volatility may be spread around enough to have only limited impact on any particular economy, but trade would likely decline overall if the risk materializes.

1.1.19 GDP growth by subregion

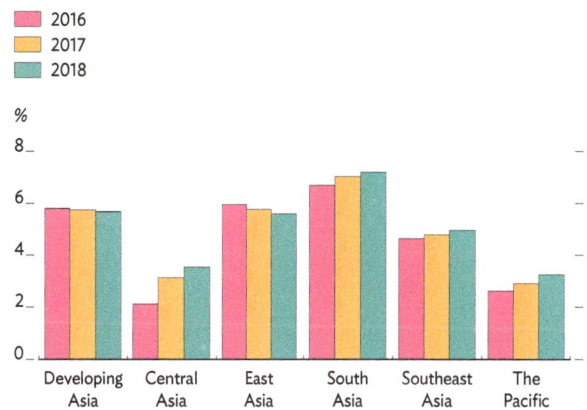

Source: *Asian Development Outlook* database.

1.1.20 GDP growth, developing economies

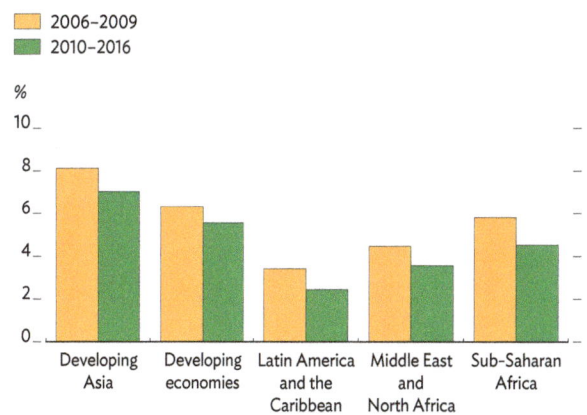

Note: Latin America and the Caribbean, Middle East and North Africa, and Sub-Saharan Africa are classifications in the International Monetary Fund's *World Economic Outlook* database. "Developing economies" combine these regions with developing Asia.

Sources: International Monetary Fund, *World Economic Outlook* database, October 2016; *Asian Development Outlook* database; ADB estimates.

The final risk involves oil prices. The baseline assumptions call for a mild and steady rise in the price of Brent crude oil, averaging $56/barrel in 2017 and $58/barrel in 2018. However, anticipated deregulation of supply in the US—including the opening of the Keystone pipeline, which will allow the fast delivery of Canadian crude to oil refineries along the Gulf Coast for export to Latin America, may increase global output enough to undo the supply cutback agreed in late-2016 by the Organization of the Petroleum Exporting Countries. Developing Asia as a whole is a net importer of oil and other commodities, so low oil prices would help keep oil import bills in check, which is of particular importance to India, the Philippines, and the NIEs. On the other hand, continued low prices would delay fragile recovery in oil and gas exporters in Central Asia and the Pacific.

The following pages address the first two risks, those connected with monetary policy, and develop detailed scenarios for developing Asia if they were to materialize. Sharply higher US interest rates would likely affect the region through two channels. The first would be spillover affecting exchange rates, which would play out in different ways across Asia depending on the exchange rate regime. Economies with more flexible exchange rates would likely become more competitive at the expense of their less flexible competitors, but probably at the cost of unwelcome inflation. The second channel would be abrupt capital outflows from the region in search of higher returns. This could destabilize financial sectors in some regional economies, particularly those with high corporate and consumer debt, but central banks would likely be able to respond promptly and effectively.

Risk of sharper US interest rate hikes

Before the March 2017 increase in the Fed funds rate, the US Federal Reserve had raised its benchmark policy interest rate only twice since it set the rate at its historic low in October 2008. The first hike was in December 2015 and the second in December 2016. On all three occasions, the Fed funds rate was raised by only 25 basis points, which still leaves it ultralow, perpetuating accommodative monetary policy. The question remains: How fast will the Fed raise interest rates going forward? The opinion of the Federal Open Market Committee is fluid. It projected in March last year much faster interest rate increases for 2017 and 2018 than it did in March this year (Figure 1.2.1). If, however, emerging economic conditions warrant a trajectory of steep policy rate rises—one more like the March 2016 projection than the March 2017 projection—the effects will ripple across the global economy and affect the outlook for developing Asia.

1.2.1 Range of Fed interest rate projections, March 2016 versus March 2017

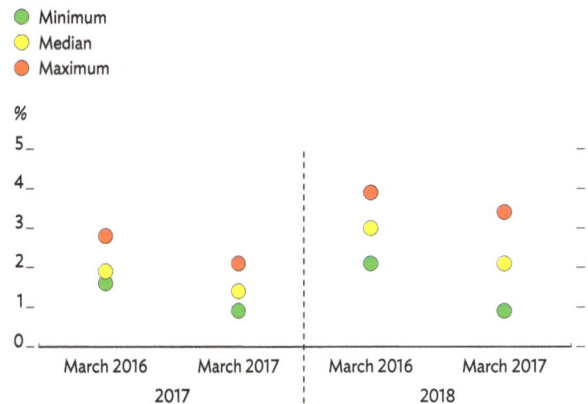

Sources: Board of Governors of the Federal Reserve System, Federal Open Market Committee. March 2016 and March 2017.

How fast will the Fed normalize rates?

The most recent Fed funds rate increase did little to quell a debate about whether the Fed is behind the curve in its monetary policy. Some analysts argue that recent trends, bringing higher inflation and lower unemployment as the economy recovers, leave the current interest rate too low if one considers lessons learned in an inflation surge in the mid-1960s. Others agree that Fed's current policy is behind the curve but base their assessment on the Taylor Rule. Introduced in Taylor (1993), it describes a likely policy rate given the deviation of inflation from its target, the neutral interest rate (the equilibrium real interest rate when the economy is operating at its potential), and the deviation of output from its potential or trend.

Fed policy makers have repeatedly countered that their monetary policy is responsive to data. Some observers agree. In an historical analysis of error in forecasts of the Fed funds rate, Nechio and Rudebusch (2016) argued that the rates set by the Fed in 2016 were not unusually low relative to what was projected at the end of 2015. That is, the distance between the policy rate and its higher projection appears to be consistent with what the Fed has done historically in response to evolving economic data. It also argued that the neutral interest rate is currently lower than what it was in Taylor (1993). Therefore, it concludes, with appropriate adjustments to the interest rate policy rule, the Fed does not seem to be behind the curve.

While the debate on this issue is inconclusive, a look at how the Fed policy rate has related to inflation in the recent past provides valuable insights about the likely future trend for the Fed funds rate.

Following the burst of the dot-com bubble in early 2001, the Fed slashed its benchmark interest rate repeatedly to stimulate the economy. The Fed funds rate fell from 6.5% in December 2000 to a low of 1.0% in June 2003 (Figure 1.2.2). As inflationary pressures returned in mid-2004, the Fed actively lifted its benchmark policy interest rate. Within 2 years, the Fed funds rate was raised by 425 basis points. This period of low interest rates had passed, but not before it contributed to the housing bubble that eventually triggered the global financial crisis of 2008–2009.

In response to the global financial crisis of 2008–2009, the Fed again aggressively brought down its benchmark interest rate to an historic low approaching zero percent and then kept it there until the end of 2015. During this episode, international oil prices reached more than $100/barrel and caused headline inflation in the US to shoot up. Inflation was seen as externally driven, however, at a time of benign domestic price pressures. It therefore did not trigger a policy reaction from the Fed. When international oil prices fell in 2015, headline inflation in the US followed suit.

Although oil prices have not climbed back up to anywhere near their peak in 2011–2014, US inflation has recently been back on the rise, suggesting that domestic factors have a role in pushing up aggregate prices. Under these circumstances, the Fed can be expected to start raising its benchmark rate, but the speed at which US interest rates will rise remains an open question. The *Asian Development Outlook 2017* (*ADO 2017*) baseline assumptions have the Fed funds rate increasing only gradually to the forecast horizon (Figure 1.2.2). A much faster increase in interest rates is possible, however, especially if concerns of a repeat financial crisis come to the fore. If this were to happen, what would the global implications be?

Modeling spillover from US monetary policy

The following pages consider two alternative scenarios to the *ADO 2017* baseline with faster US interest rate hikes. The analysis examines each scenario's first-round effects, should they materialize, on economies other than the US. The two alternative simulations are conducted using the Global Projection Model appropriately calibrated to accommodate *ADO 2017* baseline assumptions (Box 1.2.1). Discussion begins with the scenario of interest rate increases accelerating independently, then follows up with a scenario in which acceleration is induced by a large increase in aggregate demand in the US. The analysis suggests that neither scenario is likely to materialize.

Faster hikes in US interest rates

To model US interest rate hikes occurring much faster than expected, the assumptions mirror the period observed prior to the global financial crisis of 2008–2009, which saw interest rates raised by 425 basis points over 2 years. The target range of the Fed funds rate is assumed to be

1.2.2 Interest rate and inflation, United States

- Headline inflation
- Interest rate
- Interest rate in the *ADO 2017* baseline

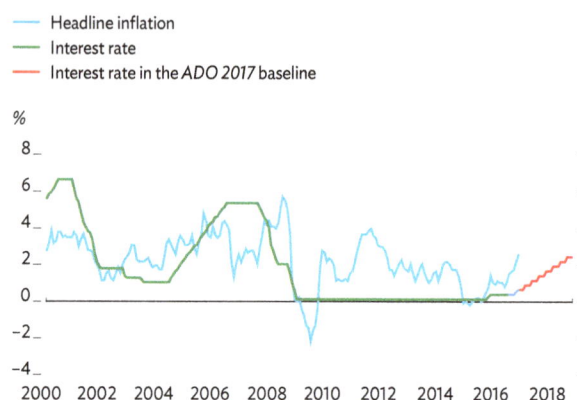

Sources: Haver Analytics (accessed 24 March 2017); ADB estimates.

1.2.1 The Global Projection Model

The Global Projection Model (GPM7) is a quarterly model for seven global regions currently used by many central banks and international organizations for forecasting and policy analysis.[a] The regional blocks covered by GPM7—the US, the euro area, Japan, the PRC, Latin America, emerging Asia (excluding the PRC), and "remaining countries"—together account for 85% of global GDP. Emerging Asia consists of India, Indonesia, the ROK, Malaysia, the Philippines, Singapore, Thailand, Taipei,China, and Hong Kong, China. The PRC and emerging Asia together account for over 90% of developing Asia's GDP in purchasing power parity terms. GPM7 focuses on a few variables that interest policy makers the most: output, inflation, interest rates, exchange rates, and global commodity prices.

Each region is described by four behavioral equations familiar and interpretable to policy makers: an output gap equation that measures the difference between actual and potential GDP, a Philips curve that shows the inverse relationship between the unemployment rate and the inflation rate, a Taylor rule that stipulates how much a monetary authority should change the nominal interest rate in response to changes in inflation and output, and an uncovered interest parity condition with risk premiums, which links real interest rates with real exchange rates.

For the advanced economies—the European Union, Japan, and the US—the model also incorporates linkages between finance and the real economy by including relevant indicators of bank lending tightness. These linkages can proxy for global financial shocks as they can be correlated across regions and have spillover beyond the advanced economies. The PRC is modeled somewhat differently from other regions as interest rate and exchange rate responses have historically been more persistent than in other economies.

GPM7 is often described as a "gap model" because it uses deviations from equilibrium values—potential output, the nonaccelerating inflation rate of unemployment, the equilibrium real interest rate, and the equilibrium real exchange rate—in the behavioral equations mentioned above. Equilibrium values are unobserved and specified as stochastic processes, with lead–lag structures and stochastic shocks to both levels and growth rates. Finally, GPM7 includes world commodity prices for oil, food, and metals, which are functions of the world output gap and affect inflation and output across regions.

[a] GPM7 was developed and is maintained by the International Monetary Fund and Centre pour la Recherche Économique et ses Applications with support from a network of members in many countries. The approach used in GPM7, which is described in detail in Blagrave et al. (2013), attempts to strike a balance between fully micro-founded dynamic stochastic general equilibrium models, which are theoretically sound but only at the cost of empirical accuracy, and time-series models, which are empirically accurate but only at the cost of theoretical consistency.

Source: Blagrave P., P. Elliott, R. Garcia-Saltos, D. Hostland, D. Laxton, and F. Zhang. 2013. *IMF Working Paper* 13/256. International Monetary Fund. www.imf.org/external/pubs/ft/wp/2013/wp13256.pdf

hiked to 4.75%–5.00% by the end of 2018 with rate increases especially fast in the last 3 quarters of 2017, followed by a more measured distribution of hikes in 2018 (Figure 1.2.3).

Table 1.2.1 shows the likely consequences of the shocks in terms of GDP growth and inflation deviating from *ADO 2017* baseline assumptions. Much more rapid interest rate increases in the US would squeeze liquidity in the domestic market and bring down inflation within the forecast horizon. The combination of higher interest rates and lower domestic inflation would cause the US dollar to appreciate against other currencies as demand for the currency grows.

This faster pace of US interest rate hikes would be costly for the US. The model indicates that, relative to the *ADO 2017* baseline projection, GDP growth would be suppressed by 0.2 percentage points in 2017 and slashed by 0.6 percentage points in 2018. Such deductions from growth would risk widening the output gap and hurting economic recovery, which would contradict the Fed policy of sustaining healthy economic growth. Consequently, a faster hike in US interest rates is unlikely, occupying on the risk curve a distant point at the tail end.

1.2.3 US interest rates, baseline assumption versus faster hike scenario

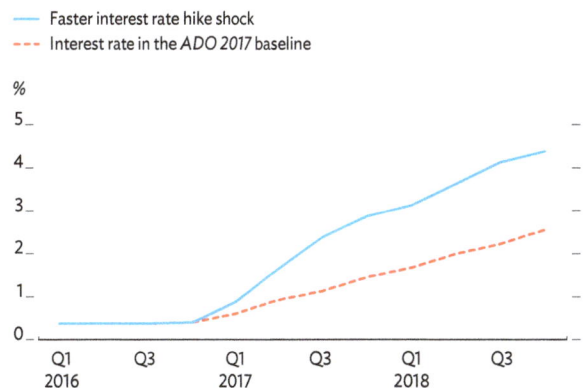

Q = quarter.
Source: ADB estimates.

1.2.1 Effects of faster US interest rate hikes
(deviations from the baseline, percentage points)

	GDP		Inflation	
	2017	2018	2017	2018
United States	−0.2	−0.6	−0.1	−0.5
Euro area	0.0	0.1	0.0	0.1
Japan	0.0	0.0	0.0	0.1
People's Republic of China	0.0	−0.2	0.0	0.0
Emerging Asia	0.0	0.1	0.1	0.4

Note: Emerging Asia includes India, Indonesia, the Republic of Korea, Malaysia, the Philippines, Singapore, Thailand, Taipei,China, and Hong Kong, China.
Sources: Asian Development Outlook database; ADB estimates.

Assuming this tail-end risk nevertheless materializes, the euro area and Japan would not be substantially affected, as they would maintain their easy monetary policy to keep stimulating growth in their own economies. GDP growth and inflation would not deviate much from what the baseline suggests (Table 1.2.1). Interest rate differentials would likely induce capital flight, causing the euro and the yen to depreciate against the US dollar. This would eventually improve real effective exchange rates in the euro area and Japan and thus their price competitiveness against the US and other economies with less responsive exchange rates.

The likely implications for emerging Asia are slightly different. Economies that manage their currencies to maintain a stable exchange rate vis-à-vis the US dollar, like the PRC for example, would tend to experience less currency depreciation than those that historically have experienced more volatile currency movements. While dampening excessive currency volatility helps manage country risks, these economies would tend to lose out in terms of price competitiveness and have to sacrifice part of their global market share to economies with more exposed currencies.

Most economies in emerging Asia have flexible exchange rates. Consequently, they would tend to be among those that benefit from improved real effective exchange rates. However, this benefit comes with a cost. As most economies in emerging Asia already operate at or near their potential, inflation would shoot up rapidly in line with a faster rate of currency depreciation. This might imperil domestic economic stability, requiring the authorities to tighten domestic liquidity.

Interest rate hikes induced by aggregate demand

A somewhat more likely scenario is that faster US interest rate increases occur in response to a surge in aggregate demand. The new US administration intends to raise the annual growth rate to 3.5%–4.0%. To assess the implications of such a boost to the economy, the analysis assumes faster growth in the US starting in the third quarter of 2017 that lifts GDP growth by almost 0.2 percentage points above the baseline for that year and brings the growth rate to 3.5% in 2018, or 1.1 percentage points above the baseline projection (Figure 1.2.4).

An aggregate demand shock raises inflation by about 0.4 percentage points in 2018 above the baseline (the blue bar in Figure 1.2.4b). To fend off such inflationary pressure, the Fed is assumed to raise interest rates at the same rate as the independent interest rate shock discussed above. This move from the Fed mitigates the inflationary effect of the aggregate demand shock but at the cost of slower growth (the orange bars in Figure 1.2.4a). After the Fed's response, US growth in 2018 will be up by only about 0.5 percentage points from the baseline, but with inflation relatively unaffected.

The aggregate demand shock in the US would tend to strengthen the US dollar further. Absent any worsening of trade friction globally, this should benefit US trade partners and stimulate growth elsewhere, including in Asia. This effect could be accompanied by intensified inflationary pressure in economies whose currencies depreciate. The global implications of the Fed's faster interest rate increases in response to domestic demand pressures in the US are similar to the effects discussed above in the section *Faster Hikes in US Interest Rates*. In short, the benefit of increased aggregate demand accompanied by faster monetary tightening in the US would be shared unevenly by trading partners depending on how rigid their exchange rates were, and the inflationary cost of resulting currency movements would tend to be greater in economies that already operated at or near their potential.

A catch is that a surge in aggregate demand in the US would not necessarily follow from a public spending binge there, which itself is less than likely given the slow pace of the budgetary approval process, particularly when considering appropriations large enough to deliver a surge in aggregate demand of the magnitude envisaged here.

Accelerated capital outflow from Asia?

This analysis argues that, absent any domestic policy responses, economies with more flexible exchange rate regimes and more open capital accounts would tend to benefit at the expense of those with more closely managed currencies. As the open economies became more price competitive in trade, the managed economies would sacrifice global market share.

Such an outcome would call for policy responses in economies outside the US. The responses would complicate economic relations globally, but these second-round effects are beyond the scope of this analysis. An obvious possible response would be intervention to adjust the exchange rate to maintain price competitiveness. This is consistent with Benigno et al. (2016), for example, which argues that an exchange rate policy that has no cost in terms of efficiency may be the best option. However, this analysis also shows that policy intended to limit the unwanted implications of currency depreciation may be required when exchange rate policy does entail efficiency costs such as a surge

1.2.4 Effects of US aggregate demand boost

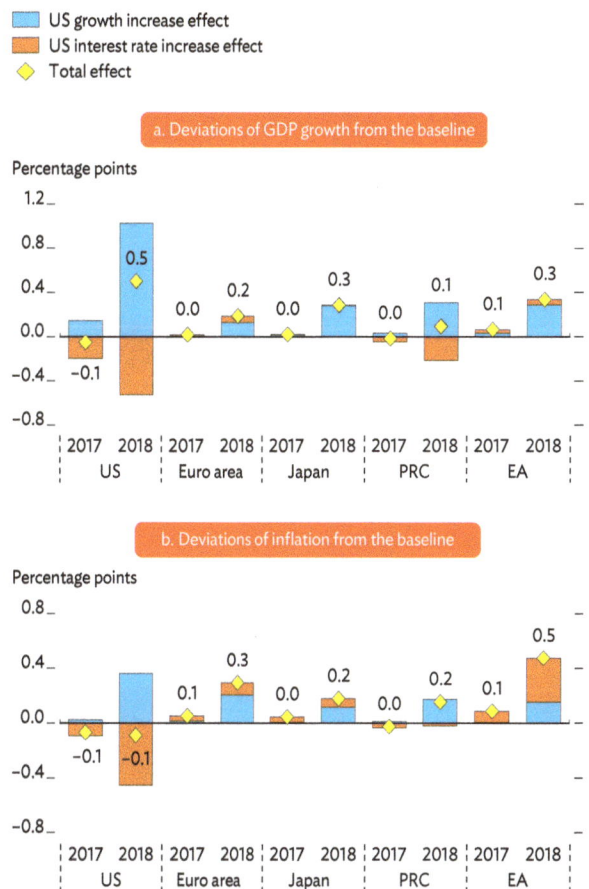

■ US growth increase effect
■ US interest rate increase effect
◆ Total effect

a. Deviations of GDP growth from the baseline

EA = emerging Asia, PRC = People's Republic of China, US = United States.
Note: Emerging Asia includes India, Indonesia, the Republic of Korea, Malaysia, the Philippines, Singapore, Thailand, Taipei,China, and Hong Kong, China.
Sources: Asian Development Outlook database; ADB estimates.

in inflation. The inflationary impact of such policies, for example, may then be addressed through appropriate adjustments to monetary and fiscal policies.

Faster interest rate hikes in the US could further drain foreign investment from emerging Asia but to varying degrees in individual economies. As international capital flows are typically sensitive to the US dollar exchange rate, different rates of currency depreciation may influence the volume and destinations of capital flows. A multitude of factors may enter into an explanation for this trend, but investment movements are essentially driven by changes in expected returns, which depend fundamentally on expected movements in interest and exchange rates.

Capital flows and financial risks

The normalization of US monetary policy discussed in the preceding section raises the prospect of capital outflows from developing Asia. If Asian central banks follow suit and raise their own interest rates, highly leveraged households could be compromised, posing a risk to financial stability. However, the risks from capital flows and household debt appear to be manageable in the short term, and continued vigilance by policy makers promises to further strengthen financial stability and resilience.

Region facing capital outflows

Higher US interest rates may pose risks to financial stability in emerging Asia. Along with better US economic prospects, higher interest rates and a consequently strong US dollar may tilt global investor sentiment such that capital flows out of Asian markets, exerting downward pressure on asset prices in emerging Asia. Because international capital flows are sensitive to the US dollar exchange rate, emerging Asia has in the past experienced net capital inflows when the dollar was weak and, this time since the second half of 2014, outflows when the dollar strengthened (Figure 1.3.1a). Additional interest rate hikes in the US could further drain foreign investment from emerging Asia.

Net capital flows to large economies in emerging Asia—the PRC, India, Indonesia, the ROK, Malaysia, the Philippines, Singapore, Thailand, Viet Nam, Taipei,China, and Hong Kong, China—have declined since the second quarter of 2014. While net flows of foreign direct investment (FDI) into the region held up initially, they too started to reverse and flow out of the region beginning in the second half of 2015. This last episode of capital outflow has notably affected the PRC but not every other economy in emerging Asia, some of which were still receiving positive net flows of FDI in the third quarter of 2016.

Capital began flowing out of the PRC in the second quarter of 2014 in the amount of $35 billion that quarter. Outflows picked up the pace to exceed $130 billion in the third quarter of 2016 (Figure 1.3.1b). Most of these outflows involved banking activities (the "other investments" category) and portfolio investment. Since the second half of 2015, they have included net outflows of FDI. In the rest of emerging Asia, net portfolio outflows amounted to $38 billion in the third quarter of 2016. However, FDI recorded a

1.3.1 Capital flows from selected Asian economies

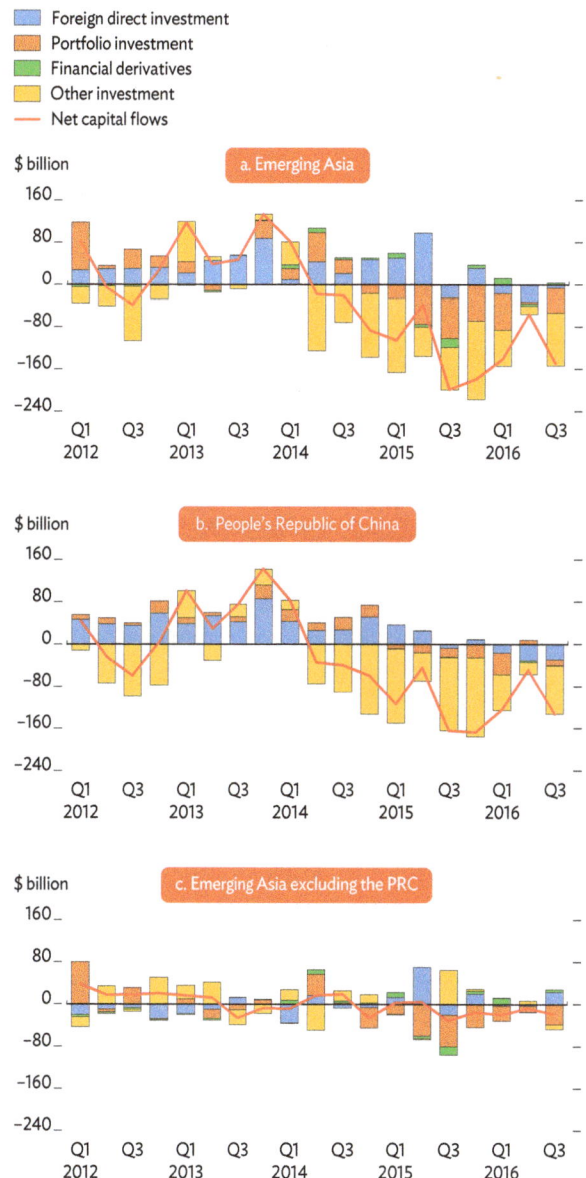

- Foreign direct investment
- Portfolio investment
- Financial derivatives
- Other investment
- Net capital flows

a. Emerging Asia

b. People's Republic of China

c. Emerging Asia excluding the PRC

PRC = People's Republic of China, Q = quarter.
Note: Emerging Asia includes the PRC, India, Indonesia, the Republic of Korea, Malaysia, the Philippines, Singapore, Thailand, Viet Nam, Taipei,China, and Hong Kong, China.
Source: Haver Analytics (accessed 24 March 2017).

net inflow of $24 billion during the quarter, reducing the total net outflow to $19 billion after accounting for outflows from banking activities (Figure 1.3.1c). Despite the broad negative trend in net flows, some variation has occurred in emerging Asia. India, Indonesia, and Singapore received net capital inflows after recovering in the fourth quarter of 2013 from investors' response to the Federal Reserve announcement that it was tapering purchases of government and mortgage-backed securities. Viet Nam has received net inflows as well since the fourth quarter of 2015. India, Indonesia, and Viet Nam are still benefiting from net flows of FDI into their economies.

Net capital outflows from economies in emerging Asia are expected to continue this year and next. The *Asia Bond Monitor* (ADB 2017) identifies three potential risks to Asia's financial stability. First, a pickup in the global economy, particularly in the US, and uncertainty surrounding the global economic landscape will become a key theme for investors in 2017. Second, policy and political uncertainty in the US and the euro area may influence the global economic outlook and become a key risk to financial markets in emerging Asia. Third, although unlikely, a sharp depreciation of the PRC renminbi would pose a risk to economies and financial markets elsewhere in emerging East Asia.

Higher US interest rates may exert further downward pressure on local currencies. Although many regional authorities are adopting a wait-and-see approach and keeping their monetary policy stable, worsening depreciation pressures may push central banks to tighten their domestic monetary stance. Because many emerging Asian economies have accumulated substantial foreign and local currency debt in the low-interest-rate environment prevailing since the global financial crisis, the possible tightening of monetary policy could undermine their financial stability. Higher domestic interest rates may also add pressure on highly leveraged households in Asia (see below). Nevertheless, solid economic prospects and sufficient international reserves should cushion the impact of possible shocks.

Emerging Asia faces uncertainty concerning the domestic monetary stance of many economies that have lowered policy rates over the past 2 years to support investment and growth. Tighter monetary policy in the US may affect these economies, especially those with open capital accounts and flexible exchange rate regimes. If currency depreciation accelerates, central banks may want to follow the Fed in tightening policy. Policy rates in emerging Asia have historically been strongly correlated as common external shocks elicited parallel responses, and now with growing regional integration. Rising interest rates may adversely affect liquidity across the region. At the same time, the authorities in emerging Asia may want to delay monetary tightening to maintain growth momentum. Although emerging Asia faces risks from an uncertain liquidity environment, they appear to be manageable in the short term. Moreover, differences in monetary policy among the major industrial economies suggest that the era of easy global liquidity may not yet be over.

Concerns over political and policy uncertainty in the US and the euro area have influenced the global economic outlook, creating risks for financial markets in emerging Asia. The new US administration has mooted possible radical changes to tax and trade policies, raising questions about US commitment to the open movement of goods and capital. The United Kingdom invoked Article 50 of the Lisbon Treaty on 29 March 2017, but this did nothing to clarify the timing or outcome of Brexit negotiations between the United Kingdom and the European Union. The euro area still faces major unresolved problems such as Greek sovereign debt and fragile banks in Italy. These concerns add to the vulnerability of recovery in the euro area. Despite global recovery, prices for safe-haven assets such as gold remain robust, reflecting investor concern about political risks and the sustainability of economic recovery in the advanced economies. Asian financial markets may adjust further, pricing in these risks, which would exacerbate volatility.

A weaker renminbi might curb exports from emerging East Asia to the PRC, the region's largest trader, and intensify competition for export markets in the US and other economies. In the unlikely case of rapid renminbi depreciation, capital outflow from the PRC could undermine asset prices there and the balance sheets of financial institutions, challenging highly leveraged investors in the PRC. Any negative investor sentiment that results could spill over into other markets in emerging Asia, further driving capital out of the region.

Risks from highly leveraged households in Asia

Abundant global and local liquidity since 2008 has boosted commercial and household borrowing in developing Asia, more so than in other emerging regions. Macroeconomic vulnerability has worsened in some economies as a result, causing capital flow reversals and financial market volatility. The Fed's tightening cycle has intensified fiscal and financial risk in the region, particularly in economies with highly leveraged private sectors. This requires close attention from policy makers.

Besides commercial debt (discussed at length in *ADO 2016 Update*), growing household debt has been a primary cause of rising leverage in the region. Fueled by the global availability of relatively cheap and abundant credit, consumer debt has surged in many Asian economies toward purchases of property, cars, and motorcycles, as well as many other consumer goods financed without collateral. Mortgage loans comprise the bulk of household debt in Asia.

Of some concern has been the speed with which household leverage has spiked in recent years. In the ROK, the ratio of household debt to GDP rose from 74% in late 2008 to nearly 91% in the third quarter of 2016. Thailand's household debt ratio jumped by 26 percentage points in the same period, and Malaysia's by 21 points, both reaching about 71%. In addition, the PRC, Singapore, and Hong Kong, China saw household debt increase substantially. In other economies where data are available, including India and Indonesia, debt ratios grew less and remain low (Figure 1.3.2).

In Malaysia, sustained economic growth in recent years has boosted household incomes and consumer confidence, encouraging debt acquisition. Buoyant credit demand has come from a relatively young workforce and the influx of a more affluent population in urban areas, as home purchases continue to account for the largest portion of household debt. Government policies instituting fiscal incentives for homebuyers, streamlined and reduced duties on cars, and a government-sponsored property lender have further spurred demand for household credit.

Thailand's debt levels also reflect the impact of quasi-fiscal measures. Following floods in 2011, the government introduced a program for first car buyers in 2012 to support the hard-hit auto industry, raising demand for auto loans (IMF 2016). The program has since expired, but its impact on household debt lingers. Households have relied on credit cards to smooth consumption, further raising their debt. A survey conducted in September 2016 confirmed that recent increases in average household debt resulted mainly from purchases of vehicles and other consumer products, often using credit cards (University of the Thai Chamber of Commerce 2016).

Household leverage in some Asian economies has reached high levels seen in mature economies, which sets the region apart from the rest of the developing world, where households are generally less indebted. By itself, household debt is unlikely to trigger financial crises in the region, at least not if unemployment stays low, asset prices remain fairly stable (Figure 1.3.3), and banks continue to be profitable and well capitalized (Figure 1.3.4). None of these parameters currently poses a problem for highly leveraged economies in the region. In Malaysia, for example, households' capacity to service debt has been supported by stable domestic employment and a favorable income outlook. Heightened market volatility has caused a small decline in the value of household equity investments, but the aggregate household balance sheet remains healthy, with household financial assets valued at double their debt in the past 5 years. Further, stress tests suggest that potential bank losses are limited in Malaysia and easily covered by banks' capital buffers.

Ratios of nonperforming mortgage loans have remained low in the region. This is true even in Thailand, where delinquencies have increased in recent years, mostly involving younger people (Figure 1.3.5). The balance sheets of Thai commercial banks remain healthy, though other specialized financial institutions are more exposed to lower-income households. A recent Bank of Thailand assessment of these institutions found no imminent systemic risks but recommended heightened vigilance about sector risk exposure.

However, households, financial systems, and central banks are bound to feel it this year when rising US interest rates exert upward pressure on local borrowing costs, which have been fairly stable in the past 5 years (Figure 1.3.6). Higher rates will challenge households' ability to service debt, particularly in economies such as Malaysia that have seen household debt service ratios rise (Figure 1.3.7). Loan delinquency will increase as a result, and households' financial struggles may depress private consumption. In this situation,

1.3.2 Household debt

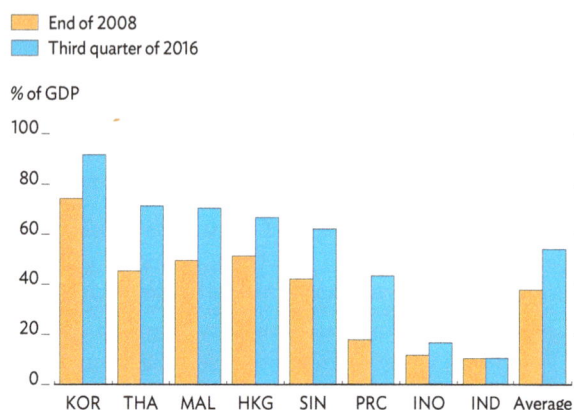

HKG = Hong Kong, China, IND = India, INO = Indonesia, KOR = Republic of Korea, MAL = Malaysia, PRC = People's Republic of China, SIN = Singapore, THA = Thailand.
Source: Bank for International Settlements. BIS total credit statistics database.

1.3.3 Real property prices

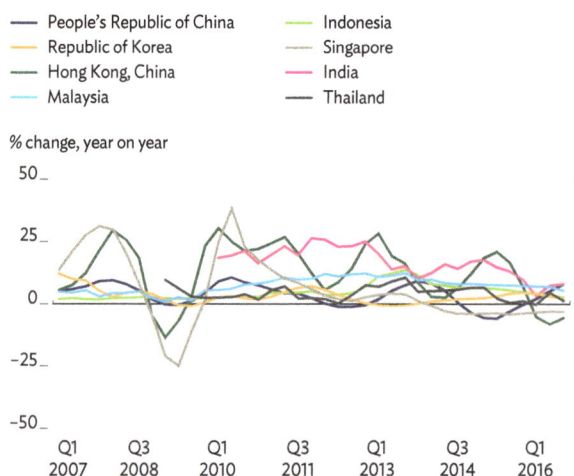

Q = quarter.
Source: Bank for International Settlements. BIS residential property database.

central banks could find themselves torn, wanting on the one hand to lower interest rates to support growth and householder balance sheets, but on the other to raise rates to stem capital outflow and support national currencies.

This could be the case in the ROK, where low interest rates and government stimulus that eased property regulations have lifted household leverage ratios to the highest in developing Asia. Although delinquency ratios remain low, at 0.5% for bank loans and 2.7% for nonbank loans, the pressure on households and the financial system is rising fast. The June 2016 *Financial Stability Report* from the Bank of Korea, the central bank, shows that nearly a third of household debt is held by households in distress, whose net financial assets are less than zero and who spend at least 40% of their disposable income on debt servicing. With 62% of mortgages at floating rates and another 30% with adjustable rates that shift to floating rates a certain point, the sector is highly vulnerable to a sharp hike in interest rates, particularly if combined with a growth slowdown and rising unemployment that would complicate central bank intervention.

To stem the risks from raising interest rates, the government has raised the target share of fixed-interest loans in bank portfolios; borrowers are encouraged to use them to refinance their adjustable-rate loans. In August 2016, it further tightened banks' loan-screening requirements and lending by mutual finance institutions. This followed a more comprehensive package to manage household debt implemented the year before that sought to improve household loan quality, sharpen the assessment of borrowers' repayment ability, and strengthen banks' ability to respond to shocks and absorb losses.

Other policy makers in the region have been monitoring rising household debt for the past several years and enacting macroprudential policies to strengthen household and bank financial health. For example, Bank Negara Malaysia recently tightened limits on loan-to-deposit ratios and unsecured lending. It also required domestic banks to improve the asset quality of their balance sheets. The Bank of Thailand has been using loan-to-value ratios to limit household leveraging and property speculation.

In some other economies, though, macroprudential policies remain relatively loose, and across the region the sensitivity of household debt to changing interest rates remains a risk to financial stability. This requires policy makers to stay vigilant and tighten policy where warranted. In particular, the authorities should assess the scope for further tightening loan-to-value and debt-to-income ratios and requirements that banks set aside special reserves and actively monitor and account for debt service ratios in their lending decisions. Further interventions may be needed in some housing markets to cool speculative demand and avoid asset bubbles.

1.3.4 Capital adequacy ratio

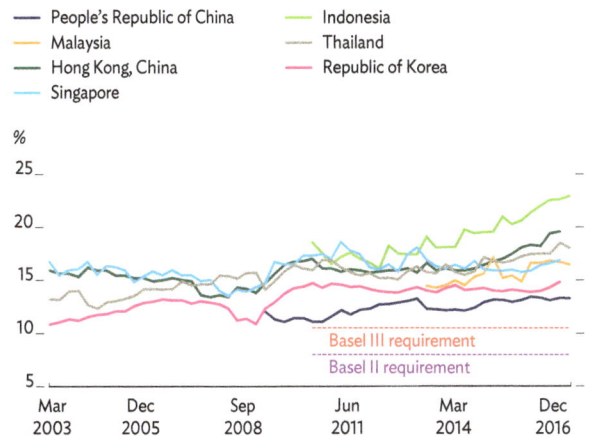

Source: CEIC Data Company (accessed 14 March 2017).

1.3.5 Mortgage nonperforming loan ratios

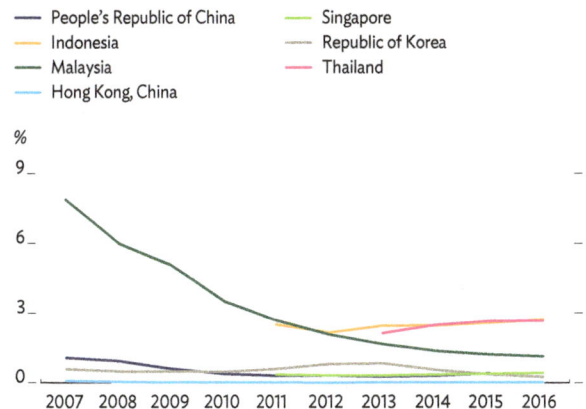

Note: Ratio for Hong Kong, China refers to the 6-month delinquency ratio of property loans; for the Republic of Korea, 1-month delinquency ratio of property loans; for Thailand, ratio of nonperforming loans to loans for personal consumption.

Source: CEIC Data Company (accessed 14 March 2017).

Strong growth momentum and the transition to high income

Developing Asia continues to perform well despite policy uncertainty in the advanced economies. Growth projected at 5.7% in both 2017 and 2018 means that Asia will continue to be the fastest-growing region of the world and make a significant contribution to global growth. It is true that regional growth has, along with growth in the world economy, languished somewhat since the global financial crisis of 2008–2009. To some extent, the regional slowdown reflects global factors, in particular the global trade slowdown since the crisis. Another major cause is the slowdown of the PRC, which is a normal and welcome transition to a somewhat slower growth trajectory that is more sustainable but still robust. Exceptionally rapid growth has lifted the PRC to upper-middle income, at which growth typically decelerates. These considerations help to keep the region's less-stellar post-crisis growth performance in perspective.

This broader perspective suggests that developing Asia's strong growth prospects in the short run basically extend from its impressive growth performance in recent decades. Rapid growth has transformed the region from mostly low income to mostly middle income within a single generation. This naturally gives rise to a long-term structural question: Can developing Asia make the transition from middle income to high income—just as it successfully completed the journey from low income to middle income—in a relatively short period of time? Asia's past performance and short-run prospects give plenty of cause for optimism. In addition, many economies in developing Asia have sound macroeconomic policies and invest heavily in physical and human capital. Yet past success is no guarantee of future success, and a growth paradigm that worked well at low income may need to adjust and evolve after an economy reaches middle income. The failure of many middle-income economies in Latin America and elsewhere to reach high income quickly and smoothly suggests that the transition from middle to high income can be challenging.

The following theme chapter of *ADO 2017* examines the issue of what developing Asia, now an overwhelmingly middle-income region, must do to reach high income. Some prerequisites for growth, such as macroeconomic stability, are universal and apply to all income levels. A stable macroeconomic environment at home mitigates the adverse impact of global shocks such as higher global interest rates and militates against the emergence of domestic imbalances such as excessive household debt. At the same time, the landscape of economic growth evolves as an economy develops. Above all, productivity growth comes to the fore as an economy approaches high income.

1.3.6 Short-term interest rates

- People's Republic of China
- Singapore
- Hong Kong, China
- Thailand
- Indonesia
- India
- Malaysia
- Republic of Korea

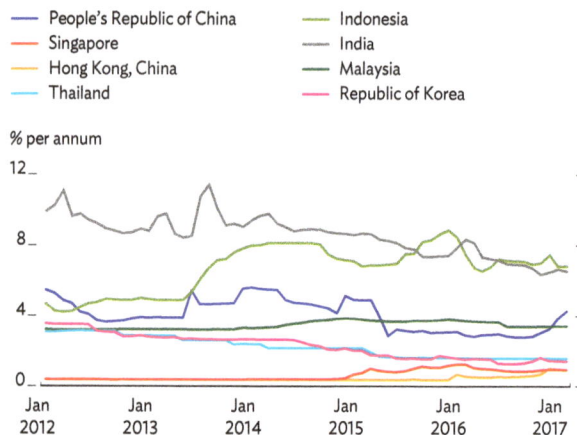

Note: Interest rate for the PRC uses the 3-month Shanghai interbank offered rate; for Hong Kong, China, the 3-month interest settlement rate; for Indonesia and Malaysia, the 3-month interbank rate; for Singapore, the 3-month Singapore interbank offered rate; for India, the 3-month Mumbai interbank offered rate; for the Republic of Korea, the 3-month interbank offered rate.
Source: CEIC Data Company (accessed 14 March 2017).

1.3.7 Debt service ratios of households

- People's Republic of China
- Republic of Korea
- Hong Kong, China
- Malaysia
- India
- Singapore
- Indonesia
- Thailand

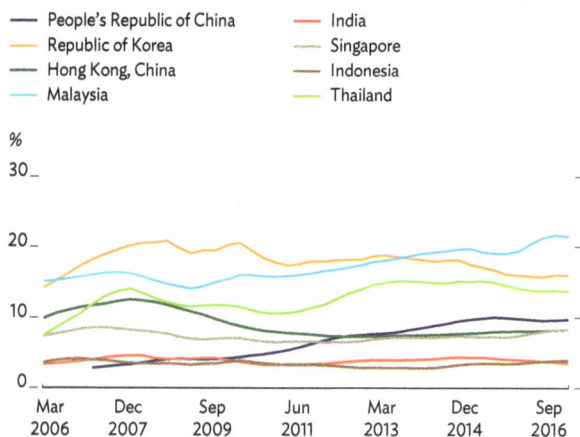

Notes: Debt service ratios are 4-month moving averages. Ratios were computed using methodology from the Bank for International Settlements.
Sources: CEIC Data Company (accessed 14 March 2017); Bank for International Settlements.

Further, in middle-income economies, productivity growth relies to a great extent on innovation, which is supported by human capital and infrastructure. These challenges are perhaps epitomized by the PRC in its current quest to transition seamlessly from investment-led growth to innovation-led growth as it bends toward a more sustainable growth path. Whether the PRC and developing Asia successfully make the final transition has enormous implications for the region and beyond.

References

ADB. 2017. *Asia Bond Monitor* (March). Asian Development Bank.

Bank of Korea. 2016. *Financial Stability Report No. 23* (June). http://www.bok.or.kr/down.search?file_path=/attach/ eng/2578/2016/08/1472627575964.pdf&file_name=Financial+Stabili ty+Report%28June+2016%29.pdf

Benigno, G., H. Chen, C. Otrok, A. Rebucci, and E. R. Young. 2016. Optimal Capital Controls and Real Exchange Rate Policies: A Pecuniary Externality Perspective. *Journal of Monetary Economics* 84 (1).

IMF. 2016. Thailand: 2016 Article IV Consultation Staff Report. *International Monetary Fund Country Report* No. 16/139. International Monetary Fund.

Nechio, F., and G. D. Rudebusch. 2016. Has the Fed Fallen behind the Curve This Year? *FRBSF Economic Letter* 2016-33. 7 November. http://www.frbsf.org/economic-research/files/el2016-33.pdf

Taylor, J. B. 1993. Discretion versus Policy Rules in Practice. *Carnegie-Rochester Conference Series on Public Policy* 39 (1).

University of the Thai Chamber of Commerce Center for Economic and Business Forecasting. 2016. *Thai Household Debt Status in 2016* (in Thai). 15 September. http://cebf.utcc.ac.th/upload/poll_file/ file_th_74d15y2016.pdf

Annex: Cautious optimism for a modest rebound

In 2016, economic growth slowed in the United States, the euro area, and Japan, with expansion decelerating in all three and the aggregate growth rate slipping from 2.2% to 1.6% (Table A1.1). The US is expected to add 0.8 percentage points and grow by 2.4% in 2017 and 2018 on strong private consumption and investment, lifting growth for the group to 1.9% in both years. Firm labor markets will help modest expansion to continue in the euro area, but the outlook for the currency union is clouded by upcoming elections in several large economies, with euro skeptics potentially gaining ground, and by the risk of Greek default. Rising exports should help to sustain modest growth in Japan, but prospects could be undermined by possible changes to US trade policy. With growth accelerating in the US, the Federal Reserve is expected to continue its incremental policy tightening. In the euro area and Japan, by contrast, accommodative monetary policy is likely to the forecast horizon in 2018.

A1.1 Baseline assumptions on the international economy

	2015	2016	2017	2018
	Actual		ADO 2017 Projection	
GDP growth (%)				
Major industrial economies[a]	2.2	1.6	1.9	1.9
United States	2.6	1.6	2.4	2.4
Euro area	1.9	1.7	1.6	1.6
Japan	1.2	1.0	1.0	0.9
Prices and inflation				
Brent crude spot prices (average, $ per barrel)	52.4	44.0	56.0	58.0
Food index (2010 = 100, % change)	−15.4	1.6	3.0	2.0
Consumer price index inflation (major industrial economies' average, %)	0.2	0.7	1.7	1.8
Interest rates				
United States federal funds rate (average, %)	0.1	0.4	1.0	2.0
European Central Bank refinancing rate (average, %)	0.1	0.0	0.0	0.1
Bank of Japan overnight call rate (average, %)	0.1	0.0	−0.1	−0.1
$ Libor[b] (%)	0.2	0.5	1.0	2.0

ADO = Asian Development Outlook, GDP = gross domestic product.

[a] Average growth rates are weighted by gross national income, Atlas method.

[b] Average London interbank offered rate quotations on 1-month loans.

Sources: US Department of Commerce, Bureau of Economic Analysis, http://www.bea.gov; Eurostat, http://ec.europa.eu/eurostat; Economic and Social Research Institute of Japan, http://www.esri.cao.go.jp; Consensus Forecasts; Bloomberg; CEIC Data Company; Haver Analytics; and the World Bank, Global Commodity Markets, http://www.worldbank.org; ADB estimates.

Recent developments in the major industrial economies

United States

Although the growth rate slowed, economic performance improved as the year proceeded. After a weak start in the first half of 2016, economic activity in the US strengthened noticeably in the third quarter. In the fourth quarter, a drop in exports slowed growth again, but GDP still expanded at a seasonally adjusted annualized rate (saar) of 2.1%, with private investment rising by 9.4% and contributing 1.5 percentage points (Figure A1.1). Private consumption, the main source of expansion, contributed 2.4 percentage points. While government outlays remain unchanged from the previous quarter, net foreign trade experienced a sharp correction in exports and a jump in imports, dragging output down. GDP expanded by 1.6% in the full year, 1.0 percentage point less than in 2015. While the economic performance for the whole year looks less vibrant than in 2015, a trend reversal during the year encourages optimism.

Private consumption remained the backbone of growth in 2016. After a disappointing 1.6% expansion in the first quarter, it jumped by 4.3% in the second quarter and subsequently posted stellar figures. The trend in consumer confidence also turned positive during the year (Figure A1.2), particularly in the second half, and remained high as wage growth accelerated. The consumer confidence index surpassed its 2007 reading in November 2016 and has continued rising since then, reaching 111.1 in February 2017, the highest since July 2001. Retail sales also rose throughout the year. These trends suggest, as does accelerating income growth, that private consumption will remain strong and likely be an important driver of future growth.

Investment declined in the first half of 2016 but improved in the second half on a rise in inventory. Industrial production remained flat but edged toward growth near the end of the second quarter as economic activity turned up after declining since the last quarter of 2015. The purchasing managers' index showed a similar trend, but its readings have never recently foretold contraction in US production. Manufacturing is gradually recovering from sharp appreciation of the dollar in 2014 and 2015, and global manufacturing conditions also improved. Industrial production and the purchasing managers' index both rose in the last quarter of 2016 and continued rising in the first 2 months of 2017, suggesting continuing recovery in US production.

The labor market strengthened in 2016 and the first 2 months of 2017. The number of nonfarm jobs rose by more than 235,000 in both January and February 2017, outpacing job growth of 155,000

A1.1 Demand-side contributions to growth, United States

- Private expenditure
- Private investment
- Government expenditure & investment
- Net exports
- Gross domestic product

Percentage points, seasonally adjusted annualized rate

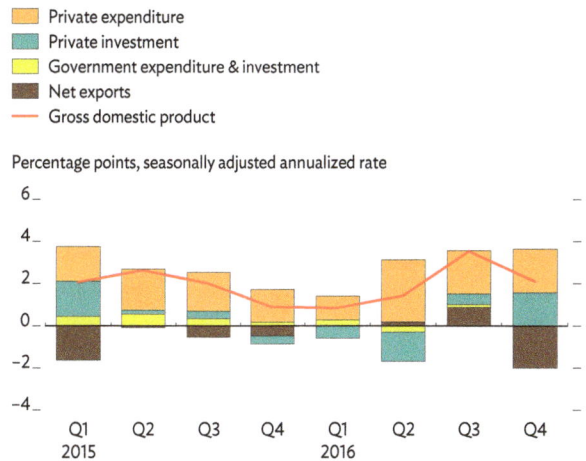

Q = quarter.

Sources: US Department of Commerce. Bureau of Economic Analysis. http://www.bea.gov; Haver Analytics (both accessed 31 March 2017).

A1.2 Business activity and consumer confidence indicators, United States

- Consumer confidence
- Industrial production
- Retail sales
- Purchasing managers' index

2007 = 100   50 = no change

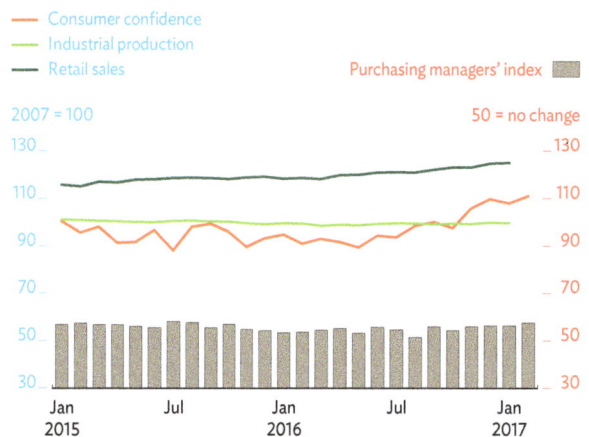

Note: For the purchasing managers' index, a reading below 50 signals deterioration of activity, above 50 improvement. The index is compiled by the Institute for Supply Management.

Source: Haver Analytics (accessed 10 March 2017).

in December 2016. The surge in employment pushed the unemployment rate down to 4.7% in February 2017 despite higher labor force participation. Moreover, the average duration of unemployment shortened to 25 weeks in February 2017 from 29 weeks at the start of 2016 (Figure A1.3). Average hourly earnings also rose in February, by 2.8%, following 2.6% growth in January 2017.

Headline inflation, on a rising trend since 2015, accelerated further in 2016 from an annual rate of 0.8% in July to 2.1% in December, reflecting in part the rise in global commodity prices. The trend continued in 2017 with inflation climbing to 2.5% in January, its highest rate since March 2012, driven mainly by higher prices for gasoline, clothing, and footwear. Core inflation rose at a slower rate but hovered just above 2.0% throughout 2016 and accelerated to 2.3% in January 2017 (Figure A1.4), suggesting that less volatile components are propping up aggregate prices.

The Federal Reserve raised the target range of the federal funds rate by 25 basis points in December 2016 and by another 25 basis points in March 2017. Given the expectation for sustained growth in the US, continuing gradual increases are expected during the next 2 years, bringing the rate to about 1.4% by the end of 2017 and about 2.4% at the end of 2018. Higher interest rates will likely strengthen the US dollar, discouraging exports, encouraging imports, and making it hard for trade to contribute much to growth. Despite the interest rate increases, inflation is expected to quicken to 2.3% in both 2017 and 2018, reflecting a robust economy.

Underlying strength in private consumption and investment points to growth at 2.4% in both 2017 and 2018. Risks to the forecasts seem to be mainly on the upside, considering the possibility of fiscal expansion from the new US administration. However, the probability of an accelerating rise in interest rates and lingering global uncertainty temper optimism.

Euro area

After a blip in the second quarter of 2016 that coincided with the Brexit referendum in the United Kingdom, growth strengthened in the euro area for the rest of the year. In the fourth quarter, GDP rose by 1.6% saar to bring annual growth to 1.7% (Figure A1.5). This was less than the 1.9% recorded in 2015, however, as protracted uncertainty on both the economic and the political front weighed on market sentiment. Domestic demand remained the primary growth driver, supported by accommodative monetary and fiscal policies, as well as an improving labor market and steady incomes. Recovery in exports remained fragile, despite recent weakness in the euro. Investment recovered notably in the fourth quarter to contribute 0.8 percentage points to growth, close to the private consumption contribution of 1.0 percentage point. Both helped offset a negative contribution from external trade.

A1.3 Unemployment rate and average duration, United States

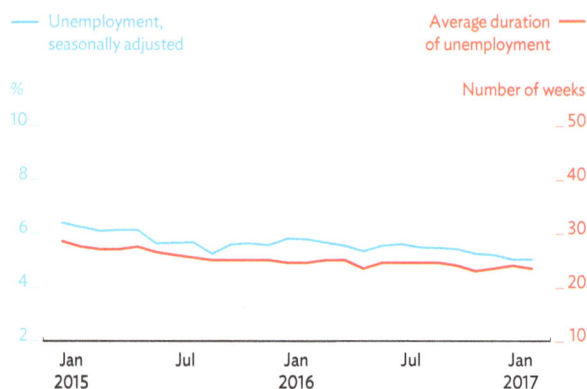

Source: Haver Analytics (accessed 10 March 2017).

A1.4 Inflation, United States

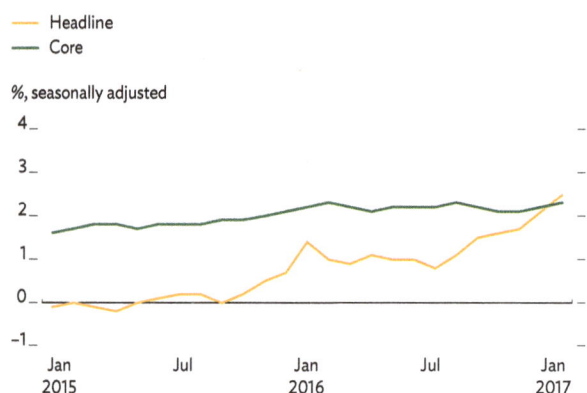

Source: Haver Analytics (accessed 10 March 2017).

Performance varied across the major economies. In the fourth quarter, only France and Germany managed to augment their growth rate—both expanding by 1.7%—but growth in Spain was sustained at 2.8%. Portugal slowed to 2.7%, while Italy's expansion weakened to 0.7% because of internal risks. Greece contracted by 4.8%, reversing earlier sustained growth.

The United Kingdom's decision to leave the European Union seems to have slowed regional growth less than expected so far, and economic sentiment appears to be positive, however fragile. Retail sales improved somewhat in the fourth quarter of 2016 after stagnating in the third quarter, helped by low inflation and falling unemployment. Unemployment inched down further to 9.6% in December, the lowest since April 2009, helping to boost consumer confidence (Figure A1.6). Company sentiment also appears to have improved. The composite purchasing managers' index reached a 5-year high in December, suggesting that company activity is expanding. Although industrial production contracted unexpectedly in December, as Germany saw its biggest drop since January 2009, it has already rebounded in January, and new orders signal accelerating production in the coming months. Leading indicators suggest that growth momentum in the latter half of 2016 is likely to continue. Economic sentiment rose further in February to its highest in almost 6 years, while consumer sentiment remained upbeat despite upcoming political change in the region. The March purchasing managers' index neared a 6-year high, indicating continued robust activity (Figure A1.7).

While inflationary pressures were mostly weak in 2016, inflation finally returned to the euro area, rising from zero in 2015 to 0.2% for the full year. In December, inflation accelerated sharply to 1.1%, the highest since August 2013, after averaging 0.2% in the previous 11 months. The causes were a marked rise in energy prices and higher prices for food, alcohol, and tobacco. In February 2017, inflation accelerated further to 2.0% from a bigger jump in energy prices.

The European Central Bank kept its interest rates unchanged at its March 2017 meeting. It extended its quantitative easing program from the planned March 2017 close to the end of the year, aiming to buoy inflation and market liquidity over the continuing growth doldrums. However, from April it will curtail its monthly purchases of bonds from $80 billion to $60 billion.

In 2017, GDP is forecast to expand moderately by 1.6% as improving labor markets keep consumption robust and export growth accelerates with a euro weakened by divergence between monetary policies on either side of the Atlantic. However, a delayed and fragile recovery in business and investment could offset the gains from improved external trade. A surge in inflation could dampen real incomes and spending, further depressed by uncertainty with the approach of national elections

A1.5 Demand-side contributions to growth, euro area

- Net exports
- Government consumption
- Total investment
- Private consumption
- Gross domestic product

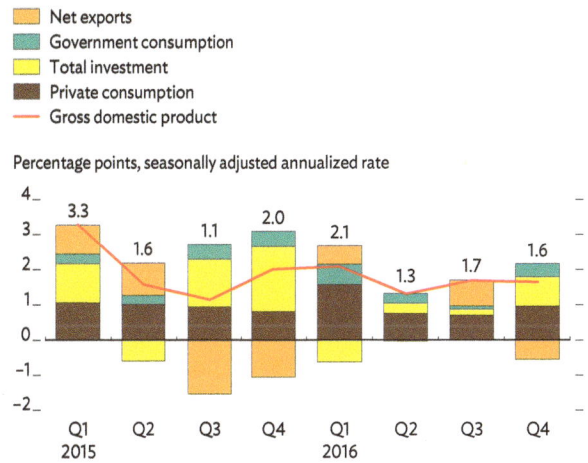

Percentage points, seasonally adjusted annualized rate

Q = quarter.
Source: Haver Analytics (accessed 14 March 2017).

A1.6 Selected economic indicators, euro area

- Industrial production
- Retail trade
- Consumer confidence

% change, month on month

Seasonally adjusted balance, %

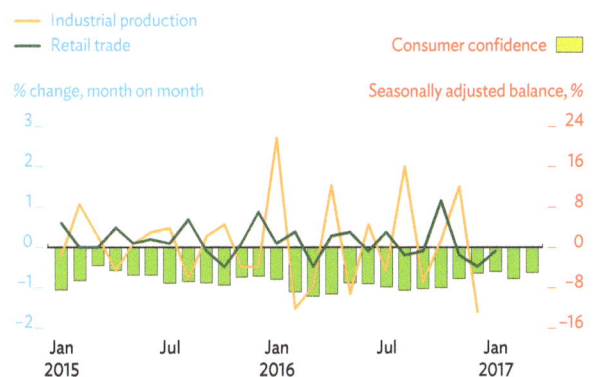

Source: Haver Analytics (accessed 29 March 2017).

in France, Germany, and possibly Italy. Victory for euro skeptics in any of them could spell a continental Brexit redux, seriously jeopardizing the European Union. Moreover, markets are responding again to fears of a Greek default because of a debt repayment looming in July and the current impasse with quarreling creditors (Box A1.1). In Italy, the government's creation of a €20 billion fund in December to recapitalize its third-largest bank and a number of smaller regional lenders currently awaits European Union approval, dependent on compliance with rules limiting governments' ability to pump state money into banks. Besides these internal challenges, difficult and complex negotiations on the separation of the United Kingdom from the union will start this year and are likely to complicate growth prospects in the euro area. Many investment decisions will probably be delayed until at least some matters have been resolved, and trade with the United Kingdom, an important trading partner, is bound to drop significantly.

In 2018, barring adverse systemic shocks, expansion will likely remain modest at 1.6%. Employment growth is seen to provide solid support for consumer demand. Inflation is expected to rise but will likely remain below the European Central Bank target. Improving growth in major trading partners should boost the region's exports, assuming that world trade has not been slowed by radical shifts in US trade policy. And while constrained by uncertainty, investment will continue to benefit from low financing costs and the coming online of projects under the European Union's new programming period and the Investment Plan for Europe.

Japan

Japan's economy recorded positive growth in every quarter of 2016, but annual growth slipped to 1.0% from 1.2% in 2015 (Figure A1.8). The introduction of new national income accounting standards in December 2016 prompted an upward revision of growth estimates for the past 3 years and early 2016. Expansion was thus revised as stronger in the first half of the year. Growth at 1.9% saar in the first quarter was driven by consumption and net exports. Growth at 2.2% in the second quarter was driven by private investment but softened in the latter portion. Private investment dragged growth down to 1.2% in the third quarter. In the fourth quarter, GDP growth was unchanged but this time kept slow by public investment. Private and government consumption languished, but private investment rebounded for a positive contribution. GDP growth slowed despite a boost to net exports from a weakening yen, which compensated only partly for weak domestic demand.

Monthly indicators suggest that recovery in the external sector started benefiting domestic industrial activity and business conditions toward the end of last year.

A1.7 Economic sentiment and purchasing managers' indexes, euro area

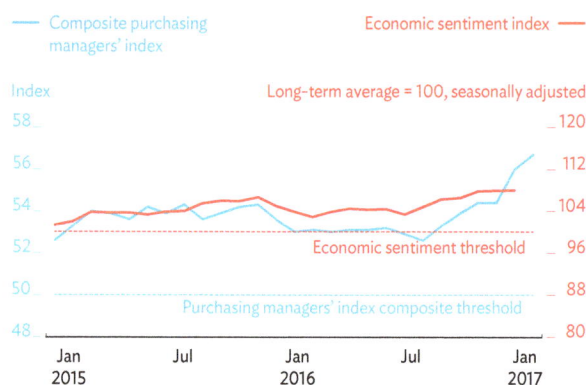

Sources: Bloomberg; Haver Analytics (both accessed 29 March 2017).

A1.8 Demand-side contributions to growth, Japan

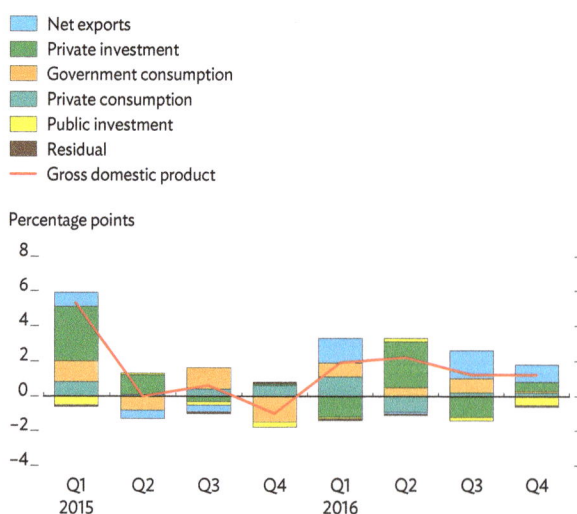

Q = quarter.
Source: Haver Analytics (accessed 8 March 2017).

A1.1 Uncertainty over a third Greek bailout

The Greek bailout is back in the news, pushing up yields on Greek sovereign debt at the start of the year (box figure 1). The European Commission, euro area governments, and the International Monetary Fund (IMF) disagree about the country's economic performance, outlook, and how to achieve debt sustainability. The latest debt sustainability analysis from the IMF describes public and external debt ratios higher than in previous projections and concludes that even with the full implementation of policies agreed under the European Stability Mechanism, "public debt and financing needs will become explosive in the long run" (box figure 2).

The IMF has long argued that sustainability requires substantial new debt relief but also strict compliance with fiscal pledges. Changes to debt maturities and interest rates granted by European creditors have not satisfied the IMF, which has given Greece no disbursements in 3 years. The IMF refuses to join the third program without a change in European requests and macroeconomic and fiscal assumptions. Meanwhile, the IMF asked that Greece pre-legislate additional fiscal measures that would be triggered automatically if austerity targets are missed, which the Greek government has so far failed to do.

The president of the euro area financial ministers' body Eurogroup argues that the IMF debt sustainability analysis and its conclusions do not reflect improved growth and fiscal progress in Greece. The managing director of the European Stability Mechanism contends that the IMF ignores the long-time support and financial assistance that the mechanism provides. Neither argument has yet convinced the IMF Executive Board, which has not ruled out participating in the third program but may finally do so. This is a serious problem in view of parliamentary requirements in Germany and other states that the IMF endorse and oversee any Greek program. With elections looming in Germany, the impasse risks jeopardizing parliamentary approvals in time for the release of bailout funds.

Greece has enough funds to last until July without additional aid but will need bailout money to meet payments of nearly €7 billion falling due then. Investor confidence is eroding, and all parties know that a solution must be found rapidly. To reach a deal, Greece must adopt additional policy measures to meet program targets, Germany and other European countries must grant real debt relief and ease their request for a 3.5% primary surplus in the medium term, and the IMF must admit that its debt sustainability analysis will keep showing Greek public and external debt unsustainable without some compromise in its assumptions. Common ground may be found eventually. A promising sign is that the latest meeting between the Greek authorities, euro area finance ministers, and the IMF, on 20 February 2017, ended with preliminary agreement that the Greek government would legislate structural reform, including pension cuts and income tax measures if necessary, to meet agreed fiscal targets. However, details about the size of additional debt relief or the exact role of the IMF in the program have yet to emerge. Pressure has nevertheless eased somewhat on Greek sovereign bonds, and markets appear to be appeased for the time being.

1 Yield on 10-year bonds issued by the Greek government

Source: Bloomberg.

2 Greek public debt and external debt

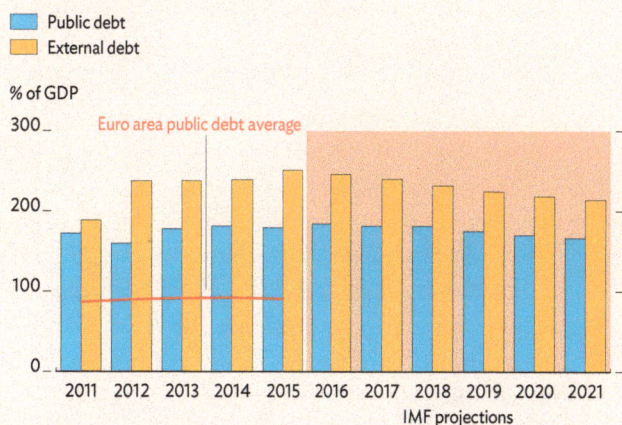

Source: International Monetary Fund. *Staff Report for the 2016 Article IV Consultation.*

Following 8 quarters of decline, manufacturing started expanding in the third quarter of 2016 and strengthened further in the fourth (Figure A1.9). However, a drop in January, by 0.7% month on month, saw 2017 begin more slowly. Machinery orders, considered a leading indicator of capital spending and hence of nonresidential investment, rebounded strongly in the fourth quarter. Further, the Nikkei flash manufacturing purchasing managers' index crossed the threshold of 50 in September last year, signaling expansion in manufacturing, and rose further to 53.3 in February, for the highest reading since March 2014. Business sentiment, as reflected in Tankan surveys, appears to be generally optimistic, supported by accommodative monetary policy and financial conditions. Owing to government stimulus, the Bank of Japan projects that public investment will increase through fiscal 2017 and thereafter remain relatively high as preparations begin for the Olympic Games in 2020.

In the national accounts, private consumption expanded fairly strongly in the first 3 quarters of 2016 but barely grew in the fourth. Monthly retail sales also slumped toward the end of the year. Although sales rose by a seasonally adjusted 0.5% in January and consumer confidence approached a 3-year high, the recovery in consumption seems restrained as real household spending declined in January by 1.2% year on year. The unemployment rate in January was, at 3.0%, the lowest since the mid-1990s. Despite a tight labor market, wage growth has been moderate and could be a factor limiting consumer spending. With domestic demand fragile, the government delayed from April 2017 to October 2019 its consumption tax hike, which was originally slated for October 2015.

Inflation picked up only slowly from 0.3% saar in December 2016 to 0.5% in January, reflecting higher energy prices. Core inflation, which excludes food and energy, turned negative in December but then rose as well in January, to 0.1%. In its March meeting, the Bank of Japan announced that it would continue as necessary its quantitative and qualitative monetary easing with yield curve control, which it introduced last year, to achieve its 2.0% inflation target in a stable manner. Accordingly, the short-term policy interest rate was kept at −0.1%, and the target for 10-year Japanese government bond yields is zero percent.

Merchandise exports recorded positive year-on-year growth in June 2016 for the first time in several months on strengthening external demand. They ended the year with a robust 8.9% rise in the fourth quarter, as the yen had begun weakening against the US dollar in September (Figure A1.10). Most recent data suggest that export growth continued with a 4.4% rise in January. Imports also grew strongly by 11.8%, generating a trade deficit of $9.5 billion in January.

The economy is expected to continue expanding at a modest pace, above its technical potential in the short term, with growth forecast at 1.0% in 2017. But the recovery is precarious, relying excessively

A1.9 Consumption and business indicators, Japan

PMI = purchasing managers' index.
Source: Haver Analytics (accessed 6 March 2017).

A1.10 Trade growth and exchange rate, Japan

Source: Haver Analytics (accessed 6 March 2017).

on higher exports. A weak yen and an uptick in global demand have boosted exports and domestic manufacturing, but a decline in manufacturing at the start of the year sounded a note of caution. Additionally, consumer spending could hesitate under strengthening price pressures as the effects of low energy prices wane and the depreciating yen raises import prices. Moreover, uncertainty attached to emerging US trade policies casts a shadow over buoyancy in the external sector. The forecast for 2018 is therefore lower at 0.9%.

Australia and New Zealand

The Australian economy expanded by 4.4% saar in the fourth quarter of 2016, recovering from 2.0% contraction in the previous quarter (Figure A1.11). Fixed capital formation was the main driver of growth, contributing 2.6 percentage points, with consumption adding 2.1 points and net exports 0.7 points, while change in inventories deducted 0.6 points. Seasonally adjusted retail sales expanded by 0.4% in January 2017, an improvement from 0.1% contraction in December 2016. The consumer sentiment index rose to 99.6 in February from 97.4 in January, still slightly below 100, the line dividing pessimism from optimism. The seasonally adjusted unemployment rate declined marginally to 5.7% in January from 5.8% in December. The Australian Industry Group's performance of manufacturing index jumped to 59.3 points in February from 51.2 in the previous month, well above the threshold at 50 that indicates expansion in manufacturing. Seasonally adjusted inflation accelerated to 1.5% in the fourth quarter of 2016 from 1.3% in the previous quarter, still less than the central bank target of 2.0%–3.0%. Even with meager expansion in mining hampering growth, rising commodity prices and non-mining business investment will sustain expansion this year. Panelists for the FocusEconomics Consensus Forecast expect GDP to grow by 2.5% in 2017, marginally above last year's 2.4%, and accelerate further to 2.8% in 2018.

New Zealand's economy grew by 5.7% in the third quarter of 2016, outperforming 5.0% growth in the previous quarter. Consumption was the biggest contributor to growth, adding 4.5 percentage points. Also boosting growth were fixed capital, contributing 1.4 percentage points, and change in inventories, contributing 2.0 points, while net exports subtracted 2.4 points (Figure A1.12). Retail sales expanded by 4.7% in the fourth quarter, slightly above the 4.6% rise in the third quarter. The seasonally adjusted performance of manufacturing index declined to 51.6 in January 2017 from 54.2 in December 2016, staying above the threshold of 50 indicating expansion. The business confidence index, which subtracts the percentage of pessimists from that of optimists, dropped to 16.6 in February from 21.7 in December but stayed in positive territory. Consumer confidence also remained

A1.11 Demand-side contributions to growth, Australia

Net exports
Change in inventories
Gross fixed capital formation
Consumption
Gross domestic product

Percentage points, seasonally adjusted annualized rate

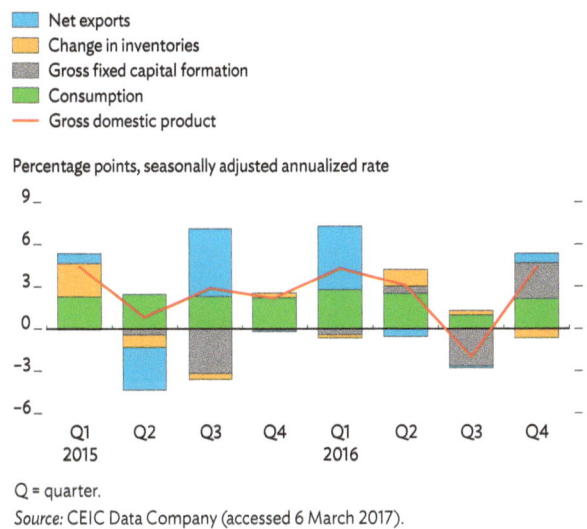

Q = quarter.
Source: CEIC Data Company (accessed 6 March 2017).

A1.12 Demand-side contributions to growth, New Zealand

Net exports
Change in inventories
Gross fixed capital formation
Consumption
Gross domestic product

Percentage points, seasonally adjusted annualized rate

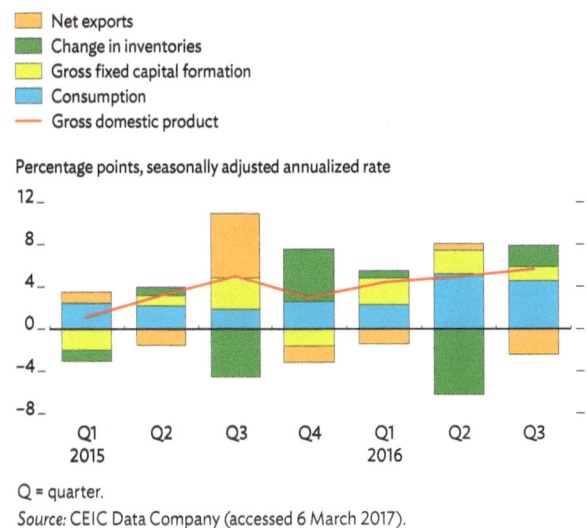

Q = quarter.
Source: CEIC Data Company (accessed 6 March 2017).

positive above the threshold at 100, rising by 5.1 points to 113.1 in the fourth quarter of 2016. Inflation was stable at 0.4% in the first three quarters of 2016 but jumped to 1.3% in the fourth quarter, satisfying the Reserve Bank of New Zealand target of 1.0%–3.0% for the first time since the third quarter of 2014. The seasonally adjusted unemployment rate rose to 5.2% in the fourth quarter from 4.9% in the previous quarter. Weighing an accommodative monetary policy, higher dairy prices, and a robust domestic economy, the FocusEconomics Consensus Panel projects GDP expanding by 3.1% in 2017 and 2.8% in 2018.

Commodity prices

Average commodity prices continued their decline in 2016, albeit at a much slower pace than in the previous year. International oil prices remained low with improved supply and weak demand. They are expected to recover in the next 2 years as the global oil market rebalances. Food prices are similarly forecast to rise with increased demand and higher oil prices, but the rise will be tempered by good supply.

Oil price movements and prospects

Brent crude oil prices averaged $44/barrel in 2016, 16% lower than the average price of $52/barrel in 2015 (Figure A1.13). Relatively high production and stocks constrained oil prices throughout most of 2016. However, upward pressure on prices came in the second half of the year from negotiations and eventual agreement among members of the Organization of the Petroleum Exporting Countries (OPEC) to cut crude oil production, reinforced by similar pledges from some key producers outside of OPEC. Consequently, Brent crude ended 2016 at just above $55/barrel, coincidentally 55% above its price a year earlier.

   Global oil supply continued to grow in 2016, albeit much more slowly than in the previous year. In 2016, global oil supply increased by only 0.4 million barrels per day (mbd), a fraction of the 3.1 mbd rise in the previous year. After increasing by 1.5 mbd in 2015, non-OPEC supply declined by 0.8 mbd in 2016. The US accounted for most of the decrease as its crude oil production fell by 5.7%, from 9.4 mbd to 8.9 mbd. Supply from OPEC, by contrast, rose by 1.2 mbd. Most of the increase came from Iran, Iraq, and Saudi Arabia, whose combined additional output accounted for 91% of the rise in OPEC production. World oil demand increased by 1.6 mbd in 2016, down from the 5-year-high 2.0 mbd increase in 2015, when oil prices fell sharply. However, growth in 2016 still exceeded the 5-year average of 1.3 mbd in 2011–2015. With the rise in oil demand outpacing supply growth, expansion in global oil inventories eased to 0.4 mbd in 2016, or one quarter of the inventory buildup in 2015.

A1.13 Price of Brent crude

Sources: Bloomberg; World Bank. Commodity Price Data (Pink Sheet). http://www.worldbank.org (both accessed 9 March 2017).

Oil prices have been relatively steady since 30 November, when OPEC and a number of non-OPEC producers agreed to cut production by 1.8 mbd in the first half of 2017. The agreement to cut production has improved sentiment in global oil markets, and oil price volatility has been ebbing since December. In February, Brent crude oil traded at $53.50–$56.90/barrel, the narrowest monthly range since January 2005. Although oil prices have risen by more than 10% since the announcement of the production cut, they have been unable to stay above $55/barrel for long because upward price pressures from the OPEC-led production cuts are countered by concerns over renascent US shale production.

In its *Oil 2017* report, the International Energy Agency predicted a tightening of the oil market in the next 5 years. Underpinned by the projected acceleration of global economic growth, world oil demand is expected to rise by 1.4 mbd in 2017 and 1.3 mbd in 2018. However the forecast increase is lower than the increase in 2016 as oil consumption is constrained by factors like the persistent strengthening of the US dollar, a stronger focus on cleaner energy, and slowing growth in the People's Republic of China (PRC).

World oil supply this year and next depends on how current restraint on output plays out. According to initial reports, adherence so far has been high. OPEC production in February decreased by nearly 1.1 mbd from December production, to average 32.0 mbd. Gabon, Kuwait, Iraq, Saudi Arabia, and the United Arab Emirates reduced production by more than what was required. Preliminary estimates show the 11 non-OPEC producers that together committed to cut production by 558,000 barrels/day having delivered 60% of the agreed cuts. Outside of the production agreement, other non-OPEC producers—Brazil, Canada, and the US—are expected to significantly increase their output. The largest increase will come from the US, whose oil production reportedly bottomed out in early October 2016 and is now forecast to increase by 0.4 mbd in 2017 and 0.6 mbd in 2018.

Oil price movements over the rest of the year will depend mostly on supply developments. Cuts in oil production will accelerate the drawdown of the large oil stock overhang that has weighed on markets since mid-2014. An extension of the agreement to cut production after 6 months will exert further upward pressure on the oil price. With a tighter oil market, any supply disruption that occurs exerts upward pressure on prices. According to the Energy Information Agency, 2.1 mbd were removed from oil markets in February 2017.

Meanwhile, US inventories have started to rise again. In the week ending on 3 March alone, US crude inventories climbed by 8.2 million barrels. If US shale output starts rising briskly, OPEC may be forced to cancel its production cuts to protect market share. This possibility exerts further downward pressure on oil prices, as do forecast production increases from other major oil producers. The pressure can be seen in futures markets that show Brent crude trading below $60/barrel to the forecast horizon (Figure A1.14). Market expectations that production restraint will not be

A1.14 Brent crude futures and spot prices

— Average spot price
--- 11 March 2016
--- 12 December 2016
--- 23 January 2017
--- 8 March 2017

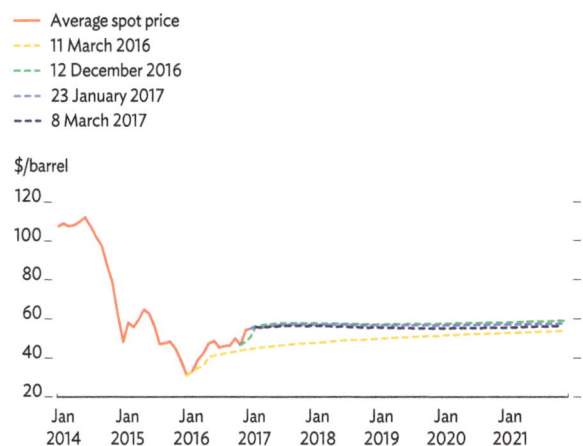

Source: Bloomberg (accessed 9 March 2017).

extended can be seen in the futures curve, which shows a sharp increase in short-term prices but relatively little movement further out. Barring major supply disruptions, the price of Brent crude is forecast to average $56/barrel in 2017 and reach $58/barrel in 2018.

Food price movements and prospects

Agricultural prices fell for a fifth consecutive year in 2016. The index averaged 89.1 points, 0.2% below its 2015 average, but the drop was much smaller than in 2015 because higher food prices largely offset a price fall for beverages and raw materials. Still, the 2016 agricultural index was 27% below its peak in 2011 as downward price pressures from favorable supply and low energy prices have negated upward pressure from higher demand.

After falling for 3 consecutive years, food prices rose by 1.6% in 2016. Increased prices for edible oils and other foods more than compensated for lower grain prices (Figure A1.15). The price index for edible oil and meal rose by 5.2%, driven mostly by higher prices for palm products, coconut oil, and soybean. Disappointing harvests in Malaysia and Indonesia helped raise palm prices, while rising soybean prices reflected weather concerns in Argentina and forecast demand increases for biodiesel. Coconut oil production has fallen as bad weather caused by El Niño tightened supplies of copra, from which coconut oil is drawn. After falling in 2015, the "other food" category rose by 5% in 2016, mainly reflecting a sharp 34% increase in sugar prices after 4 consecutive years of declines. Sugar prices soared because of reduced production in both Brazil and India, and as a strengthening Brazilian real against the US dollar encouraged sugar farmers to retain their stocks rather than sell them. Excepting rice, prices for all other components of the grain index fell in 2016, reflecting ample supply from good crop yields. Wheat and barley prices dropped by more than 18%, and maize prices were down by 6%. Prices for rice rose by 2.6% as inclement weather worsened crop prospects, particularly in the PRC and Viet Nam.

The rise in food prices has continued in 2017, with the index up by 10.9% in the first 2 months of the year on increases for most subindexes. The supply of sugar stayed tight, but the edible oil index turned down in February, marking its first month-on-month decline since October 2016. Better crop prospects and slowing global import demand put downward pressure on edible oil prices. Grain prices continued to decline year on year, the grain price index now at half of its April 2008 peak. The decline in grain prices reflects news of bumper rice crops in most East Asian rice producers and expectations for better wheat and maize harvests.

Global supplies of the three major grains—combining stocks and production of maize, rice, and wheat—remain healthy. The latest prospects, as reported in March 2017 by the US Department of Agriculture, show global supplies of these crops reaching 2.8 billion tons in the 2016/17 crop year, 4.9% above the previous year.

A1.15 Food commodity price indexes

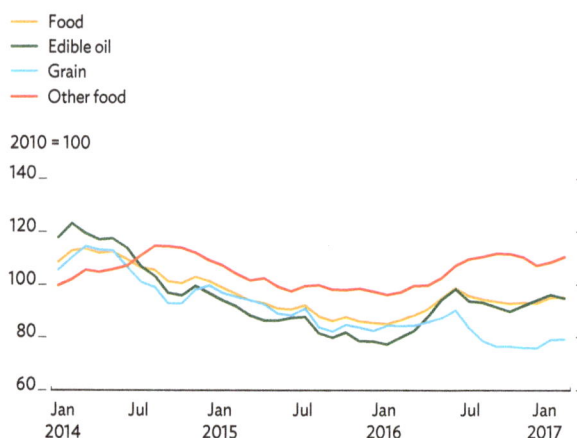

Source: World Bank. Commodity Price Data (Pink Sheet). http://www.worldbank.org (accessed 9 March 2017).

Global production of wheat is expected to be 2.2% higher in 2016/17, driving a 15-year high in the ratio of stock to use (Figure A1.16). Similarly, the market for maize is forecast to loosen, with global production in 2016/17 increasing by 8.3%, thanks to higher crop yields in Argentina, Canada, India, Mexico, South Africa, and Ukraine. Despite increased production, higher consumption is projected to leave the ratio of stock to use only marginally higher. Recovering from El Niño, global rice production is expected to expand by 1.7%. Output from major rice exporters India, Pakistan, Thailand, and Viet Nam is forecast to rise by 3.3%, but the ratio of stock to use will remain close to its 10-year average at 24.6%.

The outlook for edible oil and meal remains positive, with supplies projected to rise in 2016/17 by 4% after a slight fall in the previous crop year. Supplies are expected to remain high because of elevated stock carryover, especially for soybeans, which experienced a production increase in 2015/16 by 12% from 2013/14, when high carryover began.

Regarding La Niña, which usually follows El Niño, the 9 February 2017 update from the US National Oceanic and Atmospheric Administration found La Niña conditions no longer present, which bodes well for crops. Upward price pressures will stem from increased demand, higher oil prices, and inevitable unfavorable weather in some areas. However, with adequate supply in most food commodity markets, food prices are forecast to rise by only 3.0% in 2017 and 2.0% in 2018.

External environment in sum

With the industrial economies recovering, albeit at different speeds, developing Asia should be able to experience a pick up in external demand. Fiscal adjustment and structural reform in some economies will pay off with sustained growth as external demand from the industrial economies picks up. An assumption is that growth will remain steady in the region as the PRC continues its controlled deceleration but is countered by slightly higher growth in the rest of developing Asia, particularly in South Asia. Improved consumer and business confidence is reflected in a recent turnaround in exports. Uncertainty nevertheless clouds the medium-term outlook for export growth given the unknown direction of trade and financial policies in the US and Europe.

A very mild pickup in inflation reflects mostly higher commodity prices, but inflationary expectations are well anchored. The Federal Reserve is likely to increase interest rates, but if the increases are gradual and anticipated by markets, they will help maintain financial stability in the PRC and the region as a whole.

A1.16 Ratio of stock to use

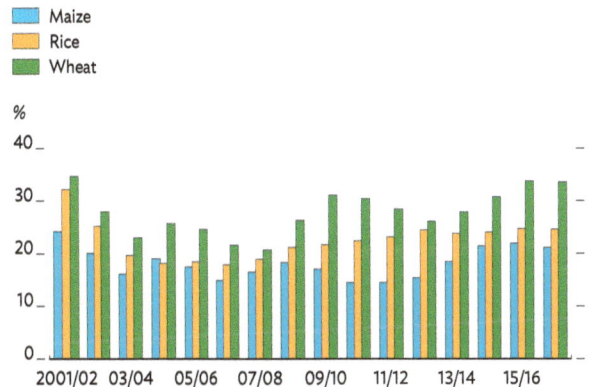

Note: Years refer to crop years.
Source: US Department of Agriculture. Production, Supply, and Distribution Online. http://www.fas.usda.gov/psdonline/psdQuery.aspx (accessed 9 March 2017).

2

TRANSCENDING THE MIDDLE-INCOME CHALLENGE

Transcending the middle-income challenge

Developing Asia has transformed itself through sustained rapid growth from a largely low-income region to a largely middle-income one. The vast majority of the region's population now lives in middle-income economies, presenting a remarkable turnaround. As recently as 1991, more than 90% of Asians lived in low-income economies, half again the world average of less than 60% (Figure 2.0.1). The region continues to grow at a healthy pace, its strong growth momentum motivating optimism about the region's ability to eventually reach high income. However, the transition from middle income to high will not be driven by the same factors that lifted economies out of low income. Further, the historical track record is mixed. Some middle-income economies have been at this stage for a very long time—notably in Latin America—and only a handful of economies have successfully made the final transition, most famously Asia's four newly industrialized economies (NIEs): the Republic of Korea (ROK), Singapore, Taipei,China, and Hong Kong, China.

This chapter explores some key development challenges that middle-income Asian economies face and presents some policy options for tackling them. While the middle-income challenge has many dimensions, the central theme is the need to foster productivity to sustain economic growth. Focusing on three interlinked productivity-enhancing factors—encouraging innovation and technological progress, upgrading human capital quality, and investing in information and communication technology (ICT) and other advanced infrastructure—can support economic growth in middle-income economies as they aspire to graduate to high income.

In many ways, the transition from middle income to high is fundamentally different from the transition from low to middle. The government typically plays a more nuanced role in the economy in the more advanced transition, especially as the private sector becomes more developed. Moreover, as an economy matures, productivity growth has to come increasingly from innovation rather than the more basic sources of productivity growth, such as reallocating workers from low-productivity agriculture to higher-productivity manufacturing and services. To successfully make the transition to high income, middle-income economies therefore need to shift their attention to areas that foster innovation and create positive productivity spillover.

2.0.1 Population share by income groups, developing Asia and world

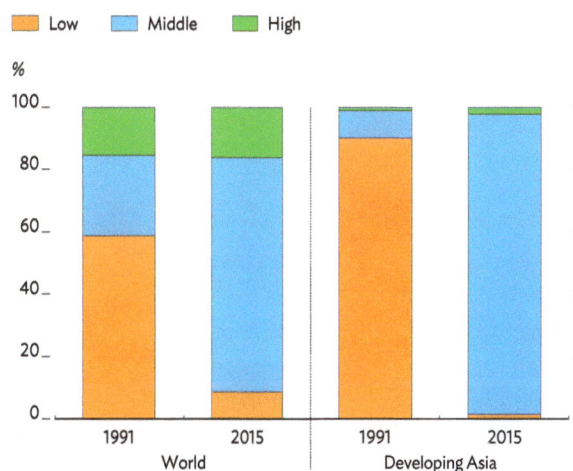

Source: Estrada et al., forthcoming.

This chapter was written by Donghyun Park, Abdul Abiad, Gemma Estrada, Xuehui Han, and Shu Tian of the Economic Research and Regional Cooperation Department, ADB, Manila. Contributions from Era Dabla-Norris and Minsuk Kim of the International Monetary Fund, Guillermo Felices of the London School of Economics, Andrew Powell of the Inter-American Development Bank, Christos Sakellariou of Nanyang Technological University, and Jesus Felipe of the Economic Research and Regional Cooperation Department, ADB, Manila, are gratefully acknowledged.

Sustaining growth at middle income

Developing Asia's transition out of a low-income state is almost complete, with virtually the whole region now considered middle income. The region's relatively smooth and rapid transition, as well as its robust current growth, encourage optimism about prospects for the next milestone: moving from middle to high income. However, international historical experience suggests that this transition may be more challenging. It also suggests that, while human and physical capital accumulation continues to matter at middle income, more rapid productivity growth is essential to achieving high income. Innovation supported by human capital and infrastructure offers a promising pathway to productivity and economic growth.

Asia's transformation to middle income

Over the past 50 years or so, developing Asia has undergone a dramatic shift from a region consisting mainly of low-income economies to one dominated by middle-income economies. Income classification constructed relative to per capita income in the United States in 1960 indicates developing Asia's dynamic transition since the 1960s. The income classification is based on 2011 US dollars adjusted for purchasing power parity (PPP) using Penn World Tables 9.0 and covers 107 economies from 1960 to 2014, of which 15 are in developing Asia.[1]

Figure 2.1.1 shows that income distribution across the world gradually shifted over the decades from being largely low or middle income to one dominated by either middle or high income. While there were 56 low-income economies in 1960, constituting about half of all countries with data, their number dropped to 24 by 2014, only about a fifth of the total. The number of high-income economies—defined as

2.1.1 Distribution by income class

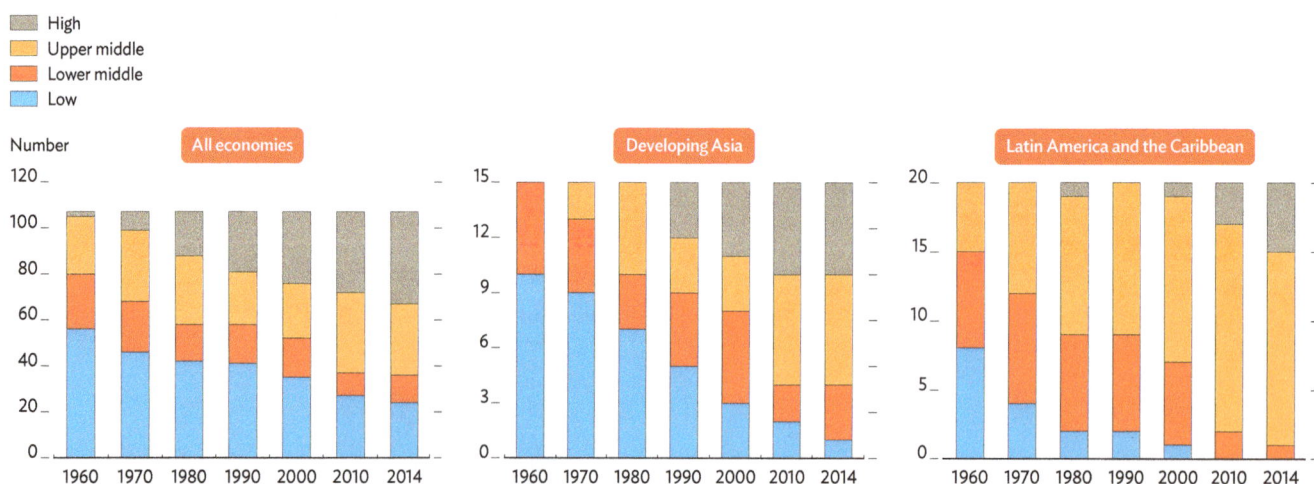

Source: Estrada et al., forthcoming.

those that surpassed US per capita income in 1960—increased remarkably from only 2 to 40 during the period.

In 1960, fully 10 of the 15 large economies in developing Asia were considered either extremely low or low income, while the rest were lower-middle income. By 1980, slightly over half of Asian economies had reached middle-income status. Toward the end of the 1980s, three economies had already achieved high per capita income: Singapore, Taipei,China, and Hong Kong, China. The ROK, the fourth NIE, later joined their ranks in the mid-1990s. By 2014, however, 9 of the 10 low-income economies in developing Asia had moved out of that income group, while 5 economies—the NIEs and Malaysia—had transitioned to high income (Figure 2.1.2).

Standard income classification from the World Bank shows a similar dynamic shift in the region and the world in more recent years (Figure 2.1.3). While the World Bank database covers more economies and is updated to 2015, income classification starts only in the late 1980s (Box 2.1.1). Based on the World Bank classification, 49.3% of all economies in the world today are middle income. Only 14.2% are low income, and 36.5% are high income.[2]

Developing Asia now has a much greater proportion of middle-income economies than does the world, comparing aggregate data. While only half of world economies are considered middle income, counting large states and small, 80% of economies in developing Asia are so classified, for the highest proportion among developing regions. Viewed by population, the favorable transition of Asia's most populous economies—the People's Republic of China (PRC), India, and Indonesia—means that more than 95% of Asia's population now lives in middle-income economies. Only 2 of the 45 developing Asia economies in the sample remain low income, while 7 have already achieved high-income status.

2.1.2 GDP per capita, PPP (2011 $)

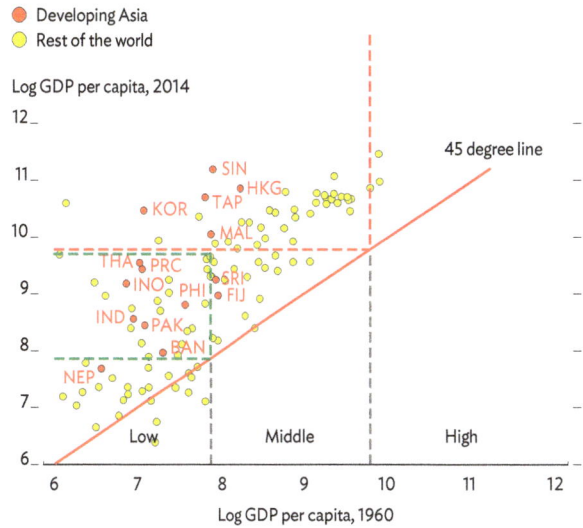

BAN = Bangladesh, FIJ = Fiji, HKG = Hong Kong, China, IND = India, INO = Indonesia, KOR = Republic of Korea, MAL = Malaysia, NEP = Nepal, PAK = Pakistan, PHI = Philippines, PPP = purchasing power parity, PRC = People's Republic of China, SIN = Singapore, SRI = Sri Lanka, TAP = Taipei,China, THA = Thailand.

Note: The region defined by red dashed lines is successful transition from middle or low income to high income. The region defined by green dashed lines is successful transition from low income to middle income.

Source: Estrada et al., forthcoming.

2.1.3 World Bank's classification of economies, 1991 and 2015

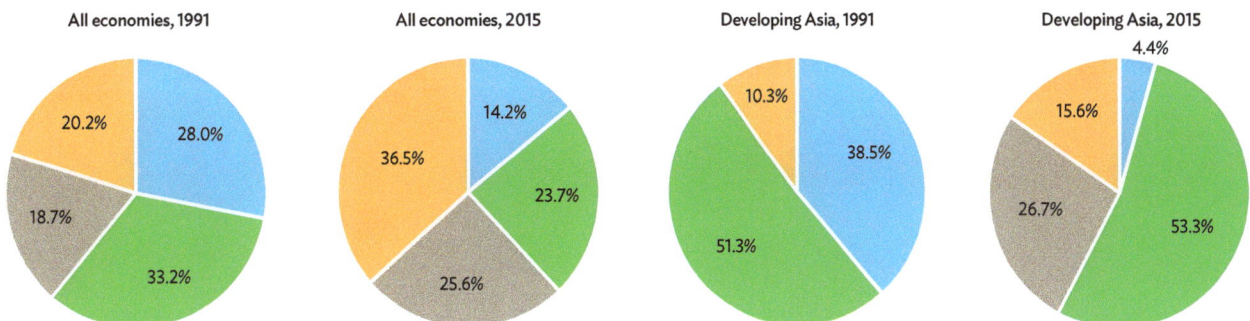

Source: Estrada et al., forthcoming.

2.1.1 Comparing income groupings from Penn World Tables 9.0 and World Bank datasets

In examining Asia's transformation over the past several decades, two sets of data are used: Penn World Tables 9.0 (PWT 9.0) and the World Bank. Income classification constructed from PWT 9.0 ranks economies based on gross domestic product (GDP) per capita at purchasing power parity (PPP) in constant 2011 dollars. The groups are as follows: (i) low income at less than $2,586, (ii) lower-middle income from $2,586 to $5,351, (iii) upper-middle income from $5,352 to $17,600, and (iv) high income above $17,600. Following Han and Wei (2015), cutoff lines are derived by making PWT 9.0 GDP per capita data at PPP in 2011 dollars compatible with the World Bank thresholds for income groupings that are in gross national income (GNI) per capita denominated in US dollars, having converted from local currency using the World Bank Atlas method.[a] Adjustments are made to make US per capita GDP in 1960 the threshold for classifying high-income economies. In addition, the thresholds for lower-middle and upper-middle income are calibrated so that there are about the same number of countries in both categories in 1960.

The World Bank classifies economies based on GNI per capita in US dollars into four income groups: low, lower middle, upper middle, and high. Economies are grouped on 1 July each year using estimates of their GNI per capita in the previous calendar year. The World Bank recognizes that while GNI per capita does not completely summarize a country's level of development, it is considered an easily available indicator that is closely related with nonmonetary measures of the quality of life such as life expectancy at birth, child mortality, and school enrolment rates. The thresholds are revised annually with an adjustment for inflation based on the change in the special drawing rights (SDR) deflator, compiled from inflation measures for the euro area, Japan, the United Kingdom, and the US. In July 2016, the World Bank released its income

classification for 2015 as follows: (i) low income less than $1,026, (ii) lower-middle income from $1,026 to $4,035, (iii) upper-middle income from $4,036 to $12,475, and (iv) high income above $12,475. Because these thresholds are applied only to current GNI per capita in 2015, and other years have their own thresholds, they are not directly comparable with the PWT thresholds that are applied on GDP per capita at PPP in constant 2011 dollars across all years. The World Bank has data since 1987, but at least 20% of the 218 economies in its sample were not classified annually before 1990.

Relative to World Bank data, PWT covers more years but fewer economies. PWT allows comparison of income status since 1960, though only 107 of its 182 economies can be tracked beginning in 1960. The World Bank covers 218 economies but has data starting only in 1987, with close to 90% of the sample classified annually beginning only 1991.

Some economies are classified differently under the two data sets. For example, a middle-income economy that graduated to high income in PWT may still be classified as middle income in the World Bank data. Malaysia is one case. In PWT, its per capita GDP exceeded from 2007 constant 1960 US per capita GDP at PPP and thus could be considered high income by this measure beginning in 2007. However, in the World Bank data, it remains middle income. Kazakhstan and Turkmenistan are two other Asian economies that are classified as high income by PWT data but not by World Bank data. Despite the differences, both data sets show developing Asia's dynamic transition from primarily low income to largely middle income.

[a] The ratios of the average GNI per capita to GDP per capita at PPP in constant dollars per income group were applied to the thresholds in GNI per capita to get the equivalent thresholds in GDP per capita at PPP.

The high-income hurdle

Developing Asia's transition from low income to middle income has been swift and smooth, but does this necessarily guarantee a similar transition from middle income to high income? Some clues to answer this question can be drawn from international historical experience and the economics literature. The evidence from both indicates that such a transition is within Asia's reach, but achieving it will require the region to confront a different set of challenges.

Time in middle income

Past research suggests that it may take some time for an economy to reach high income even though it has successfully grown out of low income. Grouping economies as low, lower-middle, upper-middle, and high income by applying World Bank income classifications to long time series data from Maddison (2010), Felipe, Kumar, and Galope (2017) found the transition to be quite lengthy—about 64 years for economies on average that had reached lower-middle income before World War II. The Netherlands, for example, was the first economy to break out of low income in the study, reaching the lower-middle threshold in 1827 and remaining there for 128 years until 1955.

While similar marathons of 80 years or more at lower-middle income are common historically, the pace of transition accelerated markedly in the postwar period as the median number of years in lower-middle income declined to 28 years, largely the result of the fast transition experienced by East Asian economies, without which the median is 52 years. The shift from upper-middle to high income was much faster both before and after 1950, usually 15–20 years.

In some ways, the postwar Asian experience raises expectations of rapid transition to high income for today's middle-income economies. Japan's reconstruction and recovery propelled it into upper-middle income in 1968 and into high income in 1977. Japan was quickly followed by the NIEs: Hong Kong, China graduating to high income in 1983, Singapore in 1988, Taipei,China in 1993, and the ROK in 1995. The NIEs completed the full transition from low income to high in 3 decades on average. The high-income Latin American economies, in contrast, had transition speeds closer to the global average. Argentina, Chile, and Uruguay were already lower-middle-income economies before 1900 but had to wait until the first decade of the 21st century to become high income.

Replicating the approach of Felipe, Kumar, and Galope (2017) using PPP 2011 data from PWT 9.0 for the period 1960–2014 yields similar results across regions. The rapid transition of the NIEs is evident: the ROK made a swift 23-year transition from low income to high, while Taipei,China managed it in 27 years (Figure 2.1.4). Singapore and Hong Kong, China, which both began the period as lower-middle income, broke into high income in the 1980s. By contrast, the Latin American economies—even those that today are high income—spent much of the period of analysis as middle income. Brazil and Colombia have been upper-middle income since the 1960s but have yet to reach high income, after 54 years for Brazil and 55 years for Colombia.

In general, the shifts in income classification proceeded more quickly in Asia than in the rest of the world, whether the transition was from lower-middle to upper-middle income or from upper-middle income to high income. Differentials in regional growth rates account for the different transition speeds. Middle-income Asian economies grew by an average annual rate of 4.8% during 1960–2014, almost double 2.6% growth in middle-income Latin America. What is not yet clear is what lies behind the higher growth rates of rapidly transitioning economies.

The middle-income challenge: literature review

In response to the failure of many middle-income economies to move smoothly to high income, a large and growing literature has sprung up to examine whether economic growth slows at middle income.

2.1.4 Years as middle income, 1960–2014

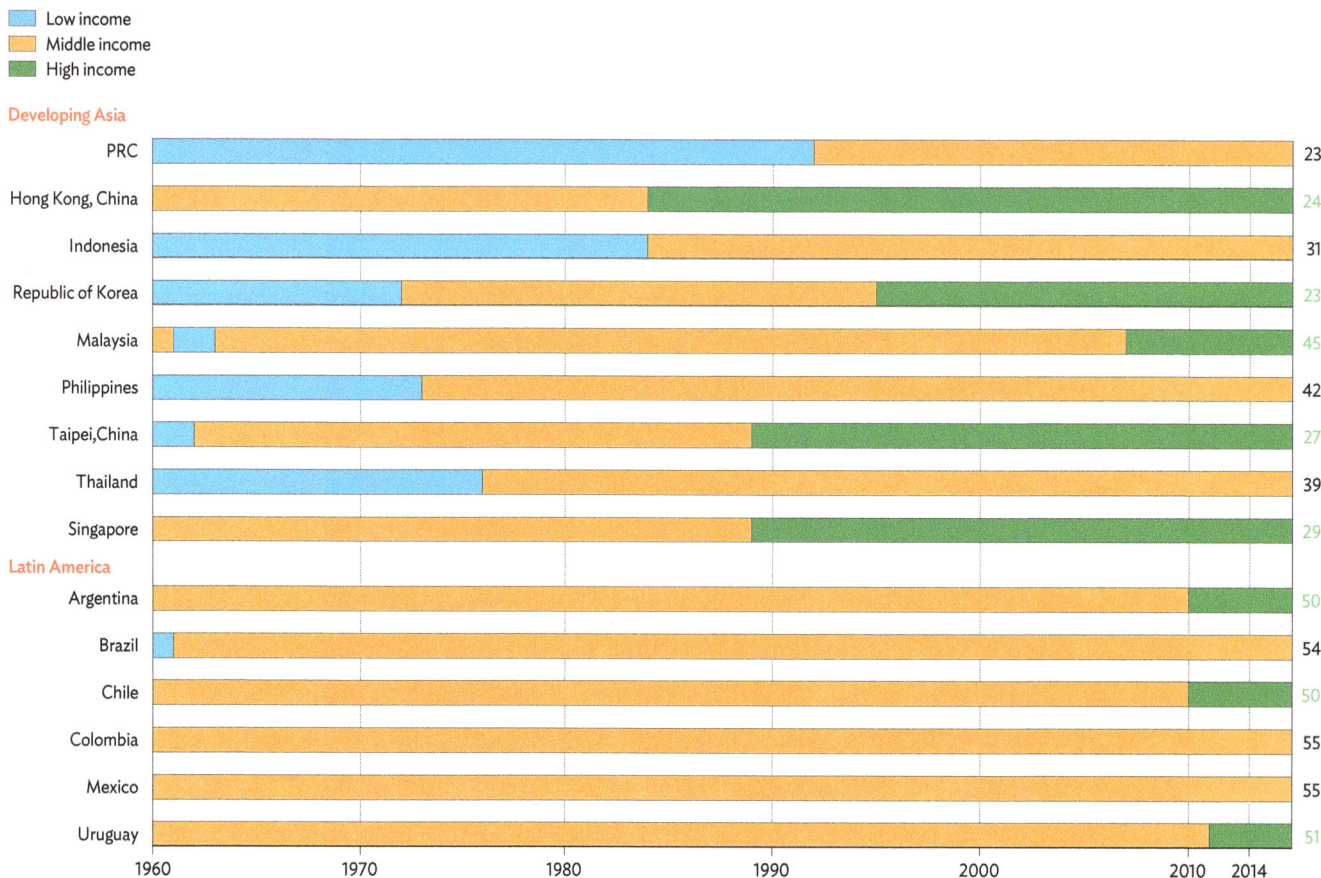

- Low income
- Middle income
- High income

Developing Asia

PRC	23
Hong Kong, China	24
Indonesia	31
Republic of Korea	23
Malaysia	45
Philippines	42
Taipei,China	27
Thailand	39
Singapore	29

Latin America

Argentina	50
Brazil	54
Chile	50
Colombia	55
Mexico	55
Uruguay	51

1960   1970   1980   1990   2000   2010 2014

PRC = People's Republic of China.

Note: Numbers beside the horizontal bars are the years as middle income between 1960 and 2014. Highlighted in green font are those who have reached high income based on the income classification using purchasing power parity in constant 2011 dollars from Penn World Tables 9.0.

Source: Estrada et al., forthcoming.

A number of studies have confirmed that growth does indeed slow at that point. More specifically, these studies find that growth typically slows when economies reach upper-middle income. Spence (2011) used the term "middle-income transition" to specify the phase in the growth process when an economy's per capita income enters the range of $5,000–$10,000. Agénor, Canuto, and Jelenic (2012) argued that economic growth is likely to slow tangibly when an economy's income reaches around $15,000–$16,000. Income variance across economies is often attributed to a "middle-income trap" characterized by sharp deceleration in gross domestic product (GDP) and productivity growth.

Eichengreen, Park, and Shin (2012) examined the eventual slowdown of fast-growing economies. The research showed that such economies slow considerably when their per capita income reaches about $17,000 in 2005 constant international prices. It found growth slowdowns to be positively associated with rapid growth in the preceding period, a high senior citizen dependency ratio, and very high investment rates.

Extending the earlier study, Eichengreen, Park, and Shin (2014) analyzed the incidence of growth stagnation in middle-income economies. Their evidence suggested that many economies experience slowdowns in two ranges of per capita income: one is $10,000–$11,000 and the other is $15,000–$16,000. If found that slowdowns are less likely in economies where the share of population with secondary and tertiary education is relatively high. However, this was not true for education in general, suggesting that high quality human capital matters more for avoiding growth slowdown. The study pointed out that advanced education is vital for middle-income countries seeking to shift production toward technologically sophisticated products and services. In addition, slowdowns are less likely to occur where high-technology accounts for a relatively large share of exports, indicating the importance of moving up the technology ladder to avoid a middle-income slowdown.

The findings of Eichengreen, Park, and Shin (2014) are consistent with the conceptual framework of the middle-income challenge put forth by Aghion and Bircan (forthcoming). According to this framework—which is ultimately based on Schumpeter's notion of creative destruction as new technologies and products drive out old technologies and products (page 62)—graduating to high income requires a shift from investment-led growth to innovation-led growth as an economy approaches the global technology frontier. Innovation-led growth is rooted in innovative entrepreneurship, in which dynamic new businesses and startups bristle with fresh ideas and different ways of doing things. Institutions and policies must evolve to lubricate the shift toward a more innovative economy.

While the studies cited above support the notion of a middle-income trap, other studies do not. For example, Barro (2016), Im and Rosenblatt (2015), Han and Wei (2015), and Bulman, Eden, and Nguyen (2014) found that moving from middle income to high income is not very different from moving from low income to middle income. Barro (2016) argued that there have been no special patterns or trends of dispersion regarding GDP growth since 1870 in the 25 economies studied. No evidence was found in this study that the second transition, moving from middle to high income, is more difficult than the transition from low to middle income. Im and Rosenblatt (2015) similarly found no difference. Likewise, Han and Wei (2015) found that middle-income economies are no more likely to be stuck in the same income group than low-income or high-income economies. According to these studies, the growth patterns of middle-income economies do not present any distinctive pattern that can be easily categorized as a "trap."

In sum, evidence of a supposed middle-income trap is mixed. Some studies found evidence that economies are more likely to slow down at middle income than at high or low income, but others did not. The much more pertinent question, however, is what factors enable middle-income economies to sustain rapid growth and reach high income relatively quickly? This is the central question examined in the balance of this chapter.

A need for a new growth model?

One way that middle-income economies are structurally different from their low-income counterparts is that they have more human and physical capital. This suggests that productivity—the efficiency with which an economy uses capital, labor, and all other inputs to produce output—is likely to become a more significant driver of growth. The data indicate that this is indeed the case. Meanwhile, productivity growth seems to be the litmus test of an economy's ability to make the final jump. Fostering productivity growth must therefore be an integral component of any growth model that will successfully guide Asia toward high income.

Different structures at middle income

The economic structure of middle-income economies differs fundamentally from low-income economies, indicating room for catchup growth to reach high income. The box-and-whisker plots in Figure 2.1.5a show the heterogeneity of demographic structures among different income groups, as well as variations within each income group. Low-income economies tend to have a lower proportion of elderly, with a median of about 3.0%, than do middle-income economies, at 4.8%. Although middle-income economies may still have some demographic dividend to reap compared with high-income economies, which have a median 11.9% share of elderly population, this needs to be complemented by other critical factors that can boost growth.

While demographic structures tend to be less favorable at higher incomes, human capital tends to improve. The median number of years of schooling is 6.1 for middle-income economies, more than double the 2.5 years for low income economies, though still considerably lower than the 9.7 median for high-income economies (Figure 2.1.5b). Given the important contribution of human capital to growth, low-income and middle-income economies need to close gaps in years of schooling. As shown in the section on human capital below, narrowing differences in educational quality is even more critical in boosting growth.

Physical capital is considered important to driving productivity growth. As with human capital, middle-income economies tend to have accumulated more physical capital than have low-income economies but not as much as have high-income economies. Middle-income economies on average have more capital per capita, $31,260 in PPP 2011 terms compared with $4,374 in PPP 2011 terms for low income.[3] One finds the same pattern using direct measures of infrastructure development suggested by Calderón, Moral-Benito, and Servén (2014). The median length of paved roads in middle-income economies is only 3.2 kilometers per thousand workers, substantially shorter than 21.3 kilometers in high-income economies but only somewhat better than the case of low-income economies, for which the paved road median is less than 0.1 kilometers (Figure 2.1.5c). Electricity generating capacity in gigawatts per thousand workers and total length of rail in kilometers per thousand workers show the same wide gaps.

The financial sector in middle-income economies, while more developed than in low-income economies, also lags behind high-income economies in terms of depth and efficiency. Domestic credit to the private sector has a median of 26.4% of GDP in middle-income economies, far lower than 78.5% in high-income economies. In low-income economies, the corresponding figure is 13.3%.

2.1.5 Structural features by income group

a. Demographic structure

Population 65 and above, share in %

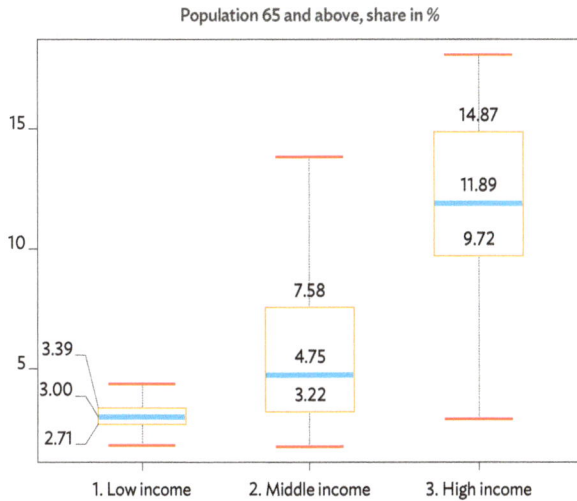

b. Human capital

Years of schooling

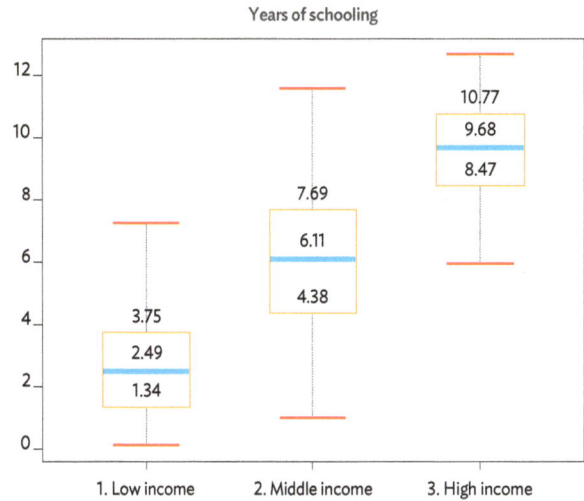

c. Infrastructure

Electricity generating capacity, gigawatts/thousand workers

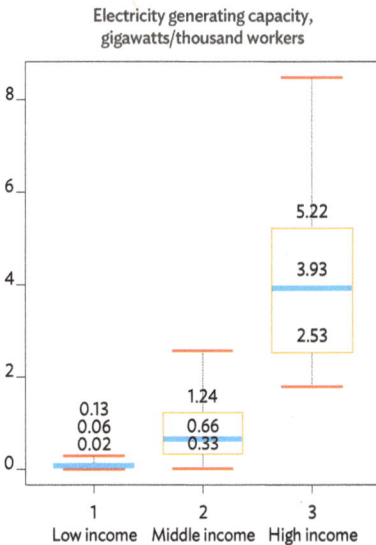

Paved road in kilometers/thousand workers

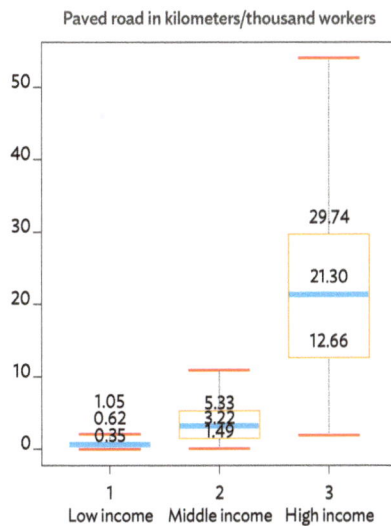

Railway in kilometers/thousand workers

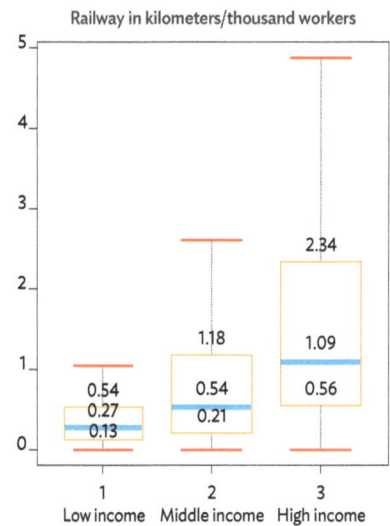

Note: Vertical lines show in each category the whole range of data. The boxes on each line corral the middle half, with the blue line indicating the median value of the whole range, the bottom border of the box indicating the first quartile (the median of the bottom half, with 25% of the whole sample below and 75% above), and the top border indicating the third quartile.

Source: Estrada et al., forthcoming.

Considered a measure of financial sector efficiency, the bank lending–deposits spread is 6.5% for middle income, which lies between 4.2% for high income and 8.3% for low income.

Structural differences suggest that closing gaps with the high-income group through the accumulation of physical and human capital remains important in driving growth. However, middle-income economies already have a larger stock of both types of capital relative to the low-income group. This suggests a bigger role for improved total factor productivity, or growth in production not accounted for by greater input use, in enabling growth in middle-income economies and the transition to high income.

Productivity growth at middle income

In growth accounting, total factor productivity (TFP) is the residual that captures the share of GDP growth that cannot be explained by the observable factors of production: physical capital stock, human capital stock, and labor. It is at best a broad, first-order measure of productivity but nevertheless is widely used in empirical studies and serves as a proxy for the efficiency with which the inputs are combined to produce output.

Table 2.1.1 reports growth accounting for aggregate GDP in economies of different income classes. TFP is calculated in PWT 9.0 using labor hours, not number of employees, as the measure of labor input.[4] Economies are categorized based on per capita income at the beginning of each decade and if they moved to another category over the remainder of that decade. Of special interest are middle-income economies that remained middle income and those that graduated to high-income status. However, the results for other economies—those that remain low income and those that move from low to middle income—are also reported for reference.[5]

Growth accounting can be useful in that it provides clues on whether some components of GDP growth are more important than others in enabling economies to move up the income ladder. The figures reveal that middle-income economies able to transition to high income experience positive TFP growth in every decade (Table 2.1.1e). Human capital input also rises quite strongly in these economies, probably reflecting relatively heavy investment in education. Physical capital stock likewise tends to grow rapidly in successful middle-income economies.

Some interesting patterns emerge when comparing the results for middle-income economies that successfully rise to high income with results for those unable to do so (Table 2.1.1d). Physical capital and human capital play a similar role in the growth of both groups, but labor plays a visibly smaller role in the growth of graduating economies. More importantly, TFP growth appears visibly slower in economies that remain at middle income and accounts for a much lower share of GDP growth. More precisely, TFP contributed 1.2 percentage points (TFP share times GDP growth) to the 4.3% growth recorded for the entire sample period in economies able to transition to high income. In contrast, it contributed only 0.4 percentage points to 4.1% growth in economies unable to move out of middle income.

The decompositions suggest that economies that successfully achieve high-income status exploit multiple advantages, including relatively rapid growth in TFP and human capital, and relatively high fixed investment. The clear difference between middle-income economies that graduate to high income and those that do not is the larger TFP growth in the former, in both absolute and relative terms. It is therefore worthwhile to take a closer look at the determinants of TFP growth in the next section.

The growth accounting exercise above suggests that, although investment in physical and human capital will continue to matter as middle-income economies grow richer, productivity growth will become more important as a driver of economic growth. For middle-income economies to graduate to high income, they need to achieve rapid productivity growth. Georgiev et al. (forthcoming), for example, pointed out that emerging Europe experienced relatively rapid income convergence fueled primarily by rapid TFP growth in individual economies. Failure to achieve productivity growth, on the other hand, can doom economies to a long stay in middle income (See Box 2.1.2). In sum, productivity growth appears to be pivotal to the transition.

2.1.1 Growth accounting for aggregate GDP by income class

a. All economies

	Observations	Aggregate output growth (%)	% contribution to output growth			
			Capital	Labor	Human capital	Total factor productivity
1960s	69	5.39	39.4	14.4	8.5	37.6
1970s	81	4.77	58.4	22.0	10.9	8.8
1980s	92	2.87	58.9	39.7	20.9	−19.5
1990s	105	2.65	61.3	33.8	18.8	−13.9
2000s	114	3.96	48.4	16.4	9.8	25.4
2010–2014	113	3.38	60.1	22.8	11.5	5.6
Total	630	3.90	51.5	22.1	11.5	14.9

b. Low-income economies that stay low income in the ensuing decade

	Observations	Aggregate output growth (%)	% contribution to output growth			
			Capital	Labor	Human capital	Total factor productivity
1960s	17	4.71	30.7	21.2	7.2	40.9
1970s	15	4.02	50.5	35.1	8.5	6.0
1980s	21	2.85	42.0	54.2	19.9	−16.1
1990s	20	2.61	46.2	62.6	22.5	−31.3
2000s	14	5.09	32.6	26.1	8.3	33.0
2010–2014	12	5.29	58.8	32.7	11.7	−3.2
Total	99	3.91	42.6	36.9	12.3	8.2

c. Low-income economies that rise to middle or high income in the ensuing decade

	Observations	Aggregate output growth (%)	% contribution to output growth			
			Capital	Labor	Human capital	Total factor productivity
1960s	6	6.60	37.3	16.7	7.3	38.8
1970s	7	6.71	53.7	23.7	9.7	13.0
1980s	5	6.23	49.4	29.4	17.2	4.0
1990s	3	5.14	50.8	27.2	15.8	6.2
2000s	9	5.77	40.6	10.7	8.0	40.7
2010–2014	3	4.79	51.1	30.5	−5.6	24.0
Total	33	6.04	46.0	20.5	9.3	24.2

d. Middle-income economies that stay middle income in the ensuing decade

	Observations	Aggregate output growth (%)	% contribution to output growth			
			Capital	Labor	Human capital	Total factor productivity
1960s	40	5.63	43.0	10.8	8.5	37.7
1970s	34	5.35	60.2	20.4	9.7	9.7
1980s	38	2.75	67.9	44.5	24.8	−37.2
1990s	42	2.68	69.8	34.3	20.1	−24.3
2000s	43	4.17	48.6	15.6	10.3	25.5
2010–2014	46	4.04	57.3	23.1	11.9	7.7
Total	243	4.07	55.5	21.9	12.8	9.8

e. Middle-income economies that rise to high income in the ensuing decade

	Observations	Aggregate output growth (%)	% contribution to output growth			
			Capital	Labor	Human capital	Total factor productivity
1960s	5	4.51	37.7	21.5	15.1	25.7
1970s	14	4.04	57.4	2.7	13.4	26.5
1980s	4	5.57	49.8	12.9	10.8	26.5
1990s	9	3.83	56.7	15.7	12.0	15.7
2000s	11	4.22	36.5	5.5	9.5	48.6
2010–2014	7	4.44	58.8	14.6	7.9	18.7
Total	50	4.27	50.0	10.3	11.4	28.3

Note: Growth accounting is based on data collected from Penn World Table 9.0. To examine income-level dynamics, a country's income level at the initial year is compared to that at the final year of each period.

Source: Eichengreen, Park, and Shin, forthcoming.

2.1.2 Productivity growth and the middle-income trap in Latin America and the Caribbean

Very few economies in Latin America and the Caribbean have managed to move from middle income to high income.[a] Why has the middle-income trap been so pernicious for that region? What were the main challenges and how have policy makers managed to address them?

One fundamental reason for the middle-income trap in Latin America and the Caribbean has been low productivity growth. While the 1980s is referred to as the lost decade in terms of growth, it was even worse in terms of productivity, with the region never fully recovering ground lost in its debt crisis.

Normalized global share of GDP per capita

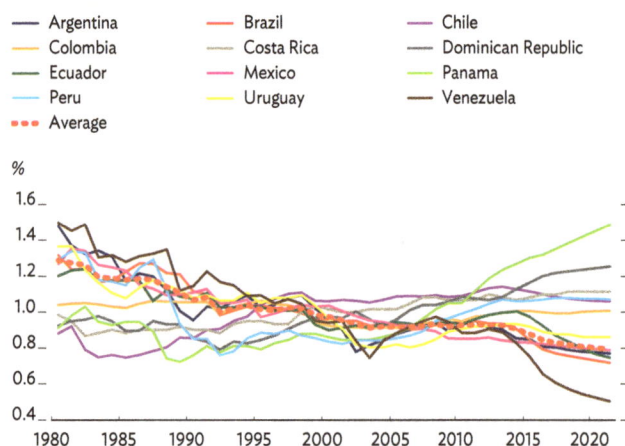

Note: Each line is normalized by the average of that economy such that if the GDP per capita share stayed constant the result would be a horizontal line at 1.0. The average is the simple average of the 26 countries that borrow from the Inter-American Development Bank. Based on underlying dollar values using PPP exchange rates.
Source: Inter-American Development Bank using data from International Monetary Fund. 2016. *World Economic Outlook*. October.

The poor performance of the region in the 1980s is evident in the box figure, which plots global shares of per capita GDP. Although the 1990s featured a strong reform agenda that saw trade and capital accounts liberalized in many economies and widespread privatization, the results were mixed. Growth spurts in some economies ending in financial crises, an outcome arguably related to volatile global capital flows and the opening of capital accounts even while financial systems remained relatively weak. The 2000s saw some progress as commodity exporters were aided by a boom in commodity prices and many economies enjoyed a demographic bonus from fast growth in the working-age population.[b]

The relatively low growth of productivity in Latin America and the Caribbean has several facets. Estimates indicate significant inefficiency in the allocation of resources, including the expansion of low-productivity services and the presence of very small and often informal firms that drag down measures of economic efficiency. In the formal sector, there appear to be inefficiencies even in manufacturing for lack of large and highly productive companies and the persistence of less efficient smaller firms. Some sectors have seen relatively high productivity growth, however, notably agriculture.[c]

[a] The World Bank counts high-income economies as those with a gross national income per capita of $12,476 or more in 2015. By this classification, Chile and Uruguay are the two countries among the 26 that borrow from the Inter-American Development Bank that transitioned from upper-middle to high income in recent years.

[b] A growth accounting exercise is presented in Inter-American Development Bank. 2014. *Latin American and Caribbean Macroeconomic Report*, Appendix A. http://www.iadb.org/en/research-and-data/publication-details,3169.html?pub_id=IDB-AR-109

[c] A general review of productivity in Latin American and the Caribbean is available in Inter-American Development Bank. 2010. *The Age of Productivity: Transforming Economies from the Bottom Up*. http://www.iadb.org/en/research-and-data/dia-development-in-the-americas-idb-flagship-publication,3185.html?id=2010

Source:
Inter-American Development Bank using data from International Monetary Fund. 2016. *World Economic Outlook*. October.

Setting a course for high income

The preceding analysis points to productivity growth as key to paving developing Asia's pathway to high income. While economic growth is intrinsically multidimensional and country-specific, the vital role of productivity growth in middle-income growth suggests that innovation, human capital, and infrastructure may be especially important for economic growth.

All three factors contribute to TFP improvement. Innovation fosters technological progress, which improves the productivity of capital and labor. As an economy becomes richer, innovation becomes a more important driver of productivity growth as other sources, such as the reallocation of labor from agriculture to manufacturing and services, are gradually exhausted. Human capital contributes directly to higher output and higher productivity, with skilled workers better equipped to use advanced technology and create new technology. Infrastructure adds directly to a country's stock of physical capital while improving the productivity of capital, labor, and all other inputs. Road improvement, for instance, reduces economy-wide transportation costs, while the internet reduces economy-wide information and communication costs.

Innovation, human capital, and infrastructure are no doubt closely related. This helps explain why middle-income economies able to graduate to high income, such as Asia's NIEs, tend to be strong on these points. It is no accident that successful economies tend to perform well in all three areas. Human capital in particular is an indispensable component of innovation. Quality human capital accumulation and adaptive education policies enabled the ROK to shift to more innovation-based growth. Infrastructure investment can boost growth by promoting both innovation and human capital. Knowledge reinforces both innovation and human capital, while certain types of advanced infrastructure such as mobile telephone and broadband networks are vital for creating and disseminating knowledge.

Several studies document the positive and significant effect of innovation, human capital, and infrastructure on TFP growth. For example, in a review of the literature on the determinants of TFP growth, UNIDO (2007) found that the most significant factors are education, health, and infrastructure. Human capital enhances the capacity to absorb new technology, which fosters technological progress and innovation. Development at the technology frontier also strongly drives TFP growth, implying an important role for innovation. McMorrow, Röger, and Turrini (2010), for example, found that industries with higher expenditures on research and development (R&D) and adoption rates for information and communication technology (ICT) experience the fastest TFP growth. Similarly, Cardarelli and Lusinyan (2015), a study of TFP growth in the US, observed how states with higher educational attainment and greater investment in R&D often lie closer to the production frontier.

In a comprehensive, sector-level empirical analysis, Dabla-Norris et al. (2015) studied the role of innovation, human capital, and infrastructure in TFP growth and document how the intensive use of high-skilled labor and ICT capital inputs, and higher spending on R&D, tend to be associated with higher productivity growth.

Econometric analysis clarifies the relationship between TFP growth on the one hand and innovation, human capital, and infrastructure on the other (Box 2.1.3). While the results are far from definitive and leave wide scope for further research, they provide empirical support for the positive contribution these three factors make to productivity.

The successful middle-income growth model clearly emphasizes productivity. Innovation becomes more important after economies fully reap the benefits of using existing resources efficiently. Even in the accumulation of physical and human capital, the focus shifts to areas with positive productivity spillover such as advanced infrastructure and higher education. All of this must be underpinned, of course, by a supportive policy environment and a stable macroeconomy.

2.1.3 The sources of total factor productivity growth: econometric analysis

In a comprehensive study, Bosworth and Collins (2003) attempted to synthesize the findings of the large and growing literature on growth regressions and growth accounting. Constructing a consistent series of growth accounts for a wide set of economies, they adopted a growth regression framework to examine the different correlates of TFP growth. Using cross-sectional data for 84 advanced and developing economies during 1960–2000, they found average TFP growth to be negatively associated with per capita income (the convergence effect) and positively associated with health as measured by life expectancy, population size, and institutional quality as measured by a composite of indicators from the International Country Risk Guide.[a] Other factors, such as trade openness, inflation, and government budget balance were not found to be significantly associated with TFP growth.

This box extends the Bosworth and Collins (2003) regressions, adding the three variables of interest—human capital, infrastructure, and innovation—to examine their role as potential correlates of TFP growth. Human capital is measured using average total years of schooling in the population, with series obtained from the dataset of Barro and Lee (2013). Infrastructure is represented by a composite index, constructed as the first principal component of five different types of indicators of infrastructure provision, taken from Calderón, Moral-Benito, and Servén (2014). Innovation is denoted by growth in the per capita capital stock in R&D using data obtained from Kim and Park (forthcoming). Additional controls include per capita income relative to the US, life expectancy relative to the US, population size, and trade openness defined as exports and imports as a share of GDP. The sample is an unbalanced panel covering 64 economies from 1975 to 2014.[b]

The following regression is estimated, with results summarized in the box table:

$$\Delta ln(TFP)_{it} = \beta_0 + \beta_1 humancap_{it} + \beta_2 infra_{it} + \beta_3 (\text{R\&D stock/worker})_{it} + y'Z + \varepsilon_{it}$$

The results confirm that human capital, infrastructure, and R&D growth are significantly associated with TFP growth. Interpreting the coefficients, for an economy

Correlates of total factor productivity, 10-year average growth

Variables	Coefficient
Human capital, 10-year average	0.0180*** (0.0046)
Infrastructure (composite), 10-year average	0.0022*** (0.0008)
Research and development capital stock per worker growth, 10-year average	0.0254* (0.0134)
Log of per capita GDP relative to the United States, initial year	−0.0070*** (0.0025)
Life expectancy relative to the United States, initial year	−0.0081 (0.0185)
Population, initial year	−0.0007 (0.0008)
Openness, 10-year average	0.0000 (0.0000)
Constant	−0.0444*** (0.0104)
Observations	145
R-squared	0.220

Note: *** indicates significance at 1%, ** at 5%, and * at 10%. Standard errors are in parentheses.
Source: ADB estimates.

with average educational attainment, an additional year of schooling is associated with a 0.3% increase in TFP growth. Raising physical infrastructure from the level of Indonesia, which is close to the 25th percentile by this indicator, to that of the ROK, which is near the 75th percentile, is associated with a 0.5% increase in TFP growth. Finally, a 5 percentage point increase in the growth rate of R&D capital stock is associated with a 0.13% increase in TFP growth.

[a] The PRS Group. *International Country Risk Guide.* http://www.prsgroup.com/about-us/our-two-methodologies/icrg

[b] To focus on the fundamental drivers of TFP growth and abstract from fluctuations in the business cycle, and because the variables of interest are slow-moving, 10-year nonoverlapping averages are used. The slow-moving nature of the variables of interest implies that most of the variation is cross-sectional or between economies, rather than within a single economy. For this reason, ordinary least squares method was applied, rather than a fixed-effects specification.

Innovation for diversifying and upgrading production

As other sources of productivity gains are exhausted—such as the shift of labor from agriculture to manufacturing—innovation inevitably plays a bigger role in generating productivity growth, especially for middle-income economies hoping to rise to high income. As economies move closer to the technology frontier, productivity growth becomes driven largely by this key element of productivity, implying a need for economies to switch from investment-led to innovation-based growth. In this scenario, it becomes increasingly useful to understand the nexus between innovation and entrepreneurship, which is crucial for promoting the entry of firms with new ideas or technology. Ultimately, middle-income economies aspiring to reach high income need to diversify and upgrade their production structure, a goal that can be facilitated by government policies promoting innovation.

The previous section showed how successful middle-income economies, those that eventually graduate to high income, tend to have relatively fast TFP growth. The importance of innovation in productivity growth naturally implies that successful middle-income economies will be innovative economies. The data seem to bear out this prediction. Examining R&D behavior in middle-income economies, with the sample divided into lower-middle income and upper-middle income, Kim and Park (forthcoming) found that those able to cross to a higher income group typically performed better on standard indicators of innovation intensity: R&D stock per worker, ratio of R&D investment to GDP, and patent applications per million persons (Figure 2.2.1). R&D investment measures inputs to the innovation process, while patent applications measure outcomes of innovative activities.

2.2.1 Innovative intensity in middle-income economies

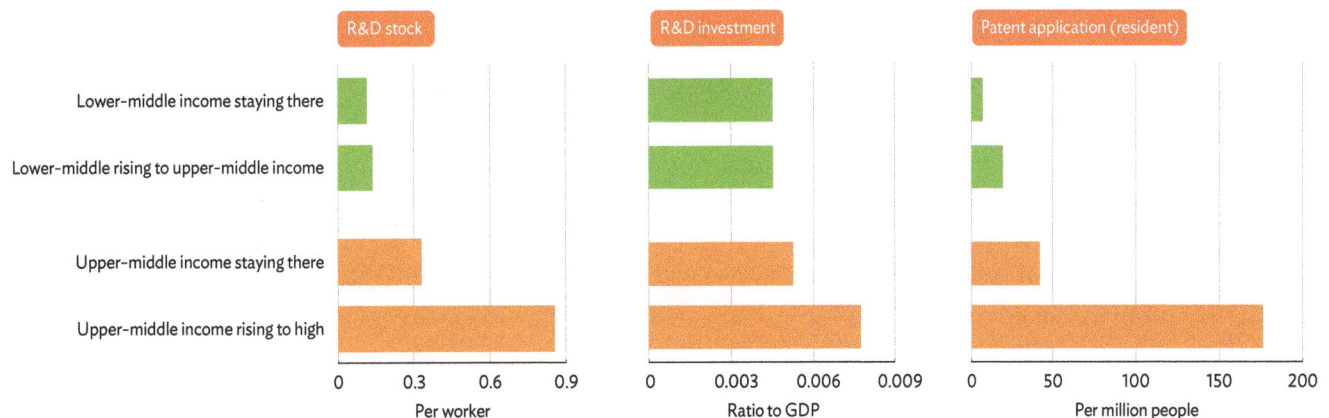

R&D = research and development.
Note: The entire sample covers 1975–2014 that is divided into nonoverlapping ten-year intervals, except for the last 9-year period: 1975–1985, 1985–1995, 1995–2005, and 2005–2014. To examine income-level dynamics, a country's income level at the initial year is compared to that at the final year of each interval. R&D data are available only in post-1980.
Source: Kim and Park, forthcoming.

Interestingly, the difference in innovation intensity between transitioning economies and those remaining in the income category is much larger for the transitions from upper-middle to high than for the transition from lower-middle to upper-middle. Upper-middle-income economies that eventually graduate to high income have more than 2.5 times the R&D stock per worker than their peers. This suggests that innovation is a critical ingredient of the final income transition.

From investment-led to innovation-led growth: literature review

A brief literature review on the shift from investment-led growth to innovation-led growth provides a better understanding of the central role of innovation in the transition to high income. Improved understanding leads in turn to a better conceptual understanding of the challenges facing middle-income economies in their quest to become innovative, high-income economies.

Growth through creative destruction

In his classic theory of economic growth, Joseph Schumpeter proposed three main ideas (Schumpeter 1942).

First, innovation plays a central role in long-run growth. It is the natural counterpart of the conclusion in Solow (1956) that long-run growth requires sustained technological progress.

Second, risk-taking entrepreneurs are central to the fostering of innovation, and these individuals respond to incentives that are influenced by economic policies and institutions. In particular, those incentives influence entrepreneurial investments in R&D, training, and computer purchases that foster innovation. In contrast, an unfavorable environment that suffers poor protection of property rights or hyperinflation, for example, can discourage innovation-based growth by damaging the profitability of innovation. Using country–industry panel data obtained from the Organisation for Economic Co-operation and Development (OECD), Aghion, Howitt, and Prantl (2013) found evidence supporting the complementary roles of patent protection and competition policy in encouraging R&D investment and innovation.

Third, according to the notion of creative destruction, new products and technologies constantly replace old products and technologies. Creative destruction is essentially a competitive process between the old and the new. Incumbent firms and interests try to prevent or delay the entry of new competitors into their industry, while new firms and interests try to enter the industry and expand their market share. The efforts of incumbents to hinder new competitors require assistance from governments and therefore become factors in the political economy.

Productivity, innovation, and competition

In most sectors of an economy, one can think of essentially two types of firms (Aghion and Bircan, forthcoming). First are "frontier firms" that lie close to the current technological frontier. Second are "laggard firms," which lie far below. Faced with greater competition, frontier firms will innovate more to escape competition, while laggard firms will be discouraged by increased product market competition and thus innovate less. Figure 2.2.2 summarizes the relationship between competition and enterprise growth for these two groups of firms.

Acemoglu, Aghion, and Zilibotti (2006) suggested that, as economies get closer to the technology frontier, cutting-edge innovation replaces capital accumulation and technological catchup as the main engine of growth. It further showed that low trade openness and high entry barriers become increasingly detrimental to growth as the country approaches the frontier. According to Aghion and Bircan (forthcoming), many middle-income economies fail to achieve fast growth because their institutions and policies fail to evolve in tandem with their stage of economic development.

This scenario is best captured by the concept of a non-convergence trap in Schumpeter's growth theory. Specifically, the concept refers to the level of development, or distance to the technological frontier, at which an economy fails to switch from an investment-based growth strategy to an innovation-based growth strategy even though the threshold for switching has been reached. An economy that is trapped in this sense stops converging to the frontier (Acemoglu, Aghion, and Zilibotti 2006).

As shown in Figure 2.2.3, economies often grow at rapid rates and converge toward the technological frontier through investment-based strategies when they are between points A and B. However, between points B and C they must switch to an innovation-based strategy to continue their productivity convergence. Developing Asia as a whole has experienced a relatively smooth and rapid transition from A to B. Going forward, the question looming for the region is how to strengthen innovation and move from B to C.

The People's Republic of China (PRC) is perhaps a good example of an economy that has been growing at a very high rate for a long time but is now slowing down and fears getting stuck as it approaches the technological frontier. For many decades, the PRC growth model has used high rates of investment and net exports that are mostly funded and enabled by the state. GDP per capita in the PRC increased from the equivalent of 5% of US GDP per capita in 1980 to almost 25% in 2015. However, PRC convergence has started to slow in the past 5 years. The next stage of development will likely have to come from innovation-led growth, which will require policies and institutions that are quite different from the ones that were so successful in helping the PRC move out of low-income status.

2.2.2 Growth and competition, frontier versus laggard firms

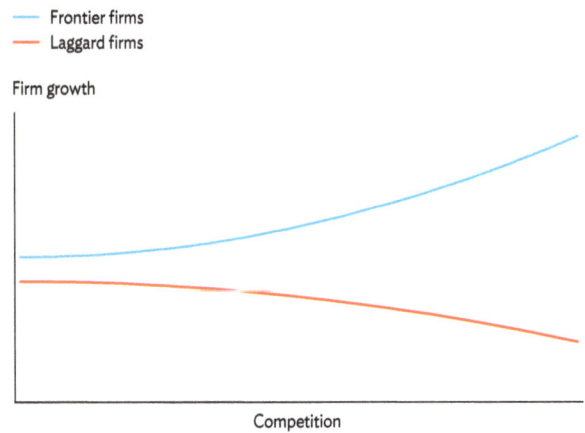

Source: Aghion and Bircan, forthcoming.

2.2.3 Innovation versus investment-led growth

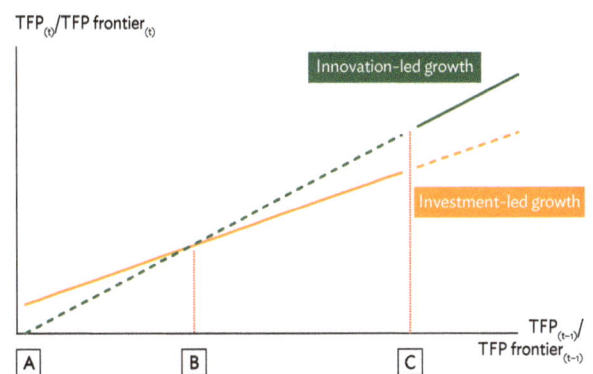

TFP = total factor productivity.
Source: Aghion and Bircan, forthcoming.

Implications for developing Asia

What can emerging economies in Asia do to innovate their way out of middle income? The literature suggests a few priorities going forward. First, the process of technological diffusion, or spillover, is an important factor behind convergence across economies. While imitation of existing technologies drives technological diffusion at lower stages of development, economies need more cutting-edge technology and frontier innovation as their income rises to sustain knowledge diffusion. Hence, greater investment in human capital and R&D becomes essential for middle-income economies. The rising stock of patents and other innovative activity in Asia, particularly in the PRC, is a promising sign in this regard.

Second, in light of the importance of state-of-the-art technology, economies need to ensure that more productive enterprises can engage in and reap the benefits of the latest innovations. One step in this regard is better protection of intellectual property rights, which should extend to reducing the scope of expropriating successful entrepreneurs. Another is a level playing field for access to finance. If innovations can be funded only by the retained earnings of producers or cheap credit through the state, R&D and patenting are unlikely to be allocated to the most efficient enterprises. Developing Asia still has a long way to go in terms of both protecting intellectual property rights and efficiently allocating R&D.

Finally, policy must allow innovative enterprises to grow to an efficient scale. Innovative entrepreneurs should be encouraged to start up and grow, and less productive entrepreneurs should be allowed to fail. This relates to the political economy dimension of Schumpeter's growth theory. Institutions and policies that favor large incumbent firms at the expense of new entrepreneurial firms and startups should be dismantled. Creative destruction is possible only with enabling institutions, which play more important roles as an economy approaches the technology frontier. In practical terms, this means that middle-income economies in Asia should encourage the creation of new businesses by lowering barriers to entry and strengthening the rule of law. Stronger competition policies can help to level the playing field for new entrants as well and contribute in this way to competition and innovation.

Role of entrepreneurship in innovation

The concept of creative destruction holds the entry of new enterprises central to innovation, and there is ample empirical evidence to support this. Akcigit and Kerr (2010), for instance, found that new firms tend to seek more radical innovations to expand their production, while incumbent firms seem content to pursue incremental innovations that rely largely on existing products and processes. Lentz and Mortensen (2008) echoed this result and showed how more than half of total factor productivity (TFP) growth in industry can be attributed to the entry of new firms. Aghion et al. (2009) extended the analysis and argued that incumbent firms may innovate more when in competition with new firms, especially in high-technology industries.

These findings have initiated further research on the impact of firm entry on productivity growth and the different channels of impact. However, studies typically assume that new firms are a single homogeneous group when looking at their contribution to innovation. Analysis differentiating the motivations behind entrepreneurship and innovation attributes across income groups remains very limited. But such differentiation may be important. As seen in the theme chapter of the International Monetary Fund *Fiscal Monitor* published in April 2016, necessity-driven entrepreneurship tends to negatively correlate with GDP per capita, while opportunity-driven entrepreneurship tends to positively correlate. Necessity-driven entrepreneurship is propelled by economic need when work opportunities are scarce, while opportunity-driven entrepreneurship involves the development of new ideas or technology. Put simply, street vendors are examples of necessity-driven entrepreneurship, fueled by the need for survival, but tech startups exemplify opportunity-driven entrepreneurship fueled by potential profits from innovation.

The following pages argue that emerging markets and developing economies need to increase the share of opportunity-driven entry and make it a development goal. Along these lines, analysis considers whether middle-income and high-income economies differ in the extent to which innovation motivates entrepreneurship. This investigation uses two relevant indicators—one called the entrepreneurship motivational index and the other being the innovation type of early-stage entrepreneurship.

The first measure, the entrepreneurship motivational index, comes from the Global Entrepreneurship Monitor dataset. The index surveys early-stage entrepreneurs, defined as 18–64 years old and either nascent entrepreneurs or owner-managers of new businesses. The percentage of individuals who are seeking improvement-driven opportunities is divided by the percentage who are motivated by a basic need to be employed. A ratio greater than one means that there are more opportunity-driven entrepreneurs than necessity-driven entrepreneurs in a population.

What does it mean? A higher entrepreneurship motivational index may indicate that more new firm owners are driven by the prospect of developing new ideas or technology than by a lack of job options. This reflects opportunity-driven initiatives where an entrepreneur has a new creation or invention that cannot hit the market unless the entrepreneur starts a business to take advantage of the opportunity. A lower reading, on the other hand, implies greater necessity-driven entrepreneurship, which may indicate that there are no other job options available to the entrepreneur, who has to start a new business to find employment.

Charting this index across economy income status reveals a distinctly positive relationship for economies that already enjoy high incomes. As the left panel of Figure 2.2.4 shows, high-income economies have a relatively high ratio of opportunity-driven to necessity-driven early-stage entrepreneurship, nearly double that of middle-income economies. The ratio shows that, in high-income economies, startups driven by new opportunities are 3.4 times as numerous as those driven by necessity. In middle-income economies, they are little more than half as prevalent, at 1.8 times as numerous.

2.2.4 Innovation-related entrepreneurship and income status

Ratio of opportunity-driven over necessity-driven early entrepreneurship

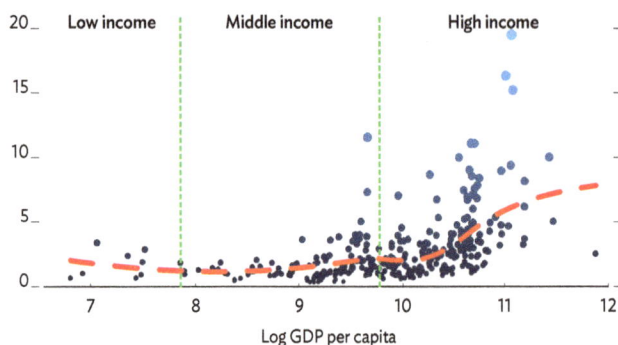

Ratio of innovation type of early-stage enterpreneurship

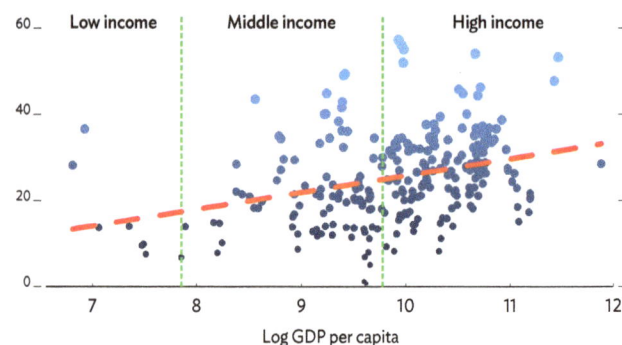

Note: Global Entrepreneurship Monitor is constructed by surveying sampled individuals. The survey covers 17 years of data from 182 economies in an unbalanced way. Total early-stage entrepreneurial activity is the percentage of the population aged 18–64 who are either nascent entrepreneurs or owner-managers of a new business. Within this set, opportunity-driven/ necessity-driven early-stage entrepreneurship (the motivational index) is the percentage of those who seek improvement-driven opportunity divided by the percentage of who are motivated by necessity. The innovation type of early-stage entrepreneurship is the percentage of the set who indicated that their product or service is new to at least some customers and that few or no other businesses offer the same product.
Sources: Global Entrepreneurship Monitor; ADB estimates.

The second measure, which captures the innovation type of early-stage entrepreneurship, is calculated as the percentage of early-stage entrepreneurs who indicate that their product or service is new to at least some customers and that few or no existing businesses offer the same product or service. As shown in the right panel of Figure 2.2.4, high-income economies clearly enjoy a higher share of early-stage innovators. On average, 28% of early-stage entrepreneurs in high-income economies indicate that their business belongs to the innovation type, but only 21.8% of early-stage entrepreneurs in middle-income economies do so. Again, the clear implication is that the relationship between entrepreneurship and innovation is demonstratively stronger in high-income economies.

To achieve high-income status, middle-income economies may therefore be well advised to nurture and promote entrepreneurs who engage in new businesses to pursue opportunities based on new ideas, especially startups that aim to provide innovative products or services that do not yet exist on the market. Such a policy would naturally be in addition to the more traditional goal of fostering a macro-environment that does not force individuals into entrepreneurship for lack of other employment options.

Economy and product complexity versus innovation

Another way to understand how innovation can help an economy graduate to high income is through the notion of structural transformation. As suggested by the development economics literature, this entails changing what an economy produces and exports by diversifying and upgrading its product mix.

In this vein, Hidalgo and Hausmann (2009) explained economic development as a process of learning how to produce and export more complex products. Complexity is a characteristic of both products and of economies. Product complexity refers to the capabilities required for producing a product. Economy complexity refers to the capabilities available in it. Development requires acquiring new sets of capabilities to move toward new activities associated with higher productivity.

These capabilities include the human and physical capital, legal system, institutions, and other factors needed to produce a product; the know-how or working practices held collectively by the group of individuals comprising a firm; and the organizational abilities that provide the capacity to form, manage, and operate activities involving large numbers of people.

To calculate measures of product and country complexity, Hidalgo and Hausmann (2009) devised the method of reflections, which looks at trade data as a network connecting two mutually exclusive sets: the set of economies and the set of products they export with revealed comparative advantage.[6] To make this method operational, diversification is defined as the number of products that a country exports with revealed comparative advantage, and ubiquity as the number of economies that export the product with such an advantage. Diversification is the simplest measure of complexity in an economy, and ubiquity the simplest measure of lack of complexity in a product.

According to these definitions, an economy that exports more goods with revealed comparative advantage, and so is more diversified, is more complex than an economy that exports fewer goods with revealed comparative advantage, or is less diversified. Meanwhile, a product exported by fewer economies with revealed comparative advantage, and so is less ubiquitous, is more complex than a product that is exported with revealed comparative advantage by more economies (more ubiquitous). The intuition behind these interpretations is simple. An economy can export a certain product only if it possesses the necessary capabilities in terms of labor skills, institutions, machinery, public inputs, and tradable inputs. An economy with more capabilities is more complex. Similarly, a product that is less ubiquitous is more complex in terms of requiring more exclusive capabilities.

To sum, complexity is associated with the set of capabilities required by a product (product complexity) or with the set of capabilities that are available to an economy (economy complexity). The implication for middle-income economies is that upgrading export structures toward more diversified and complex products is critical to foster rapid growth and eventually reach high income.

Recent data from the Atlas of Economic Complexity, a research initiative of the Center for International Development at Harvard University, indicate that in 2014 the top 10 economies by economic complexity were Japan, Germany, Switzerland, the ROK, Sweden, Austria, the Czech Republic, Finland, Hungary, and the United Kingdom. Among economies in developing Asia, only the ROK made the top 10.

While not in the top 10, other economies in developing Asia have improved their ranking from 1995 to 2014. The PRC was ranked 19 in 2014, well up from its 1995 ranking of 48. Other Asian economies have seen their ranking improve over the period, though not as much as the PRC. Malaysia rose from 44 to 28, and Indonesia moved up from 78 to 56 (Figure 2.2.5).

Looking now at product complexity, Table 2.2.1 shows the 10 most complex products and the 10 least complex products, ranked from a total of 1,240 products. It also shows the major exporters and their share of world exports of the product. The table indicates that the most complex products are chemicals, machinery, and metals, and the major exporters of these products are the advanced economies. The exception is the PRC, which has become a major exporter of some of the most complex products. The right-hand side of the table shows the 10 least complex products such as textiles and agricultural products. Their major exporters are developing economies, some of them from Asia.

Product complexity likewise appears to correlate well with economy income. For instance, Felipe et al. (2012) showed that the top exporters of the most complex products are all high-income economies: Germany, Japan, the Netherlands, the United Kingdom, and the US.[7] By contrast, the top exporters of the least complex products include Cameroon, Congo, Equatorial Guinea, Gabon, and Malaysia. Further, the 100 most complex products accounted for 8%–10% of all exports from Germany and Japan, the two top economies in terms of economic complexity. The corresponding shares in many middle-income economies in the region such as Indonesia, the Philippines, Thailand, and Viet Nam were all less than 1%.

Table 2.2.2 summarizes the top five products that the PRC, Indonesia, and Malaysia export. The products exported by the PRC in 1995 exhibited low complexity, such as toys and footwear, but the composition of its top exports had dramatically changed by 2014. The top five exports by then were largely much more complex machinery and electronics. Indonesia did not change the composition of its top five exports much, consisting mainly of much less complex petroleum and other natural resource products. Although Malaysia improved its index of complexity standing from 1995 to 2014, the composition of its top five exports shifted from largely machinery to predominantly oil products.

Although many Asian economies have managed to improve their economic complexity ranking, the progression of the PRC is remarkable as it has acquired the capabilities necessary to produce a more varied and sophisticated range of products. Acquiring the necessary set of capabilities to produce more complex products apparently enabled it to achieve faster growth than other economies in the region.

Analysis suggests that, to reach high income, middle-income economies need to manufacture the most complex products. This inference seems to be backed by empirical evidence. Felipe et al. (2012), for example, divided 5,107 products into six groups by product complexity and found a positive and statistically significant relationship between export share in the four product groups 1–4 (the more complex products) and income per capita, and a negative and statistically

2.2.5 Index of economic complexity

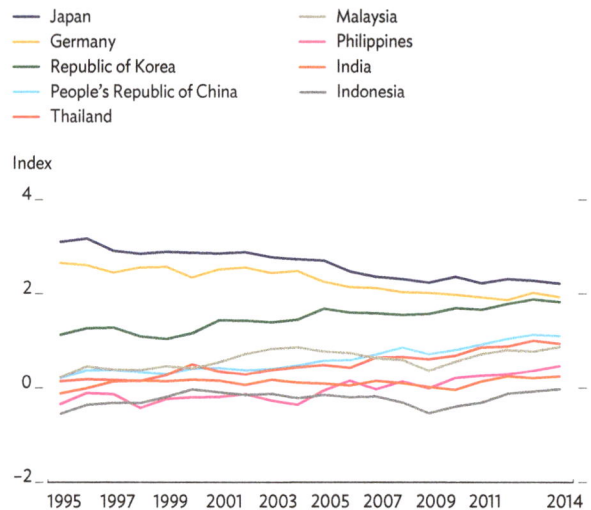

Source: Center for International Development at Harvard University. *The Atlas of Economic Complexity.* http://www.atlas.cid.harvard.edu (accessed 31 January 2017).

2.2.1 The 10 most complex and 10 least complex products and their top exporters, 2014

10 most complex products			10 least complex products		
HS4 classification	**Top exporters (export share of product)**	**GDP per capita, PPP (2011 $)**	**HS4 classification**	**Top exporters (export share of product)**	**GDP per capita, PPP (2011 $)**
(7805) Lead tubes, pipes, and fittings	Japan (96.7)	35,359	(5303) Jute and other textile fibers	Bangladesh (62.7)	2,885
	ROK (2.9)	35,104		Tanzania (16.6)	2,213
	PRC (0.4)	12,473		India (10.3)	5,224
(8444) Machines to extrude, cut manmade textile fibers	Germany (48.9)	45,961		Belgium (1.9)	43,668
	Japan (24.1)	35,359		PRC (1.2)	12,473
	PRC (10.5)	12,473	(1801) Cocoa beans, whole	Cote d'Ivoire (37.5)	na
	Switzerland (3.3.)	58,469		Ghana (24.0)	3,570
	Italy (2.9)	35,807		Cameroon (6.2)	2,682
(9204) Accordions and similar instruments	Germany (78.5)	45,961		Nigeria (6.7)	5,501
	PRC (10.3)	12,473		Ecuador (6.1)	10,968
	United States (6.3)	52,292	(2615) Niobium (columbium), tantalum, vanadium, or zirconium ores	Australia (30.9)	43,071
	Barbados (4.8)	14,220		South Africa (20.9)	12,128
(8457) Machining centers for working metal	Japan (45.6)	35,359		Rwanda (11.3)	1,565
	Germany (19.1)	45,961		Brazil (3.7)	14,871
	Hong Kong, China (5.9)	51,808		Russian Federation (2.9)	24,039
	ROK (4.6)	35,104	(714) Manioc (cassava)	Thailand (56.5)	13,967
	United States (4.2)	52,292		Viet Nam (13.5)	5,353
(8113) Cermets (composites of ceramic and metal)	Germany (25.4)	45,961		United States (5.1)	52,292
	Austria (17.1)	47,745		Costa Rica (3.5)	14,186
	PRC (15.7)	12,473		Cambodia (3.0)	2,995
	United States (8.9)	52,292	(2609) Tin ores	Myanmar (38.0)	5,344
	Japan (7.3)	35,359		Rwanda (15.3)	1,565
(7507) Nickel tubes, pipes, and tube or pipe fittings	Japan (25.2)	35,359		Australia (14.0)	43,071
	United States (16.2)	52,292		Dem. Rep. of Congo (6.5)	1,217
	France (10.4)	39,374		Nigeria (4.4)	5,501
	Germany (10.2)	45,961	(5310) Woven fabrics of jute or of other textile bast fibers	India (49.3)	5,224
	Italy (9.8)	35,807		Bangladesh (25.0)	2,885
(2812) Halides and halide oxides of nonmetals	Germany (28.6)	45,961		PRC (8.3)	12,473
	Japan (16.6)	35,359		Nepal (6.8)	2,173
	United States (11.4)	52,292		Germany (1.4)	45,961
	ROK (11.9)	35,104	(6704) Wigs	PRC (77.7)	12,473
	PRC (11.5)	12,473		Indonesia (8.6)	9,707
(3705) Photographic plates and film, exposed and developed, not motion-picture film	Japan (23.6)	35,359		United States (1.3)	52,292
	ROK (12.3)	35,104		Philippines (1.1)	6,659
	United Kingdom (9.4)	40,242		Bangladesh (1.0)	2,885
	Belgium (8.3)	43,668	(4106) Tanned skins of animals (other than fur skins)	India (33.7)	5,224
	PRC (8.3)	12,473		Pakistan (12.3)	4,646
(9027) Instruments and apparatuses for physical or chemical analysis	United States (23.2)	52,292		Italy (11.5)	35,807
	Germany (16.9)	45,961		Nigeria (10.9)	5,501
	Japan (13.0)	35,359		Kenya (3.1)	2,769
	PRC (6.5)	12,473	(801) Coconuts, Brazil nuts, and cashew nuts	Viet Nam (25.5)	5,353
	Singapore (5.5)	72,583		India (17.9)	5,224
(9022) Apparatuses based on the use of x-rays or of alpha, beta, or gamma radiation	Germany (23.7)	45,961		Cote d'Ivoire (13.2)	na
	United States (19.9)	52,292		Indonesia (6.4)	9,707
	Japan (9.5)	35,359		Philippines (5.6)	6,659
	PRC (7.5)	12,473	(2709) Petroleum oils, crude	Saudi Arabia (16.8)	48,025
	Netherlands (7.3)	47,240		Russian Federation (13.5)	24,039
				United Arab Emirates (6.2)	64,398
				Canada (5.7)	42,352
				Iraq (5.3)	12,096

na = data not available, PRC = People's Republic of China, ROK = Republic of Korea.

Source: Center for International Development. The Atlas of Economic Complexity. http://www.atlas.cid.harvard.edu (accessed 31 January 2017).

2.2.2 Top five exports of selected Asian economies, 1995 and 2014

PRC, top five export products, 1995	$ billion	Share (%)	PRC, top five export products, 2014	$ billion	Share (%)
Total exports	219.0	100.0	Total exports	2,340.0	100.0
Toys, scale models, puzzles	8.5	3.9	Automatic data-processing machines	193.0	8.2
Trunks or cases of any kind	7.6	3.5	Transmission apparatus for radio, telephone, and TV	150.0	6.4
Footwear, with leather body	6.7	3.0	Telephones	103.0	4.4
Reception apparatus for radio broadcasting	6.3	2.9	Parts and accessories for office machines	45.1	1.9
Other footwear of rubber or plastics	5.6	2.6	Electrical transformers	31.3	1.3
Indonesia, top five exports, 1995			**Indonesia, top five exports, 2014**		
Total exports	48.1	100.0	Total exports	189	100.0
Petroleum oils, crude	4.8	10.0	Coal, briquettes	19.9	10.5
Petroleum gases	4.4	9.1	Palm oil, crude	17	9.0
Plywood, veneered panels, and similar laminated wood	3.4	7.0	Petroleum gases	14.2	7.5
Natural rubber	2.0	4.2	Petroleum oils, crude	9.46	5.0
Gold content	1.4	2.9	Natural rubber	5.17	2.7
Malaysia, top five exports, 1995			**Malaysia, top five exports, 2014**		
Total exports	78.6	100.0	Total exports	284.0	100.0
Electronic integrated circuits	10.4	13.2	Electronic integrated circuits	53.7	18.9
Automatic data processing machines	5.6	7.1	Petroleum oils, refined	25.8	9.1
Reception apparatus for radio broadcasting	4.3	5.5	Petroleum gases	18.1	6.4
Palm oil, crude	3.5	4.4	Palm oil, crude	12.7	4.5
Parts and accessories for office machines	2.9	3.7	Petroleum oils, crude	12.0	4.2

PRC = People's Republic of China.

Source: Center for International Development. The Atlas of Economic Complexity. http://www.atlas.cid.harvard.edu (accessed 31 January 2017).

significant relationship regarding the least complex products in group 6. These significant relationships when considering the top and bottom product groups are clear in Figure 2.2.6.

The conclusion of this analysis is that to move up the development ladder, Asia's middle-income economies need to change their production and export structures, diversifying and upgrading their product lines to make their structures more complex. Developing Asia has made significant progress in this regard, and the experience of the PRC since the mid-1990s is exceptionally successful. Economies need to study what they produce and export and situate their basket in the product complexity ranking accordingly, deciding judiciously how far up they can go in terms of structural change.

The important question is how an economy diversifies and upgrades its economic structure. It cannot simply leapfrog into more complex products. Diversification and upgrading are path-dependent processes in which history matters greatly. Economies upgrade to products that require capabilities similar to those they already possess, by learning and doing. They do not switch to products utterly alien to their capabilities. History shows that today's advanced economies did not simply follow their comparative advantage, though, in the sense of letting the market decide, when making decisions to diversify and upgrade their production structures. Instead, active governments facilitated and induced this process through industrial policy.

2.2.6 Shares of the most and least complex exports

Share of most complex exports (log)

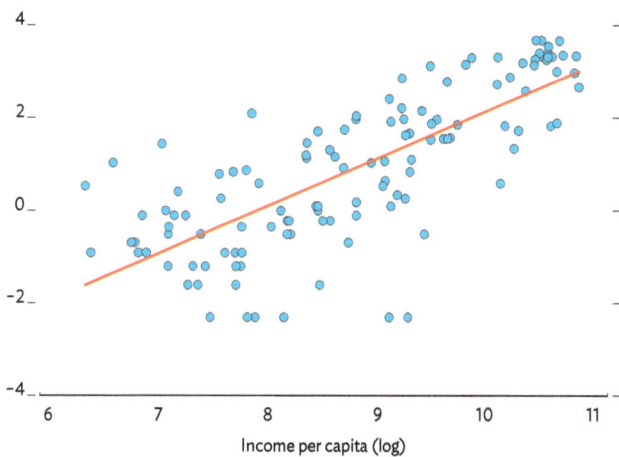

Income per capita (log)

Share of least complex exports (log)

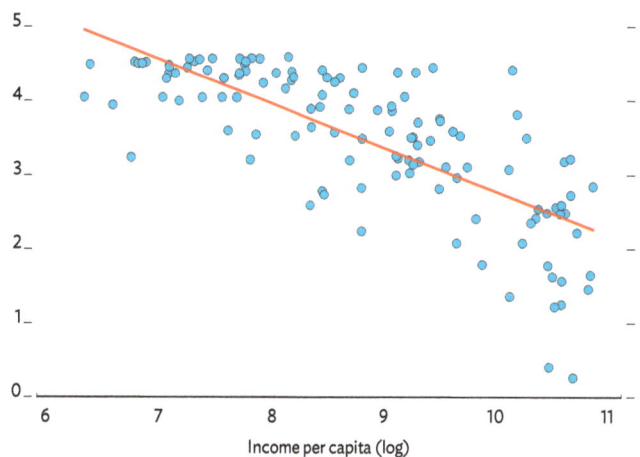

Income per capita (log)

Notes:

1. The equation for the share of most complex exports is as follows: Export share = –12.707 + 1.026 GDP per capita (log)
   t-stat: (–17.81) (12.77)

2. The equation for the share of least complex exports is as follows: Export share = 4.150 – 0.600 GDP per capita (log)
   t-stat: (9.58) (–12.29)

Source: ADB estimates based on data in Felipe et al. (2012).

This has also been the case of Asia's most advanced economies. Although it is virtually impossible to use the same policy tools today that these economies used decades ago, governments in today's middle-income economies can still play a significant role in advancing and supporting structural transformation. For successful structural transformation, two fruitful strategies are innovation, particularly in R&D, and education.

In a discussion of how the governments of modern middle-income countries can think about how to move into more complex products and sectors through innovation, Felipe and Rhee (2014a, 2014b) posited that these economies will have to increase their R&D spending, both public and private. However, the structure of R&D in these economies reflects a model not conducive to commercial success, either because the private sector plays only a limited role in knowledge generation, or because market-driven demand for technology is weak, as evidenced by low R&D spending. For this reason, middle-income economies typically do not have many high-technology sectors. Meanwhile, the public sector is ill-equipped to lead R&D efforts because it lacks the private sector's incentive to commercialize R&D outcomes. However, initiating R&D consortiums with the private sector in targeted industries can be an effective strategy by which governments jumpstart R&D investment.

Foreign direct investment (FDI) is a particularly important element in industrial diversification, as many middle-income economies rely on it to acquire advanced business skills and technology. However, if not managed properly, preferential treatment and R&D incentives given to multinational corporations can disproportionately increase the profitability of their operations without effecting the transfer of technology to domestic firms. Policy should thus focus more on the acquisition of advanced technology through strategic FDI. Sometimes simply buying technology and paying royalties may be the most effective approach to developing domestic technology bases.

Besides innovation, education is another area that appears especially relevant to middle-income economies looking to climb into high income. These economies often suffer from shortage of skilled professionals, particularly professional managers. Without a steady supply of high-skilled labor, upgrading an economy's industrial structure is impossible. Education that endows high school graduates with strong cognitive skills, especially in math and science, can be more important for development through export diversification than simply increasing the quantity of education available. As the next section will further show, economies committed to growth through human capital accumulation need to refocus their efforts on improving education quality.

Human capital for emerging marketplace needs

A skilled workforce is indispensable for creating new knowledge and technology. It can be considered the core of an innovative economy. Skilled workers are better able to learn, use, and adapt advanced technology. Given the wide gap in human capital between developing Asia and the advanced economies, there remains wide scope for expanding human capital investment in the region. This not only helps boost the region's growth but can also improve economic equity. That Asian populations are aging further strengthens the case for investing in human capital.

As seen in the previous section, middle-income economies that graduate to high income are more innovative than other middle-income economies. As human capital is an indispensable ingredient of innovation, it is reasonable to expect them to have superior human capital as well. Indeed, the data show that middle-income economies that reach high income invest more in human capital than their peers (Figure 2.3.1). The difference is more pronounced for the transition from upper-middle income to high income than from lower-middle income to upper-middle income. And, significantly, it is more pronounced for secondary and tertiary education than for primary education. This suggests that education, particularly post-primary education, is especially important for upper-middle-income economies seeking to reach high income.

Human capital spending, inequality, and growth

Spending on human capital development raises productivity and may play a pivotal role in promoting growth, as the experience of the Asian NIEs has shown. The ROK, Singapore, Taipei,China, and Hong Kong, China all enjoyed exceptionally high growth rates from the mid-1960s to the 1990s, allowing them to achieve high income within the period. This feat is partly attributed to an environment that fostered human capital accumulation, especially of knowledge capital, and the efficient allocation of these resources (e.g., Mankiw, Romer, and Weil 1992, Barro 2001, Aghion and Howitt 2009, Hanushek and Woessmann 2016). Human capital accumulation also promised to help mitigate income inequality and promote equity, which has become a growing concern worldwide, including in developing Asia. Public investment in human capital could be a potent way to improve incomes in the region, provided it does not harm public finances.

2.3.1 Average schooling in middle-income economies

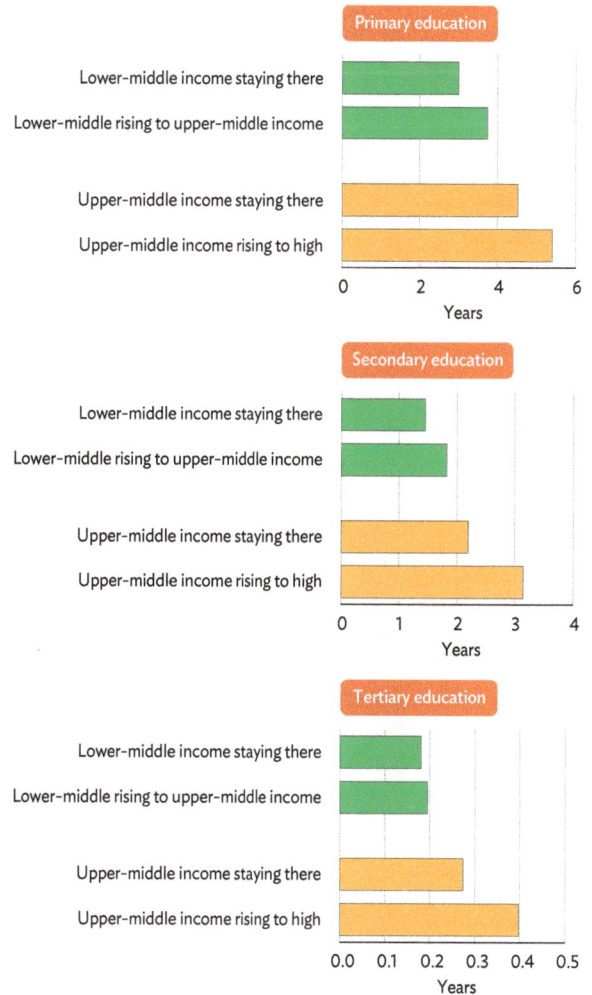

Note: The entire sample covers 1975–2014 that is divided into nonoverlapping ten-year intervals, except for the last 9-year period: 1975–1985, 1985–1995, 1995–2005, and 2005–2014. To examine income-level dynamics, a country's income level at the initial year is compared to that at the final year of each interval.

Source: Kim and Park, forthcoming.

Impact of human capital spending: empirical analysis

Recent empirical research has focused on how the demographic transition can affect the aggregate economy. Highlighting the role of greater investment in children, specifically in their human capital, Lee and Mason (2010) and Mason, Lee, and Jiang (2016), for example, found that fertility decline that is accompanied by an increase in human capital spending can substantially boost economic growth.

A change in an economy's population age structure can have two effects on growth. The first demographic dividend is a very direct quantitative effect on income and consumption from a decline in fertility. Over the past half century, long-term fertility decline in Asia and in the rest of the world has caused radical and important changes in the population age distribution. In the medium term, economies in the early stage of the transition have benefited from an increasing share of the working-age population relative to the young and elderly (Bloom and Williamson 1998, Kelley and Schmidt 2001, Mason 2001, Mason and Lee 2007). The same demographic forces may also have improved fiscal health in developing Asia (Lee, Kim, and Park 2016).[8]

The second demographic dividend, likewise owing to fertility decline, stems from a scaling up of human capital investment and is often associated with three main effects: higher consumption growth, greater physical capital per worker, and augmented human capital. Mason, Lee, and Jiang (2016) estimated these effects and found human capital to be a highly significant channel of this demographic dividend.

To gain better understanding of the issues, the following pages empirically examine the impact of human capital investment on productivity, inequality, and fiscal health in developing Asia. The data and empirical methodology are described in Box 2.3.1. Human capital can change as fertility changes, but the observed outcomes are also influenced by education policy, parental investment in children, the nature of the job market, and other socioeconomic factors. The goal of the exercise is not to estimate the effect of a fertility decline on human capital, though, but to compare the different scenarios in the absence of fertility changes.

The main channel of the economic impact of demographic transition is an increase in labor income because of higher human capital spending. With expanding incomes, governments may directly benefit in turn from the expansion of their tax base as more income can be taxed and it can be taxed at higher rates.

Impact of human capital investments: simulation results

Figure 2.3.2 plots lifetime public and private human capital investments in developing Asia and in other economies where NTA estimates are available. For comparability across economies, values are normalized relative to the average labor income of people aged 30–49 to control for national

2.3.2 Public versus private human capital spending in developing Asia

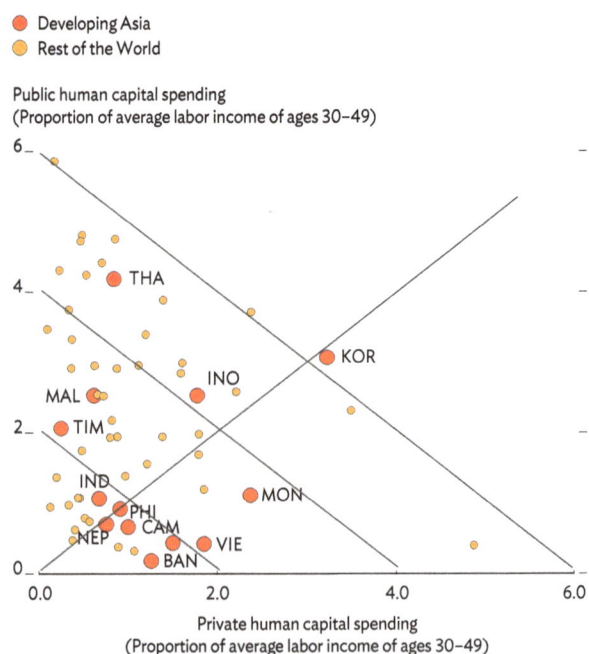

● Developing Asia
● Rest of the World

Public human capital spending
(Proportion of average labor income of ages 30–49)

Private human capital spending
(Proportion of average labor income of ages 30–49)

BAN = Bangladesh, CAM = Cambodia, IND = India, INO = Indonesia, MAL = Malaysia, MON = Mongolia, NEP = Nepal, PHI = Philippines, KOR = Republic of Korea, THA = Thailand, TIM = Timor-Leste, VIE = Viet Nam.

Note: Lifetime public and private human capital spending is based on a synthetic cohort measure of health and education spending based on NTA data for a recent year. It is calculated as the sum of public and private per capita health consumption for ages 0–17, and of public and private per capita education consumption for ages 3–27.

Source: Abrigo, Lee, and Park, forthcoming.

2.3.1 Data and model for estimating the impact of human capital

This box attempts to simulate the impact of human capital on the economy in a manner similar to Lee and Mason (2010). The major source of data is the National Transfer Accounts (NTA) (www.ntaccounts.org). The NTA is an accounting framework to document economic flows across populations of different ages in a manner consistent with the United Nations System of National Accounts (United Nations 2013).

Economic life cycles are estimated from household surveys and government administrative data and are scaled to match aggregate controls compiled using the United Nations System of National Accounts. The NTA provides a detailed measure by age of how much people consume and produce, and how the gap in their consumption and production is funded through other sources, namely transfers and asset-based reallocations.

Data on human capital spending and labor income are based on NTA life-cycle estimates in 12 Asian economies along the whole range of incomes: Bangladesh, Cambodia, India, Indonesia, Malaysia, Mongolia, Nepal, the Philippines, the ROK, Thailand, Timor-Leste, and Viet Nam. Human capital investments are measured based on NTA estimates of public and private education and health expenditures by single year of age. The NTA measure on human capital expenditure contains some useful information about the quality of human capital, which is an important dimension of it. It also allows an examination of both public and private human capital investment.

Following Lee and Mason (2010), education expenditures for people aged 0–26 are included in the analysis. Health care expenditure for those aged 0–17 meanwhile excludes spending related to reproductive health. It is important to note that the NTA estimate of human capital spending captures only those goods and services available from the market and does not include the opportunity cost of students' time or the value of services provided by parents and other family members, which also contribute to human capital.

Analyzing fiscal impacts necessarily requires estimates of tax profiles. The NTA distinguishes public transfer flows to and from households by purpose, such as education or pension, and by source, such as labor income tax, consumption tax, and so on. These estimates are not available, however, for many Asian economies in the sample. As an alternative, country-specific tax schedules levied on personal income are used and applied to labor income.

The economy is modeled as a human capital-augmented Cobb-Douglas production function. Human capital investments can be made by either governments or households. Public and private human capital investments are initially assumed to be equally effective. The analysis then looks at how the results vary when public human capital investment becomes more effective relative to private investment. The model also introduces heterogeneity among economies and among individuals within them. Heterogeneity permits analysis of the distributional impacts of targeted human capital spending interventions. The simulated method of moments is used to simulate the impact of increasing human capital investment on inequality, productivity, and the fiscal health of Asian economies. Abrigo, Lee, and Park (forthcoming) explained the methodology in detail.

differences, including the labor costs that are prominent in the delivery of education services (Mason, Lee, and Jiang 2016). Estimates below the 45-degree line indicate a greater share for the private sector in financing human capital spending, while values above it indicate a greater share for the public sector. Estimates that are closer to the origin at the bottom left signify smaller human capital spending in total.

Human capital spending in developing Asia varies greatly from economy to economy both by amount and financing source. Thailand, for instance, invests on average about 5 years of prime-age labor income on human capital for each person. In Bangladesh, by contrast, average lifetime human capital spending per person is only 1.4 years of prime-age labor income. Viet Nam and Timor-Leste spend about 2.3 years of labor income on human capital per person, but Viet Nam relies largely on private rather than government spending. These variations are determined to some extent by each economy's stage of economic development.

2.3.3 Human capital spending and GDP per capita

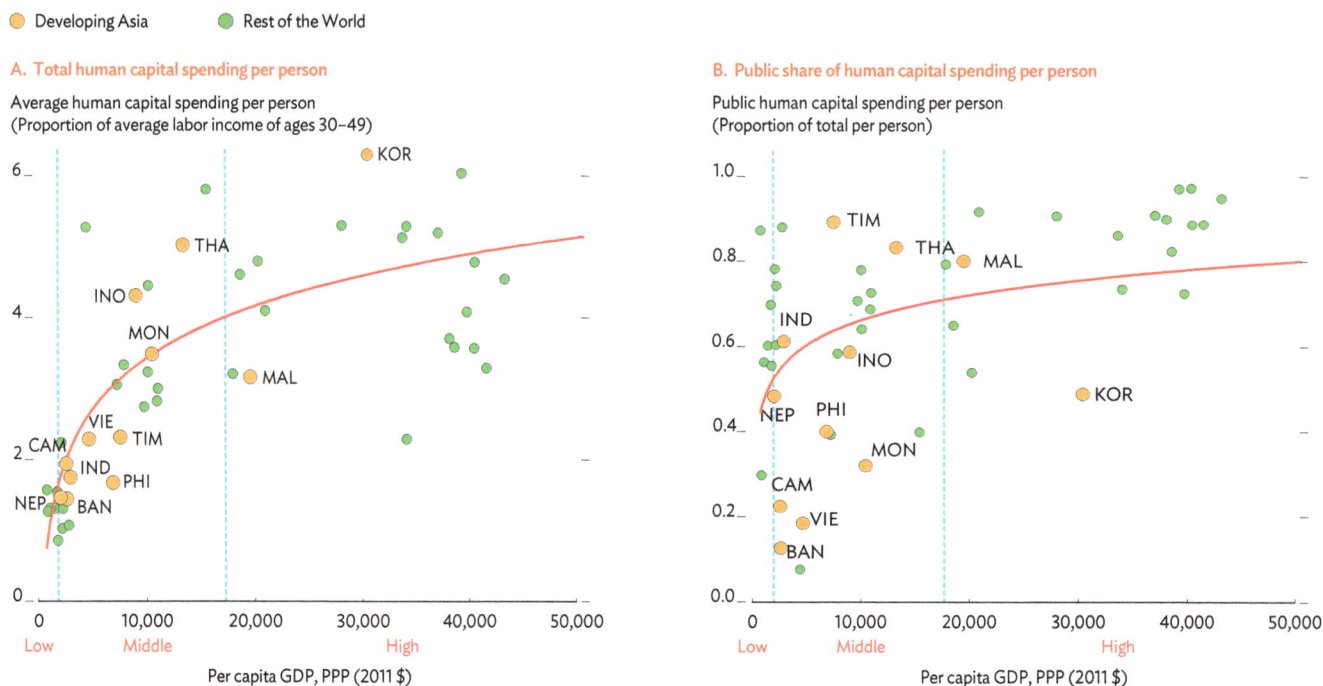

● Developing Asia   ● Rest of the World

A. Total human capital spending per person

Average human capital spending per person
(Proportion of average labor income of ages 30–49)

B. Public share of human capital spending per person

Public human capital spending per person
(Proportion of total per person)

BAN = Bangladesh, CAM = Cambodia, IND = India, INO = Indonesia, KOR = Republic of Korea, MAL = Malaysia, MON = Mongolia, NEP = Nepal, PHI = Philippines, PPP = purchasing power parity, THA = Thailand, TIM = Timor-Leste, VIE = Viet Nam.

Note: Lifetime public and private human capital spending is based on a synthetic cohort measure of health and education spending based on NTA data for a recent year. It is calculated as the sum of public and private per capita health consumption for ages 0–17, and of public and private per capita education consumption for ages 3–27.

Source: Abrigo, Lee, and Park, forthcoming.

Figure 2.3.3 plots each economy's average lifetime human capital spending against its per capita GDP. Two observations are apparent. First, higher-income economies invest more on human capital per person (Panel A). The importance of investing in human capital to promote economic growth is well emphasized in the literature. While most regional economies in the sample invest the average amount for their income, if not more, some economies, such as Malaysia, the Philippines, and Timor-Leste, spend substantially less.

Second, the public sector contribution to human capital spending intensifies as economies develop (Panel B). While there is wide variation in the government's share in human capital spending among developing economies, an upward trend is clear as per capita GDP increases. This shift toward a larger role for governments in financing human capital investment has also been observed recently in health-care spending (e.g., Fan and Savedoff 2014) and much earlier in financing general consumption in general (e.g., Peacock and Wiseman 1961).

Figure 2.3.4 presents the simulated impacts of a universal 20% increase in human capital spending per capita on labor productivity growth (Panel A) and income inequality (Panel B) in 13 developing and industrialized Asian economies. These economies were selected for the availability of data needed to estimate the structural model presented in the previous section. The simulated increase in human capital spending per person roughly equals the magnitude of the projected drop in average births per woman in developing Asia over the next 3 decades.

2.3.4 Simulated impact of increased human capital spending per capita

A. Labor productivity growth

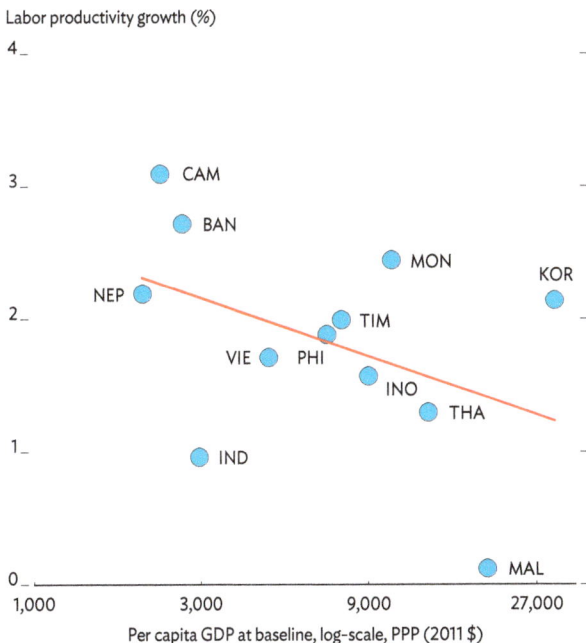

B. Income inequality

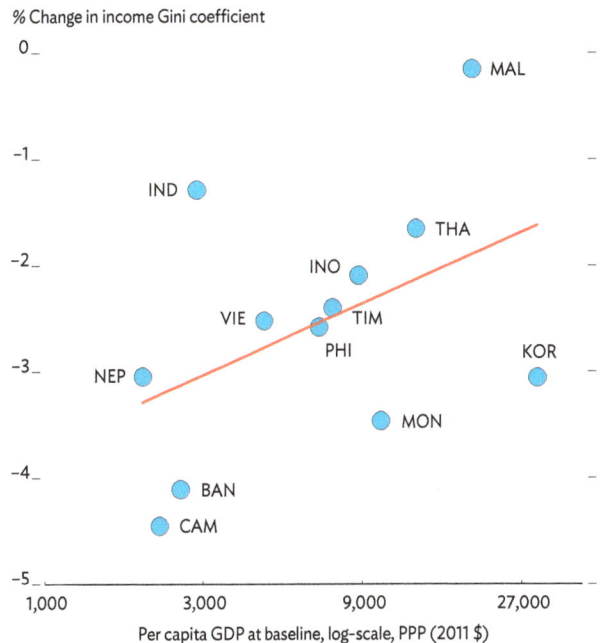

Labor productivity growth (%)

% Change in income Gini coefficient

BAN = Bangladesh, CAM = Cambodia, IND = India, INO = Indonesia, KOR = Republic of Korea, MAL = Malaysia, MON = Mongolia, NEP = Nepal, PHI = Philippines, PPP = purchasing power parity, THA = Thailand, TIM = Timor-Leste, VIE = Viet Nam.

Note: Simulated impact estimates are responses to a 20% increase in per capita human capital spending by age.

Source: Abrigo, Lee, and Park, forthcoming.

The projected impact in different economies shows some interesting patterns. Lower-income economies seem likely to benefit more from increased human capital spending. Labor productivity in economies with lower incomes, such as Bangladesh, Cambodia, and Nepal, is projected to increase by up to 3.1% as a result of a 20% expansion of human capital spending per person. In more developed economies such as Malaysia and Thailand, the projected impact is more modest. It is quite interesting that in economies at similar economic stages, such as Bangladesh and India, the projected impact of human capital spending per capita on labor productivity can differ quite substantially, reflecting the peculiarities of their age profiles and resulting productivity. On the other hand, the simulated impact on productivity growth in the ROK and Nepal are about the same, despite the large development disparity between them. This suggests that expanding human capital spending may also benefit higher-income economies despite the usual downward trend in impact as per capita income rises.

Greater human capital spending significantly narrows inequality. Again, the impact is greater in lower-income economies than in more developed ones. In Bangladesh, Cambodia, Nepal, and Viet Nam, increased human capital spending per capita is projected to bring down income Gini coefficients by 3%–5% from baseline values. In more developed economies like Thailand and Malaysia, the decline is smaller at 1%–2%.

2.3.1 Simulated impact of human capital spending on productivity growth and inequality, selected Asian economies

Country	Change in inequality (%)		Productivity growth rate by income quintile (%)					
	Human capital	Labor income	Q1 (poorest)	Q2	Q3	Q4	Q5 (richest)	All groups
Middle income								
Bangladesh	−6.7	−4.1	7.5	5.7	4.0	2.4	0.6	2.7
Cambodia	−7.2	−4.5	7.4	6.1	4.6	2.8	0.8	3.1
India	−3.7	−2.1	3.4	3.3	2.8	2.0	0.3	1.6
Indonesia	−2.3	−1.3	2.3	2.2	1.9	1.3	0.2	1.0
Malaysia	−0.3	−0.2	0.3	0.3	0.3	0.2	0.0	0.1
Mongolia	−5.8	−3.5	5.7	4.9	3.9	2.5	0.6	2.4
Philippines	−4.3	−2.6	4.7	4.2	3.3	2.1	0.4	1.9
Thailand	−2.9	−1.7	2.6	2.6	2.5	1.9	0.3	1.3
Timor-Leste	−4.5	−2.4	3.5	3.5	3.3	2.8	0.6	2.0
Viet Nam	−4.1	−2.5	4.7	3.9	2.9	1.7	0.3	1.7
Others								
Nepal (low income)	−5.1	−3.1	4.7	4.3	3.5	2.4	0.5	2.2
ROK (high income)	−5.1	−3.1	4.9	4.3	3.5	2.3	0.5	2.1

ROK = Republic of Korea.

Source: Abrigo, Lee, and Park, forthcoming.

The welfare effects of increased human capital spending may be traced to its greater impact on poorer households, especially in lower-income economies (Table 2.3.1). In Bangladesh and Cambodia, for instance, labor productivity among households in the poorest income quintile is projected to increase by 7%–8% because of greater investment in human capital. The impact on higher-income households is substantial as well, but less so.

Public finances and human capital investment

Higher worker productivity can directly benefit the government. The fiscal impact of greater human capital spending depends as much on tax structure as on government involvement in boosting human capital spending and on the impact on productivity. Personal income taxes per capita in Cambodia and Timor-Leste, for example, are projected to increase by at least 3%. In other economies, the projected impact on government revenues may be insignificant despite large gains in labor productivity.

There are many different ways governments can intervene to increase human capital spending aside from a universal increase in government provisions. Governments may increase human capital spending for targeted vulnerable groups while maintaining current amounts for the mainstream. An alternative strategy is to improve the efficiency with which public spending is translated to human capital without increasing appropriations. These strategies are not mutually exclusive but may be combined to create more targeted strategies.

To further investigate the issue, this subsection considers three types of targeted strategies. Strategy 1 assumes that governments increase human capital spending by 20% per person for each age group.

This strategy assumes no change in spending efficiency. Strategy 2 assumes a 20% improvement in the efficiency of translating public spending inputs to human capital, while the amount of public spending is kept at the baseline value. Strategy 3 considers both a 20% increase in government human capital spending and a 20% improvement in efficiency. These three scenarios are combined with three different government targeting schemes: a universal program where every household benefits from the public interventions on human capital, a targeted program that is available only to households belonging to the lower 40% by income, and a targeted program available only to those in the lower 60% by household income.[9]

In all the strategies considered, government revenues are projected to increase with expansion of the tax base, with labor income per capita growing by as much as 3%–5% in some scenarios in certain economies. Increasing both the efficiency and amount of public human capital spending seems to increase tax collection per capita more than the interventions implemented separately, if they can be added together. There is only a modest decline in effective tax rates, indicating household labor income will grow faster than the amount the government collects from these households in taxes.

The fiscal impact of public spending on human capital per capita depends on the government strategy employed to raise human capital. In general, strategies that improve efficiency without increasing inputs have little or no positive effect on the fiscal rate of return from public human capital spending. Increasing public spending is projected to lower the fiscal rate of return, though rates remain positive in all scenarios.

In summary, simulations in individual economies using the NTA database show that increasing human capital spending promotes inclusive growth by improving labor productivity and narrowing income inequality. Government-led human capital investment appears to be more inclusive than human capital accumulation led by the private sector.[10] Lower-income economies and poorer households within economies tend to benefit more from increased human capital spending, which argues for early investment. Interestingly, investing in human capital not only promotes growth and equity but may also improve government budgets in developing Asia in the long run.

This outcome is not guaranteed, as it depends partly on how human capital spending is transformed to actual productive labor in each economy. Other government policies and the economic environment are also important. Moreover, the government interventions on human capital spending that the simulation exercise considered—either a universal increase in human capital spending, a targeted increase only for vulnerable groups, and improved efficiency in human capital spending—are not mutually exclusive and can be combined to create more targeted strategies.

The aging of Asia's population further strengthens the case for human capital accumulation and puts a spotlight on the quality of education. Intuitively, more productive workers can offset the negative economic impact of having fewer workers. The share of the elderly population is rising across developing Asia as a whole, though the speed and current status of population aging varies a lot across the region. Populations in India and the Philippines are still relatively young, while the PRC and Thailand have significantly older populations. Richer economies such as the ROK and Singapore, meanwhile, are at an advanced stage of demographic transition. Notwithstanding such heterogeneity, there is a clear regional trend toward older populations, and even in many younger Asian populations, demographic dividends associated with relatively large working-age cohorts are set to decline in the foreseeable future (ADB 2011).

The pace of demographic transition is very rapid in some Asian economies, especially in East Asia. A transition that took rich Western economies more than a century is occurring in these economies in just a few decades. For example, from 2000 to 2050, the old-age dependency ratio will increase by a factor of 6 in the ROK and by a factor of 4 in the PRC. According to Ha and Lee (forthcoming), in the absence of significant human capital investments, many aging middle-income Asian economies may see their growth rates fall sharply. At a minimum, deteriorating demographics should add a sense of urgency to improving Asia's human capital.

Prioritizing educational quality

A study by ADB (2015) showed that education can promote growth effectively only if it is sufficiently high quality to significantly raise cognitive skills, the thinking skills that enable individuals to learn, solve problems, and create new knowledge. Increasing the average years of schooling can boost economic growth, but this also requires that schooling build cognitive skills.

The ADB study indicated that the additional growth obtained from raising the average years of schooling to 11.6, the OECD average, would be relatively low (scenario 1 in Figure 2.3.5). Growth would be more rapid if economies focused on achieving basic cognitive skills that are comparable with the average in OECD economies. In Figure 2.3.5, this is shown as scenario 2, in which 85% of students score at least 400 on international tests of cognitive skills for mathematics and science.[11] Scores around 400 indicate that a student has reasoning skills and can do simple mathematical or science procedures. Economies with higher cognitive skills, in which 85% of students achieve at least 400 and 15% achieve at least 600 in the tests (scenario 3 in Figure 2.3.5), achieve even faster growth when compared with growth obtained from raising basic skills. These economies are considered to have a critical mass of students who possess top-level skills and demonstrate the ability to solve complex problems, reason, and strategize, and thus would likely become innovators.

2.3.5 Growth projections from 2015 to 2045 under different education and skills scenarios

Scenario 1

Raising average years of schooling in Asian economies to the OECD average

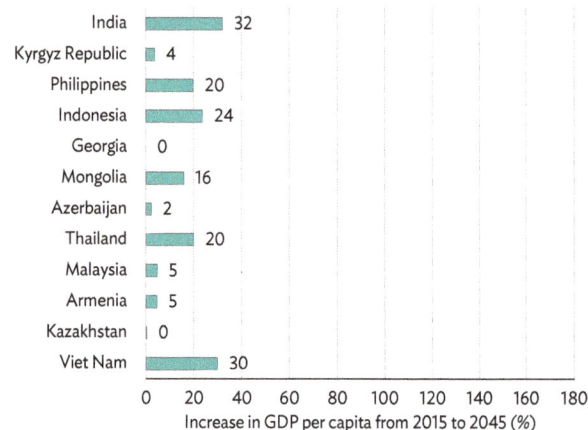

Economy	Increase in GDP per capita from 2015 to 2045 (%)
India	32
Kyrgyz Republic	4
Philippines	20
Indonesia	24
Georgia	0
Mongolia	16
Azerbaijan	2
Thailand	20
Malaysia	5
Armenia	5
Kazakhstan	0
Viet Nam	30

Scenario 2

Raising the share of students scoring 400+ to the OECD average

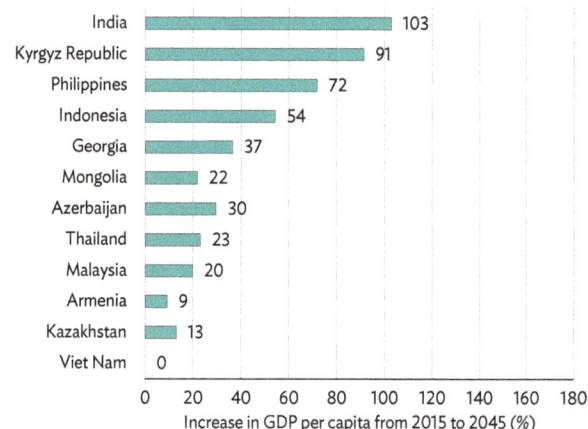

Economy	Increase in GDP per capita from 2015 to 2045 (%)
India	103
Kyrgyz Republic	91
Philippines	72
Indonesia	54
Georgia	37
Mongolia	22
Azerbaijan	30
Thailand	23
Malaysia	20
Armenia	9
Kazakhstan	13
Viet Nam	0

Scenario 3

Raising the share of students scoring 400+ and 600+ to the OECD average

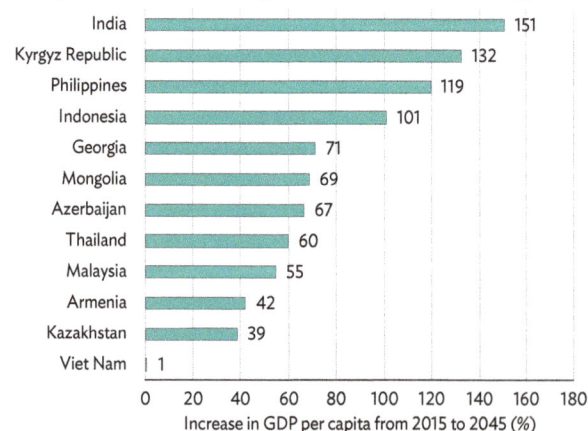

Economy	Increase in GDP per capita from 2015 to 2045 (%)
India	151
Kyrgyz Republic	132
Philippines	119
Indonesia	101
Georgia	71
Mongolia	69
Azerbaijan	67
Thailand	60
Malaysia	55
Armenia	42
Kazakhstan	39
Viet Nam	1

OECD = Organisation for Economic Co-operation and Development.
Note: Projections assume that educational reform takes 15 years and that fully replacing the workforce with skilled workers takes another 40 years. Scenario 1 simulates raising the average years of schooling in Asian economies to the OECD average of 11.6 years. Scenario 2 simulates raising the share of students who score above 400 to the OECD average of 85%. Scenario 3 simulates additionally raising the share of students who score above 600 to the OECD average of 15%.
Source: ADB. 2015. *A Smarter Future: Skills, Education, and Growth in Asia.* In *Key Indicators for Asia and the Pacific 2015.*

If education systems that build cognitive skills offer higher growth prospects, the question becomes what features of education systems can deliver better cognitive skills? Evidence suggests three important ones. First is having information systems that conduct quality data collection and provide relevant, timely, and credible data on schooling inputs and skills outcomes. These systems enable governments to reach evidence-based policy decisions and hold schools and teachers accountable for learning outcomes. Further, providing information to parents on student and school performance can empower families to demand better educational quality. Second is curriculum content that matches student capabilities and fosters the development of critical skills, in particular problem-solving and noncognitive skills emphasizing basic digital and financial skills. Basic education curricula, especially at the secondary level, ideally focus on developing skills that are highly transferable. Third is value placed on early childhood education, as this can foster substantial improvement in skills outcomes. Evidence shows that early childhood education is associated with higher cognitive skills and educational attainment, which facilitate other positive outcomes.

Key to middle-income economies' achievement of faster economic growth and movement up to high income is a greater emphasis on the quality of education, to ensure that education systems deliver more skills that are relevant in the labor market. It is fundamentally the quality and not just the quantity of education that delivers more rapid growth.

Related to this—and as suggested at the outset of this section—higher education built on a foundation of sound primary education may become more important as an economy approaches the global technology frontier. Evidence from the US indicates that, in states close to the technology frontier, returns on education that features research are higher than returns on 2-year college education. In stark contrast, as Figure 2.3.6 shows, the returns on basic education exceed the returns on research education in states that are distant from the frontier. The lesson for middle-income Asian economies is that they ought to increase their investment in research-type education as they grow richer and catch up.

Closing education gaps

The profitability of investing in education is indisputable, and supporting evidence continues to grow. The long history of estimating returns on education in all regions of the world and almost all economies has shown that the size of the return on education rivals and often exceeds that of investment in most forms of physical capital. A dollar invested in increasing education by 1 year, especially for girls, generates an increase in earnings and other benefits, such as in health, of $4 in lower-middle income economies and as high as $10 in low-income economies (Jamison and Schäferhoff 2016). Understanding the pattern of returns on education in different settings can inform understanding of the relative benefits of investing in different levels of education.[12]

2.3.6 Long-term growth effects of spending $1,000 per person on higher education, US states

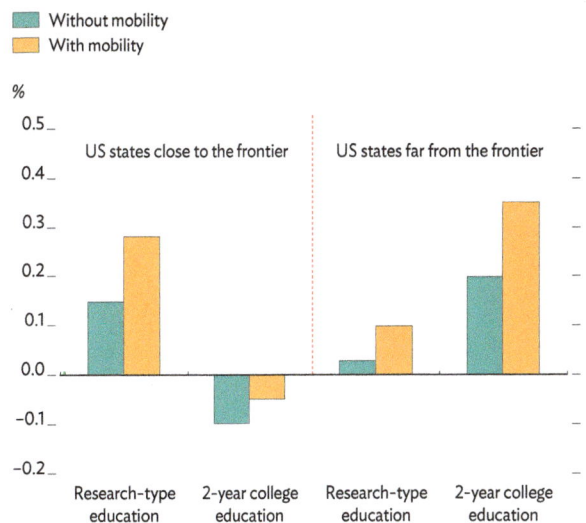

Source: Aghion and Bircan, forthcoming.

Until the 1980s, intuition, as well as evidence based on thousands of estimates of rates of return,[13] pointed to higher returns for low-income economies than for high-income economies and higher returns for primary than for tertiary education, especially in low- and middle-income economies. However, since the 1990s, there has been mounting evidence of significantly higher returns on post-primary and especially tertiary education from studies spanning most parts of the world, including low- and middle-income economies in Asia, Latin America, and Africa (Schultz 2004, Kingdon, Patrinos, Sakellariou and Soderbom 2008, Patrinos, Ridao-Cano, and Sakellariou 2006, Riboud, Savchenko, and Tan 2006). This pattern reversal is hardly a surprise for two reasons. One is the widespread expansion of primary education across the world, including in low- and middle-income economies, thus increasing the supply of low-skilled workers. The other is skill-biased technological change that reduces demand for low-skilled labor.

These findings naturally alter the policy implications of public spending on education for poverty reduction. Subsidies to tertiary education need not to be very large or universal, as those who can afford higher education will pay as needed. Governments can focus instead on correcting credit market failures to ensure that the poor have access to education (Colclough, Kingdon, and Patrinos 2009). Meanwhile, efforts to make primary education universal need to be continued to build a strong foundation for tertiary education.

Although bridging the gap in post-secondary education completion rates between high-income and low- and middle-income economies is necessary (Figure 2.3.7), precedence arguably goes to bridging another gap, in education quality rather than quantity. Successful education systems provide quality education and equip graduates with marketable skills. Working with panels of international test scores, Hanushek and Woessmann (2008) found strong evidence that it is skills relevant to the labor market, such as numeracy, literacy, and problem solving, that have the strongest association with high individual earnings, high economic growth, and equitable distribution of income.

2.3.7 Average schooling years by income group

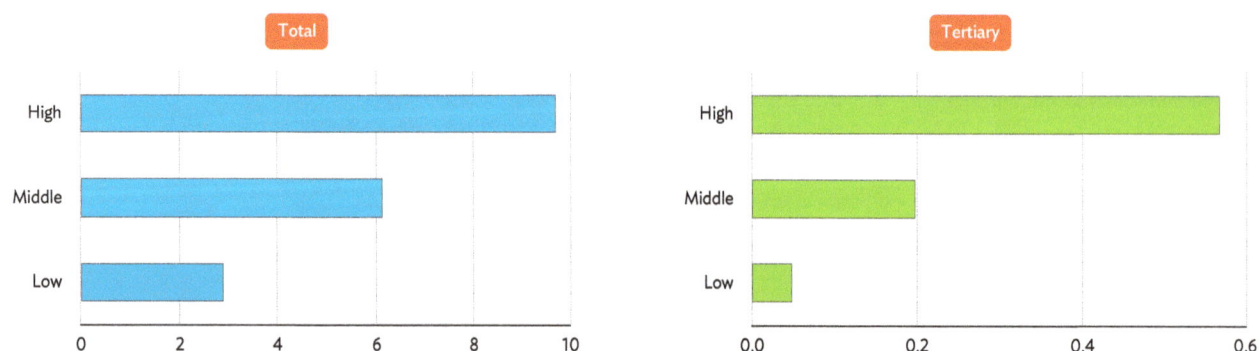

Source: ADB estimates based on data from Barro and Lee (2013).

Yet, international surveys such as the Programme for International Student Assessment and Trends in International Mathematics and Science Study continue to reveal stark differences in the quality of learning between students in most low- and middle-income economies and economies that are more economically and educationally advanced. While substantial educational attainment differences persist, especially in the proportion of tertiary education graduates (Figure 2.3.8), the gap in educational performance, indicating quality of education, is spectacular (Figure 2.3.9). The average proportion of 15-year-old students in OECD economies who score high on mathematics and science tests is 4 to 5 times greater than in middle-income economies, and the proportion of low performers in middle-income economies on the same subjects is more than 2 times the OECD average. In developing Asia, an exception like Viet Nam, which ranks at 8 among the 72 economies covered, tends to indicate that the gap can be closed with sound education policies.

2.3.8 Educational attainment, middle income versus advanced economies

Legend: Advanced economies; Middle income

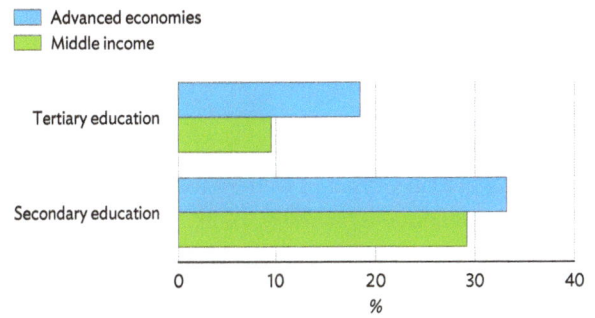

Source: Barro and Lee 2013.

2.3.9 Performance on standardized math and science tests, middle income versus OECD economies

Legend: Middle income; Organisation for Economic Co-operation and Development

A. Math

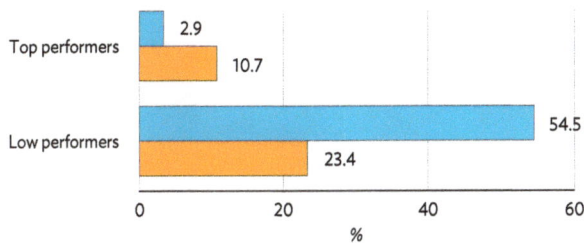

B. Science

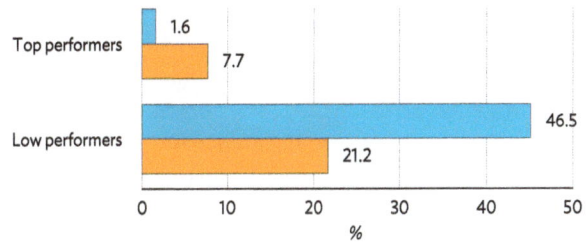

Note: Top performers are students that are proficient at level 5 or 6. Low performers are those that rate below level 2, the baseline level of proficiency.
Source: Organisation for Economic Co-operation and Development. 2015. Programme for International Students Assessment.

Building successful education systems, ones that enable better student learning, remains a challenge. Such systems do, however, share certain characteristics. One is an effective assessment system that frequently measures student learning and provides timely information to students, teachers, and policy makers. Another is accountability and effective oversight that requires schools to take responsibility for the performance of the school and of the individual student. Yet schools need a degree of autonomy in planning and the management of school budgets and personnel.

Infrastructure investment for facilitating structural change

Infrastructure typically refers to the basic structures that facilitate and support economic activity. Here, the term is used to denote network infrastructure—transport by road and rail, electricity, water supply and sanitation, and telecommunications by landline, mobile phones, and internet systems. Providing essential services and connecting markets, infrastructure is essential to the smooth functioning of the economy. It is highly complementary to labor and other types of capital, and as such its contribution to output gains is potentially large.

Infrastructure differs from other types of capital in a few important ways. Infrastructure projects are often big and capital intensive, making them natural monopolies. They have large upfront costs, but benefits accumulate over very long periods. Infrastructure also tends to generate positive externalities as social returns often exceed private gains. Because of these peculiarities, which make the private financing and provision of infrastructure hard, infrastructure is still commonly provided by governments. Given the budget constraints faced by many low- and middle-income economies, infrastructure often remains underprovided no matter how badly it is needed.

By helping to boost output, infrastructure investment can play a critical role in sustaining growth in middle-income economies, including in developing Asia. ADB reported in 2017 that Asia will need to invest $1.7 trillion per year in infrastructure to maintain its growth momentum (ADB 2017). The type of investment undertaken is important as an economy's infrastructure needs change as it develops. While the transition from low to middle income corresponds to a basic shift from sectors with low to higher productivity, most commonly from agriculture to manufacturing, the transition to high income is more complex, requiring economies to diversify into a wider set of products, innovate rather than just imitate, and upgrade to more complex products with higher value added.

The empirical literature to date is sparse on whether infrastructure plays a special part in overcoming the development challenges faced by middle-income economies. To understand the issue, this section first investigates whether an economy's infrastructure needs alter across its stages of development. It then explores whether infrastructure investment has a causal impact on output and whether this differs for middle-income economies.

On the whole, the analysis reveals a clear pattern in the sectoral provision of infrastructure across development stages, with basic infrastructure such as for transport and for water supply and sanitation more important in the early stages and more advanced infrastructure such as for electric power generation and information and communication technology (ICT) becoming more important in later stages. Faster-growing middle-income economies invest more in infrastructure and tend to have a greater share of infrastructure in ICT than their slower-growing peers. The causal analysis finds as well a strong and sustained impact from public infrastructure investment on output growth in middle-income economies, which further underscores the possible benefits of an infrastructure push for this income group.

Evolution in infrastructure needs

In thinking about the role of infrastructure at different stages of economic development, it is useful to provide a sketch of how an economy transitions from one income group to another. In a standard dualistic development model, low-income economies are able to reach middle-income status through sectoral shifts—primarily by moving workers out of low-productivity agriculture to higher-productivity manufacturing—and by adopting or imitating foreign technology. These sources of high growth tend to peter out, however, once upper-middle income is reached, as the pool of underemployed labor shrinks, causing wages to rise and competitiveness to decline.

Maintaining growth becomes increasingly difficult at middle income unless an economy finds other ways to raise productivity. This would require, for instance, strong investment in innovation that generates new ideas, processes, and technologies and a shift to industries with ever higher value added. Infrastructure may be central to this process. Agénor and Canuto (2015) argued that sufficiently large investments in advanced infrastructure such as high-speed communication networks promote innovation and encourage additional human capital accumulation, which helps a developing economy to escape a middle-income slowdown.

One can draw from this a few hypotheses about the role of infrastructure in development. One is that the infrastructure required would evolve as the economy progresses, with more rudimentary infrastructure such as for transport and for water supply and sanitation critical during the earlier stages of development and more sophisticated infrastructure required for industrialization and subsequently innovation, such as reliable power supply and ICT, likely to be important in the later stages, particularly when an economy reaches middle income.[14] Another hypothesis is that economies that are better at providing the necessary infrastructure tend to perform better.

This subsection documents stylized facts regarding infrastructure provision in the various income groups to allow a comparison of middle-income economies with others.[15] All country-year observations in the sample are initially classified in three income groups: low income, lower-middle income, and upper-middle income. As mentioned above, these income groups are based on income thresholds set by the World Bank and are applied to GDP data from the Penn World Table 9.0.

Within each income group, the economies are further classified based on geometric mean per capita GDP growth within a particular income group, with "top25" representing the fastest-growing quartile, "mid50" the middle 50%, and "low25" the slowest-growing quartile. This is done to see if differences in infrastructure provision are associated with differences in growth performance within each income group.

Figure 2.4.1 shows a strong positive correlation between an economy's stage of development and physical measures of infrastructure. This is not surprising and has been documented elsewhere (e.g., International Monetary Fund 2014). The more novel finding is that economies that grow faster than their peers in the same income group tend to have more of certain types of infrastructure. This is true of transport and ICT. For electricity, water supply, and sanitation, however, there seems to be little or no association between growth performance and infrastructure provision.

While all types of infrastructure tend to increase as economies develop, their relative importance changes, as measured by their share in the overall stock of infrastructure. To explore this conjecture, different types of infrastructure are aggregated using unit costs of production drawn from Fay and Yepes (2003). Examining the patterns of provision of the different infrastructure types, it is evident that, as hypothesized, middle-income economies tend to switch their focus away from basic infrastructure such as for transport and toward more advanced infrastructure such as for ICT.

2.4.1 Infrastructure, income, and growth performance

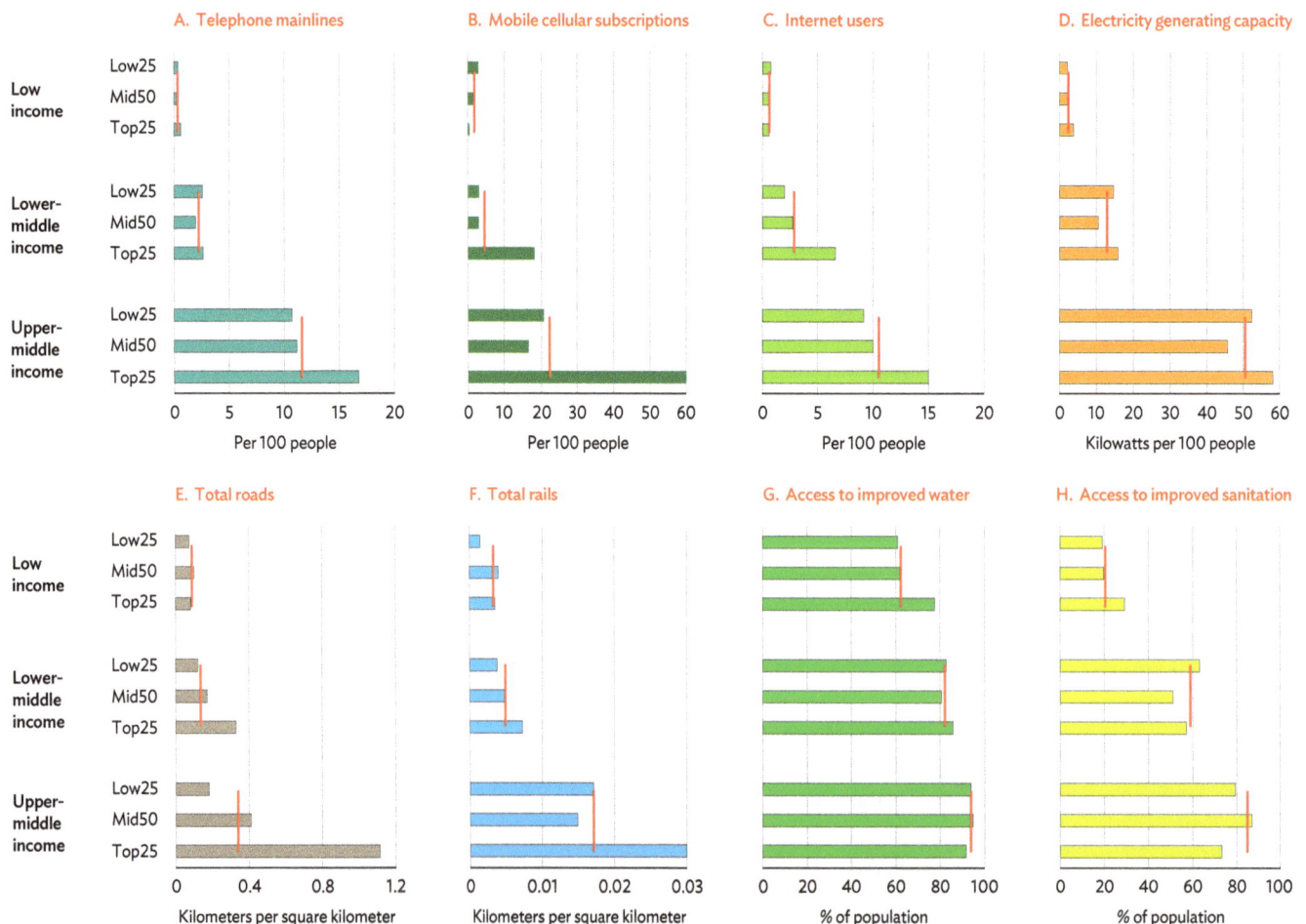

Note: Horizontal bars show median infrastructure stock in each quartile of each income group. Vertical lines show median infrastructure stock for a whole income group.
Source: Abiad, Debuque-Gonzales, and Sy, forthcoming.

2.4.2 Shares of different types of infrastructure in total infrastructure stock

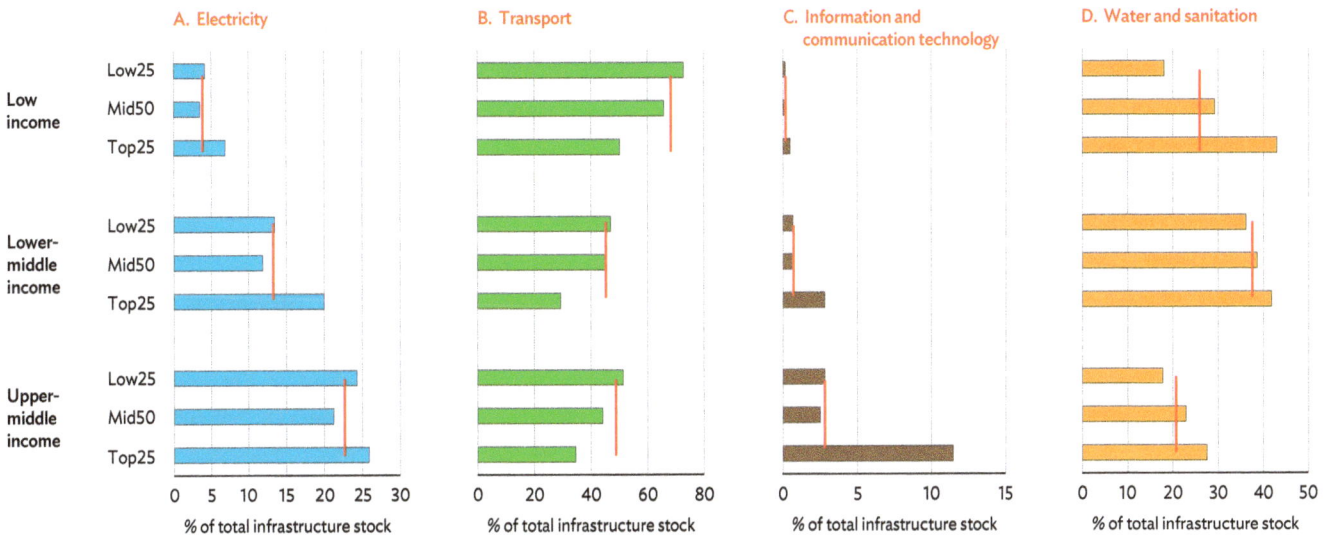

Note: Horizontal bars show median infrastructure shares in each quartile of each income group. Vertical lines show median infrastructure shares for a whole income group.
Source: Abiad, Debuque-Gonzales, and Sy, forthcoming.

Figure 2.4.2 shows that, as income improves, the share of transport in total infrastructure stock declines while that of energy and ICT rises. The latter trend is particularly true for the fastest-growing middle-income economies (top25). The figure also shows that the share of water supply and sanitation drops as an economy reaches the upper middle-income phase. This is not surprising, as providing water and sanitation is a top priority when economies are starting to develop. As Figure 2.4.1 shows, by the time economies reach middle income, access to water is already high. The share of electric power supply climbs steadily as an economy progresses. This may reflect industrialization, as industry uses more power than agriculture, but it may also reflect higher energy consumption in homes. The results indicate that the power requirements of an economy remain relatively large even at higher income.

Figure 2.4.3 summarizes infrastructure stock by income group and mobility. It shows that economies moving successfully up the income ladder tend to have more infrastructure than their peers, just as they invest more in innovative activities and human capital. They have more of different types of infrastructure: telephone fixed lines, mobile telephones, internet, electricity, roads, railroads, water supply, and sanitation. Further, the differences between graduating economies and their peers are statistically significant in most cases (Table 2.4.1).

2.4.1 Group mean t-test for differences in infrastructure across income-transition country groups

Infrastructure indicator	Lower-middle income staying there versus lower middle rising to upper-middle income	Upper-middle income staying there versus upper-middle income rising to high
Telephone mainlines per 100 people	*	**
Mobile phone subscriptions per 100 people	**	**
Internet users per 100 people		**
Total roads per sq km	*	**
Total rails per sq km	**	**
Electricity generating capacity per 100 people	**	**
Water access (% of population)		**
Sanitation access (% of population)		**

** = group mean t-test significant at 5%, * = group mean t-test significant at 10%, sq km = square kilometer.
Note: The entire sample covers 1975–2014 that is divided into nonoverlapping ten-year intervals, except for the last 9-year period: 1975–1985, 1985–1995, 1995–2005, and 2005–2014. To examine income-level dynamics, a country's income level at the initial year is compared to that at the final year of each interval. Data availability varies by indicator.
Source: ADB estimates.

2.4.3 Infrastructure by income group and mobility, middle-income subgroups

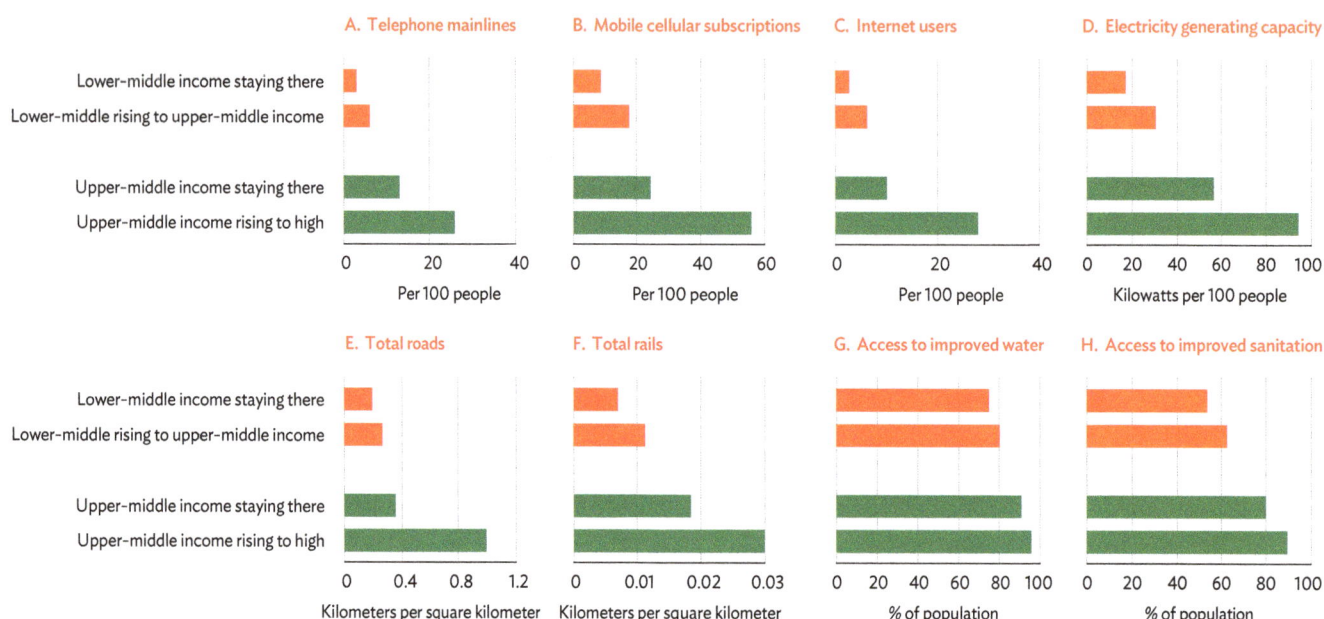

A. Telephone mainlines
B. Mobile cellular subscriptions
C. Internet users
D. Electricity generating capacity

Lower-middle income staying there
Lower-middle rising to upper-middle income
Upper-middle income staying there
Upper-middle income rising to high

Per 100 people
Per 100 people
Per 100 people
Kilowatts per 100 people

E. Total roads
F. Total rails
G. Access to improved water
H. Access to improved sanitation

Lower-middle income staying there
Lower-middle rising to upper-middle income
Upper-middle income staying there
Upper-middle income rising to high

Kilometers per square kilometer
Kilometers per square kilometer
% of population
% of population

Note: The entire sample covers 1975–2014 that is divided into nonoverlapping ten-year intervals, except for the last 9-year period: 1975–1985, 1985–1995, 1995–2005, and 2005–2014. To examine income-level dynamics, a country's income level at the initial year is compared to that at the final year of each interval. Data availability varies by indicator.
Source: ADB estimates.

To examine differences in infrastructure investment, a measure of total infrastructure investment is computed that sums the ratios of public investment and private infrastructure investment as a share of GDP.[16] From this overall measure of infrastructure investment, it is evident that infrastructure spending does not differ substantially across income groups (Figure 2.4.4). Interestingly, though, faster-growing economies invest more in their infrastructure. Examining the breakdown of overall infrastructure investment into public and private components, one can see that the public component is larger in fast-growing economies. Higher infrastructure investment is not driven by higher incomes, as the compared economies are in the same income group. There are two possible explanations for the positive association between infrastructure investment and growth performance. It could be that infrastructure investment enables or causes higher growth, or infrastructure investment could be simply responding to higher growth. The issue of causality is investigated more systematically below.

2.4.4 Total infrastructure investment

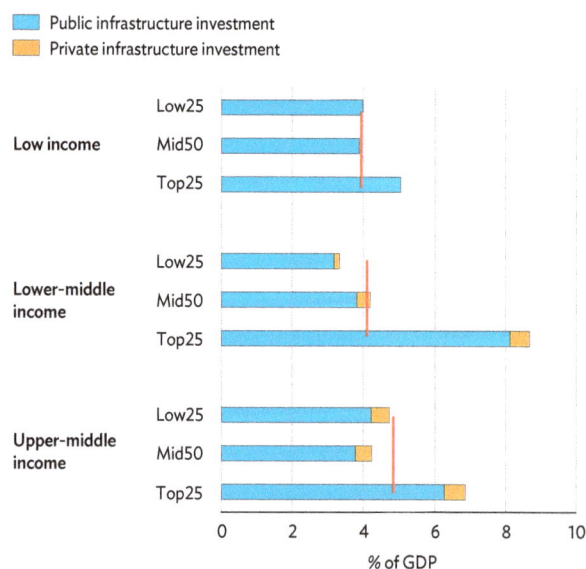

■ Public infrastructure investment
■ Private infrastructure investment

Low income
  Low25
  Mid50
  Top25

Lower-middle income
  Low25
  Mid50
  Top25

Upper-middle income
  Low25
  Mid50
  Top25

% of GDP

Note: Horizontal bars show median infrastructure investment in each quartile of each income group. Vertical lines show median infrastructure investment for a whole income group.
Source: Abiad, Debuque-Gonzales, and Sy, forthcoming.

A closer look at infrastructure provision

While highly informative about the empirical regularities regarding infrastructure provision across income groups, the analytical approach used to this point does not take into account the role of other factors, nor does it make any formal inferences about the observed empirical relationships. To deal with these shortcomings, more rigorous methods

2.4.1 Determinants of infrastructure: empirical methodology

Panel regressions can control for factors other than level of development that may influence infrastructure provision in an economy. In the various specifications, the dependent variables are the different types of infrastructure stock. The key explanatory variables enter the regressions as dummy variables, representing income groups (with low-income economies serving as the omitted group) and growth performance (with the slowest-growing economies serving as the omitted group).[a] Following papers on the determinants of infrastructure provision such as Fay and Yepes (2003) and Ruiz-Nuñez and Wei (2015), the following equation is estimated (inclusive of a standard set of controls):

$$I_{i,t} = \beta_0 + \gamma_1 LMIC_{i,t} + \gamma_2 UMIC_{i,t} + \gamma_3 HIC_{i,t} + \delta_1 mid50_{i,t} + \delta_2 top25_{i,t} + \beta_1 A_{i,t} + \beta_2 P_{i,t} + \beta_3 U_{i,t} + \beta_4 D_i + \beta_5 D_t + \varepsilon_{i,t}$$

In this specification, $I_{i,t}$ is the log of the level of infrastructure stock in country i at time t (except for water and sanitation access, which are in percent of population); $LMIC_{i,t}$, $UMIC_{i,t}$, and $HIC_{i,t}$ which are the income group dummies corresponding to lower-middle income, upper-middle income, and high income, respectively; $mid50_{i,t}$ and $top25_{i,t}$ are the growth performance dummies; $A_{i,t}$ is the percent share of agriculture in GDP; $P_{i,t}$ is log of population density, defined as population per square kilometer of land area; $U_{i,t}$ is the degree of urbanization, defined as urban population as a percent of total population; and D_i and D_t are respectively the economy and time fixed effects.[b] Measures of economic structure (percent share of agriculture in GDP), population density, and degree of urbanization are included as more industrialized, more densely populated, and more urbanized economies can be expected to have more infrastructure. Country and time fixed effects are included to control for systematic unobserved heterogeneity across economies and over time.

[a] For completeness, dummies are introduced for high-income economies with GDP per capita at PPP in constant 2011 dollars ≥ $17,600. Results are similar when regressions are estimated on a sample that excludes high-income economies.

[b] The results are similar when GDP per capita and its square are used in place of income group dummies. See Abiad, Debuque-Gonzales, and Sy (forthcoming) for details.

are adopted in this subsection to better examine the relationship between infrastructure, stage of development, and growth performance. The methodology is outlined in Box 2.4.1.

What do the results of this exercise reveal? The regressions confirm that lower-middle-income economies tend to have greater infrastructure stock than low-income economies, and that upper middle-income economies tend to have higher infrastructure stock than both groups (Table 2.4.2). This is true for most types of infrastructure.

A few results stand out that add nuance to the previous observations on infrastructure provision across development stages. One is the continued accumulation of mobile, internet, and energy infrastructure throughout and beyond the middle-income stage, as evidenced by the increasing size of the country income dummy coefficients.[17] The other, also based on these coefficients, is the tendency for telephone line, transport, and water supply and sanitation provision to level off following a run-up during the upper middle-income phase.

Regarding roads, a possible explanation is that, during early stages of development, the focus is on expanding the road network, or building new roads where none existed. At later stages of development, however, the focus shifts to improving the quality and capacity of existing roads by widening and by converting provincial into national roads then into limited-access highways. This is not captured in the indicator, which measures only the length of the road network. Access to water supply and sanitation also tends to rise during early middle-income stages, and expansion in these services naturally tapers as access becomes nearly universal by the time an economy reaches high income or even upper-middle income.

2.4.2 Sectoral infrastructure regressions using income group dummies

Variables	Telephone mainlines (1)	Mobile phones (2)	Internet users (3)	Total roads (4)	Rails (5)	Electricity (6)	Water access (7)	Sanitation access (8)
Lower-middle income	0.518***	0.892***	0.760***	0.300***	−0.013	0.327***	3.540***	5.007***
	(0.049)	(0.125)	(0.162)	(0.023)	(0.016)	(0.031)	(1.363)	(0.798)
Upper-middle income	0.900***	1.390***	1.602***	0.339***	0.067**	0.485***	4.917***	7.665***
	(0.064)	(0.164)	(0.213)	(0.042)	(0.027)	(0.046)	(1.753)	(0.885)
High income	0.817***	1.845***	1.880***	0.277***	0.069**	0.600***	4.027*	6.390***
	(0.072)	(0.244)	(0.268)	(0.046)	(0.031)	(0.054)	(2.163)	(1.011)
Mid 50% for growth	0.030	0.017	0.336***	−0.037*	0.033*	−0.079***	1.994	1.498**
	(0.039)	(0.129)	(0.124)	(0.020)	(0.017)	(0.026)	(1.470)	(0.684)
Top 25% for growth	0.231***	0.500***	0.268*	−0.138***	−0.011	−0.081**	3.861**	1.953***
	(0.053)	(0.184)	(0.161)	(0.033)	(0.020)	(0.040)	(1.578)	(0.632)
Agriculture, share of GDP	−0.033***	−0.081***	−0.071***	−0.011***	0.000	−0.012***	−0.095	−0.148***
	(0.003)	(0.009)	(0.010)	(0.001)	(0.001)	(0.0020)	(0.081)	(0.027)
Population density	0.164**	6.941***	5.482***	0.274***	0.045	−0.302***	21.519***	6.401***
	(0.076)	(0.515)	(0.447)	(0.042)	(0.038)	(0.049)	(3.094)	(1.017)
Urbanization	0.027***	−0.003	0.044***	0.005***	0.002*	0.020***	0.308***	0.440***
	(0.003)	(0.012)	(0.014)	(0.002)	(0.001)	(0.002)	(0.102)	(0.043)
Constant	−1.161***	−35.147***	−32.377***	−2.219***	−4.120***	3.009***	−24.508*	31.082***
	(0.320)	(2.480)	(2.166)	(0.198)	(0.127)	(0.270)	(13.818)	(4.790)
Observations	3,249	2,016	1,779	3,291	3,225	3,713	525	2,045
R-squared	0.968	0.915	0.931	0.978	0.981	0.978	0.965	0.993
Formal test of differences in coefficients:								
Upper middle > Lower middle	Yes	Yes	Yes	Yes	Yes	Yes	No	Yes
High income > Upper middle	No	Yes	Yes	No	No	Yes	No	No
Top 25% > Mid 50%	Yes	Yes	No	No	Yes	No	Yes	No

*** = $p < 0.01$, ** = $p < 0.05$, * = $p < 0.1$.

Note: All regressions include economy and year fixed effects.

Source: Abiad, Debuque-Gonzales, and Sy, forthcoming.

The regressions confirm the positive association between growth performance and certain types of infrastructure stock. Most notably, better performers in the top 25% tend to have more ICT infrastructure. Economies in the top quartile for growth tend to have 25%–50% more telephone mainlines, mobile subscriptions, and internet usage than those in the bottom quartile. Fast-growing economies also seem to have 2%–4% more access to water supply and sanitation. Exceptions to the positive relationship are rail provision, which seems unrelated to growth performance, and energy and roads, where fast-growers seem to have 8%–14% less provision. Coefficients on the control variables generally hold the correct signs in both sets of regressions, with higher population density and higher degree of urbanization associated with significantly more infrastructure and greater share of agriculture with significantly less.

To see which set of economies is responsible for the relationship between good growth performance and the accumulation of certain types of infrastructure, a similar set of regressions is estimated using

2.4.3 Sectoral infrastructure regressions for the middle-income subsample

Variables	Telephone mainlines (1)	Mobile phones (2)	Internet users (3)	Total roads (4)	Rails (5)	Electricity (6)	Water access (7)	Sanitation access (8)
Lagged GDP per capita	0.599***	0.125	0.761**	−0.151***	−0.012	0.234***	3.242	0.912
	(0.063)	(0.253)	(0.307)	(0.047)	(0.027)	(0.048)	(2.398)	(0.946)
Mid 50% for growth	0.244***	0.353**	0.745***	0.081**	0.038	0.119***	1.031	2.505***
	(0.056)	(0.162)	(0.220)	(0.033)	(0.024)	(0.039)	(2.294)	(0.675)
Top 25% for growth	0.491***	0.810***	0.953***	−0.414***	−0.134***	0.026	3.765*	3.901***
	(0.094)	(0.226)	(0.209)	(0.130)	(0.036)	(0.071)	(2.160)	(0.749)
Observations	1,351	860	755	1,314	1,327	1,496	218	863
R-squared	0.943	0.954	0.938	0.966	0.969	0.947	0.928	0.987

*** = $p < 0.01$, ** = $p < 0.05$, * = $p < 0.1$.

Note: All regressions include economy and year fixed effects. Control variables not reported above are share of agriculture, population, and urbanization.

Source: Abiad, Debuque-Gonzales, and Sy, forthcoming.

subsamples representing the different income groups.[18] Consistent with the earlier stylized facts, the relationship appears to be primarily driven by the faster-growing middle-income economies in the case of ICT (Table 2.4.3). This group of economies also seems to be largely behind the positive association between growth performance and access to water supply and sanitation.

All things considered, the stylized facts and regression results suggest a hierarchy of needs where economies are more likely to invest in basic infrastructure such as water supply and sanitation, roads, power, and telephone mainlines during early stages of development. Economies then seem to turn their attention to advanced infrastructure such as mobile and internet connections when they reach the upper-middle income, with power continuing to be a priority. Fast-growing economies within each income group tend to have higher infrastructure stock than their slower-growing counterparts for certain types of infrastructure, notably ICT.

The macroeconomic effects of public investment

Discussions above have established an association between infrastructure provision and investment, on the one hand, and stage of development and growth performance on the other. But the bivariate charts and multivariate regressions cannot shed light on the direction of causality. The positive relationship could arise from output responding to infrastructure investment as the latter boosts demand in the short term or the productivity of existing factors of production in the long term. It could arise as well from infrastructure responding to output, either because higher output makes it easier to pay for infrastructure or because expectations of higher growth induce greater investment in infrastructure. This is a problem that has long plagued the literature on the macroeconomic effects of infrastructure investment.

The challenge is to identify changes in infrastructure investment that are not driven by contemporaneous or lagged output, nor by expectations of future output growth. To tackle this issue, the following pages adopt the empirical strategy of Corsetti, Meier, and Müller (2012), which relies on the idea that significant parts of government spending are likely to be determined by past information and cannot easily respond to current economic conditions. Based on this assumption, one can estimate a fiscal policy rule for public investment and from this obtain a series of exogenous shocks to public investment.[19] The estimated policy shocks can then be used to trace the dynamic effects of public investment on output.

In principle, the assumption that public investment cannot easily respond to current economic conditions may not hold for two reasons. First, public spending can automatically respond to cyclical conditions. This should not pose a problem for public investment, however, because automatic stabilizers work mostly through revenues and social spending. Second, discretionary public investment spending can occur in response to output conditions. As discussed in Corsetti, Meier, and Müller (2012), the relevance of this concern relates to the precise definition of contemporaneous feedback effects. Although it is typically assumed in the literature that government spending does not react to changes in economic activity within a given quarter (Blanchard and Perotti 2002), whether it may respond in a period longer than a quarter is an open question. Recent evidence for advanced economies suggests that the restriction that government spending does not respond to economic conditions within a year cannot be rejected (Beetsma, Giuliodori, and Klaassen 2009, Born and Müller 2012). Box 2.4.2 describes the empirical methodology for estimating the macroeconomic impact of infrastructure.

The results suggest that public investment has a positive and persistent impact on output in developing economies (Figure 2.4.5, Panel A). The contemporaneous effect of an increase in public investment equal to 1% of GDP is a 0.3% increase in output. This gradually increases to 1.2% in the 7th year after the shock, with an impact significantly different from zero in both the short and the long run.

2.4.5 Effect of public investment on output

A. Developing (low and middle income)

B. Low income

C. Middle income

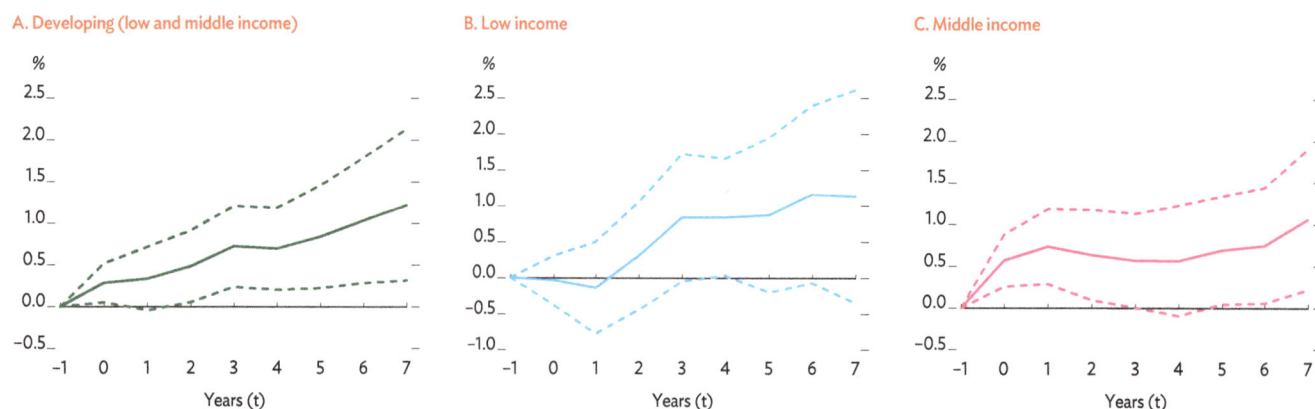

Notes: t = 0 is the year of the shock. Dashed lines denote 90% confidence bands. Shock represents an exogenous increase in public investment spending equal to 1% of GDP.
Source: Abiad, Debuque-Gonzales, and Sy, forthcoming.

2.4.2 Impact of infrastructure on output: empirical methodology

A two-step regression is involved in this approach. In the first step, an annual time series of public investment shocks is estimated using a fiscal policy rule that assumes public investment as a share of GDP to be related to its own lag, past indebtedness and output growth, stage of development, growth performance, and expectations about current economic activity, according to the equation:

$$i_{i,t} = \alpha_i + \varphi_t + \beta i_{i,t-1} + \sigma d_{i,t-1} + \theta g_{i,t-1} + \gamma_1 LMIC_{i,t} + \gamma_2 UMIC_{i,t} + \gamma_3 HIC_{i,t} + \delta_1 mid50_{i,t} + \delta_2 top25_{i,t} + \mu E_{i,t-1}(g_{i,t}) + e_{i,t}$$

where $i_{i,t}$ refers to public investment as a share of GDP, α_i and φ_t are respectively the economy and time fixed effects, d is the debt-to-GDP ratio, g denotes output growth, $E(g)$ is the expectation about current economic activity (proxied by the *World Economic Outlook* growth forecasts as of October in the previous year), and e represents the measure of public investment shocks.

In the second step, following the "local projections" approach proposed by Jordà (2005) in estimating impulse response functions, the impact of public investment innovations ($\hat{e}_{i,t}$) on output is estimated through the equation

$$y_{i,t+k} - y_{i,t} = \alpha_i^k + \varphi_t^k + \beta^k PUBINV_{i,t} + \varepsilon_i^k$$

where y is the log of output, α_i and φ_t are respectively the country and time fixed effects, and *PUBINV* represents the shocks ($\hat{e}_{i,t}$) derived from the fiscal policy rule in the first step. This equation is estimated for each k (= 1, 0, 2, 3, ..., 7) representing the time horizon after a shock. Impulse response functions are computed using the estimated coefficients β^k, and the confidence bands associated with the impulse response functions are generated using the estimated standard coefficients of β^k based on clustered robust standard errors.

This approach is applied to explore the macroeconomic effects of infrastructure investment in developing economies and, more specifically, to examine whether macroeconomic effects are different in middle-income economies relative to low-income economies.[a] The dataset is an unbalanced panel that covers 72 developing economies from 1991 to 2014. To compare the country income groups, impulse response functions are generated for each income group separately.

---

[a] Abiad, Furceri, and Topalova (2016) examine the macroeconomic effects of public investment using a more precise measure of shocks to public investment, namely forecast errors in public investment from OECD economic reports. This approach is not feasible for this investigation of developing economies for lack of similar forecast data.

When splitting the developing economy sample into low-income and middle-income economies, one sees a difference in effects (Figure 2.4.5, Panel B versus Panel C). In low-income economies, public investment shocks do not raise output immediately. There is an increase in long-term output of 1.1% after 7 years, but with increasing size of the standard error as time passes after the shock, the estimated impact is not significantly different from zero. In middle-income economies, public investment shocks raise output by 0.6% immediately, and the effect is significantly different from zero. Over time, the impact increases to 1.1% in the 7th year after the shock, and this long-run effect is also significantly different from zero. Although the patterns in the middle-income and low-income subsamples are noticeably different, given the large error bands around the estimated effects, one cannot reject that the impact in both types of economies is the same.

The somewhat weaker impact of public investment in low-income economies may seem counterintuitive but is consistent with evidence from studies, such as Warner (2014) and Kraay (2012). This is an important point: Infrastructure investment can have a wide range of outcomes, and even though the positive association between infrastructure provision and development is clear, positive causal effects from infrastructure investment to output require the right conditions. Failure of public investment to lead to sustained output growth is often attributed to poor investment efficiency that inhibits the conversion of dollar spending into productive capital stock. Another cited reason for weak output gains is the limited absorptive capacity of certain economies, with marginal returns likely to decline as investment outlays are scaled up (Presbitero 2016). One can reasonably expect absorptive capacity constraints, which occur during a rapid acceleration and ratcheting up of public investment, to be more severe in low-income economies. Governments also tend to focus on basic infrastructure such as water supply and sanitation in earlier development stages. Such investments, while vital, may not be particularly growth-enhancing and are therefore unlikely to catalyze substantial output gains. A final explanation is that the marginal productivity of infrastructure investment may not be higher in low-income economies despite the more acute shortage of infrastructure there, because complementary factors of production—human capital, private capital, and the right institutions—are in similarly short supply.

Invest more, and in the right kinds of infrastructure

What role does infrastructure play in middle-income economies? The analysis uncovered several noteworthy results. Looking at the stylized facts, one finds that the stock of infrastructure tends to rise with income, and with growth performance. Infrastructure type systematically varies with an economy's stage of development, reflecting a clear hierarchy of requirements. Transport, basic communications, water supply, and sanitation are more important at early stages of development, while reliable electricity supply and ICT become more important as economies advance.

Better-performing economies, especially among middle-income economies, differ from others in their income group in two important ways. Faster-growing economies tend to have more of certain types of infrastructure—especially ICT—than their peers. They also invest a bigger share of GDP in infrastructure. The strong positive association of certain types of infrastructure with growth at different stages of development suggests a potential policy lever for governments grappling with the middle-income challenge of sustaining growth. It is not enough to simply raise the amount of infrastructure investment, economies also need to invest in the right types of infrastructure, which depend on their current stage of development. While it may be beneficial for a low-income economy to focus initially on basic infrastructure such as water supply and sanitation, for instance, analysis finds that they should shift attention to more advanced infrastructure such as ICT during their middle-income stage, and especially during their upper middle-income stages.

The experience of the Republic of Korea (ROK) is illustrative. The ROK was on the cusp of transitioning to high income in the mid-1990s, and by some measures it crossed the threshold in 1995. But shortly thereafter, it was hit hard by the Asian financial crisis, imperiling its newfound status as a high-income economy. Several studies, including Lee (2003), Oh and Larson (2011), Bae (2011),

Yeo et al. (2014), and Lee (2015), document how the ROK government deliberately targeted the development of ICT infrastructure in the late 1990s. Even though broadband services were first launched in the ROK only in 1998, by the early 2000s, the broadband penetration rate in the ROK was the highest in the world (Bae 2011). As a result, Oh and Larson (2011) noted: "In 1997 the ICT sector contributed only about 12 percent to the nation's GDP growth. By 2003, that percentage had risen to about 40 percent and it remained substantial through 2009." The world-leading ICT infrastructure of the ROK likely contributes to the economy being ranked the most innovative in the world (Bloomberg 2015).

A positive association between infrastructure and growth performance in middle-income economies cannot be the basis for policy, as causality can run either way—or both. The additional analysis in this section moves in this direction by showing how exogenous shocks to public investment have significant positive and persistent effects on output, particularly in middle-income economies. This provides reassurance that at least part of the causality between infrastructure provision and development runs from infrastructure to national output and income. The slightly bigger and more sustained impact of infrastructure investment on output in middle-income economies indicates the potentially strong benefits of increased infrastructure investment in them. That said, further research is needed to determine the precise relationship between infrastructure and economic growth. Better data on ICT infrastructure investment, in particular, would help researchers definitively identify the benefits of that particular type of investment.

Reaching toward high income

Decades of rapid economic growth transformed developing Asia from a low-income region to a middle-income region. The vast majority of the population now lives in middle-income economies. The region continues to grow at a healthy pace, and its NIEs have reached high income in record time. However, the experience of many middle-income economies in Latin America and elsewhere suggests that graduation from middle income to high income can be challenging. Further, middle-income economies are structurally different from low-income economies, and the transition from low to middle income differs in important ways from the transition from middle to high income. This is a good time to take stock of the challenges facing the middle-income region as it seeks to build on its past success.

An examination of middle-income challenges reveals that while the accumulation of physical and human capital continues to matter a lot for sustaining healthy growth, productivity comes to the fore. Total factor productivity (TFP), the growth in production not accounted for by increased use of inputs, plays a bigger role in middle-income economies' growth, particularly those successfully reaching high income. The successful middle-income growth model emphasizes productivity and innovation. Innovation becomes more important after economies fully reap the benefits of using existing resources efficiently. Even in the further accumulation of physical and human capital, the focus shifts to areas with positive productivity spillover like advanced infrastructure and higher education. Finally, all of this must be underpinned by a supportive policy environment and stable macroeconomy.

Stepping up innovation requires a skilled workforce capable of creating new knowledge and technology. Middle-income economies should increase human capital investment, which not only fuels growth but also promotes equity. When building human capital, the focus should be on educational quality to enhance cognitive skills, in particular science and math capabilities, which enhances the chances of students becoming innovators.

Advanced infrastructure is an important investment to foster innovation and human capital accumulation. As middle-income economies develop, their infrastructure needs evolve from basic infrastructure to advanced infrastructure. The combination of advanced infrastructure, a skilled workforce, and innovation can help sustain productivity growth and pave the way for a steady transition to high income.

Sound policies and institutions

Sound policies and institutions will play a vital role in the broad transition from middle to high income, as it did in Asia's transition from low to middle income. The role of the government will necessarily evolve as economies progress. The development of the private sector in particular demands a more nuanced economic role for the government.

More generally, the government must provide an environment conducive to innovative entrepreneurship by promoting investment in education and infrastructure. The quality of education and higher education in particular becomes more important as economies grow richer, as does advanced infrastructure such as ICT. The experience of Asia's newly industrialized economies highlights the role of innovation, human capital, and infrastructure in sustaining TFP growth at middle income.

In terms of innovation, middle-income economies must prioritize institutions and policies that level the playing field for the new firms that play major roles in innovation. Strong intellectual property rights ensure that new entrepreneurs can capitalize on commercially useful new ideas, products, or technologies without fear of expropriation by large incumbent firms or other parties. This gives them the confidence to invest their time and effort in innovative activities. Access to finance on reasonable terms enables entrepreneurs to transform new ideas into novel products and services. Effective competition laws, and more broadly strong rule of law, limit the scope for large incumbents to abuse their market power toward hindering the entry and expansion of innovative newcomers.

With respect to human capital, analysis indicates that, as an economy converges on the global technology frontier, the quality of education increasingly takes precedence over the quantity of education. Education policy and reform should be geared toward producing technically competent workers who are capable of absorbing and using new knowledge. Augmenting the pool of cognitive skills such as math and science is key to upgrading the workforce to one that is capable of creating the new technology and knowledge that are the cornerstones of innovation-led growth. There is also a case for investing more in higher education that features research, built on a solid foundation of basic education.

Analysis also indicates that infrastructure investment will be no less important during developing Asia's transition from middle to high income than during its past success in moving up from low to middle income. The region should therefore continue to prioritize investment in infrastructure of all types, from roads to electricity. Since energy and advanced infrastructure such as ICT seem to be especially important for the final transition, economies should expand investments in these areas as they approach high income.

The case can be made for more direct government intervention in a selective and targeted way to foster a more diverse and sophisticated output mix, as shown in Peru's successful experience with industry–government coordination (Box 2.5.1). The case for intervention is stronger when the government has adequate institutional capacity, as Berglof and Cable (forthcoming) and Bruszt and Campos (forthcoming) emphasize. Within the region, Thailand's success in becoming Southeast Asia's hub for automobile manufacturing is revealing. Instead of trying to foster a national champion, Thai policy makers pursued a more nuanced, market-oriented strategy of attracting foreign auto firms. Extensive dialogue between government and industry was vital to fostering a critical mass of local auto parts suppliers, an indispensable pillar of any auto industry (Hill and Kohpaiboon 2017).

2.5.1 Product diversification through industry–government coordination in Peru

The Peruvian government embarked in 2014 on a coordinated industrial policy to facilitate the emergence of a more diversified economy with the aim of boosting Peru's growth exports and growth potential. Peru has comparative advantages in natural resources, so activity naturally concentrated in fishing, cotton, and mining, which together account for some 43% of exports. This left Peru's economy exposed to exogenous shocks, as prices for these commodities are volatile.

The government realized that productive diversification could bring Peru closer to the world technology frontier. In early 2014, the Ministry of Production started to introduce measures to nurture productive diversification. Progress was made in three key areas: expanding across sectors the scope of such public goods as access to affordable finance, higher quality standards, and improved infrastructure; providing ample public goods to selected sectors to boost their productivity; and subsidizing activities with positive externalities such as R&D investment, training, and technology transfer. The set of industrial policies buoyed innovation by identifying sectors with high growth potential, promoting coordination between stakeholders in the public and private spheres, facilitating access to financing, investing in training and tertiary education, and fostering technological transfer.

Implementation targeted a few selected sectors with great economic potential, emphasizing an agile and interactive approach. Sectorial working groups were created to help remove growth barriers in five industries: forestry, aquaculture, textiles, food and beverages, and creative industries. Public–private coordination was introduced in the form of temporary public–private executive boards that seek to boost productivity by eliminating bottlenecks, whether they were sector specific or affected multiple sector, such as logistics. These boards coordinate agents in the public and private sectors, combining their limited expertise to assemble enough know-how to clear bottlenecks affecting their industries.

This practice helps identify promising economic sectors, list relevant stakeholders, analyze the major challenges they face, and provide possible solutions and action plans. Forestry, for example, has great potential in terms of area available for plantations, conditions for quick tree growth, and export prospects. Compared with Chile, whose forestry exports are worth $5.5 billion, Peru exports much less, only $150 million, but has potential to generate $10 billion in exports and create 1 million jobs—and this with plantation trees reaching maturity in half the time. To achieve this potential, the forestry board passed new legislation to foster investment in the sector and comply with environmental standards. This dramatically reduced the time required to register privately owned land that was appropriate for plantations and to get extraction permits, shortening it to a few days from what had been up to 12 months. Finance was improved with adaptions appropriate for the sector, adjusting payment timing to align it with forestry business cash flows and not requiring firms to use their land as collateral because ill-defined property rights makes this impossible. With these hurdles overcome, loans for forestry projects rose to stand today at $60 million. Such a surgical approach effectively activates the potential of underperforming sectors, achieving results rapidly at relatively low cost.

Importance of macroeconomic stability

One vital element of a growth-conducive environment is macroeconomic stability. Evidence has emerged since the global financial crisis of 2008–2009 that growth in individual economies has become more dependent on such global factors as global growth, oil prices, and financial volatility (Aizenman et al. forthcoming). This indicates that the region may be more vulnerable to external shocks.

Empirical evidence indicates that when an economy reaches middle income, its growth rate is more vulnerable to threats to macroeconomic stability—such as whether a banking or currency crisis, large capital inflows other than foreign direct investment, and high government debt relative to GDP. Exploring the determinants of growth in a global dataset from 1960 to 2014, Eichengreen, Park, and Shin (forthcoming) confirmed the importance of a number of variables: initial income, years of schooling, investment share, demographic characteristics, infrastructure, financial development indicators, and governance. The study also included variables related to macroeconomic stability: flows of foreign direct investment, the occurrence of banking or currency crises, and government debt.

Interestingly, the study found that the economic factors associated with per capita income growth do in fact differ between middle-income and other economies. The critical distinction is between low and middle income. For example, in middle-income economies, the lending–deposit rate spread matters less than in low-income economies. This suggests that inefficiencies in the financial system matter less in relation to other factors as economies move up the income scale. Similarly, the gender ratio is no longer as important as before, suggesting the diminishing importance of demographic determinants with graduation to middle-income status.

So what are the factors that come to the fore when an economy reaches middle income? The study found that growth in middle income is more vulnerable to those that affect macroeconomic stability. More specifically, in middle-income economies a banking or currency crisis can significantly hinder growth, as can capital inflows other than foreign direct investment and high government debt as a share of GDP. The region should therefore stay vigilant about protecting macroeconomic stability, as it has done in the past through sound fiscal and monetary policies. The brief reversion of the ROK from high income to middle income during the Asian financial crisis of 1997–1998 serves as a stark reminder of the high cost of macroeconomic instability.

The evidence in this chapter indicates that sustaining rapid growth will not be easy, but it is within the reach of middle-income Asia. Many factors that served the region well at low income, such as macroeconomic stability and high investment, still serve it well at middle income. At the same time, the pattern of growth will have to evolve if Asia is to sustain rapid growth and eventually reach high income. In particular, innovation, human capital, and infrastructure will have to play vital roles. The region's dynamic track record and the transition of the region's most advanced economies provide some cause for optimism about sustaining rapid growth at middle income.

Learning from regional success stories

One group of Asian economies that was able to shift from investment-led growth to innovation-based growth is the newly industrialized economies (NIEs): the ROK, Singapore, Taipei,China, and Hong Kong, China. The output mix of these economies became more diverse and sophisticated as they graduated from middle to high income, having initially specialized in labor-intensive products during the early stages of their industrialization but gradually shifting to a wide range of products requiring advanced skills and technology.

In 1960, Singapore and Hong Kong, China were both lower-middle income, while the ROK and Taipei,China were both low income. From that year, Hong Kong, China labored for 24 years and Singapore for nearly 30 years in middle income before reaching high income. Taipei,China took 27 years to transition from middle to high income, 10 years ranked as lower-middle income and 17 years as upper-middle income. For the ROK, the road to high income spanned 23 years, including 10 years in lower-middle income and 13 years in upper-middle income. The record of the NIEs shows that innovation, human capital, and infrastructure all played vital roles in their remarkable transition from middle to high income.

Innovation and infrastructure spur technological development

An important factor that enabled NIEs to achieve high and steady growth is the innovation that drove their rapid technological progress. Both the ROK and Taipei,China sustained productivity increases through local firms' development of new technologies (Cherif and Hasanov 2015, Agénor, Canuto, and Jelenic 2012). The drive toward innovation was supported by strong protection of intellectual property rights. In 1990, or 5 years before the ROK graduated to high income, its number of patent applications was already comparable to that of Germany and the US (Figure 2.5.1).

Direct government support played a key role in spurring innovation among NIEs. In Taipei,China, the authorities had a direct hand in creating innovative firms. The government helped foster close and long-term relationships between small and medium-sized enterprises and multinational corporations, enabled public and quasi-public research institutes to spin off firms and create new technologies, and invested heavily to train engineers overseas. In the ROK, the government pushed several conglomerates to enter several industries simultaneously and export almost immediately to create global brands. State support included access to credit that was conditional on explicit and quantifiable export targets, pushing companies such as Hyundai to accelerate its R&D and technological upgrading (Cherif and Hasanov 2015).

In addition to innovation, advanced infrastructure networks facilitated NIEs' rapid transition. Setting up high-speed communications and broadband technology was aided by the liberalization of telecommunication networks and regulatory reform. A strong drive toward global competitiveness in communication technology catalyzed in the ROK and Taipei,China the emergence of robust broadband and multimedia industries in their own domestic markets. In Singapore and Hong Kong, China, advanced infrastructure networks supported their use as regional headquarters for large foreign multimedia companies (Agénor, Canuto, and Jelenic 2012).

2.5.1 Patent applications in selected economies, 1990 and 2014

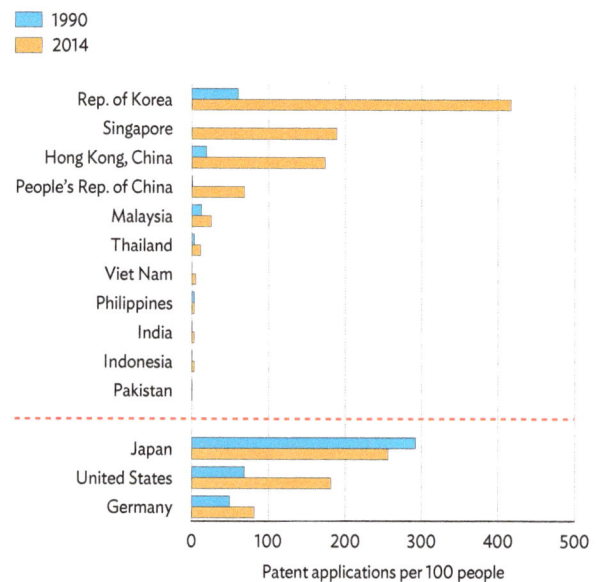

Source: World Bank, World Development Indicators online database. http://databank.worldbank.org/data/home.aspx (accessed 4 October 2016).

Human capital toward knowledge-based economies

Human capital accumulation facilitated innovation among NIEs and enabled them to transform into knowledge-based economies. Shifting to a knowledge economy requires a development approach that emphasizes the quality of education and includes R&D investments in science and technology. Figure 2.5.2 illustrates how NIEs in general have a stronger position in research and knowledge creation than middle-income economies.

The NIE experience shows that combining R&D and human capital investments can shift an economy from investment-led growth to innovation-led growth, provided there is a sound institutional environment that provides incentives for the efficient use of knowledge.

2.5.2 Knowledge production, selected Asian economies

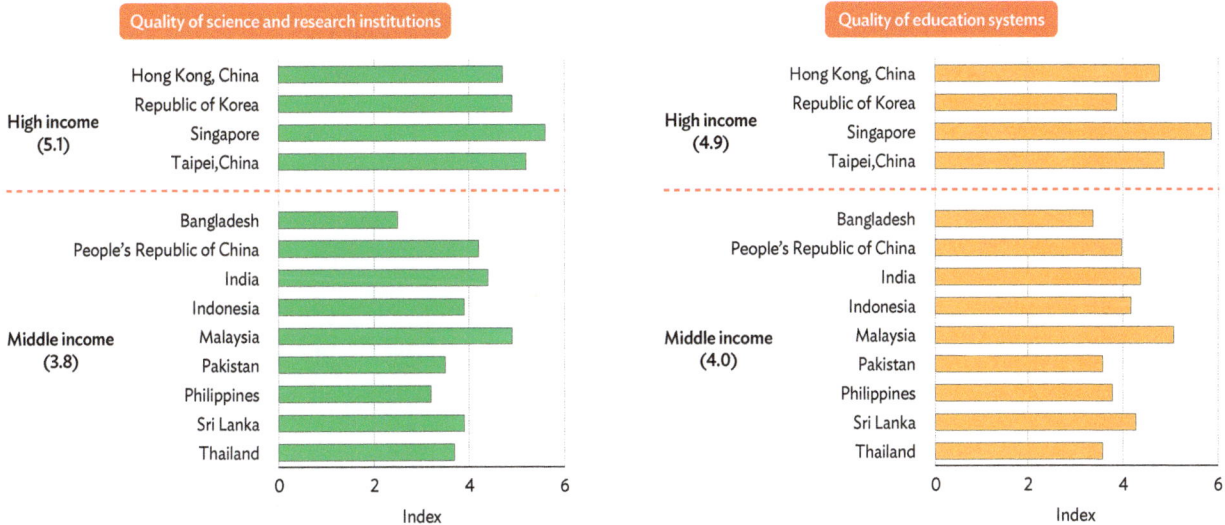

Quality of science and research institutions

High income (5.1)	Hong Kong, China
	Republic of Korea
	Singapore
	Taipei,China
Middle income (3.8)	Bangladesh
	People's Republic of China
	India
	Indonesia
	Malaysia
	Pakistan
	Philippines
	Sri Lanka
	Thailand

Index

Quality of education systems

High income (4.9)	Hong Kong, China
	Republic of Korea
	Singapore
	Taipei,China
Middle income (4.0)	Bangladesh
	People's Republic of China
	India
	Indonesia
	Malaysia
	Pakistan
	Philippines
	Sri Lanka
	Thailand

Index

Note: Figures in parentheses are averages.

Sources: World Economic Forum. 2012. *The Global Competitiveness Report 2012–2013*; INSEAD, Global Innovation Index 2012.

One good example of such a transformation is the ROK, which moved to high income on the basis of innovation, human capital, and infrastructure.

Government support for human capital accumulation through education reform played a critical role in the ROK transition to a knowledge-based economy. During the 1960s and 1970s, secondary education was made universal, and vocational and technical schools were established to meet skills demand from manufacturing industries. The ROK also established science and technology institutes, adopting US-style graduate education and research system. In the early 1980s, the ROK further expanded tertiary education to prepare for the transition into advanced industry. Alongside education reform, the ROK strengthened R&D capacity to boost human capital. During the transition to upper middle income, knowledge production in the ROK increased tremendously, with the number of scientific and technical journal articles multiplying sixfold in the decade to 1994, from 424 to 2,931.

In the 1980s, the government encouraged the private sector to participate in R&D through incentives like tax subsidies. Even small and medium-sized enterprises were actively involved in R&D, with some allocating as much as 10% of sales income to R&D. The transformation of the ROK into a knowledge-based economy enabled it to move toward the production of high-technology goods. From 1988 to 1994, its ratio of high-technology exports to all manufactured exports increased from 15.9% to 22.7%. This feat was achieved before the ROK graduated to high income in the mid-1990s.

2.5.3 Infrastructure provision in newly industrialized economies

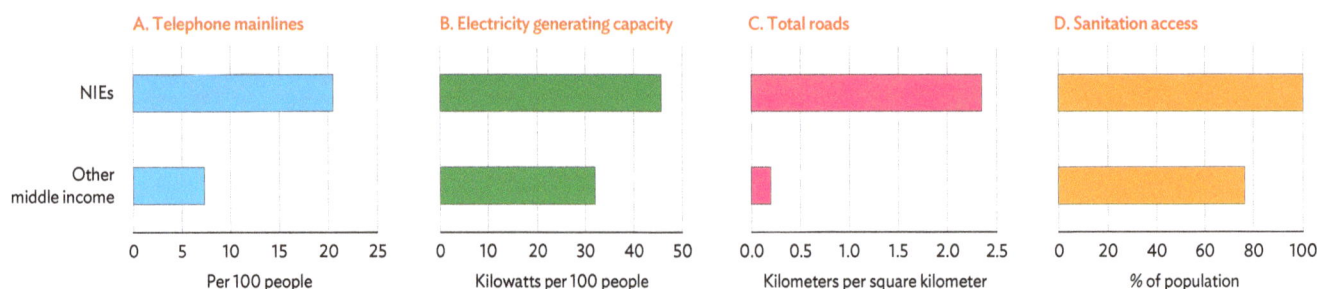

| A. Telephone mainlines | B. Electricity generating capacity | C. Total roads | D. Sanitation access |

NIEs = newly industrialized economies (Republic of Korea, Singapore, Taipei,China, and Hong Kong,China).
Note: The colored bars show the median infrastructure stock when the NIEs were still middle income.
Source: ADB estimates.

Solid foundations built on strong basic infrastructure

While heavy investment in advanced infrastructure contributed to the more recent success of the NIEs, no less important was their earlier heavy investment in basic infrastructure, which provided the quartet with a solid foundation for economic takeoff. The NIEs invested more in basic infrastructure than did other middle-income economies (Figure 2.5.3). The NIEs had 3 times as many telephone mainlines per 100 people than other middle-income economies, for example, and 40% more electricity generating capacity per capita. Significantly, the NIEs' provision of basic infrastructure was already virtually universal even when they were middle income. By contrast, today in other middle-income economies, almost a quarter of the population still lacks basic sanitation.

Behind this higher rate of infrastructure provision lay higher infrastructure investment rates. Public investment in the NIEs when they were middle income was substantially higher, equaling nearly 8% of GDP, than in their peers, at 4% of GDP. Public investment was probably more efficient in these economies as well. In the ROK, infrastructure investment was an explicit priority beginning with the First Five-Year Plan, 1962–1966, and infrastructure was geared toward developing the ROK as an export-oriented economy. New power plants were built to supply electricity for manufacturing, and new expressways and expanded ports provided good logistics at low cost.

Clearing the final hurdle

Having been transformed from a low-income region to a middle-income region quickly, developing Asia now faces the final transition, from middle to high income. Just as the transition from low to middle income required rapid growth sustained over decades, the transition from middle to high income will also require that rapid growth is sustained. Sustaining rapid growth will not be easy but is within the reach of middle-income Asia. Many factors that served the region well at low income, such as macroeconomic stability and high investment, will serve it well at middle income. Some key ingredients of economic growth will persist.

At the same time, the pattern of growth will have to evolve if Asia is to sustain rapid growth and eventually reach high income. The structures of middle-income economies are different from those of low-income economies—with, for example, higher stocks of human and physical capital—so it is only natural that the contours of growth will be somewhat different. In particular, the analysis indicates that productivity growth will have to play a larger role in the transition. Productivity growth rests in turn on the three pillars of innovation, human capital, and infrastructure. Therefore, the central mandate of Asian policy makers must be to foster more innovative economies by strengthening education and investing in infrastructure.

The region's dynamic track record gives cause for optimism that the authorities can adapt their growth models to overcome the middle-income challenge. While completing the journey to high income is far from guaranteed, there is every reason to believe that good institutions and policies can lift developing Asia to high income.

Endnotes

1   Bangladesh; the People's Republic of China; Fiji; Hong Kong, China; India; Indonesia; the Republic of Korea; Malaysia; Nepal; Pakistan; the Philippines; Singapore; Sri Lanka; Taipei,China; and Thailand.

2   The shares are based on 219 economies, of which 218 are from the World Bank database. Data on one economy, the Cook Islands, come from the *Asian Development Outlook* database.

3   Capital per capita is calculated for each economy for 2014 based on the PWT 9.0 database, which divides capital stock at current PPP by population size.

4   For economies that do not report labor hours, it is assumed that average labor hours change the same way as in the US over the period.

5   See Eichengreen, Park and Shin (forthcoming) for results for other subgroups, such as high-income economies that remain high income.

6   An economy exports a product with revealed comparative advantage if the share of the product in its total exports is larger than the share of the product on the world market.

7   Felipe et al. (2012) documented that, by category, the most complex products are machinery, chemicals, and metals, while the least complex products are raw materials and commodities, wood, textiles, and agricultural products.

8   Over the longer term, however, older populations will place significant strain on finances in Asia, not only in countries with especially generous public support systems for the elderly but also in those that rely heavily on labor income taxes to finance public consumption.

9   The study of Abrigo, Lee, and Park (forthcoming) has quantitative estimates of the fiscal impact of different public investments in human capital in the 12 economies in developing Asia.

10   This analysis leaves for a future study a deeper probe into how effectively productivity is boosted by human capital spending growth from the government versus from the private sector.

11   These were the Programme for International Student Assessment and the Trends in International Mathematics and Science Study.

12   This section is based on material contributed by Christos Sakellariou.

13   Largely credited to George Psacharopoulos. For a recent update, see Psacharopoulos and Patrinos (2004) and Montenegro and Patrinos (2014).

14   Because of congestion, pollution, and other problems associated with the urbanization that occurs in the middle-income phase, certain urban infrastructure also becomes more important for middle-income economies. However, lack of comprehensive data across economies on urban infrastructure such as mass transit prevents further analysis here.

15   The complete list of data sources used in this section can be found in Abiad, Debuque-Gonzales, and Sy (forthcoming). The sample period of the data starts in 1960 but is subject to data availability.

16   Data on public investment is from the Investment and Capital Stock Dataset of the International Monetary Fund Fiscal Affairs Department, and private infrastructure investment is from the World Bank Private Provision in Infrastructure Database. In the absence of more direct measures, public investment often proxies for government infrastructure spending. Public investment can include investment in non-infrastructure items such as machinery and equipment, inventories, valuables, and land. More disaggregated data on public infrastructure investment is available only for OECD economies. The Private Provision of Infrastructure Database covers infrastructure investment by firms at least 20% privately owned.

17   Formal tests of differences in coefficients support these conclusions.

18   To save space, only the table for the middle-income subsample is presented.

19   This identification strategy is very similar to the structure embedded in fiscal policy vector autoregressions. The fiscal policy rule links the change in government spending to its lags, lagged growth, current and lagged public indebtedness, and expectations of growth next year.

Background papers

Abiad, A., M. Debuque-Gonzales, and A. L. Sy. Forthcoming. *The Role and Impact of Infrastructure in Middle-Income Countries: Anything Special?* Asian Development Bank.

Abrigo, M., S-H. Lee, and D. Park. Forthcoming. *Human Capital Spending, Inequality, and Growth in Middle-Income Asia.* Asian Development Bank.

Aghion, P. and C. Bircan. Forthcoming. *The Middle-Income Trap from a Schumpeterian Perspective.* Asian Development Bank.

Aizenman, J., Y. Jinjarak, G. Estrada, and S. Tian. Forthcoming. *Flexibility of Adjustment to Shocks: Economic Growth and Volatility of Middle-Income Countries Before and After the Global Financial Crisis of 2008.* Asian Development Bank.

Berglof, E. and V. Cable. Forthcoming. *Back in Business: Industrial Policy for Emerging Economies in the New Globalization.* Asian Development Bank.

Bruszt, L. and N. F. Campos. Forthcoming. *Deep Economic Integration and State Capacity: A Mechanism of Avoiding Middle-Income Trap?* Asian Development Bank.

Eichengreen, B., D. Park, and K. Shin. Forthcoming. *The Landscape of Economic Growth: Do Middle-Income Countries Differ?* Asian Development Bank.

Estrada, G., X. Han, D. Park, and S. Tian. Forthcoming. *Asia's Middle-Income Challenge: An Overview.* Asian Development Bank.

Georgiev, Y., S. Guriev, P. Nagy, and A. Plekhanov. Forthcoming. *Structural Reform and Productivity Growth in Emerging Europe and Central Asia.* Asian Development Bank.

Ha, J. and S-H Lee. Forthcoming. *Population Aging and the Possibility of a Middle-Income Trap in Asia.* Asian Development Bank.

Kim, J. and J. Park. Forthcoming. *The Role of Total Factor Productivity Growth in Middle-Income Countries.* Asian Development Bank.

References

Abiad, A., D. Furceri, and P. Topalova. 2016. The Macroeconomic Effects of Public Investment: Evidence from Advanced Economies. *Journal of Macroeconomics* 50.

Acemoglu, D., P. Aghion, and F. Zilibotti. 2006. Distance to Frontier, Selection, and Economic Growth. *Journal of the European Economic Association* 4(1).

Agénor, P-R. and O. Canuto. 2015. Middle-Income Growth Traps. *Research in Economics* 69.

Agénor, P-R., O. Canuto, and M. Jelenic. 2012. Avoiding Middle-Income Growth Traps. *Economic Premise* No. 29. Poverty Reduction and Economic Management Network. World Bank.

Aghion, P. and P. Howitt. 2009. *The Economics of Growth.* MIT Press.

Aghion, P., R. Blundell, R. Griffith, P. Howitt, and S. Prantl. 2009. The Effects of Entry on Incumbent Innovation and Productivity. *The Review of Economics and Statistics* 91(1).

Aghion, P., P. Howitt, and S. Prantl. 2013. Revisiting the Relationship between Competition, Patenting, and Innovation. *Advances in Economics and Econometrics* 1.

Akcigit, U. and W. R. Kerr. 2010. Growth through Heterogeneous Innovations. *NBER Working Paper* No. 16443. National Bureau of Economic Research.

ADB. 2011. *Asian Development Outlook: Preparing for Demographic Transition.* Asian Development Bank.

——. 2015. *Key Indicators for Asia and the Pacific 2015 Special Chapter: A Smarter Future: Skills, Education, and Growth in Asia.* Asian Development Bank.

——. 2017. *Meeting Asia's Infrastructure Needs.* Asian Development Bank.

Bae, K. Y. 2011. ICT and Broadband in Korea. http://unpan1.un.org/intradoc/groups/public/documents/ungc/unpan047290.pdf

Barro, R. 2016. *NBER Working Paper* No. 21872. National Bureau of Economic Research. www.nber.org/papers/w21872

Barro, R. J. 2001. Human Capital and Growth. *The American Economic Review* 91(2).

Barro, R. J. and J-W. Lee. 2013. A New Data Set of Educational Attainment in the World, 1950–2010. *Journal of Development Economics* 104(C).

Beetsma, R., M. Giuliodori, and F. Klaassen. 2009. Temporal Aggregation and SVAR Identification, with an Application to Fiscal Policy. *Economics Letters* 105(3).

Blanchard, O. J. and R. Perotti. 2002. An Empirical Characterization of the Dynamic Effects of Changes in Government Spending and Taxes on Output. *Quarterly Journal of Economics* 107(4).

Bloom, D. E. and J. G. Williamson. 1998. Demographic Transition and Economic Miracles in Emerging Asia. *World Bank Economic Review* 12.

Bloomberg. 2015. The Bloomberg Innovation Index. http://www.bloomberg.com/graphics/2015-innovative-countries/

Born, B. and G. Müller. 2012. Government Spending Shocks in Quarterly and Annual Time Series. *Journal of Money, Credit and Banking* 44(2–3).

Bosworth, B. P. and S. M. Collins. 2003. The Empirics of Growth: An Update. *Brookings Paper on Economic Activity* 34(2).

Bulman, D., M. Eden, and H. Nguyen. 2014. Transitioning from Low-income Growth to High-income Growth—Is There a Middle-Income Trap? *Policy Research Working Paper* No. 7104. World Bank.

Calderón, C., E. Moral-Benito, and L. Servén. 2014. Is Infrastructure Capital Productive? A Dynamic Heterogeneous Approach. *Journal of Applied Econometrics* 30(2).

Cardarelli, R. and L. Lusinyan. 2015. US Total Factor Productivity Slowdown: Evidence from the US States. *IMF Working Paper* WP/15/116. International Monetary Fund.

Cherif, R. and F. Hasanov. 2015. The Leap of the Tiger: How Malaysia Can Escape the Middle-income Trap. *IMF Working Paper* WP/15/131. International Monetary Fund.

Colclough, C., G. Kingdon, and H. Patrinos. 2009. The Pattern of Returns to Education and its Implications. *Policy Brief No. 4, Research Consortium on Educational Outcomes and Poverty.* The University of Edinburgh, UK.

Corsetti, G., A. Meier, and G. J. Müller. 2012. What Determines Government Spending Multipliers? *Economic Policy* 27(72).

Dabla-Norris, E., S. Guo, V. Haksar, M. Kim, K. Kochar, K. Wiseman, and A. Zdzienicka. 2015. The New Normal: A Sector-Level Perspective on Productivity Trends in Advanced Economies. *IMF Staff Discussion Note* SDN/15/03.

Eichengreen, B., D. Park, and K. Shin. 2012. When Fast Growing Economies Slow Down: International Evidence and Implications for China. *Asian Economic Papers* 11.

——. 2014. Growth Slowdowns Redux. *Japan and the World Economy* 32.

Fan, V. Y. and W. D. Savedoff. 2014. The Health Financing Transition: A Conceptual Framework and Empirical Evidence. *Social Science and Medicine* 105.

Fay, M. and T. Yepes. 2003. Investing in Infrastructure: What is Needed from 2000 to 2010? *Policy Research Working Paper* No. 3102. World Bank.

Felipe, J. and C. Rhee. 2014a. Issues in Modern Industrial Policy (I): Sector Selection, Who, How, and Sector Promotion. In Jesus Felipe, ed. *Development and Modern Industrial Policy in Practice. Issues and Country Experiences.* Edward Elgar.

——. 2014b. Issues in Modern Industrial Policy (II): Human Capital and Innovation, and Monitoring and Evaluation. In Jesus Felipe, ed. *Development and Modern Industrial Policy in Practice. Issues and Country Experiences.* Edward Elgar.

Felipe, J., U. Kumar, A. Abdon, and M. Bacate. 2012. Product Complexity and Economic Development. *Structural Change and Economic Dynamism* 23.

Felipe, J, U. Kumar, and R. Galope. 2017. Middle-income Transitions: Trap or Myth? *Journal of the Asia Pacific Economy.* http://dx.doi.org/10.1080/13547860.2016.1270253

Han, X. and S. J. Wei. 2015. Re-examining the Middle-income Trap Hypothesis: What to Reject and What to Revive? *ADB Economics Working Paper Series* No. 436. Asian Development Bank.

Hanushek, E. and L. Woessmann. 2016. Knowledge Capital, Growth, and the East Asian Miracle. *Science* 351(6271).

——. 2008. The Role of Cognitive Skills in Economic Development. *Journal of Economic Literature* 46(3).

Hidalgo, C. and R. Hausmann. 2009. The Building Blocks of Economic Complexity. *Proceedings of the National Academy of Sciences of the United States of America* 106(26).

Hill, H. and A. Kohpaiboon. 2017. "Policies for Industrial Progress," not "Industry Policy:" Lessons from Southeast Asia. In L. Y. Ing and F. Kimura, eds. *Production Networks in Southeast Asia.* Routledge.

Im, F. G. and D. Rosenblatt. 2015. Middle-income Traps: A Conceptual and Empirical Survey. *Journal of International Commerce, Economies and Policy* 6(3).

International Monetary Fund. 2014. Is it Time for an Infrastructure Push? The Macroeconomic Effects of Public Investment. *World Economic Outlook*, Chapter 3. October.

——. 2016. *Fiscal Monitor: Acting Now, Acting Together.* April.

Jamison, D. and M. Schäferhoff. 2016. Estimating the Economic Returns of Education from a Health Perspective. Background Paper for the Education Commission. SEEK Development.

Jordà, O. 2005. Estimation and Inference of Impulse Responses by Local Projections. *American Economic Review* 95(1).

Kelley, A. C. and R. M. Schmidt. 2001. Economic and Demographic Change: A Synthesis of Models, Findings, and Perspectives. In N. Birdsall, A. C. Kelley, and S. Sinding, eds. *Population Matters: Demographic Change, Economic Growth, and Poverty in the Developing World*. Oxford University Press.

Kingdon, G., H. Patrinos, C. Sakellariou, and M. Soderbom. 2008. International Pattern of Returns to Education. Mimeo, World Bank.

Kraay, A. 2012. How Large is the Government Spending Multiplier? Evidence from World Bank Lending. *The Quarterly Journal of Economics* 127(2).

Lee, R. and A. Mason. 2010. Fertility, Human Capital, and Economic Growth over the Demographic Transition. *European Journal of Population* 26(2).

Lee, S. H., J. Kim, and D. Park. 2016. Demographic Change and Fiscal Sustainability in Asia. *Social Indicators Research*. doi:10.1007/s11205-016-1424-0

Lee, S. M. 2003. South Korea: From the Land of Morning Calm to ICT Hotbed. *The Academy of Management Executive* 17(2).

Lee, Y. H. 2015. ICT as a Key Engine for Development: Good Practices and Lessons Learned from Korea. *World Bank Note*. http://siteresources. worldbank.org/INTEGOVERNMENT/Resources/NoteKoreaICT.doc

Lentz, R. and D. T. Mortensen. 2008. An Empirical Model of Growth through Product Innovation. *Econometrica* 76(6).

Maddison, A. 2010. *Historical Statistics of the World Economy: 1–2008 AD*. http://www.ggdc.net/MADDISON/oriindex.htm

Mankiw, N. G., D. Romer, and D. N. Weill. 1992. A Contribution to the Empirics of Economic growth. *Quarterly Journal of Economics* 107(2).

Mason, A. ed. 2001. *Population Change and Economic Development in East Asia: Challenges Met, Opportunities Seized*. Stanford University Press.

Mason, A. and R. Lee. 2007. Transfers, Capital, and Consumption over the Demographic Transition. In R. Clark, N. Ogawa, and A. Mason, eds. *Population Aging, Intergenerational Transfers and the Macroeconomy*. Edward Elgar.

Mason, A., R. Lee, and J. X. Jiang. 2016. Demographic Dividends, Human Capital, and Saving. *The Journal of the Economics of Ageing* 7.

McMorrow, K., W. Röger, and A. Turrini. 2010. Determinants of TFP Growth: A Close Look at Industries Driving the EU–US Productivity Gap. *Structural Change and Economic Dynamics* 21.

Montenegro, C. and H. Patrinos, 2014. Comparable Estimates of Returns to Schooling Around the World. *Policy Research Working Paper* 7020. World Bank.

Oh, M. and J. F. Larson. 2011. *Digital Development in Korea: Building an Information Society*. Routledge.

Patrinos, H., C. Ridao-Cano, and C. Sakellariou. 2006. Estimating the Returns to Education: Accounting for Heterogeneity in Ability. *Policy Research Working Paper* 4020. World Bank.

Peacock, A. T. and J. Wiseman. 1961. *The Growth of Public Expenditure in the United Kingdom*. Princeton University Press.

Presbitero, A. F. 2016. Too Much and Too Fast? Public Investment Scaling-up and Absorptive Capacity. *Journal of Development Economics* 120.

Psacharopoulos, G. and H. Patrinos. 2004. Returns to Investment in Education: A Further Update. *Education Economics* 12(2).

Riboud, M., Y. Savchenko, and H. Tan. 2006. The Knowledge Economy and Education and Training in South Asia: A Mapping Exercise of Available Survey Data. Draft. World Bank.

Ruiz-Nuñez, F. and Z. Wei. 2015. Infrastructure Investment Demands in Emerging Markets and Developing Economies. *Policy Research Working Paper* No. 7414. World Bank.

Schultz, T. P. 2004. Evidence of Returns to Schooling in Africa from Household Surveys: Monitoring and Restructuring the Market for Education. *Journal of African Economies* 13(2).

Schumpeter, J. 1942. *Capitalism, Socialism and Democracy*. Harper & Row.

Solow, R. M. 1956. A Contribution to the Theory of Economic Growth. *The Quarterly Journal of Economics* 70(1).

Spence, M. 2011. *The Next Convergence. The Future of Economic Growth in a Multispeed World*. Farrar, Straus, and Giroux.

UNIDO. 2007. Determinants of Total Factor Productivity: A Literature Review. *Research and Statistics Branch Staff Working Paper* 02/2007. United Nations Industrial Development Organization.

United Nations, Department of Economic and Social Affairs, Population Division. 2013. National Transfer Accounts Manual: Measuring and Analyzing the Generational Economy.

Warner, A. M. 2014. Public Investment as an Engine of Growth. *IMF Working Paper* 14/148. International Monetary Fund.

Yeo, Y. H., S. K. Kim, J. H. Bae, and B. G. Kim. 2014. The Assessment of Information and Communication Technology (ICT) Policy in South Korea. *Advances in Computer Science and its Applications* 279.

ECONOMIC TRENDS AND PROSPECTS IN DEVELOPING ASIA

3

CENTRAL ASIA

ARMENIA
AZERBAIJAN
GEORGIA
KAZAKHSTAN
KYRGYZ REPUBLIC
TAJIKISTAN
TURKMENISTAN
UZBEKISTAN

Armenia

Weak domestic demand and the onset of deflation slowed growth to 0.2% in 2016 despite a higher fiscal deficit and a narrower trade deficit. With demand likely to remain weak and no room for fiscal stimulus, projections for 2017 and 2018 are for modest growth, low inflation, and further balancing in the current account. Policy should promote export-oriented industries and innovation.

Economic performance

The economy grew by a mere 0.2% in 2016 following growth at 3.0% in the previous year. On the supply side, declines in agriculture and construction were the main causes for the slowdown, while services and industry excluding construction expanded (Figure 3.1.1).

Bad weather caused agriculture to contract by 5.8% in 2016, reversing double-digit growth in 2015. Industry excluding construction expanded by 5.1%, mainly on higher output in mining and in food, beverages, and tobacco. Construction contracted by 11.3%, recording a fourth consecutive year of decline as organizations and households continued to pull back. Services, which account for more than half of GDP, contributed the most to growth, expanding by 4.0% after no growth in 2015. Much of the expansion was in recreation, transport, finance, and insurance.

On the demand side, growth came mainly from a modest rise in total consumption and a halving of the deficit in net exports of goods and services to an estimated 6.0% of GDP in 2016 from 12.2% a year earlier. Growth in private consumption was a lackluster 0.3%, reflecting weak household spending, though public consumption grew by an estimated 6.0% as expansionary fiscal policy aimed to stimulate the economy. Gross fixed capital formation contracted by 6.2% because of sluggish public and private investment.

Monetary policy was accommodative throughout the year. Considering weakened growth prospects and a deflationary environment, the Central Bank of Armenia gradually relaxed its policy rate from 8.75% in December 2015 to 6.00% in February 2017. Despite this monetary easing, weak aggregate demand and lower commodity prices caused consumer prices to decline. Reversing average inflation of 3.7% in 2015, deflation averaged 1.4% in 2016 and stood in December at 1.1% year on year (Figure 3.1.2). Falling prices for food, which account for two-thirds of the consumer basket, outweighed higher prices for services. The central bank inflation target is 2.5%–5.5%.

3.1.1 Supply-side contributions to growth

- Agriculture
- Industry excluding construction
- Construction
- Services including indirect taxes and other items
- Gross domestic product

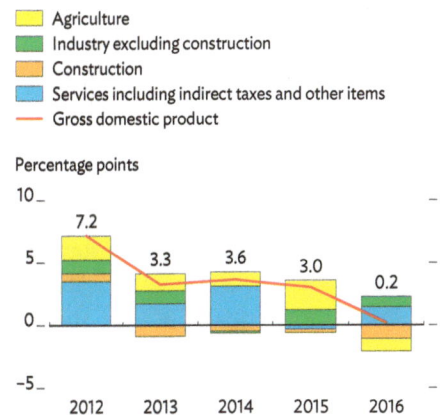

Source: National Statistical Service of the Republic of Armenia. http://www.armstat.am (accessed 3 March 2017).

3.1.2 Inflation

- Overall
- Food
- Other goods
- Services

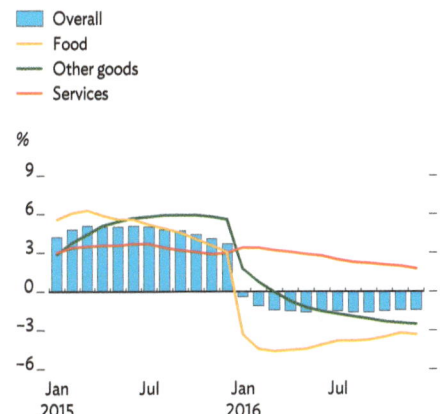

Source: National Statistical Service of the Republic of Armenia. http://www.armstat.am (accessed 3 March 2017).

This chapter was written by Grigor Gyurjyan of the Armenia Resident Mission, ADB, Yerevan, and Dominik Peschel of the Central and West Asia Department, ADB, Manila.

The slack economy, deflation, and expansionary fiscal policy all undermined the government budget in 2016, causing the deficit to widen to 5.4% of GDP from 4.8% in 2015 (Figure 3.1.3). As tax revenue declined by 4.4%, total budget revenue fell 2.6% short of its target, slipping to the equivalent of 22.8% of GDP from 23.2% in 2015, while budget expenditure was below the planned amount by 3.7%, equal to 28.2% of GDP.

The higher budget deficit pushed public debt to 56.7% of GDP at the end of 2016 from 48.8% a year earlier. External public debt increased to 45.9% of GDP from 41.5% in 2015, while domestic debt rose to 10.9%, up by 3.5 percentage points (Figure 3.1.4). The ratio of public debt to the previous year's GDP stood at 57.1% at the end of 2016, breaching the 50% ceiling in the Public Debt Law for the first time.

The current account deficit narrowed marginally to an estimated 2.6% of GDP in 2016 from 2.7% in 2015 (Figure 3.1.5). Rising exports and declining imports that reflected weak domestic demand reduced the trade deficit to an estimated 8.8% of GDP in 2016 from 11.3% in 2015. An expanding deficit in investment income and further shrinkage of surpluses in personal transfers and employee compensation from abroad were the main reasons why the overall income surplus narrowed. Remittances, measured as net inflow of private noncommercial transfers through banks, declined by 17.8% to $716 million in 2016, the third consecutive year of contraction (Figure 3.1.6).

Higher government borrowing helped keep international reserves at acceptable levels. Gross international reserves at the end of 2016 stood at $2.2 billion, equal to 6.2 months of estimated imports (Figure 3.1.7).

Strong export performance and large inflows of foreign financing caused the Armenian dram to appreciate in nominal effective terms against a basket of major currencies by 3.1% month on month in December 2016. Meanwhile, domestic deflation and inflation in Armenia's main trading partners caused the dram to depreciate in real effective terms by 0.5%.

Economic prospects

GDP growth is projected at 2.2% in 2017 and 2.5% in 2018 (Figure 3.1.8). External risks to the forecast arise mainly from developments in the Russian Federation, with which Armenia has strong economic links. The forecast assumes some recovery there and a resulting rebound in remittances. Domestic risks to the economic outlook reflect low fiscal and external buffers and subdued investor enthusiasm ahead of parliamentary elections due in April 2017. On the positive side, tariff reductions in early 2017 for gas and electricity—with especially steep decreases for certain vulnerable households and, regarding gas, for food processing firms and greenhouses—should support growth. The expected rise in demand could, however, spur inflation.

On the supply side, all sectors are seen growing moderately in 2017 and 2018. Industry excluding construction is projected to expand by 6.2% and somewhat more in 2018, again mainly on expansion in mining and in food, beverages, and tobacco. Announced government initiatives—such as renewed efforts to spur export and innovative industries

3.1.3 Fiscal indicators

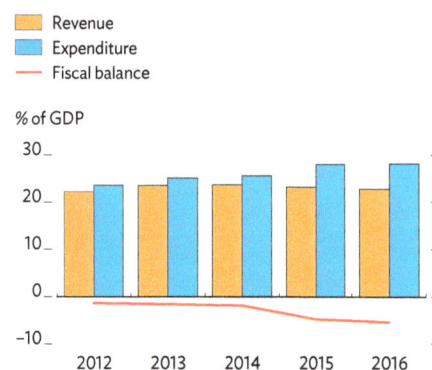

■ Revenue
■ Expenditure
— Fiscal balance

% of GDP

Sources: Ministry of Finance. http://www.minfin.am; National Statistical Service of the Republic of Armenia. http://www.armstat.am (accessed 3 March 2017).

3.1.4 Public debt

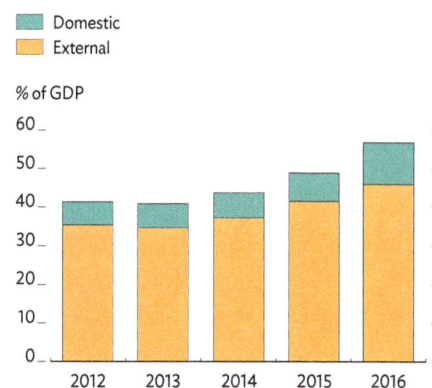

■ Domestic
■ External

% of GDP

Sources: Ministry of Finance. http://www.minfin.am; National Statistical Service of the Republic of Armenia. http://www.armstat.am (both accessed 3 March 2017).

3.1.5 Current account components

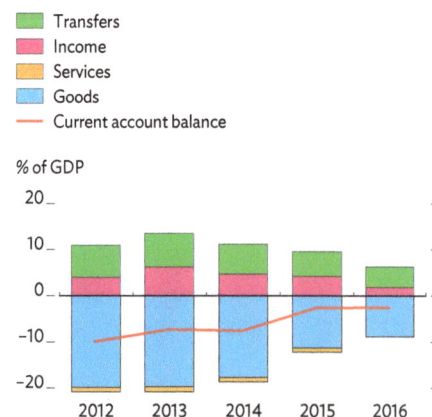

■ Transfers
■ Income
■ Services
■ Goods
— Current account balance

% of GDP

Sources: Central Bank of Armenia. http://www.cba.am (accessed 3 March 2017); ADB estimates.

through new mechanisms and tools, the creation of a free-trade zone on the border with Iran, and the establishment of a joint investment fund with the Russian Federation for financing Armenia's priority economic sectors—are considered essential to promote industrial expansion. Copper production could support growth if the price remains relatively high. However, construction is projected to contract by a further 6.4% in 2017 in view of a significant decline in capital spending in the 2017 state budget and slackening construction funded by remittances. The rate of contraction will likely moderate again in 2018.

With normal weather, agriculture is projected to recover by 8.6% in 2017 and possibly more in 2018. Additional support could come from the government's efforts to foster the construction and expansion of greenhouses, through the favorable gas prices for greenhouses beginning this year. Services are expected to grow by only 2.4% in 2017 and slightly more in 2018, constrained by sluggishness in remittance-supported trade.

On the demand side, the main drivers of growth will probably be further narrowing of the deficit in net exports of goods and services (though less than in 2016) and a slight rebound in private consumption.

Monetary policy is likely to remain accommodative. With moderate output growth, weak domestic demand, and only modest inflationary pressures expected from abroad, average annual inflation is projected to turn positive but remain low at 1.2% in 2017 before edging up to 1.8% in 2018.

Significant and sustained fiscal consolidation will be crucial over the medium term. To reduce debt-related vulnerability and contain fiscal risk, the 2017 budget envisages halving the budget deficit to 2.8% of GDP in 2017, mainly through cuts in capital spending and measures to contain public wages and pensions. The adoption of a new tax code in 2016, its provisions to be introduced gradually during 2017–2021, should facilitate fiscal consolidation by strengthening tax administration and broadening the tax base.

Provided the decline in income and transfers abates, the current account deficit is projected to narrow further to 2.3% in 2017 and 2.0% in 2018 as domestic demand remains sluggish and exports of goods and services outpace imports (Figure 3.1.9). To attract foreign direct investment, the government has undertaken several initiatives. These include establishing a strategic initiatives center, introducing a single platform for investment proposals, and revising business regulation. The successful implementation of these measures should raise inward foreign direct investment, thereby helping to strengthen the current account.

The trade deficit is expected to narrow further. Exports are forecast to expand by 6.5% in 2017 and a further 5.0% in 2018, underpinned by rising exports of agricultural products, nonferrous metals, and precious stones and metals. Constrained by only moderate recovery in domestic demand, imports are projected to grow modestly by 2.5% in both 2017 and 2018. The services account will remain relatively balanced.

3.1.6 Remittances and their sources

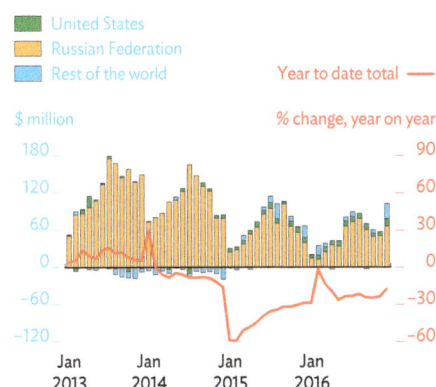

Source: Central Bank of Armenia. http://www.cba.am (accessed 3 March 2017).

3.1.7 Reserves and effective exchange rates

Sources: Central Bank of Armenia. http://www.cba.am; International Monetary Fund. International Financial Statistics online database (accessed 3 March 2017).

3.1.8 GDP growth

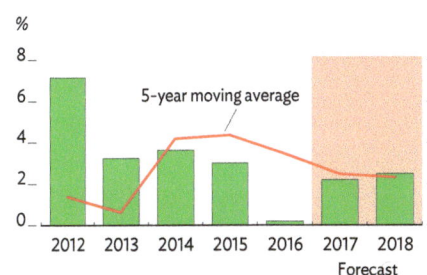

Sources: National Statistical Service of the Republic of Armenia. http://www.armstat.am (accessed 3 March 2017); ADB estimates.

Policy challenge—export diversification

Accelerating reform that promotes exports and diversifies domestic output is essential to make economic growth broad based and more inclusive and, ultimately, to alleviate macroeconomic imbalances, in particular the budget deficit and public debt, both of which are relatively high and have worsened since late 2015. Despite a marked narrowing of the trade deficit, exports remain a small share of GDP, estimated at 17% in 2016, and highly concentrated in terms of both content and destination.

The government's strategy to pursue export-led industrial development, approved in 2011, targets 11 subsectors with export potential. It has played an important role in setting long-term objectives and framing dialogue between the public and private sectors. The strategy has triggered some dynamism in manufacturing, though much of the progress has been in high-input food processing, rather than in precision engineering, textiles, footwear, or other areas able to capitalize on skills and innovation.

Activities to encourage investments that improve productivity could catalyze export diversification by fostering innovation. The government's initiative to collect business proposals on a single platform for presentation to investors is a way to mobilize much-needed resources for the structural transformation of the economy. The many proposals collected from private firms and local communities across the country are expected to be financed from various sources including the state budget, local community budgets, and the private sector. Even partial implementation of these investments would help channel know-how and innovation into production processes, expand the variety of exports, and add value to existing products—ultimately creating new, highly productive jobs.

The other initiatives under way include, as mentioned above, the further improvement of institutional and regulatory frameworks for export promotion, introduction of new instruments for export promotion and export insurance, establishment of the joint investment fund with the Russian Federation, and creation of the free-trade zone on the Iranian border.

Support for innovation and technology is another way to transform Armenia into a knowledge-based economy and add value to production. During the past decade, effective public–private collaboration has brought sustained growth in information technology. The creation of technology parks and incubators, after-school learning centers, and engineering laboratories in pilot schools has, along with the entry of international companies, significantly improved educational resources for specialist training. Armenia can boost its total factor productivity and enhance economic growth by scaling up these existing initiatives and orienting them toward industries that produce technologically sophisticated products, thereby leveraging its competitive advantage in highly skilled and low-cost labor in such fields as engineering and computer science.

3.1.1 Selected economic indicators (%)

	2017	2018
GDP growth	2.2	2.5
Inflation	1.2	1.8
Current account balance (share of GDP)	-2.3	-2.0

Source: ADB estimates.

3.1.9 Current account balance

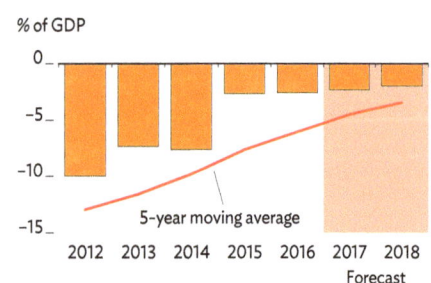

Sources: National Statistical Service of the Republic of Armenia. http://www.armstat.am (accessed 3 March 2017); ADB estimates.

Azerbaijan

Continued weak oil prices helped cause GDP to contract by 3.8% in 2016 and the current account to fall into deficit. Meanwhile, inflation accelerated to 12.4%. GDP is forecast to decline by a further 1.1% in 2017 and then recover by 1.2% in 2018, and higher oil prices should return the current account to surplus. Combatting unemployment is a major challenge.

Economic performance

GDP contracted by 3.8% last year following 1.1% growth in 2015 (Figure 3.2.1). The decline reflected weak oil prices and lower oil production, but also a falloff in domestic demand, including less public investment, that caused the economy outside of the large oil sector to shrink by 5.4%.

On the supply side, industry contracted by 7.1%, much more than the 1.9% decline in 2015, mainly because construction plummeted by 27.6% as the government slashed public investment in response to plunging revenues. Manufacturing declined by 1.4%, reversing 7.7% growth in 2015 as the production of construction materials fell by 10.6% and of petrochemicals by 9.1%. Oil output edged down by 1.3% in 2016, but gas extraction rose by the same percentage, albeit from a much smaller base. Slowing transport and financial services caused services to contract by 0.7% after a 4.5% increase in 2015. Meanwhile, agriculture expanded by 2.6% on growth at 2.8% in livestock and 2.5% in key crops, though managing less than half of the 6.6% pace achieved in 2015.

On the demand side, growth in consumption slowed with depreciation of the Azerbaijan manat and reduced consumer lending. Net exports fell by more than 50%, following a 72% decline in 2015, as lower hydrocarbon output reduced export volume.

The inflation rate tripled to 12.4% from 4.0% in 2015 as the impact of currency depreciation in 2015 lingered (Figure 3.2.2). Prices for food rose by 14.7%, other goods by 16.7%, and services by 5.8%.

Fiscal policy tightened in 2016 as the state budget deficit narrowed to the equivalent of 0.4% of GDP from 1.2% in 2015. Revenue equaled 29.2%, down from 31.5% in 2015, as transfers from the sovereign wealth fund were reduced by 6.3% to conserve assets and lessen the budget's dependence on oil income. In February 2016, the authorities revised the budget, cutting expenditure to ensure long-term fiscal sustainability. Outlays fell to 29.6% of GDP from 32.7% in 2015 as lower capital spending offset a sharp rise in interest payments due to earlier devaluations and 10% increases for public wages, pensions, and social protection. Public and publicly guaranteed debt rose to equal 20.4% of GDP at the end of 2016 from 19.8% a year earlier.

3.2.1 GDP growth by sector

- Agriculture
- Industry
- Services
- Gross domestic product

% change, year on year

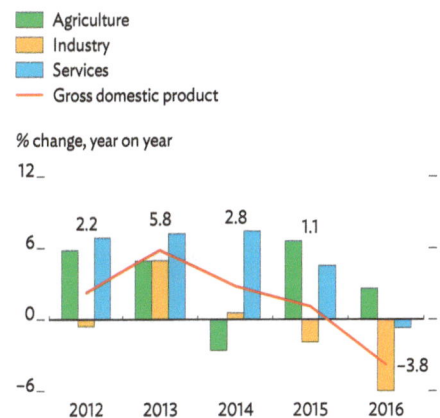

Source: State Statistical Committee of the Republic of Azerbaijan.

3.2.2 Monthly inflation

- Overall
- Food
- Other goods
- Services

% change, year on year

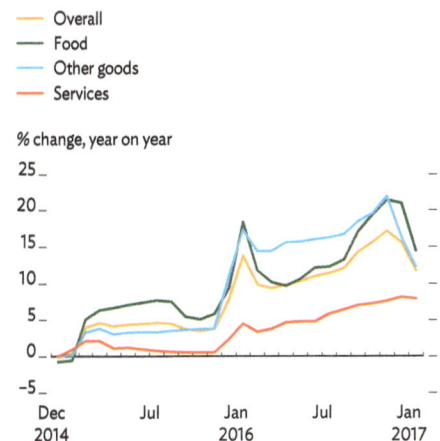

Sources: State Statistical Committee of the Republic of Azerbaijan; Haver Analytics (accessed 13 March 2017).

This chapter was written by Nail Valiyev of the Azerbaijan Resident Mission, ADB, Baku, and Dominik Peschel of the Central and West Asia Department, ADB, Manila.

Monetary and financial policy in 2016 aimed to limit inflation and restructure the banking system in the wake of steep currency depreciation in 2015. In response to high inflation, the central bank raised the policy interest rate in four steps to 15.0% in September 2016 from 3.0% in September 2015. Broad money shrank by 4.9%, four times the 1.1% contraction in 2015 (Figure 3.2.3), and central bank international reserves declined by 20.8% (Figure 3.2.4). Moreover, deposits fell by 10.0%, contributing to a 19.6% falloff in loans to borrowers outside of the government. After the central bank adopted a floating exchange rate at the end of 2015, the manat depreciated by a further 12.0% against the US dollar in 2016, aggravating balance sheet and liquidity risks (Figure 3.2.5). To restore confidence in the local currency, the authorities provided in March 2016 full deposit insurance that guarantees repayment of local currency deposits at an interest rate of 15%, versus 3% for foreign currency deposits. Dollarization nevertheless remained high with 75.2% of deposits in foreign currency at the end of 2016, albeit down from 81.6% a year earlier.

The current account deficit widened to an estimated 2.1% of GDP in 2016, from a deficit of 0.4% in 2015. Lower oil prices and output cut exports by a further 15.8% on top of the 44.8% decline a year earlier. Imports declined by 12.7%, reversing a 4.7% pickup a year earlier, mainly because of lower imports of cars, tobacco, and pharmaceuticals. The services deficit narrowed by 28.4% as receipts from tourism improved by 22.8% and imports of construction services declined.

Economic prospects

GDP is projected to contract by 1.1% in 2017 with a further decline in oil production. Tightened fiscal policy will limit public investment. However, GDP is forecast to turn up by 1.2% in 2018 with the onset of production from the Shah Deniz gas field and some recovery anticipated among private firms (Figure 3.2.6).

On the supply side, industry is forecast to contract by 0.5% in 2017 as oil production, which accounts for 65% of total industry, declines further. However, gas condensate from new Shah Deniz gas field will help industry expand by 1.0% in 2018. Construction is projected to fall by a further 10.0% in 2017, reflecting planned cuts in public investment, and then expand by 1.0% in 2018 as the economy recovers and the government accelerates the implementation of its social housing program. Government efforts to stimulate non-oil exports, in particular through its Made in Azerbaijan promotion, should catalyze growth in agriculture at 3.0% in 2017 and 4.0% in 2018. Services are projected to show little change in 2017 as retail trade and transportation decline, then expand by 1.0% in 2018 as transportation recovers and tourism improves.

On the demand side, private consumption is predicted to contract in 2017 in response to higher inflation and remain subdued in 2018. Investment is expected to fall in 2017 as tightened fiscal and monetary policy curb both private and public investment. Net exports are forecast to improve in 2017 and particularly in 2018 as gas production increases.

3.2.3 Contributions to money supply growth

- ▢ Net foreign assets
- ▢ Credit to the economy
- ▢ Net claims on government
- ▢ Net other items
- — Broad money (M3) growth

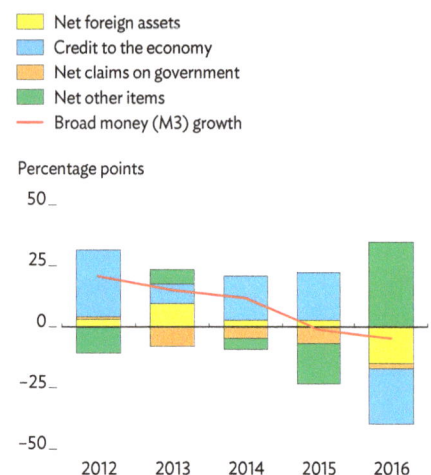

Source: Central Bank of the Republic of Azerbaijan.

3.2.1 Selected economic indicators (%)

	2017	2018
GDP growth	–1.1	1.2
Inflation	9.0	8.0
Current account balance (share of GDP)	5.9	11.4

Source: ADB estimates.

3.2.4 State fund and central bank reserves

- ▢ State Oil Fund of Azerbaijan
- ▢ Central bank reserves
- — Total

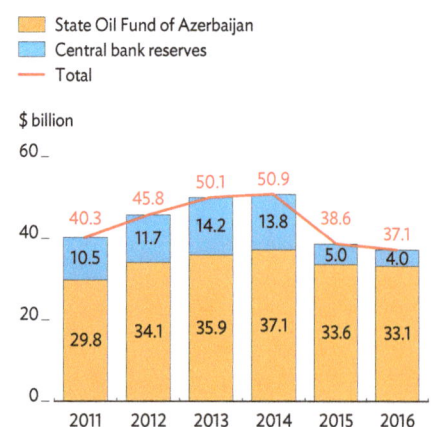

Sources: Central Bank of the Republic of Azerbaijan; State Oil Fund of Azerbaijan. http://www.oilfund.az (accessed 13 March 2017).

Inflation is projected to moderate to 9.0% in 2017 with less currency depreciation, despite tariff increases for electricity and gas, then slow further to 8.0% in 2018 barring further adjustment to utility prices or resurgent depreciation (Figure 3.2.7). Inflation will remain a key challenge over the forecast period, and containing it will require coordinated efforts from monetary and fiscal authorities.

Fiscal policy will aim to limit deficits in the next 2 years. Including transfers from the sovereign wealth fund, the government anticipates state budget deficits equal to 1.0% of GDP in 2017 and 0.9% in 2018 (Figure 3.2.8). Constrained imports will limit revenue from custom duties, while slow economic activity holds down domestic tax receipts. Expenditure will be restrained to contain the deficit. With real GDP declining in 2017 and growing little in 2018, revenue is forecast at 25.2% of GDP in 2017 and 25.6% in 2018. Expenditure is projected at 26.2% of GDP in 2017, reflecting higher current outlays and a further 41.1% cut in capital spending, and at 26.4% in 2018. Public and publicly guaranteed debt is expected to increase in 2017 and 2018 to allow the government to complete the expansion of the Shah Deniz gas field and to improve agriculture.

Monetary policy will likely focus on curbing inflation. As the central bank continues to tighten policy, private credit growth will slow. In addition, growing demand for foreign currency may further weaken the manat unless the central bank intervenes. Dollarization in banking will remain high, limiting liquidity in the local currency. Manat depreciation will crimp borrowers' repayment capacity, possibly pushing the share of nonperforming loans above 10%. The combined impact of continued currency depreciation, tightened monetary policy, and a stagnant private sector is expected to create serious risks for domestic banks.

The current account balance is forecast to record surpluses equal to 5.9% of GDP in 2017 and 11.4% in 2018 as the trade surplus in goods widens and the services deficit narrows (Figure 3.2.9). Total exports are projected to grow by 22.6% in 2017 with the projected improvement in oil prices and expand by a further 15.0% in 2018 as the Shah Deniz gas field starts producing. Imports are expected to contract by 6.2% in 2017 because of further manat depreciation and a temporary ban on government imports, then expand by 12.5% in 2018 as the ban is lifted. The services deficit is forecast to expand by 15.6% in 2017, reflecting payment for construction, and then narrow by 20.0% in 2018 on gains from transportation and tourism. Remittances, an important source of income for the rural population, are forecast to rise in 2017 and 2018 as the Russian Federation recovers. Gross reserves including assets in the sovereign wealth fund are projected at $30.1 billion in 2017 and $31.5 billion in 2018.

Policy challenge—reducing unemployment

Recession has weakened Azerbaijan's labor market. As lower turnover caused many state and private enterprises to lay off workers, the number of unemployed rose by 2.5% in 2015 and 14.5% in 2016, after falling by an average of 2.0% annually from 2010 to 2014 (Figure 3.2.10).

3.2.5 Exchange rate and average crude oil price

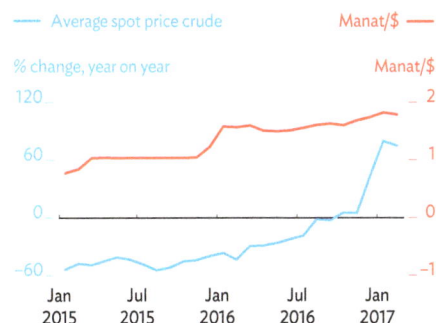

Note: An increase in the exchange rate indicates a depreciation.
Sources: Central Bank of the Republic of Azerbaijan; Haver Analytics (accessed 13 March 2017).

3.2.6 GDP growth

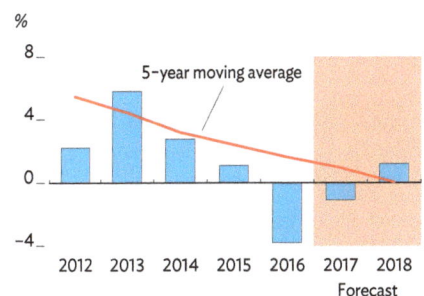

Sources: Central Bank of the Republic of Azerbaijan; ADB estimates.

3.2.7 Annual inflation

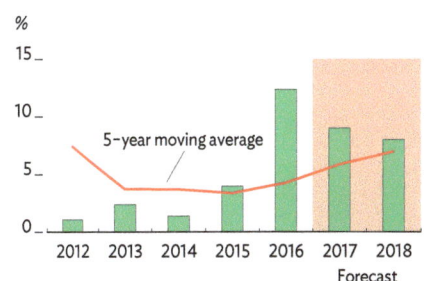

Sources: Central Bank of the Republic of Azerbaijan; ADB estimates.

More fundamentally, joblessness reflects low labor productivity and a shortage of marketable skills. Currently, agriculture employs 36.3% of workers to produce only 6.2% of GDP, while industry employs only 6.9% of workers to produce 47.0% of GDP.

To date, the government has relied mainly on regional socioeconomic development programs to combat joblessness. These programs helped cut the unemployment rate from 7.2% in 2005 to 4.9% in 2014, though many of the jobs created were temporary. The unemployment rate subsequently rose to 5.6% at the end of 2016. To ease the impact of the recession and minimize social discontent, the government took further measures in 2016 to promote employment and hired 35,000 workers on a temporary basis. In addition, to address shortages in technical qualifications and gaps in professional retraining, it established an agency to coordinate technical and vocational education. To support rural employment, a new project was launched to help family firms produce goods and deliver them to markets. In addition, a social housing program was launched with the goal of creating 10,000 jobs by 2020. To strengthen agriculture and agro-processing, farmers were given 179,000 hectares of arable land for additional cotton, hazelnut, and tea production, which should provide more rural jobs and limit migration to urban areas. Through the National Entrepreneurship Support Fund, the state budget provided $100 million to expand small and medium-sized enterprises and create an additional 12,600 jobs. In December 2016, the government adopted a roadmap program that prioritizes 11 sectors, emphasizes the provision of sustainable employment, and sets an ambitious goal of creating 450,000 jobs by 2025.

To augment these measures, the authorities should pay more attention to job promotion for younger workers, as the youth unemployment rate has risen especially rapidly. They could consider additional measures to better link vocational education with the labor market, develop the job skills needed to raise productivity in the private sector, provide small and medium-sized enterprises with more affordable financing, and open centers to provide agricultural support services. The privatization of inactive state-owned enterprises should reactivate them and create jobs.

3.2.8 Fiscal balance

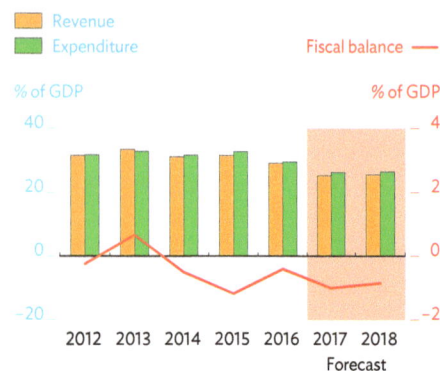

Source: Ministry of Finance of the Republic of Azerbaijan.

3.2.9 Annual current account balance

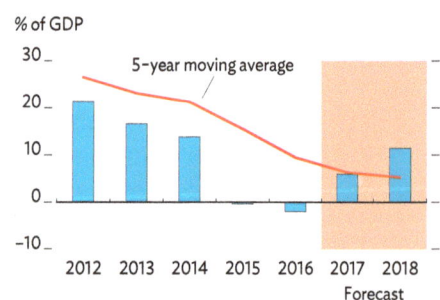

Sources: Central Bank of the Republic of Azerbaijan; ADB estimates.

3.2.10 Growth in total unemployment

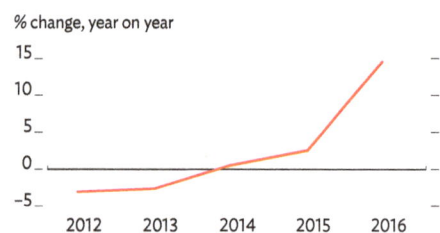

Source: State Statistical Committee of the Republic of Azerbaijan.

Georgia

External factors held growth at 2.7% in 2016, but higher capital spending and corporate tax reform should permit growth to reach 3.8% in 2017 and 4.5% in 2018. Inflation, low in 2016, will likely rise to 4.2% in 2017 under currency depreciation and an excise tax increase. Skills mismatch in the labor market is an important constraint on long-term growth.

Economic performance

Continued shocks from trade partners limited growth in 2016 to an estimated 2.7% despite fiscal stimulus. On the supply side, 8.0% expansion in construction and 4.8% in manufacturing drove growth in industry as increases of 9.9% in tourism and 9.2% in finance lifted services (Figure 3.3.1). On the expenditure side, growth came mainly from a 17.1% surge in consumption, led by the government, and a 3.5% rise in investment, notably in public infrastructure to promote trade and tourism.

Inflation averaged 2.1% in 2016, driven by 13.1% higher prices for such excisable goods as tobacco and alcoholic beverages, though low import prices limited overall inflation (Figure 3.3.2). Lower fuel costs kept the rise in transport prices to 2.2%. However, in anticipation of an increase in the fuel tax effective on 1 January 2017, fuel prices started rising in December 2016, and in January 2017 monthly inflation reached its highest rate since the end of 2015. Despite pressure on the Georgian lari, the National Bank of Georgia, the central bank, cut the policy interest rate gradually from 8.0% at the end of 2015 to 6.5% in September 2016 before restoring it to 6.8% in early 2017 in response to rising inflation expectations (Figure 3.3.3). The average interest rate on loans fell in 2016 by 1.6 percentage points to 12.7%, and for deposits by 0.8 points to 4.5%, as the central bank pursued a more accommodative monetary policy.

Currency in circulation grew by 19.8%, following near-zero growth in 2015, to contribute to a 20.2% rise in broad money, which pressed down on the lari but helped lift inflation toward the central bank's 2016 target of 5.0%. Beginning in October, credit growth accelerated to 22.3% from 19.4% in 2015 (Figure 3.3.4). Nonperforming loans remained modest at less than 4%, and bank profits rose by 26.4%. Meanwhile, the percentage of deposits in foreign currency climbed by 2 percentage points to 70%, well above the 57% prevailing in October 2014, before the start of significant currency depreciation.

The fiscal deficit rose to 4.5% of GDP in 2016 from 3.8% in 2015 (Figure 3.3.5) with a planned large increase in expenditure, though tax collections and total revenue exceeded targets. Total revenue rose by 7.9% to equal 28.5% of GDP, up from 28.2% in 2015. External public debt,

3.3.1 GDP growth by sector

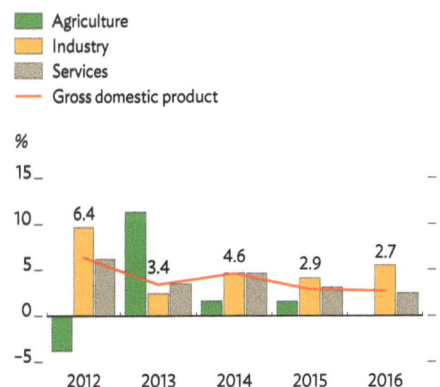

- Agriculture
- Industry
- Services
- Gross domestic product

Source: National Statistics Office of Georgia. http://www.geostat.ge (accessed 3 March 2017).

3.3.2 Monthly inflation

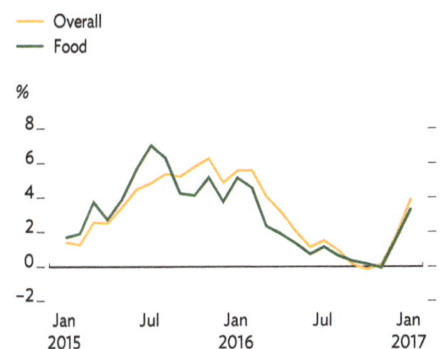

- Overall
- Food

Source: National Statistics Office of Georgia. http://www.geostat.ge (accessed 3 March 2017).

This chapter was written by George Luarsabishvili of the Georgia Resident Mission, ADB, Tbilisi, and Dominik Peschel of the Central and West Asia Department, ADB, Manila.

accounting for 78% of total public debt, rose from 32.9% of GDP in 2015 to 33.9%, while total public debt grew from 41.4% of GDP in 2015 to 43.0%.

The current account deficit widened to an estimated 13.1% of GDP in 2016, up from 11.9% a year earlier, largely because of recession in the Russian Federation and slow growth in other trading partners. These effects appeared to wane toward year-end as tourism, remittances, and exports started to recover. Exports of goods fell by about 4.0%, mainly because of lower prices. Imports excluding medication financed by grants decreased by about 1.0%, reflecting a weaker lari and lower oil prices. Remittances rose by 6.6%, as higher inflows from Europe and the United States—up by 11.2% from Italy, 5.8% from Greece, and 27.6% from the US—countered an 8.8% decline from the Russian Federation. Foreign direct investment (FDI) rose by 5.2% in 2016, with a significant rise in reinvested FDI, from 9.3% in 2015 to 31.6% in 2016, going mostly to construction, energy, manufacturing, and especially transport and communication to supply an expansion of the South Caucasus Pipeline.

The lari depreciated in 2016 by 10.5% against the US dollar and 7.2% against the euro (Figure 3.3.6). The depreciation reflected Georgia's large current account deficit and the outflow of foreign exchange to pay for imports. Meanwhile, the lari strengthened in nominal terms against the currencies of some key trading partners, notably Turkey and Azerbaijan, though the real exchange rate was stable, preserving Georgia's competitiveness. Central bank net sales of foreign exchange were about zero as foreign exchange sales in the second half of the year offset purchases in the first half. Gross international reserves at the end of the year amounted to $2.8 billion, or cover for 2.9 months of imports.

Economic prospects

Increased capital outlays are expected to push growth to 3.8% in 2017 and 4.5% in 2018, when the impact of infrastructure spending is expected to be greatest (Figure 3.3.7). Higher domestic consumption and a modest recovery in exports will contribute to growth and employment in 2017. The government estimates that corporate tax reform could add as much as 1.5 percentage points to growth in the next 2 years, especially in 2017 but also in 2018, by encouraging higher private investment (Box 3.3.1). Two pacts with European countries—the Deep and Comprehensive Free Trade Area and the European Free Trade Association—and the expected ratification by mid-2017 of a free trade agreement with the People's Republic of China should expand Georgia's access to markets engaged in a third of world trade, thereby bolstering its export potential along established routes.

Inflation is expected to reach 4.2% in 2017 and 4.5% in 2018 (Figure 3.3.8). Higher oil prices, currency depreciation, and heightened inflationary expectations will kindle inflation on the supply side. Moreover, a higher fuel excise tax from January 2017 is projected to add some 0.8 percentage points to the inflation this year, and higher inflation will render a lower policy interest rate unlikely before next year. Monetary policy is expected to move toward a more neutral stance in 2018, once the effect of the fuel excise increase on prices has dissipated and the central bank has moved to increase lending in lari.

3.3.3 Interest rates

- Policy
- Deposit
- Lending

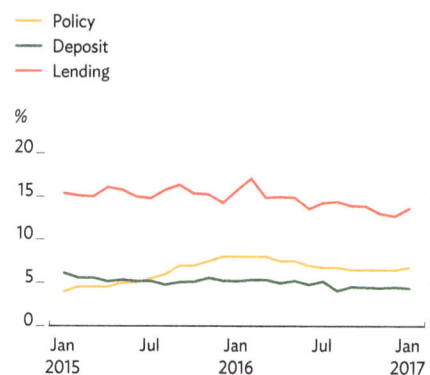

Source: National Bank of Georgia. https://www.nbg.gov.ge (accessed 3 March 2017).

3.3.4 Contributions to M3 broad money growth

- Net foreign assets
- Net claims on government
- Credit to the economy
- Net other items
- Broad money (M3) growth

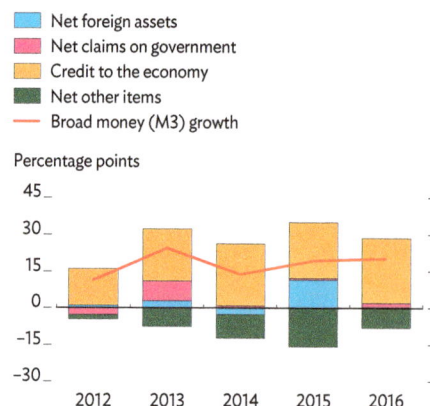

Source: National Bank of Georgia. https://www.nbg.gov.ge (accessed 3 March 2017).

3.3.5 Fiscal indicators

- Nontax revenue and grants
- Tax revenue
- Total expenditure
- Fiscal balance

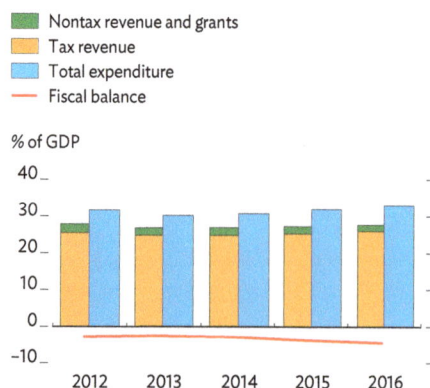

Sources: International Monetary Fund. www.imf.org; Ministry of Finance of Georgia. www.mof.ge (both accessed 3 March 2017).

3.3.1 Reforms implemented since late 2016

The new government that took office following the October 2016 parliamentary elections has introduced wide-ranging reforms. It significantly accelerated infrastructure spending financed by excise tax increases. It introduced from 1 January 2017 the Estonian corporate income tax model, which gives resident companies tax exemption for retained or reinvested earnings. A de-dollarization strategy allows borrowers with income in Georgian lari to convert outstanding US dollar-denominated loans of up to $100,000 that were issued before 1 January 2015 into lari-denominated loans at a preferential exchange rate.

Relatively low inflation should support the lari in the medium term as the economic impact of external shocks dissipates. Broad money (M3) is expected to grow by 15% in 2017 and 19% in 2018.

On the fiscal side, the introduction of an Estonian-type corporate income tax is projected to reduce revenue by the equivalent of 1.5% of GDP a year in 2017 and 2018. To compensate for the revenue loss, excise taxes on fuel, tobacco, and automobiles were raised on 1 January 2017, current spending was trimmed, and one-time measures were implemented, such as collecting certain taxes earlier. With these offsets, revenue is projected to equal 29.7% of GDP in 2017 and 29.1% in 2018. Although capital spending is set to increase by 24.5% because of new infrastructure projects, the government aims to reduce the budget deficit to 4.1% of GDP in 2017 and 4.0% in 2018. Achieving this will require every component of the government strategy to work as intended, with expenditure kept to 33.8% of GDP in 2017 and 33.1% in 2018. The deficit could prove higher if other elements of the program are not achieved, or if growth turns out slower than envisaged. Because of depreciation, the ratio of public debt to GDP is projected to reach 44.0% in 2017 and 2018, with some shift to a higher share of domestic debt (Figure 3.3.9).

The current account deficit is projected to narrow to 12.0% of GDP in 2017 and 11.5% in 2018, to be financed mainly through FDI (Figure 3.3.10). Exports of goods and services are expected to rise by 8.9% in 2017 and 9.8% in 2018 on higher service exports. Imports of goods and services are forecast to grow by 4.8% and then 5.8% with higher service imports in particular and modest rises in energy prices. Remittances are also expected to increase slightly by 4.2% in 2017 and 4.8% in 2018.

The main risks to growth are continuing sluggishness in external demand and further lari depreciation. Continued regional instability and weak economic activity in Georgia's key trading partners would hurt exports, remittances, and GDP growth. The ambitious nature of government plans creates a downside risk that some of its goals may not all be achieved, notably the anticipated rise in private investment in response to the Estonian-type corporate income tax. However, prudent monetary and fiscal policies should support economic growth while fostering more lending, investment, and consumption. Stronger FDI and other foreign inflows could boost business confidence and augment growth.

3.3.1 Selected economic indicators (%)

	2017	2018
GDP growth	3.8	4.5
Inflation	4.2	4.5
Current account balance (share of GDP)	−12.0	−11.5

Source: ADB estimates.

3.3.6 Exchange rate

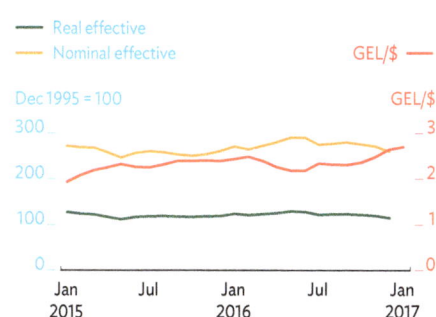

Source: National Bank of Georgia. https://www.nbg.gov.ge (accessed 3 March 2017).

3.3.7 GDP growth

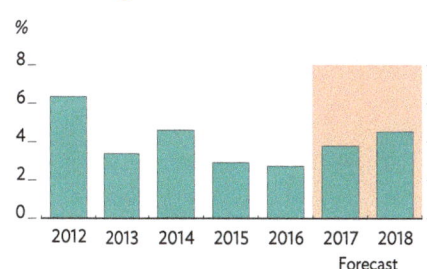

Source: Asian Development Outlook database.

3.3.8 Inflation

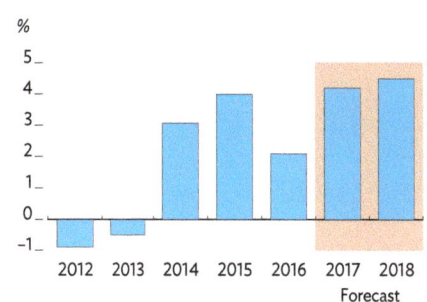

Source: Asian Development Outlook database.

Policy challenge—addressing the mismatch in labor supply and demand

Despite wide-ranging reforms undertaken by the recently installed government, important challenges remain. One is a shortage of well-trained labor, even as growth occurs mainly in skills-intensive services rather than in manufacturing (Figure 3.3.11). The mismatch between labor demand and labor supply limits productivity while raising business costs. Addressing the mismatch would help Georgia diversify its economy away from low-yield subsistence activities by enabling the reallocation of labor to more productive enterprise.

The government has taken a number of steps to address this challenge, in particular by reforming vocational education. In 2013, it adopted a vocational education strategy for 2013–2020 along with an action plan for 2013–2017 to implement it. Reform aims to improve the ability of stakeholders to develop and carry out vocational education, thereby ensuring the quality of vocational education programs and their relevance to labor market requirements. The plan focuses on quality assurance and occupational standards to meet the changing needs of employers and includes a counselling system to support students in transition to employment. It enhances students' facility with information and communication technology through modular coursework applied in concert with workplace learning and company-based practice. It includes professional and skills development for teachers and new education standards. The vocational education and training curricula and related materials have been reviewed for compliance with certain minimum standards.

In addition to these measures, the government has launched a labor market information portal. Assessment of demand for various skills and improved labor market facilities that use this assessment can help remedy the mismatch between workforce skills and market demand. Further, the government has established a framework for professional competence in line with market trends and demand for professional qualifications.

More could be done, however, to develop skills and alleviate labor shortages: giving firms financial and tax incentives, expanding training, and promoting certain career pathways. Doing so would involve introducing or rethinking unemployment insurance or targeted subsidies in the labor market to encourage job seekers to seek further training rather than accept jobs for which they are poorly trained. The government could encourage firms to support e-learning programs for skills development and to adopt more advanced technology that would productively use the skills of newly trained workers.

3.3.9 Public debt

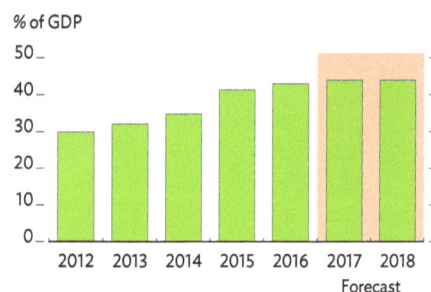

% of GDP

Sources: Ministry of Finance of Georgia. www.mof.ge; International Monetary Fund. www.imf.org (accessed 3 March 2017); ADB estimates.

3.3.10 Current account components

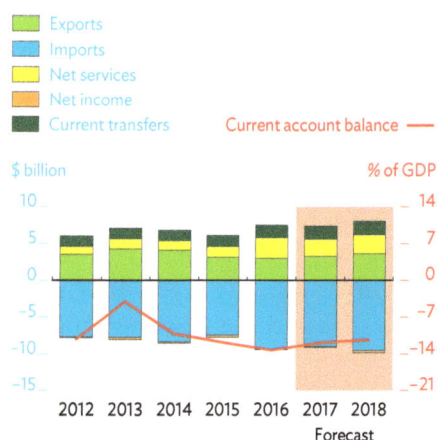

Sources: National Bank of Georgia. https://www.nbg.gov.ge (accessed 3 March 2017); ADB estimates.

3.3.11 Employment share

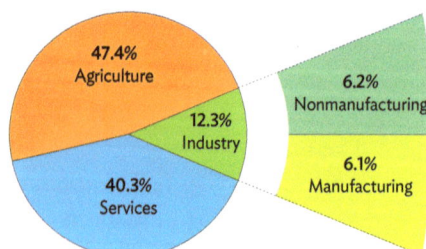

47.4% Agriculture
12.3% Industry
40.3% Services
6.2% Nonmanufacturing
6.1% Manufacturing

Source: National Statistics Office of Georgia. http://www.geostat.ge (accessed 3 March 2017).

Kazakhstan

Low revenues from oil exports cut growth to 1.0% in 2016 and widened the current account deficit, while the lagged effect of depreciation in 2015 pushed average inflation to 14.6%. As oil price recovery boosts development spending, growth is forecast at 2.4% in 2017 and 2.2% in 2018. The current account is expected to improve and inflation to fall in 2017 and 2018. The banking system needs strengthening.

Economic performance

Growth slowed to 1.0% in 2016, the third consecutive year of deceleration largely because of weak prices for oil, the economy's main export. Heavy government spending kept growth from falling more.

On the supply side, industry contracted by 1.1% with a continued decline in mining, though less than the 1.4% drop registered in 2015. Services expanded by 0.8%, less than the 3.1% rise in 2015, as declines in communications and trade weighed on gains in transport and other services. Construction is estimated to have expanded by 7.9%, up from 4.4% in 2015, thanks to sizable government outlays. Agriculture reversed contraction of 3.5% in 2015 to grow by an estimated 5.5% on increases of 7.8% for crops and 2.7% for livestock.

On the demand side, for which data are available only for the first 9 months, consumption rose by 1.4%, slower than the 2.4% increase in the same period of 2015. Private consumption rose by only 1.0%, constrained by currency depreciation, but higher government spending boosted public consumption by 2.7%, more than the 2.5% gain in 2015. Fixed investment expanded by 4.0%, up from 3.1% in 2015, as higher public investment offset a slowdown in private investment. Net exports fell by 21.3% as reduced exports of oil and gas condensate caused total exports to fall more than imports (Figure 3.4.1).

Average inflation jumped to 14.6% from 6.6% in 2015, reflecting currency depreciation in the last quarter of 2015. However, year-on-year inflation eased in December to 8.5% from 13.6% in 2015 with the stabilization of the exchange rate. Prices rose by 9.7% for food, 9.5% for other goods, and 6.1% for services (Figure 3.4.2).

The state budget balance recorded a deficit equal to 1.6% of GDP, down from 2.2% in 2015. Revenue rose to 20.4% of GDP from 18.7% in 2015, while expenditure, including net lending and financial asset transactions, came to 22.0% of GDP, up from 20.9% in the previous year (Figure 3.4.3). The revenue increase reflected the impact of currency depreciation on import duties and earnings from the oil sector, as well as inflation, but also improved tax administration.

3.4.1 Demand-side contributions to growth

- Private consumption
- Public consumption
- Gross fixed investment
- Net exports of goods and services
- Gross domestic product

Percentage points

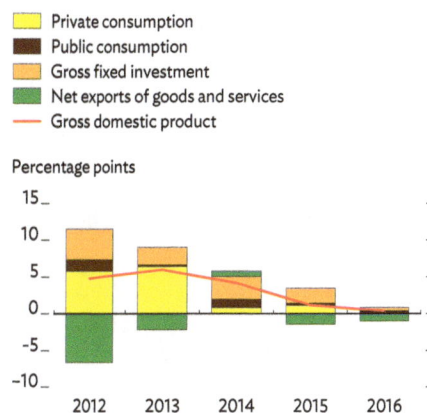

Note: 2016 is for the first 9 months.
Source: Republic of Kazakhstan. Ministry of National Economy. Committee on Statistics.

3.4.2 Monthly inflation

- All goods and services
- Food, beverages, and tobacco
- Other goods
- Services

% change, year on year

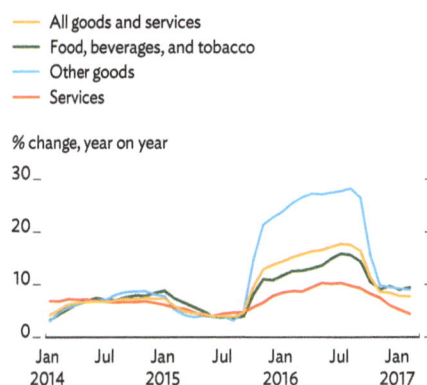

Source: Haver Analytics (accessed 23 March 2017).

This chapter was written by Nurlan Sakuov, consultant, Kazakhstan Resident Mission, ADB, Astana, and Dominik Peschel of the Central and West Asia Department, ADB, Manila.

Expenditure was higher because of increased current outlays and spending for anti-crisis programs and development projects.

The National Bank of Kazakhstan, the central bank, continued to target interest rates with the goal of cutting inflation to 6%–8% in the medium term and 3%–4% in the long term. It nevertheless lowered the base interest rate from 17% in February 2016 to 12% in November and 11% in February 2017 to maintain growth. Broad money in local currency (M2) rose dramatically by 46.4% during the year, versus 7.9% in 2015 (Figure 3.4.4). Total broad money including foreign currency deposits grew more slowly, by 15.7% versus 34.3% in 2015, as policy measures to address dollarization made holding Kazakh tenge more attractive and expectations of further depreciation abated, reducing the share of deposits in foreign currency to 54.6% from 69.0% a year earlier (Figure 3.4.5).

Credit to nonfinancial entities in the private sector grew by 1.2% in 2016, down from 4.6% in 2015, with short-term loans growing faster than long-term credits to reach 62.6% of all loans at the end of the year. Foreign currency loans rose by 10.0%, while local currency loans rose by only 4.0% despite the adoption of measures, including interest rate subsidies, to encourage lending in tenge. Average rates for commercial bank loans to companies rose by 1.5 percentage points to 17.2% for loans in tenge and by 0.3 percentage points to 7.6% for loans in foreign currency.

The current account deficit is estimated to have doubled to 6.1% of GDP from 3.0% in 2015. Exports fell by 20.0%, reflecting weak oil prices, while imports declined by 17.6% as lower incomes and tenge depreciation curtailed household purchasing power and demand for imported goods and services. The estimated trade surplus fell by 25.5% to $9.4 billion. The services deficit narrowed by 6.4%, but the deficit in the income account widened by 9.1% on larger net profit outflows. Since late January 2016, the exchange rate against the US dollar has stabilized, and oil prices trended upward, albeit with fluctuations, through the end of 2016.

Total international assets decreased by 0.6% in 2016 to $90.7 billion, of which $61.0 billion comprised sovereign wealth fund assets (Figure 3.4.6). Using end-of-period exchange rates, external debt including intercompany loans equaled 120.7% of GDP at the end of September 2016, down from 128.0% in December 2015, as the tenge strengthened during the period. Excluding intercompany loans, external debt equaled 54.7% of GDP at the end of September 2016, down from 59.7% at the end of 2015 (Figure 3.4.7).

Economic prospects

Growth is forecast to rise to 2.4% in 2017 and slow slightly to 2.2% in 2018 with a smaller fiscal deficit. Domestic demand is expected to be the main source of growth, reflecting continued fiscal spending for consumption and investment and higher earnings from oil exports.

On the supply side, industry is forecast to expand by 2.4% in 2017 and 2.2% in 2018 with higher infrastructure spending and increased production of oil and gas condensate (Figure 3.4.8). Oil production

3.4.3 Fiscal indicators

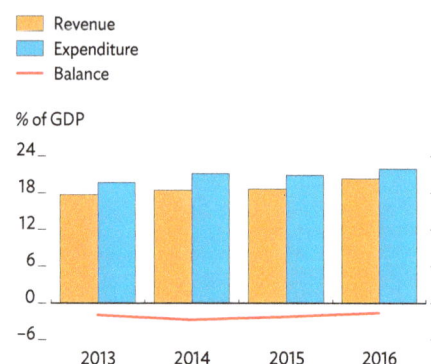

Sources: Ministry of Finance; Ministry of Economy; National Bank of the Republic of Kazakhstan.

3.4.4 Broad money

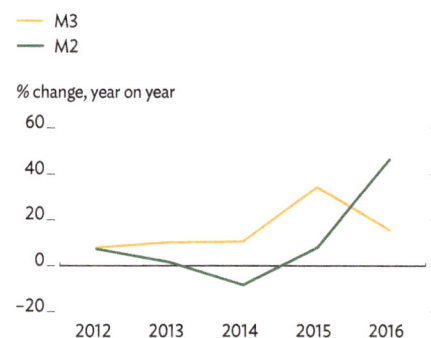

Source: National Bank of the Republic of Kazakhstan.

3.4.5 Dollarization in the banking system

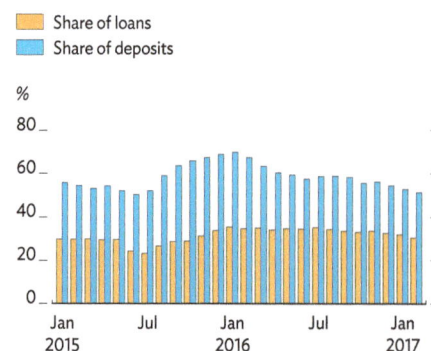

Source: National Bank of the Republic of Kazakhstan.

in 2017 is expected to rise by 3.8% to 81 million tons, with 5 million tons likely to be produced at the Kashagan oil field. In addition, a $36.8 billion expansion of the Tengiz oil field planned since 2016 is projected to raise crude oil production by 260,000 barrels per day. Agriculture is expected to grow by 3.5% in 2017 and 4.0% in 2018, reflecting a new state support program that should boost wheat and livestock production. Services are projected to rise by 1.9% in 2017 and 1.8% in 2018 with higher outlays for social programs and growth in wholesale and retail trade forecast at 1.7% in 2017 and 1.5% in 2018.

On the demand side, a slight improvement in household consumption and higher public spending are projected to raise overall consumption, while expanded infrastructure outlays should boost investment. With total exports of goods and services expected to increase faster than imports, net exports should add to growth.

Average annual inflation is projected at 8.0% in 2017 and 7.0% in 2018 (Figure 3.4.9), within the government's target range of 6%–8%, as the authorities adjust the policy rate, use open market operations to control monetary growth, and maintain price controls. Imports other than food are expected to remain the chief source of inflation.

Fiscal policy is expected to remain expansionary. The state budget is projected to record a deficit equal to 2.9% of GDP in 2017, with plans to reduce it to 1.2% in 2018. Revenue is expected to rise to 22.6% of GDP in 2017 and then decline to 18.2% with smaller transfers from the sovereign wealth fund. The government's plan is to reduce the share of receipts from the sovereign wealth fund to 29.2% of total revenue by 2019. Expenditure including net lending and financial asset transactions is forecast at the equivalent of 25.7% of GDP in 2017 and 19.3% in 2018, including planned spending for countercyclical measures. Public and publicly guaranteed debt should remain below 27% of GDP at the end of 2017. Kazakhstan is planning to introduce ceilings on the combined debt of the government and state-owned companies, which by 2020 should not exceed 25% of GDP.

The authorities are expected to maintain the current floating exchange rate regime. Monetary policy is anticipated to focus on containing inflation while retaining some flexibility to support growth in the event of a slowdown and protect the tenge against serious depreciation. Growth in local currency broad money is projected to remain high in 2017 at 43.8% and slow somewhat to 42.4% in 2018. This will likely contribute to continued inflationary pressures.

The current account is projected to record deficits equal to 3.4% of GDP in 2017 and 3.0% in 2018 as some improvement in oil prices boosts exports (Figure 3.4.10). Exports are forecast to grow by 15.2% in 2017 with oil prices above $50 per barrel and oil production as planned. A further increase of 4.8% is projected for 2018 with the expectation of an additional rise in oil prices. Imports are projected to increase by 5.0% in 2017 and 3.0% in 2018. Import demand will likely come mostly from public infrastructure spending and anti-crisis measures, as well as oil and gas development projects. The estimated value of the sovereign wealth fund is forecast to exceed $65 billion at the end of 2017 and $66 billion at the end of 2018 as higher petroleum exports help to replenish it.

3.4.1 Selected economic indicators (%)

	2017	2018
GDP growth	2.4	2.2
Inflation	8.0	7.0
Current account balance (share of GDP)	–3.4	–3.0

Source: ADB estimates.

3.4.6 Foreign currency reserves and oil fund assets

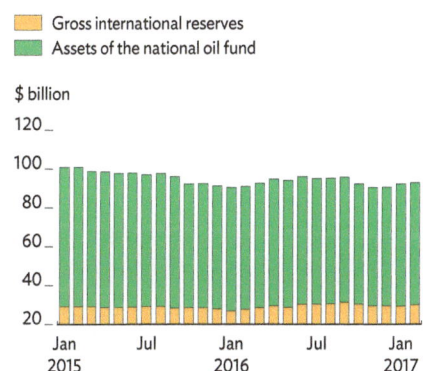

Source: National Bank of the Republic of Kazakhstan.

3.4.7 External debt

Note: 2016 is as of September.
Sources: National Bank of Kazakhstan; ADB estimates.

Policy challenge—strengthening the banking sector

Kazakhstan's economic slowdown has brought renewed attention to its troubled banking sector, which has yet to recover from the global financial crisis of 2008–2009. The central bank reported nonperforming loans (NPLs) at only 6.7% of all loans as of 1 January 2017. However, this figure simply aggregates NPLs reported by individual banks, which may differ in how they identify and report impaired loans. Banks need not report NPLs on a consolidated basis, and some have moved troubled loans off their balance sheets. Further, NPL counts exclude loans restructured by "evergreening," or adding unpaid principal and interest to loan balances rather than declaring the loans delinquent.

The central bank and the government increasingly recognize that a significant share of the massive total of restructured loans may be unrecoverable. In 2016, Moody's estimated NPLs including restructured loans at 37%, and Standard & Poor's estimated them in the range of 25%–30%. Moreover, poor portfolio quality has undermined banks' profitability and liquidity. In 2016, the central bank provided more than $1 billion in liquidity support to Kazkommerzbank (KKB), the country's largest bank in asset terms, to facilitate its acquisition of Bank Turan Alem, 90% of whose assets are troubled.

The government has supported the banking sector through subsidized loans from the budget, Kazakhstan's Problem Loans Fund, and a national pension fund, as well as by placing government and public enterprise deposits in selected financial institutions at low interest rates. It also provided more than $5 billion from the sovereign wealth fund during 2009–2015 to purchase bank shares, refinance mortgage loans, and provide loans to the private sector.

The central bank postponed until 2017 introducing more stringent capital adequacy requirements because of the deteriorating business environment for banks and the slowdown in the economy. Though average capitalization in the banking sector in terms of core capital (Tier I) stood at 14.3% in 2016, some banks are expected to fall below current capital adequacy requirements if needed to write off NPLs. The central bank also eased its timetable for adopting Basel III regulatory standards, moving the deadline for full compliance from 2019 to 2021. Thus, banks were not required in 2016 to increase capital adequacy ratios or meet international standards for consolidated bank reporting.

Unresolved asset quality problems prompted the authorities in February 2017 to inject $3.4 billion into the Problem Loans Fund, expanding the 2017 republican budget by 24%. The transfer is expected to enable the restructuring of KKB by allowing the fund to purchase the NPLs held by the KKB subsidiary Bank Turan Alem, which has most of the NPLs in the banking system. The fund's acquisition of these NPLs would enable Halyk Bank, Kazakhstan's second-largest bank, to purchase the remaining KKB assets and become the country's largest bank. Separately, Tsesna Bank, Kazakhstan's third-largest financial institution, aims to purchase an estimated 41.8% of Bank CenterCredit, Kazakhstan's fifth-largest bank, from Kookmin Bank of the Republic

3.4.8 Supply-side contributions to growth

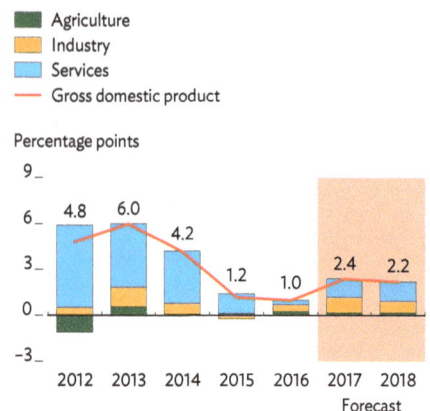

Sources: Republic of Kazakhstan. Ministry of National Economy. Committee on Statistics; ADB estimates.

3.4.9 Inflation

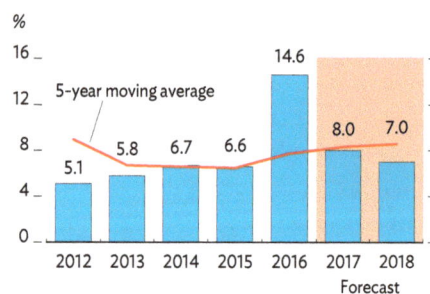

Source: Asian Development Outlook database.

3.4.10 Current account balance

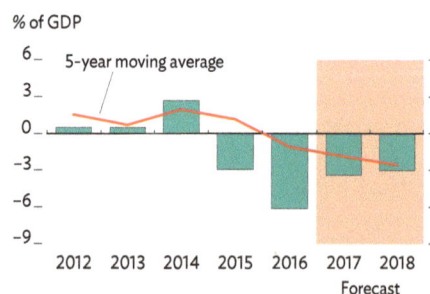

Source: Asian Development Outlook database.

of Korea. In sum, proposed acquisitions would leave Kazakhstan's top three banks holding about 53% of bank assets in the country.

Early in 2017, the central bank moved to undertake asset quality reviews of systemically important banks through an international firm using international standards, and then to enforce measures to either restore banks' solvency or proceed with their liquidation. Moreover, the central bank is expected to begin stress-testing this year, using the exercise to identify which banks need additional capital and how much, as well as to inform an assessment of their handling of impaired loans and provisioning practices, and ultimately improve it.

Although the government has spent significant amounts on resolving problem loans and bank recapitalization, many banks remain undercapitalized. Moreover, further accumulation of NPLs can be expected in view of the weak economy. The high share of real estate loans in NPLs is a problem because collateral is not regularly revalued and is often overstated. In addition, banks are not allowed to transfer NPLs collateralized with real estate, the usual collateral, to the Problem Loans Fund. Broadening the fund mandate to include such assets is therefore important.

On top of the measures already taken, the authorities would do well to relax bank secrecy rules on loans to allow more precise loan appraisals and better assessment of the likelihood of future loan difficulties, and to use international standards when conducting asset quality reviews. Also helpful would be greater clarity about regulatory plans as part of a broader effort to strengthen monetary policy by improving central bank transparency and communication with the public and financial markets.

Kyrgyz Republic

Strong performance in gold mining and trade overcame an early slump to bring 3.8% expansion in 2016. Currency appreciation and higher remittances curbed inflation and the current account deficit. Growth is projected to slow to 3.0% in 2017 before recovering to 3.5% in 2018 with faster regional growth. Higher inflation and a wider current account deficit are likely. Eurasian Economic Union membership poses both challenges and opportunities.

Economic performance

Growth slowed marginally to 3.8% in 2016 from 3.9% in 2015 as strong performance in gold mining and trade offset a slowdown in manufacturing, as well as spillover from recession in the Russian Federation and slower growth in Kazakhstan (Figure 3.5.1). Growth in industry jumped to 5.9% from 2.9% in 2015 as gold production more than doubled, offsetting declines in textiles, apparel, and electricity generation. Agriculture increased by 3.0% thanks to gains in crops and livestock, though well below the 6.2% expansion in 2015. Services growth slowed to 3.0% from 3.7% in 2015 although trade growth increased to 7.6% from 7.1%. Construction rose by 7.4%, down from 16.3% in 2015, as growth in capital investment slowed even more to 3.8% from 14.0%.

On the demand side, a 22.0% rise in remittances boosted private consumption.

Average inflation plunged to 0.4% in 2016 from 6.5% the previous year as consumer prices fell by 0.5% from December 2015 to December 2016 (Figure 3.5.2). This resulted from currency appreciation by 9.6% against the US dollar, a 5.0% decline in food prices, and unexpectedly small price adjustments following the country's accession to the Eurasian Economic Union (EEU). Prices for other goods rose by 1.6% and for services by 5.2%.

Despite a shortfall in tax revenues, the government managed to limit the fiscal deficit to the equivalent of 4.6% of GDP, albeit up from 1.5% in 2015, by underspending on goods and services. Revenue slipped to equal 28.5% of GDP, compared with 29.8% in 2015, while expenditure rose to 33.1% of GDP from 31.3% in 2015. However, external government debt eased with currency appreciation.

With inflation low as the Kyrgyz som appreciated to Som69.23 to the US dollar by year-end from Som75.89 on 1 January (Figure 3.5.3), the central bank reduced the policy interest rate in several steps from 10.0% at the start of 2016 to 5.5% as of February 2017. The policy rate will likely rise if inflation accelerates, but monetary policy has limited impact

3.5.1 GDP growth by sector

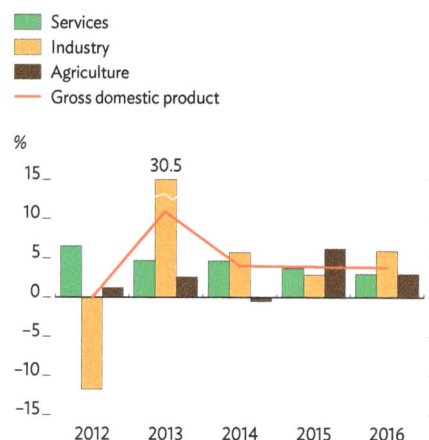

Source: National Statistics Committee of the Kyrgyz Republic. http://www.stat.kg (accessed 3 March 2017).

3.5.2 Monthly inflation

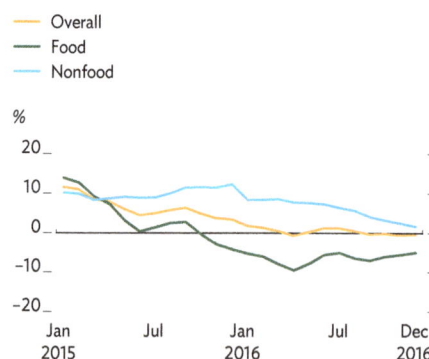

Source: National Statistics Committee of the Kyrgyz Republic. http://www.stat.kg (accessed 3 March 2017).

This chapter was written by Gulkayr Tentieva of the Kyrgyz Resident Mission, ADB, Bishkek.

under extensive dollarization, with 44.5% of loans and 53.4% of deposits in foreign currency at the end of 2016. The average deposit interest rate declined by 0.2 percentage points to 4.5%, while the average lending rate fell by half a point to 18.3%. Deposits rose by 5.0%, and credit fell by 0.5%, while broad money grew by 14.6%, slightly less than the 14.9% in 2015. The nonperforming loan rate worsened to 8.8% at the end of 2016 from 7.1% a year earlier.

The current account deficit is estimated to have narrowed to the equivalent of 10.0% of GDP from 15.2% in 2015, reflecting a somewhat better external environment. Imports declined by 3.7%, mainly reflecting lower imports of vehicles and machinery, while exports increased by 5.1% on higher exports of gold, as well as increased exports of agricultural products to the Russian Federation, and despite falling exports of textiles and apparel. Accession to the EEU and better treatment accorded to migrants under the treaty boosted remittances from the Russian Federation by 22.0% despite recession there and ruble depreciation (Figure 3.5.4). At the end of 2016, international reserves reached $2.0 billion, cover for 4.6 months of imports, up from $1.8 billion at the end of 2015.

With currency appreciation, external debt as a percentage of GDP is estimated to have fallen slightly to 59% from 63% at the end of 2015, all of it public or government guaranteed. The ratio could rise again, however, if the local currency weakens more (Figure 3.5.5).

Economic prospects

Growth is projected to slow to 3.0% in 2017 because of a high base in 2016 and an expected decline in output from Kumtor, the main gold mine. It is expected to recover to 3.5% in 2018 with some improvement in the domestic economy and higher growth in the country's main regional partners, Kazakhstan and the Russian Federation (Figure 3.5.6).

On the supply side, gains in agro-processing, light industry, and construction should sustain growth. On the demand side, higher remittances may further raise household incomes and private consumption, particularly in 2017.

Inflation is forecast to return to 5.0% in 2017 because import tariffs must rise to EEU mandates, and then ease to 4.0% in 2018 with limited additional adjustment in tariffs. Inflation could be higher if further depreciation of the Kazakh and Russian Federation currencies causes the som to weaken.

If prices rise as projected, the central bank will probably raise interest rates over the next few years. It will likely maintain a flexible exchange rate policy, intervening less often to smooth exchange rate volatility.

The fiscal deficit is projected to narrow to the equivalent of 3.0% of GDP in 2017 and 2.5% in 2018 as the government strives to restrain expenditure, despite a presidential election in November 2017, and to boost revenue by reforming tax policy and administration. Tax receipts could be higher if EEU accession yields more customs revenue than now forecast.

3.5.3 Exchange rate

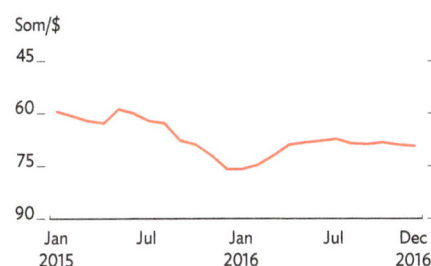

Som/$

Source: National Bank of the Kyrgyz Republic. http://www.nbkr.kg (accessed 3 March 2017).

3.5.4 Remittances

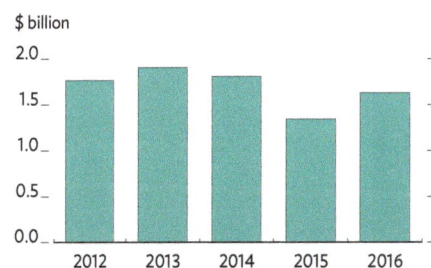

$ billion

Source: National Bank of the Kyrgyz Republic. http://www.nbkr.kg (accessed 3 March 2017).

3.5.5 External debt

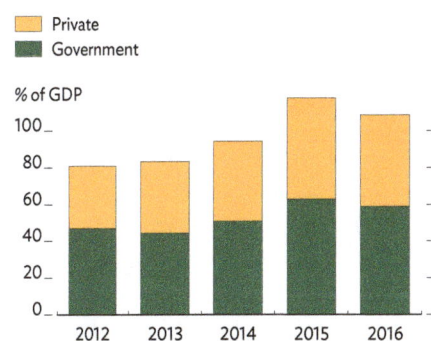

■ Private
■ Government

% of GDP

Note: Government debt is both government and government-guaranteed debt.
Sources: Ministry of Finance; National Statistics Committee. http://www.stat.kg; National Bank of the Kyrgyz Republic. http://www.nbkr.kg (both accessed 3 March 2017).

The current account deficit is forecast to widen to 13.0% in 2017 and 13.5% in 2018, reflecting some improvement in trade with the EEU and significantly lower exports to countries outside the EEU, notably the People's Republic of China (PRC) (Figure 3.5.7). Exports are forecast to grow by 6.0% in 2017 and 5.5% in 2018, mainly from gains in agriculture and textiles. However, weak demand in 2017 within the EEU could worsen the trade outlook, as could the failure of Kyrgyz products to comply with EEU veterinary and phytosanitary standards. Using $1 billion from a joint development fund with the Russian Federation, the government is working to restructure the economy by supporting export-oriented industries and taking other measures to smooth entry into the EEU.

Imports are expected to grow by 10.0% in 2017 and 5.5% in 2018 to meet the needs of planned infrastructure projects. Remittances will likely rise by another 20%–25% in 2017, reflecting some recovery in the Russian Federation and the favorable conditions for the Kyrgyz labor migrants under the EEU treaty.

The Kyrgyz Republic is very close to being rated at high risk of debt distress. External public debt, propelled by heavy public investment, could surpass 63% of GDP during the next 2 years if the currency depreciates, though debt will likely decline in subsequent years. International reserves are forecast to be kept at around $2.0 billion in 2017 and 2018.

Policy challenge—opportunities and challenges under the Eurasian Economic Union

The Kyrgyz Republic became a full member of the EEU in August 2015, expecting membership to boost external trade, allocate labor and capital more efficiently, and reduce nontariff trade barriers over the long term (Box 3.5.1). In the short term, however, accession has fueled uncertainty and shown that adjusting to EEU membership will take the Kyrgyz Republic several years.

The main benefits from accession thus far have been higher labor remittances from other EEU members, mainly the Russian Federation, and loans to local firms from a $1 billion joint development fund with the Russian Federation. By the end of 2016, about $200 million in loans had been disbursed, mainly for agriculture, textiles, other manufacturing, mining and metals, infrastructure development, tourism, and medicine. Trade benefits in 2016 were negligible, however, because demand for Kyrgyz exports languished as regional currencies weakened and recession persisted along with low oil prices. This compounded the effect of lower demand from the PRC and other trading partners outside the EEU.

The main challenge facing the Kyrgyz Republic is its poor compliance with EEU veterinary and phytosanitary standards. Veterinary checkpoints have been placed along the Kyrgyz–Kazakh border pending the release of data on possible epidemics and the introduction of an electronic identification system for Kyrgyz livestock. The government response so far has been an effort to improve outdated laboratory equipment and the poor quality of cross-border trade statistics.

3.5.1 Selected economic indicators (%)

	2017	2018
GDP growth	3.0	3.5
Inflation	5.0	4.0
Current account balance (share of GDP)	–13.0	–13.5

Source: ADB estimates.

3.5.6 GDP growth

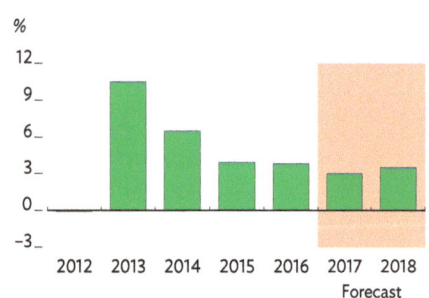

Sources: National Statistics Committee of the Kyrgyz Republic. http://www.stat.kg (accessed 3 March 2017); ADB estimates.

3.5.7 Current account balance

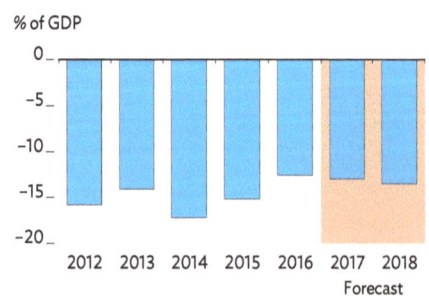

Sources: National Bank of the Kyrgyz Republic. http://www.nbkr.kg (accessed 3 March 2017); ADB estimates.

3.5.1 History and goals of the Eurasian Economic Union

The treaty establishing the EEU was signed on 29 May 2014 by the presidents of Belarus, Kazakhstan, and the Russian Federation and came into force on 1 January 2015 with the signing of the EEU customs union agreement. Armenia became an EEU member on 2 January 2015. The Kyrgyz Republic joined the same year on 29 March, and its accession took effect on 12 August 2015, opening its borders with Kazakhstan.

The fundamental goals of the EEU are to promote economic integration among its member countries and enable them to become more competitive, accelerating trade and growth. The EEU presents economic opportunities to the Kyrgyz Republic in the form of a larger market embracing a combined population of 185 million and guaranteeing the free movement of goods, services, capital, and labor, as well as the eventual elimination of customs controls and nontrade barriers. In particular, EEU accession should ease restrictions faced by migrant workers in EEU countries. Over the longer term, benefits should come from significantly lower nontariff trade barriers.

In 2017, the Kyrgyz Republic became chair of the EEU Board. While serving as chair, the government aims to deepen economic integration with other EEU members and remove barriers to cross-border trade among them. Also this year, negotiations for free trade agreements are planned with India, Iran, the Republic of Korea, the PRC, some Arab countries, and Europe through its Generalized System of Preferences.

As the EEU Board chair, the government will lead the start of negotiations to harmonize member countries' obligations under the EEU and World Trade Organization agreements. To stimulate exports, discussions are exploring ways to encourage joint ventures between small and medium-sized enterprises across the EEU countries and in the PRC. In addition, negotiations will start on revising the EEU treaty to reflect newly arising issues, both regional and global.

The government is receiving advisory technical assistance to smooth its adaptation to EEU membership, realize the opportunities offered, and address the risks. Over the long term, the country is expected to benefit from customs cooperation and the development of a common EEU market for industry, agriculture and agro-processing, energy, finance, information technology, and other services.

Tajikistan

Strong public investment enabled growth to reach 6.9% despite weak remittances, low private investment, and other shortfalls. Troubled banks and continued weak remittances are projected to moderate growth to 4.8% in 2017 despite better performance in the Russian Federation and other regional partners, followed by recovery to 5.5% in 2018. Healthier banks would boost credit growth and enhance private investment.

Economic performance

Growth reportedly accelerated to 6.9% in 2016 from 6.0% a year earlier thanks to higher public investment (Figure 3.6.1). Growth would have been higher if not for weakening private investment, budget shortfalls, lower prices for aluminum and cotton exports, and 13% depreciation of the Tajik somoni. Continued recession in the Russian Federation made 2016 the third consecutive year with a decline in the number of Tajik migrants working there (Figure 3.6.2), causing a 13.1% drop in remittances.

On the supply side, industry expanded by 16.0%, up from 11.2% in 2015 as value added in mining more than doubled and growth in manufacturing reached 12.8%. Electricity generation and exports grew by 3.7% and higher crop yields boosted agriculture growth to 5.2% from 3.2% in 2015. Meanwhile, services contracted by 0.3% as lower remittances curbed consumer spending, following 7.1% contraction in 2015.

On the demand side, a 17.4% rise in capital investment attributable to public spending was the main source of growth, partly offset by lower private consumption resulting from weak remittances and currency depreciation.

Inflation accelerated to 6.1% from 5.1% in 2015 (Figure 3.6.3). This reflected the lagged impact of currency depreciation in 2015 and early 2016 on import prices despite lower global prices for petroleum and wheat (Figure 3.6.4). Prices rose by 6.8% for food, 5.7% for other goods, and 4.5% for services. Public sector wage increases of 10%–20% in July 2016 and then a 16.5% hike in average electricity tariffs in November also fueled inflation.

The government budget recorded a deficit equal to 1.7% of GDP, less than the 2.3% in 2015 (Figure 3.6.5). Shortfalls in revenue, reflecting weak collection of domestic taxes and customs duties, forced the authorities to cut spending in June 2016, though the budget was able to accommodate higher salaries and pension payments. Still, total revenues reached 32.1% of GDP, up from 30.1% in 2015, as firms felt more pressure

3.6.1 GDP growth by sector

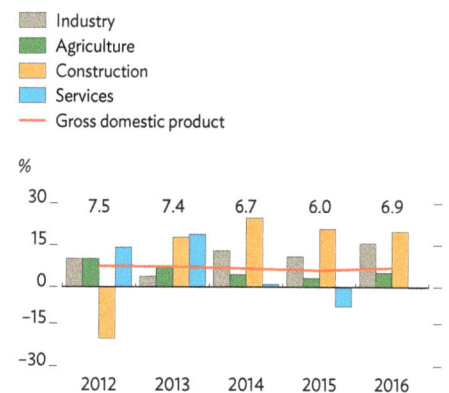

Source: Tajikistan State Statistical Agency.

3.6.2 Migration trend in Tajikistan, 2012–2016

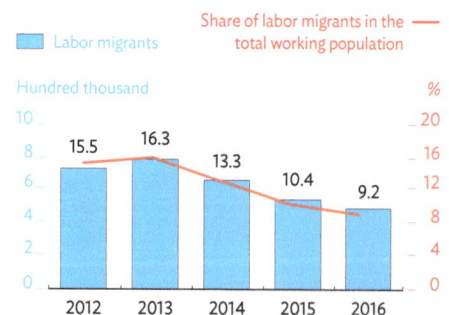

Source: Ministry of Labor, Employment, and Migration of the Republic of Tajikistan.

This chapter was written by Muhammadi Boboev of the Tajikistan Resident Mission, ADB, Dushanbe.

to pay taxes and tax administration improved. Expenditure rose to 33.8% of GDP from 32.4% in 2015 as the government maintained social programs and used foreign financing to expand capital investment. Public and publicly guaranteed debt climbed to 32.7% of GDP from 27.8% a year earlier, owing to external borrowing and currency depreciation that raised external liabilities in local currency terms.

Monetary policy aimed to maintain currency stability and combat inflation. To limit depreciation, the National Bank of Tajikistan, the central bank, required from February 2016 that all remittances in rubles be converted to somoni and that banks immediately sell to it half of the rubles converted. Together with tightened foreign exchange controls, these measures helped stabilize the exchange rate for the rest of the year and reduce the share of deposits in foreign currency from 71.5% at the end of 2015 to 62.5% a year later.

To combat inflation, the central bank raised the refinancing rate in four steps, from 8.0% to 9.0% in March 2016, then to 11.0% in July, to 12.5% in February 2017, and finally to 16.0% in March 2017. In addition, in March 2017, it increased reserve requirements. The central bank also increased the interest rate for liquidity support loans to 2 percentage points above the interbank rate and introduced overnight financing, a short-term refinancing tool, at the refinancing rate plus 2 percentage points. Further, it increased its sales of central bank securities and Treasury bills of the Ministry of Finance to sterilize the impact of the ruble conversion requirement on liquidity, selling in 2016 the equivalent of 7.9% of GDP, double the 3.7% of GDP sold in 2015. As banks bought more of these securities, they reduced credit to the private sector. In February 2017, all Tajiks were required to register their foreign accounts.

Despite these moves and a 13% drop in the stock of credit to the private sector, which also reflected weak demand and problems in the financial sector, broad money grew by 27.9%, up from 18.7% in 2015, as higher international reserves and a sharp rise in demand for local currency raised reserve money (currency in circulation plus banks' reserves) by 36.8%, more than double the rise in 2015 (Figure 3.6.6). Further efforts to consolidate microfinance organizations by raising their minimum capital requirements thinned their numbers by 15% through mergers and license withdrawal. In addition, the share of loans classified as nonperforming rose sharply from 29.9% at the end of 2015 to 54.7% at the end of September 2016, prompting bank recapitalization (Figure 3.6.7).

The current account deficit narrowed to an estimated 4.8% of GDP from 5.9% in 2015 despite a further decline in remittance inflows. Exports rose by 0.9% mainly on higher domestic output and despite lower world prices for the country's main exports. Imports fell by 11.8% because of lower private consumption and subdued global food prices. External debt rose to the equivalent of 32.7% of GDP at year-end from 27.8% at the end of 2015, reflecting depreciation and higher borrowing for capital spending. Gross international reserves rose in the first 9 months of 2016 by 50% as a result of the purchase of domestically produced gold, higher gold prices, and the conversion of private savings from foreign to local currency (Figure 3.6.8).

3.6.3 Sources of inflation

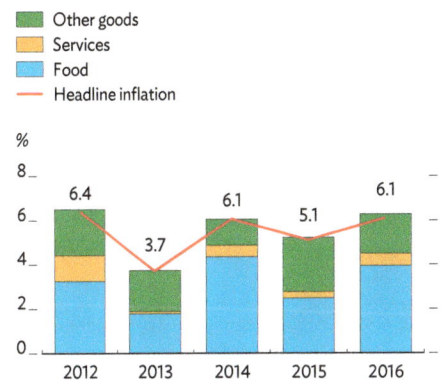

Source: Tajikistan State Statistical Agency.

3.6.4 Exchange rate fluctuations, Tajikistan and its main trade partners

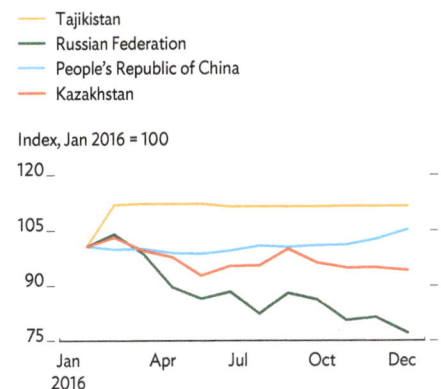

Note: Change in the official exchange rate against the US dollar, January 2016 = 100.
Source: Bloomberg.

3.6.5 Fiscal balance and public debt

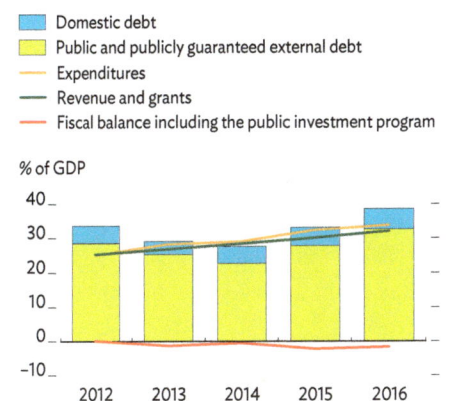

Sources: National Bank of Tajikistan; Tajikistan State Statistical Agency.

Economic prospects

Growth is forecast to moderate to 4.8% in 2017 as high loan losses limit bank lending and weak remittances curb consumption, despite some recovery in the Russian Federation and slightly better performance in other regional partners. Greater pressure on firms to meet tax collection targets will limit growth. Additional tightening of monetary policy and foreign exchange controls could inhibit lending and private investment, further constraining expansion. Growth is expected to recover to 5.5% in 2018 with higher externally financed public investment.

On the supply side, industry is forecast to expand in 2017 as construction on the Rogun Hydropower Plant picks up and accelerate in 2018 with gains in mining and manufacturing and the opening of the Tajikistan segment of a gas pipeline from Turkmenistan to the People's Republic of China. Agriculture is expected to rise modestly as some migrants return to the land. Some growth in remittances is projected to boost services moderately.

On the demand side, growth will depend on higher public investment because low foreign exchange earnings and likely further depreciation of the currency will constrain private consumption and investment.

Inflation is projected to accelerate to 8.0% in 2017 and then slow to 7.0% in 2018 (Figure 3.6.9). The rise will reflect higher liquidity as troubled banks are recapitalized, as well as a 16.5% rise in electricity tariffs from November 2016, a 25% rise in the cost of other public services from January 2017, the lingering impact of the July 2016 public salary hike, and continued currency depreciation. Inflation could be even higher if depreciation exceeds expectations or the authorities institute a more freely floating exchange rate regime.

Over the next 2 years, fiscal policy is expected to be expansionary in view of plans for infrastructure spending. The budget deficit is projected to remain at 2.5% of GDP in 2017 and 2018 as weak imports limit customs receipts. The deficit could be higher with faster currency depreciation or a requirement that the government clear arrears at state-owned enterprises. Revenues are forecast at 30.3% of GDP in 2017 and 30.8% in 2018, and expenditures at 32.8% in 2017 and 33.3% in 2018, as the government strives to improve tax administration and continues to maintain social expenditure and raise capital outlays. Public and publicly guaranteed domestic and external debt are projected to exceed their respective legal ceilings of 7% and 40% of GDP with bank recapitalization, additional foreign-financed public investment, and currency depreciation. Higher public debt may impair Tajikistan's long-term development plans (Box 3.6.1).

Monetary policy will likely strive to contain inflation and limit depreciation while preventing a downturn. Money growth could accelerate further in 2017 and 2018 with reserve accumulation, higher foreign exchange deposits, and further liquidity support to underpin local currency loans, though weak demand will limit the rise in private credit. The central bank may make further changes in the refinancing rate if needed to contain inflation.

The current account deficit is forecast to expand to the equivalent of 5.5% of GDP in 2017 and 6.0% in 2018 (Figure 3.6.10) as higher infrastructure spending sharply increases outflows of net income.

3.6.6 Monetary indicators

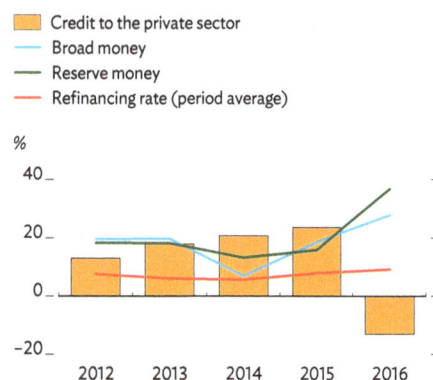

Sources: National Bank of Tajikistan; Tajikistan State Statistical Agency.

3.6.7 Indicators of banking system soundness

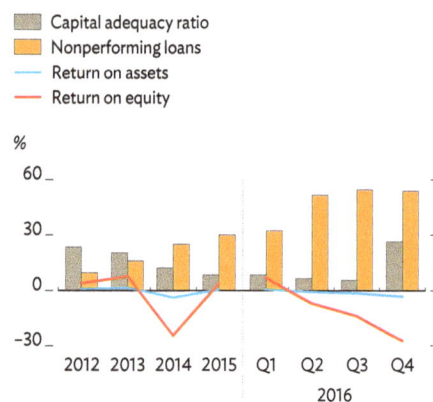

Q = quarter.
Source: National Bank of Tajikistan.

3.6.8 Gross international reserves

Q = quarter.
Source: National Bank of Tajikistan.

3.6.1 Tajikistan's long-term development goals

Tajikistan attained lower-middle-income status in 2014 with gross national income per capita estimated under the Atlas method at $1,080. However, growth has come with high economic vulnerability to international commodity prices and developments in the Russian Federation. Tajikistan's goal in the medium-to-long term is to catch up with its neighbors and reach upper-middle-income status. Convergence will be difficult, however, because of fiscal constraints and the economy's narrow base, with production limited in quantity and restricted to products with little value added, highly concentrated exports, low private investment, and dependence on remittances and other external factors.

The government's National Development Strategy to 2030 has ambitious targets to achieve average real GDP growth of 8%–9% annually, which would raise real GDP by 250% to around $24.2 billion measured in 2016 prices. Economic diversification and a sharp increase in exports of goods and services are identified as the main avenues for attaining this goal. Gross domestic savings are to rise from 8.5% to 30.0% of GDP, and the private investment share of GDP is to soar eightfold from 3.0% to 25.0%. Industrialization is to raise the GDP share of industry from 12.3% to 22.0%, thereby expanding output and exports. The GDP share of services is to remain unchanged, but services are to become more sophisticated. Moreover, the index of export concentration in the three largest items is to fall from 83% to 58%. Attaining these goals would help expand the middle class, defined as households with per capita spending for monthly consumption at TJS230–TJS294, from less than a quarter of the population to half. The cost of financing the programs needed to attain these objectives is estimated at $118.1 billion.

Independent analysis suggests that, given average population growth of 2.3%, attaining by 2030 the targeted GDP per capita of $7,000 (at purchasing power parity in current US dollars) from the 2015 estimate of $2,970 would require an annual growth rate of at least 8.8%, well above the 6.9% recorded in 2016. If growth averaged 7.5%, the target would be reached in 2035.

Exports are projected to grow by 5% in 2017 and 10% in 2018 as depreciation boosts competitiveness and industrial output rises. Imports are expected to contract a further 5% in 2017 and stabilize in 2018. The decline will reflect lower demand and import substitution, and will come despite higher capital spending and some growth in remittances with recovery in the Russian Federation (Figure 3.6.11).

Policy challenge—strengthening banks through finance reform

A banking sector that effectively channels savings into investment is crucial to private sector development, but Tajikistan has a poor record of providing firms access to finance. In its *Global Competitiveness Report 2016–2017*, the World Economic Forum ranks Tajikistan at 105 among 138 economies for financial market development. In *Doing Business 2017*, the World Bank ranks it at 118 among 190 for getting credit, down from 109 in 2016.

Over the past 3 years, Tajikistan's banking system has recorded losses and a sharp rise in nonperforming loans has reduced bank capital. The rise in toxic assets has multiple causes: weak corporate governance, poor risk management, cronyism in lending to companies and individuals, a high concentration of loans in risky sectors such as construction and agriculture, large transaction costs, and a lack of diversity in banking products. Several large banks have suffered from inadequate provisioning and a fall in the value of collateral. Bank weakness has made it hard for households to access deposits and withdraw money from payroll accounts. In addition, firms have had trouble meeting contract obligations, paying taxes, and borrowing at reasonable rates. High interest rates and short loan maturities have kept many firms from undertaking productive investment.

3.6.9 Inflation

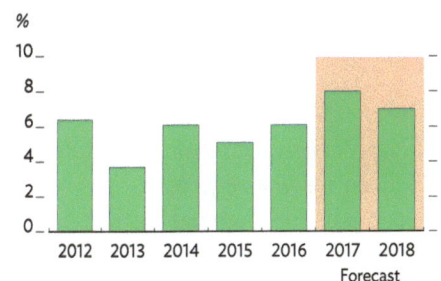

Sources: Tajikistan State Statistical Agency; ADB estimates.

3.6.1 Selected economic indicators (%)

	2017	2018
GDP growth	4.8	5.5
Inflation	8.0	7.0
Current account balance (share of GDP)	–5.5	–6.0

Source: ADB estimates.

3.6.2 Recapitalization of four Tajik banks in 2016

On top of a business slowdown, the depreciation of the Tajik somoni by nearly 50% since the beginning of 2015 has brought a sharp rise in nonperforming loans, from 29.9% of Tajikistan's sector total at the end of 2015 to 54.7% at the end of September 2016. Moreover, the average ratio of bank capital to risk-weighted assets fell to 5.4%, less than half the required 12.0%. Four banks faced possible insolvency, limiting access to deposits and preventing the timely settlement of payments and tax liabilities. To maintain confidence in the banking system, the government recapitalized the four banks in December 2016 at a cost of nearly $500 million, equal to 7.1% of GDP. Five-year Treasury bills with a concessional 2% interest rate were issued to the four banks in exchange for selected bank assets. The banks could use these securities to obtain liquidity from the central bank for new lending (box figure). To prevent currency pressures and limit inflation, the resources of certain state budget organizations that the Ministry of Finance previously placed in the troubled banks, notably those of the agency that handles social insurance and pensions, must be returned to the Central Treasury at the ministry.

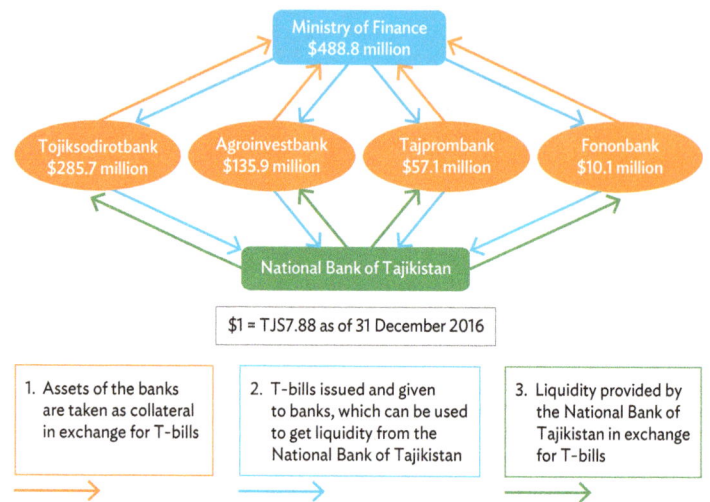

Ministry of Finance
$488.8 million

Tojiksodirotbank $285.7 million Agroinvestbank $135.9 million Tajprombank $57.1 million Fononbank $10.1 million

National Bank of Tajikistan

$1 = TJS7.88 as of 31 December 2016

1. Assets of the banks are taken as collateral in exchange for T-bills

2. T-bills issued and given to banks, which can be used to get liquidity from the National Bank of Tajikistan

3. Liquidity provided by the National Bank of Tajikistan in exchange for T-bills

Moreover, with more than 70% of loans denominated in foreign currency, firms bear the risk of currency mismatch. These problems contributed to the 13% drop in the stock of credit to the private sector in 2016.

The government took several steps to address the problem in 2016: recapitalizing four troubled banks (Box 3.6.2), strengthening bank supervision, and tightening foreign exchange controls. In addition, it eased reserve requirements applicable to both local and foreign currency deposits for financial institutions that met capital adequacy standards. It worked to facilitate cashless transactions and increase deposit insurance coverage. An entrepreneurial support fund was established to provide local currency loans at concessional rates to borrowers in remote areas. Finally, the authorities introduced a law on Islamic banking and facilitated the creation of two credit information bureaus.

Beyond the measures already undertaken, several other reforms could help Tajikistan improve firms' access to finance in the short run. They include obtaining a sovereign country rating to promote foreign inflows, strengthening bank supervision, preventing cronyism in lending, enhancing the affordability and accessibility of financial services, and helping eligible financial institutions provide financing to farmers and rural food processors in local currency to reduce their exposure to foreign exchange risk.

Over the medium term, further regulatory measures are needed: raising the capital adequacy ratio to enhance confidence in the banking system, establishing credit insurance and guarantee schemes to facilitate export financing, introducing more convenient and up-to-date banking facilities, and requiring banks to disclose their ownership and financial results. In addition, the authorities should develop an effective stress-testing framework, introduce long-term foreign exchange risk hedging, and take steps to establish inflation targeting that could support the currency over the medium-to-long term.

3.6.10 Current account balance

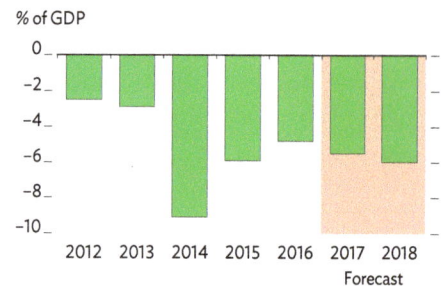

% of GDP

Forecast

Sources: International Monetary Fund; National Bank of Tajikistan; ADB estimates.

3.6.11 Remittances and GDP growth

— Russian Federation GDP growth
— Tajikistan GDP growth
Personal remittances received —

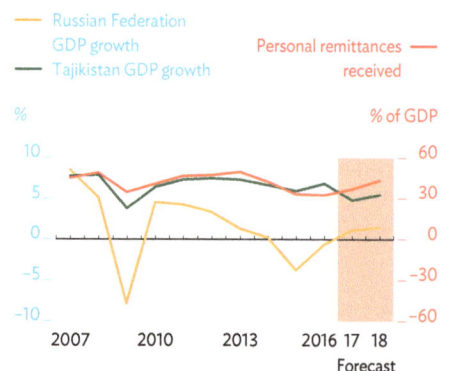

%　　% of GDP

Forecast

Sources: World Bank, World Development Indicators online database; National Bank of Tajikistan; ADB estimates for Tajikistan GDP growth and remittance inflows.

Turkmenistan

Growth moderated to 6.2% in 2016. While inflation also declined slightly, the current account deficit was wider, driven by higher service imports and lower hydrocarbon exports. Growth is projected to return to 6.5% in 2017 and accelerate to 7.0% in 2018, with some rise in inflation and a narrower current account deficit as prices for hydrocarbons improve. Private sector development is key to diversifying growth.

Economic performance

The government reported GDP growth at 6.2% in 2016, slightly below the 6.5% recorded a year earlier (Figure 3.7.1). The slowdown reflected lower global energy prices, weaker demand for hydrocarbons from trade partners, worsening terms of trade, and a slowing of investment.

On the supply side, Turkmenistan's large hydrocarbon economy expanded by 2.8%, the same as in 2015. Growth came from the non-hydrocarbon economy, which expanded in 2016 by 6.6%. This was less than last year's 8.5% as industry, traditionally the country's key growth driver, expanded by only 1.2%, down from 3.1% in 2015 and 11.4% in 2014 as the contraction in hydrocarbons reduced sector growth. Services grew by 11.0%, improving on last year's 10.0% with increases of 14.2% in trade, 10.4% in transport and communications, 4.4% in construction services, and 9.7% in other services. Agriculture reportedly grew by 12.0% as the strategic crops cotton and wheat met production targets.

On the demand side, investment drove growth. The International Monetary Fund (IMF) estimated gross investment equal to 39% of GDP in 2016, of which 13 percentage points was foreign direct investment (FDI), mainly for gas, oil, and chemical processing. Growth in consumption, particularly private consumption, was less robust as inflation and currency depreciation weakened household real incomes despite a 10% rise in salaries, pensions, and stipends.

No official estimate of inflation in 2016 is available. An IMF estimate in October 2016 put inflation at 6.4% in 2015 and 5.5% in 2016, though it may have slowed only to 6.0% (Figure 3.7.2). Sustaining inflation were depreciation pressure on the Turkmen manat last year against the US dollar that was factored in domestic prices, higher utility tariffs as public utility subsidies are being phased out, and rising prices for imported consumer goods because of higher import duties. To keep inflation within projections, the government continued to administer price controls and support import substitution, aiming to ensure that supplies of locally produced consumer goods were sufficient and affordable. In addition, the Central Bank of Turkmenistan kept strict

3.7.1 GDP growth

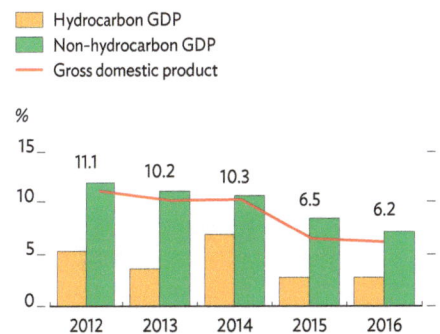

- Hydrocarbon GDP
- Non-hydrocarbon GDP
- Gross domestic product

Sources: International Monetary Fund. 2016. *Regional Economic Outlook, Middle East and Central Asia.* October; ADB estimates.

3.7.2 GDP growth and inflation

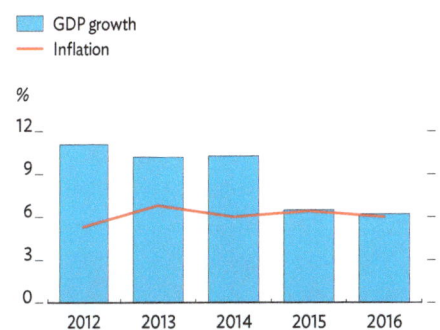

- GDP growth
- Inflation

Sources: International Monetary Fund. 2016. *Regional Economic Outlook, Middle East and Central Asia.* October; ADB estimates.

This chapter was written by Jennet Hojanazarova of the Turkmenistan Resident Mission, ADB, Ashgabat.

control of cash in circulation by limiting foreign exchange conversion and by promoting noncash payments through debit cards, the Milli card denominated in manat, and the Visa card in dollars. Tighter monetary policy, reduced bank lending, and more stringent financial operations helped slash broad money growth to 7.2% from 16.1% in 2015.

The state budget is estimated to have incurred a small deficit equal to 0.8% of GDP in 2016, similar to the 0.7% deficit in 2015 (Figure 3.7.3). Revenue, estimated at 15.1% of GDP, was in line with the state budget, while expenditure was reported at 15.9% of GDP, which was 13.5% less than planned. Over 80% of spending went to social programs and a 10% rise in salaries, pensions, and stipends. Outlays for investment rose by 1.2% in 2016, much less than the 7.8% in 2015, as the government rationalized capital spending and prioritized large investment programs. (This does not take into account quasi-fiscal operations, which are believed to be large.) As industry outside of hydrocarbons improved its performance, the fiscal deficit derived from the non-hydrocarbon sector gradually shrank from 11.2% of non-hydrocarbon GDP in 2014 to 8.2% in 2015 and 6.8% last year. The Stabilization Fund helped smooth revenue volatility and offset contraction from lower energy exports.

The current account deficit is estimated to have widened to 18.5% of GDP as higher FDI-related imports of services and factor income payments combined with lower hydrocarbon exports, which account for 85% of all exports. Exports of goods fell by 15.4% while imports of goods contracted by 16.7% (Figure 3.7.4). According to estimates from the United Nations Conference on Trade and Development, the stock of FDI rose to $32.1 billion in 2015 from $13.4 billion in 2010, when last reported. FDI inflows reached $4.3 billion in 2015, up from $3.6 billion in 2010 (Figure 3.7.5). This made Turkmenistan the largest FDI recipient among landlocked economies in transition. Most FDI went to boost processing and value added in oil, gas, and chemical production. External debt, all of it public, remained low at 23.2% of GDP, and an IMF debt-sustainability assessment characterized debt as "resilient to most shocks." According to figures from the Bank for International Settlements, foreign exchange reserves remained at a comfortable 30 months of import cover.

Economic prospects

Growth is projected to rise slightly to 6.5% in 2017 and 7.0% in 2018, led by government investment, strong FDI, and consumption, both public and private. An expected recovery in global energy prices should boost income and fiscal revenue.

On the supply side, a recovery in hydrocarbons is projected to help industry expand by 4.0%–5.0%, supported by growth in food processing, agro-industry, light industry, construction materials, and chemicals—all targets for import substitution. With extensive government support for farmers, agriculture is expected to grow by 10.0% in both 2017 and 2018. Demand for services is projected to grow by more than 10.0% in both years thanks to a boost from the Fifth Asian Indoor and Martial Arts Games, which are expected to attract participants from 62 countries in Asia and Oceania to the capital Ashgabat in September 2017.

3.7.3 Government fiscal balances

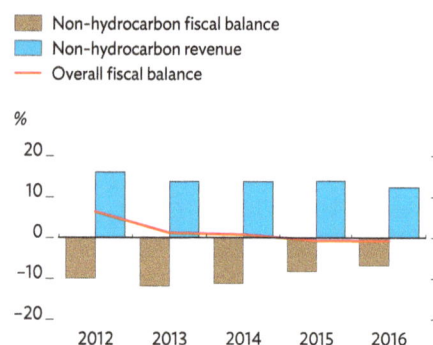

Note: Fiscal data refer to general government. Non-hydrocarbon fiscal balance and revenue are percentages of non-oil gross domestic product, and the overall fiscal balance is a percentage of total gross domestic product.
Sources: International Monetary Fund. 2016. *Regional Economic Outlook, Middle East and Central Asia.* October; ADB estimates.

3.7.4 GDP growth and exports

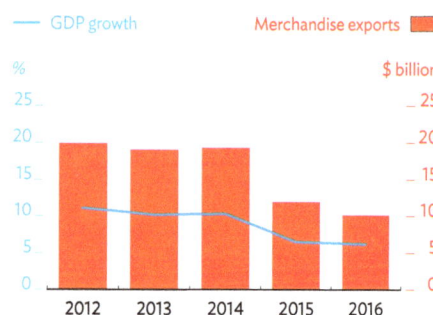

Sources: International Monetary Fund. 2016. *Regional Economic Outlook, Middle East and Central Asia.* October; ADB estimates.

3.7.1 Selected economic indicators (%)

	2017	2018
GDP growth	6.5	7.0
Inflation	6.0	6.0
Current account balance (share of GDP)	–15.0	–13.0

Source: ADB estimates.

The authorities aim to limit inflation by maintaining a tight monetary policy that includes a fixed exchange rate, price controls, and strict foreign exchange regulations. However, directed lending will remain significant to support import substitution and agriculture. Inflation is projected at 6.0% in 2017 and 2018, assuming no further currency depreciation. Broad money growth is projected to reaccelerate to 8.2% in 2017, reflecting credit expansion for the private sector (Figure 3.7.6).

The state budget projects a deficit equal to 0.4% of GDP in 2017 and a surplus of 0.5% in 2018 as higher energy prices and expansion in the non-hydrocarbon economy raise revenue (Figure 3.7.7). The government plans to continue supporting social programs and build industrial infrastructure in the regions to create jobs and raise incomes in rural areas, thereby smoothing urban–rural disparities.

With some recovery in global energy prices, exports are forecast to rise by 12.0%, outpacing import growth of 10.3%. Despite the assumption of large FDI-related service imports and factor income payments, the current account deficit is expected to narrow to 15.0% of GDP in 2017 and 13.0% in 2018. External debt is projected to rise slightly to 23.4% of GDP in 2017 and then decline to 18.0% in 2018 with the repayment of some debt for hydrocarbon investment.

Policy challenge—diversifying growth through private sector development

The government's growth model uses hydrocarbon revenue to finance public investment for development. This model has generated strong growth, averaging 12% in the past decade, which enabled the country to reach upper-middle-income status in 2012. However, the decline in energy prices since late 2014 requires rethinking this approach and seeking alternative sources of growth through diversification (Figure 3.7.8). Developing the private sector is particularly important as a way to diversify the economy, attract investment, and support incomes through job creation.

The National Program of Socio-Economic Development, 2011–2030 aims to raise the private sector share of the non-hydrocarbon economy to as much as 70% by 2020 from 56% in 2012. The program stipulates a three-phase privatization program to 2020 that uses FDI to privatize construction, energy, transport, and communications.

Developing small and medium-sized enterprises (SMEs) is an effective way to expand the private sector. The government has initiated a number of measures to speed SME development through job creation, import substitution, and export promotion. To this end, legislation was revised to provide SMEs with stronger legal, financial, and capacity-building support (Box 3.7.1). According to the government, the private sector share of non-hydrocarbon GDP surpassed 65% in 2016.

Further improvement of the business climate beyond current programs would facilitate economic transformation and diversification. The *Transition Report 2016–17* from the European Bank for Reconstruction and Development surveyed progress away from central planning toward an industrialized market economy and found it limited, evident in only

3.7.5 Foreign direct investment

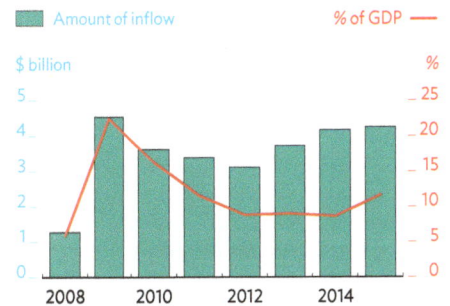

Sources: United Nations Conference on Trade and Development. 2016. *World Investment Report.* New York and Geneva; United Nations; ADB estimates.

3.7.6 Money supply and inflation

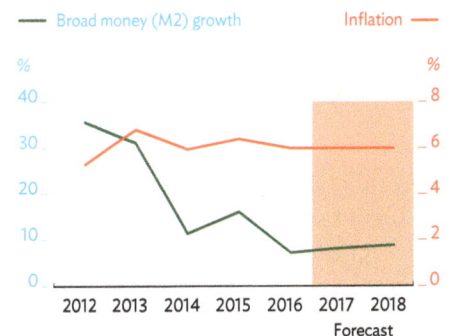

Sources: International Monetary Fund. 2016. *Regional Economic Outlook, Middle East and Central Asia.* October; ADB estimates.

3.7.7 Fiscal indicators

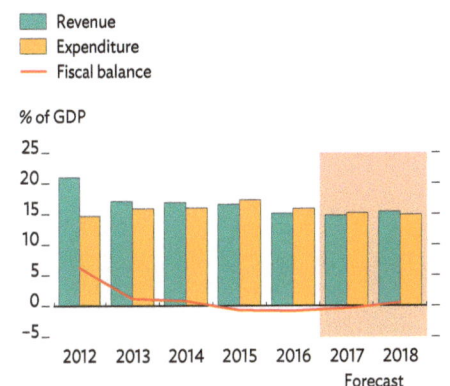

Sources: International Monetary Fund. 2016. *Regional Economic Outlook, Middle East and Central Asia.* October; ADB estimates.

3.7.1 Support for small and medium-sized enterprises

Since 2011, the government has taken several steps to support SME development. One was a new law that simplified SME registration and provided to SMEs favorable taxation, special financing programs, capacity building, and other support. As a consequence, the tax code introduced a single tax rate of 2% on the incomes of entrepreneurs, streamlined the paperwork required from firms, and simplified tax reporting and payments.

The State Development Bank was created in 2011 to direct to public projects the central budget surpluses that had accumulated in the Stabilization Fund. The bank was authorized to make concessional loans to enterprises and private entrepreneurs that implement projects to develop and modernize production facilities and create jobs. In the same year, the government established the Union of Industrialists and Entrepreneurs. In 2012, it created the country's first private bank, Rysgal, which received a 10-year interest-free loan equal to $100 million to pass on as soft loans to SMEs.

Government support helped increase the number of legal entities with private ownership by 40% from 2011 to 2016. In addition, the private sector share of non-hydrocarbon GDP grew by 60% from 2010. Sectors with expanding private participation include agriculture, agro-industries, transport, construction, food and other light industry, textiles, construction materials, and tourism.

2 of 15 sectors. The report noted development gaps in the business environment, business skills, and the financial sector, including bank financing, the related legal framework, and nonbank financing.

In addition, tremendous potential exists for gains from modernizing education. Private entrepreneurs need to enhance their skills in innovation and entrepreneurship to produce and export competitive and sophisticated products that benefit from Turkmenistan's comparative advantage. This calls for more investment in education and professional programs that are higher quality and more relevant, as training for workers and students must improve to meet international standards and the demands of the labor market. More support for science, research, and technology would foster collaboration between academia and industry to find innovative ways to diversify the economy, promote long-term competitiveness, and create better-paying jobs.

3.7.8 GDP growth and energy prices

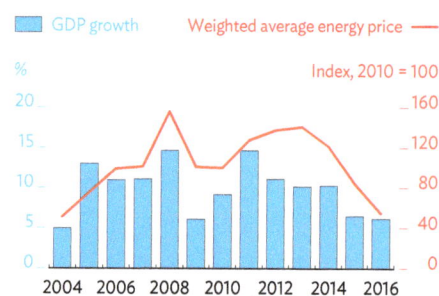

Note: Average energy price uses weights of 85% for natural gas and 15% for crude oil.

Sources: World Bank. Commodity Price Data (Pink Sheet); ADB estimates.

Uzbekistan

Reported growth slowed to 7.8% in 2016 from 8.0% the previous year. Inflation was marginally lower at 8.4%, and the current account recorded a small surplus. Growth is projected at 7.0% in 2017 and 7.3% in 2018, with some improvement in the current account. Currency depreciation and government spending are forecast to raise inflation to 9.5% in 2017 and 10.0% in 2018. The financial sector needs reform.

Economic performance

The government reported GDP growth sustained by investment at 7.8% in 2016, albeit down from 8.0% in 2015 (Figure 3.8.1). Growth was expected to be lower in view of protracted economic weakness in Uzbekistan's key trading partners. Industry and agriculture each grew in 2016 by 6.6%, down from 8.0% and 6.8%, respectively, mainly because of the weak external environment. Services expanded by 10.7%, up from 9.8% in 2015, reflecting buoyant finance, trade, and telecommunications. Public investment in infrastructure and housing contributed to a 12.8% rise in construction.

On the demand side, investment was the main source of growth. According to government statistics, gross fixed capital formation expanded by 9.4%, slightly below the 9.9% rise in 2015. This likely reflected less financing from commercial banks and the Fund for Reconstruction and Development, the sovereign wealth fund, as more investment in modernization by state-owned enterprises and private firms offset a 20% decline in investment financed by state-run specialized funds, which focus mainly on roads and social projects. The share of foreign funding in total investment rose to 21.9% in 2016 from 20.4% in 2015 as the government secured investor participation, mainly from Asia and the Russian Federation, in energy and petrochemicals.

The government reported the fiscal budget with a surplus of 0.1% of GDP in 2016 (Figure 3.8.2). It used national reporting standards without making public any detailed breakdown of revenues and expenditures. Using the International Monetary Fund (IMF) approach to government finance statistics, the budget is estimated to have been in deficit equal to 1.0% of GDP, similar to the estimated deficit of 0.9% for 2015. Factoring in the balance of the sovereign wealth fund, the augmented budget is estimated to have recorded a surplus of 0.2% of GDP, unchanged from 2015. Consolidated budget revenue declined from the equivalent of 33.3% of GDP in 2015 to an estimated 32.9% in 2016, presumably reflecting smaller inflows to the sovereign wealth fund from

3.8.1 Supply-side contributions to growth

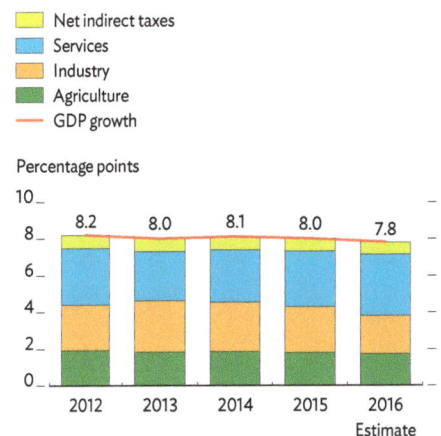

Sources: State Statistics Committee; ADB estimates.

3.8.2 Fiscal performance

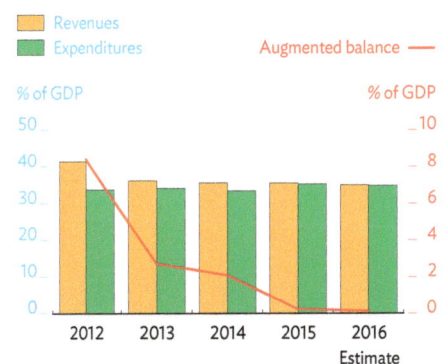

Note: Augmented budget includes the Fund for Reconstruction and Development.
Sources: International Monetary Fund; ADB estimates.

This chapter was written by Iskandar Gulamov of the Uzbekistan Resident Mission, ADB, Tashkent.

exports of key commodities and thus smaller transfers to the budget. Consolidated budget expenditure including outlays for net lending also declined, from 34.2% of GDP in 2015 to an estimated 33.9%, as public sector wages and pensions rose by the equivalent of 3.4% annually, less than the nominal increase in GDP. Government debt, all of it external, rose to 13% of GDP in 2016 from 11% in 2015 as foreign borrowing increased to finance infrastructure development.

The government reported average inflation at 5.7% in 2016, well within the monetary authority's target range. Using the same data but a different methodology, the IMF estimated inflation at 8.4% (Figure 3.8.3). Despite public wage and pension increases, tariff hikes, and faster depreciation of the Uzbek sum against the US dollar, inflation slowed in 2016 largely because of global food price deflation and lower import costs. Growth in broad money also slowed, to 14.9% in 2016 from 20.7% in 2015.

The latest exchange rate developments point to less currency depreciation against the US dollar on both the official and the parallel market. The sum depreciated in official terms by 15% in 2016, slightly less than the 16% depreciation in 2015 (Figure 3.8.4). The pace of depreciation on the parallel market appeared to slow far more, to 19% in 2016 from 60% in 2015.

The current account surplus narrowed to the equivalent of 0.1% of GDP from 0.3% in 2015 (Figure 3.8.5). Excluding services, the trade balance recorded a deficit of $2.0 billion, up from $1.7 billion in 2015. Exports of goods and services fell by 2.4% in 2016, mainly because of a sharp 48% decline for energy and a 19% drop for food. Exports of natural gas, the country's largest export, suffered from lower global prices and decreased demand from the People's Republic of China (PRC) and the Russian Federation. Limited data make it hard to explain the decline in food exports.

Imports of goods also declined, by 1.2%. Imports of food dropped by 9.2% and of energy by 18.8%, mainly from tighter import controls and lower import costs. Machinery and equipment remained the largest import category, representing 44% of all imports. Service imports fell by 7.2% as weak external trade reduced demand for imported logistics and cargo services.

The slowdown in the PRC and Kazakhstan, Uzbekistan's main trading partners, continued to affect the domestic economy in 2016. Exports of goods and services to the PRC fell by 28%, and to Kazakhstan by 46%, reflecting lower exports of natural gas and consumer goods. The weak economic situation in the Russian Federation reduced labor demand in that country's construction and logistics sectors, the main employers of Uzbek migrants, depressing remittances to Uzbekistan. Remittance inflows in the first 9 months of 2016, the latest for which data are available, amounted to $1.8 billion, down from $2.0 billion in the comparable period of 2015 and $4.0 billion a year earlier.

3.8.3 Broad money and inflation

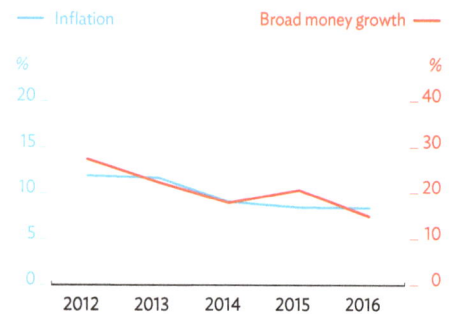

Source: International Monetary Fund.

3.8.4 Exchange rate

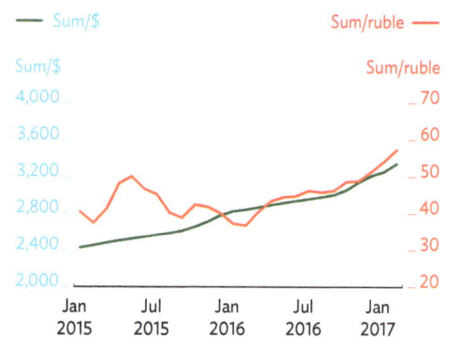

Source: Central Bank of the Republic of Uzbekistan, www.cbu.uz (accessed 17 March 2017).

3.8.5 Current account components

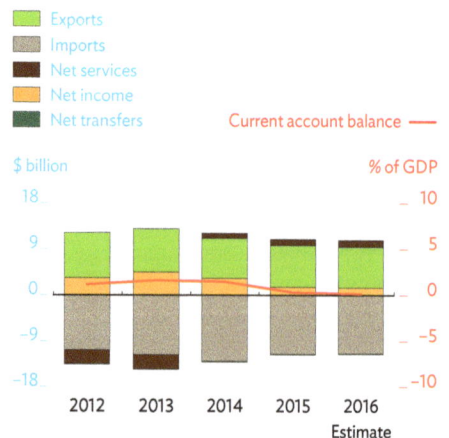

Sources: International Monetary Fund; ADB estimates.

Economic prospects

Growth is forecast at 7.0% in 2017 and 7.3% in 2018, driven by an improving external outlook and higher investment, including infrastructure (Figure 3.8.6). On the supply side, investment-led industry is expected to remain a key driver of growth, with higher external demand for the country's main export commodities providing additional impetus for annual expansion in industry by 6.0% in 2017 and 6.4% in 2018. Planned wage and pension increases that outpace inflation should sustain private consumption, supporting growth in services at 8.8% in 2017 and 9.1% in 2018. However, remittance inflows are projected to remain considerably below historical amounts, limiting the potential for increased household consumption. Agriculture is expected to expand by 6.8% in 2017 and 7.1% in 2018, reflecting higher production of fruit and vegetables from major horticulture and agro-processing development programs initiated in 2017.

Inflation is forecast at 9.5% in 2017 and 10.0% in 2018 (Figure 3.8.7). Inflationary pressures will come mainly from higher government spending and continued depreciation of the currency against the US dollar. The government has announced that it intends in the near future to liberalize the exchange rate, most likely establishing a managed floating regime, and to ensure the market-based allocation of foreign exchange. Pending further information, forecasts project annual depreciation at about 15% against the US dollar in 2017 and 2018. Rising global food prices and potentially higher import costs will add to inflationary pressures. Managing inflation will therefore remain a key policy challenge, requiring close coordination of monetary and fiscal policies.

Broad money is projected to grow by 17.5% in 2017 and 18.6% in 2018 in line with the rising net foreign assets of the monetary authority. Capital accumulation in commercial banks and their relatively high net interest margins should encourage growth in credit extended to the economy. The Central Bank of the Republic of Uzbekistan is expected to expand its sterilization activities to limit growth in the monetary base, but its policy (or refinancing) rate is expected to remain at 9.0%.

The government projects a consolidated budget deficit equal to 0.9% of GDP in 2017 and 1.0% in 2018 to support economic expansion. Including expected surpluses in the sovereign wealth fund, the augmented budget is projected to be in balance in 2017 and to post a small deficit of 0.2% of GDP in 2018. Consolidated budget revenues are set to decline modestly, reflecting greater exemptions for the private sector, to the equivalent of 32.5% of GDP in 2017 and 32.2% in 2018. The government is expected to raise expenditure to support a new national development strategy, which includes higher spending for health, education, and social security (Box 3.8.1). This increase will likely be offset by savings elsewhere in the public sector. Consolidated budget outlays are forecast at 33.5% in 2017 and 33.2% in 2018.

The current account surplus is forecast to widen to the equivalent of 0.2% of GDP in 2017 and 0.4% in 2018 (Figure 3.8.8). Recovering global trade and a gradually improving economic situation in the Russian Federation and the PRC should promote bilateral trade and transfers. Merchandise exports are projected to rise by 2.0%

3.8.1 Selected economic indicators (%)

	2017	2018
GDP growth	7.0	7.3
Inflation	9.5	10.0
Current account balance (share of GDP)	0.2	0.4

Source: ADB estimates.

3.8.6 GDP growth

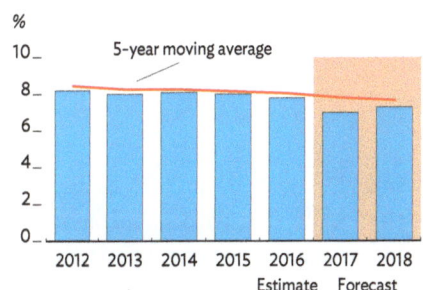

Source: Asian Development Outlook database.

3.8.7 Inflation

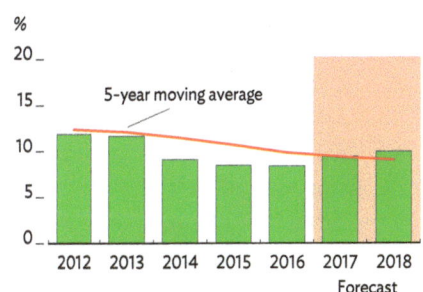

Source: Asian Development Outlook database.

3.8.1 New development strategy for 2017–2021

In February 2017, following Uzbekistan's first change in leadership in 25 years, the government adopted a 5-year national development strategy for 2017–2021. It sets five priority areas for reform: (i) governance and public administration, (ii) the rule of law and the judicial system, (iii) economic development and liberalization, (iv) social development, and (v) security, tolerance, and foreign policy. The strategy identifies inclusive growth and continued economic diversification as key to its reform objectives.

Under this strategic framework, during the next 5 years the government envisages undertaking business-conducive policy measures that provide affordable financing for firms, address insolvency, enhance legal mechanisms to enforce contractual obligations, improve access to electricity, simplify procedures for obtaining construction permits, and ease business registration. On 9 February 2017, the government approved a new streamlined system for registering new businesses, introducing registration at a single window. From 1 April 2017, business owners will be able to register online and receive approval within 30 minutes. To ensure full coverage, the government will establish 194 physical single-window centers across the country. These measures are expected to promote the development of micro and small enterprises.

Another initiative promotes agricultural diversification and the development of high-value horticulture through farm mechanization, improved infrastructure, and more productive use of land and water. More market-oriented agricultural policies and the development of agribusiness promise to make farms more financially stable. The government has prepared a sector development plan through 2020 that envisages further reductions in cotton and wheat production and their replacement with more varied horticulture crops. The strategy aims to improve logistics and processing and enable more exports.

in 2017 and 3.0% in 2018 as merchandise imports rise by 3.0% and then 4.0% (Figure 3.8.9). Import demand will come mostly from ongoing infrastructure spending and the industrial modernization program, as well as from the purchase of capital goods for the recently approved agriculture diversification program. Given the large external borrowing component of these programs, external debt is set to increase to 18% of GDP in 2017 and 2018 (Figure 3.8.10).

Policy challenge—reforming the financial sector

Stability in Uzbekistan's financial sector is closely linked to the country's macroeconomic performance and sovereign finance. The financial system is dominated by banks, which control over 95% of sector assets. In 2015, eight state-owned banks controlled 75% of banking assets and provided most credit to state-owned entities. These banks prioritize large export-oriented and manufacturing firms—a reflection of active public spending channeled through public banks. Smaller private banks lend mainly to small and micro enterprises. The government also plays a significant role in financial sector liquidity. It provides about 20% of all deposits, second only to corporate deposits amounting to 40%, of which a portion comes from state-owned enterprises.

The sector fails to provide sufficient financing to the economy, in particular to small and medium-sized enterprises. At the same time, the prolonged market dominance of state-owned banks poses a major vulnerability. Serious concerns include the concentration of banking assets, their questionable quality, and banks' continued receipt of public funding. While the sector's exposure to global risks is limited, it remains largely ineffective at promoting financial intermediation. The rate of financial intermediation, measured as the monetization ratio of broad money to GDP, is estimated at 23% of GDP. This is far below

3.8.8 Current account balance

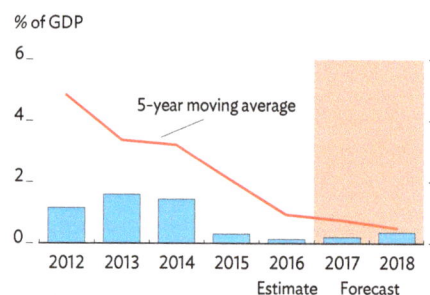

Source: Asian Development Outlook database.

the ratio of 54% in Honduras, 79% in India, or 138% in Viet Nam, all economies with per capita income similar to Uzbekistan's. Exacerbating this problem is an underdeveloped capital market. According to the IMF, total activity in 2014 was only $7.6 million, of which only 2.8% involved individual investors.

The government has stated its intention to strengthen private sector access to finance and financial services. It has identified small business development as a priority and aims to improve legislation to facilitate the establishment and operation of small businesses by reducing taxes and simplifying registration, licensing, and reporting requirements. The government's medium-term strategy for developing the financial sector anticipates that lending to small firms will increase by 120% from 2015 to 2020, though inflation will mean a smaller real increase.

In December 2015, the authorities announced plans to sell at least a 15% stake in some state-owned banks to foreign investors. Progress to date has been mixed. International rating agencies have noted possible understatement of nonperforming loans, officially reported at less than 1% of all loans though Moody's has estimated them at 6%. In addition, foreign investors have voiced concern about inadequate access to foreign exchange, as many firms have reported difficulty in obtaining hard currency for current international transactions, with delays extending up to 12 months. The central bank has noted the concerns of rating agencies and is working with commercial banks to address the situation. To improve sector capitalization and liquidity, the central bank plans to introduce Basel III standards and recommendations gradually but in full by 2019. In 2017, the government announced its intention to improve access to hard currency by developing the domestic foreign exchange market and adopting a market-based exchange rate policy.

While the government has taken major initiatives, more is needed to promote financial sector development. The main challenges are to relax, if not eliminate, restrictions on cash and foreign exchange transactions and to stop channeling loans to specific borrowers and sectors. Current regulations prohibit the use of cash to buy raw materials and other inputs, and they delay cash withdrawal from bank accounts. Small businesses often fail to meet requirements for bank credit because of inadequate financial documentation, limited fixed assets, and high reliance on cash flow revenue. Further, limited trust in the formal financial system has prompted the holding of substantial savings in cash or real estate, constricting the financial sector's role in intermediation. At the end of 2016, bank deposits equaled only 23.6% of GDP, one of the lowest ratios in Central Asia. Reform to address these impediments is thus essential to allow other measures—including improvements in supervision, risk management, credit infrastructure, credit information systems, and nonbank financial institutions—to bring about financial inclusion and broad-based economic development.

3.8.9 Growth in exports and imports of goods

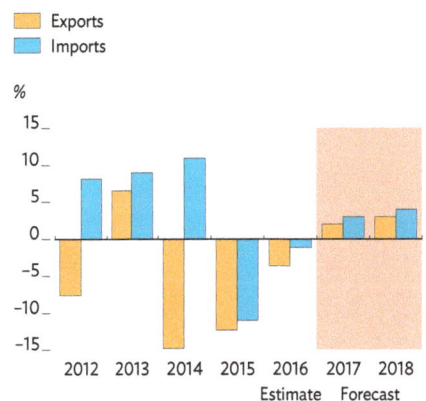

Source: Asian Development Outlook database.

3.8.10 External debt

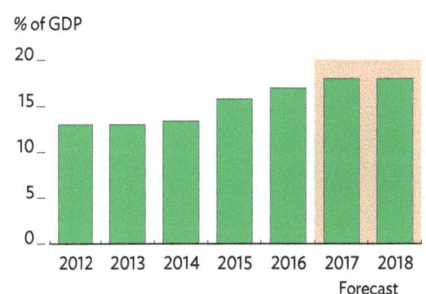

Source: Asian Development Outlook database.

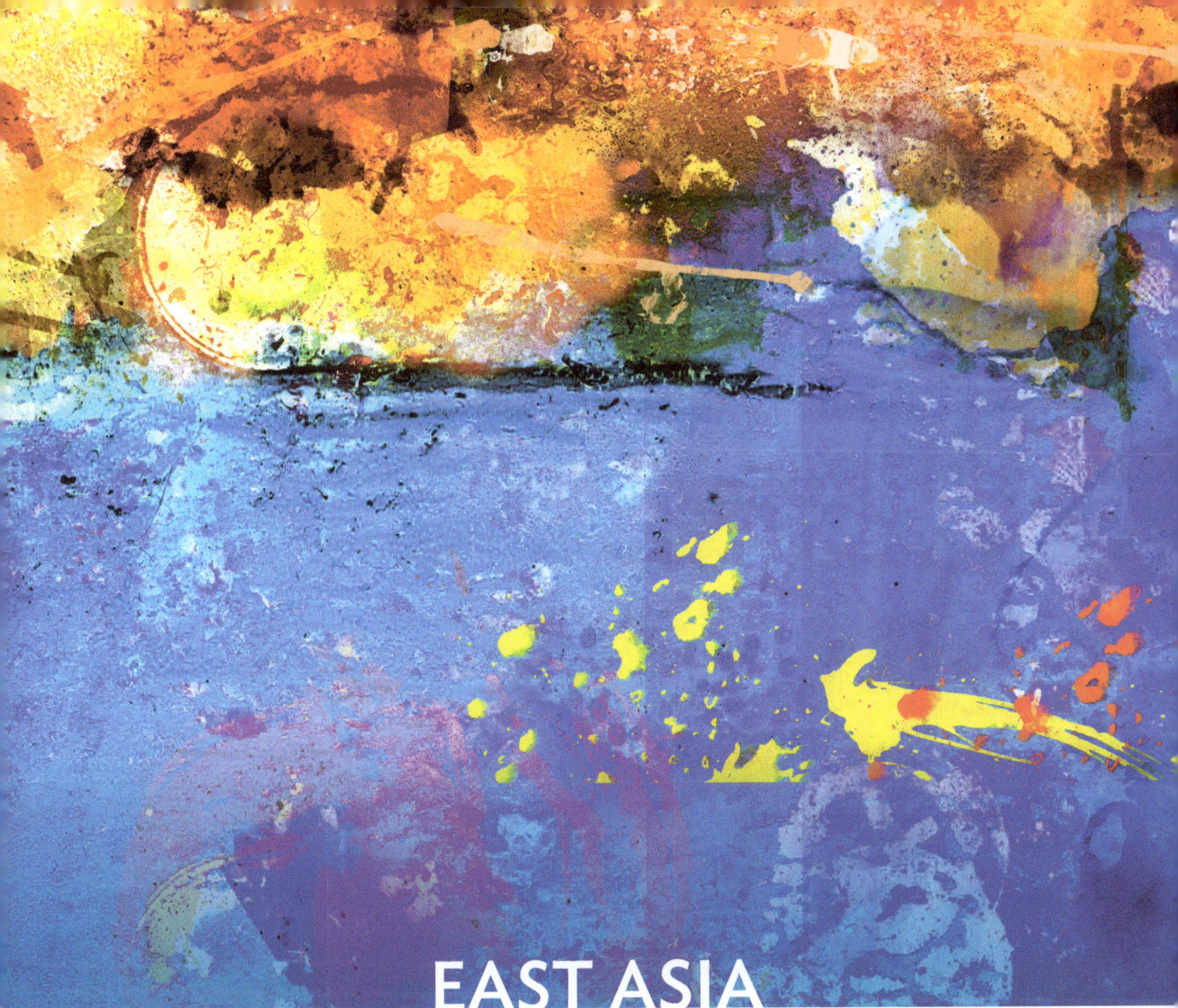

EAST ASIA

PEOPLE'S REPUBLIC OF CHINA
HONG KONG, CHINA
REPUBLIC OF KOREA
MONGOLIA
TAIPEI,CHINA

People's Republic of China

Growth in this restructuring economy continued to decelerate in 2016, but the government ensured stability through targeted fiscal and monetary support. Inflation started to rise, and the current account surplus narrowed but remained sizeable. These trends will continue in 2017 and 2018. Structural reform needs to be accelerated to boost productivity and sustain growth as outlined in the current 5-year plan.

Economic performance

GDP growth slowed further from 6.9% in 2015 to 6.7% in 2016, continuing a trend since 2010 as the economy of the People's Republic of China (PRC) changes its growth model toward one driven mainly by consumption and services (Figure 3.9.1). The government continued to provide strong monetary and fiscal support to smooth structural transformation and ensure economic, financial, and social stability. This boosted investment in infrastructure and real estate, spilled over into other parts of the economy, and kept growth higher than the average of 6.5% called for in the Thirteenth Five-Year Plan, 2016–2020.

On the supply side, services remained the main growth driver as real estate services boomed and other services registered strong growth, though growth in the whole sector slowed to 7.8% from 8.2% in 2015. The share of services in GDP further increased from 50.2% in 2015 to 51.6%, or 11.8 percentage points above that of industry. Industry expanded by 6.1% in 2016, a rate close to 2015, as growth in manufacturing picked up due to spillover from invigorated real estate activity, a jump in car production stimulated by a cut in the sales tax, and robust construction that lifted demand for heavy industry and energy. Energy consumption per unit of GDP nevertheless fell by 5.0%, cumulatively easing energy intensity by more than 37% since it peaked in 2005. Agriculture grew by only 3.3%, down from 3.9% in 2015 because of adverse weather and despite heavy investment. The contribution of services to GDP growth increased to 3.9 percentage points while that of industry fell to 2.5 points and agriculture's contribution remained 0.3 points (Figure 3.9.2).

Heavy industry continued to report job losses, but the labor market remained stable nationwide with the creation of 13.1 million new urban jobs—many more jobs than the estimated 800,000 lost in the steel and coal industries. During the fourth quarter of 2016, the ratio of urban job openings to job seekers rose to its highest since 2014. This maintained some pressure on wages, but migrant workers, a particularly vulnerable segment of the workforce, saw wage growth decelerate to 6.4% in 2016 from 9.5% in 2015.

3.9.1 Economic growth

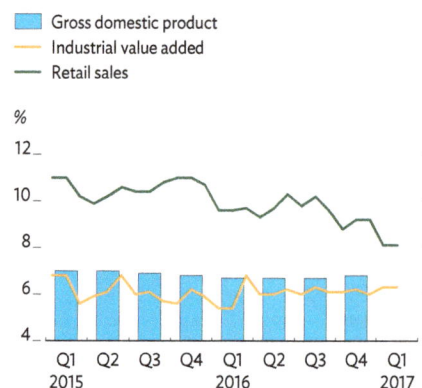

Q = quarter.
Note: GDP data for the first quarter of 2017 are not yet available.
Source: National Bureau of Statistics.

3.9.2 Supply-side contributions to growth

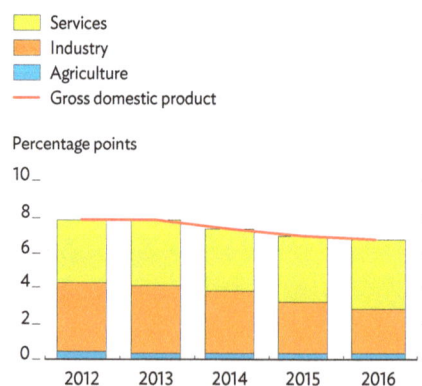

Source: National Bureau of Statistics.

This chapter was written by Jurgen Conrad and Jian Zhuang of the People's Republic of China Resident Mission, ADB, Beijing.

On the demand side, the contribution of consumption to growth increased to 4.3 percentage points, that of investment fell to 2.8 percentage points as the economy became less investment driven in line with government objectives, and that of net exports declined further to subtract 0.5 percentage points (Figure 3.9.3). As can be expected in an urbanizing country with rising incomes, strengthening social insurance, and an aging population, the household savings rate continued to fall. Thus, consumption outpaced GDP despite real disposable income growth slipping to 6.3% from 7.4% in 2015 and below the GDP growth rate.

In contrast, total industrial investment plummeted in response to excess capacity in heavy industry and mining, high corporate debt, and an uncertain business outlook. This retreat was almost fully compensated, however, by rising infrastructure and real estate investment, as well as large outlays by emerging high-value technology firms. Infrastructure investment was supported off budget through policy banks and public–private partnerships, imposing further contingent liabilities on the government. Real estate investment expanded strongly from a low base as easier mortgage interest rates and down-payment requirements fueled housing sales and provided incentives for new investment by reducing floor space awaiting sale, particularly in larger cities (Figure 3.9.4). When some local property markets overheated, purchase restrictions returned in many larger cities since September 2016 and moral suasion on banks tightened access to mortgages. These restrictions have dampened sales growth but not yet housing investment.

Consumer price inflation averaged 2.0% in 2016, up from 1.4% in 2015 but still below the government ceiling of 3.0% (Figure 3.9.5). This increase mainly reflected higher food, service, and administered prices. Core inflation, which excludes food and energy, remained stable at 1.6%. Real estate prices rose by an average of 6.4% in the largest 70 cities, though the restrictions introduced in September helped to moderate price increases and in some cases reverse them. Average producer price deflation moderated from 5.2% in 2015 to 1.3% in 2016 as industrial input costs—heavily weighted in the PRC producer price index—increased with rising global commodity prices and cuts to domestic capacity in upstream industries. This boosted corporate profit and ability to service debt. Producer price inflation continued to trend upward in early 2017, but consumer price inflation remained moderate.

Budgetary stimulus came mainly through tax cuts. Consolidated revenue collected by the central and local governments grew less rapidly at 4.8% in 2016, down from 8.5% in 2015 and 3.4 percentage points below nominal GDP growth. However, as growth in budget expenditure plummeted from 15.9% in 2015 to 6.9% in 2016, growth in the budget deficit was contained at 3.8% of GDP, only marginally up from 3.4% in 2015. Expenditure data do not include off-budget spending, for which timely data are unavailable. It has been sizeable in the past.

Responding mainly to the loss of liquidity caused by capital outflows, the authorities cut reserve requirements in March 2016 and injected liquidity through open market operations and refinancing facilities for selected banks. Interbank market rates remained low for most of 2016 (Figure 3.9.6). Broad money grew by an average of 12.0% year on year,

3.9.3 Demand-side contributions to growth

- Net exports
- Investment
- Consumption
- Gross domestic product

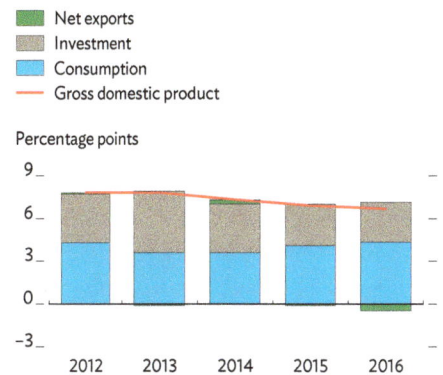

Source: National Bureau of Statistics.

3.9.4 Real estate markets

- Floor space sold
- Floor space waiting for sale
- Growth of real estate investment in residential building

Sources: National Bureau of Statistics; ADB estimates.

3.9.5 Year-on-year inflation

- Overall consumer price inflation
- Core consumer price inflation
- Producer price inflation

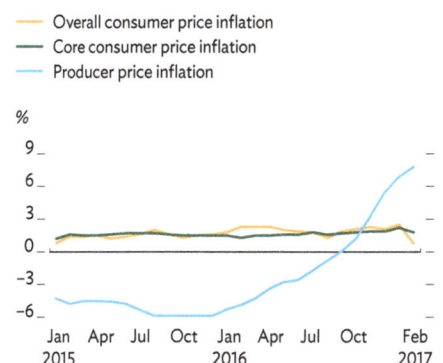

Source: National Bureau of Statistics.

down from 12.3% in 2015. Credit growth substantially exceeded nominal GDP growth in 2016 (Figure 3.9.7), and debt and associated risks therefore continued to mount. The stock of total social financing, which includes bank credit and financing from nonbank financial institutions and capital markets to households and enterprises, expanded by an estimated 13.4%, faster than broad money but down from 14.3% in 2015. The share of capital market financing through bond and equity issuance in total social financing increased in 2016 while that of loans provided by banks and nonbank financial institutions declined. In early 2017, the share of nonbank financing again increased following government efforts to curb bank credit (Figure 3.9.8). Local government bond issuance—introduced in 2015 to reduce funding costs and lengthen maturities—increased strongly in 2016 at the expense of borrowing by local government financing vehicles. The former is not included in the total social financing, while the latter is. Therefore, with local government bond issuance factored in, financing expanded even faster than total social financing suggests.

To counter financial vulnerability arising from high credit growth, the People's Bank of China, the central bank, reduced net injection of liquidity through open market operations in September, edging interbank rates higher and tamping down credit growth. Other reasons to act were rising price pressures in the housing market and capital outflows, as well as confidence by September that the growth target for 2016 would be met. An increase in rates for two medium-term and several short-term lending facilities in January, February, and again in March 2017 confirmed that the rate-easing cycle had ended in the PRC and signaled that the authorities are prepared to hike rates to contain credit growth and support the renminbi, at least as long as growth remains sufficiently strong.

Preliminary balance-of-payments data indicate that the current account deteriorated in 2016. Exports of goods fell by 7.2% year on year. However, real export growth was stronger than US dollar figures suggest, given the weakness of other invoicing currencies. Imports declined by 4.6% even as prices for commodity imports stabilized or increased. The merchandise trade surplus thus fell from $567.0 billion in 2015 (5.1% of GDP) to $485.2 billion in 2016 (4.3%). As the services deficit further widened, mainly on $341.2 billion spent by outbound tourists, the current account surplus narrowed to equal 1.9% of GDP, down from 3.0% in 2015 (Figure 3.9.9). The deficit on the capital and financial account remained sizeable in 2016. Persistent drivers of capital outflow were renminbi depreciation, easy credit, residents' desire to diversify their portfolios internationally, and a continued surge in outbound direct investment.

Indeed, net foreign direct investment flows turned negative in 2016 for the first time in the recent history of the PRC. Under the government's opening-up policy, which deregulates investment abroad and provides credit support, outbound direct investment more than tripled from $65.0 billion in 2012 to $211.2 billion in 2016. By contrast, inflows of foreign direct investment plummeted from $241.2 billion to $152.7 billion over the same period as the business environment deteriorated for foreign companies in the PRC.

3.9.6 Interest rates and interbank offered rate

Source: People's Bank of China.

3.9.7 Money supply and nominal GDP

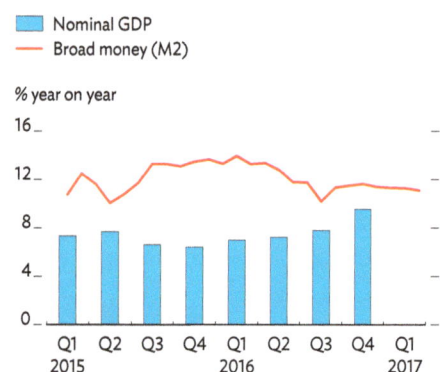

Q = quarter.
Note: GDP data for the first quarter of 2017 are not yet available.
Sources: National Bureau of Statistics; People's Bank of China; ADB estimates.

3.9.8 Total financing provided

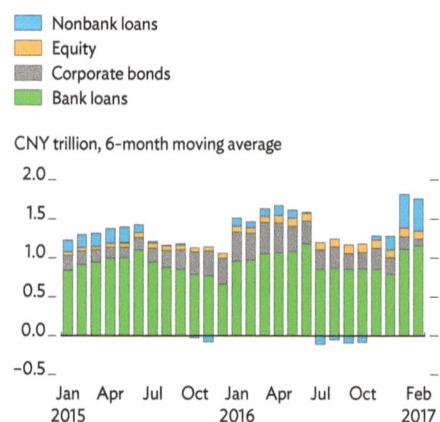

Sources: People's Bank of China; ADB estimates.

The smaller current account surplus and sizable net capital outflows drained official reserves in 2016 by $443.6 billion (excluding valuation changes) but nevertheless left $3.1 trillion by year-end. As the decline in reserves was overcompensated by an increase in other claims on foreign countries, total foreign assets increased from $6.2 trillion in 2015 to $6.5 trillion in September 2016. Deducting liabilities, net foreign assets increased from $1.6 to $1.8 trillion over the same period. The PRC thus remained the world's largest creditor nation.

Since late 2015, the authorities have managed renminbi exchange rates with reference to a number of indicators including the renminbi–US dollar closing rate of the previous day, and changes in the renminbi's real effective exchange rate. Amid increased volatility, the renminbi depreciated against the US dollar in 2016 by 6.8% on average and by over 4% in both nominal effective (trade-weighted) and real effective (inflation-adjusted) terms (Figure 3.9.10). The renewed strengthening of the US dollar since October 2016 and the resulting weakening of the renminbi triggered capital outflow that risked fueling expectation of further depreciation. The authorities swiftly stabilized the situation through tightened capital controls, open market operations, and a clampdown on renminbi provided through various lending facilities. As a result, the renminbi appreciated again in early 2017.

Economic prospects

GDP growth is expected to moderate further in line with the controlled deceleration of the past couple of years to 6.5% in 2017 and 6.2% in 2018 (Figure 3.9.11). The official growth target for 2017 is "about 6.5%." The government has clarified that growth could be lower if efforts to achieve the target would entail excessive risk to the economy or the financial sector. Nevertheless, it is likely that sufficient monetary and fiscal support will be provided to keep growth at or even above 6.5% until the Nineteenth Party Congress scheduled for autumn 2017.

The forecast assumes that the government may allow growth to slip below 6.5% in 2018, which would widen its scope for tackling credit growth and accelerating structural reform, in particular to roll up highly indebted enterprises and further cut excess industrial capacity. However, the government will certainly continue to provide selective policy support to ensure that adjustments remain socially acceptable. Fiscal support for infrastructure investment will play a key role here, provided mainly through policy banks and public–private partnership.

On the demand side, consumption will remain the main driver of growth over the forecast period. Support comes from continued wage growth that results from a solidly growing economy with a stagnant or shrinking workforce and therefore a tight labor market despite layoffs in industries with excess capacity. Consumption will be further bolstered by more generous social spending on health, education, and pensions as the government addresses income inequality and improves access to social services nationwide. Overall income growth will likely continue to moderate slightly in line with the trend in recent years, but this should

3.9.9 Current account balance

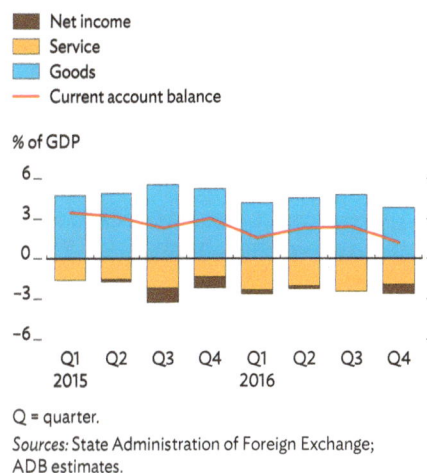

Q = quarter.
Sources: State Administration of Foreign Exchange; ADB estimates.

3.9.10 Exchange rates

Sources: China Foreign Exchange Trading Center; Bank for International Settlements.

3.9.11 GDP growth

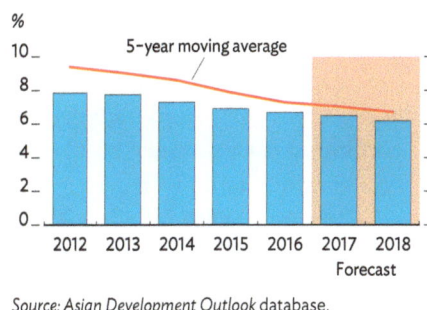

Source: Asian Development Outlook database.

be countered by a falling savings rate as consumer confidence remains strong and, according to central bank surveys, the propensity to spend strengthens.

Several factors indicate that investment will likely be less robust in the forecast period than in 2016 and that its share of GDP will continue to shrink. A strong rebound in housing investment peaked in May 2016, stocks of unsold housing in many smaller cities remain high, access to mortgages has tightened, and purchase restrictions have been reintroduced in larger cities. It is thus unlikely that real estate will contribute as much to growth in 2017 as it did in 2016. Investment in manufacturing and services stabilized in mid-2016 but remains weak. Again, there is no reason to believe that 2017 will bring major improvement as the business outlook for export-oriented industries remains uncertain and credit growth is decelerating. Further, newly emerging industries with growth potential are generally less capital intensive than the old declining industries where investment remains constrained by persistent excess capacity despite some progress in reducing steel and coal production capacity in 2016.

The government will continue to mitigate the drag on growth from economic restructuring by investing in infrastructure, which in any case is urgently needed to support rapid urbanization. However, infrastructure accounts for only one-fifth of total investment and cannot fully compensate for the falloff in investment elsewhere. Investment growth overall will thus lag GDP growth over the forecast period. This is in line with the objectives of changing the country's growth model, reducing financial vulnerability, and ensuring sustainable long-term growth.

The forecasts for 2017 and 2018 have to take into account likely developments in international trade relations, which are currently highly unpredictable. Stronger growth is expected globally and should be a boon for PRC exporters, but optimism must be tempered by the rising specter of protectionism, which can only spell trouble for the world's biggest exporter. On balance, net exports are expected to detract slightly from growth over the forecast period, and the falling trend in the share of exports in GDP, from a peak above 32% in 2006 to 18% in 2016, will continue.

On the supply side, services will remain the key driver despite a weaker contribution from real estate services. The economy's service sector is diverse, and subsectors such as health, education, entertainment, tourism, and industrial support services have huge growth potential, which will be slowly realized as the government further deregulates and opens more of the service sector to private and foreign investment. Industry—burdened by excess capacity, slowing real estate investment, and high debt—will grow more slowly than in 2016, continuing a trend since 2010, though consumer-oriented manufacturing will continue to do well.

Consumer price inflation is forecast to accelerate to 2.4% in 2017 and 2.8% in 2018, coming closer to the government ceiling of 3.0%, now reconfirmed for 2017 (Figure 3.9.12). Key drivers are strong consumer demand, higher wages, continued price deregulation, some spillover from the weaker renminbi, and global commodity price

3.9.1 Selected economic indicators (%)

	2017	2018
GDP growth	6.5	6.2
Inflation	2.4	2.8
Current account balance (share of GDP)	1.8	1.7

Source: ADB estimates.

3.9.12 Inflation

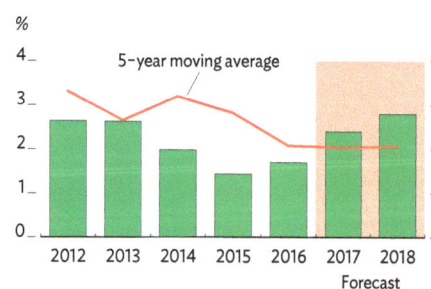

Source: Asian Development Outlook database.

increases. To keep funding costs stable in an environment of rising inflation, the authorities will have to further increase policy interest rates over the forecast period. This is necessary as well to keep the gap between domestic and US interest rates from widening too much, which could trigger additional capital outflow, and to slow credit growth and thus contain financial risk.

If looming tensions in trade relations can be contained, the PRC trade surplus should remain broadly unchanged as the share of exports with higher value added continues to grow. The current account surplus will remain sizeable but fall below the 2016 surplus with a widening deficit in the services balance. The overall balance of payments will likely remain in deficit because of net capital outflow, dragging official reserves to below $3 trillion in 2017. This amount will likely be adequate for an economy with an increasingly flexible exchange rate regime and persisting capital controls.

The downside risks to the outlook include, from the external perspective, heightened protectionism and increasing capital outflow. Although the PRC enjoys adequate international reserve buffers to mitigate the impact of any risks that may materialize within the forecast period, the authorities may consider containing the outflow to protect reserves, especially if it approaches the $100 billion/month drain seen in late 2015 and early 2016 (Figure 3.9.13). In that case, they would likely opt for further tightening of capital controls before considering hiking interest rates or floating the currency. Hiking interest rates substantially would constrain growth but cannot be ruled out if capital controls prove to be less effective than in the past, or if US rates rise faster than expected. Floating the currency risks creating a vicious cycle of further depreciation expectations and additional outflow, destabilizing the foreign exchange market. It would also contravene the government's stated goal of keeping the renminbi basically stable in 2017 relative to a basket of currencies.

A fully flexible exchange rate has been a government strategic objective for years, consistent with its desire to further open up the economy and advance renminbi internationalization, but these priorities have been in retreat since mid-2015. The share of foreign trade settlements denominated in renminbi peaked above 30% in September 2015 but has since halved to below 15% with concerns over the exchange rate outlook and tighter capital controls. Renminbi deposits abroad and their role in foreign exchange transactions have been eroding for the same reason. To reverse these trends, further exchange rate liberalization remains a possibility over the forecast period, particularly if foreign exchange markets and the balance of payments become more stable.

The principal domestic risk is peril to the asset quality of banks and nonbank financial institutions posed by persistently rapid credit expansion, including credit to inefficient firms, in an environment of decelerating economic growth. Troubled loans classified as nonperforming or with overdue interest payments already occupy almost 7.0% of banks' loan portfolio, and strong credit growth may mask more serious repayment problems, potentially undermining financial stability and investor confidence. Tackling credit expansion is thus essential but

3.9.13 Official reserves and capital flows

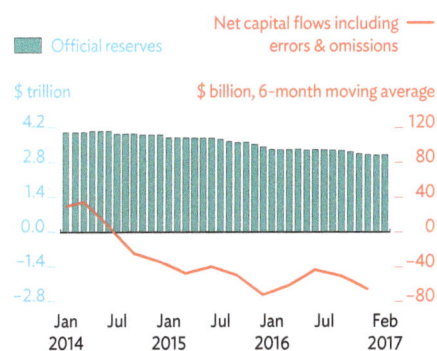

Sources: People's Bank of China; State Administration of Foreign Exchange.

itself poses risks as the failure of individual financial institutions could quickly spread across the system, especially as intermediation channels between banks and nonbank financial institutions are opaque and poorly understood, and if liquidity shortages are not swiftly addressed. The government's Financial Sector Work Conference, which is held every 5 years and due in 2017, will likely mitigate this risk by deciding how sector regulators can better work together to head off incidents and contain their fallout.

Policy challenge—raising investment productivity

The PRC investment rate, or gross fixed capital formation over GDP, jumped from 40% in 2008 to 45% in 2009 and stayed at this elevated level until 2013 (Figure 3.9.14). This was the result of the debt-financed and investment-oriented stimulus deployed to support economic growth during the global financial crisis. Until 2008, the PRC investment rate aligned with East Asian and Western norms and was thus not unusually high. However, the 5 percentage point jump has created inefficiency and distortion in resource allocation and vulnerability in the financial system. Against this background, the authorities have embarked on rebalancing the economy toward consumption. As a result, the investment contribution to GDP growth has gradually declined as the consumption contribution returned to its long-run level of about two-thirds.

From a supply-side perspective, the contribution to economic growth from declining investment volume can be maintained only with productivity gains. Only 5% of investment today is undertaken by enterprises or administrative units subordinate to central government ministries, offices, or companies. Local government investment accounts for less than one-third of the remaining 95%. Improving the productivity of investment thus poses three challenges.

The first challenge is to improve the efficiency of the one-third of total investment that is still undertaken by government agencies. This includes most investment in public utilities, construction, transportation, information technology, finance, environmental facilities, education, health, and culture. Reforms to public–private partnership and mixed ownership are already under way for that purpose, but outright privatization should also be considered, especially where local government enterprises engage in commercial activities. No modern market economy, and no high-income economy in particular, has state-owned enterprises as dominant as they are in the PRC.

The government's policy goals include structural changes to investment that boost private investors' involvement in the provision of services and replace industry with services as the main driver of growth. The service sector share of investment declined from 62.2% in 2003 to 54.6% in 2008 and then gradually recovered to 58.0% in 2016 (Figure 3.9.15). Further opening of sectors dominated by state-owned enterprises such as transport, telecommunication, and finance to private investors, as announced by the government, will support this trend over the forecast period and reduce the state's share in overall investment.

3.9.14 Share of gross fixed capital formation in GDP

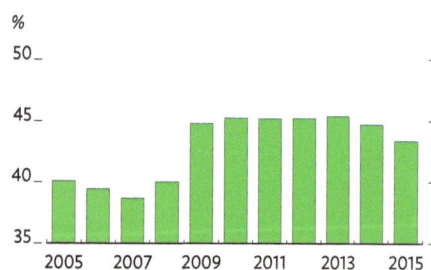

Source: National Bureau of Statistics.

3.9.15 Sectoral share of fixed asset investment

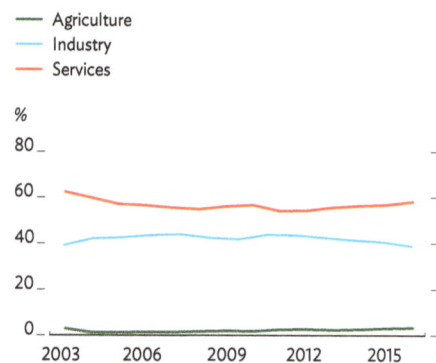

Source: National Bureau of Statistics.

Second, the government has to further improve conditions for the two-thirds of investment that is not directly subordinated to a government agency but rather undertaken by private enterprises (corporate and individual), companies with mixed ownership, and foreign-funded companies (Figure 3.9.16). Ensuring that these enterprises are fully market driven requires, among other things, continued financial reform to attract savings to the most productive investment projects, encouraging investment in innovation and movement toward the higher-technology end of the production chain, and alleviating constraints on skilled labor supply. The government is indeed attempting to push investment toward innovation and technology-driven production, as outlined in the Thirteenth Five-Year Plan and other strategies, by providing fiscal, financial, and regulatory incentives to selected high-tech industries to turn the PRC into a "manufacturing superpower."

Cross-sector analysis confirms that profitability and market demand are major determinants of investment, but other factors can be obstructive in individual industries. These factors include formal and informal industry-specific policies and/or constraints imposed by local governments to protect privileged enterprises in their jurisdiction, notably through discriminatory nontariff barriers and price setting, prohibitions on the sale of nonlocal goods and services, government procurement and compulsory trading that favor local enterprises, and compulsory takeovers and collusive cartels. Strengthening competition policies and their enforcement through strong institutions is crucial to overcoming such constraints, as are industrial policies that are market friendly and implemented without discrimination, and that allow weak companies to fail.

Although the share of the private sector in total investment has been on the rise, reaching 51% in 2016 from 40% in 2008, the share of foreign investment (including from Taipei,China and Hong Kong, China) in total investment has dropped from 11% to less than 4%, and foreign investment has become concentrated in very few sectors. This pattern may reflect a newly found ability of domestic enterprises to invest and innovate across all sectors, but it suggests as well that the current foreign investment regime hampers innovation and economic growth. To address this issue, the government announced in January 2017 that the environment for foreign investments will be liberalized to align with that for domestic investment.

The third challenge is to ensure that investment stimulus provided to stabilize economic growth does not compromise efforts to make investment more productive. Measures should thus be designed to focus on regions where support is most needed and on sectors that are new growth drivers. Further, stronger private sector involvement in investment would empower market forces to enhance the outcomes of stabilization efforts.

3.9.16 **Share of ownership in fixed asset investment**

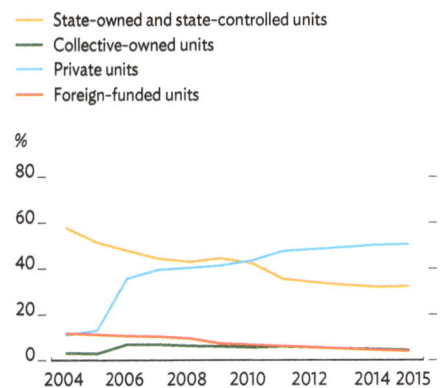

Source: National Bureau of Statistics.

Hong Kong, China

Growth moderated in 2016 for a third year in a row but will recover modestly in 2017 and 2018, helped by a stable labor market, durable incomes, and fiscal support. Inflation will moderate further, and the current account surplus will remain stable. Sharp increases in US interest rates could, if instituted, derail economic recovery, with the property market particularly at risk.

Economic performance

GDP growth slowed to 1.9% in 2016 from 2.4% in 2015, though growth in the fourth quarter reached 3.1% year on year. Resilient domestic demand underpinned the expansion in 2016. Supported by steady real incomes, low inflation, and a stable labor market, private consumption grew by 1.6% and contributed 1.1 percentage points to GDP growth, while government consumption added another 0.3 percentage points (Figure 3.10.1). Investment rebounded in the second half of 2016 on strong inventory restocking and resilient construction outlays to contribute 1.1 percentage points to GDP growth. Trade benefited from improving regional trade flows in the latter part of the year, with exports growing year on year by 0.9% and imports by 1.2% (Figure 3.10.2). Net exports staged a turnaround in the last quarter of 2016 but still ended up shaving 0.5 percentage points off overall growth. Construction and services were the primary drivers from the supply side. Construction grew by 2.4% in 2016, while services expanded by 2.3%, despite a lackluster performance by retail trade owing mainly to a decline in tourist arrivals.

The current account surplus widened to equal 4.5% of GDP in 2016. A narrower merchandise trade deficit reflected in part a fall in retained imports in the first half of the year and partly a pickup in the value of goods exports in the latter part of the year. An increase in the net inflow of primary income offset shrinkage in net service receipts as exports of travel services declined more steeply. With net outflow of portfolio capital, the overall balance of payments surplus in 2016 equaled 0.4% of GDP. Gross official reserves rose to $386.2 billion at the end of 2016, or cover for 7.8 months of imports.

Consumer price inflation slowed to 2.4% (Figure 3.10.3). External price pressures remained benign with subdued international prices for food and other commodities and a weak renminbi holding down imported inflation from the People's Republic of China (PRC). Steady labor costs and subdued rent increases helped contain domestic costs. Residential property prices fell by 11% year on year in late 2015 and early 2016, but they rebounded and by December 2016 were slightly above their September 2015 peak (Figure 3.10.4).

3.10.1 Demand-side contributions to growth

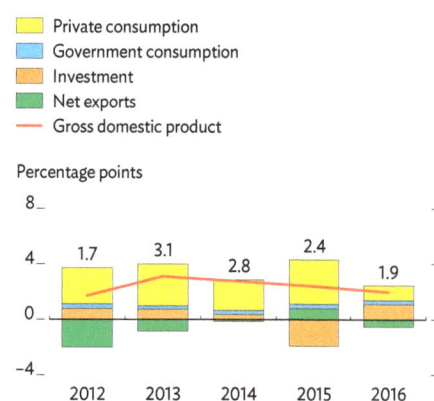

Private consumption
Government consumption
Investment
Net exports
— Gross domestic product

Percentage points

Source: CEIC Data Company (accessed 25 February 2017).

3.10.2 External trade

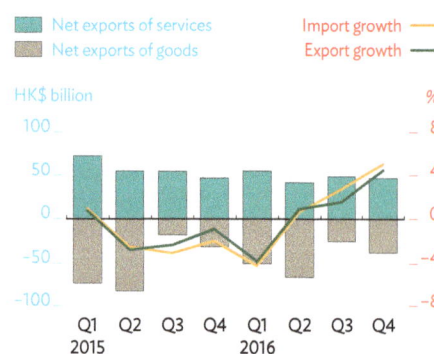

Net exports of services
Net exports of goods
Import growth
Export growth

HK$ billion   %

Q = quarter.
Source: CEIC Data Company (accessed 25 February 2017).

This chapter was written by Benno Ferrarini and Marthe Hinojales of the Economic Research and Regional Cooperation Department, ADB, Manila.

The government revised the estimate of the budget surplus for FY2016 (ended 31 March 2017) to the equivalent of 3.7% of GDP from an initial budget forecast of 0.5% (Figure 3.10.5). The higher revised surplus resulted from additional receipts of HK$81.5 billion, equal to 3.3% of GDP and mainly revenues from land sales and stamp duties from a buoyant property market. Government expenditure continued to increase modestly, primarily on higher provision for social welfare and capital works projects, but is likely to be lower than initially budgeted. Fiscal reserves on 31 March 2017 were expected to stand a tad higher at 37.6% of GDP.

Monetary conditions remained accommodative, though the Hong Kong Monetary Authority (HKMA) adjusted its benchmark base rate twice in December 2016 and March 2017, cumulatively from 0.75% to 1.25% in tandem with increases in the US federal funds rate. Domestic credit grew by 7.3%, and growth in broad money supply (M2) accelerated to 7.7%. The local equity market staged a rebound after the sharp correction in early 2016, falling to a 4-year low in February but ending the year 0.5% higher than in 2015 (Figure 3.10.6). Hong Kong, China remained in 2016 the top market for initial public offerings even though the total funds raised dropped to a recent low.

Economic prospects

GDP growth is projected to pick up to 2.0% in 2017 and recover further to 2.1% in 2018 (Figure 3.10.7). Domestic demand supported by building and construction will remain the engine of growth. Private consumption will benefit as well from continued stable employment and strong incomes. Large public infrastructure projects will lift overall investment, but private investment will remain sluggish. Business sentiment remains fragile, weighed down by moderation in the PRC, developments in the euro area, and the normalization of US interest rates. The purchasing managers' index slipped back into contraction in the first 2 months of 2017 after finally and briefly breaching in December 2016 the threshold at 50 indicating expansion. Business surveys in the first quarter of 2017 showed pessimism still entrenched, particularly in retailing and construction (Figure 3.10.8). On the supply side, growth will come from construction and services, in particular financial and professional services, the latter benefiting especially from strengthening ties with financial markets in the PRC and opportunities arising from the Belt and Road development initiative.

Inflation will moderate this year and next to about 2.0%. A strong local dollar will dampen imported inflation, while local cost increases will be contained by a negative output gap and moderate economic growth. Together, these factors will dampen upward pressure from rising global prices for oil and other commodities.

The FY2017 budget includes a package of pro-growth fiscal measures equal to 1.3% of GDP that the government forecasts will prop up 2017 GDP by 1.1%. The package includes one-off tax reductions for households and firms, waivers of rates, and extra social security allowances and, more permanently, recurrent social benefits and a tax reduction for

3.10.3 Inflation

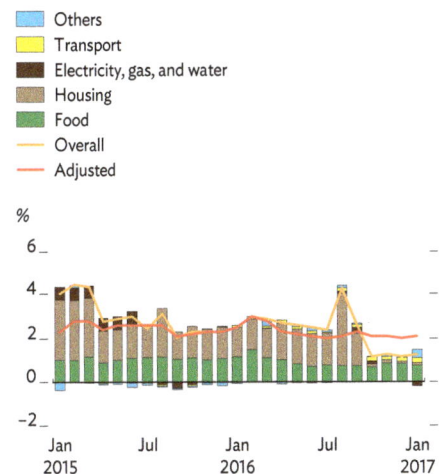

- Others
- Transport
- Electricity, gas, and water
- Housing
- Food
- Overall
- Adjusted

Note: Adjusted overall inflation refers to the rate once the effects of temporary subsidies by the government are removed.
Source: CEIC Data Company (accessed 11 March 2017).

3.10.4 Property market indicators

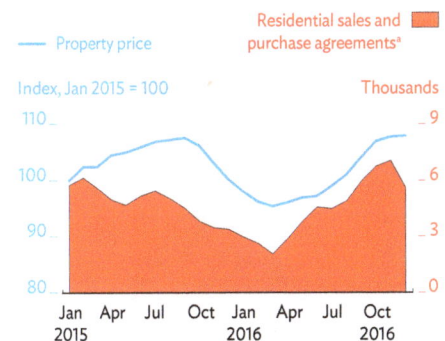

— Property price
Residential sales and purchase agreements[a]

a 3-month moving averages.
Source: CEIC Data Company (accessed 28 March 2017).

3.10.5 Fiscal indicators

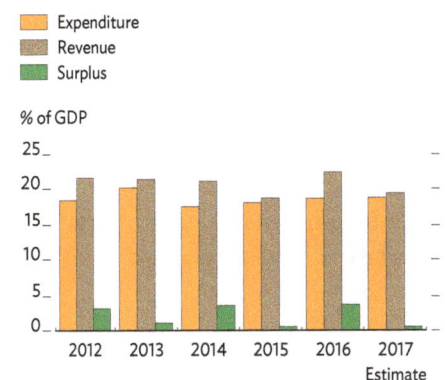

- Expenditure
- Revenue
- Surplus

Note: Years are fiscal years ending 31 March of that year.
Sources: The Government of the Hong Kong Special Administrative Region of the PRC. The 2016–2017 Budget, and other years. http://www.budget.gov.hk; Hong Kong Monetary Authority; *Asian Development Outlook* database.

home loan interest. When compared with the revised estimate of FY2016, the budget further includes a 0.7% increase of capital outlays. On balance, budgetary revenues are estimated to fall by 9.3% and expenditures to rise by 5.3%, shrinking the FY2017 fiscal surplus to the equivalent of 0.6% of GDP. This is a step in the right direction given the negative output gap and the need to counter monetary tightening resulting from expected US interest rate hikes.

The stabilization of global demand and growing demand in the PRC for high tech products, especially semiconductors, should offer some support to exports of goods and services in 2017. However, further strengthening of the US dollar, to which the local dollar is tied, could limit export gains. Imports are likely to return to growth as the decline in investment continues to moderate and a depreciating renminbi lifts import demand. The resulting trade deficit will be offset by an improving surplus in the services account as tourist numbers begin to revive and demand for professional and financial services grows. On balance, the current account surplus is forecast to remain stable at 3.1% this year and next.

Despite the recent decline in offshore renminbi activity in response to prevailing expectations of renminbi depreciation, the role of Hong Kong, China as the premier center for offshore renminbi trading remains secure. Trading will most likely be further strengthened by the December 2016 launch of a cross-boundary investment channel with the Shenzhen Stock Exchange in the PRC, following the launch in 2014 of a similar channel with the Shanghai Stock Exchange.

The main risks to the outlook are negative spillover from monetary tightening in the US, given the currency link between the two economies, and the potential impact of changes in US trade policy, which could hurt exports and undermine Hong Kong, China as a regional trading hub. Deepening integration with the PRC is beneficial on the whole, but it renders Hong Kong, China more vulnerable to adverse economic developments in the PRC. However, if any of these risks materialize, the government has ample fiscal and macroprudential tools to limit the buildup of systemic vulnerabilities.

Policy challenge—responding to rising US interest rates

Because of the linked exchange rate system by which the local dollar is pegged to the US dollar yet freely exchangeable, monetary policy in Hong Kong, China must track that of the US. When the US Federal Reserve raises its interest rates, the HKMA has to follow suit soon thereafter to avoid pressure on the peg. Banks may not immediately raise their rates in response, as long as there is ample liquidity available in the local banking system for lending, but they will have to raise rates eventually if there is less liquidity as a result, for example, of fund outflows from Hong Kong, China. A gradual rate increase, as currently anticipated, would have only limited effect on the economy, with mild movements of interbank and bilateral exchange rates that should prove easily manageable. The local property sector would feel the impact,

3.10.1 Selected economic indicators (%)

	2017	2018
GDP growth	2.0	2.1
Inflation	2.0	2.1
Current account balance (share of GDP)	3.1	3.1

Source: ADB estimates.

3.10.6 Stock market

Index, July 1964 = 100

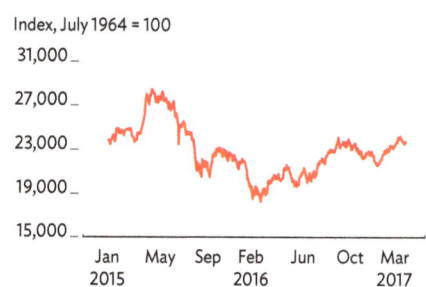

Source: Bloomberg (accessed 11 March 2017).

3.10.7 GDP growth

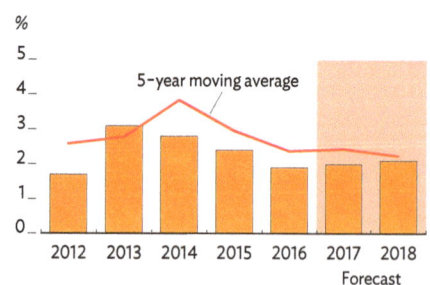

Source: Asian Development Outlook database.

but large upward adjustments in mortgage rates are unlikely as long as the banking system retains sufficient liquidity to continue offering low-interest mortgages.

However, if the Fed were to enact this year more than the expected two or three increases of 25 basis points each, local interest rates would have to climb higher, hurting domestic demand. A feedback effect on consumption from resulting negative wealth effects could force down asset prices, especially for property. Further, if higher interest rates strengthen the US and local dollars, this would undercut export competitiveness and create headwinds for tourism, thus compounding the damage to economic growth, at least to the extent that price flexibility in the service sector cannot mitigate the effect.

Local banks are well capitalized and have prudently managed mortgage financing risks by applying prudent loan-to-value ratios and assessing individual borrowers' repayment ability (Figure 3.10.9). The HKMA also conducts stress-testing regularly to assess resilience in the banking sector. However, the International Monetary Fund noted that an increase in the ratio of nonfinancial corporate debt to GDP might make companies more vulnerable in the event of a sharp interest rate hike.

Hong Kong, China has a strong policy framework and ample buffers in place to navigate shocks. Fiscal reserves equal to 37% of GDP allow additional fiscal stimulus if needed, and the crises-tested linked exchange rate system continues to be a credible anchor for the local economy and financial system. Meanwhile, progress is being made in reform to improve transparency and mitigate counterparty risks in the over-the-counter derivatives market, in which mandatory clearing began in September 2016. With sound fundamentals and policies in place, the main task will be the continued exercise of risk management and countercyclical prudential policy to contain any adverse impacts from wide fluctuations in financial markets. Policy measures include ensuring that banks maintain adequate liquidity and countercyclical capital buffers in line with Basel III rules, respect the caps on loan-to-value ratios and debt-servicing ratios that measure the ability of mortgage holders to service their debt, and comply with requirements limiting concentration of exposure to single borrowers, industries, and sectors.

3.10.8 Business tendency surveys

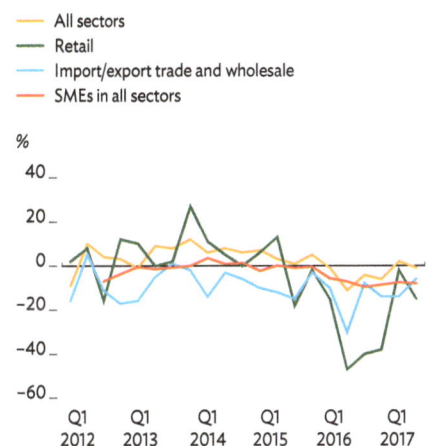

- All sectors
- Retail
- Import/export trade and wholesale
- SMEs in all sectors

Notes: Except for the small and medium-sized enterprise (SME) index, indicators represent the difference between the percentage of establishments expressing a better sentiment about the business situation and those expressing a worse sentiment. A positive reading denotes an improvement in the expectation of the business situation.

The SME variable was computed to represent the distance of the quarter's Standard Chartered Hong Kong SME leading business index from the 50-threshold mark, where a negative number represents predominantly pessimistic sentiment.

Sources: CEIC Data Company (accessed 22 January 2017); Standard Chartered Hong Kong SME Leading Business Index, Standard Chartered and Hong Kong Productivity Council.

3.10.9 Loan-to-value ratios of new mortgage loans (% average)

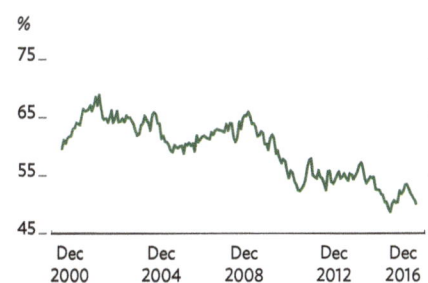

Source: CEIC Data Company (accessed 28 March 2017).

Republic of Korea

Strong private consumption early in the year and robust private investment sustained growth in 2016 despite lackluster exports. Growth will likely slow a little in 2017 but pick up in 2018 as political uncertainties recede and exports recover. The current account surplus will shrink in 2017 and 2018, but inflation will pick up moderately. Strategies exist to counter emergent trade policy uncertainty.

Economic performance

Economic growth accelerated marginally to 2.7% in 2016 from 2.6% in 2015, driven by strong expansion in consumption expenditure (Figure 3.11.1). Consumption increased by 2.8% and contributed 1.8 percentage points to growth, mostly reflecting faster growth in private expenditure. Stimulus measures including tax discounts for car purchases helped lift consumer spending in the first half. Then, undermined by a political crisis and subdued employment prospects, consumer sentiment plunged to a 7-year low in November, causing growth in consumer spending to soften in the second half (Figure 3.11.2). The unemployment rate rose to 3.7% from 3.6% in 2015 with the first falloff in manufacturing employment since 2009 and further job losses as the shipping and shipbuilding industries endured corporate restructuring.

Investment expanded by 5.4% in 2016 and contributed 1.6 percentage points to GDP growth (Figure 3.11.3). Investment growth accelerated in the second half as lower interest rates pushed up private investment, which provided 79.7% of gross capital formation. Construction investment expanded by 11.0%, accounting for over 90% of investment growth and outweighing a 2.4% decline in investment in machinery and transport equipment. External demand, by contrast, remained subdued. Net exports subtracted from growth again in 2016 as export growth was less than half of import growth in real terms, at 1.4% versus 3.0% (Figure 3.11.4).

On the supply side, services grew by 2.5%, owing mainly to expansion in wholesale and retail trade, and health and social services, contributing 1.4 percentage points to GDP growth. Manufacturing expanded more slowly, at 1.7%, held back by lingering weakness in exports and the impact of corporate restructuring, as well as by production cuts following the recall of the Samsung Note 7.

Average consumer price inflation rose to 1.0% in 2016, picking up in the second half along with higher food and global oil prices (Figure 3.11.5). By contrast, core inflation, which excludes agricultural and petroleum products, slowed to 1.6% from 2.2% in 2015.

3.11.1 Quarterly GDP growth

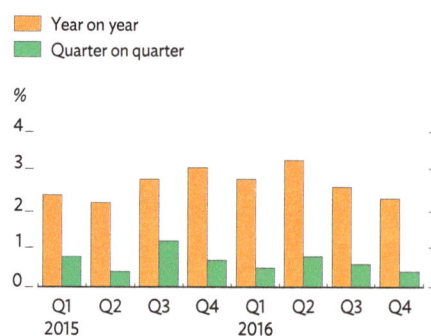

Q = quarter.
Source: Bank of Korea, Economic Statistics System, http://ecos.bok.or.kr/EIndex_en.jsp (accessed 14 February 2017).

3.11.2 Growth in private consumption

Q = quarter.
Source: Bank of Korea, Economic Statistics System, http://ecos.bok.or.kr/EIndex_en.jsp (accessed 14 February 2017).

This chapter was written by Gemma Esther Estrada and Donghyun Park of the Economic Research and Regional Cooperation Department, ADB, Manila.

Reflecting the mild inflation environment, monetary policy was accommodative, especially toward the second half of 2016 when the Bank of Korea, the central bank, cut its policy rate to a record low of 1.25% in June to support economic activity. With interest rates low, household debt continued to rise, equaling 82.8% of GDP at the end of 2016. Home mortgages accounted for 41.8% of debt.

Fiscal policy was likewise expansionary in 2016 to support growth. In September, the government approved a $10 billion supplementary budget to counter the impact of tepid external demand and support provincial economies hit by corporate restructuring. Nevertheless, the fiscal deficit including the supplementary budget amounted to only 2.4% of GDP, unchanged from 2015. Government debt recorded a small uptick.

Customs data indicate that exports continued to contract in US dollar terms last year but less quickly. Total exports dropped by 5.9% in 2016 as exports to all major partners declined. Exports to the People's Republic of China (PRC), which took one-fourth of the total, fell by 9.3% in 2016, even more steeply than in 2015, and exports to the US fell by 4.8%, compared with only a 0.6% drop in 2015. Shipments declined as well to the Association of Southeast Asian Nations, which accounts for 14.7% of all exports, and to the European Union, another key market, but by less than in 2015. Imports also sank in US dollar terms but by only 6.9%, much less than the 16.9% drop in 2015. With the merchandise trade surplus shrinking to the equivalent of 8.7% of GDP and the services deficit unchanged at 1.1%, the current account surplus shrank to 7.1% of GDP.

Despite global capital shifting out of emerging markets, the net capital position of the Republic of Korea (ROK) improved as net outflows abated owing to a recovery in foreign equity investment and an increase in inward foreign direct investment. The current account surplus contracted but remained large, and foreign exchange reserves rose by $3.2 billion to reach $361.7 billion at the end of 2016. The ROK won, which had been appreciating against the US dollar until early August, reversed course with heightened capital outflow in the fourth quarter. By December, it was 3.0% weaker against the dollar than at the end of 2015. In real effective terms, it appreciated by 0.6% during the year, just as it did the previous year.

Economic prospects

GDP growth is expected to slow from 2.7% in 2016 to 2.5% in 2017, the lowest since 2012 (Figure 3.11.6). Domestic demand will soften with weaker private consumption, but a recovery in exports can be expected to support growth. In 2018, growth is likely to bounce back to 2.7% as the impact of the political crisis fades and improved consumer and business sentiment boosts domestic demand.

Growth in private consumption will slow in 2017, tamped down by rising household debt and unfavorable consumer sentiment (Figure 3.11.7). However, fiscal measures to support job creation—such as subsidies to support new business establishment, larger budgetary allocations to promote job creation in information technology, and higher financial support to companies that retain employees after

3.11.3 Demand-side contributions to growth

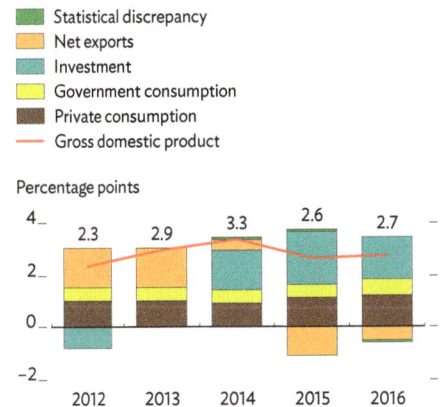

Percentage points

Source: Bank of Korea, Economic Statistics System, http://ecos.bok.or.kr/EIndex_en.jsp (accessed 14 February 2017).

3.11.4 Merchandise exports and imports

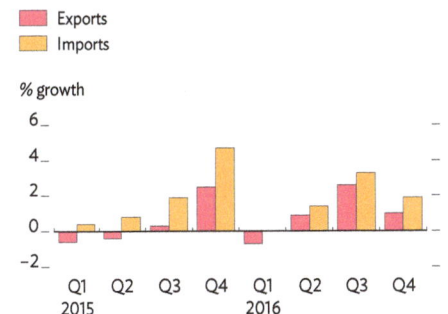

% growth

Q = quarter.
Source: Bank of Korea, Economic Statistics System, http://ecos.bok.or.kr/EIndex_en.jsp (accessed 14 February 2017).

3.11.5 Monthly inflation

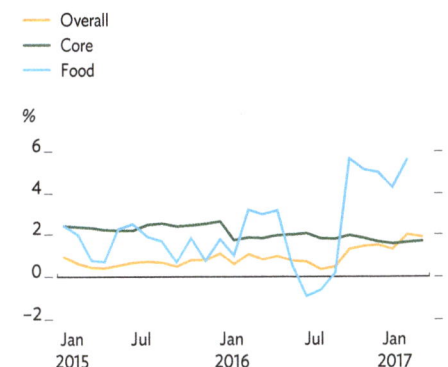

%

Source: CEIC Data Company (accessed 14 February 2017).

maternity leave—may counterbalance these effects to allow a 2% increase in private consumption.

Growth in investment will be held down by decelerating construction investment in 2017, as indicated by recent weakness in leading indicators such as construction starts and orders. Tighter property market restrictions introduced in August and November last year to manage household debt have kicked in to contain growth in residential construction. Further, the planned cut in the government budget for social overhead capital, which funds infrastructure such as bridges and roads, will curb civil engineering investment. However, deceleration in investment growth will likely be countered by recovery in machinery and transport equipment investment induced by the expected rise in external demand.

The planned fiscal impulse will be smaller than in 2016, but to counter prevailing uncertainty the government plans to frontload budgetary outlays this year such that over 30% of spending is in the first quarter, targeting job creation and the completion of public infrastructure projects. Government expenditures are projected to increase by 3.7% as revenues grow by 6.0%, so the fiscal deficit is projected to shrink to 1.7% of GDP in 2017 from 2.4% in 2016. Given ample fiscal resources, authorities are likely to draw a supplementary budget if economic conditions deteriorate in the second half of the year.

The rise in consumer inflation above 2.0% in January 2017 for the first time in 51 months indicates that inflation will be higher this year. It is forecast to average 1.7% as global commodity prices rise and 1.8% next year as domestic demand recovers. As a huge importer of oil, however, the ROK is vulnerable to unexpected movements in global oil prices, as is this forecast.

An expansionary monetary policy will likely continue despite rising concerns about high household debt (Figure 3.11.8). Benign inflation is allowing the central bank to maintain low interest rates, thereby supporting mortgage and property markets and borrowers' capacity to meet repayments.

Higher exports are forecast for the coming 2 years. After contracting in all but 1 of 21 months running, exports to the PRC began to rise in November 2016, and total exports grew by double digits in January and February 2017. These trends and expected higher growth in the advanced economies—especially the US, the second largest trading partner after the PRC—indicate that recent export momentum is likely to be sustained. As with exports, imports have started to pick up after an extended period of decline, partly reflecting higher oil prices, and are expected to rise further as growth improves. On balance, the current account surplus is forecast to narrow to the equivalent of 5.8% of GDP in 2017 and 5.3% in 2018.

The forecast faces a number of downside risks. First, the continued appreciation of the ROK won, which rose by 6.7% against the US dollar in the first 2 months of 2017, will be bad news for exporters on top of growing trade policy uncertainty in the US. Second, upward price pressures are building and may push inflation beyond the forecast rate at a time when, according to some estimates, actual output appears to be trailing potential output by a widening margin, raising the specter of

3.11.1 Selected economic indicators (%)

	2017	2018
GDP growth	2.5	2.7
Inflation	1.7	1.8
Current account balance (share of GDP)	5.8	5.3

Source: ADB estimates.

3.11.6 GDP growth

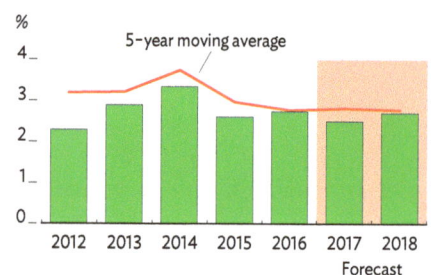

Sources: Bank of Korea, Economic Statistics System, http://ecos.bok.or.kr/EIndex_en.jsp (accessed 14 February 2017); ADB estimates.

3.11.7 Business and consumer confidence

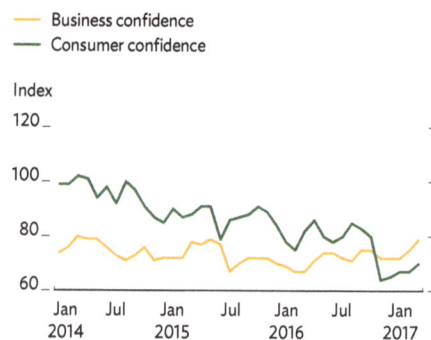

Note: A reading below 100 means that more respondents answered negatively than positively.
Source: Bank of Korea, Economics Statistic System, http://ecos.bok.or.kr/EIndex_en.jsp (accessed 1 March 2017).

3.11.8 Household debt to GDP

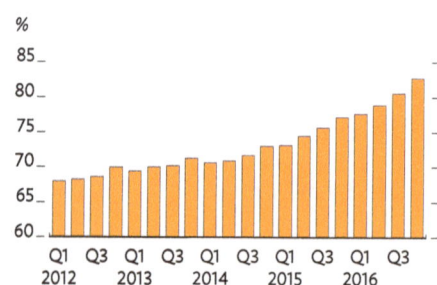

Q = quarter.
Source: Bank of Korea, Economics Statistic System, http://ecos.bok.or.kr/EIndex_en.jsp (accessed 1 March 2017).

stagflation (Figure 3.11.9). Third, persistent political uncertainty could undercut growth. A unanimous court verdict in March 2017 to remove the President could pave the way for political stability to return, but the resulting snap election could be highly contentious, delaying its return until a new government is formed. While policy paralysis is unlikely, an unsettled political situation would dent business and consumer confidence. Further, geopolitical risks arise with provocations from the Democratic People's Republic of Korea, which test fired ballistic missiles in February and March 2017.

An upside risk to the forecast is export recovery that is more robust than forecast, especially if growth gains momentum globally and in particular in the US. On the ROK domestic front, a smooth and orderly resolution of the political crisis would likely improve business and consumer confidence, strengthening domestic demand more than forecast. The balance of risks tilts to the downside with growth underperforming, but the government has ample fiscal resources to respond.

Policy challenge—coping with uncertainty in US trade policy

As the US is an important export market, taking 13.4% of ROK exports in 2016, a more restrictive trade policy there could have major adverse implications (Figure 3.11.10). The number of US trade measures recently targeting ROK exporters totaled 2,025 before the latest US election, so any hint of further US policy change heightens concerns for the ROK economy (Figure 3.11.11).

The most immediate and direct impact of US policy change would be felt through lower exports to the US. However, ROK firms may be hurt indirectly by new US policy change against other countries. Most crucially, trade friction between the US and the PRC would crimp ROK exports to the latter, which are mostly intermediate goods used in products that the PRC assembles and exports to the US. Further, the impending renegotiation of North American Free Trade Area agreement with Canada and Mexico could restrict or increase the cost of access to the US markets for goods originating in Mexico, causing losses for ROK firms that invested in Mexico for its easy access to the US market. These investments grew to $5.5 billion annually in 2015.

The persistent ROK trade surplus with the US, which has exceeded $20 billion every year since 2013, could place the KORUS Free Trade Agreement (FTA), concluded between the US and the ROK in 2012, among those targeted for renegotiation. The FTA eliminated 95% of the tariffs between the two markets and created additional protections for financial and other service firms. The KORUS FTA is the largest FTA the US has in Asia and one of the two largest for the ROK, the other being with the European Union. Given substantial opposition to the FTA before it was agreed—not only from US firms but also on the ROK side, notably from farmers—renegotiation could spell the end of it.

A preliminary empirical analysis found that annual ROK exports to the US would fall by as much as $13 billion in 2017–2020, at the cost

3.11.9 GDP gap and consumer inflation

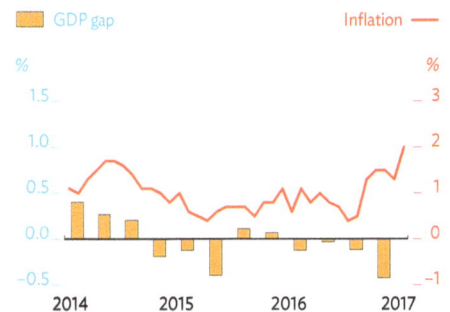

Source: Hyundai Research Institute.

3.11.10 Exports to and trade surplus with the United States

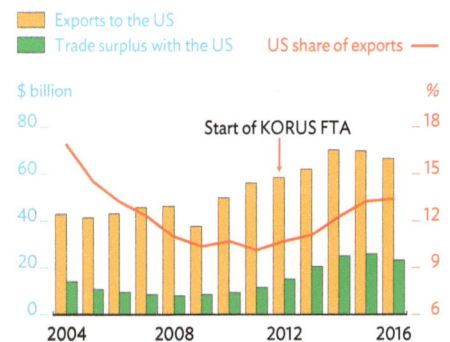

KORUS FTA = free trade agreement between the Republic of Korea and the United States.
Source: CEIC Data Company (accessed 14 February 2017).

3.11.11 US trade measures affecting ROK exports

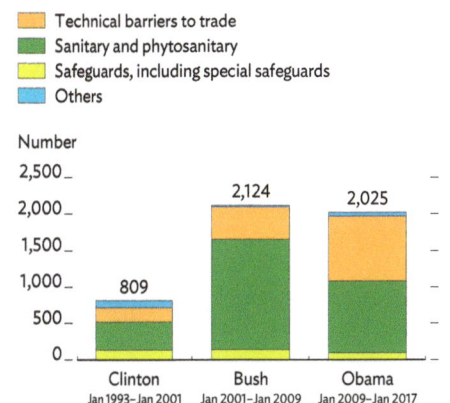

Note: Others include antidumping, countervailing measures, export subsidies, quantitative restrictions, and tariff quotas.
Source: World Trade Organization, Integrated Trade Intelligence Portal. https://www.wto.org/english/res_e/statis_e/itip_e.htm (accessed 9 March 2017).

of 127,000 jobs in the ROK, if the KORUS FTA collapsed (Table 3.11.2). The average yearly export loss of $3.3 billion equals 5% of ROK exports to the US in 2016. Further, a 10% drop in the PRC exports to the US would cause a 1.5% drop in ROK exports to the PRC. The combined impact of restrictive policies targeting the ROK and the PRC would lower ROK export proceeds by $5.2 billion, or 1% of the total in 2016.

Effectively meeting the potential challenge of US policy uncertainty requires three sets of policies. First, government and industry can take preventive action together to reduce trade friction and prepare for any policy change that nevertheless materializes. To this end, the government announced in late January plans to expand imports from the US. However, industries that are likely to be hit hard by annulment of the KORUS FTA, such as autos, electronics, and machinery, should prepare strategic contingency plans to comply with possible new trade regulations and develop new export markets.

Second, policy makers should closely monitor domestic financial market instability associated with mounting uncertainty regarding US trade and other economic policies. In light of the highly open capital account in the ROK, potentially volatile foreign capital flows are of particular interest. The ROK has adequate buffers to mitigate the impact of large capital outflows, but the authorities must be prepared to act promptly to dispel any concerns about the balance of payments.

Third, ROK policy makers can actively explore ways to extend the two countries' robust security alliance into the economic arena. An effective approach to defusing trade frictions would be to negotiate a broad economic partnership that brings together the government, industry, and other stakeholders in both countries. This task would be enormously complicated, but achieving such a partnership would be well worth the effort.

3.11.2 Projected export and employment losses with KORUS FTA annulment

	Decline in exports to the US ($ billion)	Decline in employment (1,000)
2017	3.09	30
2018	3.20	31
2019	3.31	32
2020	3.42	33
Total	13.01	127
Average	3.25	32

KORUS FTA = free trade agreement between the Republic of Korea and the United States.

Note: The projections are based on empirical analysis that assumes that United States tariffs on goods from the Republic of Korea revert to levels before the KORUS FTA.

Source: Hyundai Research Institute.

Mongolia

Growth will accelerate this year on large mining investments, then moderate in 2018 as coal production reaches full capacity. Inflation will rise in both years, and the current account will remain in deficit on the surge of imports for mining works. Cooperation with the international community is key to addressing financing gaps and preserving economic and social stability. Strengthening the management of natural resources revenue remains a major challenge.

Economic performance

The economy slowed to 1.0% growth in 2016 from 2.4% in 2015 with a sharp fall in construction and declining household consumption. GDP growth fell by 6.2% in the third quarter, but the economy recovered in the fourth quarter as an unexpected hike in coal prices prompted a steep increase in coal production. This lifted growth in transportation and storage services, raising the service sector contribution to growth to 0.8 percentage points (Figure 3.12.1). Agriculture added 0.6 percentage points as livestock herds grew despite a harsh winter. However, continued decline in construction by 15.9%—the result of oversupply caused by lending subsidized by the Bank of Mongolia, the central bank—dragged down industrial output, subtracting 0.4 percentage points from GDP growth.

External demand was the driver of growth in 2016. Exports rose by 14.7% as coal and gold exports surged (Figure 3.12.2). With imports rising more slowly, net exports grew, adding 1.3 percentage points to GDP growth (Figure 3.12.3). Meanwhile, domestic demand dragged on growth. Consumption contracted by 5.5%, subtracting 3.9 percentage points from growth, as household spending slumped because of lower agricultural incomes as meat prices fell, and because of lower wages and salaries with downsizing in construction and transport, which together provide 10.6% of employment. Meanwhile, gross capital formation reversed the falling trend of the previous 2 years to increase by 14.3% as restocking of inventories surged, adding 3.6 percentage points to growth.

Average consumer price inflation fell to 1.1% in 2016 as meat prices dropped by 8.2% on higher supply resulting from the accelerated culling of cattle. The Mongolian togrog depreciated by 24.8% against US the dollar, mostly in the second half of 2016, but the pass-through to prices started to emerge only this year, with inflation rising by 2.1% year on year in February (Figure 3.12.4).

Fiscal policy remained expansionary. Budgetary expenditure rose by 33.4% to equal 39.9% of GDP as capital expenditure surged before the

3.12.1 Supply-side contributions to growth

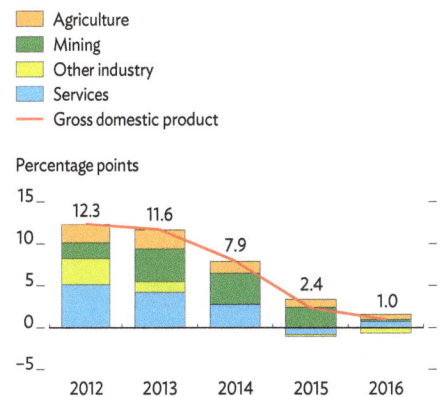

- Agriculture
- Mining
- Other industry
- Services
- Gross domestic product

Percentage points

Source: National Statistics Office of Mongolia. 2017. Monthly Statistical Bulletin. January. http://www.nso.mn

3.12.2 Components of merchandise exports

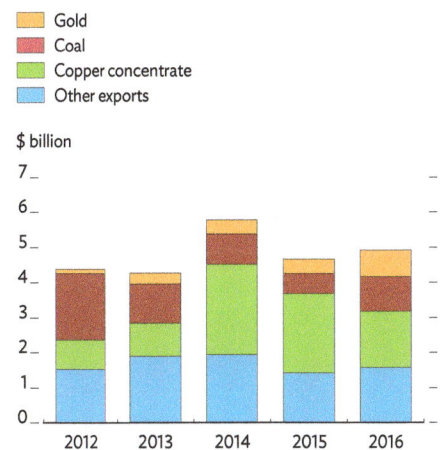

- Gold
- Coal
- Copper concentrate
- Other exports

$ billion

Sources: National Statistics Office of Mongolia. 2017. Monthly Statistical Bulletin. January. http://www.nso.mn; Bank of Mongolia.

This chapter was written by Akiko Terada-Hagiwara of the East Asia Department, ADB, Manila, and Amar Lkhagvasuren of the Mongolia Resident Mission, ADB, Ulaanbaatar.

election in June and large off-budget spending was consolidated into the budget by the newly elected government. Revenue meanwhile slid by 2.2% on lower income tax receipts to equal 24.5% of GDP. The fiscal deficit widened to 15.4% of GDP. However, including off-budget government expenditure financed by loans from the Development Bank of Mongolia, the deficit soared to 17.7% of GDP. Interest payments on government bonds accounted for more than 10% of total expenditure in 2016, a jump from 1% in 2010. Total public debt including the central bank's foreign liabilities reached the equivalent of 111% of GDP (Figure 3.12.5). As debt rose, the Fiscal Stability Law was amended again in 2016 to lift the government debt ceiling from 55% of GDP to 88%, with the requirement that it should be gradually lowered to 60% by 2021.

The togrog depreciated sharply in the face of balance-of-payment pressures, prompting the central bank to terminate all off-budget activities except for the subsidized mortgage program and to raise the policy rate by 450 basis points to 15% in August (since then reduced to 14%). Nevertheless, net domestic credit increased by 15.0% in 2016. In addition, through its practice of purchasing gold from the local mining companies, the central bank added to domestic liquidity. Broad money (M2) rose by 10.4% in the year.

Rapid credit growth without strict bank supervision or adequate reserve provisioning has eroded the quality of bank assets, undermining their soundness. The nonperforming loan rate has doubled since 2014, reaching 7% of all loans outstanding at the end of 2016 (Figure 3.12.6).

The current account deficit narrowed to 4.0% of GDP by the end of the year as the merchandise trade balance improved. Foreign borrowing at high cost staved off the risk of a crisis in the balance of payments, but it added to the problem of long-term debt sustainability. The current account deficit has been financed increasingly by external borrowing owing to capital flight and plummeting foreign direct investment. Thus, net foreign assets declined by 19.5% to a liability of $3.2 billion. However, gross international reserves remained unchanged at $1.3 billion at the end of 2016, supported by external borrowing.

Economic prospects

The outlook is for improvement enabled by higher commodity prices, the successful refinancing of a $580 million bond in March 2017, and the expected approval of an economic adjustment program supported by the International Monetary Fund (IMF) and the international community at large. Continued efforts by the new government to preserve economic and social stability remain key. Growth is forecast to accelerate to 2.5% this year but moderate slightly to 2.0% in 2018 on the base effect of the surge in coal production in 2017 (Figure 3.12.7). The forecast assumes that investment in the second phase of the Oyu Tolgoi mine will rise from $200 million last year to $1.0 billion in 2017 and $1.2 billion in 2018. However, large household debt and income contraction will depress household consumption, and fiscal consolidation will drastically reduce public capital expenditure and some transfers. Net exports will add to growth in 2017 as strong momentum in coal exports continues

3.12.3 Demand-side contributions to growth

- Private consumption
- Government consumption
- Total investments
- Net exports
- Gross domestic product

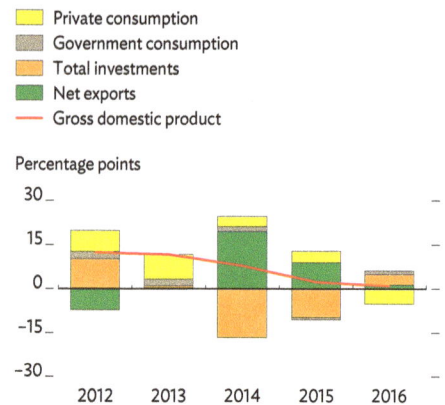

Source: National Statistics Office of Mongolia. 2017. Monthly Statistical Bulletin. January. http://www.nso.mn

3.12.4 Inflation and exchange rate

— Change in MNT/$ Inflation —

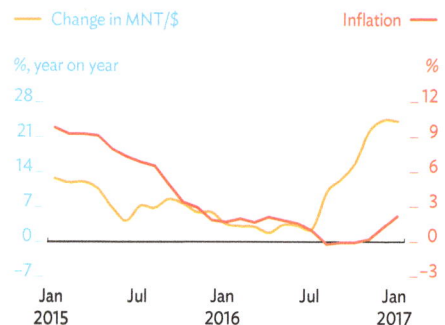

Source: Bank of Mongolia. 2017. Monthly Statistical Bulletin. http://www.mongolbank.mn

3.12.5 Public debt

- Domestic debt
- External debt
- Interest payments —

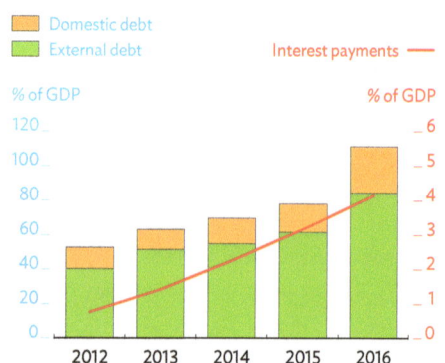

Source: Ministry of Finance. http://www.mof.gov.mn; Bank of Mongolia. http://www.mongolbank.mn

before subtracting from it in 2018 as coal exports level off and imports rise on capital-intensive investment in Oyu Tolgoi.

On the supply side, agriculture and services are expected to support growth modestly during the forecast period. Steady growth in livestock will be the major driver of growth in agriculture, while services will benefit from higher demand for transport and storage from rising coal exports and imports for Oyu Tolgoi. Construction will likely remain flat as the increase in mining-related construction offsets an expected reduction in subsidized mortgage lending, following the reformulation of the program by the new government. As coal production reaches full capacity in 2017, growth in 2018 will be driven by steady expansion in agriculture and services, as well as a pickup in construction.

Average inflation will rise to 3.5% in 2017 and 3.9% in 2018 as prices for imported goods increase when converted into a weaker currency (Figure 3.12.8). Fuel prices will edge higher as excise taxes are raised, but meat prices are expected to remain stable on the combined effect of improved supply and the depletion of government reserves.

Fiscal policy will be less expansionary during the forecast period. The budget under the proposed revision targets a deficit equal to 8.8% of GDP in 2017. Monetary policy will also be less expansionary this year and the next. Money supply growth must halve in 2017 from 2016 to remain consistent with macroeconomic objectives agreed under the IMF program.

The current account deficit will narrow to 2.1% of GDP in 2017 on strong coal exports but widen again to 6.3% in 2018 as imports continue to expand while exports stabilize. The expected larger inflows evidenced from a pickup in foreign direct investment at the end of 2016 will ease pressure on the balance of payments.

Downside risks to the outlook derive from uncertainty regarding macroeconomic management. Borrowing options will narrow, and costs will rise, if debt obligations are not met, or in the absence of a firm commitment to policy reform or agreement on the IMF program, or if there is slippage in program implementation. Any of these risks would necessitate additional fiscal retrenchment and weaken growth. The proliferation of nonperforming loans presents another risk to the outlook as it can threaten financial stability. There is also a risk that the Oyu Tolgoi investments may be delayed, undercutting economic activity.

Policy challenge—enhancing the management of natural resources revenue

Mongolia's abundant natural resources include 10% of known coal reserves globally and the world's fourth-largest copper reserves. They are expected to last at least 100 years, but their eventual depletion raises intergenerational equity issues. At the same time, the economy is subject to the boom-and-bust cycles that commonly affect commodity-dependent economies. Designing appropriate policies and institutions that respond to these constraints is a major challenge for the government.

3.12.6 Banking indicators

Note: Loan growth excludes government.
Source: Bank of Mongolia. 2017. *Monthly Statistical Bulletin.* http://www.mongolbank.mn

3.12.7 GDP growth

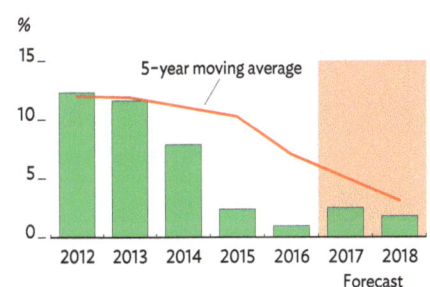

Source: Asian Development Outlook database.

3.12.1 Selected economic indicators (%)

	2017	2018
GDP growth	2.5	2.0
Inflation	3.5	3.9
Current account balance (share of GDP)	−2.1	−6.3

Source: ADB estimates.

Most resource-rich countries establish sovereign wealth funds, but Mongolia's two earlier attempts to do so did not succeed for lack of resources commensurate with mandated obligations and because of pro-cyclical fiscal policies. Indeed, revenue management has not brought wealth accumulation but rather rising public debt. In a new effort, the government established the Fiscal Stability Fund in 2010 to manage commodity boom-and-bust cycles and the Future Heritage Fund in 2017 to set aside funds for future generations.

For this new effort to succeed, the extractive sector must yield more fiscal revenues. These revenues, which include mainly royalty payments and exploration and permit fees, have averaged over the past 5 years less than 3% of GDP or 10% of revenue (Figure 3.12.9). By comparison, other resource-rich economies in the region such as Malaysia and Kazakhstan collect almost 10% of GDP. Receipts from taxes on mining company profits are likely to increase as commodity prices trend up during the forecast period. However, sizeable increases in mineral-related fiscal revenues require both changes in arrangements for the royalties, fees, and taxes, which may be politically difficult to adopt, and improved efficiency in tax collection and the elimination of tax avoidance. Further resources can be raised for the two funds by allocating to them a portion of fiscal revenues unconnected with mining, which are well above 25% of GDP in Mongolia, or more than double the usual percentage in countries with similar income.

It is crucial to avoid pro-cyclical fiscal policies. Studies show that commodity exporters are prone to pro-cyclical policies especially if booms are caused by high world commodity prices. The Fiscal Stability Law was expected to discourage pro-cyclical policies by limiting the budget's structural deficit to the equivalent of 2% of GDP. However, the rule has not been enforced, and off-budget spending has provided a way around it.

Future Heritage Fund resources including accumulated profit and interest should be considered a replacement for natural resources as they become depleted. They should be used in the meantime only in extreme emergencies. The current requirement that 10% of fund profits be automatically transferred to the budget creates a loophole for their depletion, as does the use of fund resources for social transfers. Both practices should be avoided. Regarding the Fiscal Stability Fund, clear rules are needed to govern its use to smooth expenditures over boom and bust years. Transfers to the budget should be allowed only if budgetary resources prove inadequate to meet nondiscretionary expenditure.

The overarching condition required for the successful management of these funds is a budgeting process with assured integrity. This requires, most crucially, that the annual budget include all government payment obligations and be prepared taking into account medium-term macroeconomic objectives. Further, Fiscal Stability Law ceilings must be respected and off-budget expenditure avoided.

3.12.8 Inflation

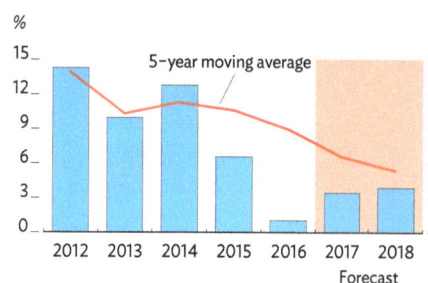

Source: Asian Development Outlook database.

3.12.9 Revenue by economic classification

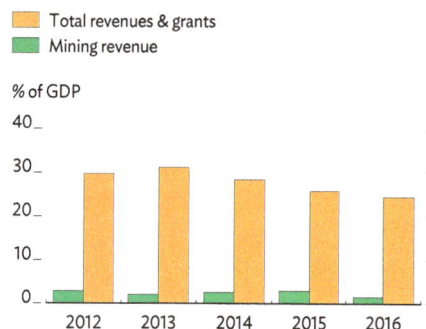

Note: Mining revenue includes receipts from taxes on profits, other taxes on large price increases for exported minerals, exploration and mining permit fees, and royalties.
Source: Ministry of Finance. http://www.mof.gov.mn

Taipei,China

Economic growth accelerated in 2016, inflation rose, and the current account surplus narrowed. Growth will likely accelerate further in 2017 and 2018 on higher government and private expenditure. Inflation will trend downward on lower food prices, and the current account surplus will narrow further on rising imports. A well-designed incentive scheme is needed to attract innovative enterprises with strong potential for job creation.

Economic performance

GDP growth doubled to 1.5% in 2016 as domestic spending grew (Figure 3.13.1). Private consumption remained the main driver of growth, rising by 2.1% mainly on higher fuel and car purchases to contribute 1.2 percentage points to GDP. Government consumption added another 0.4 percentage points to growth, as did total investment (Figure 3.13.2). Exports declined in the first half of the year owing to tepid external demand but rebounded in the second half to record 2.1% annual growth as semiconductor market conditions improved and international prices for agricultural and raw materials increased. However, as imports expanded more rapidly, net exports subtracted 0.7 percentage points from GDP growth.

On the supply side, industry and services drove growth. Rising manufacturing output propelled growth in industry to 1.9%, adding 0.7 percentage points to GDP growth. Semiconductor production rose significantly on higher demand for use in smart technology products and as technological advances in Taipei,China made its semiconductors more competitive. Services grew by 1.3% on rising tourist arrivals, adding 0.8 percentage points to growth. The year nevertheless saw growth in tourist arrivals slow by more than half from 2015, with a drop in visitors from the People's Republic of China (PRC) only partly compensated by higher arrivals from Japan, Southeast Asia, and the US (Figure 3.13.3). Agriculture contracted by 6.9% because of unfavorable weather, subtracting 0.1 percentage points from growth.

The consumer price index rose by 1.4% year on year in 2016, pushed up by food price inflation as agriculture stagnated (Figure 3.13.4). Core inflation, which excludes food and energy, rose to 0.6%, but wholesale price deflation persisted until late in the year. Responding to tame inflation and slow growth, the central bank cut the discount rate in two steps from 1.625% in February to 1.375% in July. The money supply (M2) grew by 3.6%, and credit to the private sector rose by 4.3%.

Despite anemic growth, fiscal policy was hardly expansionary, the budget deficit equal to 0.3% of GDP. Central government revenue grew

3.13.1 Demand-side contributions to GDP growth

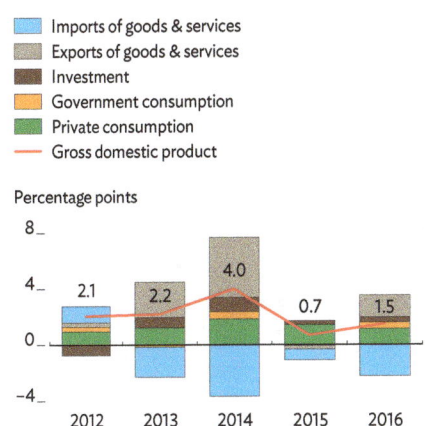

- Imports of goods & services
- Exports of goods & services
- Investment
- Government consumption
- Private consumption
- Gross domestic product

Percentage points

Source: Haver Analytics (accessed 16 March 2017).

3.13.2 Contributions to growth from gross fixed capital formation

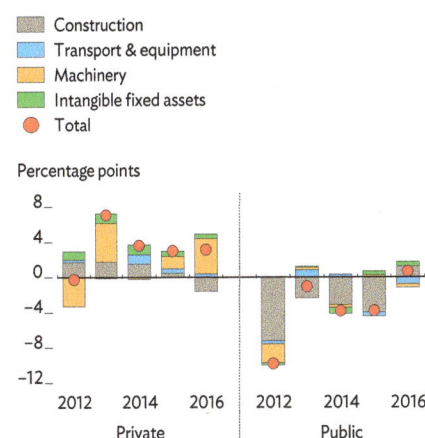

- Construction
- Transport & equipment
- Machinery
- Intangible fixed assets
- Total

Percentage points

Source: Haver Analytics (accessed 16 March 2017).

This chapter was written by Xuehui Han and Nedelyn Magtibay-Ramos of the Economic Research and Regional Cooperation Department, ADB, Manila.

by 0.8% as tax revenue exceeding the budgeted amount by 4.7% of total revenue, while expenditure rose by 2.8%. Since 2014, the government has pursued expenditure and revenue reform to raise tax revenue, reduce the ratio of the deficit to GDP, and ensure that debt does not grow faster than the average GDP growth rate over the previous 3 years. Reflecting these policies, the ratio of outstanding government debt to nominal GDP decreased from 34.1% in 2012 to 31.5% in 2016.

The current account surplus narrowed to 13.4% of GDP in 2016 from 14.3% in the previous year owing to slippage in the trade surplus and lower net service receipts (Figure 3.13.5). This, together with contraction in the capital and financial account, narrowed the overall balance of payments surplus. Gross reserves decreased by 29% to $10.7 billion. The local dollar depreciated by 1.3% against the US dollar but appreciated by 10.0% against the renminbi, partly because of capital repatriated from the PRC by investors in Taipei,China. In real effective terms, the local dollar appreciated by 1.8%.

Economic prospects

GDP growth is forecast to accelerate to 1.8% in 2017 and 2.2% in 2018 on major public infrastructure investments, robust private consumption, and rising private investment. The National Development Council is preparing what it calls a "forward-looking infrastructure investment program" with private sector participation. Even including planned spending under this multiyear NT$1 trillion program, the budget deficit will rise to only 0.8% of GDP in 2017. Government debt at a sound 31.5% of GDP leaves substantial finances for higher expenditure to further boost the economy.

The implementation of the government's proposed new industrial policy is expected to energize private investment. Under this policy, seven major innovative industries have been selected as the core group to lead growth through innovation and high technology. The programs for the defense and recycling industries have yet to be finalized, but those for the smart machinery industry and Asian Silicon Valley, which aspires to turn the island into an innovative startup destination for young Asians, have been prepared, as have the programs for green energy technology, the biotech industry, and industrial agriculture, which aims to boost value added to agricultural products and services. The plans include measures to create an enabling environment, especially through appropriate regulation, and to attract international talent.

Encouraged by the industrial policy initiative, private investment will remain robust in 2017 and 2018. The manufacturing purchasing managers' index for January 2017 signaled strong future expansion. Investment in the airline and semiconductor industries will be especially strong, the latter driven by the sharp increase in semiconductor exports. New investments in innovative financial technology are expected from major foreign banks. Private consumption expenditure should rise in 2017 and 2018, benefiting from optimism about government policies and ongoing consumer subsidy programs such as a car-purchase and trade-in program running at least until the end of 2017.

3.13.3 Tourist arrivals

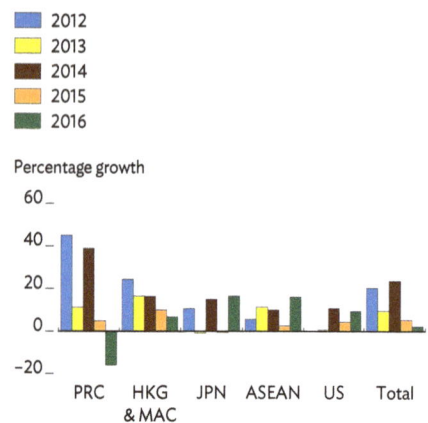

ASEAN = Association of Southeast Asian Nations, HKG = Hong Kong, China, JPN = Japan, MAC = Macau, China, PRC = People's Republic of China, US = United States.
Source: Haver Analytics (accessed 16 March 2017).

3.13.4 Inflation

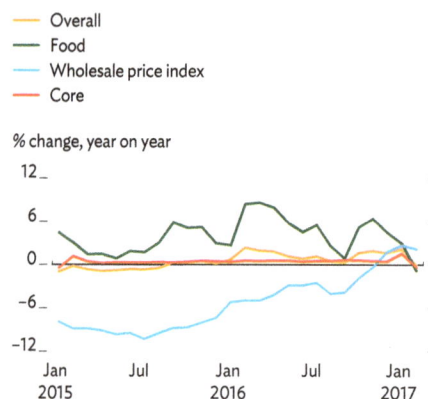

Source: CEIC Data Company (accessed 16 March 2017).

3.13.5 Current account indicators

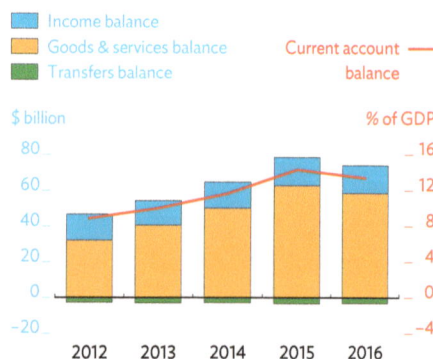

Source: Haver Analytics (accessed 16 March 2017).

Exports are expected to increase this year and next on strong demand for semiconductor components, especially for PRC branded mobile phones (Figure 3.13.6). Rising commodity prices and low base year effects are other factors. Ongoing substitution in the PRC of imports with high value added, replacing them with alternatives produced in the PRC, may moderate growth in Taipei,China exports in 2018.

Imports by export-oriented industries and the airline industry will show a corresponding increase in both years, while terms of trade are likely to deteriorate as prices for imports recover from sharp declines since 2015. The trade surplus is thus likely to trend downward, and net exports to make only a small contribution to GDP growth in both years. The current account surplus will likely shrink because exports of services are not expected to compensate for the lower surplus in goods trade.

Inflation is forecast to trend slightly lower to 1.3% in 2017 and 1.2% in 2018. Food price pressures caused by bad weather and the low base effect for the oil price will diminish, tamping down the impact of rising domestic spending supported by mildly expansionary fiscal policy and low interest rates. The local dollar is expected to remain stable against the US dollar but appreciate slightly against the renminbi during the forecast period.

External risks to the outlook are a surprisingly steep slowdown in the PRC, trade tensions caused by rising protectionism, and strong local dollar appreciation, particularly against the renminbi. To mitigate the risk of protectionism, Taipei,China intends to diversify its economic ties. The government has announced its New Southbound Policy, aiming to foster with neighboring economies closer economic and trade relations, scientific and technological cooperation, and the sharing of resources, talent, and markets. The main domestic risk to the forecast is the possible effect on consumption if forthcoming pension reform generates short-term uncertainty about benefits. The reform program, to be presented to the legislature in May 2017, aims to unify 13 pension schemes into a single plan that introduces portable accounts to improve job mobility.

Policy challenge—encouraging innovative entrepreneurship

Relatively low GDP growth rates, at 0.7% in 2015 and 1.5% last year, indicate that Taipei,China needs to raise productivity to boost growth. This is what the government's new industrial policy intends to do. The policy aligns with the findings of several studies indicating that productivity can be improved by encouraging innovative entrepreneurs (*Transcending the Middle-Income Challenge* on page 47). The entry of new enterprises encourages innovation through so-called "creative destruction." New firms have been found to engage in radical innovation to boost growth in total factor productivity. Further, older firms, especially in high-technology industries, innovate more intensively when facing competition from new firms.

3.13.1 Selected economic indicators (%)

	2017	2018
GDP growth	1.8	2.2
Inflation	1.3	1.2
Current account balance (share of GDP)	6.8	6.5

Source: ADB estimates.

3.13.6 Export orders

- — Overall
- — United States
- — PRC & Hong Kong, China
- — Japan
- — Europe
- — ASEAN-6

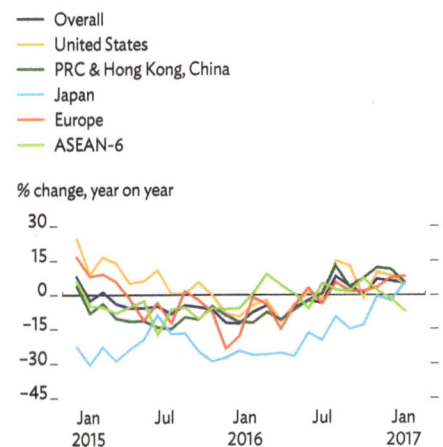

% change, year on year

ASEAN-6 = Association of Southeast Asian Nations members Indonesia, Malaysia, the Philippines, Singapore, Thailand, and Viet Nam, PRC = People's Republic of China.

Source: CEIC Data Company (accessed 16 March 2017).

Research has documented that high-income economies experience more innovative entrepreneurship than do lower-income economies. That is, high-income economies such as Taipei,China tend to have a higher ratio of opportunity-driven entrepreneurs who believe their products or services are new to the market. However, the same relationship does not necessarily exist when income differentials are replaced by growth rates. Some evidence to this effect is provided by the Global Entrepreneurship Monitor dataset, a global survey of adults aged 18–64. This dataset does not show significant correlation between the proportion of the cohort population who are entrepreneurs or owners of new businesses and the growth rate. However, it does find positive correlation between the proportion of entrepreneurs who expect to create six or more jobs within 5 years and the growth rate. Thus, in analyzing innovative entrepreneurship, entrepreneurs should not be treated as a homogeneous group but differentiated according to their motivations or expectations regarding job creation.

These data are presented in Figure 3.13.7. The plot groups middle-income and high-income economies into low-growth and high-growth categories. The four groups are plotted against the percentage of entrepreneurs who expect to create six or more jobs in 5 years, or job creator share (JCS). Each box-and-whiskers plot indicates the range of JCS in each category of economy. The plot shows that high-income economies tend to have a higher JCS and that, in the high-income group, the high-growth group has a higher JCS than the low-growth group. Also, there is a much narrower job-creation gap between high- and low-growth economies in the middle-income group than between the high- and low-growth economies in the high-income group, implying a lower correlation between JCS and growth rates in middle-income economies.

While this correlation analysis does not indicate the direction of causality—that is, whether higher income or higher growth leads to a higher JCS, or the other way around—these results provide some indication that nurturing new firms that have concrete plans for creating jobs is a promising means of improving productivity. Thus, in implementing its new industrial policy, Taipei,China should give priority to providing incentives for those start-ups that have concrete and realistic plans to create jobs.

3.13.7 Growth and entrepreneurs' job creation expectations

Percentage of entrepreneurs who expect to create 6 or more jobs in 5 years

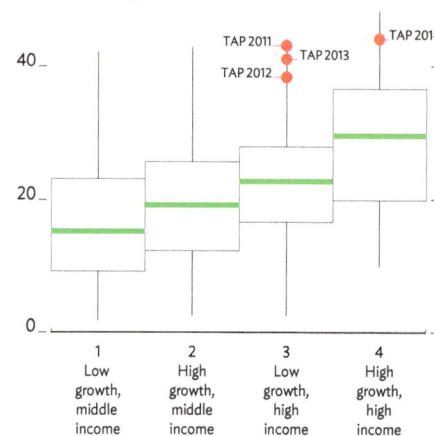

TAP = Taipei,China.

Note: Vertical lines show in each category the whole range of job creator share, the percentage of entrepreneurs who expect to create 6 or more jobs in 5 years, omitting the outliers. The boxes on each line corral the middle half, with the green line indicating the median value of the whole range, the bottom border of the box indicating the first quartile (the median of the bottom half, with 25% of the whole sample below and 75% above), and the top border indicating the third quartile. The sample data include 69 countries for box 1, 23 for box 2, 116 for box 3, and 39 for box 4.

Sources: Global Entrepreneurship Monitor dataset; ADB estimates.

SOUTH ASIA

AFGHANISTAN
BANGLADESH
BHUTAN
INDIA
MALDIVES
NEPAL
PAKISTAN
SRI LANKA

Afghanistan

Growth rose to 2% in 2016 on recovery in agriculture as industry and services slowed. Daunting challenges weigh on public confidence: an increasingly aggressive insurgency, a fragile political environment, and weak institutions. The year saw progress in strengthening public finances, and development partners reaffirmed their financial support. The outlook is for modest growth improvement even as an expected surge of refugees brings new difficulties.

Economic performance

A challenging political and security environment continued to affect economic activity in 2016. Growth is estimated to have accelerated from 0.8% in 2015 to 2.0% in 2016 (Figure 3.14.1). After falling by 5.7% in 2015, agriculture recovered and contributed to the revival in GDP growth. Growth in industry and services slowed because of pessimism across investors, the business community, and the general public. On the demand side, there was no improvement in private investment in 2016. Public investment grew slightly as the government struggled to improve its execution of a larger development budget. Weak investor and consumer confidence reflects an increasingly difficult security situation and protracted uncertainty in the political environment. Other major constraints retarding investment and business development are an inadequate business regulatory framework, lack of basic infrastructure, and limited access to financial services and utilities.

According to a survey conducted by the United Nations Office on Drugs and Crime, the area under opium cultivation increased by 10% in 2016. Most cultivation took place in the southeast and west as opium production rose to 4,800 tons in 2016, up by 45.5% from 3,300 tons in 2015. Opium prices also rose and, with higher production, increased the farm value of production in 2016 by 58% to $900 million, equal to 5% of GDP, from $570 million in 2015.

Inflation increased sharply from January to December 2016, mainly reflecting some recovery in global commodity prices. Headline consumer inflation increased in December 2016 to 4.5% year on year from 1.1% in December 2015 (Figure 3.14.2). Food prices increased by 5.8% in 2016, accelerating from 0.8% in 2015 on higher prices for meat, spices, vegetables, sugar, and sweets. Nonfood inflation rose to 3.4% from 1.4% in 2015, primarily on higher prices for tobacco, clothing, household goods and furnishings, education, and health services. Average inflation was 4.5%, reversing 1.5% deflation in 2015, when global prices for oil and other commodities plunged.

3.14.1 GDP growth by sector

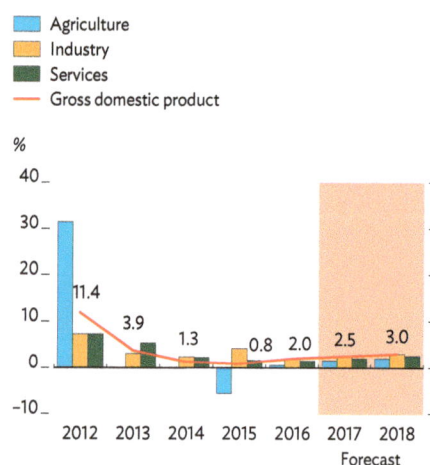

Note: Years are fiscal years ending on 21 December of the same calendar year.
Source: Asian Development Outlook database.

3.14.2 Inflation

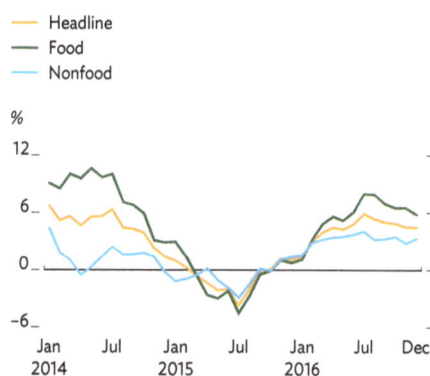

Sources: Central Statistical Office for primary data; ADB estimates for headline, food, and nonfood inflation.

This chapter was written by Rehman Gul of the Afghanistan Resident Mission, ADB, Kabul.

Revenue collection was a success story in 2016. Domestic collection grew by 24% to AF151.7 billion, 15% above the target agreed with the International Monetary Fund under its extended credit facility (Figure 3.14.3). Development budget execution remained weak, however, as only 55% of the 2016 appropriation was spent, unchanged from that in 2015. Expenditure nevertheless increased in 2016 by AF10.1 billion to AF93.0 billion. The overall budget showed a modest surplus equal to 1.6% of GDP as official grants funded 63% of expenditure, up from 56% in 2015.

Broad money (M2) expanded by 7.5% in 2016, and reserve money by 10.0%. The expansions reflected an increase in net foreign assets acquired through a strong current account surplus. Monetary policy was accommodative and credit to the private sector increased by 10% despite the weak economy and a prevailing lack of confidence.

The current account including current transfers is estimated to have sustained a surplus equal to 4.4% of GDP as high official transfers continued to generate sales of goods and services (Figure 3.14.4). Gross international reserves increased to $7.5 billion from $7.0 billion in 2015 (Figure 3.14.5). The afghani was broadly stable against the US dollar in 2016, appreciating by about 1% during the year following a 17% fall in 2015, when gross reserves fell by $300 million on strong demand for foreign currency from people wishing to emigrate (Figure 3.14.6).

Economic prospects

The economy is projected to grow by 2.5% in 2017 and 3.0% in 2018. The growth projections are based on favorable weather, a modest recovery for industry and services, continued improvement in domestic revenue collection and support from development partners, structural reform under the International Monetary Fund extended credit facility, and other reforms to improve governance and public administration and fight corruption. Poverty will persist, however, because of low labor demand, the many people internally displaced by insurgent activity, and a rapidly growing number of returning refugees—mainly from Pakistan but also Iran and, to a much lesser extent, those who sought to emigrate to Europe. Because refugee numbers are projected to increase significantly in 2017, the United Nations has appealed for $240 million in humanitarian assistance to help them.

To restore investor confidence, business regulation must be improved, especially for extractive industries. While growth in agriculture is expected to be slight because of capacity limits, growth in industry and services is projected to strengthen steadily. Afghanistan's accession to the World Trade Organization in July 2016 and the implementation of national and regional infrastructure projects such as Salma Dam in Herat Province and Chabahar Port in Iran are expected to contribute to growth and expand trade through better connectivity.

Fiscal policy will continue to pursue improved revenue collection and budget execution to improve development expenditure. Budget expenditure is projected to increase with high security spending and larger expenditure to deliver public services to an enlarging population. Government finances including grants will likely remain balanced

3.14.3 Fiscal indicators

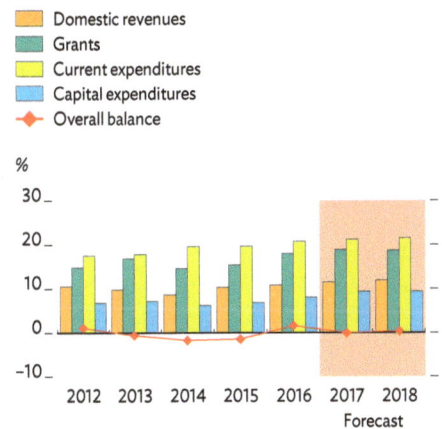

Note: Years are fiscal years ending on 21 December of the same calendar year.
Sources: International Monetary Fund Country Reports; ADB estimates.

3.14.4 Current account balance

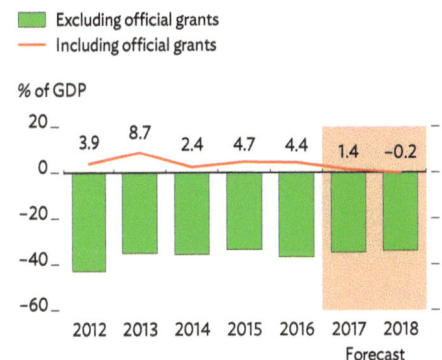

Note: Years are fiscal years ending on 21 December of the same calendar year.
Sources: International Monetary Fund Country Report No. 14/128, May 2014 for 2012; International Monetary Fund Country Report No. 15/234, November 2015 for 2013–2015; World Bank for 2016–2018.

3.14.1 Selected economic indicators (%)

	2017	2018
GDP growth	2.5	3.0
Inflation	5.5	5.8
Current account balance (share of GDP)	1.4	−0.2

Source: ADB estimates.

in the next 2 years as development partners continue to fund 62% of both recurrent and development expenditures. The ratio of domestic revenue to recurrent spending, an indicator of fiscal sustainability, is projected to slow slightly to 55.0% by 2018 from 58.3% in 2016. However, fiscal outcomes in the medium-term will depend on inflows from development partners.

Headline inflation is forecast at 5.5% in 2017 and 5.8% in 2018 as global commodity prices rise gradually and demand increases with returning refugees. The forecast assumes prudent monetary and exchange rate policies and favorable harvests. The government will maintain its managed float of the afghani to keep prices reasonable and prevent undue afghani volatility as the uncertain political and security situation exerts downward pressure on the currency.

The current account surplus including transfers is projected to shrink to the equivalent of 1.4% of GDP in 2017 and swing to a deficit of 0.2% in 2018. This reflects some reduction in current transfers that will reduce domestic demand and opportunities for employment, as well as business sales of goods and services.

Policy challenge—better execution of the development budget

Afghanistan has struggled to execute its development budget since development partners returned after the fall of the Taliban in 2001. The development budget covers spending on physical, economic, and social infrastructure. Infrastructure and natural resources occupy 55% of the development budget, followed by agriculture and rural development with a 16% share in 2016. Budget execution rates have varied from 30% to 60% in recent years and differed widely for various components. In 2016, health utilization was, at 73%, the highest accomplished rate among budget sector allocations larger than 2% (Figure 3.14.7). Infrastructure and natural resources recorded the lowest execution rate, at 44%, because poor utilization of development budget allocations has been a policy issue of long standing.

Development expenditure for infrastructure and natural resources in particular feeds directly into economic growth, job creation, and poverty reduction. Hence, improving the rate of development spending is critical. More rapid development of infrastructure would enable greater private investment, support growth, and boost employment.

The economic impact of increased capital expenditure would be high. The approved development budget was $2.6 billion in FY2016, equal to 14.2% of GDP, but the 54% execution rate diminished spending to $1.4 billion, or 7.1% of GDP. An execution rate approaching 100% would certainly accelerate growth and bring forward project assistance pledged by development partners to speed development.

Besides insecurity, the key impediment to better development expenditure execution is low capacity—in project identification and design, project costing, financial planning, procurement planning and contracting, and managing the implementation of large projects and their complex procurement contracts.

3.14.5 International reserves

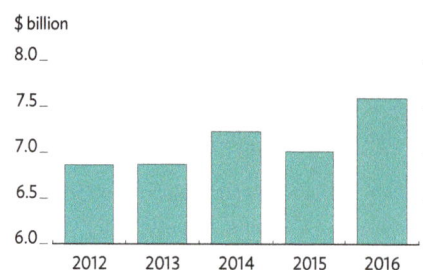

Sources: Da Afghanistan Bank. http://www.centralbank .gov.af/ (accessed 20 March 2017); ADB estimates.

3.14.6 Nominal exchange rate

Sources: Da Afghanistan Bank. http://www.centralbank. gov.af/ (accessed 20 March 2017); ADB estimates.

Other hurdles include failure of responsibility, accountability, and delegation of authority; a long procurement review and approval process; bureaucratic rigidity involving lengthy administrative processes; problems with finance controllers in line ministries; weak governance and corruption; development partner earmarking of project financing; a lack of appropriate decision-making powers; the inclusion of poorly designed projects in the national budget; and unrealistic spending plans for multiyear development projects, which means large unspent allotments carried over into subsequent fiscal years. These issues are not limited to implementing agencies. Technical barriers exist within the Ministry of Finance, and more efficient coordination with development partners in some instances could improve execution rates.

The past decade has seen noteworthy reform in budget management but not of substance with respect to development projects in implementing agencies. In consultation with development partners, the government needs to shift resources from low-priority, poorly performing projects to higher-priority projects that perform well. Slow economic growth desperately demands higher development expenditure achieved through comprehensive reform, with more attention paid to precise costing, project planning, procurement, and contract management for multiyear projects.

The government is developing policy actions to improve development budget execution.

A database for development projects will be established by the Ministry of Finance, which will cover large projects to track information on total project cost, yearly costing and funding, sources of funds, incurred expenditures, and implementation status with milestones. It will help monitor development budget performance and inform a medium-term financial framework designed to facilitate forward-looking budgets that ensure appropriate future allocations for multiyear projects and help identify financial resources available for new projects. Database estimates will facilitate recurrent budget allocations for the operation and maintenance of the new capital assets built.

The Ministry of Finance will not include any projects in the national budget unless it is fully prepared and ready for implementation. Administrative processes will be streamlined. Capacity in implementing ministries will be strengthened, and development partners will be consulted on how to make funding more flexible. Consultation with provincial authorities will seek to improve development budget execution. Finally, the Ministry of Finance will endeavor to work more closely with the seven ministries responsible for 80% of development projects.

3.14.7 Development budget execution by sector, 2016

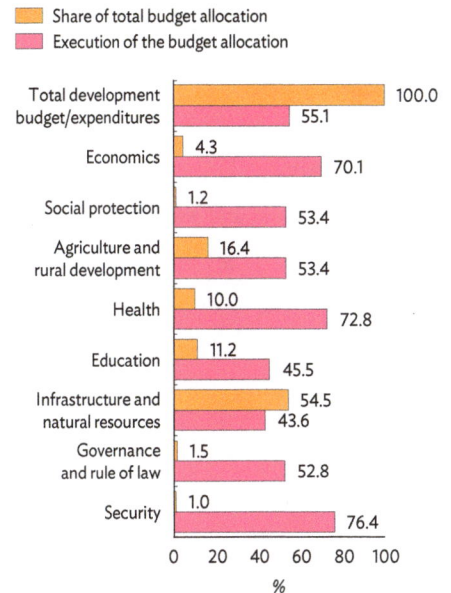

Note: Year is fiscal year ending on 21 December of the same calendar year.
Source: Budget Execution Report, Ministry of Finance.

Bangladesh

Despite global headwinds that crimped remittances, GDP recorded robust growth in FY2016 on higher private investment and exports. The current account surplus expanded, and inflation slowed. Continued high growth will require a rebound in remittances and higher exports. Productive jobs are needed in manufacturing and modern services for the large number of new entrants to the labor force and surplus farm labor and to boost female workforce participation.

Economic performance

Higher private investment, exports, and wages underpinned GDP growth acceleration to 7.1% in FY2016 (ended 30 June 2016) from 6.6% in the previous year (Figure 3.15.1). Other contributors to growth were continued political calm, improved power supply, and higher growth in credit to the private sector.

On the supply side, growth was driven by expansion in industry at 11.1%, up from 9.7% in FY2015, that mainly reflected a pickup in medium- and large-scale manufacturing aided by steady expansion in electricity generation, mining and quarrying, and construction. Supported by industry expansion, services growth accelerated to 6.2% from 5.8% in FY2015. Growth in agriculture slowed further, however, to 2.8% from 3.3% as input costs rose but farm prices remained depressed.

On the demand side, private investment was the main source of growth as public investment was constrained by low implementation capacity in line agencies. Total investment equaled 29.7% of GDP, up from 28.9%. At $2.0 billion, foreign direct investment was still less than 1% of GDP. A decline in remittance inflows curtailed consumer spending but was partly offset by higher wages in both the public and the private sector. Net exports contributed to growth with higher volumes of exports and lower imports, mainly reduced quantities of food grain and fertilizer.

Average annual inflation eased to 5.9% in FY2016 from 6.4% in the previous year, largely in response to lower global commodity prices, steady domestic supply, and a stable exchange rate between the Bangladesh taka and the US dollar that translated into taka appreciation against the currencies of most of Bangladesh's trade partners. Year-on-year inflation declined to 5.5% in June 2016 from 6.3% a year earlier (Figure 3.15.2). Food inflation slowed sharply to 4.2% from 6.3%, and nonfood inflation rose to 7.5% from 6.2%, stoked by increased prices for natural gas and electricity and higher wages.

Driven by accelerating growth in private credit, expansion in the money supply rose to 16.3% in FY2016, exceeding the target of 15.0% (Figure 3.15.3). Private investment and consumer lending pushed up private credit growth to 16.8%, exceeding the 14.8% target as political

3.15.1 Supply-side contributions to growth

- Agriculture
- Industry
- Services
- Gross domestic product

Percentage points

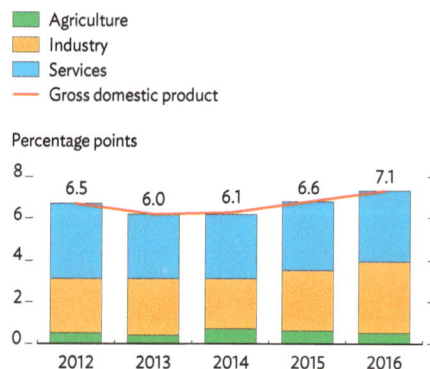

Note: Years are fiscal years ending on 30 June of that year.
Sources: Bangladesh Bureau of Statistics. http://www.bbs.gov.bd; ADB estimates.

3.15.2 Monthly inflation

- Food
- Nonfood
- Overall

% change, year on year

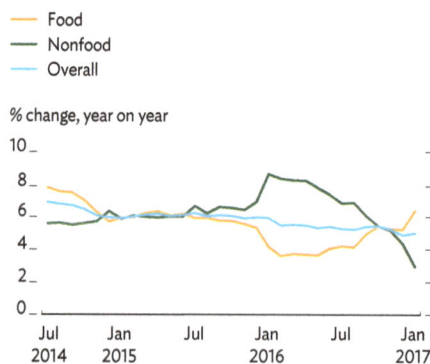

Source: Bangladesh Bank. 2017. Monthly Economic Trends. February. http://www.bb.org.bd

---

This chapter was written by Jyotsana Varma, Md. Golam Mortaza, and Barun K. Dey of the Bangladesh Resident Mission, ADB, Dhaka.

stability prevailed. While foreign financing of the fiscal deficit was lower than budgeted, growth in net bank credit to the government increased by only 3.6% in FY2016 and subsequently abated in the first months of FY2017. This trend mirrors the increased mobilization of nonbank financing in the past 2 years. Expansion in net foreign assets has stayed strong, accelerating to 23.2% in FY2016 from 18.2% a year earlier, mainly reflecting the larger surplus in the current account.

As inflation slowed, Bangladesh Bank, the central bank, lowered its repo and reverse repo rates by 50 basis points in January 2016 (Figure 3.15.4). Ample liquidity in the banking system, especially as central bank foreign exchange purchases were not fully sterilized, caused further interest rate declines. The weighted average yield on 91-day Treasury bills fell to 4.0% in June 2016 from 5.4% a year earlier. Banks' weighted average lending rate slipped to 10.3% from 11.7% in the same period. The deposit rate also declined, to 5.4% from 6.7%, narrowing banks' interest rate spread marginally by 0.1 percentage points to 4.9. The ratio of nonperforming loans (NPLs) to all bank loans rose to 10.1% at the end of June 2016 from 9.7% a year earlier. High NPLs remain a concern, especially with those at state-owned banks standing at 25.7%.

Tax collection by the National Board of Revenue grew by 14.6% in FY2016 but fell short of the ambitious budget target. Nontax revenues also missed the target, mainly because of lower contributions from Bangladesh Telecommunication Regulatory Commission profits and the Bangladesh Bank dividend. Spending was lower than budgeted as the implementation of the annual development program continued to underperform and because current spending on subsidies was lower than anticipated, as were interest payments. As a share of GDP, revenue rose to 9.9% from 9.6% a year earlier, while spending declined to 13.0% from 13.5%, curtailing the budget deficit to 3.1% of GDP (Figure 3.15.5). Domestic financing, mostly from nonbank sources, met 90% of the deficit.

Exports grew by 8.9% in FY2016, up from 3.1% a year earlier, spurred by a shift to garments with higher value added, and enabled by political stability. Garment exports, accounting for over 80% of exports, grew briskly at 10.2%, up from 4.1% in FY2015. Import payments rose by 5.5% in FY2016, nearly double the 3.0% growth in FY2015, on higher imports of petroleum products, yarn and other intermediate goods for the garment industry, capital machinery, and edible oil. Even with growth in overseas employment booming at 48.2%, remittances from workers abroad fell by 2.5% to $14.9 billion in FY2016. Lower global oil prices have forced budget consolidation in the Gulf economies that host most Bangladeshi migrant workers, undermining wages and job security. Weaker currencies, higher living costs, and new taxes further squeeze the earnings left for remittance.

The current account surplus nonetheless rose to $3.7 billion in FY2016, equal to 1.7% of GDP, from $2.9 billion in FY2015, aided by lower deficits in the trade, services, and primary income accounts (Figure 3.15.6). With net inflows in the capital and financial accounts little changed from a year earlier, the higher current account surplus pushed the overall balance of payments to a $5.0 billion surplus. Central bank gross foreign exchange reserves rose sharply to $30.2 billion at the end of June 2016, or cover for 7.9 months of imports,

3.15.3 Growth of monetary indicators

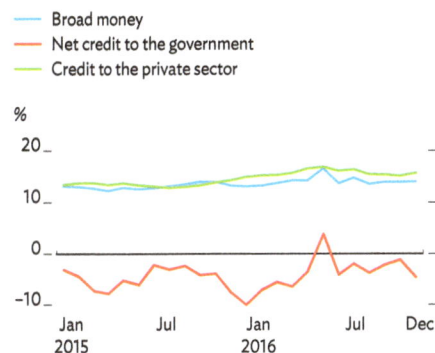

Source: Bangladesh Bank. 2017. *Major Economic Indicators: Monthly Update.* February. http://www.bb.org.bd

3.15.4 Interest rates

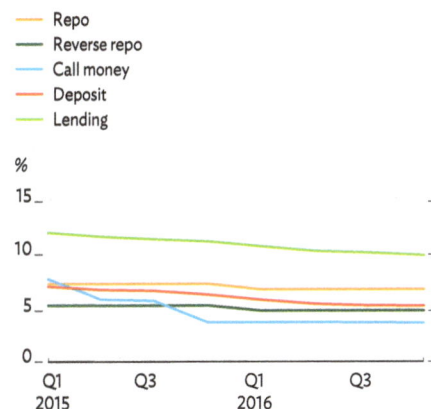

Source: Bangladesh Bank. 2017. *Major Economic Indicators: Monthly Update.* February. http://www.bb.org.bd

3.15.5 Fiscal indicators

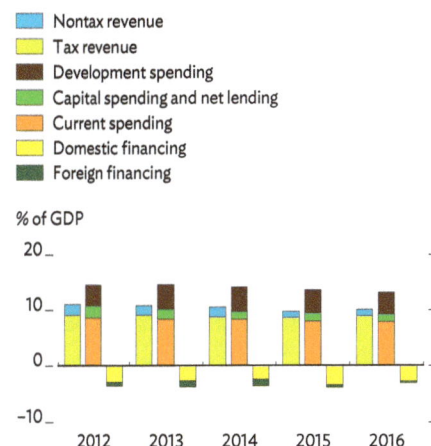

Note: Years are fiscal years ending on 30 June of that year.
Source: *Asian Development Outlook* database.

reflecting its large purchases of foreign exchange from commercial banks (Figure 3.15.7).

The higher current account surplus in FY2016 helped keep the taka broadly stable against the US dollar in nominal terms, depreciating by only 0.8% from a year earlier. Central bank exchange rate policy aims to build reserves and avoid excessive volatility in the nominal market rate, which protects garment firms whose contract pricing is denominated in foreign currencies. Bangladesh has nevertheless suffered some loss in export competitiveness, especially for minor exports, as US dollar strength against the currencies of Bangladesh's trade partners has, combined with the higher domestic inflation, brought trend appreciation in real effective exchange rate, up by 5.8% in FY2016 (Figure 3.15.8).

The Dhaka Stock Exchange broad price index stood at 4,507.6 in June 2016, registering a marginal decline of 1.6% from a year earlier (Figure 3.15.9). The market price–earnings ratio declined to 14.6 from 15.9 in the same period, while market capitalization fell by 1.9%, with only four new companies listed in FY2016. Prices then moved higher in the first half of FY2017 and appear to be broadly in line with the upward trends in other markets, both emerging and industrial.

Economic prospects

Forecasts for FY2017 and FY2018 rest on several assumptions: Political calm will continue and thus support consumer and investor confidence. The central bank will be generally mindful about keeping inflation in check while allowing ample private credit growth to support economic activity. Tax authorities will focus attention on administrative reform to boost collections and expand the tax base, and foreign financing will be available as expected for planned public investment. The government will further raise electricity and natural gas prices to cut subsidies and keep current spending in check. Finally, the weather will be normal.

GDP growth is expected to moderate to 6.9% in FY2017 as domestic demand rises more slowly and the slide in workers' remittances deepens (Figure 3.15.10). Slower export growth caused by weaker consumer demand in the euro area and the United Kingdom is expected in part because the currencies of these destination markets have depreciated against the dollar. Increases in wages and continued access to credit will help to sustain private consumption. Private investment will rise only slightly as investors turn cautious ahead of national elections in 2018. Public investment is expected to strengthen through fiscal expansion as the authorities speed up their implementation of infrastructure projects. Growth in FY2018 is expected to remain unchanged at 6.9% as the broad momentum in the previous year continues.

Agriculture is expected to slow further to 2.4% growth in FY2017 and 2.3% in FY2018, mainly because of limits on area expansion and productivity improvement. Industry growth is expected to decelerate to 10.6% in FY2017 in tandem with domestic demand. With reinvigorated domestic demand resulting from higher export income and a more moderate decline in remittances, industry growth will edge back up to 10.7% in FY2018. Services growth is expected to slow to 6.0% in FY2017, reflecting slower growth in agriculture and industry, and remain unchanged in FY2018.

3.15.6 Current account components

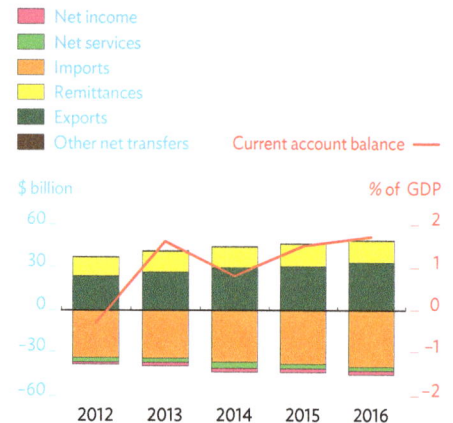

Note: Years are fiscal years ending on 30 June of that year.
Sources: Bangladesh Bank. 2017. *Annual Report 2015–2016*. https://www.bb.org.bd; ADB estimates.

3.15.1 Selected economic indicators (%)

	2017	2018
GDP growth	6.9	6.9
Inflation	6.1	6.3
Current account balance (share of GDP)	–1.0	–0.7

Note: Years are fiscal years ending on 30 June of that year.
Source: ADB estimates.

3.15.7 Gross foreign exchange reserves

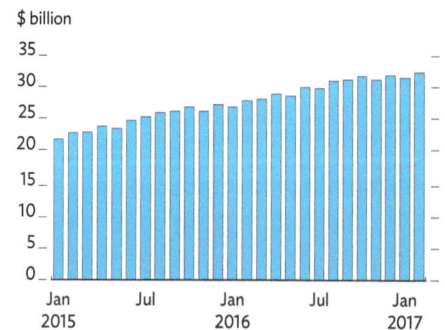

Source: Bangladesh Bank. http://www.bb.org.bd/econdata/intreserve.php

Inflation is projected to pick up in FY2017 to average 6.1% (Figure 3.15.11). It moderated from October to December 2016 as the arrival of winter vegetables and the *aman* rice crop lowered food prices. Nonfood inflation also slowed in this period, reflecting favorable international prices. Inflation is expected to rebound in the second half of FY2017, however, with likely higher global prices for oil and other commodities, upward adjustments to natural gas and electricity prices as the government continues to align prices with production costs, and the further implementation of salary hikes introduced in FY2016 for government staff and private educational institutions to adjust for inflation and improve living standards. Inflation is expected to edge up further to 6.3% in FY2018 as global fuel prices continue to rise and a new value-added tax comes into effect at the start of the year.

The monetary policy statement for the second half of FY2017 (January–June 2017) supports growth while mitigating inflation risks. The central bank kept policy rates unchanged at 6.75% for the repo rate and 4.75% for reverse repo because inflation expectations remain elevated, including for global commodity prices. It kept the July 2016 monetary policy statement growth targets to June 2017 at 15.5% for broad money and 16.5% for private credit. Considering current buoyancy in stock exchange prices, it tightened monitoring to ensure that banks abided by statutory limits on market exposure to avoid a repetition of the 2010 market run-up and collapse.

Exports grew by 4.4% in the first 7 months of FY2017, down from 8.3% in the year-earlier period. Growth in readymade garment exports was 4.1%, down from 9.1%. Export growth is expected to strengthen in the second half of FY2017 on higher projected growth in the industrial economies, but exports for the full year are expected to slow to 6.0% from 8.9% in FY2016 (Figure 3.15.12). Export growth in FY2018 is projected to edge up to 7.0% on steady external demand and improvement in the Bangladesh market share. Export forecasts assume that policy uncertainty in the US, United Kingdom, and euro area is resolved in ways not inimical to expansion in global trade flows and that the garment industry continues to improve worker safety and welfare.

Import payments rose by 8.2% in July–December 2016 with higher imports of wheat, petroleum products, capital goods, and iron, steel, and other base metals, though imports of crude oil, fertilizer, and raw cotton declined. Imports are expected to grow by 9.0% in FY2017 and 10.0% in FY2018 on broadly stable domestic demand and some pickup in global prices for commodities, especially oil.

Remittance inflows dipped by 17.6% to $6.2 billion in the first half of FY2017 as economic tightening continued in Gulf economies and newly constrained inflows from the US and the United Kingdom appeared to reflect political uncertainties there (Figure 3.15.13). Despite the 23.5% rise in jobs abroad for Bangladeshi workers in the first 6 months of FY2017, remittances are expected to sink further by 7.0% in FY2017 and 4.0% in FY2018.

Falling remittances and a larger trade deficit are expected to push the FY2017 current account into a deficit equal to 1.0% of GDP (Figure 3.15.14). The deficit is projected to shrink to 0.7% in FY2018. Capital and financial inflows will likely be sufficient to preclude any

3.15.8 Exchange rates

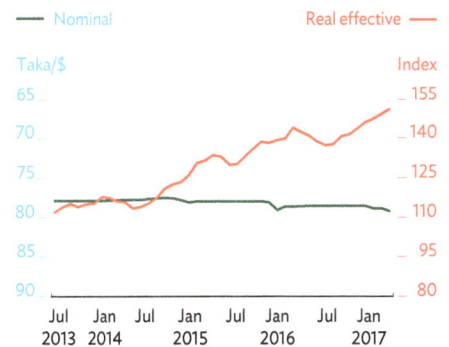

Source: Bangladesh Bank. 2017. *Monthly Economic Trends.* February. http://www.bb.org.bd

3.15.9 Dhaka stock exchange indicators

Source: Dhaka Stock Exchange. 2017. *Monthly Review.* January.

3.15.10 GDP growth by sector

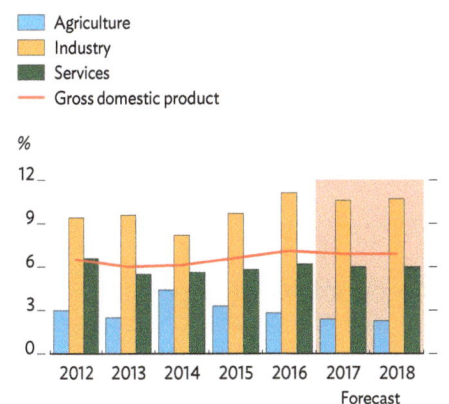

Note: Years are fiscal years ending on 30 June of that year.
Sources: Bangladesh Bureau of Statistics. http://www.bbs.gov.bd; ADB estimates.

loss of exchange reserves. The taka will likely depreciate marginally in nominal terms in FY2017 on the larger trade deficit and the continued decline in remittances.

The FY2017 budget assumes 36.8% growth in revenue, attained by raising the ratio of revenue to GDP to 12.4% from 9.9% in the previous year. Achieving this high target will be a challenge, considering that collection in the first 4 months grew by only 17.1%. Revenue from customs duties will be lower with rate cuts on several items. The collection of direct taxes could also fall short of its target in light of sluggish trends in income tax receipts from commercial banks.

Public spending was slated to grow by 28.7% to equal 17.4% of GDP in FY2017, up from 13.0% the year before. Current spending is expected to rise to 9.6% of GDP from 7.8% in FY2016, and the annual development program to 5.6% from 3.9% in FY2016. Achieving the planned large increases will demand concerted efforts. The fiscal deficit is expected to be contained within 5.0% of GDP as planned, three-fifths of it financed by domestic sources, mostly nonbanks. Implementing the new value-added tax in FY2018 will be crucial to advancing tax reform and financing higher infrastructure spending to foster growth.

As a net oil importer, Bangladesh continues to enjoy windfall gains from low global oil prices. The authorities are expected to cut retail fuel prices in FY2017 but leave enough cushion for the Bangladesh Petroleum Corporation to earn an operating profit and recoup past losses. Since the beginning of low global oil prices in 2014, the government has cut prices only once, in FY2016, as policy focused on eliminating large subsidies.

Debt indicators are generally favorable. Public debt declined to the equivalent of 27.2% of GDP in FY2016 from 27.4% in FY2015 (Figure 3.15.15). External debt declined to 11.7% of GDP from 12.2%, with a debt service ratio of only 2.0% thanks to the government's preference for concessional external borrowing. Domestic debt rose to 15.5% of GDP in FY2016 from 15.2% in FY2015 as the government met shortfalls in revenue collection largely by selling national savings certificates to the public. Interest payments were 13.8% of budget expenditure.

These projections depend on the following: Revenues need to rise quickly if the government's sizeable infrastructure development program is to be implemented. The exchange rate should be managed flexibly to offset lower remittance inflows and encourage exports. Institutional and regulatory reform needs to be accelerated, and infrastructure deficits amended, to improve the investment climate. Political stability must be maintained and security strengthened to boost investor confidence.

Policy challenge—promoting productive jobs

Bangladesh faces an employment challenge. Productive, well-paid jobs need to be created for the 1.4 million workers who join the workforce each year. Female workforce participation is still low despite sizeable employment in the garment industry, minimizing women's contribution to economic development. Productive jobs in manufacturing and modern services are needed for surplus labor currently in low-productivity agriculture (Table 3.15.2).

3.15.11 Inflation

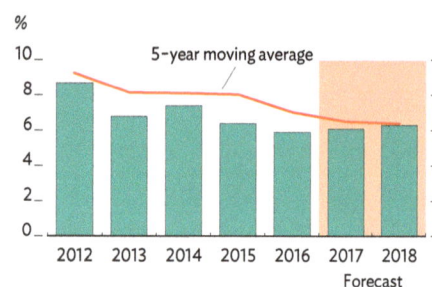

Note: Years are fiscal years ending on 30 June of that year.
Sources: Bangladesh Bank. 2017. Monthly Economic Trends. February. http://www.bb.org.bd; ADB estimates.

3.15.12 Exports growth

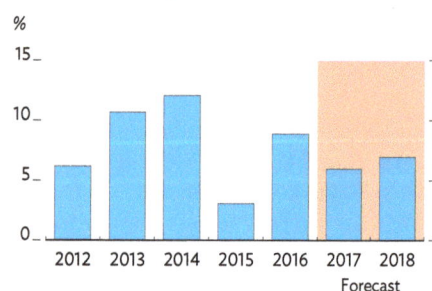

Note: Years are fiscal years ending on 30 June of that year.
Sources: Export Promotion Bureau, Bangladesh. Export performance, various issues; ADB estimates.

3.15.13 Remittances

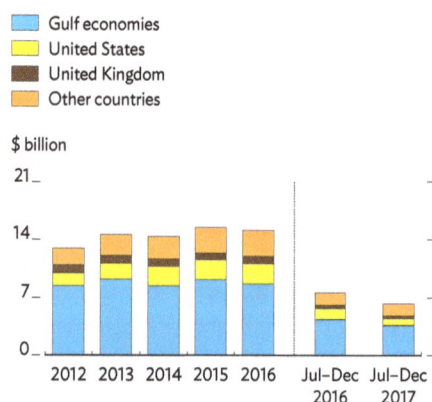

Note: Years are fiscal years ending on 30 June of that year.
Sources: Bangladesh Bank; ADB estimates.

3.15.2 Labor force participation rate, education level, and sector-productivity, 2013

	Male	Female	Total
Labor force participation aged 15 years and above (%)	81.7	33.5	57.1
Education of the employed workforce (%)			
None	21.3	21.4	21.3
Primary (1–5)	26.3	34.7	28.7
Secondary (6–10)	31.1	29.3	30.6
Higher secondary (11–12)	13.8	10.4	12.8
Tertiary (all degrees or diplomas)	7.0	3.9	6.1
Others (unknown)	0.5	0.4	0.4
	Agriculture	Industry	Services
Sector productivity[a]	0.4	1.3	1.6
Number of employed (million)	26.2	12.1	19.8

[a] Ratio of sector share in GDP and employment.

Sources: Bangladesh Bureau of Statistics. 2015. *Labour Force Survey 2013*; Bureau of Statistics. 2016. *National Accounts Statistics.* June; ADB estimates.

The government seeks to tackle the employment challenge by promoting high growth led by manufacturing and by accelerating regional development and the rural transformation.

Under the Seventh Five-Year Plan, FY2016–FY2020, the government is implementing measures to diversify the manufacturing base and identify new sources of growth and jobs. In addition to readymade garments, which supply 40% of manufacturing value added and 60% of manufacturing jobs, the government is focusing its efforts on products with high labor intensity and export potential such as footwear and leather products, jute and other agro-processed goods, electrical and electronic goods, light engineering, information technology services, medium-sized shipbuilding, ceramics, and pharmaceuticals. It is extending the duty-free import facility for raw materials and intermediate inputs used in agro-processing and shipbuilding, as well as revamping the duty-drawback system to guarantee to exporting firms world prices for imported inputs. The central bank is expanding its refinancing window to support labor-intensive small and medium-sized enterprises.

The government is reviewing import tariffs to mitigate any bias against exports, aiming to weaken effective protection for domestic manufacturers and thereby encourage them to enhance their productivity and competiveness. It has stepped up efforts to gain greater access to untraditional export markets such as the People's Republic of China, India, Japan, the Republic of Korea, and Turkey.

A government program of investment in skills for employment aims to make the skills development system more market oriented and so improve employability and productivity.

The government has decided to allow public and private entities alike to set up special economic zones toward catalyzing private investment, integrating into global value chains, and diversifying exports to create jobs. To attract private capital, these zones will provide one-stop services

3.15.14 Current account balance

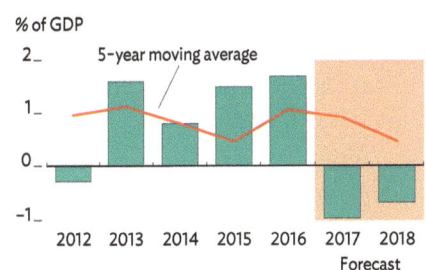

% of GDP

Note: Years are fiscal years ending on 30 June of that year.
Sources: Bangladesh Bank. 2017. *Annual Report 2015–2016.* https://www.bb.org.bd; ADB estimates.

3.15.15 Public debt

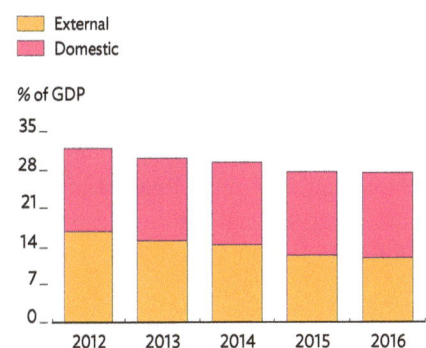

% of GDP

Note: Years are fiscal years ending on 30 June of that year.
Sources: Bangladesh Bank. 2017. *Annual Report 2015–2016.* https://www.bb.org.bd

to set up factories to produce garments and other goods and to simplify compliance with regulatory requirements, and they will be able to source raw materials readily from domestic supply chains. Several of these zones are attracting domestic and foreign investment interest and are expected to become operational in the next couple of years.

Under the Seventh Five-Year Plan, the government set a high priority on job creation in rural areas through skills training and strengthening producer and marketer cooperatives. The government is strengthening information and communication technology infrastructure in rural areas to disseminate modern techniques in agriculture, fisheries, and livestock. It emphasizes the development of agriculture value chains through private investment by encouraging the commercialization of agriculture, promoting a shift to high-value crops, and streamlining market access.

The government is developing rural areas by upgrading rural roads to reduce user costs, facilitating connectivity with railways and waterways to promote multimodal transport systems and improve logistics, and developing growth centers. It is allocating more resources to transport infrastructure and power supply improvement in the country's lagging regions in the northwest and south, with a view to promoting manufacturing and small and medium-sized enterprises through tax incentives, low-interest loans, and special economic zones. A government priority is to complete the Dhaka–Chittagong Expressway, which will substantially shorten travel time between the capital and the main port city.

The government merged the Board of Investment and the Privatization Commission into the new Bangladesh Investment Development Authority. In addition to encouraging domestic and foreign private investment, it assists in setting up industries and provides other services to investors.

To attract investment, foster rapid manufacturing-led growth, and create jobs, Bangladesh needs to reduce the cost of doing business. Most cost indicators surveyed by the World Bank—for enforcing contracts, getting electricity, registering property, getting credit, and paying taxes—rank Bangladesh in the bottom 10% of the countries covered (Figure 3.15.16). As a priority initiative, the Bangladesh Investment Development Authority is coordinating agencies' efforts to reduce the costs of doing business in Bangladesh.

To improve access to electricity, the government is investing heavily in power generation. In 2017, it expects to add another 1,840 megawatts to the current 15,350 megawatts of generating capacity. Transmission and distribution lines are being expanded and prepaid meters introduced to reduce system losses and improve management. Bangladesh is expecting to import another 500 megawatts of electricity from India by 2018. Regulations on electricity transmission and distribution tariffs announced in 2016 allow utilities to approach the Bangladesh Energy Regulatory Commission periodically for tariff review and revision to cover costs.

3.15.16 How Bangladesh ranks on *Doing Business* 2017 indicators

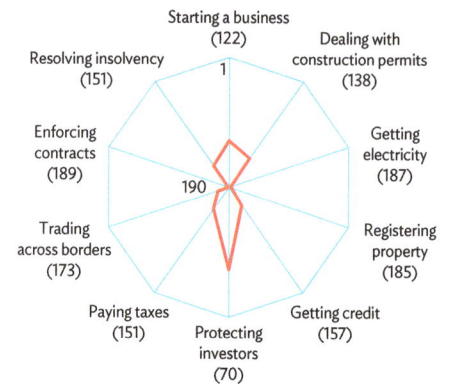

Starting a business (122)
Dealing with construction permits (138)
Getting electricity (187)
Registering property (185)
Getting credit (157)
Protecting investors (70)
Paying taxes (151)
Trading across borders (173)
Enforcing contracts (189)
Resolving insolvency (151)

Note: Numbers in parentheses show ranking out of 190 countries worldwide. 1 = best, 190 = worst.

Source: World Bank. Doing Business database. http://www.doingbusiness.org/data (accessed 26 January 2017).

Bhutan

Growth quickened in FY2016 on higher construction and investment. Inflation fell to a new low, and foreign exchange reserves strengthened. The outlook is for marked growth acceleration on expanded investment in hydropower for export, the economic mainstay, and added capacity in electricity generation. The government keenly focuses on inclusive growth. Policies to foster more adequate urban housing in the face of very rapid urbanization are a challenge.

Economic performance

The economy grew by 6.4% in FY2016 (ended 30 June 2016), slightly higher than the 6.1% a year earlier, driven mainly by accelerated construction on three major hydropower projects (Figure 3.16.1). On the supply side, industry was the main driver of higher growth, expanding by 7.3% from 6.0% a year earlier. Construction picked up, boosting demand for construction goods and so strengthening manufacturing. Even with the Dagachhu hydropower plant going into full production, electricity generation and export earnings from it declined because of weak water flows. Expansion in services slipped to 7.1% from 8.3% in FY2015. This reflected in part a 9% decline in dollar earnings from tourism, which usually contributes about 4% of GDP, as some visitors shunned the Himalayas after devastating earthquakes in Nepal in April and May 2015. Growth in agriculture improved to 4.0% from 3.5% owing to government initiatives promoting self-sufficiency and import substitution.

Consumption expanded by 5.6% in FY2016 from 1.6% a year earlier and remained the largest demand-side component of GDP (Figure 3.16.2). The acceleration was driven by higher household incomes and falling prices, as well as increased public spending, particularly on education. Investment growth edged up to 20.9% from 20.0%, primarily because of steadily expanding work on hydropower projects. Consumption and investment growth offset deterioration in net exports as export volume suffered a slight decline, while imports of construction materials and machinery increased.

Average inflation halved to 3.3% in FY2016. Prices in Bhutan broadly follow market prices in India because most imports come from there. The Indian wholesale price index dropped into deflation in January 2015 and returned to positive territory only in March 2016, suppressing inflation in Bhutan (Figure 3.16.3). Domestic food inflation was moderate in May 2016 but spiked higher in December because of destructive rains that peaked in July 2016, while there was a rise in imported food prices

3.16.1 Supply-side contributions to growth

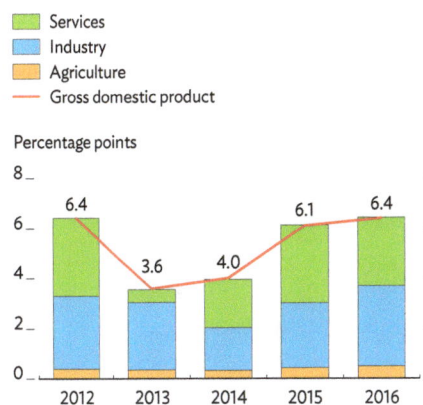

Note: Years are fiscal years ending on 30 June of that year.
Sources: National Statistics Bureau. National Accounts Statistics 2016. http://www.nsb.gov.bt; ADB estimates.

3.16.2 Demand-side contributions to growth

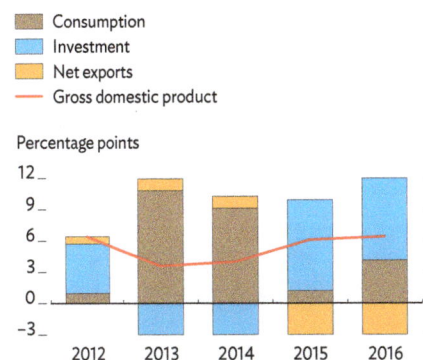

Note: Years are fiscal years ending on 30 June of that year.
Sources: National Statistics Bureau. National Accounts Statistics 2016. http://www.nsb.gov.bt; ADB estimates.

This chapter was written by Soon Chan Hong of the South Asia Department, ADB, Manila, and Danileen Parel, consultant, South Asia Department, ADB, Manila.

in the last quarter of 2016 mainly because of disruption to border trade when India demonetized most of its currency. Nonfood prices trended lower, benefitting from lower transport costs with weak global oil prices. However, they moved higher in the last quarter of 2016, mainly on a jump in rental housing costs, as did overall inflation.

Fiscal policy continued to be progressive. As FY2016 was the middle of the Eleventh Five-Year Plan, program implementation was at its highest. With increased capital spending, government expenditure grew sharply by 36.3% to the equivalent of 35.4% of GDP (Figure 3.16.4). Despite an increase in total revenue by only 1.8%, budget resources grew by 20.7% because of a 70.6% increase in grants, mainly from the Government of India, to finance infrastructure, agriculture, health, and education projects. The overall budget balance fell into a deficit equal to 3.0% of GDP, which was within the limits set by the 5-year plan and the medium-term national budget framework.

Outstanding external debt rose in FY2016 to $2.3 billion, equal to 109.5% of GDP, with new loans to expand investment in hydropower projects (Figure 3.16.5). Two-thirds of external debt is for hydropower development financed by the Government of India and linked to long-term electricity purchase contracts and explicit guarantees that cover financial and construction risks. Given this—and that the balance of external debt is largely on concessional terms—the International Monetary Fund assesses Bhutan's risk of external debt distress to be moderate.

Monetary policy aims to manage credit to avoid overheating and ensure the stability of the parity exchange rate peg to the Indian rupee. Broad money grew by 15.8% in FY2016, slightly higher than the annual average of 14.5% over the past decade (Figure 3.16.6). Growth in broad money is attributed to a 16.4% increase in net foreign assets and 14.7% expansion in credit to the private sector, little changed from a year earlier. The Royal Monetary Authority guarantees sufficient Indian rupee reserves available on demand to meet payments. Gross international reserves rose by 16.7% to $1.1 billion, cover for 11.3 months of imports, higher than the traditional rule of thumb of 3 months (Figure 3.16.7). The increase primarily reflects Indian rupee reserves expanding enough to cover 3.8 months of imports from India.

The current account deficit is high, rising even higher to 29.4% of GDP in FY2016 from 28.3% a year earlier (Figure 3.16.8). This largely reflects a widened trade deficit, in particular with India, mostly from expanded imports of capital goods and intermediates for industry. The services deficit improved slightly because of lower transport costs and a marked increase in Indian tourist arrivals, which helped compensate for the fall in tourists paying with convertible currency and larger payments for construction services. The deficit in the primary income account worsened as interest payments on hydropower debt grew, while the surplus in secondary income improved markedly because of increased Indian grants for budget support.

3.16.3 Inflation

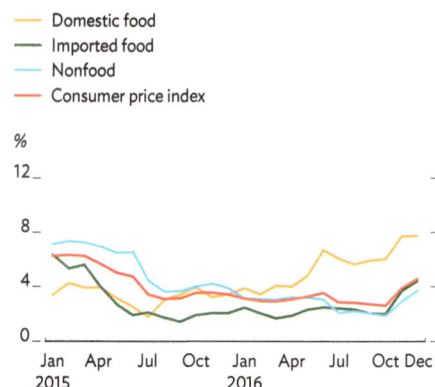

- Domestic food
- Imported food
- Nonfood
- Consumer price index

Source: National Statistics Bureau. Monthly Consumer Price Index Bulletin. December 2016. http://www.nsb.gov.bt

3.16.4 Fiscal indicators

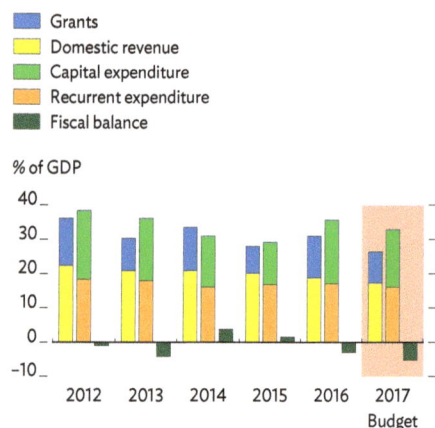

- Grants
- Domestic revenue
- Capital expenditure
- Recurrent expenditure
- Fiscal balance

Note: Years are fiscal years ending on 30 June of that year.
Source: Ministry of Finance. National Budget Financial Year 2015/16. http://www.mof.gov.bt

3.16.5 External debt

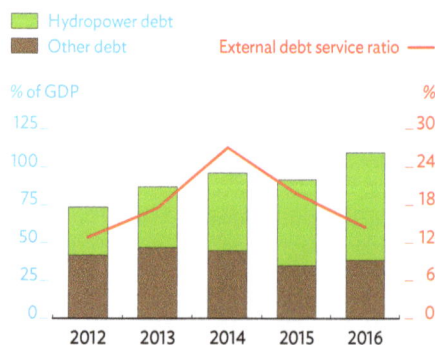

- Hydropower debt
- Other debt
- External debt service ratio

Notes: Years are fiscal years ending on 30 June of that year. The external debt service ratio excludes external debt service for loans received through an overdraft facility provided by India.
Source: Royal Monetary Authority of Bhutan. Monthly Statistical Bulletin, March 2017. http://www.rma.org.bt

Economic prospects

Growth is projected to accelerate to 8.2% in FY2017, mainly on stepped-up hydropower plant construction and the completion of projects included in the five-year plan. It is forecast to surge to 9.9% in FY2018 as electricity-generating capacity is added, provided that hydropower projects are commissioned as planned.

Industry growth is expected to strengthen markedly in FY2017 as electricity output increases with the assumed return of normal weather, work on large hydropower projects continues, and infrastructure damaged by last year's torrential rains is rehabilitated. It is expected to surge in FY2018 on much higher electricity output and exports following the completion of the Mangdechhu hydropower plant and the partial commissioning of the Punatsangchhu II hydropower plant. Services growth in FY2017 and FY2018 is projected to improve on faster expansion in industry and a recovery in tourism as worries over earthquakes in the Himalayas fade. Currency demonetization in India in November 2016 should have no lasting impact in Bhutan. With the quickened pace of hydropower investment and production, consumer incomes and spending will accelerate in FY2017 and FY2018.

Inflation is forecast to increase to 4.9% in FY2017 and 5.4% in FY2018 in line with higher wholesale prices expected in India and a 3-year domestic electricity tariff hike that started to take effect in January 2017. While the projected increase in global oil prices would increase transportation costs, continued low global prices for other commodities and India's strict monetary targeting will likely sustain broad price stability.

The government plans to slow expenditure growth sharply to 4.4% in FY2017 from over 36% a year earlier as capital expenditure drops with the completion of 5-year plan activities in the next 2 years. Investment in hydropower projects is unaffected by this decline, however, because financing and expenditure are under a public corporation. Total budget resources will slow in tandem to 4.9% with lower budgetary grants from India after the surge in FY2016. Tax revenue is projected to increase by 6.6%, mainly on higher corporate tax collection from hydropower. Notably, a much larger minimum personal income tax exemption is expected to deduct 2.5% from projected tax revenues, but it is budgeted to be offset by higher receipts from mineral royalties and rent. With growth in planned expenditure outpacing that of total revenue, the budget deficit is expected to widen to the equivalent of 5.3% of GDP in FY2017 from 3.0% last year.

Monetary policy will continue to pursue price and exchange rate stability. An accommodative monetary policy will channel credit to growth drivers. Reform of the minimum lending rate, announced by the Royal Monetary Authority in July 2016, prompted banks to slash loan interest rates and is expected to boost credit expansion temporarily before equilibrium returns in the medium term. Rules and regulations for private moneylenders, adopted in December 2016, will bring this business under the formal financial sector, supplementing other strong measures to control credit after excessive lending in FY2011 put pressure on the balance of payments.

3.16.1 Selected economic indicators (%)

	2017	2018
GDP growth	8.2	9.9
Inflation	4.9	5.4
Current account balance (share of GDP)	−27.4	−22.8

Source: ADB estimates.

3.16.6 Monetary indicators

— Credit to the private sector
— Broad money
— Net foreign assets

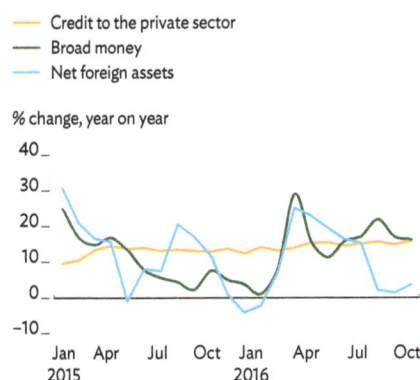

Source: Royal Monetary Authority of Bhutan. Monthly Statistical Bulletin March 2017. http://www.rma.org.bt

3.16.7 Gross international reserves

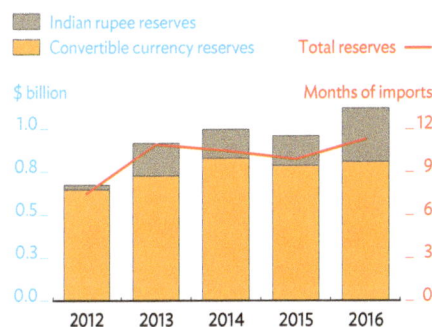

Note: Years are fiscal years ending on 30 June of that year.
Source: Royal Monetary Authority of Bhutan. Annual Report FY2015/16. http://www.rma.org.bt

The current account deficit is projected to narrow slightly to the equivalent of 27.4% of GDP in FY2017 before narrowing more substantially to 22.8% in FY2018. Imports are expected to remain high in FY2017 to supply construction goods to hydropower projects as exports grow moderately on a rebound in electricity exports with the return to normal weather and an expected increase in mineral exports. Indian demonetization in November 2016 is expected to suppress border trade somewhat through the third quarter of FY2017 but is not seen to have a long-term impact as most of Bhutan's trade with India is settled through bank drafts and checks rather than cash. The current account deficit is expected to narrow markedly in FY2018 as the new electricity generated from the Mangdechhu and Punatsangchhu II hydropower plants boosts exports to India. Improvement in the current account would have been greater if not for the further delays in the full commissioning of the Punatsangchhu II and Punatsangchhu I hydropower plants, which are now pushed further to FY2020 and FY2023, respectively.

Policy challenge—addressing the urban housing crunch

Rapid population growth and urbanization have created new housing challenges for Bhutan (Figure 3.16.9). In 2015, the population grew by 1.6% to about 760,000, with 38.6% living in urban areas, many people having migrated to where the jobs are. The result is an urban housing shortage.

Housing has consistently been the greatest area of exposure for banks. In September 2016, loans for housing amounted to Nu20 billion, or nearly one-quarter of total bank lending. These loans are made mostly to developers, however, to build multi-storey apartment blocks that are rented out to tenants. Thus, although units in these buildings are counted under home ownership, they are actually owned by a limited number of landlords. High land prices and mortgages at market interest rates with very short repayment periods make the terms for repayment impossible and home ownership inaccessible to low- and middle-income people.

The inability to purchase one's own home means heavy dependence on rental housing, limiting urban families' ability to save and build equity in their home, which in most other countries is a major personal asset. This is mainly an urban phenomenon as most rural households own their home, mostly owner built. In urban areas, only 17% of households own their home. Although the government provides some housing built by the National Housing Development Corporation, it is only for a small group of civil servants. Similarly, the quasi-governmental National Pension and Provident Fund provides housing loans but only to its members, mainly civil servants and the armed forces. These institutions solve the housing problem for only a small segment of the population.

After food, the largest expense for urban households is usually housing rental. Further, as housing construction cannot keep up with urban population growth because basic infrastructure is inadequate,

3.16.8 Current account components

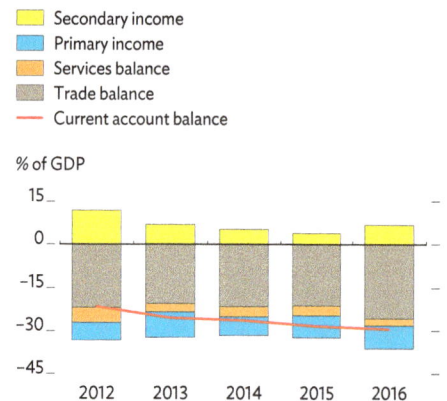

Note: Years are fiscal years ending on 30 June of that year.
Sources: Royal Monetary Authority of Bhutan. Monthly Statistics. December 2016; Annual Report FY2015/16. http://www.rma.org.bt

3.16.9 Population

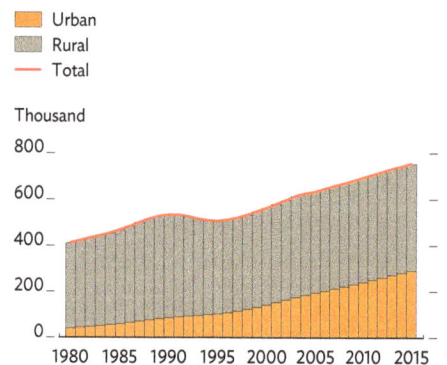

Source: National Statistical Bureau. Bhutan Statistical Yearbook 2016. http://www.nsb.gov.bt

landlords decline to make repairs or improvements, knowing that tenants will likely stay rather than look for better housing that would be more costly. This causes the condition of urban housing stock to deteriorate.

The housing crunch is being addressed by reforms and initiatives. One model is the Amochhu land development and township project of Druk Holding and Investments, a government-owned holding company, set to begin in FY2017. It will develop a 160-hectare area adjacent the Amochhu River in Phuentsholing, the second largest city in Bhutan. The project will protect the area from flooding and erosion, and establish urban infrastructure, basic services, and housing complexes.

Meanwhile, finance reform could aim to enable private developers to build for sale to individual home owners. The minimum lending rate reform in July 2016 brought more bank competition and lower lending rates, including an improved rate for noncommercial housing loans that should encourage home ownership. However, further improvements to mortgage terms are required to improve access, particularly for low- and middle-income groups, by substantially lengthening repayment periods and setting reasonable qualifying income standards and down payments.

More generally, Bhutan needs a comprehensive national land and housing policy that would provide a framework for urban development and housing. The existing national housing policy is being revised to address emerging housing issues as well as old ones. The policy, to be implemented after consultation with stakeholders, will create an enabling environment for a modern housing industry, promote finance mechanisms for middle- and low-income housing in particular, establish an agency to monitor the housing stock, and formulate strategies and legislation in response to emerging trends in the housing market.

India

Growth slowed to 7.1% in FY2016 despite recovery in agriculture. While recent GDP data may not fully capture the effects of demonetization, the slowdown did reflect a continued slump in investment. Dragging on growth were excess production capacity, problems that past overinvestment left on corporate balance sheets, and new bank lending inhibited by too many stressed assets. Moderately higher growth is projected as consumption picks up and government initiatives boost private investment.

Economic performance

In the middle of FY2016 (ended 31 March 2017), the government announced the withdrawal of legal tender status for all existing Rs500 and Rs1,000 currency notes to counter black money hoarding and counterfeiting (Box 3.17.1). This move demonetized 86% of currency in circulation by value. New Rs500 and Rs2,000 notes were introduced, but the distribution of new notes picked up only gradually, leaving a cash crunch for 2 months and straining commerce dependent on cash.

This was one reason economic growth slowed to 7.1% in FY2016, according to advance government estimates (Figure 3.17.1). This outcome was well below 7.9% growth in FY2015 and marginally above the *ADO Supplement* forecast of 7.0% issued in 2016. Much of growth came from strong agriculture and government services. Excluding government services, growth in value added dropped from 6.7% to 6.0%. Agriculture grew by a robust 4.4% as a healthy monsoon helped food grain production grow by 8.1% to new records. Livestock, forestry, and fisheries also recorded healthy growth.

After growing by 8.2% in FY2015, industry decelerated to 5.8% in FY2016. Mining slowed considerably as oil and natural gas production contracted. Manufacturing value added grew by a healthy 7.7%, though down from the 10.6% recorded a year earlier. Growth reflected robust performance by large private manufacturers, which benefited from lower input costs. However, healthy growth in manufacturing value added is at odds with the volume-based index of industrial production, which registered hardly any growth. Construction was muted, growing by 3.1% as the cash crunch possibly hit real estate activity in the second half of the fiscal year.

Services growth also moderated, to 7.9%, with notable slowdowns in finance and real estate, as well as in trade, hotels, and transportation and communication services. Anemic credit growth continued to weigh on financial services, though deposit growth picked up substantially immediately after demonetization as people deposited the discontinued banknotes. Contraction in railway ridership and tonnage,

3.17.1 Supply-side contributions to growth

- Net taxes on products
- Services
- Industry
- Agriculture
- GDP at market prices

Percentage points

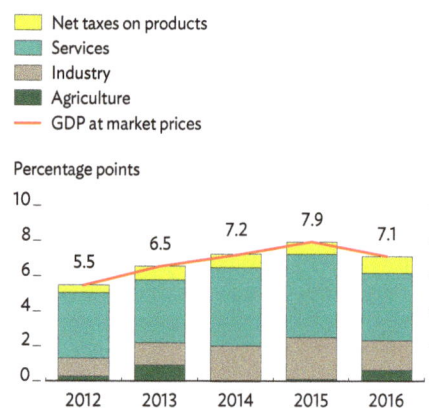

Note: Years are fiscal years ending on 31 March of the next year.
Source: Ministry of Statistics and Programme Implementation. http://www.mospi.nic.in (accessed 7 March 2017).

3.17.2 Demand-side contributions to growth

- Net exports
- Others
- Gross fixed capital formation
- Government consumption expenditure
- Private consumption expenditure
- GDP at market prices

Percentage points

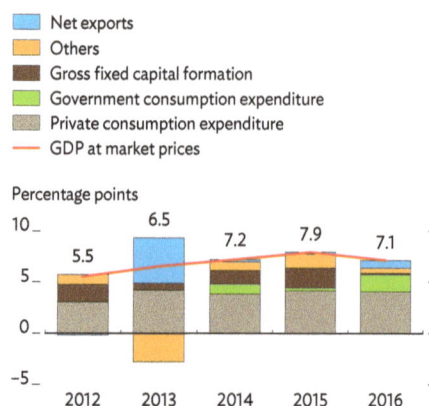

Note: Years are fiscal years ending on 31 March of the next year. Others includes valuables, changes in inventories and statistical discrepancy.
Source: Ministry of Statistics and Programme Implementation. http://www.mospi.nic.in (accessed 7 March 2017).

This chapter was written by Johanna Boestel and Abhijit Sen Gupta of the India Resident Mission, ADB, New Delhi.

and lackluster growth in commercial vehicle sales, subdued expansion in transportation services. By contrast, there was strong growth in government services, including public administration and defense, on account of salary hikes for central government employees.

Private consumption is estimated to have grown by 7.2%, much as in the previous year (Figure 3.17.2). However, this estimate may be optimistic because achieving it would require private consumption to grow by 8.2% in the second half of FY2016, significantly above the 6.1% achieved in the first half—or, for that matter, in the past few years. Government consumption is estimated to have grown at its fastest pace since FY2011 to pay the higher wages and salaries. Despite a 10.6% increase in central government capital expenditure, overall investment remained flat, growing by only 0.6%, as private investment continued to be weighed down by low capacity utilization and slow progress toward deleveraging.

GDP growth got a further impetus from a robust increase in net taxes, buoyed by strong indirect tax collection.

Inflation remained subdued for a second year, averaging 4.7% (Figure 3.17.3). While food inflation inched up in the first few months of FY2016 with rises for vegetables, pulses, and sugar, subsequent months saw prices cooled by a better monsoon and summer crop. Retail inflation is down considerably since November because of lower prices for perishable food, supplies of which tend to be ample in winter. Compounding this was a fall in demand as the cash crunch followed demonetization, forcing suppliers to sell at lower prices. Domestic fuel inflation has remained relatively subdued at 3.0%. Core inflation was also stable in FY2016, ranging from 4.5% to 5.0%. Subdued inflation allowed the Reserve Bank of India, the central bank, to reduce policy rates by 50 basis points during FY2016 for a cumulative decline of 175 basis points since January 2015 (Figure 3.17.4). Moreover, with deposit accretion far outweighing credit growth after demonetization, commercial banks lowered their lending rates by 40–90 basis points as their new deposit costs came down.

Credit growth slumped in FY2016 to its lowest in over a decade, estimated at less than 8.0%. This slowdown masked growing divergence by sector. Credit to industry has trended lower for several years and contracted in FY2016 as investment demand stayed weak and corporations actively deleveraged to strengthen their balance sheets (Figure 3.17.5). On the other hand, retail credit including housing and vehicle loans trended higher, indicating robust household demand. Demonetization was a factor in the slump for some months, deferring demand and significantly affecting cash-dependent retail trade and micro, small, and medium-sized enterprises.

Credit growth was further impeded as nonperforming loans proliferated to 9.1% of all loans in September 2016, up from 7.8% the previous March, pushing the ratio of stressed advances including restructured loans to all advances to 12.3% in September 2016 from 11.5% in March (Figure 3.17.6). Most nonperforming loans and restructured assets are concentrated in state-owned banks, where the stressed advances ratio increased to 15.8% in September from 14.4% in March. Particularly affected industries were base metals,

3.17.1 Banknote demonetization

On 8 November 2016, the government withdrew the legal tender status of all Rs500 and Rs1,000 banknotes. This demonetization intended to trip up corruption, counterfeiting, and the funding of terrorism. This decision augmented measures introduced earlier to fight corruption, including tax amnesties to encourage the disclosure of black money, agreements with other countries to share banking information, and the renegotiation of treaties to avoid double taxation. The decision was envisioned as fostering digitalization, improving tax compliance, and channeling additional savings through the formal banking system.

India is a cash-intensive society, with an estimated 78% of consumer payments concluded in cash. The initial currency crunch, caused by the slow replacement of demonetized notes, therefore hit commerce, causing a temporary drop in consumption and employment. However, steady progress in issuing new notes is expected to rapidly rectify the situation.

The temporary drop in demand helped slow inflation. The return of demonetized notes caused bank deposits to surge and lending rates to drop. Because small enterprises generate a large share of India's exports, and are highly dependent on cash, demonetization impeded exports of gems, jewelry, and garments for a few months before the situation normalized. Gold imports spiked in November, with buyers reportedly purchasing gold with discontinued notes even at large premiums.

Demonetization is likely to have a positive impact over the medium term. Along with the forthcoming implementation of the goods and services tax, demonetization will widen the tax net and improve tax compliance. With more people channeling their savings into the banking system, banks will have more money to lend at lower rates. Lower aggregate deposit costs should improve bank profitability, further increasing their lending capacity.

construction, textiles, food processing, and infrastructure development. The implementation of the new bankruptcy code is likely to modernize and expedite the bankruptcy process.

The central government budget for FY2017 was presented a month earlier than usual at the beginning of February 2016 to speed appropriations. Another aim was to counter a practice in which the government asks Parliament for enough funding to cover expenditure in the first few months until Parliament formally approves the budget. The central government succeeded in narrowing the fiscal deficit to 3.5% of GDP in FY2016 (Figure 3.17.7). Encouragingly, this reduction was accompanied by improved quality of expenditure. While capital expenditure was originally targeted to contract by 2.4% in FY2016 to compensate for higher government salaries, preliminary estimates show capital expenditure growing by 10.6%. Current expenditure grew by 12.8%. Subsidy spending continued to decline from the equivalent of 1.9% of GDP in FY2015 to 1.7% as fertilizer and petroleum subsidies fell thanks to low oil prices and the expansion of a program that pays the cooking gas subsidy directly into recipients' bank accounts to reduce leakage.

Revenue grew by a healthy 16.7% in FY2016, aided by strong growth in tax revenue and public enterprise dividends and profits. Personal income tax witnessed robust growth at 22.8% as the government introduced in FY2016 two tax amnesties to encourage income disclosure. Excise tax collection also grew strongly for a second year, partly on higher revenues from several hikes to excise rates on petroleum products in FY2015. Buoyant excise tax collections can be attributed as well to growth from other products. Meanwhile, as in previous years, income from disinvestment in public corporations was a fraction of the target.

A committee set up to review avenues to fiscal consolidation recommended sustainable debt as the principal macroeconomic anchor for fiscal policy and called for reining in the ratio of public debt to GDP from the current 67% to 60% by FY2023. To achieve this target, the committee recommended capping the fiscal deficit at 3.0% of GDP in the 3 years following the proposed FY2017 budget, which has a deficit equal to 3.2% of GDP. In line with these recommendations, the government has adopted 3.0% of GDP as the target for FY2018–FY2020.

Imports declined for a second consecutive year, contracting by an estimated 3.7% in FY2016. Although oil imports fell by nearly 2% in FY2016, much of the contraction was concentrated in the first half of the fiscal year (Figure 3.17.8). Oil prices firmed considerably in the second half, and oil imports picked up. Gold imports declined substantially in FY2016 because of softening global prices and the cash crunch following demonetization. Imports other than oil and gold were relatively steady as commodity prices stabilized and domestic demand remained muted.

As with imports, exports revived in the second half of FY2016, growing by an estimated 2.5% for the year. The revival was driven largely by a pickup in refined petroleum exports and stronger demand from the advanced economies, especially the US and Germany. In particular, exports of gems and jewelry, iron and steel, and motor vehicles picked up in the second half of FY2016. The net services trade surplus narrowed

3.17.3 Inflation

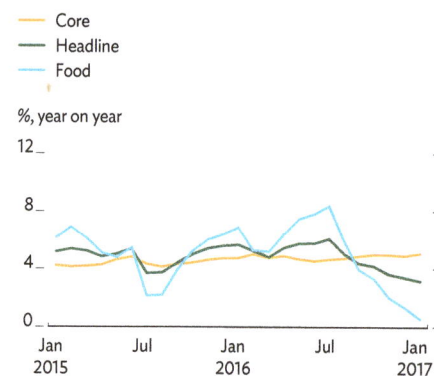

Sources: CEIC Data Company (accessed 7 March 2017); ADB estimates.

3.17.4 Policy interest rates

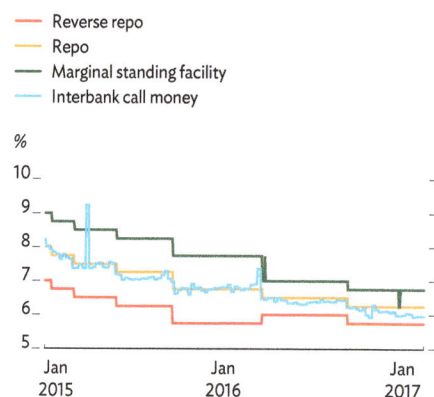

Sources: Bloomberg; CEIC Data Company (both accessed 14 March 2017).

3.17.5 Bank credit

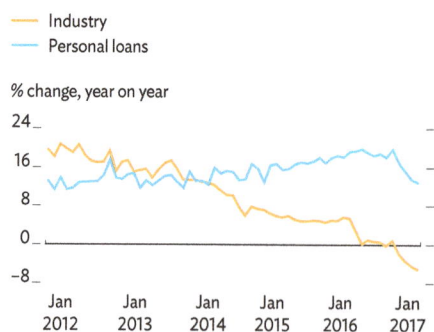

Source: Bloomberg (accessed 14 March 2017).

in FY2016, tracking a slowdown in exports of software and financial services. Remittance inflows weakened a bit in FY2016 as low crude oil prices squeezed host economies in the Middle East. In sum, the FY2016 current account deficit is estimated to equal 1.0% of GDP.

Net inflows of foreign direct investment (FDI) remained strong for a second year in FY2016 at $36.7 billion after the government simplified guidelines and allowed more FDI in real estate, airport and air transport services, and e-commerce. Net portfolio flows remained subdued by comparison. The last quarter of 2016 brought a large outflow, possibly a result of a US interest rate hike in December 2016 and uncertainty following demonetization. Net portfolio debt outflows amounted $2 billion in FY2016 (Figure 3.17.9). While varying month to month, equity inflows amounted to $7 billion in FY2016, which pushed stock prices on the Bombay Stock Exchange Sensex up by 16% over the year (Figure 3.17.10). Net deposits by nonresident Indians turned negative in FY2016 largely because of the repayment of maturing deposits that the central bank had attracted from them in FY2013. However, because these outflows were buffered by a forward sale-and-swap arrangement established earlier by the central bank, they did not significantly drain holdings of foreign reserves, which stood at $367 billion in March 2017 (Figure 3.17.11).

The Indian rupee remained stable against the US dollar in FY2016 (Figure 3.17.12). However, it strengthened by 2.4% in nominal effective terms and by 4.1% in real effective terms, raising its value against the currencies of some trading partners.

Economic prospects

The growth slowdown in FY2016 was primarily the result of sluggish investment and of consumption slowing in the second half because of the cash crunch. With the central bank printing new currency to replace the demonetized notes and lifting limits on account withdrawals in March 2017, the cash crunch eased markedly toward the end of FY2016. Consumption deferred from the second half of FY2016 by the cash crunch will likely surface in FY2017 and lift consumption growth. Consumption will receive a further boost as several state governments hike salaries and pensions for their employees in FY2017 following a similar hike for central government employees in FY2016. A good monsoon in FY2017 would allow rural consumption to grow at a healthy rate, but early forecasts indicate a monsoon still affected by El Niño.

An uptick in consumption could engage excess capacity across sectors and invite fresh investment. Public investment will continue to be an important driver of growth as private investment remains listless. The increase in central government capital expenditure targeted in the FY2017 budget augurs well for public investment, but capital spending by states is also needed to push public investment higher. Public investment is likely to receive a boost if the government receives significantly more revenue from the tax amnesties introduced in FY2016. Current deleveraging by private corporations and a rising proportion of corporate debt instruments being upgraded signal some improvement in corporate financial health, which could aid investment

3.17.6 Nonperforming and restructured loans

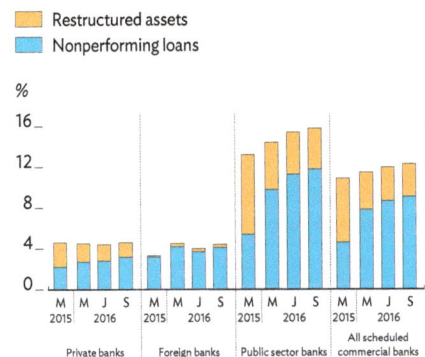

▢ Restructured assets
▢ Nonperforming loans

M = March, J = June, S = September.
Source: Reserve Bank of India. http://www.rbi.org.in

3.17.7 Federal budget indicators

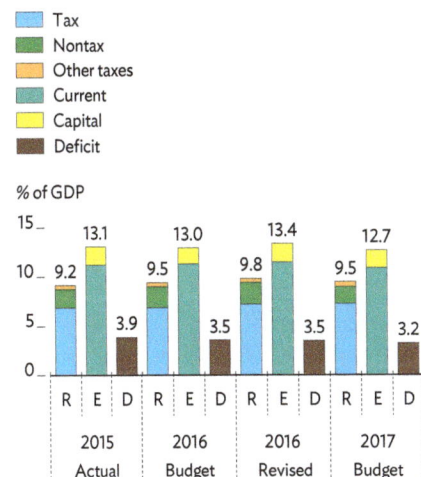

▢ Tax
▢ Nontax
▢ Other taxes
▢ Current
▢ Capital
▢ Deficit

R = revenue, E = expenditure, D = deficit financing.
Note: Years are fiscal years ending on 31 March of the next year.
Source: Ministry of Finance Union Budget 2016–2018. http://indiabudget.nic.in

recovery. The drop in commercial bank lending rates following demonetization will provide some relief to leveraged companies and reduce interest costs for productive sectors. Although the number of stalled projects inched up in the quarter ending in December 2016 from the previous quarter, it remains near a 15-quarter low. Announcements of new investment projects leveled off (Figure 3.17.13).

Various outlook surveys indicate some improvement. The services and manufacturing purchasing managers' indexes improved significantly from April to October 2016 before slipping in November and December as demonetization hit demand. However, they have recovered since January to signal a return to expansion with recovery in domestic and export orders (Figure 3.17.14).

Improved growth prospects for the advanced economies in 2017 could provide a boost to merchandise exports and to financial, telecom, business, and other tradeable services. However, this boon could be offset by any marked rise in global oil prices, considering that India meets four-fifths of its petroleum demand through imports. Resulting lower net exports could impinge on growth.

Policy options to bolster growth are limited. The central bank is unlikely to significantly reduce interest rates in the near term given the risk of inflation and of capital outflow with further US interest rate increases expected after the one on 15 March 2017. Higher oil prices and the government's commitment to further reduce the budget deficit will limit the extent to which additional fiscal stimulus can be applied.

On balance, growth is projected to pick up to 7.4% in FY2017, primarily on higher consumption. Public and private investment is expected to contribute to economic growth as the government revitalizes public–private partnerships and as deleveraging in the private sector bears fruit. Growth is expected to edge up further to 7.6% in FY2018 with continued deleveraging and as the government works to strengthen the balance sheets of state-owned banks. The implementation of a new national goods and services tax beginning in July 2017 should lower prices for capital goods, providing impetus to investment.

After easing for 4 consecutive years, consumer price inflation is expected to inch up in FY2017. With global prices for oil forecast to increase by 20% in FY2017, and with most domestic fuel prices becoming deregulated, domestic fuel inflation is forecast to rise by 10–20 basis points. Global food inflation as measured by the Food and Agriculture Organization of the United Nations started picking up in September 2016 after contracting for almost 5 years. Higher procurement prices for pulses and wheat pose, along with an uptick in rural wages, upside risks to the forecast for food inflation. The likely salary hike for state government employees in FY2017 will add further inflationary pressure. The central bank's most recent survey of inflation expectations show them falling because of steep declines for food and housing likely due to demonetization. However, the duration of low inflation expectations will likely depend on how quickly new banknotes are distributed. Moreover, even at current lows, inflation expectations continue to be almost double the 4% midpoint in the central bank target range for inflation in the medium term. Inflation is likely to average

3.17.8 Trade indicators

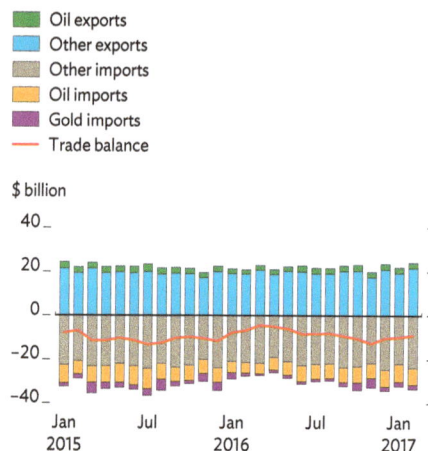

Note: Years are fiscal years ending on 31 March of the next year.
Sources: CEIC Data Company (accessed 14 March 2017); ADB estimates.

3.17.9 Portfolio capital flows

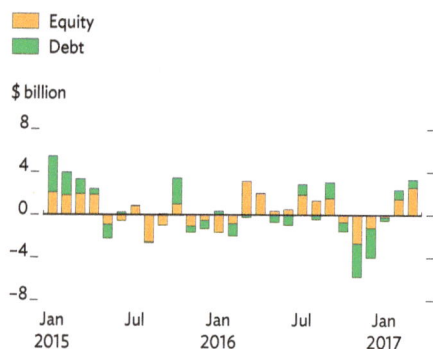

Source: Security and Exchange Board of India.

3.17.10 Stock price indexes

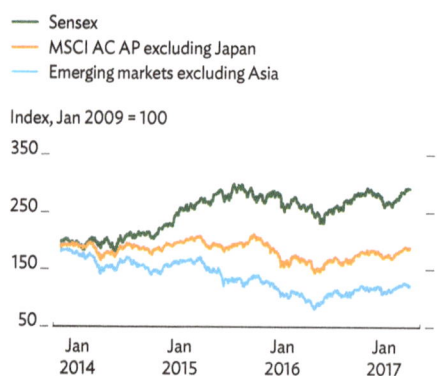

Source: Bloomberg (accessed 14 March 2017).

5.2% in FY2017, accelerating to 5.4% in FY2018 with further firming of global commodity prices and strengthening of domestic demand.

The central bank recently signaled a change in policy from accommodative to neutral, implying very limited scope for further policy rate cuts. Its focus has thus shifted to lowering inflation to the medium-term target of 4% while mindful that higher commodity prices and a stronger US dollar will tend to push inflation higher. Even though policy rates are unlikely to go lower in the near term, benign liquidity conditions allow bank lending rates to fall a bit.

The budget exhibited commitment to fiscal consolidation by targeting in FY2017 a fiscal deficit narrowed to 3.2% of GDP. However, the target of pegging the fiscal deficit at 3.0% of GDP has been put back by another year. Gross tax revenue is expected to grow by 12.2% in FY2017, yielding tax buoyancy at 1.0, which is revenue mobilization rising at par with nominal GDP growth. This is slightly lower than in recent years. Personal income tax collection is forecast to increase at a healthy rate as compliance improves because of legislative changes and tax amnesties, even though a cut in personal income tax rates for the lowest tax bracket was announced to help consumption recover. Growth in corporate tax collection is expected to be sluggish, dampened by a reduction in the tax rate for smaller companies, as is excise duty collection, inhibited by a rise in oil prices. The target for growth in services tax collection could be on the conservative side, especially if digital transactions increase. Finally, uncertainty clouds the forecast for revenues from indirect taxes with the impending implementation of the new national goods and services tax. As in previous years, the revenue target from disinvestment, equal to 0.4% of GDP, is ambitious and unlikely to be met.

The quality of expenditure is expected to improve further with capital spending in FY2017 projected to grow by 10.7%, against growth in current expenditure by only 5.9%. The budget continues to prioritize infrastructure and rural development with higher outlays on roads and highways, railways, electric power, affordable housing, and irrigation. Subsidy payments are forecast to decline as petroleum and fertilizer subsidies are curtailed. However, any significant increase in global oil prices could force up subsidy payments. Similarly, higher allowances to civil servants, a decision on which was postponed to 2017, could undermine the fiscal deficit target.

Higher oil prices will boost refined petroleum exports, which have contracted in the past 2 years. Global growth improvement would help exports, though an appreciating rupee in real effective terms could dent India's competitiveness. Price recovery for commodities like metals, chemicals, and food would lift exports, as export volumes for them have held up. Overall, exports are forecast to grow by 6.0% in FY2017. With petroleum import volume rising at an annual average of 4.4% during the last 5 years, higher global prices could push up the oil import bill considerably. Gold imports are expected to remain flat as the government's gold securities programs are expected to contain import demand. Imports of capital goods such as machinery, transport equipment, and iron and steel are likely to pick up with the revival of investment, increasing total imports by 7.5%. While remittance inflows

3.17.1 Selected economic indicators (%)

	2017	2018
GDP growth	7.4	7.6
Inflation	5.2	5.4
Current account balance (share of GDP)	–1.3	–1.5

Note: Years are fiscal years ending on 31 March of the next year.
Source: ADB estimates.

3.17.11 International reserves

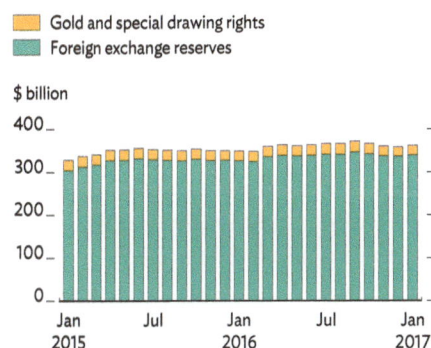

Source: CEIC Data Company (accessed 14 March 2017).

3.17.12 Exchange rates

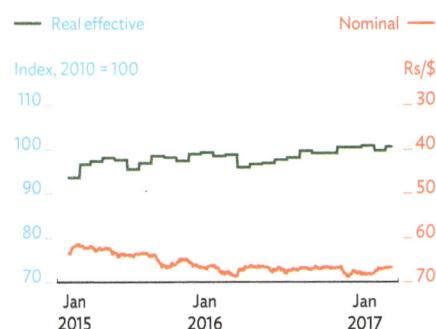

Source: Bloomberg (accessed 14 March 2017).

from oil-producing countries pick up as oil prices recover, remittances from the advanced economies could dip a bit owing to policy changes there. In sum, the current account deficit is expected to widen to the equivalent of 1.3% of GDP in FY2017.

In FY2018, export growth is expected to rise further to 7.0% as demand in the advanced economies stabilizes. At the same time, imports are projected to grow by 9.0% with higher growth and oil prices, widening the current account deficit to the equivalent of 1.5% of GDP. The current account deficit is expected to be comfortably financed by stable inflows, especially as India continues to enhance its attractions as an FDI destination by improving the ease of doing business and liberalizing regulations and sector caps for FDI.

Policy challenge—defusing the threat from high oil prices

Global oil prices have been on an upswing since early 2016, climbing by more than 75% during the year. The rise has been a result of oil exporters scaling back their output. Because India imports four-fifths of its petroleum needs, it was profoundly affected as the average import price increased by 37.6% in FY2016. A rapid increase in the price of oil challenges macroeconomic stability in numerous ways as it undermines fiscal consolidation, stokes inflation, and swells the current account deficit.

With Indian consumption of petroleum products increasing by an annual average of 5.6% over the past 5 years, any sharp increase in oil prices would widen the import bill considerably. With current import volumes, a $1 increase in oil prices raises the import bill by nearly $2 billion. However, as India exports refined petroleum products, some of the increase in the import bill is offset by higher export earnings. On balance, every $1 increase in the price of oil widens the trade and current account deficits by $1.4 billion.

Declining oil prices and price deregulation for petroleum products like gasoline and diesel have facilitated fiscal consolidation through petroleum subsidy contraction from the equivalent of 0.9% of GDP in FY2013 to 0.2% in FY2016. The government currently subsidizes cooking gas and kerosene, which comprise 14% of petroleum product consumption. To rationalize subsidies, the government has been expanding a program that pays the cooking gas subsidy directly into recipients' bank accounts and incrementally raising the price of kerosene. Despite these measures, consumption of subsidized fuels is estimated to grow by 6% annually. Higher global oil prices will raise the subsidy cost and could divert resources from growth-enhancing capital expenditure. Further, a substantial rise in oil prices could force the partial rolling back of excise duty hikes enacted in the second half of FY2015. The consequent loss of revenue would constrain fiscal consolidation.

A rise in oil prices will directly affect decontrolled prices for various fuels with a combined weight of 2.4% on the consumer price index. However, as nearly 40% of the market price of these fuels is

3.17.13 Investment projects

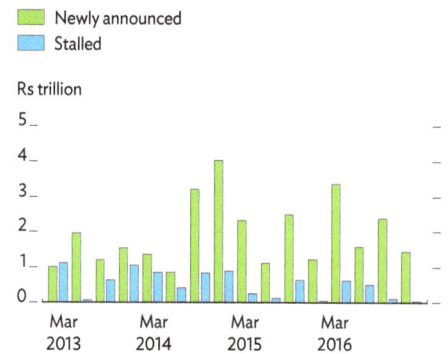

Source: Centre for Monitoring Indian Economy.

3.17.14 Purchasing managers' indexes

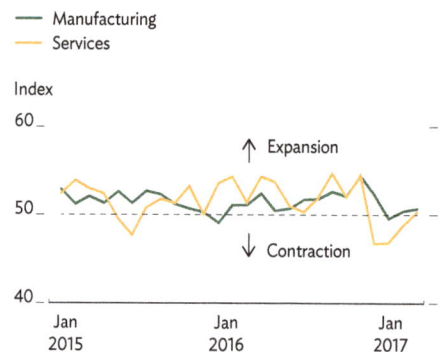

Note: Nikkei, Markit.
Source: Bloomberg (accessed 14 March 2017).

government tax that would be unaffected by higher global prices, a 20% increase in global oil prices would raise domestic prices for refined fuels by 12%, lifting retail inflation by 30 basis points. The indirect effect will be larger as higher fuel prices spillover to transportation costs. Fares for buses, taxis, auto-rickshaws, railways, and so on have a combined weight of 2.1% on the index, and the effect of a 20% increase in global oil prices would lift consumer inflation by 50 basis points.

To mitigate India's vulnerability to oil price swings, the government has proposed reducing dependence on imported oil by 10% over the next 5 years. This is to be done by making domestic production more efficient and attracting foreign and domestic private investment into the sector. A new hydrocarbon exploration and licensing policy introduced in 2016 encourages participation by placing under a single license exploration for conventional and unconventional oil and gas resources including coal bed methane, shale gas and oil, tight gas, and gas hydrates. It also introduces a revenue-sharing model that is easy to administer and frees up the marketing and pricing of the oil and natural gas produced. In addition, the government approved a policy paving the way to auction to public or private buyers 100 prospective mineral blocks. State-owned oil firms are now free to determine their own oil import policies regarding sources and pricing to enable them to compete efficiently. Also allowed now are exploration and production projects 100% financed by FDI. Meanwhile, to enhance exports of refined petroleum products, India is augmenting its refining capacity by setting up new state-owned refineries and allowing up to 49% FDI in private projects.

Maldives

Tourism recovered slightly in 2016 but remained weak for a third year, leaving growth to be sustained by expansive fiscal policy. The current account deficit widened on imports for infrastructure development. Inflation stayed low. The outlook is for continued moderate growth. Careful fiscal management is needed to ensure the success of efforts to boost tourism and develop infrastructure to foster a more diversified economy.

Economic performance

Growth picked up slightly to an estimated 3.4% in 2016 from 2.8% in 2015 as construction remained prominent, though it grew at a more moderate pace than in the previous 2 years. Tourism recovered from a decline in 2015, but its subpar performance contributed little to growth. Most of the rest of the 0.6 percentage point increase in GDP growth came from modest gains in sectors other than tourism or transport and communication and from a recovery in net indirect taxes less subsidies (Figure 3.18.1).

Continued high public investment in construction pushed imports up. Notable among imports were materials and equipment to construct the Friendship Bridge linking Malé, the capital, to the nearby island of Hulhulé.

Indicators showed some improvement in tourism, which supplies more than a quarter of GDP, but sector performance continued to be weak in 2016, mainly on account of disappointing tourist arrivals. Despite 4.2% growth, up from 2.4% in 2015, arrivals were, at 1.3 million, below target because of a further decline of 10% from the People's Republic of China, the largest single market. Visitors from Europe, the Middle East, and South Asia all increased but managed to lift sector growth by only 1.2% (Figure 3.18.2). Tourism earnings measured by bed-night occupancy recovered minimally to 2.3% growth, but the average duration of stay shortened by 3.5%.

Fisheries recovered in 2016 with fish purchases up by 7.0% following a 10.4% decline in 2015. Growth in other sectors was modest.

Following the government's decision to remove subsidies on staple goods in October 2016, except on food for the poor, food prices jumped by 70%–100% in Malé and even more on far-flung atolls despite price controls. This pushed average consumer inflation up to 1.8% in the fourth quarter of 2016, though average inflation for the whole year was still at a record low of 0.5% on account of low international prices for commodities, especially food and fuel (Figure 3.18.3).

3.18.1 Supply-side contributions to growth

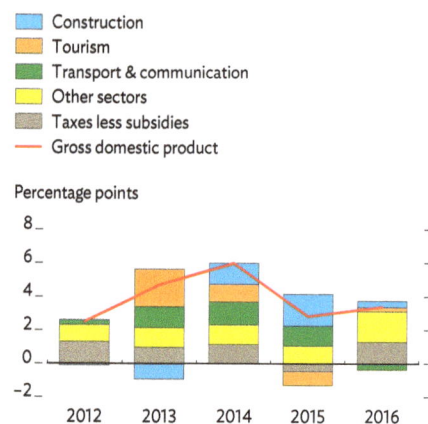

Source: Maldives Monetary Authority. 2017. *Monthly Statistics.* February. http://www.mma.gov.mv

3.18.2 Tourism indicators

Source: Maldives Monetary Authority. 2017. *Monthly Statistics.* February. http://www.mma.gov.mv

This chapter was written by Masato Nakane of the South Asia Department, ADB, Manila; and Macrina Mallari and Remedios Baes-Espineda, consultants, South Asia Department, ADB, Manila.

Lower expenditure and somewhat higher tax revenue, particularly from the newly introduced green tax and improved collection of the general goods and services tax, improved budget performance in 2016 (Figure 3.18.4). Total revenue including grants increased by an estimated 4.9% to $1.2 billion, though it fell relative to GDP by 1.5 percentage points to 31.3%. The government reprioritized spending by cutting recurrent expenditure in favor of capital spending. Recurrent expenditure fell by 5.3 percentage points to the equivalent of 26.4% of GDP, while capital expenditure rose to 12.3% from 8.9% a year earlier. Total expenditure including net lending was almost $1.5 million, falling as a share of GDP to 38.7% from 40.6% in 2015. As the quality of spending improved, the budget deficit shrank to 7.4% of GDP from 7.8%.

As in previous years, domestic debt financed most of the budget gap, or 72%, through the issuance of Treasury bonds and bills sold to commercial banks and other financial institutions. By the end of 2016, the outstanding stock of government securities had grown by 16%. Treasury bills rose by 15% year on year with increased holdings by commercial banks, while an 18% expansion in bond issuance mirrored the pension fund's conversion of Treasury bills to bonds. Treasury bills continued to be issued through a fixed-rate tap system. Interest rates were unchanged after being lowered in October 2015. More than a quarter of government debt is external, with public and publicly guaranteed debt to bilateral and multilateral organizations, commercial firms, and credit suppliers estimated at $668 million. At the end of 2016, total public debt was Rf36.7 billion, estimated to equal 63% of GDP, unchanged from a year earlier.

Low inflation allowed the Maldives Monetary Authority (MMA) to maintain an accommodative policy in 2016. Banks' required minimum reserve ratio and overnight deposit and borrowing rates were kept low. Growth in loans and advances to the private sector slowed marginally to 10.5% from 12.3% in the previous year. Growth in the money supply slowed substantially to 0.1% from 12.3% in 2015, mainly reflecting a 37% decline in MMA net foreign assets as it purchased a large bond from Maldives Airports that allowed the company to pay off a large foreign obligation (Box 3.18.1). Banks' net domestic assets grew by almost 25% on account of increased investment in securities (Figure 3.18.5).

With lower tourism receipts but a persistently large trade deficit, the current account deficit deteriorated further to the equivalent of 17.7% of GDP from 9.5% in 2015 (Figure 3.18.6). Exports fell by 14.8%, largely because re-exports of jet fuel declined. Tuna exports were broadly unchanged. Meanwhile, imports grew by 6.5% on higher demand for machinery, building materials, and electrical equipment. Payments for services, interest, and worker remittances expanded moderately.

Foreign direct investment and other financing inflows are estimated to have increased by 14% in 2016 from a year earlier but were still insufficient to plug the current account gap. The compensation payment for the cancelled airport contract reduced gross reserves in November by $200 million, pulling down usable reserves (gross reserves less commercial banks' foreign currency deposits) to cover for only 0.6 months of imports. By the end of December 2016, usable reserves

3.18.1 The airport debacle

In 2010, the government transferred responsibility for operating the Ibrahim Nasim International Airport from Maldives Airports to Grandhi Mallikarjuna Rao Male International Airport (GMIAL) for a contracted 25 years. Two years later, the next government cancelled the agreement as damaging to Maldives Airports and Maldivian citizens.

GMIAL filed a case in the Singapore International Arbitration Centre, and a settlement was reached on 25 October 2016. GMIAL had demanded $1.4 billion, but arbitration settled on an award of $208 million plus 4 years' interest and costs for a total of $271 million, equal to 7.2% of GDP.

The MMA paid GMIAL on 15 November 2016, completing the settlement quickly because the government was concerned about rising interest. The government maintains that the money did not come from the state budget but from state institutions providing what it called "generous aid."

Of the total, $140 million was raised by the sale to the MMA of Maldives Airports bonds to be repaid within 3 years at 4.9% interest. The balance of $131 million apparently came from Maldives Airports bank accounts.

3.18.3 Inflation

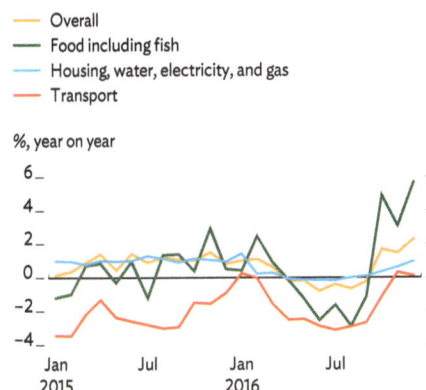

- Overall
- Food including fish
- Housing, water, electricity, and gas
- Transport

%, year on year

Source: Maldives Monetary Authority. 2017. *Monthly Statistics.* February. http://www.mma.gov.mv

were rebuilt to $200 million, unchanged from a year earlier but still less than 1 month of import cover. Gross international reserves then amounted to $467.1 million, down from $564.0 million in 2015 (Figure 3.18.7).

Economic prospects

Prospects for economic expansion in the near term will depend on the government sustaining high infrastructure investment and on the expected reinvigoration of tourism.

Growth in 2017 will come largely from robust construction as the government continues to invest in large infrastructure projects. Almost 30% of the approved $1.7 billion budget will be allocated to 704 projects under a public sector investment program. After large and persistent fiscal deficits, the government will try to cut expenditure further and expand its tax base and nontax revenue, targeting a 21% increase in budget resources including grants. The share of recurrent spending in total expenditure is programmed to drop further to 61% from 68% in 2016, while capital spending will grow to 39%, though with a reduced allocation to the public sector investment program. The government projects the fiscal deficit significantly narrower, equal to 0.5% of GDP in both 2017 and 2018. However, taking into account previous budgets, in which revenue normally fell short by 10%–12% and expenditure overshot by 5%–7%, more realistic forecasts for fiscal deficits are higher, at 6.4% of GDP in 2017 and 6.0% in 2018.

Tourism will contribute to future growth prospects as well, with recovery expected in the next few years. The government renewed its marketing campaign, Travel Trade Maldives, to run from 2016 to 2020, aiming to bring in 2 million tourists and $3.5 billion in earnings by 2020. Plans exist for 50 new resorts to be constructed in the next 4 years, 20 of them scheduled to begin operations in 2017. More flights are planned to attract more tourists from neighboring countries, and airport expansion on outlying islands is expected to boost tourism. However, slow growth in the economies of the main tourist markets could slow recovery. Moreover, further appreciation of the US dollar could weaken tourists' purchasing power. On balance, a moderate recovery of tourism is anticipated, with 5%–6% growth in arrivals.

Industries connected with construction and tourism will shape growth, as will presidential elections in 2018. The expected construction boom and a more vibrant tourism industry would have spillover on wholesale and retail trade, real estate, and transport and communications. The presidential election is expected to spur domestic spending and likewise stimulate growth, especially in 2018. However, a power struggle in the ruling party and mounting political tensions pose a risk that elections could undermine political stability and threaten growth prospects.

With growth in construction and tourism accelerating, GDP is projected to pick up to 3.8% in 2017 and further to 4.1% in 2018. In these circumstances the current account deficit would edge up to 18.9% of GDP in 2017 and 19.1% in 2018.

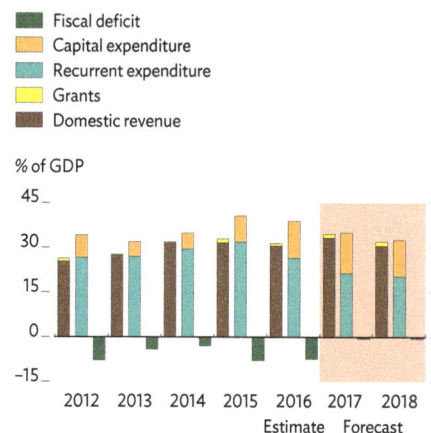

3.18.4 Fiscal indicators

Source: Maldives Monetary Authority. 2017. Monthly Statistics. February. http://www.mma.gov.mv

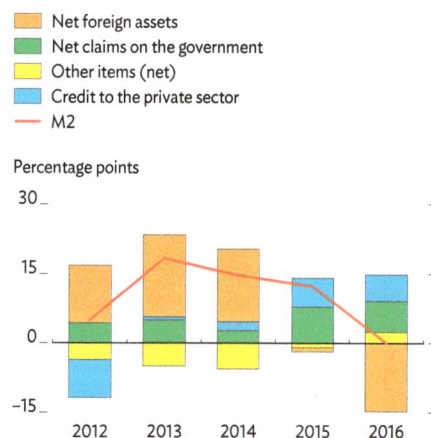

3.18.5 Contributions to money supply growth

Source: Maldives Monetary Authority. 2017. Monthly Statistics. February. http://www.mma.gov.mv

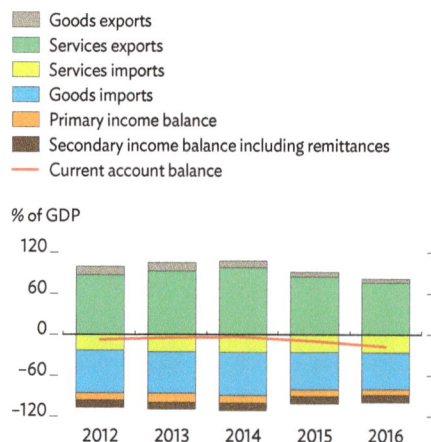

3.18.6 Balance of payments

Source: Maldives Monetary Authority. 2017. Monthly Statistics. February. http://www.mma.gov.mv

As the Maldives continues to depend heavily on imported diesel to generate electricity and power water supply, a large hike in oil prices would have a substantial impact on domestic prices. The government is trying to cut fuel consumption by introducing renewable energy. Green energy systems were slated to become operational on five islands in the first quarter of 2017, and the government aims to generate a considerable percentage of electricity from renewable sources by the end of 2018. If followed through, this would substantially lower electricity prices. However, the outlook sees higher global prices for oil and food, reduced food subsidies, and inflationary pressures from the elections edging up average inflation to 2.1% in 2017 and 2.3% in 2018.

Policy challenge—the perils of rapid urbanization

Urbanization has gathered pace in the Maldives, with more than one-third of the population now living in Malé (Figure 3.18.8). As the capital area measures less than 6 square kilometers, urban growth has brought overcrowding, high unemployment, environmental degradation, and pressure on housing and other urban infrastructure such as roads, sewage systems, and facilities to manage solid waste.

To ease the housing shortage, the government has opened the sector to private developers, introduced socialized housing programs, and embarked on ambitious land reclamation and urban development projects. Results to date have been mixed, with the number of residential units markedly higher but prices still prohibitive. Further, some residents who moved to Hulhumalé complain about a lack of jobs. To address unemployment, the government has restricted foreign workers in certain jobs and industries.

Waste management has been turned over to a state-owned company that introduced a new waste collection and management scheme last year. The government earmarked $100 million in the 2017 budget to build a waste management center for the greater Malé and the Kaafu, Alif Alif, and Vaavu atolls. Meanwhile, to control traffic in Malé, a congestion tax will be levied starting in 2017.

The socioeconomic problems brought by rapid urbanization in Malé require, however, more than one-time piecemeal solutions. Plans must be consolidated and strategies coordinated between state entities and other stakeholders. Development must reach beyond the capital and include nearby islands, ultimately creating a critical mass that would generate jobs and facilitate more efficient delivery and management of public services. The government's planned development of greater Malé is a start. The challenge is to ensure that the process is inclusive and sustainable.

3.18.1 Selected economic indicators (%)

	2017	2018
GDP growth	3.8	4.1
Inflation	2.1	2.3
Current account balance (share of GDP)	–18.9	–19.1

Source: ADB estimates.

3.18.7 Gross international reserves

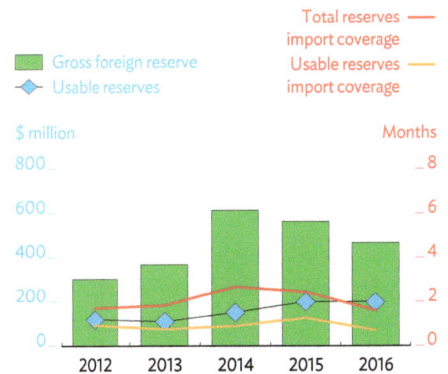

Source: Maldives Monetary Authority. 2017. *Monthly Statistics.* February. http://www.mma.gov.mv

3.18.8 Urbanization

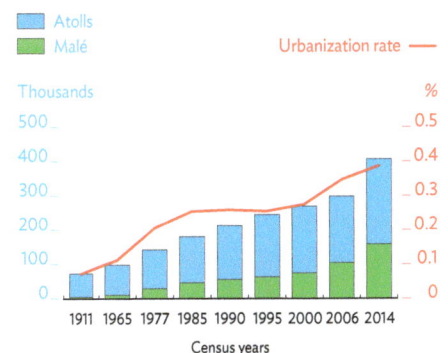

Sources: Various censuses (2000, 2006, and 2014). http://statisticsmaldives.gov.mv/census-2014/

Nepal

Growth slowed in FY2016 after devastating earthquakes late in the previous fiscal year, a weak monsoon, and trade disruptions. The outlook is for robust recovery in the next 2 years on revived agriculture and accelerated spending on reconstruction. Slow growth in worker remittances, the major source of foreign exchange, is pushing the current account into deficit. Reform to boost investment is critical to lifting the growth trajectory.

Economic performance

In FY2016 (ending 15 July 2016) GDP growth slowed to its lowest rate since FY2002 because of an unusual series of shocks to the economy: large earthquakes in April and May 2015 that demolished productive capacity and incomes, subsequent delays in earthquake reconstruction, trade and supply disruption from September 2015 to February 2016 as some groups in the southern Terai plains bordering India protested against the new constitution, and a second year of poor monsoons. Together, these events held growth to only 0.8%, well below the 4.2% average in FY2011–FY2015 and a recent high of 5.7% in FY2014 (Figure 3.19.1).

Trade disruption and delayed reconstruction shrank manufacturing and construction sharply, while agriculture and services, which supply 33% and 52% of GDP respectively, expanded slowly. Among services, trade, transport, and tourism (collectively 25% of GDP) either grew only marginally or contracted. Subsectors mostly reliant on domestic markets—such as financial intermediation, real estate, education, and community, social, and personal services (collectively 24% of GDP)—expanded slightly faster with support from overseas workers' remittances.

Inflationary pressures intensified with the earthquakes and trade disruptions and, in the second half of FY2016, weak agriculture and higher inflation in India, to whose currency the Nepali rupee is pegged. Consumer inflation averaged 9.9% in FY2016 with sharp increases for both food (44% of the consumer price basket) and other goods and services, reflecting shortages of essential commodities in the first 3 quarters of FY2016 (Figure 3.19.2). Upward deviation from inflation in India expanded to 4.7 percentage points from 1.9 points in FY2015, dampening export competitiveness.

The government budget registered a surplus equal to 1.4% of GDP in FY2016, in contrast with the anticipated 7.8% deficit to support earthquake reconstruction and much-needed investment in infrastructure and social services. While revenue continued to rise

3.19.1 Supply-side contributions to growth

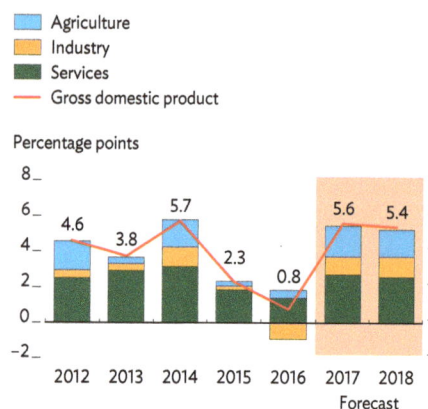

Agriculture
Industry
Services
Gross domestic product

Percentage points

Note: Years are fiscal years ending on 15 July of that year.
Sources: Central Bureau of Statistics. 2017. National Accounts of Nepal 2016/17. http://cbs.gov.np/; ADB estimates.

3.19.2 Monthly inflation

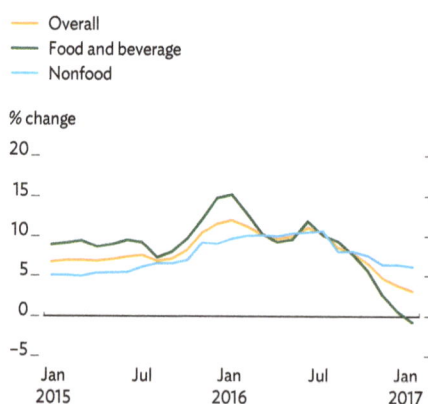

Overall
Food and beverage
Nonfood

% change

Source: Nepal Rastra Bank. 2017. Recent Macroeconomic Situation. http://www.nrb.org.np

---

This chapter was written by Sharad Bhandari and Neelina Nakarmi of the Nepal Resident Mission, ADB, Kathmandu.

and exceeded the budget target, expenditure including net lending came to 23.1% of GDP, only two-thirds of the planned 34.7% as both recurrent and capital expenditure fell short of their targets. Although capital expenditure rose to 5.2% of GDP from 4.2% in the previous year, it underperformed the 9.3% planned in the FY2016 budget, reflecting delayed operationalization of the National Reconstruction Authority, trade and supply disruption, and long-standing weaknesses in government capacity to plan, prepare, and implement projects (Figure 3.19.3).

With inflationary pressure mainly on the supply side, Nepal Rastra Bank, the central bank, pursued an accommodative monetary policy. Broad money supply (M2) rose in FY2016 at about the same rate as in the previous year. With the fiscal surplus, most of the increase was attributable to the rise in net foreign assets and credit to the private sector (Figure 3.19.4).

Trade disruption and a stronger currency in inflation-adjusted terms added to long-standing structural constraints and a 29.0% decline in FY2016 merchandise exports in US dollar terms. Imports fell by 7.1% from a higher base, narrowing the trade deficit by 1.0 percentage point to the equivalent of 30.3% of GDP. Workers remittances rose but at a much slower pace than before as migrant numbers fell; many potential migrants were needed at home after the earthquakes, and demand fell for workers in oil-exporting economies, especially in the Persian Gulf and Malaysia. The reduced trade deficit and steady remittances contributed to a larger current account surplus, equal to 6.2% of GDP (Figure 3.19.5). They also pushed foreign exchange reserves to $9.7 billion, sufficient for 14 months of imports of goods and nonfactor services (Figure 3.19.6).

Economic prospects

Economic growth is expected to revive to 5.6% in FY2017 because trade and supply disruptions from the Terai unrest have receded, the monsoon has been favorable, and earthquake reconstruction is accelerating. Other supports for growth this year are spending on local elections scheduled for mid-May 2017 and, significantly, more reliable electricity. Kathmandu has suffered very little load-shedding since October 2016, in contrast with outages of more than 10 hours per day in previous winters. Other parts of the country have also enjoyed substantially better electricity supply. Electricity consumption rose sharply with sales up by 44% in January 2017 from a year earlier, the increases strong in all segments. Improved electricity provision reflects more judicious management of demand with more equitable distribution of electricity across big industries and other consumers, stricter monitoring that reduced transmission and distribution losses by 2 percentage points to 23.8% as of mid-January 2017, and increased supply from both domestic generation and imports from India. If this trend is sustained, growth will be significantly enhanced over the medium term.

Rice production, which accounts for 16% of agricultural output, is set to increase to 5.2 million tons in FY2017, a 21% jump over last year and a new record surpassing the 5.1 million tons recorded in FY2012

3.19.3 Fiscal indicators

- Grants
- Domestic revenue
- Capital expenditure
- Recurrent expenditure
- Fiscal balance

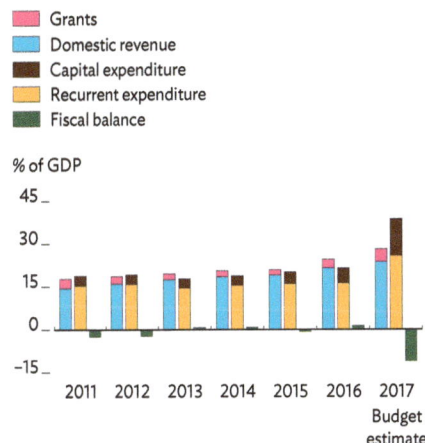

Note: Years are fiscal years ending on 15 July of that year.
Source: Ministry of Finance. Budget Speech 2017.

3.19.4 Credit to the private sector and M2 growth

- Credit to the private sector
- Money (M2) growth

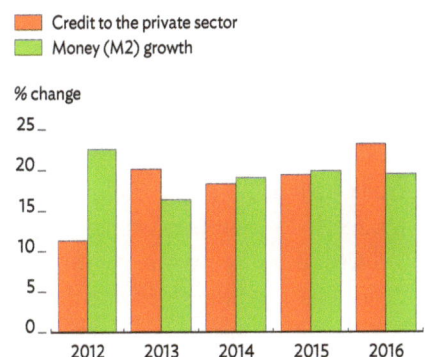

Note: Years are fiscal years ending on 15 July of that year.
Source: Nepal Rastra Bank. 2017. *Recent Macroeconomic Situation.* http://www.nrb.org.np

3.19.5 Current account indicators

- Workers' remittances
- Tourism and travel
- Non-oil imports
- Oil imports
- Exports
- Current account balance

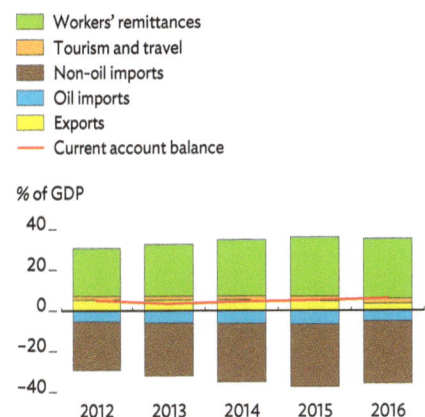

Note: Years are fiscal years ending on 15 July of that year.
Source: Nepal Rastra Bank. 2017. *Recent Macroeconomic Situation.* http://www.nrb.org.np

(Figure 3.19.7). Construction should benefit from progress in earthquake reconstruction. Of some 532,000 families eligible for housing grants in the 11 districts worst affected by the earthquakes, 476,000 had by the end of December 2016 signed grant agreements and 452,500 had received the first installment of NRs50,000 for new home foundations. The government has begun reconstructing some 8,900 classrooms (of 49,000 estimated to have been partly or completely destroyed) and 313 kilometers of roads, as well as health centers, other government buildings, and water-supply systems.

Growth in services is expected to nearly double to 5.2% in FY2017 as positive economic trends offset the effect of lackluster remittance growth. The US dollar value of remittances is projected to rise by 2.8% in FY2017, well below the 15.0% average from FY2012 to FY2015. The number of migrants going abroad is still declining, albeit more slowly after a sharp fall immediately following the earthquakes, reflecting in part weaker demand for labor in oil-exporting host countries.

Inflation is likely to subside to an average of 6.0% in FY2017 as agriculture output increases, trade normalizes, and Indian inflation abates. Higher public sector salaries and international oil prices appear to preclude a sharper decline. Food price inflation is expected to slow considerably more than nonfood inflation. As inflation slows in Nepal more than in India, the gap between the two will narrow, improving Nepal's export competitiveness. Monetary policy has aimed to restrain inflation by slowing broad money growth. Net foreign assets will rise at a slower rate with moderation in remittance growth and a higher trade deficit. Bank claims on the government for the full year may rise modestly to fund the fiscal deficit.

Credit to the private sector is likely to be significantly higher, reflecting a pickup in economic activity. Commercial bank credit to the private sector has risen steadily since the easing of trade disruptions in February 2016, while growth in deposits hovered around 20%, significantly lifting the loan–deposit ratio (Figure 3.19.8). This has exerted upward pressure on nominal and real interest rates. Moderating inflation gives the central bank scope to increase the money supply somewhat more quickly after taking into account prudential norms in the financial sector.

The FY2017 budget envisages a deficit increase to an estimated 11% of GDP with substantially higher allocations for both recurrent and capital expenditure, including earthquake rehabilitation and reconstruction. With expenditure historically falling short of allocation, the actual fiscal deficit will likely be around 1% of GDP, modestly stimulating growth. Although capital expenditure in the first half of FY2017 rose sharply from FY2016, it still fell well short of the budget target (Figure 3.19.9). Capital spending is likely to accelerate significantly in the second half of the fiscal year, as usual, then revert in FY2017 to pre-earthquake norms at about 75% of allocations. Revenue is expected to track the budget projection as economic activity picks up and a sharp increase in imports means higher duty collections, which contribute about 40% of revenue.

The trade deficit will widen significantly in FY2017 to 41.5% of GDP on the surge in imports in early FY2017 to meet pent-up demand

3.19.1 Selected economic indicators (%)

	2017	2018
GDP growth	5.6	5.4
Inflation	6.0	6.5
Current account balance (share of GDP)	–1.6	–3.2

Note: Years are fiscal years ending on 15 July of that year.
Source: ADB estimates.

3.19.6 Gross international reserves and exchange rate

Source: Nepal Rastra Bank. 2017. Recent Macroeconomic Situation. http://www.nrb.org.np

3.19.7 Rice production and agriculture growth

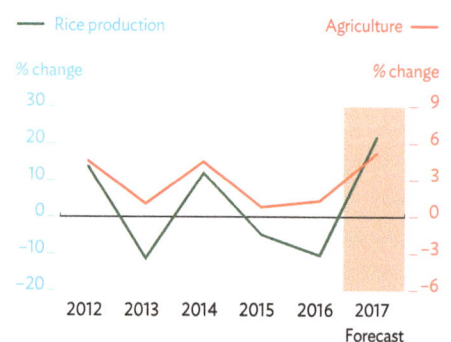

Note: Years are fiscal years ending on 15 July of that year.
Source: Ministry of Agriculture Development.

and the slower but significant earlier increase following the easing of trade disruptions. The current torrid pace of import growth will moderate after February with erosion of the base effect, imports of rice partly replaced by the rise in domestic production, and savings on oil imports as better electricity supply lessens industry reliance on diesel generators. The current account is nevertheless expected to post a deficit equal to 1.6% of GDP in FY2017, a reversal by nearly 8 percentage points from FY2016, because of the larger trade deficit and the slower rise in remittances.

GDP growth should continue into FY2018 at 5.4%. This outlook assumes a normal monsoon in 2017 and no major political or social unrest as local, provincial, and national elections are conducted and the newly elected parliament is installed by January 2018 as mandated by the constitution. Growth should be supported by buoyant agriculture, further improvement in electricity supply, increased reconstruction momentum, and a likely increase in election-related spending. Higher real interest rates and a slower rise in remittances are likely drags on growth. Inflation may accelerate modestly to 6.5% on higher domestic demand, notably from reconstruction and election-related spending, and despite improved domestic supply of agricultural staples. Even with high domestic demand, import growth will be moderate after the catchup surge a year earlier. The current account deficit is nevertheless likely to widen further to equal 3.2% of GDP in FY2018 as growth in remittances continues to languish.

Policy challenge—investment for higher sustainable growth

Nepal needs more and better investment to achieve and sustain high rates of economic growth. Fixed capital formation has languished below the 30% average in South Asia (Figure 3.19.10). Foreign direct investment is a critical conduit for financial resources and new techniques and technology but has been miniscule despite a recent rise in commitments (Figure 3.19.11). Manufacturing and tourism, two sectors with substantial potential for more productive employment, are either shrinking or stagnant. Factors constraining investment are political and policy instability, deficient infrastructure particularly for energy and transport, and inadequate formulation and enforcement of regulations to promote vibrant and competitive industries.

Since the promulgation of the constitution in 2015, the prospects for relieving constraints on investment have improved because all the main political parties agree on the need to attract investment to fuel sustainable economic growth. The reduction in electricity load-shedding is a major milestone. The government is implementing a 10-year action plan to erase the energy deficit by increasing investment in generation, transmission, and distribution infrastructure and by instituting policy and regulatory reform to level the playing field for public and private participants. Public investment in transport infrastructure has increased, and some major projects such as the Kathmandu–Tarai Fast Track expressway are being planned. Further, the government

3.19.8 Commercial bank deposits and lending

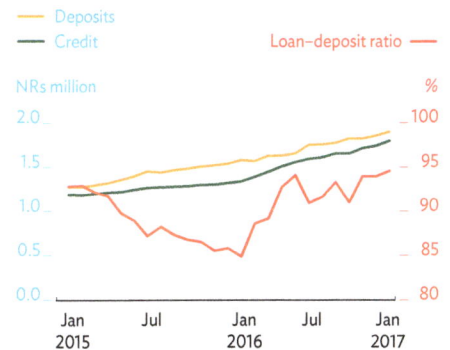

Note: Source: Nepal Rastra Bank. 2017. *Recent Macroeconomic Situation.* http://www.nrb.org.np

3.19.9 Budgeted and actual capital spending

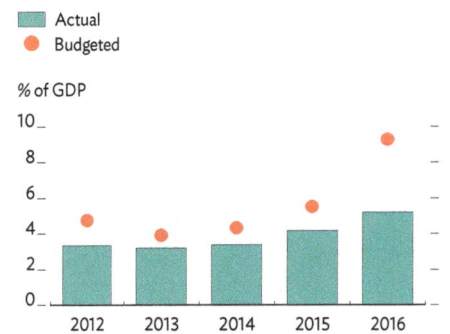

Note: Years are fiscal years ending on 15 July of that year.
Sources: Central Bureau of Statistics. http://cbs.gov.np/; Ministry of Finance. Budget speech various years.

3.19.10 Gross fixed capital formation and foreign direct investment

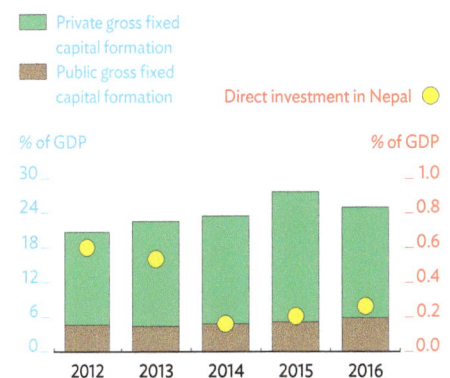

Note: Years are fiscal years ending on 15 July of that year.
Sources: Central Bureau of Statistics and Nepal Rastra Bank.

aims to complete the construction of transport and other infrastructure projects in a more timely way—to high quality and on budget—by improving project preparation, procurement, and contract management.

To attract private investment in infrastructure, the government approved a public–private partnership policy in 2015 and is currently finalizing the draft Public–Private Partnership (PPP) Act. It will establish a PPP center and streamline procedures for PPP. Capacity needs buttressing, in particular for project preparation, assessing whether a project should be public or PPP, allocating risks appropriately in PPP projects, attracting the private sector, and executing transactions.

The government recently enacted some legal changes to improve the business climate. The Industrial Enterprise Act and the Special Economic Zone Act are good starts toward making the investment environment more predictable. The former has introduced online firm registration and acceptance of digital signatures, simplified environment impact assessment, and instituted a "no work, no pay" clause to discourage ad hoc labor strikes, which have been prevalent in recent years. Similarly, the latter prohibits labor strikes or any other disruption to business operations within a special economic zone. A foreign investment act is in the final stages of enactment. The draft bill simplifies approval for foreign direct investment, portfolio investment, and equity funds. An amendment to the Company Act to ease company exit conditions is expected soon.

Despite progress, a remaining implementation challenge is to ensure that various legal provisions are consistent and coherent. For example, provisions on "no work, no pay" and related labor issues under the Industrial Enterprise Act could be superseded by the current Labor Act. Similarly, incentive schemes offered under various laws suffer inconsistent interpretation and application. Different government offices approve foreign investment depending on its size, and investors are required to get approval from both the Department of Industry and the central bank for establishment and earnings repatriation. In addition, investors are required to register with the Office of Company Registrar and the tax and immigration offices. Businesses and investors often point to a complicated web of procedures and delays they often encounter at each agency. Eliminating regulatory inconsistency and transparently enforcing rules would enhance the prospects for investment.

3.19.11 Foreign direct investment

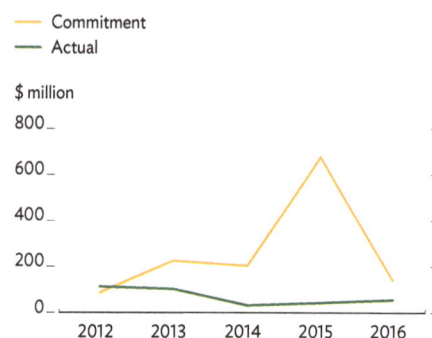

Note: Years are fiscal years ending on 15 July of that year.
Sources: Department of Industry; Nepal Rastra Bank.

Pakistan

Growth accelerated in FY2016, benefiting from major economic reforms and improved security. Low oil prices helped slow inflation markedly and keep the current account deficit moderate despite weaker exports. The outlook is for higher growth, with inflation and current account deficit edging up on higher oil prices and substantial imports for a major investment project. Continued economic reform is essential to reach a high growth trajectory.

Economic performance

Provisional estimates put GDP growth at 4.7% in FY2016 (ended 30 June 2016), driven by robust growth in services and industry (Figure 3.20.1). Growth recovery in large-scale manufacturing to 4.6% and in construction to 13.8% underpinned 6.8% expansion in industry. Automobiles, fertilizer, and cement were among manufactures with notable growth. Industry expansion, financial sector strengthening, and increasingly active trade fueled 5.7% expansion in services, which was 1.4 percentage points higher than in the previous year. GDP growth was restrained, however, by a 0.2% fall in agriculture output as adverse weather and pest infestations caused heavy losses, especially of cotton, which had knock-on effects on textile manufacturing and external trade. To cushion the impact on smallholder farmers, the government introduced a support package to subsidize agricultural inputs.

On the expenditure side, private consumption continued to drive growth, the substantial government contribution to it varying from year to year depending on the financial situation and wage adjustments (Figure 3.20.2). Investment continued to be, at 15.1% of GDP, very low when compared with similar countries in the region, constraining growth. The main causes of low investment are infrastructure deficits exemplified by crippling power outages, a difficult business environment, security issues, and bouts of macroeconomic instability. Fixed investment from the government and public enterprises increased by 12.9% to equal 3.8% of GDP, but private investment fell slightly from 10.2% of GDP to 9.8% (Figure 3.20.3). Net exports subtracted from GDP growth, but the roughly 40% plunge in global oil prices in FY2016 improved the terms of trade by 10%, allowed the US dollar value of imports to fall from the year earlier even as the government and the private sector imported markedly higher volumes of goods other than oil.

Average headline consumer inflation fell from 4.5% to 2.9% in FY2016 because of lower global prices for oil and other commodities, stable food supply, limited government borrowing, and exchange rate

3.20.1 Supply-side contributions to growth

- Services
- Industry
- Agriculture
- Gross domestic product

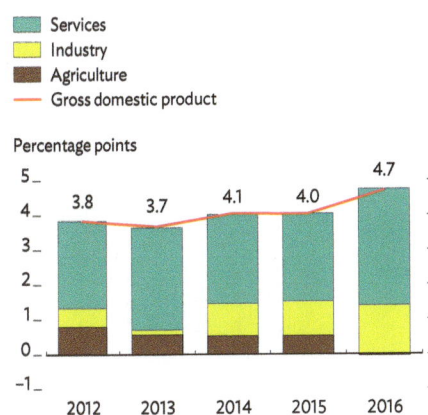

Note: Years are fiscal years ending on 30 June of that year.
Source: Ministry of Finance. *Pakistan Economic Survey 2015–16.* http://www.finance.gov.pk

3.20.2 Demand-side contributions to growth

- Net exports
- Investment
- Government consumption
- Private consumption

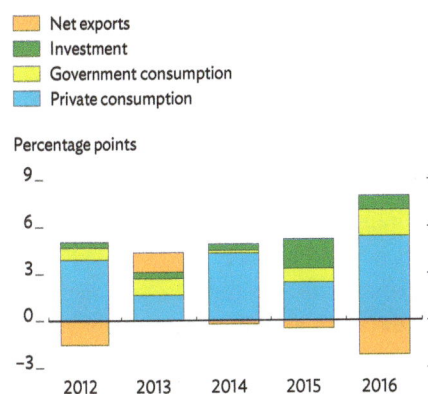

Note: Years are fiscal years ending on 30 June of that year.
Source: Ministry of Finance. *Pakistan Economic Survey 2015–16.* http://www.finance.gov.pk

This chapter was written by Guntur Sugiyarto and Farzana Noshab of the Pakistan Resident Mission, ADB, Islamabad.

stability (Figure 3.20.4). At the same time, average core inflation, other than for food and energy, improved from 6.6% in FY2015 to 4.2%. As inflation fell, the State Bank of Pakistan, the central bank, lowered its policy rate by a cumulative 75 basis points to 5.75% (Figure 3.20.5). With an improved economic environment and lower-cost borrowing, credit to the private sector doubled to PRs461 billion, the strongest expansion in recent years.

As the government improved revenue collection and restricted expenditure, the deficit in the general government budget, which consolidates federal and provincial budgets but excludes grants, narrowed by 0.8 percentage points to equal 4.6% of GDP in FY2016 (Figure 3.20.6). The Federal Board of Revenue boosted tax collection to PRs3.1 trillion, or 11.4% of GDP, and this was the major factor accounting for a 21.0% increase in tax revenue. Despite a marked decline in nontax revenue, total budget revenue increased to equal 15.0% of GDP as planned, though achieving this required the implementation of additional excise and customs taxes to cover shortfalls in oil import duties in the second half of the year.

Budget expenditure equaled 19.6% of GDP in FY2016, or 0.2 percentage points higher than in the previous year. Growth in current expenditure slowed from 10.5% in FY2015 to 6.1%. Expenditure on interest payments fell because of interest rate cuts, as did those on subsidies owing to rationalized energy tariffs. Development expenditure increased by 17.0%, reversing a 2.0% decline in the previous year. At the equivalent of only 4.4% of GDP, however, it was held below target by constraints on spending.

The lower budget deficit was financed largely from domestic sources. Domestic debt expanded in FY2016 by an amount equal to 1.7 percentage points of GDP, raising it to 46.0% of GDP and all public debt to 66.4% (Figure 3.20.7). Public external debt increased slightly to 20.4% after declining by 10.4 percentage points over the previous 5 years. The increase in external debt was largely from expanded multilateral and bilateral inflows but also reflected exchange rate adjustments. An amendment in 2016 to the Fiscal Responsibility and Debt Limitation Act, 2005 redefined public external debt as debt serviced from the consolidated fund and debt owed to the International Monetary Fund. The new definition excluded a minor category called external liabilities, which at the end of June 2016 equaled 1.3% of GDP, largely unchanged from a year earlier.

The current account deficit widened from the equivalent of 1.0% of GDP in FY2015 to 1.2% as exports declined, net interest payments increased, and growth in worker remittances slowed (Figure 3.20.8). Exports fell by 8.8% as slow growth in the major industrial economies undercut demand, the cotton crop failed, world prices fell for Pakistan's exports, and domestic production costs rose. The gains from a 32% fall in oil imports were partly offset by a 7.2% surge in other imports, especially cotton and machinery for textile production and electric power generation. Workers' remittances reached $19.9 billion, but this growth at 6.4% was less than half of the 16.0% average over the past decade (Figure 3.20.9). Remittances were nevertheless sufficient to fund the widening trade deficit. Supported by net financial account inflows of

3.20.3 Investment

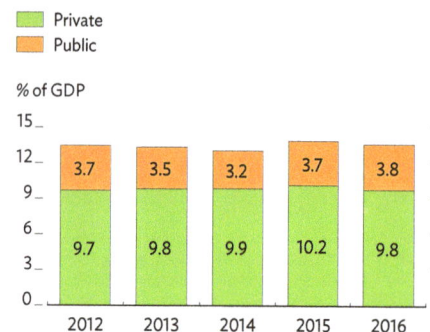

Note: Years are fiscal years ending on 30 June of that year.
Source: Ministry of Finance. *Pakistan Economic Survey 2015–16.* http://www.finance.gov.pk

3.20.4 Inflation

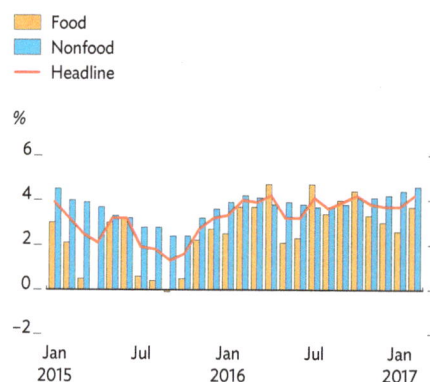

Source: State Bank of Pakistan. Economic Data. http://www.sbp.org.pk (accessed 13 February 2017).

3.20.5 Interest rates

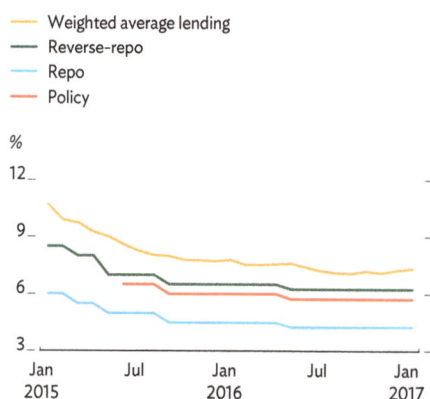

Source: State Bank of Pakistan. Economic Data. http://www.sbp.org.pk (accessed 14 February 2017).

$5.5 billion, mainly from multilateral and bilateral sources, and a near doubling of foreign direct investment to $1.9 billion, gross official foreign reserves increased to $18.1 billion, or cover for 4.3 months of imports.

Economic prospects

GDP growth is expected to edge up to 5.2% in FY2017 and 5.5% in FY2018, underpinned by higher growth in the major industrial economies. This outlook is supported by better security, macroeconomic stability, and improved economic fundamentals resulting from the continued implementation of government reform under a 3-year International Monetary Fund program completed in September 2016, as well as ongoing and planned infrastructure and other investments under an economic corridor project called CPEC, which links Pakistan with the People's Republic of China (PRC). These favorable developments are reflected in Standard & Poor's upgrading Pakistan's credit rating to B in October 2016, and Fitch doing the same in February 2017. Moreover, the Pakistan Stock Exchange scored the highest price increase in Asia in 2016 (Figure 3.20.10). Pakistan's reentry into the MSCI Emerging Market Index, scheduled for May 2017 after a 9-year hiatus, further underlines investor confidence in the economy. In this connection, a consortium of three PRC stock exchanges invested $85 million in December 2016 to acquire 40% of strategic shares in the Pakistan Stock Exchange.

Higher growth in FY2018 reflects accelerated infrastructure investment through CPEC, which is steadily lifting consumer and investor confidence and thereby further catalyzing economic activity. The government can lend policy support by maintaining macroeconomic stability and addressing structural issues that continue to inhibit exports despite the easing of regulatory constraints on doing business. With national elections scheduled for 2018, the budget to be announced in June 2017 will likely prioritize measures to foster economic expansion.

The forecast for growth in FY2017 envisages revived agriculture as recovery in cotton and sugarcane offset a forecast decline in the rice crop. The revival is underpinned by special credit facilities, subsidized fertilizer, and improved global commodity prices. Favorable weather, including timely rains in January 2017, augurs for a strong winter wheat crop. Prevailing low interest rates, improved electricity supply, and government budgetary incentives announced in June 2016 should boost large-scale manufacturing. The government announced in January 2017 a support package worth $17 billion for exports of textiles, clothing, and related raw materials. It is expected to revitalize the textile industry, which suffered from a weak cotton crop and frail global demand last year. Stronger growth in industry and agriculture will catalyze activity in the service sector.

Average consumer inflation is expected to accelerate to 4.0% in FY2017 on a rebound in oil prices, higher domestic demand, and expanded government borrowing from the central bank. Headline inflation averaged 3.8% in the first 7 months of FY2017, up from 2.3% in the same period last year, with increases for food and other goods. Core inflation, which excludes food and energy, followed the trend and

3.20.6 Government budget indicators

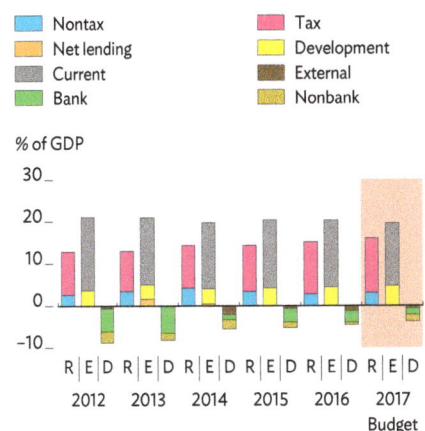

R = revenue, E = expenditure, D = deficit financing.
Notes: Years are fiscal years ending on 30 June of that year. Data refer to consolidated federal and provincial government finances. Net lending includes statistical discrepancy. Nonbank includes privatization proceeds.
Sources: Ministry of Finance. *Pakistan Economic Survey 2015–2016; Federal Budget in Brief 2016–17; Pakistan Fiscal Operations FY2016.*

3.20.7 Public debt

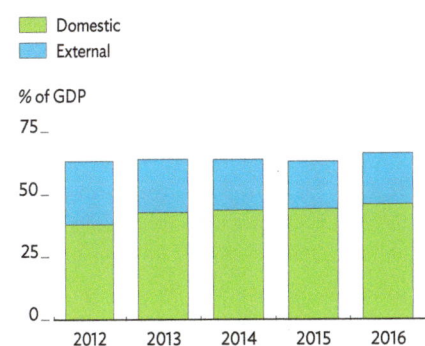

Note: Years are fiscal years ending on 30 June of that year.
Source: State Bank of Pakistan. Economic Data. http://www.sbp.org.pk (accessed 14 February 2017).

3.20.1 Selected economic indicators (%)

	2017	2018
GDP growth	5.2	5.5
Inflation	4.0	4.8
Current account balance (share of GDP)	−2.1	−2.5

Note: Years are fiscal years ending on 30 June of that year.
Source: ADB estimates.

rose by 1.1 percentage points to 5.0%. The government passed the global oil price increases on to domestic consumers by raising domestic oil prices three times from December 2016 to February 2017, after having kept them low for several months. A continued recovery in oil prices will likely accelerate inflation, which is projected to reach 4.8% in FY2018. The central bank will need to be vigilant and readjust its accommodative monetary policy if inflationary pressures intensify.

The general government budget deficit is projected to shrink to the equivalent of 3.8% of GDP in FY2017. This assumes total revenue equaling 15.8% of GDP, based on Federal Board of Revenue tax collection at 10.8% of GDP, and continued expenditure rationalization. To achieve the lower deficit, additional measures may be needed in the remaining months of FY2017 to bridge a revenue shortfall in the first half of the year, though higher imports and the pass-through of higher oil prices to consumers may be sufficient to boost indirect tax revenue. A shortfall in nontax revenue poses an additional challenge, but it should be mitigated somewhat by expected inflows under the Coalition Support Fund and, if accomplished, the budgeted sale of the 3G telecom spectrum.

Targeted expenditures in FY2017 equal 19.6% of GDP. Expenditures in the first half were, at 8.3% of GDP, about the same as last year because the government was able to contain current expenditure by curtailing domestic interest payments and spending on other categories including subsidies. Consolidated federal and provincial development spending was also low in this period at 1.5% of GDP, less than a third of the FY2017 full year target of 4.7%. Any provincial overspending in the full year, especially infrastructure development that looks ahead to the election, may challenge a key budgetary assumption that the provinces will record a cash surplus of PRs339 billion, equal to 1.0% of GDP.

The current account deficit is projected to widen to equal 2.1% of GDP in FY2017. The deficit increased to $4.7 billion in the first 7 months of FY2017, almost double the $2.5 billion deficit in the same period of FY2016. Services and income account deficits worsened as receipts under the Coalition Support Fund were delayed. Meanwhile, the workers' remittances that critically offset the large trade deficit fell for the first time in 10 years, by 1.9% to $10.9 billion, because of declining expenditures and income in oil-dependent Gulf economies.

The trade deficit widened in the first 7 months of FY2017 by 21.1% to $13 billion as imports accelerated by 9.2%, driven by an 18% increase in investment goods and a 12% rise in oil import payments as prices recovered. Investment goods accounted for 40% of the increase in imports, and oil nearly 30%. Exports continued to decline, but by only 1.3%, which was much smaller than the 11.7% plunge in the same period of FY2016. A third consecutive year of falling exports reflects weak global demand and low international commodity prices but also domestic structural issues such as power outages, scant investment in modernization, and currency appreciation in real effective terms, all of which hamper competitiveness. The nominal exchange rate was stable at PRs104.7 to the US dollar in the first 7 months of FY2017, but the Pakistan rupee continued to appreciate in real effective terms, undermining export competitiveness (Figure 3.20.11).

3.20.8 Current account components

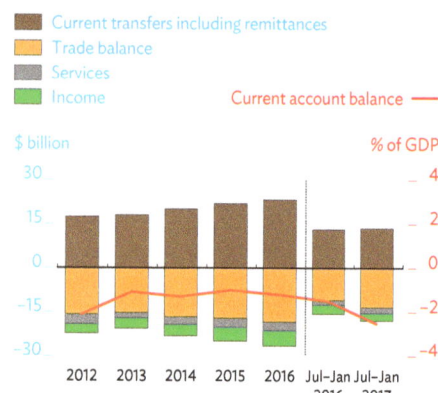

Note: Years are fiscal years ending on 30 June of that year.
Source: State Bank of Pakistan. Economic Data. http://www.sbp.org.pk (accessed 14 February 2017).

3.20.9 Remittances

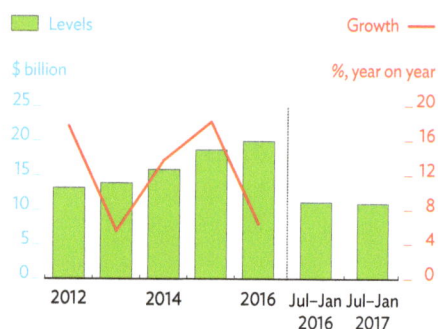

Note: Years are fiscal years ending on 30 June of that year.
Source: State Bank of Pakistan. Economic Data. http://www.sbp.org.pk (accessed 14 February 2017).

3.20.10 Stock market index: Pakistan and emerging markets

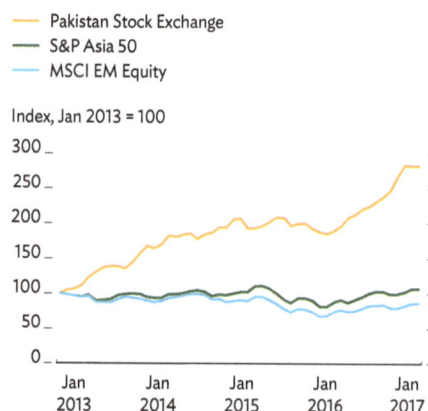

Source: Bloomberg database (accessed 8 March 2017).

The current account balance will likely deteriorate further in FY2018 to 2.5% of GDP with somewhat higher global oil prices and accelerating infrastructure investment connected with CPEC. Revived oil prices are likely to improve the prospects for remittances in the medium term as Gulf countries may relax their efforts to consolidate their finances.

A significant increase in the current account deficit could pose a risk to official exchange reserves, which peaked at $18.9 billion in October 2016 and then slid by $1.3 billion by February 2017 (Figure 3.20.12). The higher inflows to the financial account from multilateral and bilateral disbursements, along with non-debt inflows in the first 7 months of FY2017, are providing a cushion for the widening current account deficit. Portfolio investment jumped more than fourfold to $670 million, and foreign direct investment increased to $1.2 billion with investments into dairy, consumer electronics, electric power, and oil and gas. However, amortization payments on long-term government debt also increased markedly. Expected disbursements from multilateral development partners in the remaining months of the fiscal year will be needed to reverse contraction in official reserves as of February 2017.

Policy challenge—realizing potential from the economic corridor

The economic corridor project CPEC, which runs from the Xinjiang Uyghur Autonomous Region in the PRC to the Pakistani port of Gwadar on the Arabian Sea, is expected to bring substantial benefits to the economy. Announced in April 2015 as a $46 billion project, but subsequently increased to $55 billion, it provides for major investments in energy and transport infrastructure. CPEC will be financed largely by the PRC and is expected to be completed by 2030. The project will significantly address Pakistan's infrastructure deficit caused by annual spending on infrastructure at only 2%–3% of GDP in the past 4 decades.

The government has identified "early harvest" infrastructure projects that will be completed in the next few years. Of these, $21 billion will be on energy projects (Table 3.20.2). These will be financed by foreign direct investment from the PRC supported by borrowing from banks there. Independent electricity-generating firms will be offered guaranteed tariffs for their sales to distribution companies that will ensure at least 17% return on equity. About $10 billion in investments in transport infrastructure will be financed by a combination of concessional and commercial loans from the Government of the PRC.

For Pakistan, CPEC is expected to be a major opportunity to boost growth and development. CPEC is expected to provide many benefits, especially eliminating the power shortages that have held down economic growth in recent years. It will improve connectivity to domestic and international markets and so benefit Pakistan's lagging regions. The large investment in infrastructure should boost construction and related industries, spurring job creation and growth. In the long run, goods from the PRC transiting from northern Pakistan to the seaport will bolster the transport sector, further stimulating

3.20.11 Exchange rates

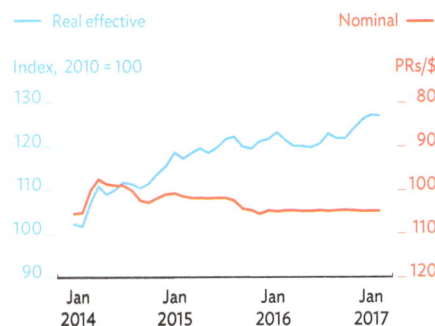

Source: State Bank of Pakistan. Economic Data. http://www.sbp.org.pk (accessed 16 February 2017).

3.20.12 Gross international reserves

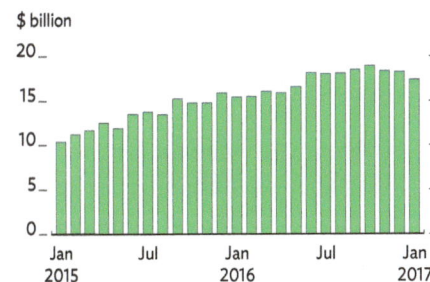

Source: State Bank of Pakistan. Economic Data. http://www.sbp.org.pk (accessed 14 February 2017).

3.20.2 CPEC priority energy projects

Project name	Installed capacity	Estimated cost ($ million)	Progress update	Estimated COD
Port Qasim 2 x 660 MW coal fired	1,320	1,980	65% of power plant and 70% of jetty completed	June 2018
Sahiwal 2 x 660 MW coal fired	1,320	1,600	Civil works 95% completed	December 2017
Engro Thar 4 x 330 MW coal fired	1,320	2,000	Construction in progress	June 2019
Thar coal surface mine, 6.5 tons per annum		1,470	IA/EA signed	2018/2019
Gwadar coal/LNG/oil fired	300	600	Expect to start work in March 2017	
Hub Power 1 x 660 MW coal fired	660	970	IA/EA signed	2018/2019
Rahimyar Khan coal fired	1,320	1,600	Feasibility in progress	
SSRL Thar coal block 1–6.5 tons per annum		1,300	Open pit mining	2018/2019
SSRL 2 x 660 MW mine mouth power plant	1,320	2,000	Independent power producer	2018/2019
Zonergy 900 MW solar park	900	1,215	Operating	August 2016
Dawood 50 MW wind farm	50	125	Construction started	January 2017
United Energy Pakistan 100 MW wind farm	100	250	61–66 turbines completed	June 2017
Sachal 50 MW wind farm	50	134	Construction in progress	June 2017
Suki Kinari hydropower station	870	1,802	Contractor mobilized to start construction	2021/2022
Karot hydropower station	720	1,420	Construction in progress	2021/2022
Matiari–Lahore transmission line		1,500	Feasibility study completed, TSA/IA initialed	2018/2019
Matiari–Faisalabad transmission line		1,500	Feasibility study completed, TSA/IA initialed	2018/2019
Total	10,250	21,466		

COD = commercial operation date, CPEC = economic corridor linking Pakistan with the People's Republic of China, EA = environmental assessment, IA = implementation agreement, LNG = liquefied natural gas, MW = megawatt, SSRL = Sino-Sindh Resources, TSA = technical service agreement.

Source: www//cpec.gov.pk

private investment and activity. Moreover, the extensive upgrading of Pakistan's infrastructure is expected to attract direct investment from abroad, including mature industries in the PRC that seek lower-cost locations.

At the same time, CPEC investments are likely to require significant increases in imports of equipment and services to implement the projects. In the medium-to-long term, these inflows will likely be followed by financial outflows as loans are repaid and profits repatriated to foreign investors. Higher foreign exchange earnings and exports will be needed to avoid pressure on the external account.

To reap the potential benefits of CPEC and shift the economy of Pakistan to a higher growth trajectory, the government must continue to address key constraints on growth. Domestic security has improved significantly in recent years, but consolidating these gains will take continued efforts. Regulation remains burdensome, requiring more reform to provide an enabling environment that facilitates business and fosters investment. Reform to boost exports by diversifying products and markets and by adopting more flexible exchange rate policies are needed to maintain external stability. Similarly, structural reform to the energy sector and state-owned enterprises are required to fully realize investments' productive potential.

Sri Lanka

Growth slowed in 2016 with a marked fall in agricultural production, but a pickup in construction and investment helped to sustain growth. Inflation was highly variable over the year but moderated in general, as did the current account deficit. The outlook is for modest recovery in growth as the government implements an economic program of fiscal reform to tackle persistent macroeconomic imbalances and a large public debt.

Economic performance

Over the past 4 years, growth has markedly slowed from the rapid pace of the economic boom that came with the end of civil conflict in May 2009. Economic growth in 2016 was affected by bad weather, with provisional estimates putting growth at 4.4% in 2016, lower than the 4.8% expansion a year earlier (Figure 3.21.1). To address persistent macroeconomic imbalances and deterioration in the balance of payments, the government in June 2016 obtained support from the International Monetary Fund (IMF) for a 3-year extended fund facility to pursue revenue-based fiscal consolidation.

On the supply side, agriculture contracted by 4.2% because of floods in May 2016 and a drought that has dragged on since August. Construction expansion at 14.9% provided the impetus for 6.7% growth in industry. Buoyant construction was driven by private sector projects supported by a rapid increase in bank credit to the private sector. Growth in manufacturing slowed from a year earlier, mainly because of weakness in the textile and garment industries. Services growth slackened to 4.2% from 5.7%, mainly with slowing in wholesale and retail trade and government-related services.

Provisional demand-side estimates of GDP show fixed investment rebounding to grow by 10%, up from 3% a year earlier, and a surge in inventory building that made these two areas the main sources of growth in 2016 (Figure 3.21.2). Consumption expenditure grew by only 1% as fiscal policies tightened following a 9% upsurge in spending fueled by highly expansive fiscal policies a year earlier, which put pressure on the balance of payments and on reserves. Net exports continued to be a sizable drag on GDP growth because a large fall in global oil prices improved the terms of trade and thus enabled other imports to expand. Export volume fell by 1% in 2016 on weak agricultural sales, reversing expanded export volumes in recent years even as prices languished.

Average annual inflation moderated to 4.0% in 2016 as measured by the national consumer price index. Food inflation pushed overall inflation higher after major flooding in May 2016, subsiding later but spiking in January and February 2017 to 10.2% partly because of a low

3.21.1 GDP growth by sector

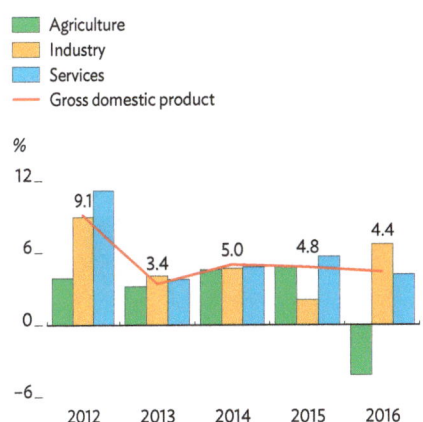

- Agriculture
- Industry
- Services
- Gross domestic product

Source: Department of Census and Statistics of Sri Lanka. http://www.statistics.gov.lk/ (accessed 16 March 2017).

3.21.2 Demand-side contributions to growth

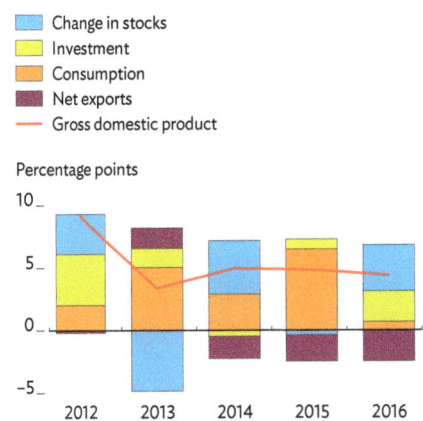

- Change in stocks
- Investment
- Consumption
- Net exports
- Gross domestic product

Source: Department of Census and Statistics of Sri Lanka.

This chapter was written by Tadateru Hayashi and Savindi Jayakody of the Sri Lanka Resident Mission, ADB, Colombo.

base effect but also as drought hit supplies (Figure 3.21.3). Nonfood inflation trended higher in the second half of the year because of Sri Lanka rupee depreciation and a value-added tax (VAT) rate hike in November 2016. Core inflation, which excludes fresh food, rice, coconuts, energy, and transport, more than doubled from 3.0% in early 2016 to 6.7% in December, further quickening to 7.1% in January and February 2017.

Monetary policy switched to tightening in 2016 to slow very rapid growth in credit to the private sector that began in mid-2014 and to ease pressure on the balance of payments and foreign exchange reserves. The Central Bank of Sri Lanka first tightened monetary policy in January 2016 by raising the statutory reserve ratio by 1.5 percentage points to 7.5%. It subsequently increased its policy rates by 50 basis points each in February and July 2016 and then again in March 2017 by 25 basis points to bring the lending facility rate to 8.75% (Figure 3.21.4). The upward adjustment in bank lending rates started to slow growth in private sector credit only in August 2016, and growth remained high at 21.9% in December 2016 (Figure 3.21.5).

Raising the country's very low revenue ratio is the major priority of fiscal consolidation under the IMF program. As the first step, the government increased the VAT rate from 11% to 15% in May 2016, but the hike was suspended in July to complete legal procedures and took effect only from 1 November. With the delay in introducing the VAT rate increase, the ratio of tax revenue to GDP in 2016 was an estimated 11.9%, a reduction of 0.2 percentage points from 2015, when revenue benefited from a one-off tax. To achieve 2016 budget deficit targets, recurrent expenditure was trimmed and public investment cut to the equivalent of 4.8% of GDP from 5.4% in the previous year. As a result, the overall budget deficit shrank to an estimated 5.6% of GDP from 7.6% in 2015 (Figure 3.21.6). Government debt increased to an estimated 79.4% of GDP in September 2016 from 77.6% in 2015 (Figure 3.21.7).

Export earnings fell in 2016 by 2.2%, improving on the 5.6% drop a year earlier. Agricultural products such as tea and spices declined by 6.3%, mainly because bad weather reduced production, though export prices firmed slightly. Garment exports, which bring in nearly half of all export earnings, increased by only 1.3% as a decline in sales to the European Union countered the benefits of expansion into new markets. Imports picked up by 2.5%, mainly on large increases for building materials and for machinery and equipment, as a 41.5% plunge in vehicle imports fully explained an 8.4% drop for consumer goods. Oil imports rose markedly during the fourth quarter, reflecting increased reliance on thermal power generation to offset hydropower losses caused by the drought. Nevertheless, the large average fall in global oil prices during the year meant a low fuel bill, which largely offset higher spending on other intermediate goods. The trade deficit in 2016 was $9.1 billion, up from $8.4 billion in 2015.

Worker remittances grew by 3.7% to $7.2 billion in 2016, posting recovery from a small decline in 2015 but languishing well below growth in earlier years. Earnings from tourism remained robust, expanding by 18.0% to $3.5 billion as visitor numbers rose by 14% to 2.1 million. Worker remittances and tourism earnings thus more than offset a

3.21.3 Inflation

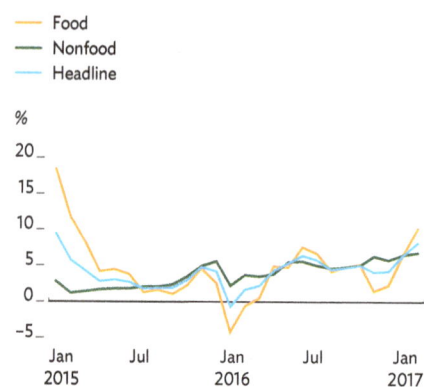

Source: Department of Census and Statistics of Sri Lanka. http://statistics.gov.lk

3.21.4 Deposit and lending rates and statutory reserve ratio

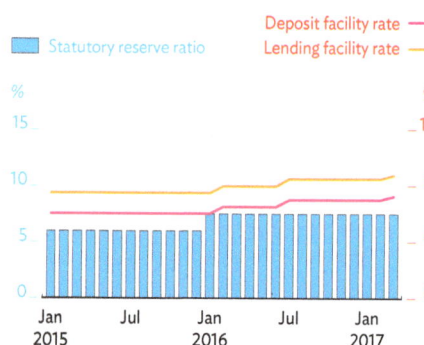

Source: Central Bank of Sri Lanka. http://www.cbsl.gov.lk (accessed 8 March 2017).

3.21.5 Interest rate, credit, and money growth

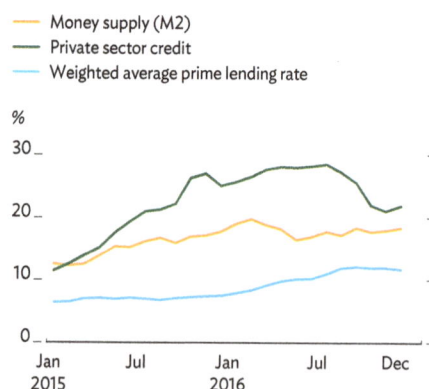

Source: Central Bank of Sri Lanka. Weekly Economic Indicators. http://www.cbsl.gov.lk

larger trade deficit by a margin of $1.7 billion, slightly improving on the $1.6 billion surplus in 2015. The current account deficit is estimated to have narrowed to the equivalent of 2.1% of GDP in 2016 from 2.5% in 2015. The official balance of payments estimate is not yet available.

While the current account remained stable, the financial account was weak despite a $1.5 billion sovereign bond issued in July 2016, as the government apparently suffered net capital outflow as foreign investors exited government securities. The 2016 overall balance of payments deficit is estimated by the central bank at $500 million, one-third of the deficit in 2015. Gross official reserves fell to $6.0 billion at the end of December 2016 (Figure 3.21.8). The rupee depreciated slightly against the US dollar, by 3.4%, mostly in the second half of the year (Figure 3.21.9). It depreciated in real effective terms by an average of 2.6% from a year earlier, suggesting improved competitiveness.

Economic prospects

Economic growth in 2017 and 2018 will be constrained by tight fiscal and monetary policies under the IMF program. Because consumption will be subdued, private investment will again have to play a primary role in maintaining economic growth. The higher VAT introduced in 2016 and improved income tax collection in 2017 will depress consumption, outweighing the positive impact of a modest increase expected in worker remittance earnings. While the March *maha* rice harvest was expected to be affected by continuing drought, an assumed return to normal rainfall promises to allow agriculture production to rebound starting in the second quarter.

Private investment is expected to continue to expand modestly in 2017. While monetary tightening has slowed the expansion of credit to the private sector, credit for productive purposes will be available even with the boost in policy rates announced in March 2017. However, further monetary tightening in response to adverse developments cannot be ruled out in 2017. Further, a substantial increase in budgeted public investment will be realized only with strong revenue performance and rationalized current expenditure to offset any increased cost of drought relief or other contingencies. Faster growth expected in the major industrial economies should lift export performance, but this will be offset to some degree by higher oil prices. On balance, GDP growth is expected to edge up to 5.0% in 2017, the rate maintained in 2018 with further consolidation reform.

Under the IMF program, fiscal policy will pursue further revenue measures to eliminate the primary deficit, which disregards interest payments. The government projected a budget deficit equal to 4.6% of GDP in 2017, down from an estimated 5.6% in 2016. The narrowing of the deficit is attributable to an expected nominal increase in tax revenue by 25%, against a 13% increase in government expenditure. The goal is for total revenue to equal 15.0% of GDP in 2017. Apart from the VAT rate increase implemented in November 2016, additional revenue is to come mainly from more efficient income tax collection with the full implementation of a new revenue administration management information system. Moreover, the tax net will be cast wider in 2017

3.21.6 Government finance

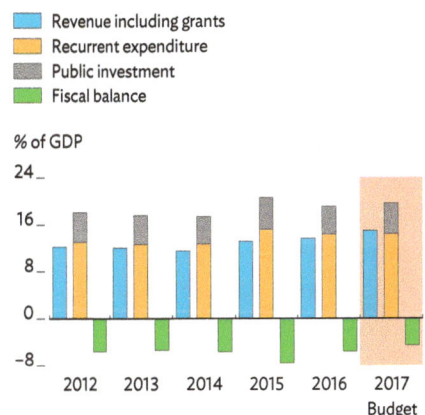

Legend:
- Revenue including grants
- Recurrent expenditure
- Public investment
- Fiscal balance

% of GDP

Source: Ministry of Finance.

3.21.7 Government debt

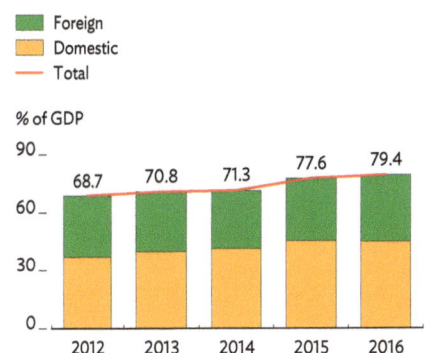

Legend:
- Foreign
- Domestic
- Total

% of GDP

Values: 68.7, 70.8, 71.3, 77.6, 79.4 for 2012–2016

Sources: Central Bank of Sri Lanka; Monthly Economic Indicators.

3.21.8 Gross official reserves

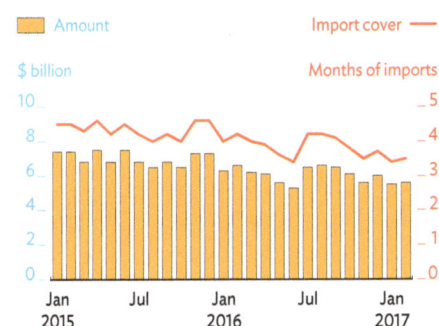

Amount   Import cover ——
$ billion   Months of imports

Sources: Central Bank of Sri Lanka; various press releases published on External Position.

under amendments to the Inland Revenue Act aiming to foster tax collection and abolish tax exemptions. Expenditure is projected equal to 19.6% of GDP, or 0.4 percentage points higher than in 2016. Higher-than-expected interest expenses from further monetary tightening or any other contingency such as payments in connection with the drought would likely cause the government to delay or cut infrastructure spending to meet the primary deficit target under the IMF program.

Inflationary pressure from the higher VAT and modest depreciation of the rupee in the second half of 2016 will add to inflation expected from slightly higher import prices. An automatic pricing formula for fuel and electricity has not yet been introduced. Inflation will be under less pressure from the demand side because growth will accelerate only slightly and the public expects fiscal austerity. Accordingly, average inflation is projected at 6.0% in 2017 and 2018.

External demand is expected to recover gradually in 2017 and 2018. Exports are projected to grow by 4% in 2017 and 5% in 2018 on the bases of gradual recovery of global demand, the renewal of concessions under the Generalized System of Preferences Plus, the removal of the European Union ban on fish imports, and the possible finalization of several free trade agreements. A larger services surplus will be driven by continued rapid expansion in tourism over the next 2 years. Worker remittances are expected to increase at a moderate pace. Projected export revenues should allow imports to expand by 5% in 2017 and 6% in 2018 without much widening of the current account deficit as a share of GDP. In addition to expected higher oil prices, imports will be on the rise because of continued imports of machinery and equipment and of building materials. The current account deficit is expected to equal 2.2% of GDP in 2017 and 2018 (Figure 3.21.10).

Policy challenge—strategies for export-oriented manufacturing

Despite reaching per capita income close to the upper-middle-income threshold, Sri Lanka persistently relies on a narrow manufacturing base. Exports are still 60% apparel and tea, and worker remittances remain a major source of foreign currency earnings. Since the end of the civil conflict in 2009, Sri Lanka has not attracted much foreign direct investment in manufacturing that could diversify production and exports.

Also important is to expand economic activity beyond Colombo and Western Province. As of 2015, Western Province, one of nine provinces, produced 41% of GDP. Further, per capita GDP in Western Province is about 1.4 times higher than in other provinces, underlining the need for regional development to make economic growth more inclusive (Figure 3.21.11).

The government recognizes the importance of diversifying the export base, and the Prime Minister's economic statement to Parliament in 2016 highlighted export-oriented foreign direct investment. A World Bank loan with parallel cofinancing from the Japan International Cooperation Agency supports reform to make the private sector more competitive.

3.21.9 Exchange rates

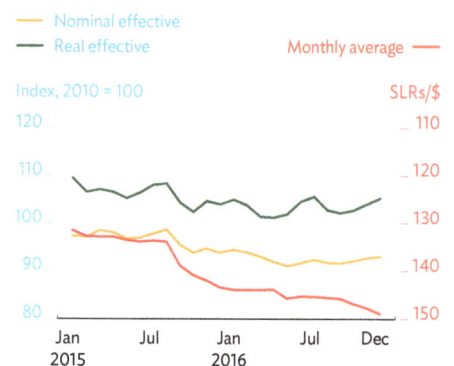

Source: Central Bank of Sri Lanka. http://www.cbsl.gov.lk

3.21.10 Current account components

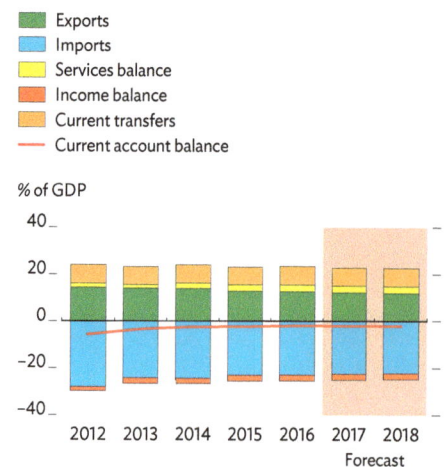

Sources: Central Bank of Sri Lanka. Annual Report 2016; ADB estimates.

3.21.1 Selected economic indicators (%)

	2017	2018
GDP growth	5.0	5.0
Inflation	6.0	6.0
Current account balance (share of GDP)	–2.2	–2.2

Source: ADB estimates.

The government is actively seeking bilateral trade agreements that would open markets for Sri Lankan products.

The government has taken up economic corridor development as a policy instrument to promote economic growth and address geographic imbalances. The Prime Minister announced the development of two economic corridors, one in the southwest and the other in the northeast. The corridors will align with major transport networks and connect urban clusters and rural areas with industrial zones. They will be publicly planned but driven by the private sector, facilitating industrial investment by easing infrastructure constraints, improving access to markets, stimulating trade, and boosting production efficiency. These corridors have potential to diversify manufacturing and agriculture production bases, help domestic firms become part of global value chains, boost productivity across sectors, and create productive jobs.

For the implementation of economic corridor development to succeed, it is imperative to identify new industrial clusters with future growth sectors and nodes along the corridors. Infrastructure requirements need to be identified to support node development. Policy reform will be needed, especially to improve the investment climate. Finding skilled labor and creating a sound regulatory framework for corridor development are among the challenges to be met. Setting up an effective institutional structure in the government is critical to coordinate line ministries and local authorities.

3.21.11 Per capita income by province

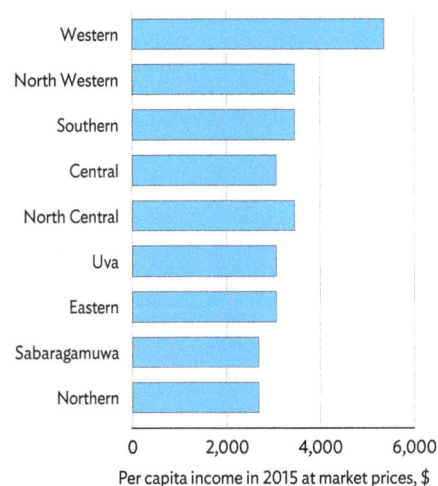

Per capita income in 2015 at market prices, $

Source: Central Bank of Sri Lanka.

SOUTHEAST ASIA

BRUNEI DARUSSALAM
CAMBODIA
INDONESIA
LAO PEOPLE'S
    DEMOCRATIC REPUBLIC
MALAYSIA
MYANMAR
PHILIPPINES
SINGAPORE
THAILAND
VIET NAM

Brunei Darussalam

After several years of declining GDP, falling consumer prices, and widening fiscal deficits, this hydrocarbon-dependent economy is poised for a mild turnaround. Large construction projects and recovering oil and gas production and prices are expected to lift GDP and inflation into positive territory and narrow the fiscal gap. Sustainable long-term growth demands substantial reform to the business environment to attract foreign investors to new industries.

Economic performance

Declining oil and natural gas production, consequently lower government revenue, and selected spending cuts caused the economy to contract for a fourth consecutive year in 2016 (Figure 3.22.1). GDP fell by an estimated 2.5%.

Oil production fell by 5% in 2016, and natural gas by 2%. Oil production has slid by 45% since 2006 as oil fields aged and suffered stoppages for repairs and maintenance (Figure 3.22.2). Last year also saw a methanol plant that uses natural gas as its main input closed for repairs for 2 months. The ripple effects of the decline in the oil industry last year were felt in the rest of the economy, which also contracted.

Reduced spending by the oil industry and the government hurt incomes and employment, curbing private consumption and causing fixed investment to fall, according to data for the first 3 quarters of 2016. Car sales, for example, fell by 12%. Net external demand dragged on GDP growth as exports of goods and services fell in real terms while real imports were relatively steady. Exports of oil and liquefied natural gas, which account for the bulk of exports, fell in 2016 by 4.6% and 1.2%, respectively, in volume terms.

Government consumption spending declined by 9% in real terms in the first 3 quarters. Government revenue, largely from oil and gas, slumped by an estimated one-third in nominal terms in FY2016 (ended 31 March 2017), following an even steeper decline in the previous year (Figure 3.22.3). Over the past 5 years, the estimated ratio of government revenue to GDP has plunged from 55% to 15%. In the meantime, despite trims to certain categories of government spending, the share of total government expenditure to GDP rose from 31% to 35%, turning budget surpluses enjoyed until 2013 into deficits. The fiscal deficit widened to an estimated 20% of GDP last year from 15% in 2015.

Consumer prices eased for a third consecutive year, with the consumer price index down by 0.7% in 2016. Bank lending to households fell by 1.7%, and lending to companies dropped by 22.2%.

3.22.1 GDP growth

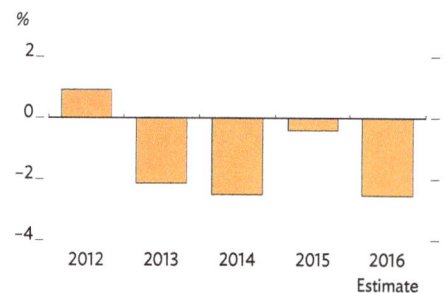

Source: Asian Development Outlook database.

3.22.2 Average daily production

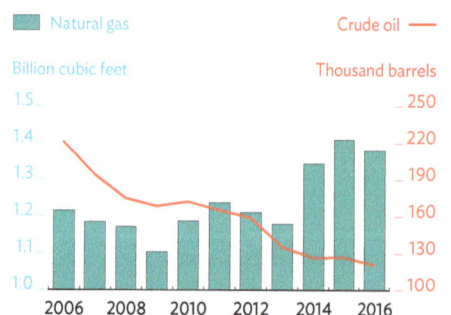

Sources: BP Statistical Review of World Energy 2016; Brunei Darussalam Department of Energy.

This chapter was written by Pilipinas Quising of the Economic Research and Regional Cooperation Department, ADB, Manila; and Anthony Patrick, consultant, Economic Research and Regional Cooperation Department, ADB, Manila.

Broad money supply increased by just 1.5% in the 12 months to December last year. Pegged at par to the Singapore dollar, the Brunei dollar depreciated by 2% against the US dollar.

Lower export volumes and prices for hydrocarbons shrank the US dollar value of merchandise exports by 20%. Merchandise imports fell by 17%. The trade surplus narrowed by 24% in 2016 for a 75% decline since 2012 (Figure 3.22.4). Declining trade surpluses have weighed on the current account, narrowing the surplus in 2016 to an estimated equivalent of 11% of GDP. International reserves at $3.3 billion covered 15 months of imports.

Economic prospects

A projected modest increase in hydrocarbon exports for higher prices should restore GDP growth this year and next. Several large construction projects will provide additional impetus if they proceed as planned. GDP is forecast to grow by 1.0% in 2017, quickening to 2.5% in 2018.

Construction is expected to swing from contraction in 2016 to expansion in 2017. A company from the People's Republic of China (PRC) plans to start building this year a $2.5 billion oil refinery and aromatics cracker plant once a bridge and jetties are completed at the site on Pulau Muara Besar. Construction is expected to take at least 2 years, with exports scheduled to start in late 2019. Public construction projects include the $1.1 billion Temburong Bridge, which will continue into 2019.

The economy is showing tentative signs of gradual diversification away from oil and gas. A company from the PRC plans to develop Muara port, and another is building a $50 million plant to make carbon steel pipe. Turkish firms have pledged to invest $1.3 billion in a project to make ammonia and urea from natural gas—starting construction this year or next and producing fertilizer for export in about 3 years— and another $30 million in a factory to make margarine from imported palm oil. Investors from Singapore and Taipei,China are developing aquaculture, an industry that is expected to expand production from this year. Brunei Darussalam has attracted in recent years a center that trains helicopter and fixed-wing pilots and other ventures that produce animal feed, halal food, and pharmaceuticals.

Consumer prices are seen turning up mainly on higher prices for food and fuel, though subsidies and price controls cushion the impact of global price movements on domestic prices (Figure 3.22.5).

Export earnings will get a lift from higher prices for hydrocarbons, but imports, too, are expected to rise as investment picks up. The current account surplus is forecast to fall to the equivalent of about 5% of GDP from 11% last year.

Higher global oil and gas prices augur well for government revenue. Nevertheless, the FY2017 budget trims nominal expenditure by 5.4% from the previous year's budget. At the same time, officials are considering how to target subsidies better and broaden the revenue base. Subsidies for household electricity consumption have been trimmed for bigger users, and progressive tariffs are expected for commercial users. A proposal to sell a new premium gasoline at market prices, if implemented, could improve the targeting of fuel subsidies.

3.22.3 Fiscal indicators

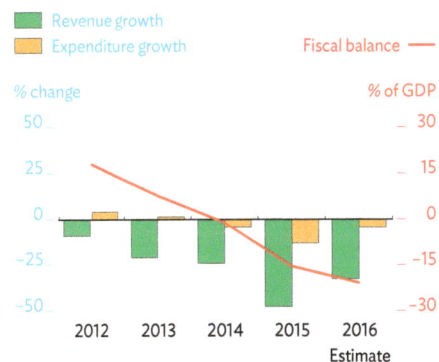

Note: Years are fiscal years ending 31 March of the next year.
Sources: *Asian Development Outlook* database; Brunei Darussalam Department of Economic Planning and Development.

3.22.4 Merchandise trade

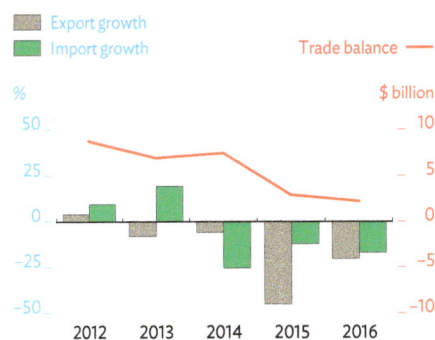

Source: CEIC Data Company (accessed 23 February 2017).

3.22.1 Selected economic indicators (%)

	2017	2018
GDP growth	1.0	2.5
Inflation	0.1	0.1
Current account balance (share of GDP)	5.3	5.5

Source: ADB estimates.

Fiscal deficits are projected to narrow over the forecast period. The deficits are financed by transfers from a fiscal stabilization fund.

Looking to the medium term, GDP growth is expected to pick up as work is completed to make existing fields more reliable and bring new gas fields on stream. Also, the oil refinery and aromatics cracker project and the fertilizer plant are scheduled to start production in 2019–2020.

Policy challenge—attracting new industries

The prolonged economic downturn demonstrates how vulnerable this small economy, the second richest in Southeast Asia, is to hydrocarbon price swings and depletion. Oil and gas directly provide more than 50% of GDP, over 90% of exports, and 80% of government revenue. Shifting growth toward other export-oriented industries will require deeper reform to the business environment to attract investment.

Encouragingly, over recent years the government has taken steps to improve the business climate: lowering the corporate income tax rate to 18.5% with tax exemptions for pioneer industries, allowing 100% foreign ownership in domestic companies, competitively pricing land and utilities in industrial parks, and establishing a special office in the Brunei Economic Development Board to fast-track foreign investment projects. It has outlined plans for a free-trade zone to attract foreign direct investment.

These reforms enabled the country to move up significantly in the latest World Bank *Doing Business* ranking, from 97 among 189 countries surveyed in 2016 to 72 among 190 in 2017. Brunei Darussalam nevertheless lags less prosperous neighbors such as Malaysia and Thailand (Table 3.22.2). Moreover, it ranked a low 142 in terms of trading across borders and 134 in property registration, behind not only Malaysia and Thailand but also Indonesia, the Philippines, and Viet Nam. It was far down the rankings in protecting the rights of minority shareholders (102) and contract enforcement (93).

Ranking Brunei Darussalam 58 among 138 economies, the *Global Competitiveness Report 2016–2017* of the World Economic Forum cited not only the country's extremely small market but also its bureaucracy as significant hindrances to doing business. Compliance with border procedures is highly time-consuming, discouraging investment in export-oriented industries. Substantial scope exists for the government to streamline procedures and make the country's non-hydrocarbon sectors more attractive to foreign investors.

3.22.5 Inflation

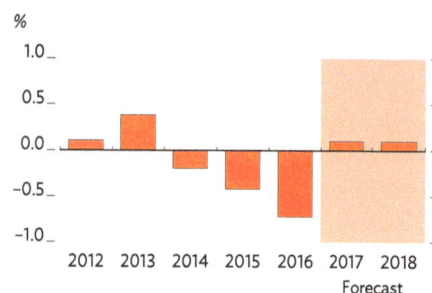

Source: *Asian Development Outlook* database.

3.22.2 Performance in *Doing Business 2017*

Country	Ranking
Singapore	2
Malaysia	23
Thailand	46
Brunei Darussalam	72
Viet Nam	82
Indonesia	91
Philippines	99
Cambodia	131
Lao People's Democratic Republic	139
Myanmar	170

Source: World Bank. 2016. *Doing Business 2017.*

Cambodia

The economy grew by an estimated 7.0% in 2016, the same pace as in the previous year. A mild slowdown in industry and services was mitigated by a slight pickup in agriculture. GDP is forecast to grow by 7.1% this year and next, with inflation edging up and the current account deficit narrowing. Reviving agriculture is critical to sustaining rapid growth and poverty reduction.

Economic performance

GDP is estimated to have grown by 7.0% in 2016 (Figure 3.23.1). Last year's strong growth came on the heels of the country graduating in 2015 from low-income to lower-middle-income status.

Though delayed, rainfall improved last year to allow agriculture to grow by an estimated 1.8% following near stagnation in 2015. Growth in industry slowed somewhat but still came in at healthy 10.5% growth last year, against 11.7% in 2015. With subdued growth in the major industrial economies, growth in garment and footwear production decelerated from 9.8% in 2015 to an estimated 7.4% last year.

Services posted 6.7% growth last year, down from the 2015 pace of 7.1% mainly because growth in wholesale and retail trade was lower, possibly indicating moderating growth in private consumption. Tourist arrivals increased by 5.0% last year, down from 6.1% in 2015 (Figure 3.23.2).

Exports posted 9.2% growth in 2016, down from 14.1% in 2015 with slower growth in garment exports, which account for some 70% of Cambodian exports. Meanwhile, import growth decelerated by half, from 12.3% in 2015 to 6.1%. As a result, the current account deficit narrowed from the equivalent of 11.1% of GDP in 2015 to 10.1% last year. The deficit was covered by official transfers and inflows of foreign direct investment (FDI). International reserves thus rose to $6.7 billion by year-end, or cover for 5.5 months of imports (Figure 3.23.3).

Net FDI rose to an estimated $2.2 billion last year, up by 30.5% from 2015, after declining by 8.1% in 2014 and 1.4% in 2015. These inflows equaled 10.7% of GDP, with construction and telecommunications posting the highest growth rates in 2016, while inflows to manufacturing declined.

Buoyant monetary and credit conditions and a turnaround in international prices for oil and other commodities drove average inflation up to 3.0% last year, more than double the previous year's 1.2%.

Money supply grew by 17.9% in 2016, up from 14.7% in 2015 and largely in line with expanded foreign currency deposits in banks (Figure 3.23.4). Although growth in credit to the private sector moderated from 27.1% at the end of 2015 to 22.5% at the end of last year,

3.23.1 Supply-side contributions to growth

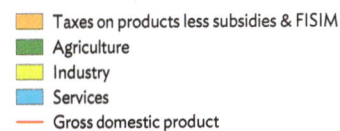

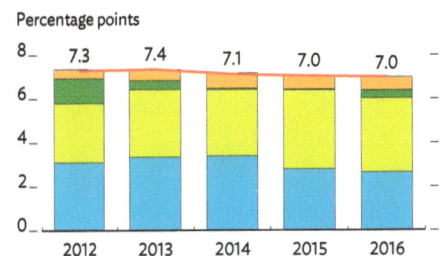

Taxes on products less subsidies & FISIM
Agriculture
Industry
Services
Gross domestic product

Percentage points

FISIM = financial intermediation services indirectly measured.

Sources: National Institute of Statistics; ADB estimates.

3.23.2 Tourism indicators

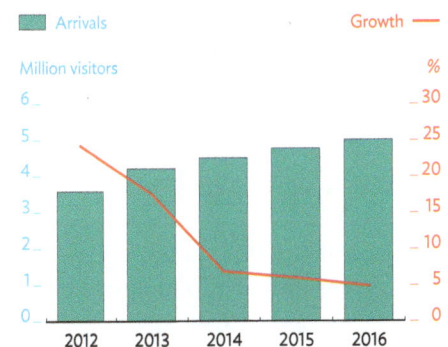

Arrivals   Growth

Million visitors   %

Source: Ministry of Tourism.

This chapter was written by Jan Hansen and Samphors Khieu of the Cambodia Resident Mission, ADB, Phnom Penh.

credit to construction, real estate, and mortgages edged up slightly last year, from 30.0% to 31.5%.

To ensure the health of financial institutions, the National Bank of Cambodia, the central bank, introduced a minimum 60% liquidity coverage ratio compliant with Basel III starting from 1 September 2016, the minimum rising to 100% by 2020. It also announced that banks and microfinance institutions would have to comply with much higher minimum capital requirements beginning in March 2018.

Continued strengthening of tax administration raised the ratio of revenue to GDP from 16.8% in 2015 to 17.6% last year (Figure 3.23.5). While current expenditure increased from the equivalent of 12.3% of GDP in 2015 to 13.0%, capital spending appears to have slowed significantly with slower disbursement of external funding for public investment projects. The fiscal deficit is therefore estimated to have been far lower than the 4.2% of GDP planned under the Budget Law 2016.

Economic prospects

Annual GDP growth is projected to be slightly higher at 7.1% this year and next (Figure 3.23.6). With growth firming up in the major industrial economies this year, Cambodia's export prospects are robust. Agriculture is seen maintaining a similar pace of growth as last year, and government spending will likely increase. Industry is projected to grow by a slightly higher rate of 10.8% this year, with growth in garment and footwear production picking up. Meanwhile, the pace of construction is likely to moderate.

Services are expected to expand by 6.7%, as in 2016. The key challenge for the tourism industry is to stay competitive as newer Southeast Asian attractions emerge, notably in Myanmar.

The potential for light manufacturing to relocate out of the People's Republic of China into lower-cost economies in the region should offer Cambodia scope to attract FDI for a variety of pursuits beyond garments and footwear.

Higher international prices for oil and other commodities should nudge inflation up to 3.4% this year and 3.5% in 2018. As Cambodia is a highly dollarized economy, it must be careful to align minimum wage adjustments with productivity increases to keep wage costs in check and stay competitive as a manufacturer for export.

As export markets firm up, exports are expected to expand by 11.0% this year, outpacing import growth at 9.0%. Tourism revenues should remain strong this year and next. The current account deficit is thus likely to narrow to the equivalent of 9.4% of GDP this year and 9.0% next. While official transfers are likely to maintain their declining trend, FDI inflows look robust in the foreseeable future. Foreign exchange reserves are seen to remain comfortable.

The Budget Law 2017 expects to further improve tax collection, with the ratio of revenue to GDP increasing to 17.4%, compared with 16.7% in the Budget Law 2016. On the expenditure side, the government continues to focus on implementing planned increases to civil servants' wages as part of civil service reform. The budget has the wage bill increasing by 20.7% in 2017. Overall public expenditure is expected to equal 21.7% of GDP, for a fiscal deficit of 4.3%.

3.23.3 Reserves and import cover

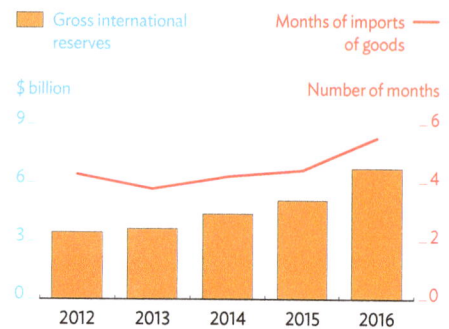

Gross international reserves

Months of imports of goods

Source: National Bank of Cambodia.

3.23.4 Money supply and private sector credit

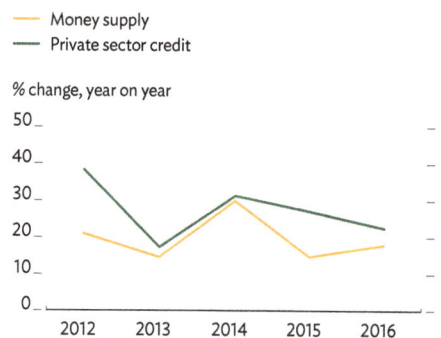

Money supply
Private sector credit

Source: National Bank of Cambodia.

3.23.5 Fiscal indicators

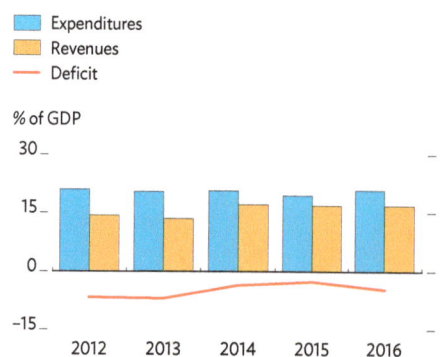

Expenditures
Revenues
Deficit

Note: 2016 refers to the Budget Law 2016 target.
Source: Ministry of Economy and Finance.

The economic outlook is subject to downside risks, both domestic and external. Domestic risks stem from vulnerabilities in the financial sector partly traceable to its rapid expansion, in particular the proliferation of microfinance institutions. On the external front, the risks are weaker growth in the euro area, a sharper-than-expected global tightening of credit, and a surge in the US dollar, which could constrain exports and stiffen competition from other low-cost producers.

Policy challenge—reviving agriculture

After growing at an average annual rate of 5.8% from 2003 to 2012, agriculture has averaged growth at just under 1.0% since 2013, even including last year's pickup (Figure 3.23.7). Adverse weather may explain part of the recent slowdown, but other problems, deep-seated ones, plague the sector. Effectively addressing them is increasingly becoming a major priority.

During the years of strong agricultural growth before the onset of the recent slowdown, farmland expansion explained 60% of growth, and only 40% came from yield increases. As most arable land is now under cultivation, there is very little scope for extending farmland without unsustainable deforestation. Future agricultural growth will thus have to come largely from productivity gains. Most smallholder farms in Cambodia have hardly improved their productivity, and agricultural commercialization is still in its infancy. Reviving agriculture requires a two-pronged effort to improve the productivity of existing crops and to diversify agriculture away from low-yielding, low-value crops toward more productive commercial crops.

A World Bank study of Cambodian agriculture in 2015 identified the key constraints on productivity improvement and diversification to be farmers' slow adoption of high-quality seeds, low fertilizer use, inadequate irrigation infrastructure, and meager agricultural extension services. Policy measures with potential impact in the short to medium term are to reduce the regulatory costs of imported fertilizer, promote the safer use of agricultural chemicals, improve farmers' access to high-quality but affordable seeds, and rehabilitate existing irrigation systems.

Over the longer term, developing a domestic agro-processing industry could give a fillip to agricultural growth by creating demand for high-quality raw materials from agriculture. Meanwhile, the Industrial Development Policy, 2015–2025 has not been implemented at the pace envisioned in the original plans. Speeding its implementation could help a vibrant agro-processing industrial base to emerge in Cambodia.

3.23.6 GDP growth

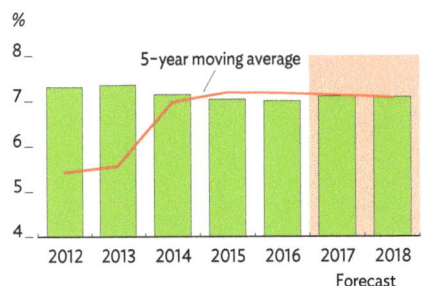

Source: Asian Development Outlook database.

3.23.1 Selected economic indicators (%)

	2017	2018
GDP growth	7.1	7.1
Inflation	3.4	3.5
Current account balance (share of GDP)	-9.4	-9.0

Source: ADB estimates.

3.23.7 Agriculture growth

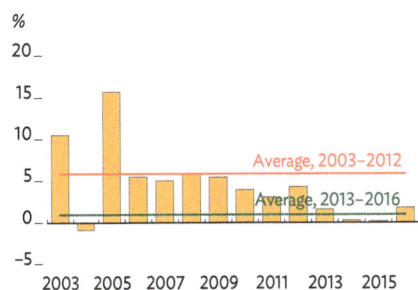

Source: Asian Development Outlook database.

Indonesia

Robust private consumption helped GDP growth reach 5.0% in 2016 even as investment weakened. Inflation was subdued, and the current account deficit narrowed. Reviving investment and external trade are likely to strengthen growth this year and next, accompanied by higher inflation and a smaller current account deficit. In addition to infrastructure development and structural reform, addressing the skills gap is one important measure needed to sustain growth over the medium to long term.

Economic performance

GDP growth firmed up last year to reach 5.0% from 4.9% in 2015. Robust private consumption supported growth even as investment slowed (Figure 3.24.1). With the strengthening of consumer confidence, private consumption also grew by 5.0% last year, marking an improvement over the previous year's 4.8%.

Growth in fixed investment slowed by 0.5 percentage points to 4.5% in 2016 despite a series of policy reforms launched by the government. Investment was dampened by delays in implementing public investment projects and weak external demand. As a share of GDP, fixed investment edged down to 32.6% (Figure 3.24.2).

Net external demand remained weak as both exports and imports continued to shrink in real terms, with imports falling faster than exports.

By sector, services contributed nearly half of GDP growth in 2016 (Figure 3.24.3). Led by buoyant banking and finance, information and telecommunications, and transportation and storage, the sector expanded by 5.6%, up from 5.5% in 2015. However, growth in manufacturing remained subdued at 4.3% in 2016, largely reflecting stalled recovery in export markets. Still recovering from forest fires and El Niño weather disturbances in 2015, agriculture grew by 3.3% last year, half a percentage point less than in 2015.

Robust growth helped the country to achieve a 3.1% rise in employment. The latest available data show that by August 2016 the unemployment rate had improved to 5.6% from 6.2% a year earlier. Partly reflecting the lower unemployment rate, the number of people living below the national poverty line in September 2016 had fallen by 1.3 million, reducing poverty to 10.7% from 11.1% a year earlier.

At 3.5%, average inflation last year remained, thanks in part to slower growth in fuel prices, near the lower end of the target range of 3%–5% set by Bank Indonesia, the central bank (Figure 3.24.4). Although food prices were elevated for some time by supply and distribution constraints, they eased after the government increased food imports.

3.24.1 Demand-side contributions to growth

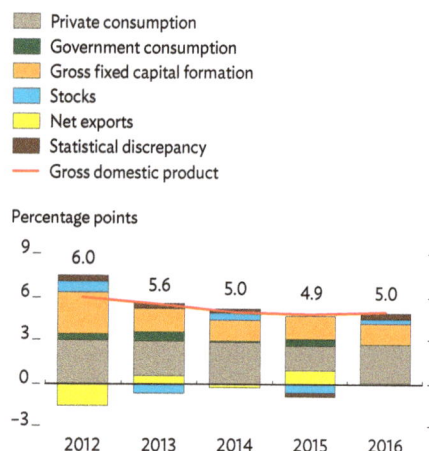

- Private consumption
- Government consumption
- Gross fixed capital formation
- Stocks
- Net exports
- Statistical discrepancy
- Gross domestic product

Percentage points

Source: CEIC Data Company (accessed 10 March 2017).

3.24.2 Fixed investment

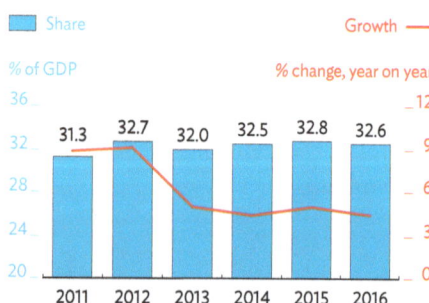

Share   Growth

% of GDP   % change, year on year

Source: CEIC Data Company (accessed 10 March 2017).

This chapter was written by Priasto Aji and Emma Allen of the Indonesia Resident Mission, ADB, Jakarta.

The declining trend of exports and imports persisted during most of 2016, except in the last quarter when it finally showed signs of turning around (Figure 3.24.5). For the year as a whole, the value of merchandise exports declined by 3.1% and that of merchandise imports by 4.5%, in neither case as steeply as in the previous year. The surplus in merchandise trade thus expanded by 9.6% last year to reach $15.4 billion. The higher merchandise trade surplus, coupled with a reduced deficit in services trade, narrowed the 2016 current account deficit to the equivalent of 1.8% of GDP from 2.0% in 2015 (Figure 3.24.6).

Increased net inflows of direct investment and portfolio capital more than offset the current account deficit last year. Foreign exchange reserves thus rose to $116.4 billion at the end of 2016, providing cover for 8.4 months of imports and repayment of official debt (Figure 3.24.7). This comfortable balance-of-payments position caused the Indonesian rupiah to appreciate last year by 2.3% against the US dollar, recovering some ground from depreciation in 2015 by more than 10.0%.

Subdued inflation allowed the central bank to pursue an accommodative monetary policy by lowering the policy interest rate by a percentage point from 7.5% to 6.5% between January and June 2016. Subsequently, with the aim of strengthening the monetary policy transmission mechanism, it adopted in August a shorter-term 7-day reverse repo rate as its new policy rate, lowering it from 5.25% in September to 4.75% in October. The central bank followed up the policy rate cuts with lower rates on its deposit and lending facilities. Despite monetary easing, though, growth in credit and the money supply remained muted most of last year.

At 2.5% of GDP, the fiscal deficit was roughly in line with the government's target of 2.4% for 2016. Fiscal containment was achieved by a cut to expenditure as revenues fell short of targets. The 9-month tax amnesty introduced in July 2016 to elicit better tax compliance and widen the tax base brought in $10.2 billion last year. Revenue excluding income garnered through the tax amnesty came in 3.7% lower than in 2015. Due to revenue shortfalls, capital spending declined by 23% and social spending by 49% from 2015.

Coupled with a favorable balance of payments, fiscal containment helped the country to reduce its external debt burden from 36.1% of GDP in 2015 to 34.0% at the end of last year. Fitch and Moody's upgraded Indonesia's rating outlook from stable to positive, confirming the country as an investment-grade issuer.

Economic prospects

The government unveiled from September 2015 to November 2016 a series of 14 economic policy packages aiming to boost investment and diversify economic activity. The packages were designed to clear regulatory bottlenecks and open up new sectors to foreign investors. They have already helped move Indonesia up by several notches in the World Bank's *Doing Business 2017* report, from 106 in the previous year to 91. Encouragingly, 527 companies had responded to the reforms by the end of 2016 with planned investments of $12.9 billion.

3.24.3 Supply-side contributions to growth

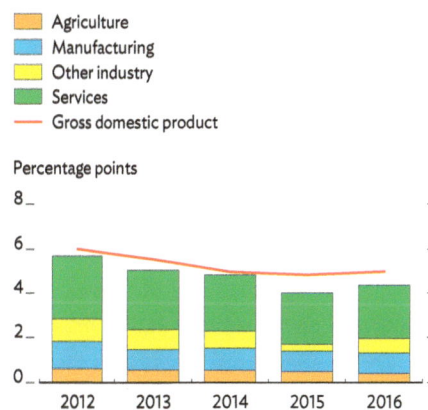

Source: CEIC Data Company (accessed 10 March 2017).

3.24.4 Monthly inflation

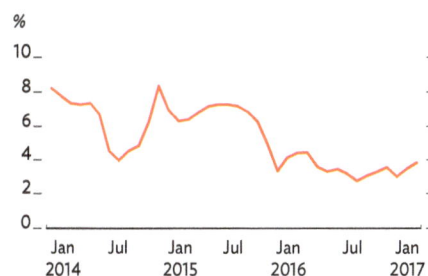

Source: CEIC Data Company (accessed 16 March 2017).

3.24.5 Merchandise trade

Q = quarter.
Source: CEIC Data Company (accessed 10 March 2017).

Along with these reform packages, the 2017 budget promotes macroeconomic stability by continuing fiscal consolidation. It establishes a fiscal deficit target equal to 2.4% of GDP. The 2017 budget sets a slightly lower limit on total government expenditure than the revised 2016 budget but with a higher allocation for infrastructure spending. A more realistic revenue mobilization target is another feature of this year's budget. The ratio of revenue to GDP is set at 12.8%, marginally higher than the 12.5% result for 2016. After the successful implementation of the tax amnesty program, the government is deepening its reform of value-added tax, income tax, and stamp duties, as well as improving tax administration. An effective implementation of the tax amnesty presents an opportunity to kick-start broader tax reform.

The 2017 budget allocates $29.1 billion for infrastructure investment, up by 22% from the revised 2016 budget, to be spent by line ministries, subnational governments, and state-owned enterprises. Subnational governments are now required to invest in infrastructure at least 25% of the resources they receive from the general allocation fund and revenue sharing. While this policy will be effective only to the extent that subnational governments have adequate implementation capacity, it should help to focus fiscal spending on infrastructure.

Monetary policy this year and next is likely to depend upon the pace at which the US Federal Reserve adjusts its interest rates. Bank Indonesia is therefore expected to be more cautious about further easing monetary policy. A banking survey it conducted in the last quarter of 2016 nevertheless showed that banks expected to increase lending by 13.1% in 2017, up significantly from 7.9% growth in 2016.

Recent structural reform and higher budget allocations for infrastructure in the 2017 budget should, along with rising income from commodity exports, give a boost to investment this year and next.

Private consumption is also expected to pick up, supported by expectations of recovery in international commodity prices. Consumption will be further supported by an 8.3% increase in the minimum wage and by enterprises' improved compliance with it. A large increase in budget allocations for the Village Fund should support rural consumption. The central bank's consumer confidence index continued to rise in February 2017 (Figure 3.24.8).

With the recovery of international prices for Indonesia's exports of copper, coal, nickel, aluminum, crude palm oil, rubber, and coffee, export prospects should improve. Moreover, in January of this year, the Indonesian government eased its 2014 ban on ore exports, which was designed to promote the development of domestic processing industries. This should boost exports of raw minerals, notably nickel ore and bauxite. The Nikkei purchasing managers' index for manufacturing showed an improving trend from late 2015 (Figure 3.24.9).

On balance, higher public infrastructure spending, a gradual improvement in investment and exports, and robust private consumption should help sustain GDP growth at 5.1% in 2017 and 5.3% in 2018.

As growth improves and international oil and commodity prices recover, average inflation is expected to pick up to 4.3% this year and 4.5% in 2018 (Figure 3.24.10). Upward adjustments to administered

3.24.6 Current account balance components

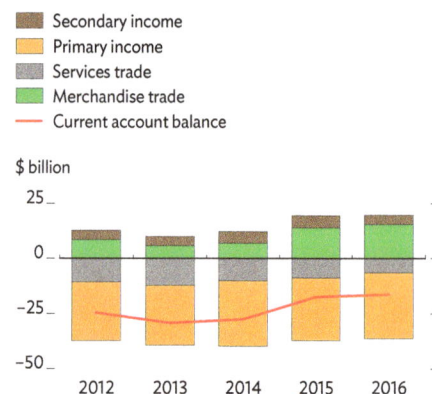

Source: CEIC Data Company (accessed 10 March 2017).

3.24.7 Gross international reserves and exchange rate

Sources: CEIC Data Company; Bloomberg (both accessed 16 March 2017).

3.24.8 Consumer and business confidence indexes

Q = quarter.
Source: CEIC Data Company (accessed 16 March 2017).

prices for fuel and electricity would contribute to higher inflation, but the rate is likely to remain within the central bank's target range.

Just as the outlook for Indonesian exports has improved, imports too are likely to grow to meet higher domestic demand, albeit at a slower pace than exports. The difference should gradually narrow the current account deficit this year and next.

Domestic risks to the forecast include possible delayed implementation of policy reform and continuing low revenues, which could prompt midyear cuts to government spending. External risks to the outlook include uncertain trade policy in the advanced economies, weaker recovery for international commodity prices and economic growth among trading partners, and accelerated adjustments to interest rates internationally. Indonesia is now in a better position to weather external shocks than in the past, with an improving economic growth, a narrowing current account deficit, a more credible fiscal framework, and a better grip on inflation.

Recent policy initiatives to increase public investment in infrastructure and improve the business environment should help to make Indonesia more competitive and spur new engines of growth. They will need to be complemented, however, by measures to close the skills gap that is increasingly a factor constraining the country from realizing its growth potential.

Policy challenge—closing the skills gap

Indonesia's workforce has improved its educational attainment in recent years. Still, almost 60% of workers, especially older ones, have not completed high school (Figure 3.24.11). Since 2002, the government has committed to education 20% of its budget, or 3.4% of GDP. While this investment has helped to improve educational attainment, education spending still lags behind that of other major economies in the region, with public spending on education in Malaysia and Viet Nam at 6% of GDP in recent years. A reflection of low educational attainment is that half of employed people today can be considered underqualified for their jobs (Figure 3.24.12).

While most of Indonesia's young people aged 15–24 years have now completed 9 years of schooling, one in four has not completed the full 12-year cycle before university. Moreover, the quality of education is a matter of continuing concern. Results from the Program for International Student Assessment of the Organisation for Economic Co-operation and Development indicate that, although Indonesia's performance has improved over time, on average Indonesia's 15-year-olds underperform their peers in other middle-income countries in Southeast Asia. For example, in the 2015 tests, Thailand and Viet Nam outscored Indonesia in all three subjects covered: science, mathematics, and reading. Meanwhile, the World Economic Forum's Executive Opinion Survey identifies a mismatch between the skills that graduates possess and those that employers require. These observations underscore the need to close the skills gap and strengthen Indonesia's human capital.

3.24.1 Selected economic indicators (%)

	2017	2018
GDP growth	5.1	5.3
Inflation	4.3	4.5
Current account balance (share of GDP)	–1.7	–1.6

Source: ADB estimates.

3.24.9 Manufacturing purchasing managers' index

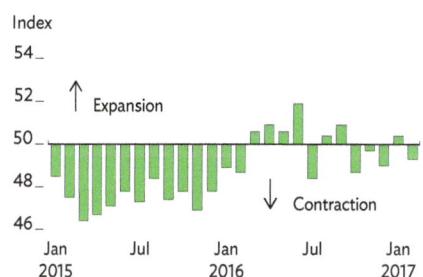

Note: Nikkei, Markit.
Source: Bloomberg (accessed 17 March 2017).

3.24.10 Inflation

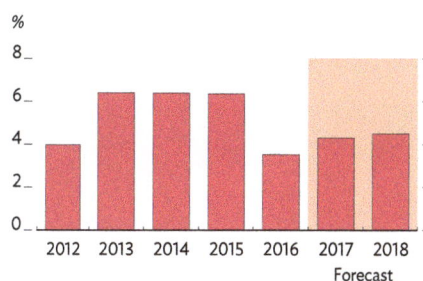

Source: Asian Development Outlook database.

The skills gap can be addressed in part through workplace training. However, at present Indonesian employers and workers invest little in skills development. Only a small percentage of workers continue training once they find employment. Data from Statistics Indonesia highlight that less than 10% of the working age population has undergone certified workplace training. Similarly, the World Bank's enterprise survey indicates that only 7.7% of firms offer formal training, one of the lowest rates among the countries surveyed. One reason that private enterprises limit their investment in human capital is labor regulation that encourages hiring people on short-term contracts.

Closing the country's skills gap requires a comprehensive program of education and training reform. It should focus on making spending on public education more efficient and developing strategies for mobilizing public and private resources for education and training. Education spending should aim not only to upgrade school infrastructure and training equipment but also raise the quality of instruction in schools by training teachers and improving the curriculum.

The reform program should facilitate much greater engagement by the government, employers, and education and training providers to ensure that graduates can meet the demands of a labor market in a middle-income country. Industry associations need to play a stronger role by developing good collaboration models that can evolve into industrywide skills-development programs, with cost-sharing initiatives to support more and better skills training. Particular focus should be placed on technical and vocational education and training. Key ingredients for success include more autonomy for providers of education and training to enable them to respond to industry needs, equipping the institutions with adequate financial and technical resources, and strengthening the industry qualification framework and the accreditation system.

Policy actions that address the reasons why private firms prefer to hire workers on short-term contracts, such as high severance pay, should encourage them to hire workers longer term. With improvements to the regulatory environment and strengthened collaboration for demand-based skills development, the private sector should be willing to shoulder greater responsibility for enabling their workers to receive high-quality training and to acquire newer skills for a fast-modernizing economy. A better safety net would protect unemployed workers as they upgrade their skills toward finding another job.

3.24.11 Educational attainment in the labor force by age group

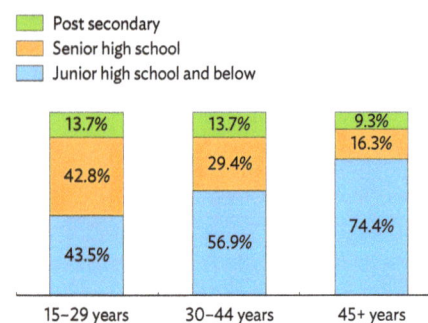

Source: CEIC Data Company (accessed 10 March 2017).

3.24.12 Mismatch in occupational skills and education, 2016

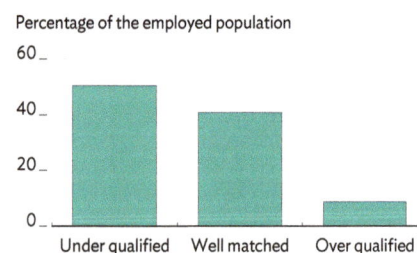

Source: Statistics Indonesia.

Lao People's Democratic Republic

Driven by solid expansion in electricity production for export and a buoyant service sector, growth held up well at 6.8% last year. Work on a major cross-border railway project should help strengthen growth this year and next. Both inflation and the current account deficit look set to rise. Major policy changes are needed to promote labor-intensive manufacturing and make the benefits of growth more inclusive.

Economic performance

Weathering a rough external environment, including lower commodity prices, the Lao People's Democratic Republic (Lao PDR) managed to maintain strong GDP growth at 6.8% last year, similar to the rate recorded in 2015 (Figure 3.25.1).

The service sector, which provides 43.0% of GDP, posted stronger growth at 9.0%, up from the 2015 figure of 8.5%. Despite a decline in tourist arrivals, most major service subsectors—wholesale and retail trade, hotels and restaurants, financial services, and telecommunications—recorded strong growth. Partly because the government changed its definition of "tourist," the number of tourist arrivals declined by 9.5%, but revenue from tourism declined only marginally (Figure 3.25.2).

Industry, which occupies 32.4% of the economy, maintained sturdy 8.0% growth last year, even as mining output declined. Electricity generation and exports, mostly to Thailand, received a significant boost as sales from the Hongsa lignite-fired electric power plant rose, as did sales from new power plants. However, low international metal prices drove down output from mining by 1.0% for copper, 1.9% for gold, and 1.7% for silver.

Despite drought early in the year, growth in agriculture picked up from 2.0% in 2015 to 2.5% in 2016 thanks to improved weather in the latter part. While rice production rose only marginally, livestock and fishery production grew by 4.2%.

Reflecting low international oil and commodity prices, inflation remained subdued at an annual rate of 1.6% last year, only marginally higher than the 2015 figure of 1.3% (Figure 3.25.3).

Growth in merchandise imports contracted further from 5.8% in 2015 to an estimated 6.7% in 2016. Meanwhile, merchandise exports grew by 12.3% in 2016, compared with a 12.9% decline in the previous year. The current account deficit thus shrank from the equivalent of 16.8% of GDP in 2015 to 14.1% last year. Foreign reserves remained precarious at $814 million at the end of December, or cover for only 1.4 months of imports.

This chapter was written by Rattanatay Luanglatbandith and Soulinthone Leuangkhamsing of the Lao PDR Resident Mission, ADB, Vientiane.

3.25.1 Supply-side contributions to growth

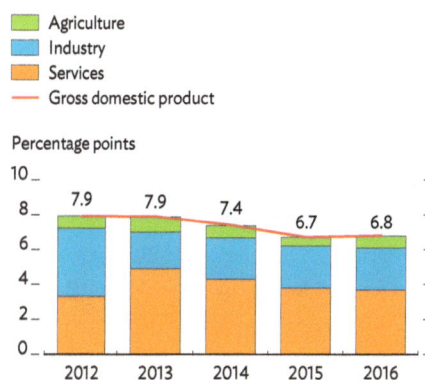

Sources: Lao Statistics Bureau; *Asian Development Outlook* database.

3.25.2 Tourism indicators

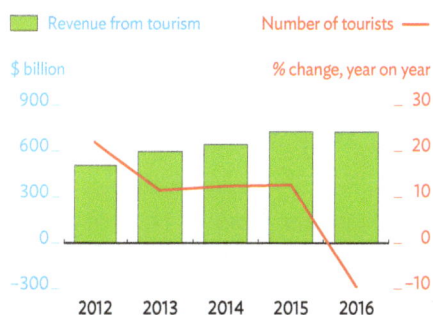

Source: National Tourism Administration.

A fiscal consolidation program that started in 2014 ran into problems last year as public expenditure outstripped budgeted amounts and revenues fell short of targets because of low metal prices, inefficient tax collection, and failure to collect huge tax arrears. As a result, the fiscal deficit for the year widened to equal nearly 6% of GDP, more than 1 percentage point higher than in 2015.

As for monetary policy, the Bank of the Lao PDR, the central bank, imposed in mid-2015 caps on deposit and lending rates for the Lao kip. This encouraged faster growth in credit, up from 16.8% in 2015 to 21.0% in 2016 (Figure 3.25.4). Broad money was estimated to have grown by about 11.0%. The kip remained stable against both the US dollar and the Thai baht.

Economic prospects

As recovery firms up in the major industrial economies and international commodity prices move higher, economic growth in the Lao PDR should edge up to 6.9% this year and 7.0% next (Figure 3.25.5).

Revenue from metal exports is expected to improve somewhat, while agricultural production—especially rice, cash crops, and livestock—should strengthen further as the rehabilitation of many old irrigation systems and the commissioning of newly completed irrigation schemes enable more dry-season cropping.

Construction began on 25 December 2016 on a railway linking the capital, Vientiane, to Yunnan Province in the People's Republic of China. This $6.8 billion project should give a boost to domestic industry. As work on the project progresses, it could spur complementary investments. Industry stands to benefit as well from other commitments of foreign direct investment to build power plants and commercial and industrial estates.

Service should stay buoyant this year and next. Although the government target of attracting 5 million tourists this year looks difficult to achieve, revenues from tourism are likely to remain strong. The composition of tourist arrivals is undergoing a promising change away from short-stay, low-spending tourists from neighboring countries toward longer-staying and higher-spending tourists from Japan, the Republic of Korea, and Taipei,China within the region and from Western Europe and North America.

With domestic economic activity getting a boost and international oil prices higher, the inflation rate is likely to rise gradually to 2.5% in 2017 and 3.0% in 2018.

As growth strengthens and inflation edges up, imports will grow faster than exports. Imports of machinery, equipment, and materials needed for the railway project, hydropower projects, and other foreign direct investments are particularly likely candidates for sharp increases. The current account deficit is thus forecast to widen to 19.0% this year and 20.0% in 2018 (Figure 3.25.6). Meager foreign exchange reserves are therefore unlikely to see much improvement soon.

The Lao PDR urgently needs to resume fiscal consolidation. Recognizing this, the government plans to cut its fiscal deficit to under 5% this year and next, leaving little scope for fiscal stimulus to support

3.25.3 Monthly inflation

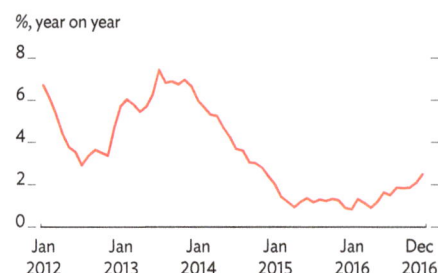

Source: CEIC Data Company (accessed 8 March 2016).

3.25.4 Monetary indicators

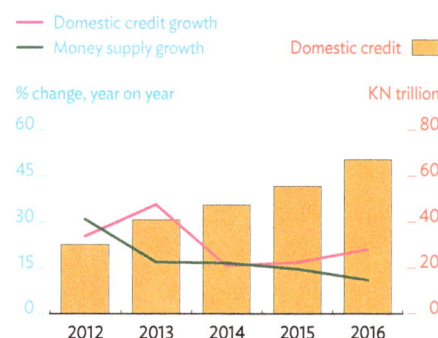

Source: Bank of the Lao People's Democratic Republic.

3.25.5 GDP growth

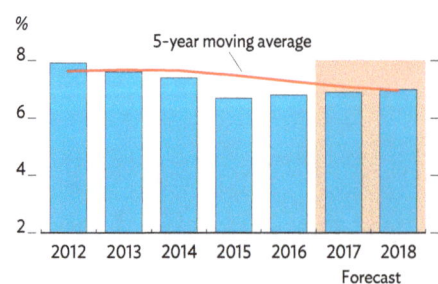

Source: Asian Development Outlook database.

growth in the near term. Monetary policy is similarly constrained in its ability to be expansionary in the immediate future because the US is expected to raise its interest rates in 2017 and 2018, and low foreign exchange reserves already put the Lao PDR in a delicate position.

Any further reversal to the fiscal consolidation program is a domestic risk to the outlook, especially as the Lao PDR is already at high risk of debt distress. The main external risk is a slowdown in the People's Republic of China that is sharper than expected.

Policy challenge—making growth more inclusive

The Lao PDR has been one of the fastest-growing economies in Southeast Asia for the past decade or so. Rapid growth enabled the country to meet its target under the Millennium Development Goals to halve extreme poverty by 2015. However, the rate of poverty reduction has not been commensurate with the strength of economic growth. To illustrate, from 2003 to 2012, every percentage point of GDP growth was matched on average by an unimpressive 0.47% decline in the poverty rate. This response is one of the smallest in Southeast Asia. Similar conclusions emerge if analysis uses international poverty lines to estimate poverty rates instead of the national poverty line used here.

The muted effect of economic growth on poverty in the Lao PDR is primarily the result of a growth pattern that relies heavily on highly capital-intensive sectors such as hydropower and mining, rather than on labor-intensive manufacturing. Mining and hydropower investments create enclaves of growth and prosperity with limited links to the rest of the economy. Even when such enclave industries grow rapidly, they create far fewer jobs than do new businesses that manufacture such labor-intensive products as garments, footwear, and consumer electronics. This isolation stymies poverty reduction even when GDP growth is strong. The key to making growth more inclusive in the future is therefore to shift the sources of growth away from extractive industries toward more labor-intensive manufacturing.

A two-pronged strategy is required to bring about such a structural transformation: liberalizing the business environment and improving the skills of young workers. The Lao PDR is ranked 139 among 190 economies surveyed for the World Bank's *Doing Business 2017*, behind every other member of the Association of Southeast Asian Nations except Myanmar (Figure 3.25.7). The country ranks poorly particularly in terms of procedures and processes for starting a business, getting an electricity connection, protecting minority shareholders, and resolving insolvency. Lack of access to finance is another factor that constrains in particular small and medium-sized enterprises in labor-intensive manufacturing.

There is thus huge scope for policy reform in these areas to attract investment, both domestic and foreign, in labor-intensive industries. Moreover, as the country also faces a skills gap that will constrain, sooner rather than later, the rise of a modern manufacturing sector, higher investment in education and training has to follow liberalization in the business environment.

3.25.1 Selected economic indicators (%)

	2017	2018
GDP growth	6.9	7.0
Inflation	2.5	3.0
Current account balance (share of GDP)	–19.0	–20.0

Source: ADB estimates.

3.25.6 Current account balance

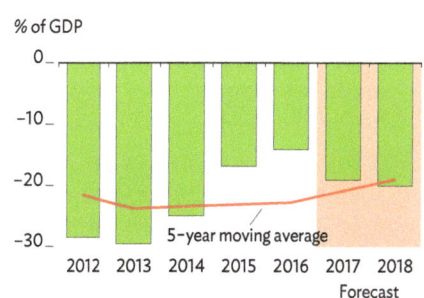

Source: *Asian Development Outlook* database.

3.25.7 Ease of doing business 2017 ranking of ASEAN members

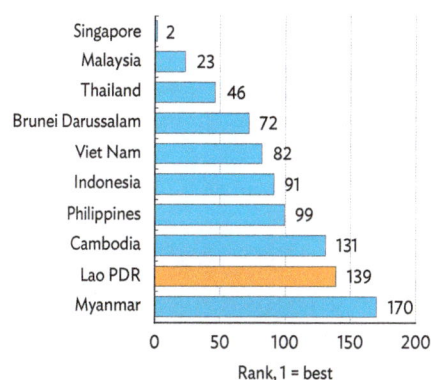

ASEAN = Association of Southeast Asian Nations, Lao PDR = Lao People's Democratic Republic.
Source: World Bank. 2016. *Doing Business 2017*.

Malaysia

A 2-year slowdown in economic growth likely bottomed out at 4.2% in 2016, with a modest recovery expected this year and next. Recovery will be accompanied by higher inflation at 3.3% and a smaller current account surplus. Sustaining growth as income rises will require higher productivity, which can be achieved through a major effort to strengthen innovation.

Economic performance

A diversified economic base and a flexible exchange rate helped to cushion the economy from a slump in global oil and commodity markets over the past 2 years. Still, economic growth slowed further to 4.2% in 2016, weighed down by decelerating fixed investment, weaker government spending, and a fall in net exports of goods and services (Figure 3.26.1). As growth slowed, the unemployment rate edged up to 3.5% in the fourth quarter of 2016 from 3.2% a year earlier.

Annual growth in private consumption, which averaged 7.2% during 2010–2014, has decelerated over the past 2 years. In 2016, it grew by a still robust 6.1% and made the largest demand-side contribution to GDP growth. Support for household spending came from increases in public sector salaries, a higher minimum wage, and government cash transfers.

Growth in government consumption spending last year braked sharply to 1.0%, and fixed investment by the government contracted for a third consecutive year, reflecting efforts to rein in the fiscal deficit. Private fixed investment grew by 4.4%, decelerating for a fourth year in a row as the outlook weakened for both domestic and external demand (Figure 3.26.2). Net external demand dragged on GDP growth as imports of goods and services rose in real terms by 0.4%, while real exports rose by 0.1%.

By sector, services grew by 5.6%, contributing the bulk of the increase in GDP last year. Wholesale and retail trade, food and accommodation, and information and communications recorded robust growth, reflecting in part expansion in consumer spending and tourism. Construction grew by 7.4%, slowing from more vigorous expansion in 2015. Growth in mining slackened to 2.7% as oil production flattened, though output in natural gas rose. Weaker demand for automobiles and a fall in palm oil processing suppressed growth in manufacturing to 4.4%, down from 4.9% in 2015. Bad weather caused agricultural output to shrink by 5.1%.

Consumer prices edged higher early in 2016 before easing later, putting average inflation for the year at 2.1%, unchanged from the preceding year (Figure 3.26.3).

3.26.1 Demand-side contributions to growth

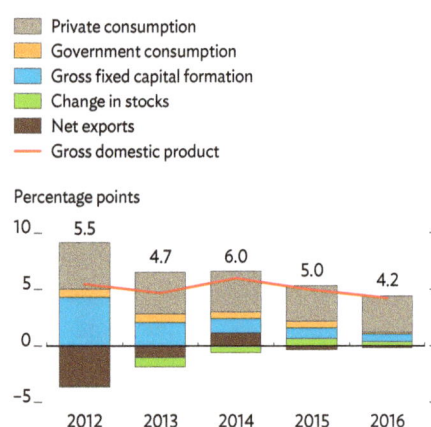

Legend:
- Private consumption
- Government consumption
- Gross fixed capital formation
- Change in stocks
- Net exports
- Gross domestic product

Percentage points

Sources: Haver Analytics; Bank Negara Malaysia. 2017. *Monthly Statistical Bulletin.* February. http://www.bnm.gov.my (accessed 16 February 2017).

3.26.2 Fixed investment growth

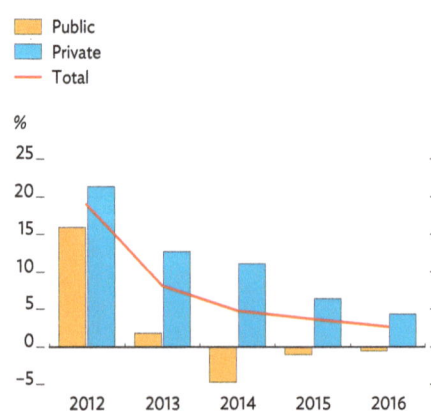

Legend:
- Public
- Private
- Total

%

Sources: Haver Analytics; Bank Negara Malaysia. 2017. *Monthly Statistical Bulletin.* February. http://www.bnm.gov.my (accessed 16 February 2017).

This chapter was written by Shiela Camingue-Romance of the Economic Research and Regional Cooperation Department, ADB, Manila; and Anthony Patrick, consultant, Economic Research and Regional Cooperation Department, ADB, Manila.

Malaysia's trade and current account surpluses continued to decline. Merchandise exports fell by 5.8% and imports by 4.4%, both in US dollar terms. In the process, the current account surplus shrank to the equivalent of 2.0% of GDP. Smaller net outflow in the capital and financial accounts enabled the overall balance of payments to post a surplus equal to 1.2% of GDP (Figure 3.26.4). Gross international reserves stood at $95 billion in February 2017, sufficient to cover 8.5 months of imports excluding imports for re-export. Viewed another way, reserves exceed the country's short-term external debt.

Last year, the Malaysian ringgit depreciated by 4.3% against the US dollar, after weakening by 19.1% in 2015, mainly on subdued exports and capital outflows. In December 2016, Bank Negara Malaysia, the central bank, required exporters to convert at least 75% of their export proceeds into ringgit, a move that helped to support the exchange rate and foreign reserves.

Sagging economic growth and subdued inflation prompted the central bank to ease monetary policy. After lowering the reserve ratio for banks from 4.0% to 3.5% in January 2016, it cut its policy interest rate by 25 basis points to 3.0% in July. Growth in bank credit nevertheless slowed from 7.7% in 2015 to 5.3% last year.

Fiscal consolidation remained on track. Revenue from a goods and services tax introduced in April 2015 went some way toward offsetting lower income from oil and gas, though total government revenue still declined by 3.0%. The government reduced expenditure by 2.0%, narrowing the fiscal deficit to 3.1% of GDP from 3.2% in 2015 (Figure 3.26.5).

Economic prospects

GDP growth is forecast to pick up this year and next but to remain well below the 5.3% average rate the country achieved in 2011–2015. Firmer growth in the major industrial economies and a mild recovery in domestic investment are likely to lift GDP growth to 4.4% this year and 4.6% in 2018 (Figure 3.26.6).

The outlook for private fixed investment is improving somewhat with higher prices for hydrocarbons, recovery in agriculture, and better prospects for semiconductors. However, concern over possible global trade disruption and the impact of the normalization of US monetary policy on capital flows to developing countries is likely to restrain recovery in investment. A pipeline of large infrastructure projects—such as the Pan Borneo Highway, the Pengerang refinery and petrochemical plant, mass rapid transport projects in Kuala Lumpur, and the East Coast rail link and high-speed rail line to Singapore—should stimulate both public and private investment. As for net external demand, its drag on GDP growth is forecast to diminish this year unless global trade is seriously disrupted.

Private consumption is expected to grow this year at around last year's pace. Rising wages are seen to underpin household spending, as are government measures to bolster incomes, including tax breaks, higher cash transfers to lower-income groups, and a reduction in mandatory employee contributions to the national retirement fund.

3.26.3 Monthly inflation

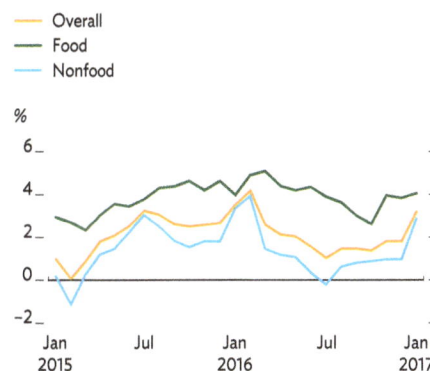

Sources: Haver Analytics; Bank Negara Malaysia. 2017. *Monthly Statistical Bulletin.* February. http://www.bnm.gov.my (accessed 14 March 2017).

3.26.4 Balance of payments components

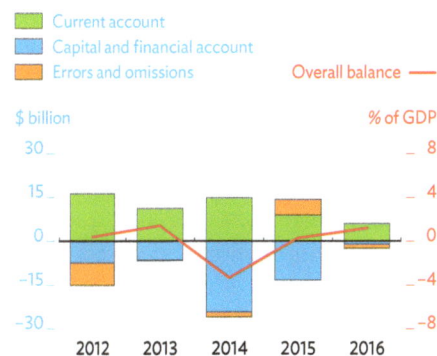

Sources: Haver Analytics; Bank Negara Malaysia. 2017. *Monthly Statistical Bulletin.* February. http://www.bnm.gov.my (accessed 14 March 2017).

3.26.5 Fiscal performance

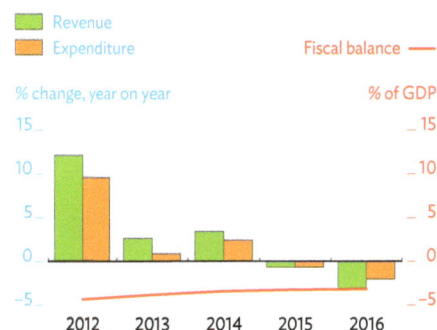

Sources: Haver Analytics; Bank Negara Malaysia. 2017. *Monthly Statistical Bulletin.* February. http://www.bnm.gov.my (accessed 14 March 2017).

Recovery in agriculture and rural subsidies will support rural incomes. However, dampeners on consumption spending include high household debt, which equals nearly 90.0% of GDP, and lackluster consumer confidence (Figure 3.26.7).

By sector, growth in services will benefit from rising inbound tourism aided by the depreciation of the ringgit. In a positive sign for industry, the purchasing managers' index indicated in February 2017 that the slowdown in manufacturing might be ending. Manufacturers reported that month that they raised production for the first time in almost 2 years (Figure 3.26.8). Demand for semiconductors will get a lift from an increase in book-to-bill ratios in North America and Japan and the launch of new mobile phone models.

Agriculture is forecast to recover this year, assuming the weather improves. Also, natural gas production is projected to rise, but oil output will likely decline as oil fields age and because of an international agreement by oil producers to temporarily trim output. Work on public infrastructure and affordable housing should give a helping hand to construction.

Higher fuel prices, cuts to subsidies, and a weaker ringgit are expected to push prices up. Inflation is forecast to rise to 3.3% in 2017 and then subside to 2.7% with the fading of the base effect from lower prices last year (Figure 3.26.9). Inflation averaged 3.9% year on year in the first 2 months of 2017. In March 2017, the central bank projected that higher global commodity and energy prices, and the impact of ringgit depreciation, would lift inflation to 3%–4% in 2017. The central bank added, however, that it did not expect these inflationary factors to have significant spillover into broader price trends, and that core inflation should increase only modestly.

Merchandise exports started 2017 on a better note, rising in January by 10.7% in US dollar terms from January 2016. All major export categories—manufactures, oil and liquefied natural gas, and agricultural products—showed improvement. Imports also rebounded in January, by 13.2%, on higher purchases of capital and intermediate goods. Growth in imports is expected to outstrip that of exports this year, narrowing the current account surplus to the equivalent of 1.8% of GDP, before the surplus edges up to 2.0% in 2018 as export growth quickens.

With inflation picking up and the current account surplus narrowing but still positive, the central bank could keep monetary policy steady for some time, though policy will be contingent on changes in US monetary policy and other external developments. Fiscal policy is expected to support economic growth. The government aims to narrow the fiscal deficit to 3.0% of GDP in 2017 but has budgeted to increase operating expenditure for the first time in 3 years and has also raised net development spending.

A significant risk to the outlook is potential disruption to global trade because Malaysia is closely integrated into the world economy. The main export markets are, in descending order, Singapore, the People's Republic of China (PRC), the US, the European Union, and Japan. Sudden tariff hikes by major partners would hamper the modest strengthening now forecast for this trade-dependent economy.

3.26.6 Annual GDP growth

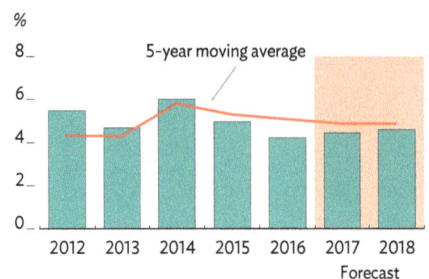

Source: Asian Development Outlook database.

3.26.1 Selected economic indicators (%)

	2017	2018
GDP growth	4.4	4.6
Inflation	3.3	2.7
Current account balance (share of GDP)	1.8	2.0

Source: ADB estimates.

3.26.7 Consumer and business confidence indexes

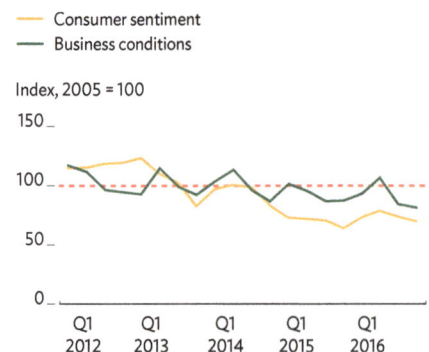

Note: Above 100 indicates improvement in business conditions and rising consumer confidence.
Sources: Malaysian Institute of Economic Research. https://www.mier.org.my; Haver Analytics (accessed 22 March 2017).

Policy challenge—fostering innovation

As Malaysia's income rises, growth will have to come increasingly from sustained gains in labor productivity through a renewed focus on innovation. Recognizing this imperative, the government has set a target of nearly doubling annual labor productivity growth to 3.7% during 2016–2020, up from the 2.0% pace in 2011–2015. Building on this plan, the government is expected to unveil a productivity blueprint in the second half of 2017.

Malaysia ranked 35 among 128 countries on the Global Innovation Index 2016, ahead of many regional peers though slipping by three places in the ranking from 2015. The innovation index is an average of two subindexes, one on innovation inputs that captures a country's institutions, human capital, infrastructure, market, and business sophistication, and another on innovation outputs that factors in knowledge and technology outputs and creative outcomes. As such, it is a proxy for the innovation potential of a country. How effectively that potential is realized is given for each country by the ratio of the output subindex to the input subindex, yielding the innovation efficiency score.

Although Malaysia outperforms many of its regional peers in terms of the composite innovation index, its innovation efficiency score is less impressive, ranking it at 59, behind such regional peers as the PRC, the Philippines, Thailand, and Viet Nam (Figure 3.26.10). The innovation index and the efficiency score may be only rough indicators, but they point to huge scope for making more of the country's high innovation potential. A 2016 survey by the Organisation for Economic Co-operation and Development highlighted that innovation in Malaysia is critically hampered by a lack of coordination across government agencies.

Interestingly, World Bank enterprise surveys have found that Malaysian firms tend to focus on innovation that involves commercial and organizational issues such as improved distribution and marketing. Only 17% invest in developing new technologies. This compares unfavorably with 27% of companies in Southeast Asia as a whole, suggesting a need for Malaysian firms to invest more in research and development and for greater effort to encourage technology transfer from multinationals to domestic enterprises.

The World Bank enterprise surveys also found that fewer Malaysian firms train their workers than do firms in other countries. Only 19% of firms in Malaysia provide formal worker training, slightly less than the average for members of the Association of Southeast Asian Nations (ASEAN) and far below the rate in high-income economies or the PRC. Such firm-level training gaps are particularly wide in manufacturing, where training programs are offered to only 44% of their workers, compared with 85% in the PRC and 60% in other ASEAN countries. Within the country's manufacturing industry, small firms offer much less formal training than do medium-sized and large firms.

How to use the country's innovation capability much more efficiently is therefore a key issue that policy makers need to address in their quest to foster innovation and boost productivity.

3.26.8 Manufacturing purchasing managers' index

Note: Nikkei, Markit.
Source: Bloomberg (accessed 22 March 2017).

3.26.9 Annual inflation

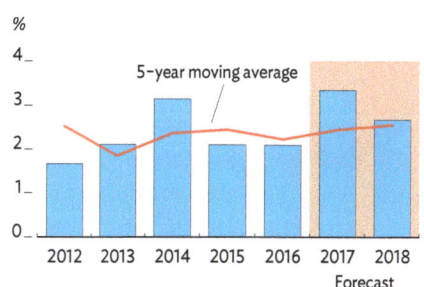

Source: Asian Development Outlook database.

3.26.10 Global innovation index and innovation efficiency ratio

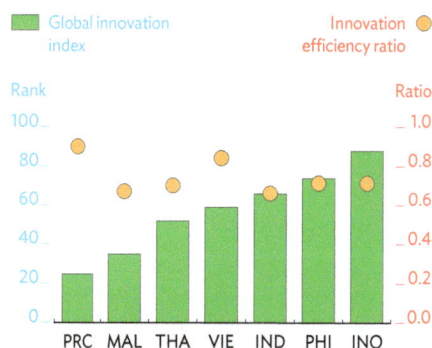

IND = India, INO = Indonesia, MAL = Malaysia, PHI = Philippines, PRC = People's Republic of China, THA = Thailand, VIE = Viet Nam.
Notes: Rank 1 = best, Ratio >1 = higher efficiency.
Source: Based on ranking from S. Dutta, B. Lanvin, and S. Wunsch-Vincent. 2016. *Global Innovation Index 2016: Winning with Global Innovation.* https://www.globalinnovationindex.org

Myanmar

GDP growth slowed to 6.4% last year from 7.3% in the previous year. Inflation eased, but the current account deficit worsened. With recovery firming in the major industrial economies, growth should accelerate this year and next, inflation edge up, and the current account deficit widen. Consolidating the country's legal and regulatory framework is crucial to develop a vibrant private sector and tap Myanmar's huge growth potential.

Economic performance

An already slowing economy decelerated further because of a weak external environment, unfavorable weather, and uncertainty about the direction economic policy will take under the newly elected government. GDP growth in FY2016 (ended 31 March 2017) came in at an estimated 6.4%, down from 7.3% in the previous year (Figure 3.27.1).

Most major sectors recorded slower growth last year. Held back by a slow recovery from floods in 2015 and subdued international commodity prices, growth in agriculture decelerated from 3.4% in FY2015 to an estimated 2.5% last year. Growth in industrial output slowed from 8.7% in FY2015 to 8.2%. Within industry, energy production suffered the most, dragged down largely by low international prices for oil and gas. Growth decelerated in services more than in other sectors, from 9.1% in FY2015 to an estimated 7.6% last year.

Reliable data on the demand-side components of GDP are not available, but investment seems to have slowed while consumption was more resilient. As private investors adopt a wait-and-see approach, approvals of foreign direct investment declined by 28% in the first 9 months of FY2016 (Figure 3.27.2).

A February 2017 report from the International Monetary Fund indicates that the value of merchandise exports hardly grew in FY2016 after declining by more than 10.0% in the previous year. Meanwhile, merchandise imports seem to have risen by more than 7.0% in FY2016 after being flat in FY2015. The current account deficit is thus estimated to have widened to the equivalent of 7.0% of GDP from 5.2% in FY2015 (Figure 3.27.3). The worsening current account deficit put pressure on the Myanmar kyat, which has depreciated by 17.0% against the US dollar in the first nine months of FY2016.

Inflation eased on subdued demand and slowing growth—and despite higher international prices for oil and other commodities, as well as kyat depreciation. It fell from a peak of 16.2% in October 2015 to less than 4.0% in October 2016. Average inflation declined to an estimated 6.5% from 11.2% in FY2015 (Figure 3.27.4).

3.27.1 Gross domestic product and sectoral growth

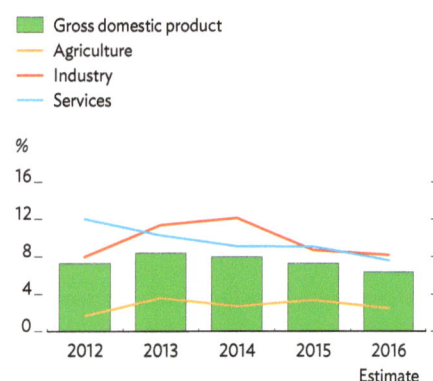

Note: Years are fiscal years ending 31 March of the next year.
Source: Planning Department, Ministry of National Planning and Economic Development.

3.27.2 Foreign direct investment

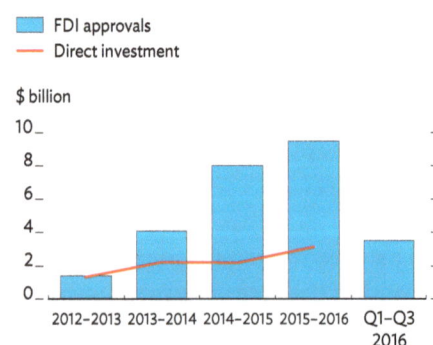

FDI = foreign direct investment.
Note: For FDI approvals, years are fiscal years ending 31 March of that year. Direct investment amounts are in calendar years.
Source: Directorate of Investment and Company Administration.

This chapter was written by Yumiko Tamura, Thi Da Myint, and Yan P. Oo of the Myanmar Resident Mission, ADB, Nay Pyi Taw.

Against the backdrop of falling inflation, monetary and fiscal policies remained accommodative to support growth. Available data indicate that credit growth continued to be strong in FY2016. The bulk of credit expansion went to finance the government's fiscal deficit, as government borrowing from the central bank without limit has been a common practice.

The International Monetary Fund report gave the fiscal deficit in FY2016 as the equivalent of 4.6% of GDP, up from 4.1% in the previous year. The ratio of government revenue to GDP continued a declining trend seen since FY2014 and is estimated to have been 17.2% in FY2016. Government expenditure had to adjust to falling revenue and is estimated to have equaled 21.8% of GDP in FY2016.

Economic prospects

Myanmar's export prospects have improved with the lifting of US sanctions in October 2016 and higher international prices for oil and other commodities. Its new investment law, effective at the beginning of April 2017, should attract more foreign investment if implemented effectively. Following recent years beset by droughts and floods, a return to normal weather would further boost agriculture, which provides nearly 30% of the GDP.

Economic performance should improve, with GDP growth at 7.7% in FY2017 and 8.0% in FY2018 (Figure 3.27.5). With normal weather and higher international commodity prices, agriculture should sustain a growth rate of around 3% this year and next. Industry and services are both likely to grow more strongly. Newly emerging demand for telecommunications should give a further fillip to the service sector. Industrial output is forecast to grow at an annual rate of around 10.0% this year and next. Growth in services is forecast to come in at a sturdy 9.0% in FY2017 and 10.0% the following year.

Exports are forecast to increase at an annual pace of 7.0% this year and next. With domestic demand gaining strength and foreign direct investment inflows responding to the implementation of the new investment law, growth in imports will outpace that in exports. As a result, the trade and current account deficits are both likely to worsen this year and next (Figure 3.27.6). Higher inflows of foreign direct investment are seen to help finance the widening current account deficit.

As growth strengthens, inflation is likely to edge up by half a percentage point this year and next, reaching 7.5% in FY2018 (Figure 3.27.7). The Central Bank of Myanmar is thus likely to face the challenging task of restraining money supply and credit to contain inflation. Encouragingly, the government has recently adopted a cap on its borrowings from the central bank, limited to not more than 40% of its total financing needs. Government loans will have market-based interest rates rather than at a flat rate of 4%, as has been past practice. This should significantly reduce pressure on the central bank to extend credit to the government, enabling it to better manage monetary conditions. Moreover, the government plans to contain the fiscal deficit to 3%–4% of GDP this year and next by strengthening revenue collection and enhancing expenditure efficiency.

3.27.3 External balances

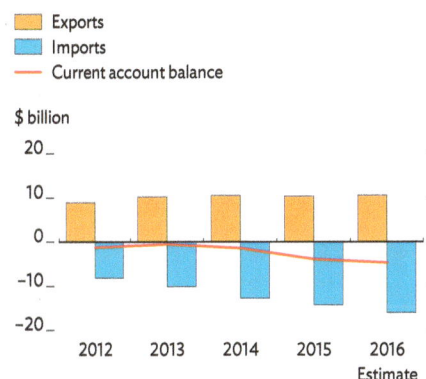

Sources: International Monetary Fund; ADB estimates.

3.27.4 Inflation

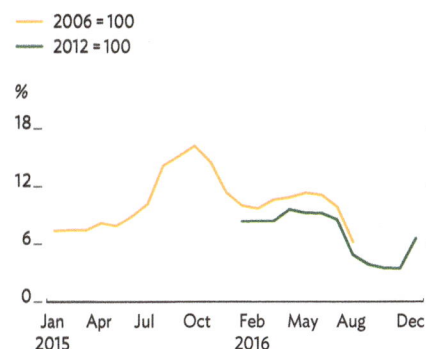

Source: Central Statistical Organization.

3.27.5 GDP growth

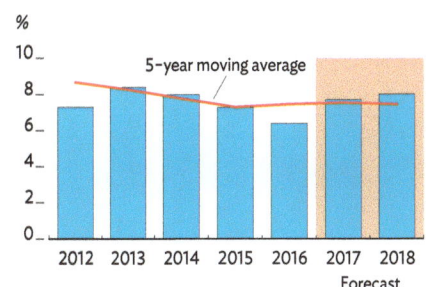

Note: Years are fiscal years ending 31 March of the next year.
Sources: International Monetary Fund; ADB estimates.

External risks to the outlook could arise from unexpectedly weak global recovery or volatility in international financial markets. Domestic risks include unclear and inconsistent policy directions, excessive credit growth, delays in implementing reform initiatives, and disruptions to social stability.

Policy challenge—developing the private sector through sound laws and regulations

A rapid transition to a market-oriented economy crucially requires the development of a sound legal and regulatory framework conducive to the private sector playing a lead role in the economy. It is encouraging that since 2011 a number of existing laws have been amended and new laws adopted to this end. More recently, two laws passed in 2012 and 2013, one for domestic investors and another for foreign investors, were merged into the unified Investment Law, slated to come into effect in April 2017. A new company law is expected to be passed in 2017 toward improving the operating and governance framework for both domestic and foreign investors.

These efforts constitute a good beginning, but Myanmar still lacks a credible and consolidated legal and regulatory framework to support the emergence of a vibrant private sector. Multiple layers of laws, regulations, and procedures often hinder investment and private business, as does their inconsistent implementation.

Major changes to the legal and regulatory framework for private business are needed to reform how laws are made, how they are translated in administrative rules and regulations, and how the rules and regulations are implemented. Laws and regulations need to be prepared with proper consultation both within the government and with other stakeholders including businesspeople. The process should ensure that the whole of government, not just one ministry alone, is involved. Rules and regulations should be fully consistent with the laws from which they are derived and easy to comply with because they satisfy the needs of business. To this end, ministries and government agencies need to deepen their understanding of modern business practice. The effective implementation and uniform enforcement of laws and regulations is as important as their formulation and enactment.

3.27.1 Selected economic indicators (%)

	2017	2018
GDP growth	7.7	8.0
Inflation	7.0	7.5
Current account balance (share of GDP)	–8.0	–8.0

Note: Years are fiscal years ending on 31 March of that year.
Source: ADB estimates.

3.27.6 Current account balance

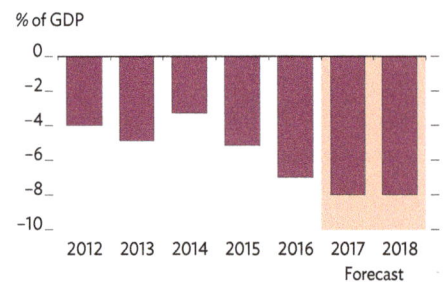

% of GDP

Note: Years are fiscal years ending 31 March of the next year.
Sources: International Monetary Fund; ADB estimates.

3.27.7 Inflation

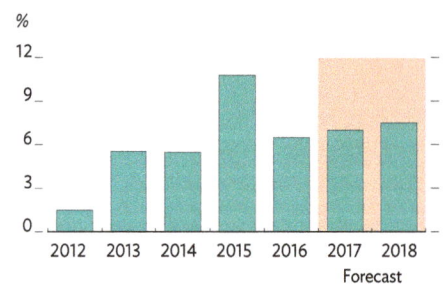

%

Note: Years are fiscal years ending 31 March of the next year.
Sources: International Monetary Fund; ADB estimates.

Philippines

Buoyant domestic demand drove economic growth up to 6.8% in 2016. Growth will moderate somewhat but still be strong at 6.4% this year and 6.6% next. Inflation is forecast to pick up, and the current account will continue to post a small surplus. Making growth more inclusive will require the effective implementation of the country's development plan for 2017–2022.

Economic performance

GDP growth accelerated from 5.9% in 2015 to 6.8% last year notwithstanding weak external demand and a reduction in agricultural production largely caused by drought. Broad-based strength in domestic demand underpinned last year's healthy growth rate, which was lifted as well by election spending.

Investment, both public and private, made the biggest contribution to growth, followed by private consumption (Figure 3.28.1). Spurred by higher outlays for durable equipment and construction (Figure 3.28.2), the ratio of fixed investment to GDP reached 23.8% in 2016, its highest in over a decade, though still behind the ratio in other Southeast Asian economies (Figure 3.28.3).

Private consumption, providing nearly 70% of GDP, grew by 6.9% last year, up from a 6.3% rise in 2015. Consumer spending benefited from higher employment and steady inflows of remittances from workers overseas. The unemployment rate declined to 5.5% in 2016, while remittances from overseas rose by 4.9% to reach $29.7 billion. Consumption got further impetus from an 8.3% rise in public spending on social programs including basic education, national health insurance and immunization, and conditional cash transfers to 4.4 million poor families, which were contingent on recipients acting to meet certain criteria. A salary increase for government staff further drove up public consumption.

By sector, services and industry were the key growth drivers. Services—the largest sector, providing over half of GDP and employment—expanded by 7.5% and generated nearly two-thirds of GDP growth last year (Figure 3.28.4). Subsectors posting strong growth were retail trade, business process outsourcing (BPO), tourism, real estate, and financial services.

Industry turned in a sturdy 8.0% growth last year, improving on 6.0% growth in 2015. Manufacturing, comprising two-thirds of the industry sector, accelerated its growth rate from 5.7% in 2015 to 7.0% last year. Benefiting from strong domestic demand, food processing, which constitutes a third of manufacturing, posted robust output gains.

3.28.1 Demand-side contributions to growth

- Private consumption
- Government consumption
- Fixed investment
- Change in inventories
- Net exports
- Statistical discrepancy
- Gross domestic product

Percentage points

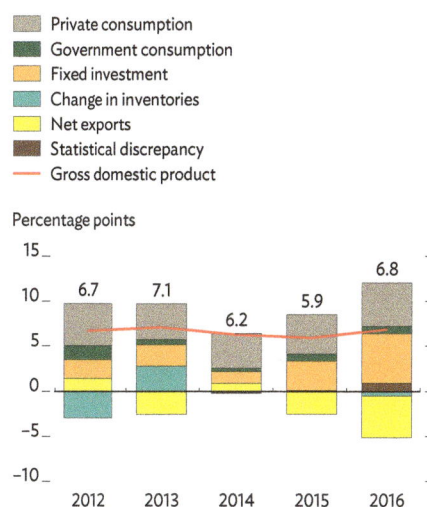

Source: CEIC Data Company (downloaded 10 March 2017).

3.28.2 Contributions to fixed investment growth

- Construction
- Durable equipment
- Others

Percentage points

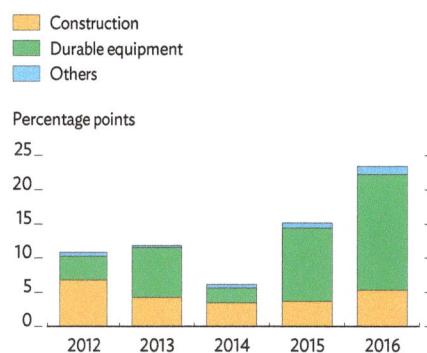

Source: CEIC Data Company (downloaded 10 March 2017).

This chapter was written by Aekapol Chongvilaivan and Teresa Mendoza of the Philippines Country Office, ADB, Manila.

A number of other industries such as chemicals, rubber products, machinery, and transportation equipment also performed well. Construction, both public and private, also contributed significantly to industry growth. Indeed, public construction expanded by 29.0% in 2016, outpacing already impressive growth of 19.0% in 2015.

Drought caused by El Niño, the periodic weather disturbance, cut agricultural output by 1.3% during the year, although there was a slight recovery in the second half. Agriculture's share in GDP has shrunk to 10%, though the sector still employs nearly 30% of working Filipinos.

Notwithstanding buoyant domestic demand, inflation remained modest, averaging 1.8% last year. This was marginally higher than the previous year's rate of 1.4% but was still lower than the target range of 2%–4% set by Bangko Sentral ng Pilipinas, the central bank. Subdued global oil prices kept the lid on inflation, and timely imports of rice augmented domestic supplies and kept food prices low.

Against the backdrop of benign inflation, monetary policy remained accommodative. The central bank kept the overnight reverse repurchase rate unchanged at 3.0%. Monetary and credit conditions thus continued to support growth, with the money supply (M3) rising by 12.7% in 2016, up from 9.4% in 2015. Demand for credit from the private sector remained the key driver of liquidity growth.

Accelerated public spending, particularly on infrastructure, widened the fiscal deficit to the equivalent of 2.4% of GDP in 2016 from 0.9% in 2015. Expenditure excluding interest payments rose by 16.8%. Nearly half of the increase in public spending was for infrastructure. Tax collection rose by 9.1% and provided 90% of revenues. The ratio of government debt to GDP declined to 42.1% in 2016, the lowest in over a decade, enabling higher spending. Debt in local currency accounted for about two-thirds of the total.

Weak external demand trimmed the current account surplus from the equivalent of 2.5% of GDP in 2015 to 0.2% last year (Figure 3.28.5). As imports rose rapidly and exports increased only marginally, the merchandise trade deficit widened to equal 11.2% of GDP, up from 8.0% in 2015. However, remittances and strong earnings from services exports, particularly BPO and tourism, managed to maintain a surplus.

In the capital account, net inflows of foreign direct investment rose to $7.9 billion, 40.7% higher year on year (Figure 3.28.6). Portfolio investments, however, registered net outflows. The overall balance of payments fell into a deficit equal to 0.1% of GDP, reversing a surplus of 0.9% in 2015. Nevertheless, by February 2017, foreign exchange reserves stood at $81.1 billion, cover for 9.2 months of imports of goods and services and income payments. The Philippine peso depreciated by 5.3% against the broadly strengthening US dollar in 2016. A continuing decline in external debt from the equivalent of 59.7% of GDP in 2005 to 24.6% in 2016 has helped strengthen the country's external payments position.

Economic prospects

GDP growth is projected to moderate to 6.4% in 2017, reflecting in part the high base effect from last year's figure but also rising commodity prices that could affect domestic demand (Figure 3.28.7). Growth is

3.28.3 Fixed investment

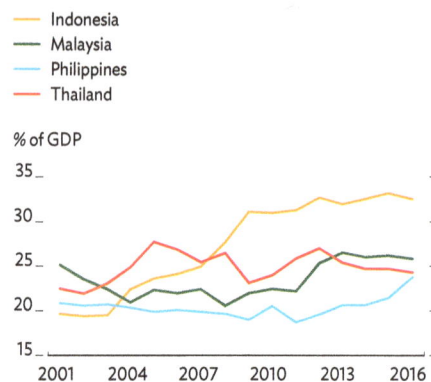

Source: CEIC Data Company (downloaded 10 March 2017).

3.28.4 Supply-side contributions to growth

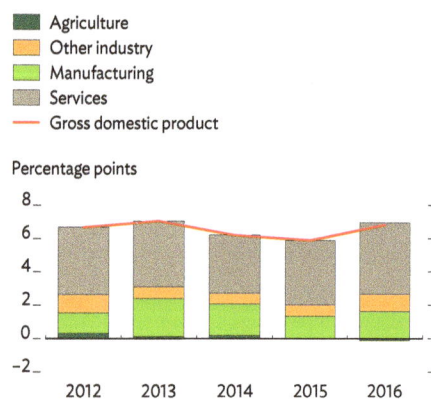

Source: CEIC Data Company (downloaded 10 March 2017).

3.28.5 Current account components

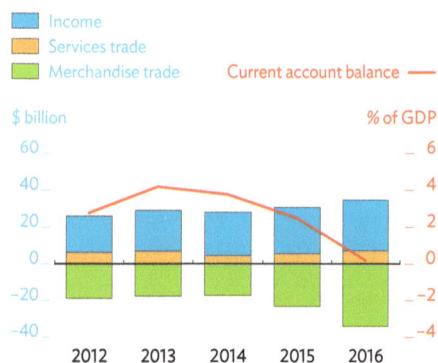

Source: CEIC Data Company (downloaded 17 March 2017).

expected to recover to 6.6% in 2018 as the government plans to further ramp up public infrastructure investment.

Private consumption will continue to rise robustly, though at a more moderate pace than last year. A central bank survey conducted in the first quarter of this year found consumers remaining optimistic, though expectations of higher inflation may temper the pace of spending (Figure 3.28.8). Similarly, investor sentiment remains broadly positive, but at the same time businesses expressed some caution arising from higher oil prices, peso depreciation, and uncertainty about global trade and monetary policies. Encouragingly, bank lending to businesses, occupying 89% of the loan portfolio, continued to grow strongly, rising by 17.5% year on year in January this year.

Net exports are expected to contract and temper GDP growth somewhat. While merchandise exports are expected to rebound from last year, imports will likely rise at a faster pace, reflecting growing consumer demand and investment.

By sector, services will remain the lead growth driver, though moderating from last year's brisk pace as growth in domestic consumption eases somewhat. BPO and tourism should continue to support services growth. International tourist arrivals rose by 11.3% last year to reach 6 million, and growth is expected to stay strong. In January 2017, tourist arrivals rose by 16.5% year on year.

Growth in manufacturing is expected to hold up well even as it slows slightly from last year's pace. The manufacturing production index rose in January 2017 by 9.3% year on year with strong gains in food processing and machinery and transport equipment. Construction-related manufactures such as metal, glass, and wood products have also sustained an upward trend. High capacity utilization also augurs well for the manufacturing sector. Spurred by public infrastructure projects, construction is forecast to remain buoyant. Private construction is also showing momentum as demand for office space, housing, and retail space stays strong.

Even as growth moderates, rising international prices for oil should nudge domestic inflation up to 3.5% this year and 3.7% next year (Figure 3.28.9). In the first 2 months of 2017, inflation edged up to 3.0% largely because of higher fuel prices and fare hikes for public transportation consequently approved in February 2017. A weaker peso following the upward adjustment of US interest rates in December will exert additional upward pressure on domestic inflation. Proposed tax reform to raise excise taxes on fuel—an important intermediate input into many economic activities—could exert still more pressure on domestic prices.

As inflation approaches the upper end of the central bank target range of 2%–4%, monetary policy will aim to strike a balance between supporting growth and containing inflation. The central bank will have to factor into this delicate balance the future course of US interest rates. A measured hike in the central bank policy rate is likely.

Current indications are for fiscal policy to remain supportive to growth. The government has raised the ceiling on the fiscal deficit from 2.0% of GDP to 3.0%, mainly to accommodate higher development spending. The 2017 national budget plans a 12% increase in spending

3.28.6 Foreign direct investment net inflows

Sources: Bangko Sentral ng Pilipinas. www.bsp.gov.ph; World Bank, World Development Indicators online database. http://databank.worldbank.org/data/reports.aspx?source=world-development-indicators (both accessed 24 March 2017).

3.28.7 GDP growth

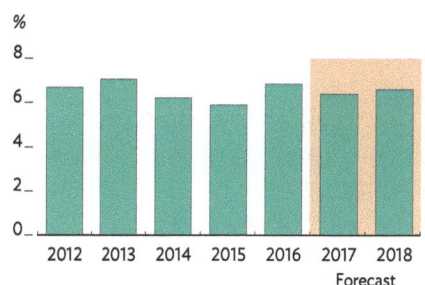

Source: Asian Development Outlook database.

3.28.8 Consumer expectations for the next 12 months

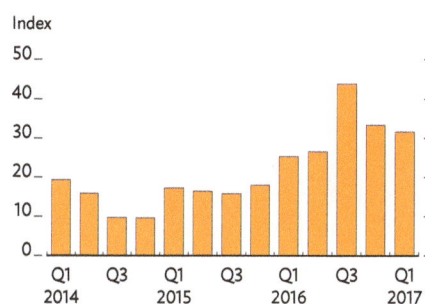

Q = quarter.
Note: The index is the percentage of households that were optimistic less those that were pessimistic. A positive index indicates a favorable view.
Source: CEIC Data Company (accessed 24 March 2017).

with significantly increased outlays for infrastructure and social programs. Allocations for social services were raised from 7.7% of GDP in 2016 to 8.4% in 2017. Infrastructure spending, including investment in roads, railways, ports, health facilities, school buildings, and agricultural works, is targeted to equal 5.3% of GDP in 2017, up from an average of 2% in the past decade. The government has developed a 3-year rolling infrastructure program that prioritizes public projects. To expedite implementation, the government has streamlined its review and approval procedures, as well as its bidding and procurement processes. Further, it launched an online portal covering details of government projects and their status to improve project monitoring.

The current account is expected to post a modest surplus equal to 0.2% of GDP in 2017, as in 2016, and 0.5% in 2018. Only modest growth is foreseen for merchandise exports because prospects for major markets are uneven. The firming up of US growth is tempered by only modest expansion in Japan and the European Union and by growth moderation in the People's Republic of China. Japan is the Philippines' biggest market, taking a fifth of all exports in 2016, followed by the US with a 15% share and the European Union with 12% (Figure 3.28.10). Higher prices for oil and other commodities will likely widen the merchandise trade deficit. Continued strength in remittances, income from BPO, and tourism receipts will, however, counterbalance the merchandise trade deficit.

Risks to the outlook could arise from two external factors: lower-than-expected growth in the Philippines' major trading partners and uncertain trade policies in the industrial economies. Domestically, realizing growth prospects will hinge on the successful implementation of the government's ambitious public investment program, especially infrastructure projects.

Policy challenge—making growth more inclusive

Improved macroeconomic fundamentals, the resumption of strong growth since 2010, and the administration's emphasis on regional development provide a foundation for the country to further reduce poverty and foster a more equal sharing of prosperity. However, income inequality and regional disparities hinder the benefits of growth from reaching poor and vulnerable sections of society.

The Gini coefficient, a measure of income inequality, improved from 0.46 in 2012 to 0.44 in 2015 but is still high for Southeast Asia (Figure 3.28.11). A government survey on family income and expenditure found that per capita income grew faster for the poorest 30% of the population than average for all income groups from 2012 to 2015. The national poverty rate fell from 25.2% in 2012 to 21.6% in 2015 but remains elevated in some regions. Families in 3 of the Philippines' 18 administrative regions—Metro Manila, Central Luzon, and Southern Tagalog—accounted for half of the national income in 2015.

Access to markets and thus economic opportunity has been hindered for the poor by underdeveloped infrastructure, including for irrigation, road transportation, and telecommunications. In *The Global Competitiveness Report 2016–2017*, the World Economic Forum ranks

3.28.9 Inflation

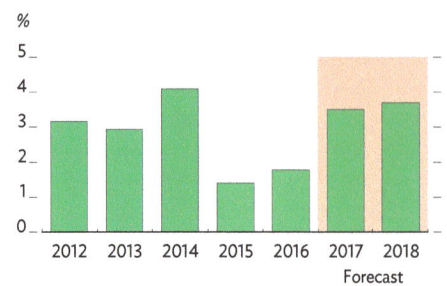

Source: Asian Development Outlook database.

3.28.10 Merchandise exports by destination, 2016

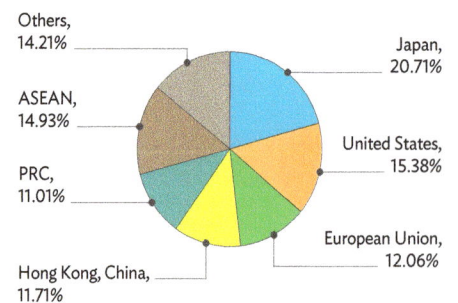

ASEAN = Association of Southeast Asian Nations, PRC = People's Republic of China.
Source: CEIC Data Company (accessed 17 March 2017).

3.28.11 Gini coefficient, 2013–2015

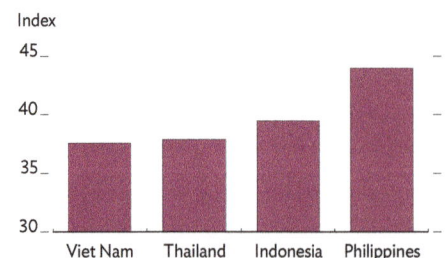

Note: Data are for the most recent year available: Indonesia 2013, the Philippines 2015, Thailand 2013, and Viet Nam 2014.
Sources: World Bank. World Development Indicators online database.http://data.worldbank.org/; Philippine Statistics Authority. www.psa.gov.ph (both accessed 24 March 2017).

the Philippines at 57 among 138 economies overall but at only 95 for infrastructure (Figure 3.28.12). Recognizing this, the government announced a 10-point socioeconomic agenda shortly after it took office on 30 June 2016. The agenda intensifies efforts to sustain strong growth and at the same time ensure that the benefits of growth are shared more across the population. Addressing this challenge requires concerted efforts to bring about more equitable access to services such as sanitation, safe drinking water, health care, and education.

Building on the 10-point agenda, the Philippine Development Plan 2017–2022, approved in February 2017, lays out the government strategy to promote more inclusive growth and development. The plan aims to bring down the poverty rate from 21.6% in 2015 to 14.0% by 2022, specifically targeting poverty in lagging regions. Rural poverty is higher at 30%, with most of the poor in low-paid informal farm work. The government aims to reduce rural poverty to 20% by 2022.

Programs to speed poverty reduction include raising agricultural productivity, building rural infrastructure such as irrigation systems and market roads, and establishing stronger links with industry and services to foster production and activities with higher value added. The plan calls for larger public investments in infrastructure, health care, education, and social protection. Infrastructure master plans will be fast-tracked and prioritize interregional connectivity toward integrating poor provinces with growth centers to improve the ease of doing business and enable the efficient delivery of public services. The share of development expenditure on social services and infrastructure is to increase from an average of 33% budgetted for 2010–2015 to 50% by 2022, boosting support for programs crucial to making growth more inclusive.

To raise more revenue to finance infrastructure and human capital investment, the government is proposing comprehensive tax reform. The Philippines has one of the lowest ratios of tax to GDP in Southeast Asia, at 13.7% in 2016. The proposed reform aims to simplify the tax system and yield more revenue. At the same time, tax burdens will be made more progressive. The first reform package, presented to Congress in January 2017, includes lowering personal income tax rates except for the highest income earners. It also seeks to expand the value-added tax base by limiting exemptions to raw food and other necessities such as education and health. Excise taxes on automobiles and oil products will be raised. To protect the poor from the impact of higher oil taxes, targeted transfers and support programs will be implemented. Further reforms being considered include adjusting excise taxes on alcohol, tobacco, and sugar-sweetened beverages and reducing the corporate income tax while rationalizing fiscal incentives for investors. These tax reforms will be supported by stricter tax administration and collection.

Key to making growth more inclusive is the effective implementation of the strategies and programs under the government's medium-term development plan.

3.28.1 Selected economic indicators (%)

	2017	2018
GDP growth	6.4	6.6
Inflation	3.5	3.7
Current account balance (share of GDP)	0.2	0.5

Source: ADB estimates.

3.28.12 Global Competitivenes ranking, 2016–2017

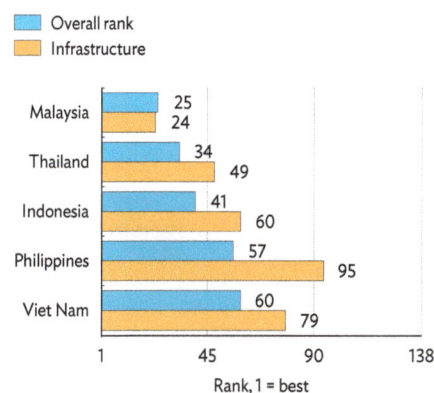

Note: Ranking in 138 economies.
Source: World Economic Forum. 2016. The Global Competitiveness Report 2016–2017.

Singapore

The economy grew faster in 2016, deflation persisted, and the current account improved. Growth is forecast to trend higher in 2017 and 2018, with the current account surplus widening in both years and prices rising for the first time since 2014. Faltering labor productivity could be improved in the coming years by encouraging small and medium-sized enterprises to innovate and adopt new technologies.

Economic performance

Recovery in manufacturing and higher government expenditure lifted the GDP growth rate to 2.0% in 2016 from 1.9% in 2015. Manufacturing reversed 5.1% contraction in 2015 with 3.6% growth led by higher output in the semiconductor and biomedical industries, contributing 0.6 percentage points to GDP growth. Construction grew by only 0.2%, slowing from 3.9% in 2015. Services grew by 1.0% and contributed 0.7 percentage points to growth, with expansion in all subsectors except business services, which declined owing mainly to a downturn in the real estate market (Figure 3.29.1).

External demand was the driver of growth in 2016. In real terms, exports of goods and services grew by 1.6% and imports by 0.3%, raising net exports by 9.8% to contribute 2.7 percentage points to growth (Figure 3.29.2). Global economic uncertainties continued to weigh on investment confidence and caused a 2.5% decline in gross fixed capital formation including change in inventories, which subtracted 0.9 percentage points from growth. Consumption expenditure grew by 1.8% on the strength of public spending, slowing from 5.3% in 2015 as household expenditure fell by 0.6% but contributing on balance 0.8 percentage points to growth.

Singapore endured more deflation in 2016 as the consumer price index declined by an average of 0.5%. Housing and utilities posted the largest decline, followed by communications and, as gasoline prices fell, private transport costs. Core inflation, which excludes accommodation and private road transport, was 0.9% because of higher costs for education services, food, and household durables (Figure 3.29.3).

Merchandise exports declined by 5.5% in 2016 as both oil and non-oil exports slumped. As oil imports shrank as well, imports fell by 5.2% to leave a trade surplus of $46.0 billion, equal to 15.5% of GDP. The current account surplus therefore rose to 19% of GDP, with the services surplus increasing by 0.5% on higher receipts from travel, transport, and insurance services. However, the overall balance of payments slipped into a deficit of $1.8 billion, or 0.6% of GDP,

3.29.1 Contributions to growth, by industry

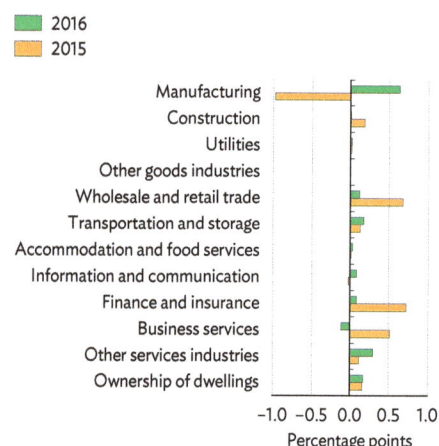

- 2016
- 2015

Manufacturing
Construction
Utilities
Other goods industries
Wholesale and retail trade
Transportation and storage
Accommodation and food services
Information and communication
Finance and insurance
Business services
Other services industries
Ownership of dwellings

-1.0 -0.5 0.0 0.5 1.0
Percentage points

Note: Excluding net indirect taxes.
Source: Ministry of Trade and Industry. Economic Survey Singapore 2016 (accessed 20 February 2017).

3.29.2 Demand-side contributions to growth

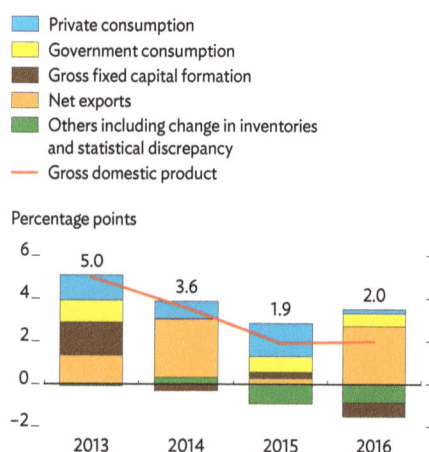

- Private consumption
- Government consumption
- Gross fixed capital formation
- Net exports
- Others including change in inventories and statistical discrepancy
- Gross domestic product

Percentage points

Source: Ministry of Trade and Industry. Economic Survey Singapore 2016 (accessed 20 February 2017).

This chapter was written by Minsoo Lee and Mai Lin Villaruel of the Economic Research and Regional Cooperation Department, ADB, Manila.

as net capital outflows increased (Figure 3.29.4). Official foreign reserves rose to $246.6 billion, or cover for 7 months of imports.

The Monetary Authority of Singapore (MAS) managed monetary conditions for price stability by keeping the policy band for the Singapore dollar's nominal effective exchange rate unchanged in 2016; while the currency strengthened by 1.1% by this measure, it weakened slightly against the US dollar in nominal terms (Figure 3.29.5). The 3-month Singapore interbank offered rate, used to price home loans, fell to 0.97% in December 2016 from 1.25% in December 2015. Credit to the private sector rose by 5.2%, pushing up total credit by 4.6%, and growth in broad money supply (M2) accelerated to 8.0%.

Fiscal policy was contractionary in FY2016 (ended 31 March 2017), with the budget recording a surplus of 1.3% of GDP. Operating revenue and expenditure both grew by 5.8%. Revenues increased mainly on higher receipts from personal income tax, motor vehicle taxes, and vehicle quota premiums as purchases of certificates of entitlement for private cars increased. Expenditures grew as outlays rose for education, national development, trade and industry, and especially health care subsidies (Figure 3.29.6).

Economic prospects

Continued restocking of technology products globally could spur expansion in both electronics manufacturing and external trade, pushing GDP growth higher to 2.2% in 2017. The purchasing managers' index for manufacturing and electronics breached the 50 threshold in September 2016, pointing to expansion in the first half of this year. However, services will weigh on growth as transport and storage lag, along with accommodation and real estate, though information and communication technology and essential social services will be robust. GDP growth is expected to improve to 2.3% in 2018 as manufacturing remains strong, and as services and construction improve (Figure 3.29.7).

Consumption will drive growth in 2017, with budgetary expenditures expected to increase by 5.2% and target education, health care, housing subsidies, and infrastructure. Investment will recover from contraction as indicated by investment commitments reported by the Economic Development Board, with fixed asset investment in 2017 forecast to reach almost S$10 billion, equal to 2.4% of GDP. Net foreign investment commitments in manufacturing reached S$1.6 billion in the fourth quarter of 2016, growing by 48.7% year on year. Government spending coupled with higher infrastructure investment, including significant investment in the Malaysia–Singapore high speed rail and a new industrial park in Jurong District, will boost growth in 2018 to 2.3%.

The deflationary trend appears to have ended as the consumer price index inched up by 0.6% in January 2017. Consumer prices are expected to rise by 1.0% in 2017, in the middle of the MAS forecast of 0.5%–1.5%, as the government increases water prices by 30% in two phases starting in July 2017 and raises diesel taxes based on volume usage. Inflation is forecast to rise further to 1.5% in 2018 on higher global oil prices, healthy wage growth, and continued increases in prices for food, utilities, and social services, especially education.

3.29.3 Inflation

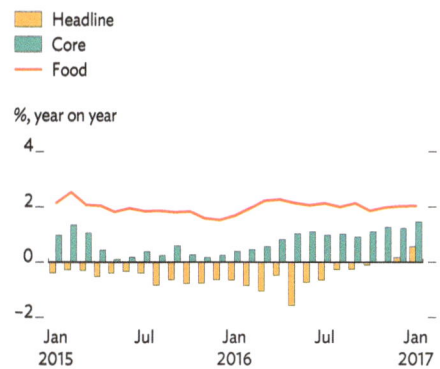

Source: CEIC Data Company (accessed 7 March 2017).

3.29.1 Selected economic indicators (%)

	2017	2018
GDP growth	2.2	2.3
Inflation	1.0	1.5
Current account balance (share of GDP)	19.5	19.8

Source: ADB estimates.

3.29.4 Balance of payments

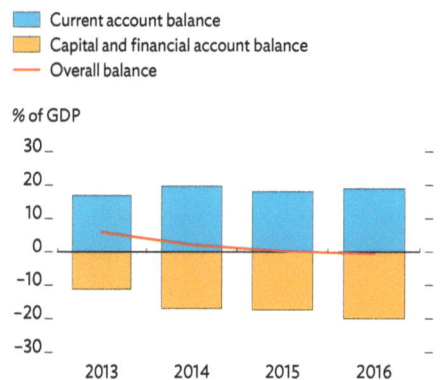

Source: Ministry of Trade and Industry. *Economic Survey Singapore 2016* (accessed 20 February 2017).

With moderate improvement in external demand in 2017 as partner economies strengthen, Singapore should see exports grow modestly (Figure 3.29.8). Merchandise exports and imports alike picked up significantly in January 2017. With some growth forecast for net services receipts as well, the current account surplus will expand modestly to equal 19.5% of GDP in 2017 and 19.8% in 2018, though the Singapore dollar is expected to appreciate marginally against the US dollar in 2017.

The MAS is expected to manage the exchange rate in response to economic developments over the forecast period to avert adverse impact on exports. Fiscal policy will continue to be prudent, with the budget surplus for FY2017 forecast to rise to the equivalent of 0.4% of GDP. Higher expenditure will be matched by rising revenue as new taxes, such as a water conservation tax on potable water, are introduced and diesel taxes are restructured.

External risks to the outlook include uncertainty regarding global economic conditions and a changing policy environment. The rising specter of protectionism has heightened these risks and can weaken sentiment in the financial markets, dampening external demand and, hence, trade-related activity. Domestically, persistent weakness in the residential property market could choke investment growth, and rising labor costs and stagnant labor productivity could hinder growth in labor-intensive sectors, slowing economic growth in the forecast period.

Policy challenge—raising labor productivity in an aging society

Over the past 3 years, labor productivity growth in Singapore, measured as average growth in value added per actual hour worked, has been nearly flat (Figure 3.29.9). It grew by a compounded annual growth rate of only 2.6% during 2009–2016. Excluding the 2010 rebound following the global financial crisis of 2008–2009, the same measure of productivity growth yielded only 1.5%, well below the government target of 2%–3% growth per annum to 2020. This stagnation is partly explained by recent changes in employment patterns. According to a recent Ministry of Trade and Industry economic survey, actual hours worked in more productive sectors, mainly the externally oriented industries that need to stay competitive in the global market, have declined relative to actual hours worked in less productive areas, including construction and food services, dragging down overall productivity (Figure 3.29.10).

Government policies have focused on raising productivity in small and medium-sized enterprises (SMEs), as they contribute about half of the GDP and employ 70% of the workforce. SMEs suffer lower productivity because of inefficient service delivery and poor management skills. They need to improve their productivity as they face stiffening competition from neighboring economies. The authorities have launched several initiatives to raise SME productivity.

3.29.5 Exchange rates

Sources: CEIC Data Company and Haver Analytics (accessed 7 March 2017).

3.29.6 Fiscal balance

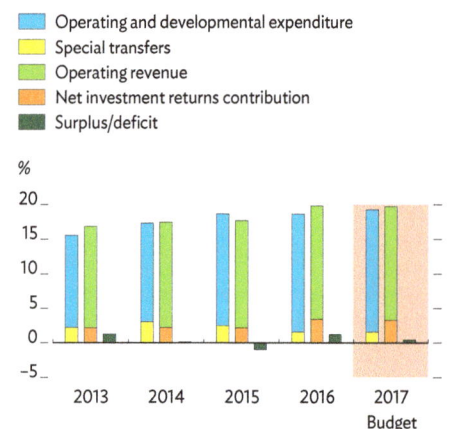

Note: The fiscal year ends on 31 March of the following year.
Source: Ministry of Finance (accessed 21 February 2017).

3.29.7 Manufacturing purchasing managers' index

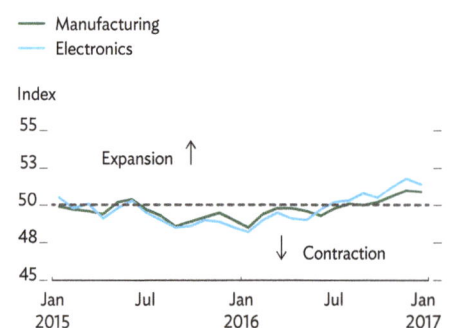

Source: CEIC Data Company (accessed 7 March 2017).

In 2016, it announced the continuation of a program that provides working capital loans to SMEs, which can be used to fund modern information technology businesses and help SMEs install digital platforms. The 2017 budget has allocated S$600 million for public partnerships with SMEs to scale up their operations and enable them to engage in international trade. SMEs can deduct from tax liability twice their expenses on market expansion and development. Other initiatives to improve SME productivity include identifying appropriate technologies tailored to SMEs' specific needs and co-investors that can help SMEs expand and internationalize.

The government-chaired Committee on the Future Economy has proposed providing SMEs with easy access to finance, catalyzing the supply of growth capital, and assisting with international trade procedures. SMEs Go Digital is a program introduced in the 2017 budget that aims to enhance digital capability in SMEs, especially in sectors with room to significantly improve productivity such as retail, food services, wholesale trade, logistics, cleaning, and security.

These and similar initiatives are bearing fruit. In the recent survey conducted by the Singapore Chinese Chamber of Commerce and Industry, 88% of SMEs have adopted measures to improve productivity, and more SMEs are attempting to change their business model toward undertaking activities with higher value added. SMEs in manufacturing and services have innovated their business practices and organization. These efforts can be enhanced by helping SMEs to streamline and harmonize business practices toward enabling them to take advantage of opportunities in the ASEAN Economic Community.

Despite these efforts, significantly improving labor productivity is a challenge in a land-constrained economy with an aging workforce and few natural resources. Policies can nevertheless be implemented to alleviate land and age constraints. Land should be allocated to activities with higher value added and those that use it efficiently. The constraint of an aging population can be addressed through retraining and senior-friendly wellness programs. The alleviation of these constraints can, combined with SME willingness to innovate, promise important productivity gains for Singapore over the medium term.

3.29.8 Merchandise trade

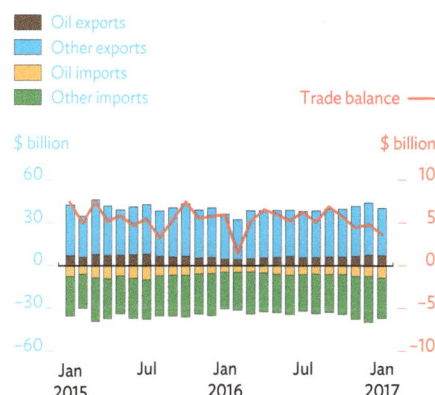

Source: CEIC Data Company (accessed 7 March 2017).

3.29.9 Growth rate of value added per actual hour worked

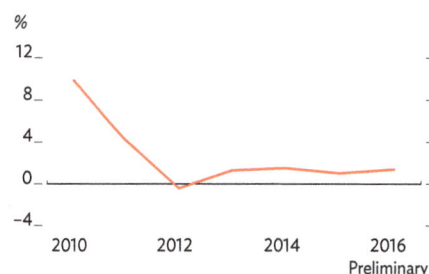

Source: Ministry of Trade and Industry. Economic Survey Singapore 2016 (accessed 20 February 2017).

3.29.10 Value added per actual hour worked, 2009–2016

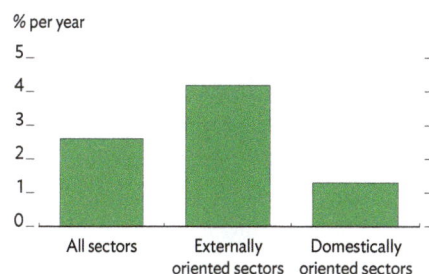

Source: Ministry of Trade and Industry. Economic Survey Singapore 2016 (accessed 20 February 2017).

Thailand

The economy grew by 3.2% last year, inflation barely slipped back into positive territory, and the current account posted a substantial surplus. Growth is likely to be slightly higher this year and next, while inflation should edge up and the current account surplus narrow. How effectively the Thailand 4.0 development agenda reignites growth will hinge on how well Thailand's youngsters upgrade their skills.

Economic performance

GDP grew by 3.2% in 2016, marginally higher than the previous year's rate of 2.9% (Figure 3.30.1). A turnaround in agriculture contributed to the mild pickup in growth, while most other major sectors either slowed or maintained their 2015 pace.

Improved weather in the second half of the year enabled agriculture to post growth at 0.6% last year, marking a significant turnaround from the previous year's 5.7% contraction. Growth in construction was a strong 8.3% but less than half of the previous year's impressive 17.0%. Construction was led by public works, especially by state enterprises. Manufacturing, which had grown by 1.5% in 2015, was still sluggish but steady with 1.4% growth last year. Aided by expansion in hotels, restaurants, and other tourism-related businesses, the service sector held up well with robust 4.7% growth, which was very similar to its 2015 pace.

On the demand side, private consumption grew by 3.1%, enabled by agriculture's turnaround to improve on 2.2% growth in 2015. Rising prices for agricultural products and the end of drought in the second half of the year boosted farm income in nominal terms by 2.8% over the whole year, reversing a steep 9.6% reduction in 2015. Also aiding private consumption, the government offered tax rebates for a few weeks of shopping and dining, initially during the Thai New Year in April and then during the Christmas season in December.

Having contracted by 2.2% in 2015, private investment picked up by an estimated 0.4% last year on a gradual recovery in business sentiment. As the government maintained an expansionary fiscal stance, public investment continued to be an important driver of growth in 2016, though it slowed from a whopping 29.3% growth in 2015 to a still sturdy 9.9% last year (Figure 3.30.2).

Partly reflecting the fragile external environment, merchandise exports hardly grew last year, having contracted by 5.6% in 2015. Encouragingly, signs of an export recovery were evident by the second half of the year. For the first time in 7 quarters, merchandise

3.30.1 Demand-side contributions to growth

- Private consumption
- Government consumption
- Total investment
- Net exports
- Statistical discrepancy
- Gross domestic product

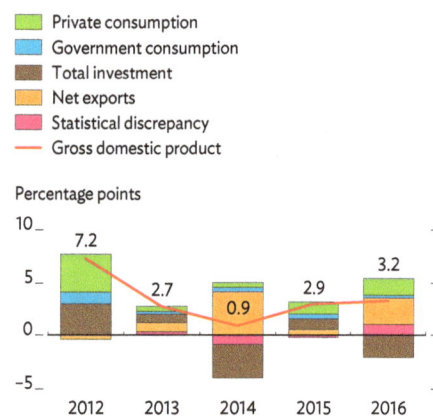

Percentage points

Source: National Economic and Social Development Board. http://www.nesdb.go.th (accessed 8 March 2017).

3.30.2 Fixed investment growth

- Private
- Public
- Total

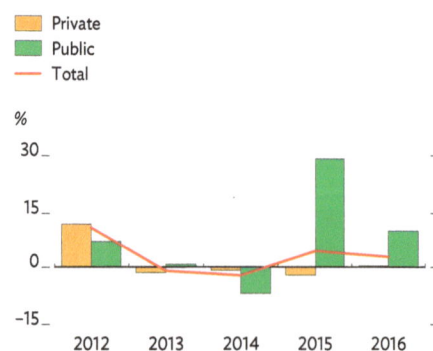

%

Source: National Economic and Social Development Board. http://www.nesdb.go.th (accessed 8 March 2017).

This chapter was written by Luxmon Attapich of the Thailand Resident Mission, ADB, Bangkok.

exports increased in the third quarter of 2016 and continued their recovery in the next quarter. Exports of manufacturing products expanded by 2.6%, led by electrical appliances, electronics, chemicals, and petrochemicals.

Meanwhile, merchandise imports continue to contract by 4.7% last year on top of a 10.6% contraction in 2015. Imports of consumer goods expanded by 5.8%, and beginning in the fourth quarter imports of capital goods also picked up. The trade balance still registered a large surplus of $35.8 billion (Figure 3.30.3). Although tourist arrivals slowed in the fourth quarter of 2016 from the same quarter in 2015 because of the mourning period for the King, who died on 13 October, and a crackdown on fraudulent tours targeting low-end visitors from the People's Republic of China (PRC), net services exports for the year as a whole posted strong growth at 26.5% (Figure 3.30.4). The country thus accumulated a current account surplus of $46.4 billion, equal to 11.4% of GDP, boosting international reserves in December to $171.9 billion, or cover for 9.4 months of imports, or 3.2 times short-term external debt.

Slack in manufacturing kept a lid on prices last year despite rising international prices for oil and other commodities. Inflation for the year as a whole came in at 0.2% (Figure 3.30.5). Consumer prices excluding food and beverages started to increase in the last quarter of 2016, following decreases for 9 quarters in succession. Inflationary pressure nevertheless remained low as drought eased and price rises for fresh food slowed in the second half.

On the fiscal front, the government implemented a number of subsidized public welfare programs: cash transfer schemes for low-income earners, housing loans at low interest rates, and soft loans for farmers, small and medium-sized enterprises, and startups, as well as tax deductions. These measures involved the government paying to special financial institutions the difference between the discount rate at which they lent to program beneficiaries and the market rate at which they raised funds. Moreover, the government injected public funds into the countryside through newly established revolving village funds.

Government revenues increased by 9.3% in FY2016 (ended 30 September 2016), pushing the ratio of revenue to GDP from 16.1% in FY2015 to 16.8%. At the same time, expansionary fiscal policy raised government expenditure by 9.0%, causing the ratio of expenditure to GDP to climb as well, from 18.4% in FY2015 to 19.1%. Of $2.4 billion in capital expenditure in FY2016, more than half was on large transport infrastructure projects under the government's transport infrastructure master plan to 2022. Adjusting for changes in the government's off-budget cash account, the overall fiscal deficit edged up from 2.5% of GDP in FY2015 to 2.7% last fiscal year.

Despite low inflation and ample foreign exchange reserves, the central bank kept its policy interest rate unchanged at 1.5% in the second half of 2016, reflecting its perception that the economy was on a recovery path in the face of global uncertainties.

3.30.3 Trade indicators

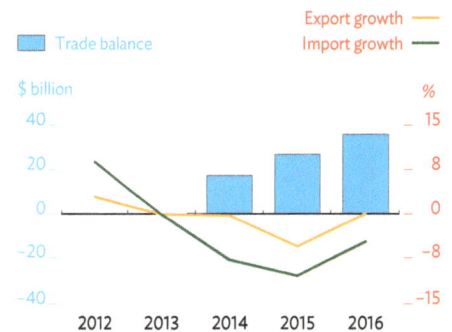

Source: Bank of Thailand. http://www.bot.or.th (accessed 8 March 2017).

3.30.4 Tourism indicators

Source: Bank of Thailand. http://www.bot.or.th (accessed 8 March 2017).

3.30.5 Inflation and policy interest rate

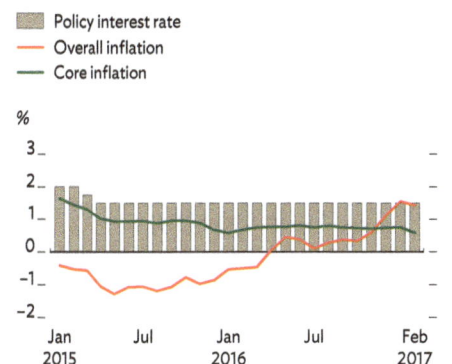

Sources: Bank of Thailand. http://www.bot.or.th; CEIC Data Company (both accessed 8 March 2017).

Economic prospects

Sustained recovery in the major industrial economies, robust domestic consumption, and the continued implementation of large public infrastructure projects should help GDP grow by 3.5% this year and 3.6% next (Figure 3.30.6). A gradual rise in the international price of rice should provide a further fillip.

Domestic consumption is expected to continue to expand, albeit modestly. Farm incomes should rise further along with commodity prices, assuming a return to normal weather. In 2018, the new personal income tax structure that allows more tax-deductible expenditures promises to lend support to consumption. The consumer confidence index plunged in October and November 2016 following the death of the King but recovered in December 2016 and continued to rise in January 2017 (Figure 3.30.7). Because high household debt remains a drag on domestic consumption, the government introduced measures to fix the longstanding problem of microfinance institutions overcharging their vulnerable borrowers. A "pico finance" license scheme went into operation in March 2017 to encourage informal lenders to conduct their business more transparently, and new legislation caps their lending rates.

Public investment will be a key driver of growth over the short term if the government expeditiously implements its planned $40 billion infrastructure investment program. Projects under the program include the construction of a double-track rail line and a major motorway and the expansion of a deepwater seaport. Bidding for several more infrastructure projects began in 2016. According to the Ministry of Transport, another 36 transport infrastructure projects worth $25.6 billion will be ready for investment this year. Financing for the projects will come from multiple sources, with the public budget providing 8.3%, loans 64.3%, public–private partnerships 22.1%, the Thailand Future Fund 4.9%, and state-owned enterprises 0.4%.

The implementation of large public infrastructure projects should spur private investment by boosting business confidence. Private investment is projected to pick up slowly this year and next as prospects for exports improve and manufacturers expand production. Although average utilization of industrial capacity is not high, standing at 60.5% in January 2017, in some subsectors—notably electronics, electrical parts, and chemical products—it exceeds 90%.

As growth edges up and international oil prices rise, inflation should rise but remain subdued at 1.8% this year and a somewhat higher rate next year (Figure 3.30.8). The combination of modest inflation and comfortable foreign exchange reserves offers scope for easing monetary policy to support growth.

Merchandise exports show signs of recovery since the end of 2016. Having increased by 3.6% year on year in the last quarter of 2016, exports of goods continued to rise in January of this year by 8.5%. Demand for electronic parts essential to the so-called "internet of things" such as integrated circuits is projected to rise this year. The gradual recovery of international oil prices should boost exports of petroleum products. Prices have risen for some agricultural products, such as rubber and sugar, so their production should increase in

3.30.1 Selected economic indicators (%)

	2017	2018
GDP growth	3.5	3.6
Inflation	1.8	2.0
Current account balance (share of GDP)	9.0	7.0

Source: ADB estimates.

3.30.6 GDP growth

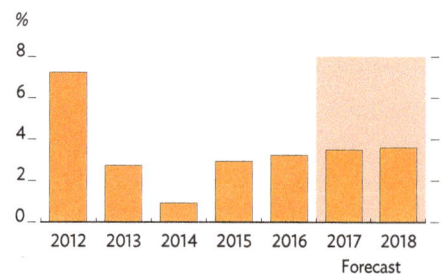

Source: Asian Development Outlook database.

3.30.7 Consumer confidence and business sentiment

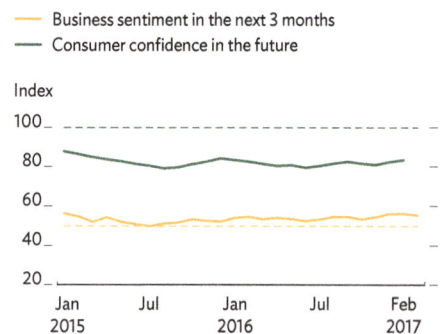

Note: A reading of less than 50 denotes a deterioration in business sentiment; a reading of less than 100 denotes deterioration in consumer confidence.
Sources: Bank of Thailand. http://www.bot.or.th; CEIC Data Company (both accessed 8 March 2017).

response. Merchandise export growth is set to return to positive territory this year and continue to strengthen next year.

Thailand's tourism sector looks strong. The adverse effects of the mourning period and the crackdown on fraudulent tours dented tourist arrivals in the last quarter of 2016, but these effects have already started to wane. The number of tourist arrivals increased in January 2017 by 6.5% year on year. A promotion begun in December 2016 that temporarily waves or reduces visa fees for the holders of selected passports could further support tourism in 2017. Tourism is expected to expand this year and next at its 2016 pace. The Tourism Authority of Thailand projects that the number of tourist arrivals will increase by 8.1% in 2017 to reach 35.3 million.

Merchandise imports are projected to grow in line with higher private investment and demand for manufacturing components, as well as higher oil prices. As imports start to grow, the current account surplus should shrink further from 11.4% of GDP last year to 9.0% this year and 7.0% in 2018 (Figure 3.30.9).

Risks to the outlook come from the potential impact of changes in US trade policy. Although the share of Thailand's exports going directly to the US is only about 11%, the Thai economy is tightly interwoven with Asian production networks and supply chains such that Thai exports could be hurt indirectly. An increase in US tariffs on imports from the PRC, for example, could translate into lower Thai exports of electronics, electrical parts, and machinery to the PRC. Volatility in capital flows is another risk, but the country's comfortable foreign exchange position should provide a good buffer. On the domestic front, undue delays in implementing the transport infrastructure program and other core components of the recently approved Thailand 4.0 development policy agenda could weigh on the economic prospects, as could a sudden discontinuity in the general direction of economic policy.

Policy challenge—reigniting growth through Thailand 4.0

With Thailand suffering subpar growth in recent years when compared with growth in its Southeast Asian peers or with its own past performance, concern is growing that the country may have slipped onto a low-growth path that leads to the middle-income trap. The economy grew at an average annual rate of 9.5% in the decade to 1996, before the Asian financial crisis of 1997–1998, then slowed to an average of 5.2% from 1999 to 2005. Since then, growth has plummeted further to an average of 3.3%. At this juncture, reigniting growth is the government's most pressing policy challenge.

Recognizing the problem, the government embarked last year on an ambitious program of strategic reform dubbed Thailand 4.0, which aims to lift the country's long-term growth path. In a nutshell, Thailand 4.0 is built on three strategic components: an agricultural transformation away from traditional farming to what it calls "smart farming," industrial restructuring to convert small and medium-sized enterprises

3.30.8 Inflation

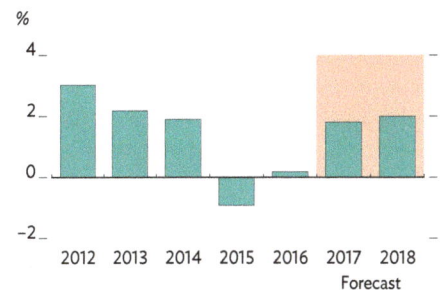

Source: Asian Development Outlook database.

3.30.9 Current account balance

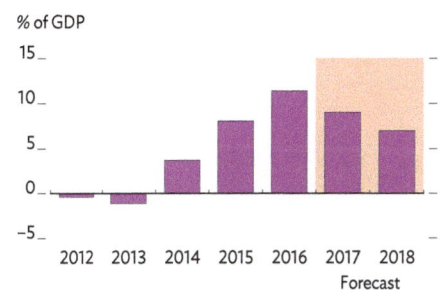

Source: Asian Development Outlook database.

into "smart enterprises," and service sector upgrading to wean tourism-related services in particular away from short-stay, low-spending tourists toward high-value guests.

Achieving the objectives of Thailand 4.0 requires a big push in infrastructure development and a substantial upgrading of the country's skills base. The government has announced that it plans to spend more than $57 billion on infrastructure development during the next 8 years. In addition to the expeditious implementation of the infrastructure program, it is crucial that policy makers address the country's growing skills gap in earnest.

A 2014 survey by the Economic Intelligence Center, the research unit of Siam Commercial Bank, showed that a shortage of skilled workers severely constrains business expansion in a number of sectors. What is more, the shortage will only worsen in the years ahead as the country's population ages rapidly and the absolute number of people of working age, from 15 to 64 years old, begins to shrink in 2018. Moreover, the survey found the quality of education and training that the country's youth receive is woefully inadequate to meet labor market needs. In a similar vein, *The Global Competitiveness Report 2016–2017* of the World Economic Forum indicates that business expansion in skills-intensive sectors is hampered by shortcomings in the Thai workforce in terms of both quantity and quality (Figure 3.30.10).

The skills gap may persist for years because Thai high school students generally underperform their peers in Viet Nam and Malaysia, for example, on standardized tests conducted by the Organisation for Economic Co-operation and Development, scoring particularly poorly in science and mathematics. Even higher education suffers a wide mismatch between the skills that education institutions impart to their students and what the labor market requires (Figure 3.30.11). Education institutions churn out many graduates in liberal arts, for whom there is limited demand, but far fewer graduates in science, technology, engineering, and mathematics, for whom demand is rapidly rising in Thailand, as in other upper-middle-income economies.

These education and training inadequacies need to be effectively addressed if the Thailand 4.0 development agenda for rapidly moving the country toward high-income status is to get much traction in the coming years. A quickly aging population makes education reform and upgrading the skills base of the young even more urgent. Education and training institutions need to engage far more with business to ensure the success of education reform.

3.30.10 Global competitiveness rankings

— Overall
— Higher education & training

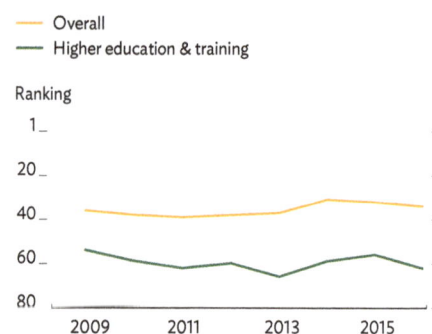

Note: Thailand ranking against 138 economies.
Source: World Economic Forum. 2016. *The Global Competitiveness Report 2016–2017.*

3.30.11 Selected education indicators

— Mean
— Expected

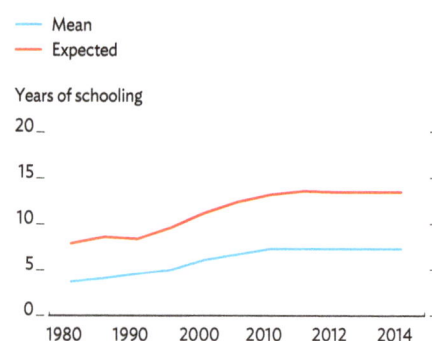

Source: United Nations Development Programme. http://hdr.undp.org/en/data (accessed 7 March 2017).

Viet Nam

Weaker agriculture and oil production offset booming services, manufacturing, and construction to slow GDP growth to 6.2% in 2016. Inflation remained modest, and the current account strengthened. A pickup in agriculture and strength in investment should boost growth this year and next. Inflation will edge up and the current account surplus shrink. Deeper agricultural transformation will be critical for sustaining strong growth in the future.

Economic performance

Economic growth slowed to 6.2% in 2016 from 6.7% in 2015 (Figure 3.31.1). Despite somewhat better weather in the second half of the year, agriculture growth slowed from 2.4% in 2015 to 1.4% as adverse weather in the first half affected production, particularly in the Central Highlands and the Mekong Delta. Field crops were the worst performers, their growth easing to 0.7%, but they were partly compensated by growth in fisheries at 2.8% and forestry at 6.1%.

Despite 4.0% contraction in mining output with continued weakness in international oil prices and aging domestic oil fields, industry and construction grew by 7.6%, albeit slowing from 9.6% in 2015. Manufacturing benefited from brisk foreign investment up by 11.9%, and high credit growth contributed to 10.0% growth in construction.

Services performed strongly, accelerating to 7.0% growth from 6.3% in 2015. The uptick was driven by a boom in tourist arrivals, which soared by a whopping 26.0% in 2016, lifting tourism-related services by 6.7%. Banking and finance also grew strongly, expanding by 7.8%.

Domestic demand remained strong, underpinned by a continuing surge in investment and a robust rise in consumption. Supported by buoyant foreign direct investment (FDI) inflows and credit, investment surged by 9.7% last year on top of a 9.0% rise in the preceding year. Although growth in private consumption eased from 9.3% in 2015, it was still robust at 7.3%. Net merchandise exports made a positive contribution to GDP growth as export growth exceeded import growth.

Inflation averaged 2.7% in 2016, up from 0.6% in 2015. Contributing to the rise were a pickup in international oil prices, rising food prices because of drought, and upward adjustments to fees for public education and health care. In the first 2 months of 2017, inflation edged up further to 5.0% in the year to date (Figure 3.31.2).

Against the backdrop of rising but moderate inflation, the State Bank of Viet Nam, the central bank, kept policy interest rates steady in 2016 while commercial lending rates were trimmed by 0.5%–1.0% in the last quarter of the year. As a result, credit grew by an estimated 19%

3.31.1 Supply-side contributions to growth

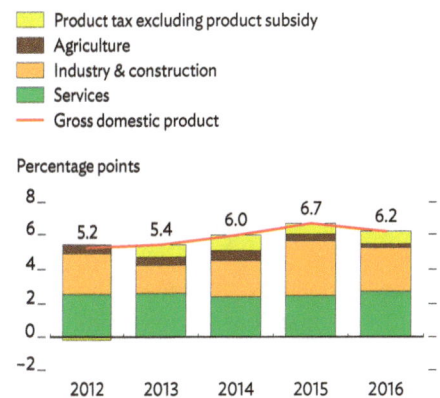

- Product tax excluding product subsidy
- Agriculture
- Industry & construction
- Services
- Gross domestic product

Percentage points

Source: General Statistics Office of Viet Nam.

3.31.2 Inflation

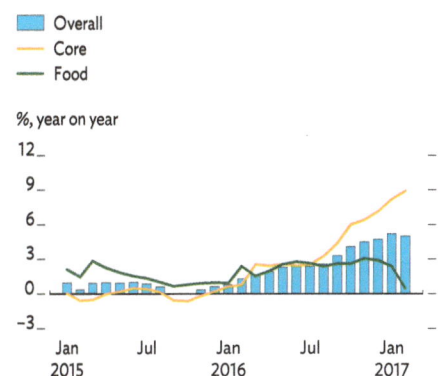

- Overall
- Core
- Food

%, year on year

Note: Core inflation excludes only food.
Source: General Statistics Office of Viet Nam.

This chapter was written by Aaron Batten, Chu Hong Minh, and Nguyen Luu Thuc Phuong of the Viet Nam Resident Mission, ADB, Ha Noi.

as money supply (M2) increased by an estimated 18% (Figure 3.31.3). The adoption of a more flexible exchange rate and the central bank's timely implementation of sterilization measures quite effectively managed external financial shocks during the year. Despite fluctuations in international financial markets, the Viet Nam dong remained relatively stable, depreciating by about 1% against the US dollar during the year (Figure 3.31.4).

The current account surplus was estimated to equal 3.3% of GDP last year, up from 0.5% in 2015, as the country posted a large trade surplus of around $14 billion, equal to 6.9% of GDP (Figure 3.31.5). Merchandise exports rose by an estimated 8.5%, while import growth slowed sharply to an estimated 4.6%. The biggest export gains were in mobile phones and their components, which increased by 14% and now comprise 20% of total exports. A 15% drop in oil imports and an 11% drop in imports of transportation equipment and spare parts slowed the pace of import growth. Reflecting both strong investment and buoyant consumption, growth in imports of electronic components and consumer goods was in the range of 9%–13%.

The capital account posted an estimated surplus equal to 3.4% of GDP, bolstered by strong FDI disbursement. The overall balance of payments surplus reached 4.2% of GDP. The strengthening balance of payments allowed the central bank to build up its foreign exchange reserves to an estimated 2.7 months of import cover, up from the 2.3 months at the beginning of 2016 (Figure 3.31.6).

Efforts to rein in the fiscal deficit had only limited success. Although government revenue grew by 12% to reach the equivalent of 23.1% of GDP, it was outstripped by expenditure growth, resulting in an on-budget deficit equal to 4.4% of GDP, significantly higher than the 2015 figure of 4.0%. This is a matter of concern, especially as public debt including government-guaranteed debt is now estimated to exceed 63% of GDP, nearing the 65% limit set by the National Assembly.

Progress in reforming the financial sector has been elusive. Although the officially reported nonperforming loan (NPL) rate in 2015 and 2016 remained low at about 2.5% of outstanding loans, this largely reflected the transfer of $12.7 billion in NPLs from banks to the state-owned Viet Nam Asset Management Company. By the end of 2016, the company had resolved only 18% of the NPLs purchased from banks. Real progress in reining in NPLs would thus depend on how fast it can resolve its impaired assets and at what cost. Moreover, progress in consolidating the banking system continues to languish, with no mergers or acquisitions completed in 2016.

Economic prospects

GDP growth is projected to be higher at 6.5% in 2017 and 6.7% in 2018 (Figure 3.31.7). With strong growth in manufacturing and services likely to continue, a modest pickup in agriculture and mining output should give an additional fillip to the economy.

Manufacturing will be boosted by the continued opening of new foreign-invested factories on the back of record FDI disbursements last year (Figure 3.31.8). Manufacturing and exports should expand

3.31.3 Credit and money supply growth

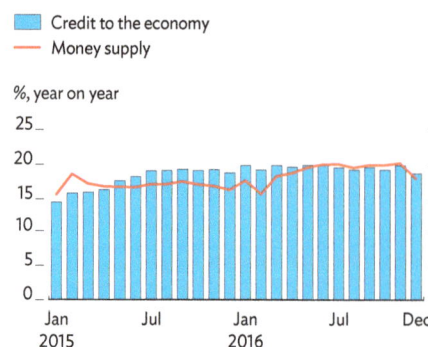

Sources: State Bank of Viet Nam; ADB estimates.

3.31.4 Exchange rate

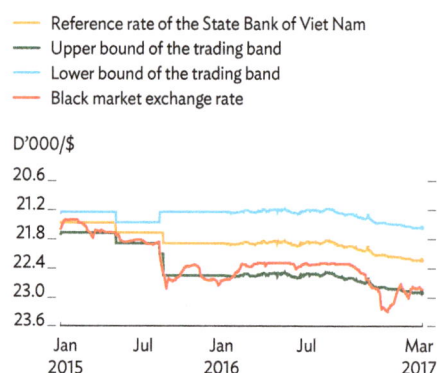

Sources: State Bank of Viet Nam; ADB observations.

3.31.5 Current account indicators

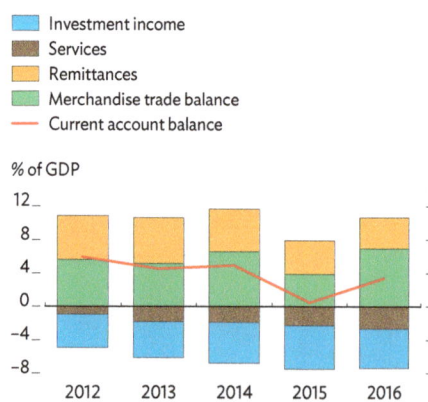

Sources: State Bank of Viet Nam; International Monetary Fund; ADB estimates.

further with continued strengthening in the US economy and the opening up of more trade opportunities with the European Union through a new free trade agreement effective at the beginning of 2018.

Construction will continue to benefit from high FDI disbursements to set up new factories, a strengthening housing sector, and continued high public investment in transport and energy.

Growth in services, strong in 2016, is projected to remain so in 2017 and 2018 with tourist arrivals further boosted by the new e-marketing campaign launched recently by the government.

Agriculture is expected to pick up somewhat in 2017 given the outlook for higher global food prices and assuming a return to normal weather. The government targets agriculture growth at 2.8% in 2017.

On the demand side, private consumption is expected to expand robustly. Consumer sentiment remains buoyant, as indicated by a November 2016 survey showing that 43% of businesses expected retail sales to improve in 2017 and another 39% expected conditions to remain stable.

Prospects for private investment look bright. Reform to business practices has helped move Viet Nam up in the World Bank's *Doing Business* rankings from 91 among 189 countries surveyed in 2016 to 82 among 190 in 2017. Ongoing reform to allow greater foreign ownership of domestic stocks and state-owned enterprises, along with reform to facilitate private participation in building infrastructure, should encourage private investment. The number of newly established enterprises hit a record high of 110,000 in 2016, up by 16.2% from 2015. The Nikkei purchasing managers' index, which measures expectations for business inventory, reached a record high in February 2017, with a particularly sharp rise in new orders to manufacturers (Figure 3.31.9).

As growth strengthens, inflation is expected to edge up to 4.0% this year and 5.0% in 2018 (Figure 3.31.10). The expected rise in global food and fuel prices, higher US interest rates, and a stronger dollar will add to imported inflation. Another likely source of inflation is the continued implementation of the government road map on administered prices for education, health, electricity and water tariffs, and minimum wages.

Higher growth and inflation will cause the current account surplus to narrow. Merchandise exports are seen rising by an annual rate of 10% over the next 2 years as new foreign-invested factories start producing and new trade agreements take effect. Imports are likely to rise even faster as larger FDI inflows draw in additional imports of capital goods and manufacturing inputs. The current account surplus is thus expected to moderate to 2.0% of GDP this year and 2.5% in 2018 (Figure 3.31.11).

Public debt pressures have prompted the government to set ambitious targets for the budget deficit, reining it in to the equivalent of 3.5% of GDP in 2017 and holding it to about 4.0% next year. Most of the reduction in the fiscal deficit would, however, be due to higher receipts from the sale of equity in state-owned enterprises, which the government treats as revenue. Excluding those receipts, fiscal deficit reduction will be much more modest. On the expenditure side, the government plans to cut recurrent expenditure by 6% while raising capital expenditure by 36%. Achieving fiscal consolidation over the

3.31.6 Gross international reserves

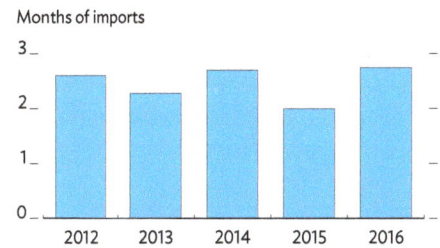

Note: Data exclude government foreign exchange deposits at the State Bank of Viet Nam and the foreign exchange counterpart of swap operations. Imports are free on board.
Sources: State Bank of Viet Nam; International Monetary Fund; ADB estimates.

3.31.7 GDP growth

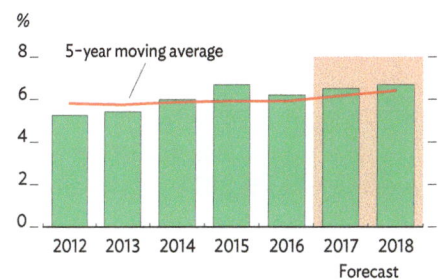

Source: Asian Development Outlook database.

3.31.8 Foreign direct investment

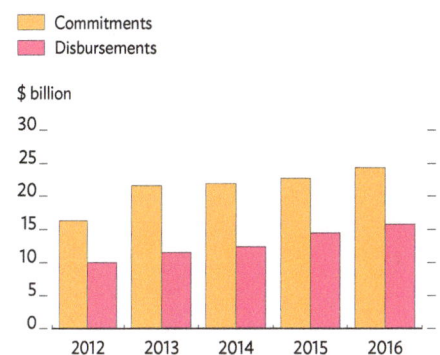

Source: General Statistics Office of Viet Nam.

medium term will be challenging and require deeper tax reform, better revenue administration, and much more efficient public expenditure.

Vulnerability in the financial sector poses a risk to the outlook. Progress on bank restructuring and NPL resolution has been slower than hoped, leaving banks exposed to large contingent liabilities. As the central bank targets credit growth at 18% in 2017, the rise of domestic lending at a faster rate than deposit growth also challenges the maintenance of adequate bank liquidity. The capital adequacy ratio was reported at an estimated 12.8% at the end of 2016, comfortably above the regulatory minimum of 9.0%, but it was not calculated according to international Basel II standards. With the government planning to have all commercial banks meet Basel II capital standards by 2020, they will likely need capital injections from foreign investors. This will require significant improvements to the legal framework, including the lifting of limits on foreign ownership of banks.

Another threat to the outlook is any sudden weakening in global demand. Slower growth in the People's Republic of China, a major trading partner, would undermine Viet Nam's trade position. Further, any worsening of global financial volatility could spill over into the domestic market even though Viet Nam's capital market is not fully open.

Policy challenge—creating a more efficient and sustainable agriculture sector

As Viet Nam begins to recover from its most severe drought in a decade, the role of agriculture in the economy and the country's ability to move up from lower-middle to upper-middle-income status have received heightened policy attention.

In the past, agriculture was a significant driver of growth and poverty reduction. The removal of trade barriers and the abolition of collective farming during the late 1980s and 1990s encouraged infusions of human and physical capital into the sector and boosted output. However, past reform to agriculture generated only one-off gains for the most part and did little to boost agricultural productivity per worker. As a result, even after 20 years of reform, Viet Nam has one of the lowest levels of agricultural labor productivity in the region (Figure 3.31.12).

Major transformation in the sector to make it more efficient and sustainable is vital to lifting GDP growth in Viet Nam and enabling it to graduate to upper-middle-income status. Achieving such a transformation requires addressing four main policy challenges.

The first is market structure and competitiveness. State-owned enterprises currently dominate input supply, postharvest processing, and the marketing of produce. State enterprises also monopolize wholesaling, which means that an unnecessarily large share of the output price is absorbed by inefficient intermediaries. This suppresses farm incomes and incentive for investment.

Secondly, rural infrastructure development needs to be expanded and more integrated to sustain strong growth in agriculture. Higher public investment is needed both to maintain existing rural infrastructure

3.31.1 Selected economic indicators (%)

	2017	2018
GDP growth	6.5	6.7
Inflation	4.0	5.0
Current account balance (share of GDP)	2.0	2.5

Source: ADB estimates.

3.31.9 Purchasing managers' index

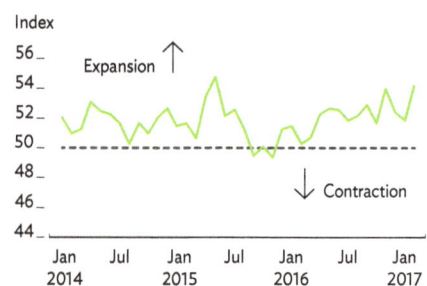

Note: Nikkei, Markit.
Source: Bloomberg (accessed 1 March 2017).

3.31.10 Inflation

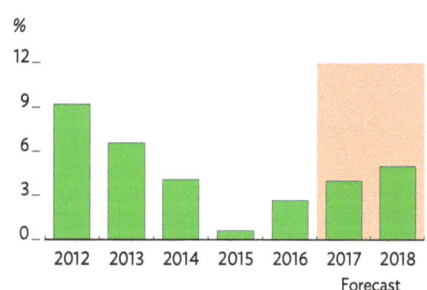

Source: Asian Development Outlook database.

3.31.11 Current account balance

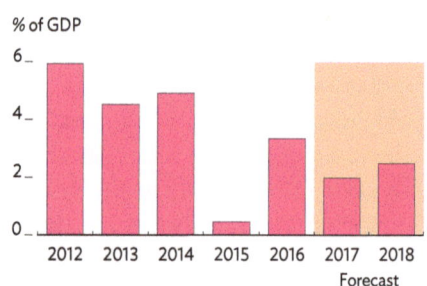

Source: Asian Development Outlook database.

and to build new infrastructure for irrigation, transport, postharvest handling, and storage. Further, farmers need to adopt improved agricultural technology and methods that are more productive and environmentally friendly. This requires stronger engagement between agricultural research institutions and farmers.

A third requirement is more sustainable natural resource management, including policies to encourage the consolidation of landholdings into larger plots. More than 80% of farms in Viet Nam are smaller than 1 hectare. Farmers rely increasingly on marginal plots and use ever-increasing quantities of chemical fertilizer to spur production with little concern for long-term environmental impacts. Worsening water quality is a particularly important concern. Agriculture already uses 82% of available freshwater in Viet Nam. Water pollution in Viet Nam's rivers is threatening the sustainability of water use for agriculture.

Finally, there is an urgent need to address the worsening impacts of climate change on agriculture. Viet Nam is among the countries most vulnerable to climate change, with agriculture particularly at risk because it relies heavily on stable agro-ecological and climatic conditions. Aside from drought, water resources will likely be affected by increasingly unreliable river flow patterns, which will force farmers to depend more on groundwater. Fisheries and other coastal resources are highly vulnerable to temperature change, uncontrolled inundation, and salinity intrusion. To adequately prepare for climate change, Viet Nam will require strong leadership that ensures climate change considerations are integrated into policy making, and to prioritize smart green investments such as improved water resource planning and more efficient water use.

3.31.12 Agriculture output per worker, 2015

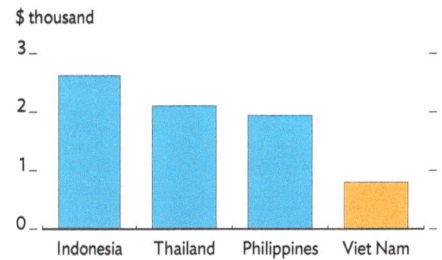

Source: World Development Indicators database (accessed 1 February 2017).

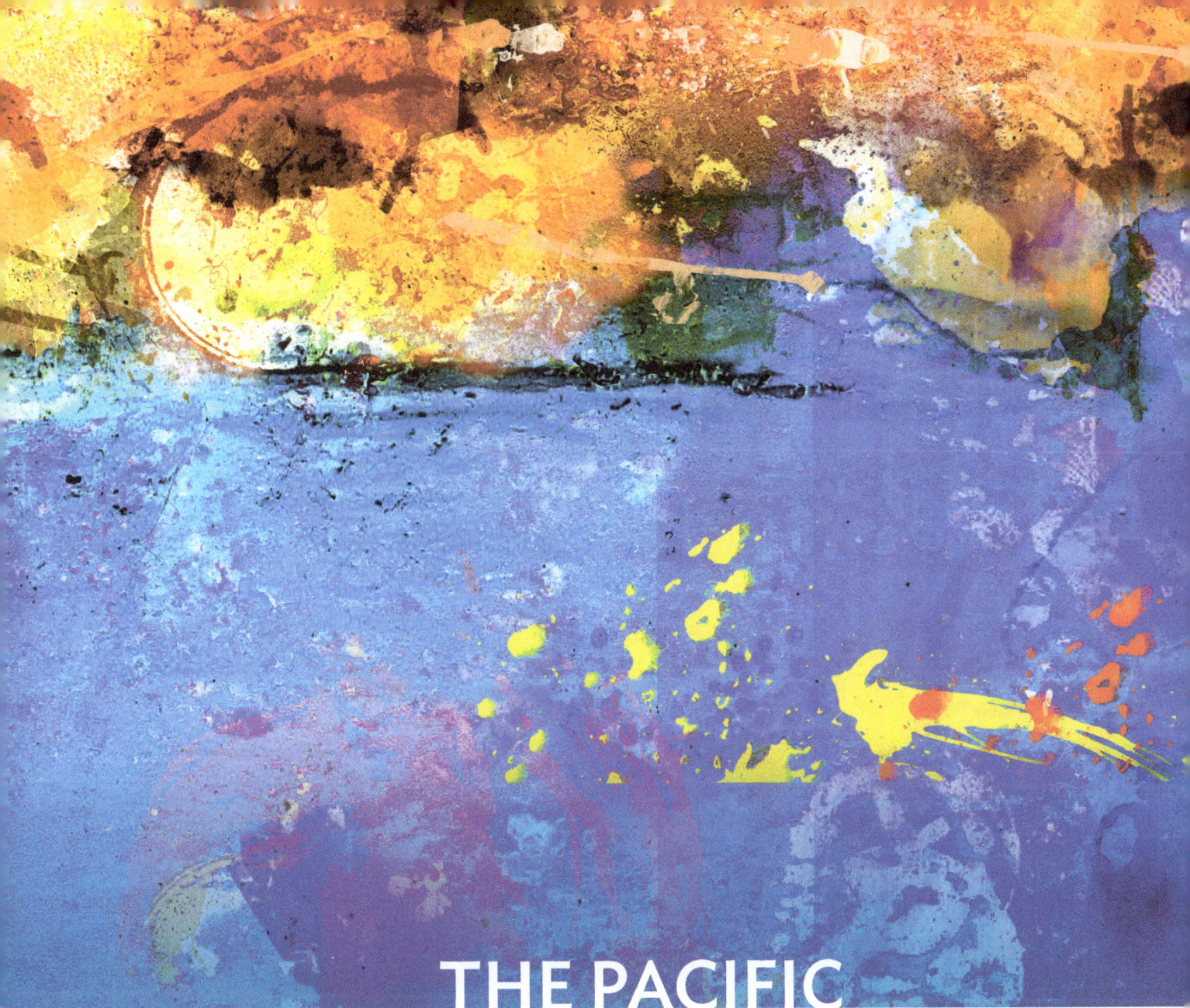

THE PACIFIC

FIJI
PAPUA NEW GUINEA
SOLOMON ISLANDS
TIMOR-LESTE
VANUATU
NORTH PACIFIC ECONOMIES
SOUTH PACIFIC ECONOMIES
SMALL ISLAND ECONOMIES

Fiji

Economic growth slowed in 2016 because of damage from Cyclone Winston estimated to equal 28% of GDP, with agriculture and forestry the hardest hit. Substantial resources from development partners supported relief and rehabilitation, and reasonable progress was made despite capacity challenges. Continuing reconstruction is expected to accelerate growth in 2017 and 2018, as will fiscal policies supporting ambitious works to develop economic infrastructure, especially roads.

Economic performance

Fiji has experienced 7 consecutive years of economic expansion, but growth slowed in 2016 as a result of substantial damage and losses sustained from Cyclone Winston in February 2016 (Figure 3.32.1). The cyclone severely affected public infrastructure, particularly in rural Fiji, and forced agriculture and forestry into recession. Sugarcane production, which contributes 27% of agricultural output and had stabilized in 2015 after 3 years of growth, plunged by 25% (Figure 3.32.2).

Other sectors reflected the resulting slowdown as well, but growth was sustained in mining and quarrying, construction, wholesale and retail trade, and professional services. Tourism continued to be the main driver of growth. Significant growth in visitor arrivals from New Zealand and Asia—the latter by 24.7% but from a fairly small base—led 5.0% growth in arrivals overall, despite a 1.9% decline from Australia, Fiji's largest market by far (Figure 3.32.3).

Significant investment to improve public infrastructure has boosted the growth potential of the economy over the long run. However, growth in credit to the private sector was, at 12.6% in 2016, down from 14.4% in 2015. This slowdown reflected weaker economic activity as a result of Cyclone Winston.

Consumption grew strongly in 2016. This was reflected by indicators such as 32% growth in new vehicle sales and 9% growth in secondhand vehicle sales during the year. Commercial bank lending for consumption expanded by 7.9%, and imports of consumer goods increased by 14.7%. Inward remittances are estimated to have risen by 10.2%, further fueling growth in consumption.

After 2 years of low inflation, the consumer price index rose by an annual average of 3.9%, mainly because of disrupted domestic food supply following Cyclone Winston but also because of higher taxes on alcoholic beverages and tobacco. Declines in prices for fuel, transport, communication, household equipment and furnishings, recreation, and miscellaneous items could not offset the increases.

3.32.1 GDP growth

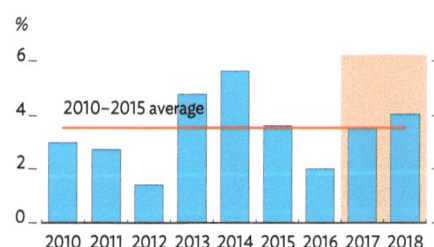

Sources: Fiji Bureau of Statistics; ADB estimates.

3.32.2 Sugarcane production

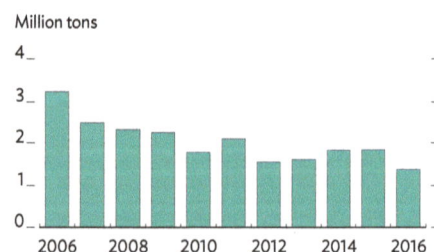

Source: Fiji Bureau of Statistics.

This chapter was written by Shiu Raj Singh of the South Pacific Subregional Office, ADB, Suva.

After Cyclone Winston, the government changed its fiscal year from the calendar year to one ending on 31 July of the year for which it is named. Although there was significant reallocation of budgetary resources following the cyclone to meet immediate relief and rehabilitation needs, the deficit for FY2016 came to the equivalent of only 1.6% of GDP, substantially lower than deficits of 4.1% in 2014 and 3.2% in FY2015 (Figure 3.32.4). The reduced fiscal deficit resulted from higher direct and indirect tax revenues and lower-than-expected capital expenditure. At the end of July 2016, public debt equaled 47.9% of GDP, more than 70% of it domestic. The Fiji National Provident Fund holds 46.9% of government debt.

Monetary policy remained accommodative with the policy interest rate at 0.5%. Commercial bank lending rates are still low by historical standards, but recent liquidity developments have stirred interest rates for deposits. Liquidity fell by 7.5% in 2016 as commercial banks' demand deposits with the central bank declined. Average rates for time deposits of more than 24 months edged upward to 2.95%, an increase of 25 basis points over the previous year. This could induce commercial banks to increase their lending rates.

Imports fell in 2016 despite strong consumer demand and cyclone reconstruction. This allowed robust growth in earnings from tourism and remittances to push the current account surplus excluding aircraft to the equivalent of 3.4% of GDP in the first 3 quarters of 2016. Foreign reserves stood at $960 million at the end of the year, sufficient to cover 5.4 months of retained imports of goods and nonfactor services.

Economic prospects

As the economy recovers from Cyclone Winston, growth is projected to reach 3.5% in 2017. All sectors are expected to register positive growth given the uptick in demand, with major contributions from manufacturing, transport and storage, finance and insurance, wholesale and retail trade, accommodation and food services, and construction. Public spending is expected to rise in 2017 as the reconstruction of schools and homes damaged by Cyclone Winston picks up pace.

More building permits were issued in 2016 than in the previous year, signaling that construction will grow strongly in 2017. Further, an increase of 12.5% in visitor numbers in January augurs well for tourism in 2017. Inward remittances have been growing strongly over the past few years (Figure 3.32.5). This trend is expected to continue in 2017 with increasing labor exports, not only of seasonal workers but also of professional athletes and military personnel deployed on peacekeeping missions. Higher remittances will support higher consumption and investment, adding to economic stimulus.

Rising international prices for fuel and food will bring some inflation, but price increases will not be as significant as in 2016 (Figure 3.32.6). Higher taxes on alcoholic beverages and tobacco will continue to contribute to inflation. Domestic food prices are expected to normalize in the coming months as supplies are restored.

Exports are expected to grow strongly as agriculture recovers. With earnings from tourism and remittances higher than expected,

3.32.3 Visitor arrivals, by source

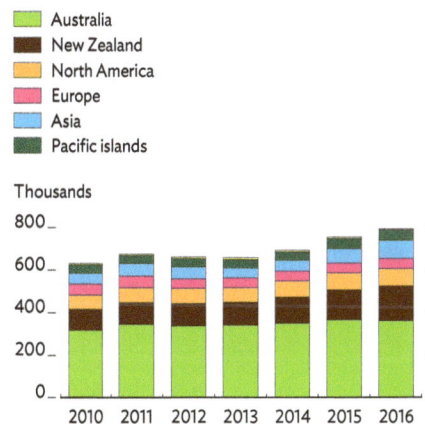

Source: Fiji Bureau of Statistics.

3.32.1 Selected economic indicators (%)

	2017	2018
GDP growth	3.5	4.0
Inflation	2.5	2.5
Current account balance (share of GDP)	3.5	3.0

Source: ADB estimates.

3.32.4 Fiscal balance

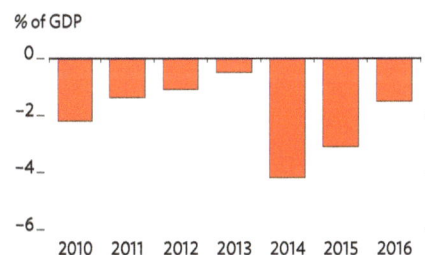

Note: Calendar years from 2010 to 2014 but fiscal years (ending on 30 July of that year) from 2015 to 2016.
Source: Fiji Ministry of Economy.

the current account will likely remain stable even with rising imports for cyclone reconstruction. Public spending is expected to remain high as rehabilitation and reconstruction pick up momentum. Beyond reconstructing public infrastructure and buildings, public expenditure will continue to support the rebuilding of homes and the restoration of livelihoods, particularly in rural areas.

On top of construction and recovery in agriculture, continued growth in tourism, transport, and public spending is expected to support growth at 4.0% in 2018.

Policy challenge—building for climate change

Fiji is, like other small island states in the Pacific, highly susceptible to climate change and extreme weather. Impacts on health care, coastal infrastructure, water resources, agriculture, forestry, and fisheries are often substantial and widespread, as shown by the aftermath of Cyclone Winston.

The country is finalizing its national development plan, which will be integrated with its Green Growth Framework to address adverse climate effects on economic assets. Climate resilience is being mainstreamed into public investment decisions.

The government's recent switch to a fiscal year that begins and ends well outside of the November–April cyclone season is intended to facilitate the timely funding of disaster response. The mainstreaming approach goes further, though, and includes shifting away from an emphasis on post-disaster emergency response toward community preparedness and disaster mitigation, and on integrating into national development planning the inevitable impacts of disasters.

A significant challenge for Fiji is to expand its infrastructure in line with economic growth, and to make it resilient under climate change so it can help sustain growth even as adverse weather becomes increasingly frequent and intense. For example, growth over the past 7 years has strained the transport network, all the more so as adverse weather hastens road deterioration. It is therefore vital that the government integrate climate resilience considerations into its public investment decisions to reduce the need for rehabilitation and reconstruction following natural disasters.

3.32.5 Remittances

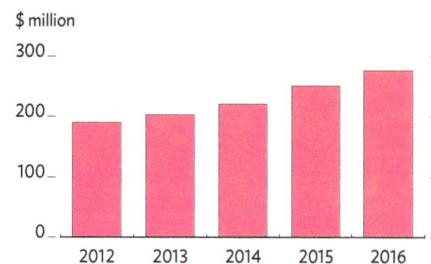

Source: Reserve Bank of Fiji.

3.32.6 Inflation

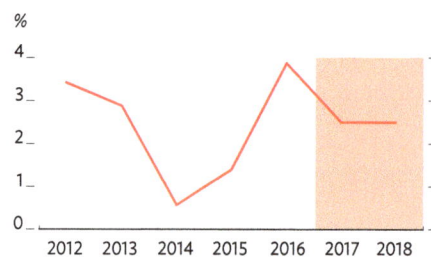

Sources: Fiji Bureau of Statistics; ADB estimates.

Papua New Guinea

Growth at 2.0% in 2016 was considerably lower than in previous years and came largely from mineral resources. The economy is expected to grow by 2.5% in 2017 and, with the hosting of the Asia-Pacific Economic Cooperation Leaders' Meeting, by 2.8% in 2018. While the short-term outlook skews to the downside, the medium-term outlook remains positive thanks to foreign investments in the pipeline.

Economic performance

The economy is estimated to have grown by 2.0% in 2016, marking a sharp slowdown from high growth rates in the previous 4 years (Figure 3.33.1). Economic growth was weighed down by slowing foreign investment, soft global commodity prices, and unfavorable weather.

Preliminary estimates show that the oil and gas sector contracted by 1.2% in 2016 as oil production declined in maturing oil fields and gas production reached full capacity. Mining and quarrying grew by 8.0% in 2016 as the Ok Tedi gold and copper mine resumed operations in the first quarter. This offset the closure of the Ramu nickel mine for several months because of noncompliance with safety standards, as well as the Porgera gold and silver mine being forced to scale down operations by a landslip and sabotage to power transmission lines.

Agriculture, forestry, and fisheries, which provide about one-fifth of economic output, grew by 3.0% in 2016. Higher copra and copra oil production came largely from higher prices, but an increase in cocoa output reflected expanded area under cultivation and improved management. Coffee production recovered from drought in the previous year.

Wholesale and retail trade, which accounts for about 12% of economic output, experienced weak sales because a shortage of foreign currency disrupted supply. Driven mostly by public investment, electricity, gas, and water grew by 3.0%. Transport, storage, and communication grew by an estimated 4.0%.

Foreign investment in Papua New Guinea (PNG) continued to fall in 2016, with net foreign assets declining by 11.5% largely because construction on a liquefied natural gas (LNG) project reached completion. Other factors include a poor investment environment outside of mining, a ban on imports of some agricultural products, and the introduction of foreign exchange controls in 2016.

The slowdown in economic growth and private business dragged down public revenue. The 2016 national budget targeted a deficit equal to 4.1% of GDP (Figure 3.33.2). However, the government's mid-year

3.33.1 Economic growth

Sources: Bank of Papua New Guinea; Papua New Guinea 2016 National Budget; ADB estimates.

3.33.2 Fiscal performance

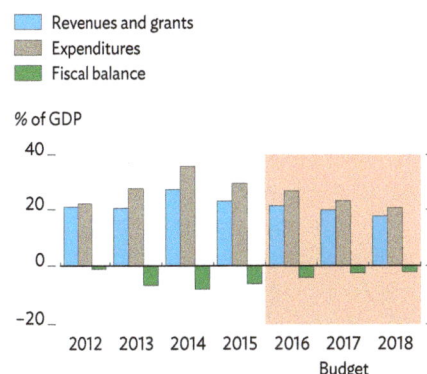

Source: National budget documents, various years.

This chapter was written by Yurendra Basnett of the Papua New Guinea Resident Mission, ADB, Port Moresby.

economic and fiscal outlook warned that because of a shortfall in revenue, the deficit would be larger than anticipated. A supplementary budget for 2016, approved in August, sought to remedy the situation by cutting expenditure and raising new financing.

Inflation is estimated at 7.0% in 2016 (Figure 3.33.3). In the first quarter of 2016, headline inflation accelerated to 6.5% from 6.2% in the first quarter of 2015, and this upward trend continued for the rest of the year. Prices rose in all the larger urban centers. The increase in domestic inflation reflects price rises across domestic goods and services, notably betel nut and mustard up by 33.5%, housing rentals 28.1%, fruit and vegetables 25.5%, hotel accommodation 18.9%, and medical services 17.0%.

The Bank of Papua New Guinea, the central bank, continued its neutral monetary policy by maintaining its policy interest rate, called the kina facility rate, at 6.25% throughout the year. Broad money supply expanded by 5.0% in 2016 largely on the continued issuance of securities to finance government expenditure. As a result, net claims on the government soared by 25.7%. Credit to the private sector rose by 3.1%.

The current account surplus, estimated to equal 9.4% of GDP in 2016, was down from 13.4% in 2015 as imports increased by 10.2% and exports were lower by 6.4% (Figure 3.33.4). The capital and financial account deficit was $1.7 billion in 2016. The overall balance of payments deficit of $121 million was financed using foreign exchange reserves, which at the end of 2016 stood at $2.2 billion, or cover for 8.8 months of imports.

Economic prospects

Growth is expected to accelerate to 2.5% in 2017, driven by output increases in mining and agriculture. The Ok Tedi gold and copper mine is foreseen returning to full capacity, and the Ramu nickel mine to 90% capacity.

Agriculture, forestry, and fishery output is forecast to grow by 3.6% with increases in both price and production, assuming favorable weather. Palm oil production is expected to recover from a slump caused by El Niño in 2015, while prevailing high prices for cocoa should add momentum to the supply response that is bringing new areas into production. Copra production will continue to increase in response to higher prices, while growth in coffee production is set to moderate in 2017 following a bumper season in 2016.

A gradual pickup in the global economy can be expected to boost commodity prices and stimulate activity in sectors outside of resource extraction. These sectors will likely enjoy further support from spending related to elections in June and July 2017, preparations for the 2018 Asia-Pacific Economic Cooperation Leaders' Meeting, and continued government investment in infrastructure.

Economic growth is expected to be 2.8% in 2018, still supported mostly by agriculture and mining.

3.33.3 Inflation

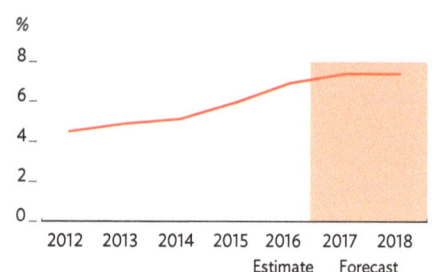

Sources: Bank of Papua New Guinea; Papua New Guinea 2016 National Budget; ADB estimates.

3.33.4 Trade performance and current account balance

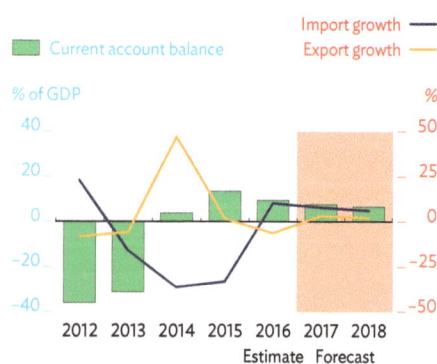

Sources: International Monetary Fund Article IV staff reports, various years; ADB estimates.

Uncertainties about global and domestic policy pose large risks to the forecast. An aggressive fiscal stance in the US could cause interest rates to surge, thereby increasing the cost of borrowing for the government and the private sector in PNG. The adoption of a more restrictive trade regime in the US could slow global trade and thus reduce demand for PNG exports. Given the importance of exports to the economy, any exogenous shock would have adverse effects on the whole economy, which has yet to recover fully from the recent downturn in commodity prices.

The government's plan to return to a balanced budget over the medium term is helping to rebuild the fiscal position necessary to absorb external shocks, and its focus on making public expenditure more effective promises better use of public resources. For 2017, the government targets a deficit equal to 2.5% of GDP, with revenue expected at $4.2 billion and expenditure budgeted at $4.6 billion. The government plans to finance the deficit through domestic and international borrowing.

The central bank is expected to continue its neutral monetary policy and leave the kina facility rate unchanged. The foreign exchange shortage is likely to persist in 2017 without substantial improvement in commodity prices. The central bank has tried to manage the shortage by selectively intervening in currency markets. The foreign exchange trading band continues to determine the speed of kina depreciation. In the absence of a freely floating kina, the economy may prove to be unable to absorb an exogenous shock. Such a shock could force a disorderly switch to a free float.

There are also important political risks to the forecast. Delays in royalty payments to landowners at LNG production sites could destabilize outputs. Reports suggest growing discontent among landowners. In December 2016, the government mobilized security forces in response to violence at production sites. How this issue is handled could affect other projects in the pipeline and substantially compromise growth.

Inflation is projected to accelerate to 7.5% in 2017 and 2018. Imported inflation is expected to rise with kina depreciation and recent increases in global oil prices. Further, spending related to the elections in 2017 and the hosting of the Asia-Pacific Economic Cooperation Leaders' Meeting will probably intensify inflationary pressures. However, these pressures will likely subside as the government continues along the path of fiscal consolidation.

The current account is projected to record a surplus of $1.4 billion in 2017, equal to 7.7% of GDP. This reflects increased output from the Ok Tedi and Ramu mines and increased exports of agricultural products in response to higher world food prices.

The current account balance is forecast to remain in surplus equivalent to 6.7% of GDP in 2018, buoyed by continued gas and gas condensate production and further increases in agriculture exports, particularly coffee, cocoa, and palm oil. These inflows are expected to be offset somewhat by large outflows in the income and financial balances to cover dividend payments to overseas investors.

3.33.1 Selected economic indicators (%)

	2017	2018
GDP growth	2.5	2.8
Inflation	7.5	7.5
Current account balance (share of GDP)	7.7	6.7

Source: ADB estimates.

Policy challenge—an effective medium-term fiscal strategy

PNG was able to withstand the global financial crisis of 2008–2009 but was severely affected by the global commodities downturn in 2014–2015. While the nature of the two shocks differed, fiscal and monetary stances preceding them provide important lessons. PNG had built fiscal buffers and reduced public debt in the years preceding the global financial crisis. However, an expansionary fiscal stance starting 2012 and the rapid depletion of fiscal and monetary reserves forced a sharp, unplanned adjustment during the commodities downturn.

The government is developing a new medium-term fiscal strategy for 2018–2022 to replace the current strategy, which expires this year. A credible and sound strategy will be important to reinforce the ability of PNG to respond to external shocks, rebuild fiscal buffers, and make public expenditure more effective. Institutions necessary to mitigate exogenous shocks, in particular a well-functioning sovereign wealth fund, are urgently needed. PNG must meet four imperatives.

The first imperative is to rebuild fiscal buffers to restore fiscal resilience under external shocks. For instance, fiscal guidelines should include a deficit target stated as a percentage of non-mining GDP. The medium-term fiscal strategy for 2008–2012 included prudent limits on the use of mineral revenues. The strategy estimated mineral revenue at the time to equal about 4% of GDP and therefore targeted a deficit for the non-mineral budget at the same 4% of GDP. Further, a 70:30 ratio governed the use of mineral revenue, with 70% earmarked for investment and 30% for repaying public debt. At the end of 2012, public debt had been retired to the equivalent of 19.1% of GDP from 31.4% in 2008 and 63.6% in 2002. These guidelines were subsequently relaxed, and the budget deficit was allowed to rise sharply on the expectation of windfall revenue (Figure 3.33.5). This made PNG less able to absorb the exogenous shock from sharply worse terms of trade experienced in 2015. To avoid a repeat of this scenario, it is important that the new medium-term fiscal strategy include strong guidelines to rebuild the fiscal buffer.

Second, the agenda for public finance reform should include getting greater value for money from public expenditure. Expenditure for health, for example, was equivalent to about 4% of GDP in 2013, well above the 1.6% average in lower-middle-income economies, but PNG has struggled to translate high public expenditure into improved social and economic outcomes. Female life expectancy at birth in PNG is 64 years, well below the lower-middle-income average of 69 years. High operating costs in a vast interior with a sparse population make cost-effective service delivery difficult. This constraint is exacerbated by institutional fragmentation and overlapping responsibilities for service delivery to the poor. The upshot is that public finance does not reach frontline service providers in an efficient and timely way.

Third, PNG should strengthen revenue collection and domestic resource mobilization. The bulk of expected annual revenue does not materialize until halfway into the year, which undermines expenditure effectiveness. This complicates cash-flow management, and the problem is magnified when a revenue shortfall occurs due to

3.33.5 Public debt

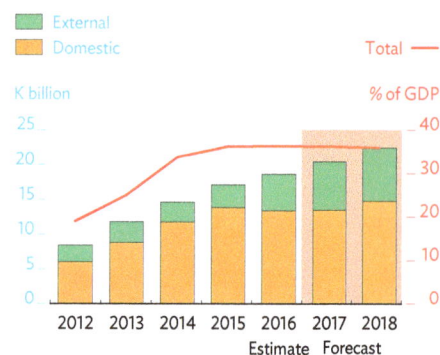

Sources: National budget documents, various years; International Monetary Fund Article IV staff reports, various years; ADB estimates.

cyclical factors such as commodity price swings or extreme weather. The situation is further complicated when the government invests in large infrastructure projects with cash needs that vary from one quarter to the next because of factors that are difficult to accurately forecast. Such issues are not very consequential when revenue collection outpaces expenditure, but the reverse situation suddenly applies the brakes, delaying investments needed for medium-term development.

Fourth, structural reform is needed to attract more private investment and participation in services. Service delivery in PNG is largely binary, public or private. A multi-institutional approach that leverages complementarity market, public, and civic solutions has a better chance of delivering lasting results. Public policy is to pursue such solutions through national development plans, but the operationalization of this policy needs further support. Many private companies and other nongovernment agencies in remote areas are involved in providing basic services. Strengthening and scaling up these services should be a policy priority. Finally, the challenge for public policy, particularly from the perspective of social equity, is to deliver such essentials as books, pencils, and medicine effectively in remote places where instant noodles and chocolates have already found markets.

Solomon Islands

Although economic growth is broadly steady, it relies on expansionary fiscal policy and unsustainable logging. Growth is likely to slow as their short-term benefits dissipate. Taking a longer view, tourism has potential as an untapped source of economic growth. Steady progress is being made in implementing a national tourism development strategy, but significant impediments remain.

Economic performance

Economic growth accelerated modestly to an estimated 3.2% in 2016 from 2.9% in 2015 (Figure 3.34.1). The government maintained its strategy of supporting growth through fiscal expansion. Aggressive logging also added significantly to growth as the industry continued to stave off expectations of eventual decline. Logging exports rose by 12.7% in 2016 to reach an annual record of 2.6 million cubic meters (Figure 3.34.2).

Exports of other commodities were mixed as fishery, cocoa, and mineral exports all contracted in volume terms while palm oil exports rose. Meanwhile, the pace of private investment appears to have slowed, with growth in credit to the private sector decelerating slightly, imports of capital goods falling, and construction softening.

The government continued to pursue an expansionary budget, taking advantage of significant fiscal reserves built up under repeated budget surpluses in the past. In 2016, the budget recorded a sizeable deficit, equal to 5.9% of GDP, as the government maintained high expenditures even as lower fishery revenue and external grant receipts dragged down total revenues. To finance the deficit, the government drew down its cash reserves held at the Central Bank of Solomon Islands, significantly eroding them to less than 1 month of cover for projected spending.

Annual inflation in 2016 is estimated at 1.1%, reversing a 0.5% decline in consumer prices in 2015 (Figure 3.34.3). Inflation for local goods and services was 3.3% but offset by a 2.1% decline in import prices, reflecting low international commodity prices. Monetary policy continued to be broadly accommodative as the central bank left the cash reserve requirement for commercial banks unchanged at 7.5% of deposits and held steady on its issuance of central bank paper.

The current account deficit almost doubled to the equivalent of 7.3% of GDP from 3.7% in 2015, mainly because lower grant inflows from development partners more than offset a slightly narrower trade deficit (Figure 3.34.4). Foreign exchange reserves are ample, however, at coverage for 10.3 months of imports. Export earnings rose by 2.1%,

3.34.1 Supply-side contributions to growth

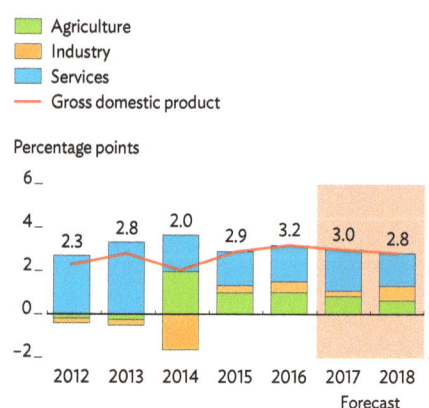

- Agriculture
- Industry
- Services
- Gross domestic product

Percentage points

Sources: Ministry of Finance and Treasury; ADB estimates.

3.34.2 Logging exports

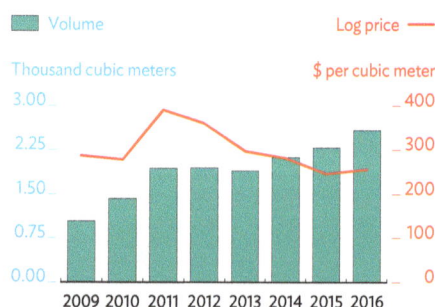

Volume — Log price

Thousand cubic meters — $ per cubic meter

Sources: Central Bank of Solomon Islands; World Bank Commodity Price Data (Pink Sheets); ADB estimates.

This chapter was written by Roland Rajah of the Pacific Liaison and Coordination Office, ADB, Sydney; and Dalcy Ilala of the Solomon Islands Extended Mission, ADB, Honiara.

driven by logging, coconut products, and palm oil. Mineral exports remain depressed following the closure of the country's sole gold mine in 2014 and a government clampdown on bauxite strip mining. The import bill was nearly flat in 2016, held to only 0.2% growth by low international commodity prices.

Economic prospects

Growth is forecast to slow to 3.0% in 2017 and 2.8% in 2018 as current short-term growth drivers fade. After 2 years of fiscal expansion, policy is set to tighten. Private investment will likely continue to moderate, and net exports are expected to detract from growth. Log export volumes are projected to decline gradually in 2017 and 2018, but logging has routinely surprised on the upside for many years, defying expectations of eventual decline. Logging therefore poses a significant risk to the outlook, especially as it accounts for a growing share of exports. Meanwhile, years of unsustainable logging heighten the risk of an eventual collapse that is more rapid and disruptive than anticipated.

The state budget is set to tighten significantly in 2017. The government is targeting a fiscal deficit equal to 1.2% of GDP, financed by further drawdowns on its cash reserves (Figure 3.34.5). The depletion of cash reserves over the past 2 years will limit the government's ability to maintain its policy of high public spending, given legal constraints on borrowing to finance recurrent budget deficits. To meet its spending targets, the government has budgeted significantly higher domestic revenue collection, projecting it to increase from the equivalent of 35.3% of GDP in 2016 to 39.9% in 2017. The budget provides little detail on how such an ambitious increase will be achieved. The risks posed by this uncertainty are counterbalanced, however, by likely underperformance on the expenditure side as the development budget continues to face implementation difficulties. In addition, low cash reserves may hinder cash-flow management and further impede effective budget implementation.

The central bank is expected to maintain a broadly accommodative stance. Higher international commodity prices are likely to feed into higher imported inflation while local inflation is forecast to pick up slowly. Inflation is projected to stay relatively subdued at 1.8% in 2017 and 2.2% in 2018. Broad money growth is expected at 8.1%, down from 9.2% in 2016, as growth in private credit slows modestly and as the government draws down cash reserves less than before and therefore injects less liquidity into the system. The current account deficit is projected to widen to the equivalent of 8.3% of GDP in 2017 as net exports deteriorate amid flat export earnings and rising import costs, and as grant inflows from development partners remain subdued. In 2018, the current account deficit will likely widen significantly to 10.7% of GDP to meet the import needs of planned major infrastructure projects, including the Tina River Hydropower Project.

3.34.3 Inflation

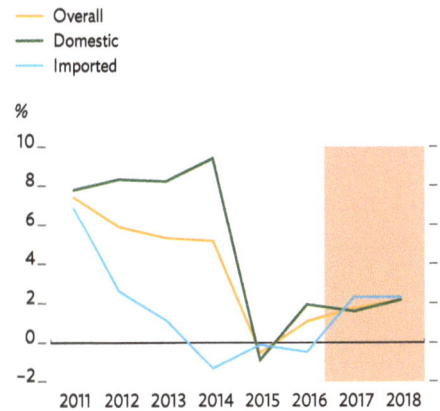

Sources: Central Bank of Solomon Islands; ADB estimates.

3.34.4 Current account balance

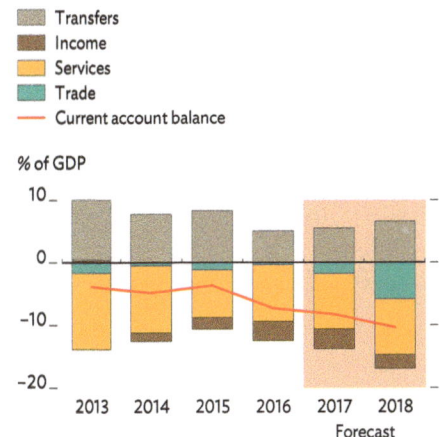

Sources: Central Bank of Solomon Islands; ADB estimates.

3.34.1 Selected economic indicators (%)

	2017	2018
GDP growth	3.0	2.8
Inflation	1.8	2.2
Current account balance (share of GDP)	−8.3	−10.7

Source: ADB estimates.

Policy challenge—unlocking tourism potential

New economic drivers are urgently needed to replace logging and external assistance, which are expected to decline over the medium term. Solomon Islands is widely considered to have world class tourism potential that remains largely untapped. Diving is currently the main attraction, but other attractions with potential include World War II historical sites, indigenous culture, bird watching, surfing, and fishing.

Visitor arrivals have been on an upwards trajectory but from a very low base. Arrivals by air rose from 19,440 in 2009 to a peak of 24,431 in 2013 (Figure 3.34.6). Severe floods in Honiara disrupted tourism in 2014, and arrivals by air have since hovered at a little over 20,000 a year. This may partly reflect substitution in favor of cruise tourism, which is growing rapidly. Visitors by sea rose from none officially recorded in 2013 to about 3,900 in 2015 and 13,400 in 2016. Contributing to this performance are stepped-up marketing by the Solomon Islands Visitors Bureau, a perception that public safety has improved somewhat, and the commencement of direct flights between Honiara and Sydney, as Australia is the major source market. Yet visitor arrivals remain far lower than in other Pacific destinations with more developed tourism infrastructure.

Numerous challenges confront efforts to unlock the tourism potential of Solomon Islands. Most fundamentally, public safety remains a concern, and key infrastructure lacking beyond Honiara includes adequate roads, reliable and affordable domestic air connections, cruise ship-capable wharves, dependable electricity supply, and modern telecommunications. Tourism is further constrained by regulatory issues, in particular the difficulty of acquiring land for tourism development. The marketing of Solomon Islands as an attractive tourism destination remains weak, recent efforts notwithstanding. There are no internationally branded or luxury hotels to create awareness and instill trust. The tourism workforce is small and needs professional development.

In 2015, the government launched its National Tourism Development Strategy, 2015–2019, which aims to develop Solomon Islands as a niche destination for small-scale adventure tourism that capitalizes on unique offerings related to its land, marine, and cultural resources. Good progress has been made in implementing the strategy in terms of restructuring the tourism ministry, increasing funding for the visitors bureau, instituting reform to support more sustainable financing, and creating an online booking portal to support small-scale tourism operators. The government has started to develop new tourism products, including cruise opportunities and niche products such as game fishing, and to profile investment-ready tourism sites.

3.34.5 Fiscal balance

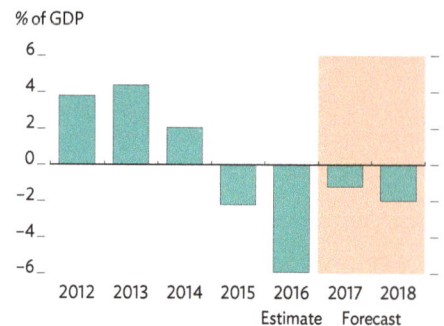

Sources: Ministry of Finance and Treasury; ADB estimates.

3.34.6 Visitor arrivals by mode of travel

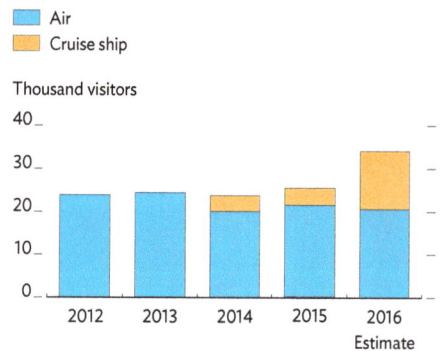

Sources: Central Bank of Solomon Islands; ADB estimates.

Timor-Leste

Growth accelerated in 2016 as the government implemented a large fiscal stimulus ahead of elections in July 2017. Growth is expected to moderate in 2017 before reaccelerating in 2018 as large public and private investments move forward. Decentralization provides an opportunity to improve public service delivery. Well-designed rules for allocating funding to municipalities will help to ensure that decentralization also promotes equity.

Economic performance

Growth picked up in 2016 as GDP excluding the large offshore petroleum sector (hereafter GDP) expanded by an estimated 5.4% (Figure 3.35.1). Public spending was the main driver of growth, rising by an estimated 17.7%. Grants from Timor-Leste's development partners fell by an estimated 3.4% and accounted for 11.7% of public spending in 2016, while government expenditures excluding grants rose by 21.2%.

The surge in public spending followed the approval of a supplementary budget in June that doubled planned capital investment and raised the 2016 budget by 25.0% to $1.95 billion, equal to 129% of GDP. Actual capital expenditure rose by 82.2% to $590 million with increased investment in transport infrastructure (Figure 3.35.2). Transfer payments, which increased by 6.3%, also contributed to the growth of public spending. Transfers to the Special Administrative Region of Oe-Cusse Ambeno rose by 57.6% to $217 million. Other components of public spending showed a modest decline, with salaries and wages down by 2.7% and payments for goods and services 3.7% lower.

The surge in public investment improved business prospects and strengthened private sector growth, as indicated by business electricity consumption rising by 17.5% year on year in the first half. Manufacturing received a boost in 2016 as Heineken completed Timor-Leste's first major brewery, but the commissioning of a new private port and a cement bagging plant was delayed. In the petroleum sector, state-owned Timor Gap initiated a multiyear program to find more oil and gas in an area of Timor-Leste's exclusive economic zone for which it has been granted an exclusive license.

Coffee production rose in 2016, but quality was harmed by rain during the harvest. In coastal areas, El Niño continued to affect agricultural production. Maize harvests fell by 8% to 21% below the average for 2011–2015, and rice production fell by 6% to 30% below the average for the period.

Increased food imports helped to offset the inflationary impact of reduced local production. Thanks to the continued pass-through of previous falls in international food prices, improved logistics, and

3.35.1 Supply-side contributions to growth

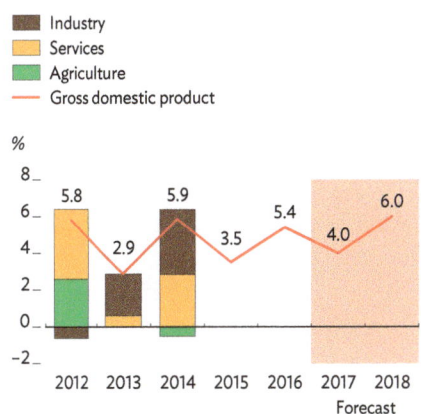

Sources: Statistics Timor-Leste; ADB estimates.

3.35.2 Fiscal outlook

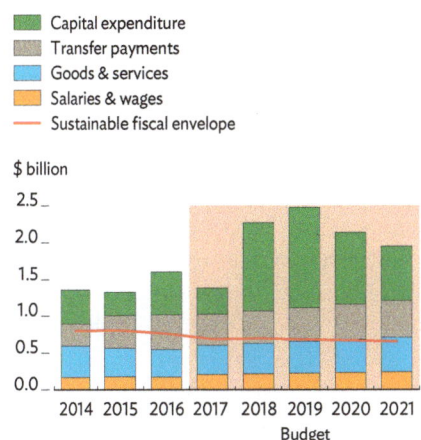

Sources: Timor-Leste 2017 State Budget; Timor-Leste Budget Transparency Portal.

This chapter was written by David Freedman, Timor-Leste Resident Mission, ADB, Dili.

increased retail competition, consumer prices fell by an average of 1.3% in 2016 (Figure 3.35.3). Deflation was more pronounced in the capital, Dili, where prices fell by 1.6%, compared with 0.5% deflation in the rest of the country.

Domestic revenue collection strengthened in 2016 by 28.6% with invigorated private business and intensified collection effort. Customs was a notable area of improvement, with revenues up by 20.9% despite a 14.4% decline in merchandise imports. Planning for fiscal reform continued in 2016 with the finalization of draft legislation for a value-added tax and the approval of legislation to restructure customs and tax administration under two new independent authorities.

Income from offshore petroleum production continued its sharp decline in 2016, when Timor-Leste received $223.9 million in taxes and royalties, down from $978.9 million in 2015 and an average of $2.5 billion per annum during 2008–2014. The fall in revenue came from both falling production, down by 6.8% in 2016, and lower oil prices, down by an average of 15.9%. Another factor was the settlement in the first quarter of 2016 of four tax disputes between the Government of Timor-Leste and ConocoPhillips, the lead operator of the Bayu-Undan oil field. The settlement terms have not been disclosed, but analysis of tax and royalty payments to Australia and Timor-Leste suggests that Timor-Leste had to forego $152.4 million in tax revenue in 2016 (Figure 3.35.4).

Lower petroleum tax income was partly balanced on paper by investments of Timor-Leste's Petroleum Fund that earned $647.7 million in 2016. The fund's equity and bond holdings both outperformed their benchmarks for an overall return on assets of 4.7%, compared with a benchmark yield of 4.0%. The fund maintained its investment strategy in 2016, but new procedures for cash management were introduced in June to reduce its exposure to losses from short-term volatility.

As in previous years, withdrawals from the Petroleum Fund financed most public spending. Withdrawals reached $1.24 billion in 2016, more than double the estimated sustainable income of $544.8 million. As a result, the fund balance declined by 2.3% in 2016, ending the year with $15.8 billion of assets, or 10.5 times GDP. The sharp decline in income from oil production and elevated spending on imported goods and services was reflected in the current account, which went from a surplus equal to 16.4% of GDP in 2015 to a deficit estimated at 49.9%.

Economic prospects

Growth is forecast to slow to 4.0% in 2017 before recovering to 6.0% in 2018 as major public and private investments move ahead. The implementation of public investments is likely to falter in 2017 as attention shifts to national elections in July and the formation of a new government. A supplementary budget may be passed immediately after the elections to reflect changes in government structure and priorities.

The 2017 budget includes new appropriations for almost $1.39 billion in expenditure this year excluding grants from development partners. This is down from an average of $1.63 billion during 2011–2016. Of the total, $361 million is for capital investment and $1.03 billion for recurrent expenditure. Recurrent expenditure includes a $172 million

3.35.3 Inflation

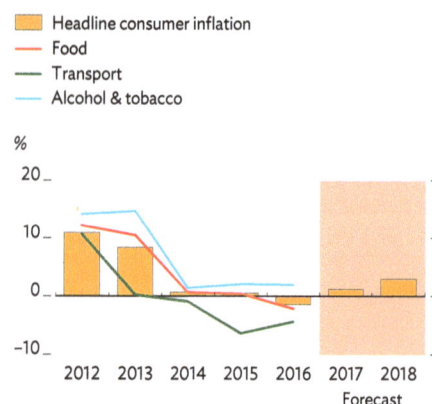

Sources: Statistics Timor-Leste; ADB estimates.

3.35.4 Actual and foregone taxes and royalties from petroleum production

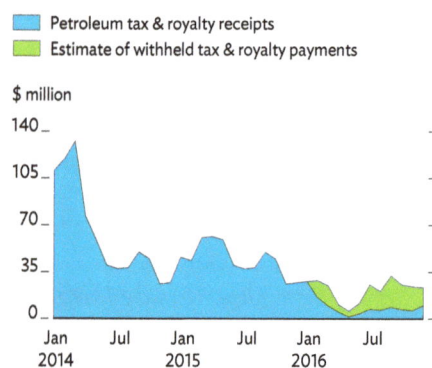

Sources: Timor-Leste National Petroleum Authority; ADB estimates.

3.35.5 Planned infrastructure fund investments

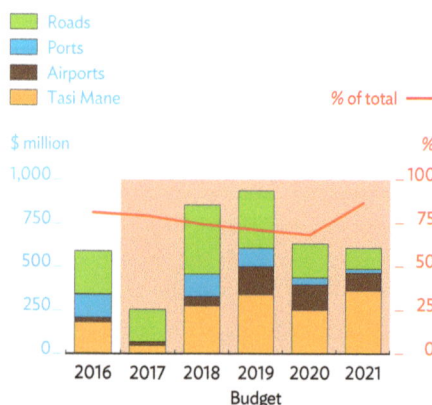

Sources: Timor-Leste Budget Transparency Portal; Timor-Leste 2017 State Budget.

transfer to Oe-Cusse Ambeno, of which 72.8% is allocated to capital works. Allocations for salaries and wages are 14.8% higher in 2017 because of increases across many ministries. However, setting aside transfers to Oe-Cusse Ambeno, the allocation for recurrent items is 3.9% lower than in 2016. Most of the savings have been achieved by allocating less for transfers and for goods and services.

The 2017 budget maintains the growth strategy in force since 2011, led by public investment. The budget for the autonomously managed Infrastructure Fund during 2017–2021 is $4.5 billion, or 3 times the GDP in 2016. Of this, 80% is allocated to roads and bridges, airports, seaports, public buildings, and the Tasi Mane project to develop a petrochemical industry on the south coast (Figure 3.35.5). An operations and maintenance program has been included in the Infrastructure Fund plan for 2017–2021 with an initial allocation of $9.6 million in 2017 and an average of $9.1 million per annum in 2018–2021. Despite the large capital budget, planned investments in water supply and sanitation, education, and health care may not be sufficient to achieve national targets for service delivery.

The discounted forecast for petroleum revenues during 2017–2022 is 44% less than in the 2016 budget, reflecting updated oil price forecasts (Figure 3.35.6). As a result, the estimated sustainable income from the Petroleum Fund has been reduced to $481.6 million, well below the $787.0 million peak in 2013. Projections for domestic revenue growth have been lifted, reflecting strong collections in 2016 and the expected impact of fiscal reform. Non-oil revenues are now projected to rise to $247.9 million by 2020, compared with a forecast of $210.3 million in the 2016 budget (Figure 3.35.7).

With revenues from oil and gas production in steep decline, the current account position is increasingly determined by income from Petroleum Fund investments and the magnitude of deficits in merchandise and services trade. The current account deficit is projected to narrow to 12.2% of GDP in 2017 as the trade deficit shrinks with lower government spending.

A current account deficit equal to 40.2% of GDP is forecast for 2018 as the trade deficit widens and income from petroleum production declines further. In the absence of new oil and gas developments or substantial fiscal consolidation, Timor-Leste is likely to see widening fiscal and current account deficits and a steady drawdown of Petroleum Fund assets in the years after 2018.

In January 2017, Timor-Leste and Australia announced their shared intention to negotiate a permanent maritime boundary between the two countries by September 2017. The termination of their revenue-sharing agreement and demarcation of a permanent border in the Timor Sea could clarify ownership of the Greater Sunrise oil field and pave the way for its development. This would not affect government revenues during the forecast period but could make fiscal consolidation less urgent.

Consumer prices are expected to increase in 2017 and 2018 with private business picking up and higher international food and fuel prices. Consumer price inflation is forecast at 1.2% in 2017, rising to 3.0% in 2018 as international food prices continue to rise and increased investment stimulates demand.

3.35.1 Selected economic indicators (%)

	2017	2018
GDP growth	4.0	6.0
Inflation	1.2	3.0
Current account balance (share of GDP)	−12.2	−40.2

Source: ADB estimates.

3.35.6 Petroleum revenues

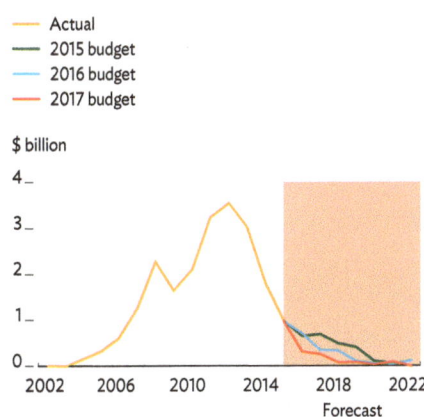

Source: Timor-Leste national budget documents, various years.

3.35.7 Domestic revenues

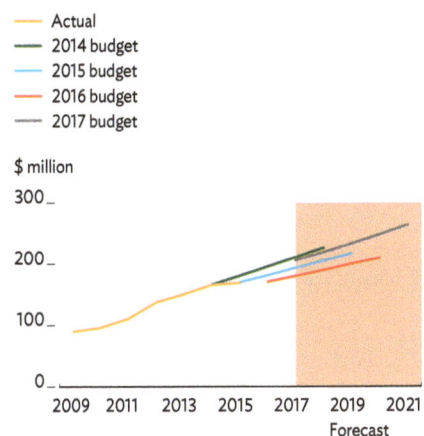

Source: Timor-Leste national budget documents, various years.

The outlook for private investment is positive during 2017 and 2018 with the Heineken brewery set to expand its operations in 2017 and the Tibar Bay port likely to garner the approvals necessary to commence construction in the second half of the year. Elections are a wild card in 2017, and final decisions could slip to 2018 regarding the development of the cement factory in Baucau and two large tourism investments near Dili.

The finalization of a range of legislative reforms could stimulate private investment and business activity. In February 2017, the National Parliament approved a package of land laws that provides the first clear framework for regulating landownership and resolving competing historical claims since Timor-Leste achieved independence in 2002. Other notable reforms targeted for completion before the 2017 elections are a new mining code, investment law, and framework for secured lending.

Policy challenge—managing the decentralization of service delivery

The decentralization program that began with establishment of the Special Administrative Region of Oe-Cusse Ambeno in 2014 is set to expand in 2017. The government approved in 2016 a new law defining the structures, roles, and responsibilities of new municipal authorities in the four largest municipalities—Baucau, Bobonaro, Dili, and Ermera—and new municipal administrations in the remaining eight municipalities.

The new law provides a framework for administrative decentralization and assigns significant responsibilities for health, education, public works, and other public services to the new municipal bodies. The law empowers central government agencies to delegate additional functions to subnational administrations and authorities.

Timor-Leste can benefit from the lessons learned in other countries as it moves forward with its own decentralization. While the legal framework has now been established, many details still need to be worked out. It will be important to ensure that the transfer of functions to subnational governments aligns with capacity in the new municipal bodies, which is currently limited, and that funding allocations from the central government are consistent with their service delivery mandates.

Fiscal policy is one area where further analysis is needed. Analysis of data from the 2014 Survey of National Living Standards and the 2015 census highlight significant regional variation in poverty rates and other human development indicators (Figure 3.35.8). While a number of government programs target poverty, current patterns of subnational spending do not reflect regional differences in poverty rates (Figure 3.35.9 and Figure 3.35.10).

Decentralization will better promote equity if fiscal rules provide a clear and objective framework for aligning funding allocations to regional variations in poverty, human development, and the cost of service delivery. It may also provide scope to incentivize service delivery by delegating selected revenue collection functions to subnational governments and establishing revenue-sharing arrangements.

3.35.8 Births attended by health professionals

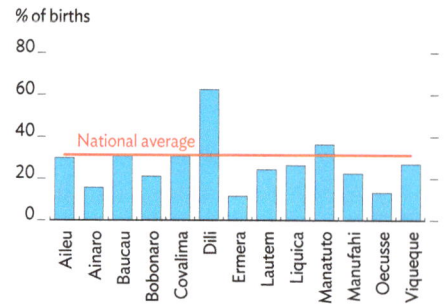

Source: Timor-Leste Population and Housing Census 2015.

3.35.9 Municipal budget allocations

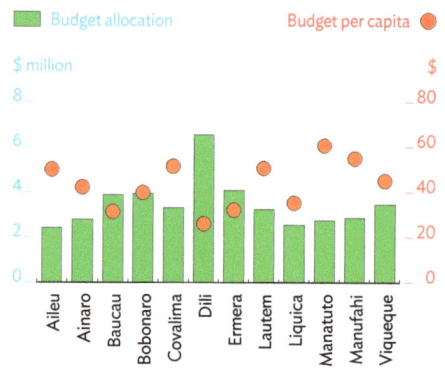

Sources: Timor-Leste State Budget, 2017; Timor-Leste Population and Housing Census 2015.

3.35.10 Municipal budget allocations and poverty rates

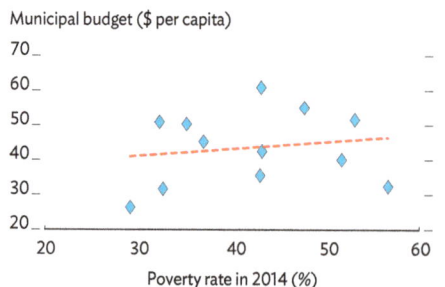

Sources: Timor-Leste State Budget 2017; Poverty in Timor-Leste, 2014.

Vanuatu

The economy is recovering after several shocks over the past 2 years, not least a devastating cyclone in 2015. Growth is driven by ongoing recovery in tourism and agriculture, cyclone reconstruction, and new infrastructure investment. However, the improved outlook faces risks from rising public debt and a legacy of policy inaction in key areas. Reform is needed to improve infrastructure management and enhance productivity for faster and more sustainable growth.

Economic performance

Growth rebounded to an estimated 3.8% in 2016, following contraction by 1.0% in 2015, as tourism and agriculture gradually recovered from a series of shocks, including Tropical Cyclone Pam in March 2015 (Figure 3.36.1). Reconstruction following the cyclone reinforced growth, as did the initiation of several large infrastructure projects.

Growth in export volumes for agricultural commodities was uneven, as cyclone damage and a long drought caused by El Niño continued to weigh on production into 2016. However, the value of exports of kava, cocoa, and copra rose significantly (Figure 3.36.2). This saw total export earnings increase by an estimated 28.2% in 2016, clawing back much of the 30.3% decline in 2015. External demand for kava increased, especially after restrictions eased in Europe and after Fiji was hit by Tropical Cyclone Winston. However, volumes for such export commodities as coconut oil, coffee, and beef continued to contract under the enduring impact of recent natural shocks and, in some cases, structural decline.

The tourism recovery in 2016 was similarly uneven as disruptions to international air services set back recovery following the cyclone. In January, two major airlines in the region, Air New Zealand and Virgin Australia, stopped flying to Port Vila over concern about the safety of the runway at Bauerfield International Airport. Qantas, a third major carrier, ended its codeshare agreement with government-owned Air Vanuatu. The government successfully completed emergency repairs by May, but only Virgin Australia resumed services. Visitors by air recovered by 5.7% in 2016 but remain 12.6% fewer than in 2014. By contrast, cruise ship arrivals rose by an estimated 28.9% in 2016, outperforming 2014 by 15.6% (Figure 3.36.3).

Government spending, including activities financed by development partners, delivered a major stimulus but resulted in a budget deficit equal to an estimated 10.6% of GDP, reversing a 6.4% surplus in 2015. The deficit financed the initiation of major cyclone reconstruction and infrastructure projects, with considerable help from development partners.

3.36.1 GDP growth

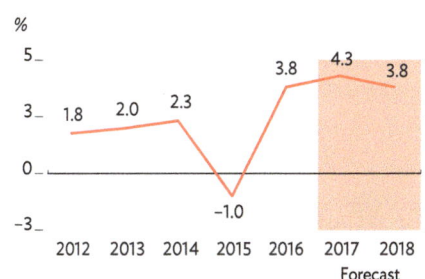

Sources: Vanuatu National Statistics Office; ADB estimates.

3.36.2 Principal exports

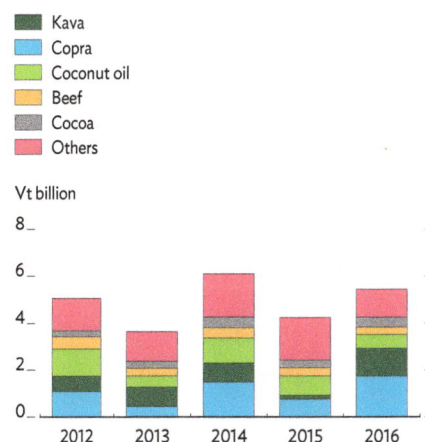

Source: Vanuatu National Statistics Office.

This chapter was written by Roland Rajah of the Pacific Liaison and Coordination Office, ADB, Sydney; and Nancy Wells of the Vanuatu Extended Mission, ADB, Port Vila.

The Reserve Bank of Vanuatu, the central bank, has kept monetary settings unchanged since raising the policy rate by 100 basis points in March 2016 as it sought to gradually wind down policy support to the banking system introduced following Tropical Cyclone Pam. Inflation decelerated to 0.9% from 2.5% in 2015 (Figure 3.36.4). Slower inflation reflected low international commodity prices and base effects from the spike in consumer prices in the immediate aftermath of the cyclone. The current account deficit widened to the equivalent of 13.8% of GDP from 9.2% in 2015, reflecting a drop in grants for emergency cyclone response and recovery, as well as higher imports to supply heightened construction activity (Figure 3.36.5). The 2016 deficit was well financed by development partners funding construction projects.

Economic prospects

Growth is expected to pick up to 4.3% in 2017 on continued recovery in agriculture and tourism and as the implementation of major reconstruction and infrastructure projects continues to ramp up. It is seen to slow slightly to 3.8% in 2018 as construction peaks and the recovery in agriculture and tourism plays out. Government plans for a significant infrastructure push are expected to drive medium-term growth prospects, with the total investment pipeline during 2016–2020 amounting to almost half of annual GDP.

Inflation is seen to remain subdued, though rising international commodity prices and heightened construction are expected to push it to 2.4% in 2017 and 2.6% in 2018. Higher imports for construction and higher international prices will likely widen the current account deficit to 17.7% of GDP in 2017, but it should be financed by inflows of external development assistance. The central bank is thus expected to maintain a broadly accommodative stance even as it continues to gradually tighten policy in line with economic recovery and rising inflation.

Despite the positive outlook, Vanuatu's economy faces acute risks from a legacy of policy inaction in several areas. Notable are deficiencies in meeting international standards for combatting money laundering and the financing of terrorism and in safeguarding the safety of vital international air and maritime transport links. Progress is being made in all these areas and needs to be pursued diligently to keep risks from becoming eventualities that could derail Vanuatu's continued recovery.

Rapid increases in public debt are another concern. The government expects to incur a consolidated fiscal deficit in 2017 equal to 16.9% of GDP. The deficit is currently being financed by the development partners that support the major infrastructure projects that drive the deficit (Figure 3.36.6). However, as the infrastructure push continues, external debt could reach over 50% of GDP by 2020, leaving Vanuatu increasingly vulnerable to shocks, including natural disasters.

Containing external debt will be essential, but equally critical will be ensuring that much-needed infrastructure investment is not crowded out by lower-quality expenditure. This places a premium on strong fiscal discipline regarding the recurrent budget, through expenditure prioritization and the mobilization of additional domestic revenue.

3.36.3 Visitor arrivals by mode of travel

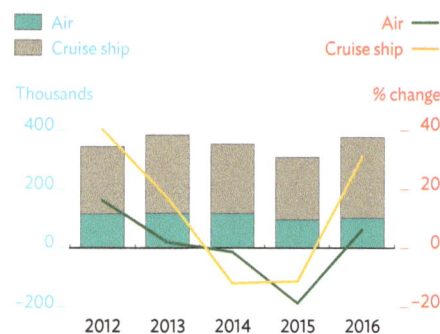

Source: Vanuatu National Statistics Office.

3.36.4 Inflation

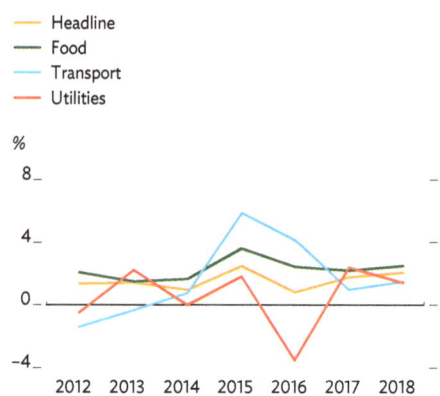

Sources: Vanuatu National Statistics Office; ADB estimates.

3.36.1 Selected economic indicators (%)

	2017	2018
GDP growth	4.3	3.8
Inflation	2.4	2.6
Current account balance (share of GDP)	-17.7	-15.0

Source: ADB estimates.

The government is consulting with the community on the introduction of personal and corporate income taxes, which if introduced would be a first in the history of Vanuatu. Such taxes would provide important new sources of domestic revenue and help to rebuild public finances while avoiding excessive reliance on more regressive taxes such as the value-added tax.

Policy challenge—delivering Vanuatu 2030

In January 2017, the government released its new national strategic development plan, Vanuatu 2030: The People's Plan. The plan sets out a vision for a "stable, sustainable, and prosperous Vanuatu." Economic growth that is higher yet sustainable will be critical to delivering on the ambitions of Vanuatu 2030. The infrastructure push currently under way is the main growth catalyst so far pursued by the government. While the infrastructure is sorely needed, it alone will be insufficient to deliver the required lift to growth.

Limited capacity for managing public investments risks undermining the benefits of the infrastructure push. The current investment pipeline amounts to over Vt10 billion each year in 2017 and 2018, equal to more than 12% of GDP. By comparison, the average annual value of public investment projects implemented during 2008–2010, the most recent previous peak in public investment, amounted to only Vt3.5 billion, not much more than 5% of GDP. The sudden scaling up could overwhelm limited project implementation capacity. Meanwhile, inadequate infrastructure planning could skew project selection, and the historical pattern of inadequate attention to maintenance threatens to undermine return on investment. There is a need to review the institutional structures for infrastructure management, including the role of the Vanuatu Project Management Unit, which manages, under the Prime Minister's Office, all projects valued at $10 million or more.

A further concern is the need for complementary reform to enhance productivity and support growth led by the private sector. Productivity growth has been deteriorating in recent years, by an average estimated at 1.5% during 2010–2014. Insufficient progress in implementing reform designed to enhance private sector development and productivity appears to be the key issue. Private investment in Vanuatu was relatively high in recent years, estimated at the equivalent of 28.0% of GDP during 2010–2014, but it did not translate into commensurate dividends in terms of economic growth.

In the absence of productivity-enhancing reform, Vanuatu's medium-term growth prospects will be constrained to 3.7% annually to 2020, delivering per capita growth of only 1.5% annually despite the planned massive increase in infrastructure investment. Moreover, growth is likely to slow thereafter because it will be difficult for the government to sustain the current high rate of public investment. Productivity-enhancing reform will therefore be critical to delivering a more prosperous Vanuatu by 2030.

3.36.5 Current account balance

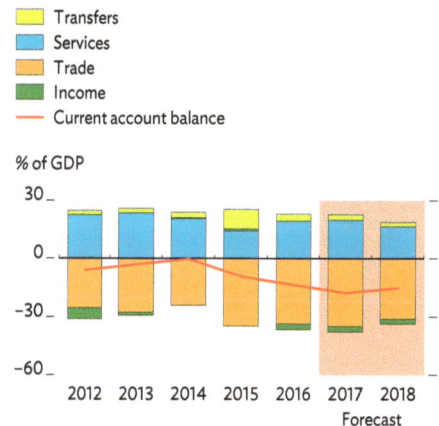

Sources: Reserve Bank of Vanuatu; ADB estimates.

3.36.6 Government expenditures

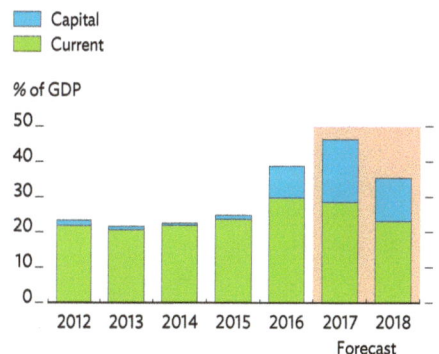

Sources: Vanuatu Department of Finance and Treasury; ADB estimates.

North Pacific economies

Growth in the North Pacific was modest in 2016. Delayed implementation of public investments slowed growth in the Federated States of Micronesia. Despite a steep drop in tourist arrivals, Palau continued to grow, supported by election-related spending. Stagnation persisted in the Republic of the Marshall Islands. While rapidly rising revenue from fishing license fees has generated structural fiscal surpluses, medium-term fiscal challenges remain.

Economic performance

The economy of the Federated States of Micronesia (FSM) is estimated to have grown by 3.0% in FY2016 (ended 30 September 2016), driven by fisheries, retail trade, and manufacturing, notably newly operating water bottling plants (Figure 3.37.1). Although infrastructure grants under the FSM Compact of Free Association with the US became available after the update of its Infrastructure Development Plan in FY2015, project implementation has been constrained by limited capacity in the national and state governments. Deflation deepened slightly in FY2016 to an estimated 0.3% from 0.2% in the previous fiscal year with lower prices for fuel imports and electricity. The national government and four state governments have recorded combined fiscal surpluses since FY2012 thanks to soaring revenues from fishing license fees. In FY2016, this consolidated fiscal surplus equaled 11.0% of GDP. High fishing license fees also helped the current account record a surplus equal to 6.0% of GDP in FY2016, as did cheaper fuel and food imports.

The Palau economy is estimated to have grown by 2.2% in FY2016 despite a significant drop in tourism (Figure 3.37.2). Visitor arrivals fell by 11.7%, mainly reflecting a 21.2% drop in visitors from the People's Republic of China (Figure 3.37.3) due to reduced charter flights and widespread trip cancellation during the drought in early 2016. However, because this segment of the tourist market spends relatively little, the sharp drop in arrivals did not push the economy into contraction. Election-related spending supported the economy. Stable food prices and lower fuel prices brought about deflation of 1.3% in FY2016 despite tax increases for tobacco products. The fiscal balance recorded a surplus equal to 2.0% of GDP, down from 4.8% in FY2015 because of slower economic growth and a rising wage bill adjusted for the cost of living. The current account has been in deficit in most recent years with deficits in goods trade more than offsetting large surpluses in trade in services and in the primary and secondary income accounts, which are buoyed by fishing license fees, official development assistance, and remittances to households. Despite lower fuel imports and higher income from fishing license fees, the current account deficit is estimated

This chapter was written by Norio Usui of the Pacific Department, ADB, Manila.

3.37.1 Supply-side contributions to growth in the Federated States of Micronesia

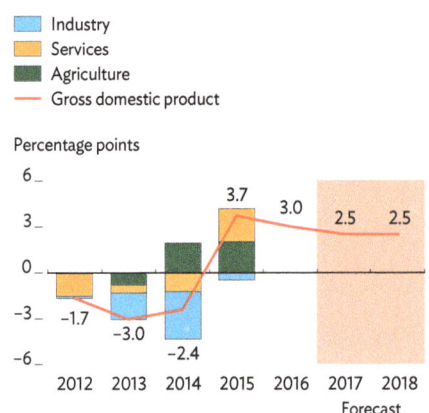

- Industry
- Services
- Agriculture
- — Gross domestic product

Percentage points

Note: Years are fiscal years ending on 30 September of the same calendar year.
Source: ADB estimates using data from the *Federated States of Micronesia FY2015 Economic Review*.

3.37.2 Supply-side contributions to growth in Palau

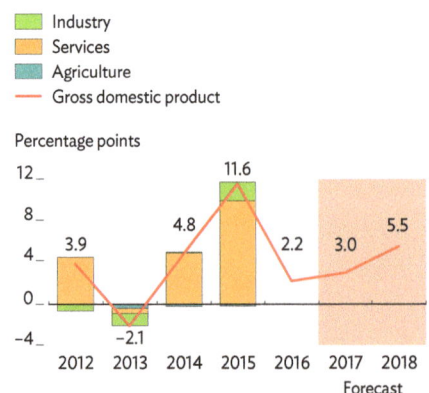

- Industry
- Services
- Agriculture
- — Gross domestic product

Percentage points

Note: Years are fiscal years ending on 30 September of the same calendar year.
Source: ADB estimates using data from the *Republic of Palau FY2015 Economic Review*.

to have widened in FY2016 to 12.0% of GDP from 3.4% as tourism receipts decreased.

GDP growth in the Marshall Islands in FY2016 improved slightly to 1.5% from 0.6% in FY2015 with fisheries strengthening and the resumption of infrastructure projects connected with the Compact of Free Association with the US (Figure 3.37.4). Reflecting lower international fuel prices and stable food prices, the Marshall Islands experienced deflation for the second successive year. The consumer price index declined by 1.3% in FY2016. Despite a 26% increase in expenditure, the FY2016 fiscal deficit was able to remain at around 2.0% of GDP thanks to a soaring fishing license fees. Subsidies to state-owned enterprises (SOEs) are estimated to have reached $11.5 million in FY2015, equivalent to 6.2% of GDP or 11.5% of total government expenditure in that year, and considerably more than government capital spending of $7.4 million (Figure 3.37.5). Lower imports and surging revenues from fishing license fees have left a current account surplus since FY2015, which in FY2016 is estimated to have reached 16.0% of GDP.

Economic prospects

The FSM economy is expected to grow by 2.5% in both FY2017 and FY2018. The national government amended legislation in FY2016 to transfer responsibility for project implementation to the states. While grants are expected to increase in the coming years, public investments will grow only gradually because of states' limited capacity to implement projects. Inflation is expected to remain low at 1.5% in FY2017 and 2.0% in FY2018, reflecting minor increases in global food and fuel prices. The strong fiscal performance of the national government is expected to continue, generating fiscal surpluses equal to 10% of GDP in the next 2 years. Current account surpluses are seen to shrink to 4.5% of GDP in both years because of higher global fuel prices.

Palau is expected to grow by 3.0% in FY2017 and 5.5% in FY2018, supported by a rebound in tourist arrivals, private investment in new resort hotels, and public investments in water supply and sanitation supported by development partners. On the demand side, growth will be boosted by capital formation, both public and private. Inflation is expected to remain low at 1.5% in FY2017 and 2.0% in FY2018 as global food and fuel prices rise modestly. The fiscal situation will likely turn around with the expected recovery in visitor arrivals and higher revenue generated by a doubling of the departure tax in FY2017 from $50 to $100. The fiscal surplus in FY2017 and FY2018 is expected to reach the equivalent of 4.0% of GDP with the forecast economic recovery. Current account deficits are expected to widen to 12.5% of GDP in FY2017 and 15.0% in FY2018 as imports of construction materials increase for tourism ventures and for infrastructure projects funded by development partners, and despite an increase of tourism receipts and stable fuel imports. These deficits will be financed with capital grants and inflows of foreign direct investment.

The Marshall Islands economy is projected to accelerate to 4.0% growth in FY2017 because of public investments funded by development partners and infrastructure grants connected with its Compact of Free Association with the US. Growth is expected to slow to 2.5% in FY2018,

3.37.3 Visitor arrivals in Palau by source

- Japan
- Taipei,China
- Republic of Korea
- People's Republic of China
- United States
- Others

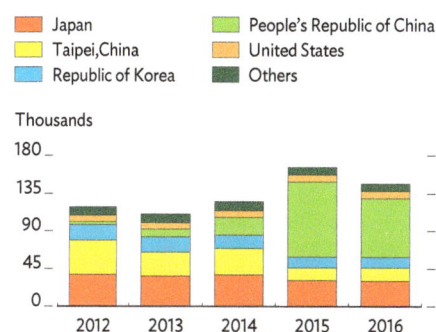

Note: Years are fiscal years ending on 30 September of the same calendar year.
Source: ADB estimates using data from the Republic of Palau FY2015 Economic Review.

3.37.1 Selected economic indicators (%)

Marshall Islands	2017	2018
GDP growth	4.0	2.5
Inflation	1.5	1.5
Current account balance (share of GDP)	4.0	4.5
Federated States of Micronesia		
GDP growth	2.5	2.5
Inflation	1.5	2.0
Current account balance (share of GDP)	4.5	4.5
Palau		
GDP growth	3.0	5.5
Inflation	1.5	2.0
Current account balance (share of GDP)	-12.5	-15.0

Note: Years are fiscal years ending on 30 June of that year.
Source: ADB estimates.

3.37.4 Supply-side contributions to growth in the Marshall Islands

- Industry
- Services
- Agriculture
- Gross domestic product

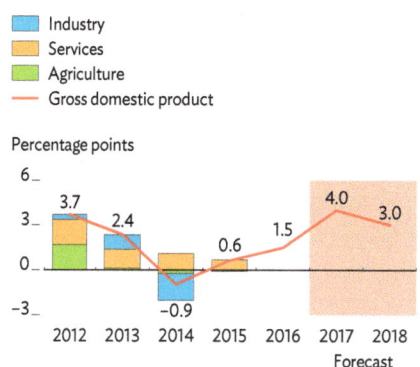

Note: Years are fiscal years ending on 30 September of the same calendar year.
Source: ADB estimates using data from the Republic of Marshall Islands FY2015 Economic Review.

however, because of limited capacity to implement projects. Inflation is projected to remain at 1.5% in FY2017 and FY2018 for the same reasons as in the FSM and Palau. Despite an anticipated increase in revenues from fishing license fees, the fiscal deficit is projected to stay at 2.0% of GDP because of slow implementation of SOE reform. Despite higher fishing license revenue, the current account surplus will narrow sharply to the equivalent of 4.0% of GDP in FY2017 because of expected increases in imports of construction materials and fuel for public investments. Then it will recover slightly to 4.5% in FY2018.

While geographic disadvantages will probably continue to limit hopes for economic diversification, adjustments are needed to spur growth and create jobs. Workers continue to leave the North Pacific economies to seek jobs abroad, even as jobs at home are filled by foreign workers. With proper matching of skills, jobs could be the key channel for distributing the benefits of economic growth to local people.

Policy challenge—ensuring fiscal sustainability

The planned cessation of compact grants in FY2023 makes fiscal sustainability over the medium term a key policy challenge for the FSM. In the past few years, the government has prudently saved a portion of its fiscal surpluses in the FSM Trust Fund. However, this fund can offset only part of the shortfall projected for the Compact Trust Fund, which is intended to generate replacement income for expiring compact grants. Since tax and tax administration reforms were repealed in FY2015, the ratio of tax receipts to GDP has languished at around 12% of GDP, one of the lowest ratios in the Pacific (Figure 3.37.6).

Challenges created by the rapid growth in tourist arrivals in Palau have confirmed that capacity constraints limit the extent to which it can depend on low-value package tourism. Restrictions on charter flights forced down tourist arrivals and temporarily allowed mounting environmental concerns to be addressed. The future is unclear. Despite a strong desire to shift toward high-end tourism, weak coordination between government bodies and with the private sector continues to prevent the emergence of coherent policies and concerted efforts. Palau needs to establish a clear and shared vision toward high-end tourism. The lack of a long-term development strategy is reflected in the composition of public spending. Even with fiscal balances in surplus since FY2011, public investments declined to the equivalent of 4.4% of GDP in FY2013–FY2015, less than half of the average of 9.2% maintained in FY2000–FY2012 (Figure 3.37.7).

In the RMI, poorly performing SOEs and social security liabilities continue to pose the major fiscal risks. Subsidies remain high for inefficient SOEs and to support social welfare in communities on outer islands and atolls. The SOE Act, approved in FY2015, has been amended to allow more public officials—politicians, ministers, and government officials—on SOE boards. This is done at the risk of continued political intervention in SOE management. An actuarial valuation in 2014 identified unfunded liabilities in the Social Security Fund amounting to $228 million, equal to 122% of FY2014 GDP. Under the current system, the fund is expected to be depleted by FY2021.

3.37.5 Subsidies to state-owned enterprises versus capital spending in the Marshall islands

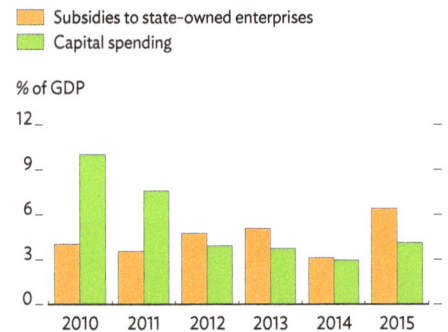

Note: Years are fiscal years ending on 30 September of the same calendar year.
Source: ADB estimates using data from the Republic of Marshall Islands FY2015 Economic Review.

3.37.6 Ratio of tax to GDP

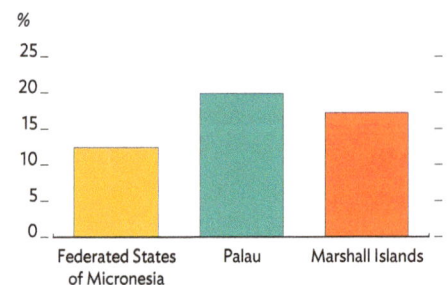

Note: Data are for FY2015 (ended 30 September 2015).
Sources: ADB estimates based on the Federated States of Micronesia FY2015 Economic Review, October 2016; Republic of the Marshall Islands FY2015 Economic Review, October 2016; Republic of Palau FY2015 Economic Review, August 2016.

3.37.7 Fiscal balance and capital spending in Palau

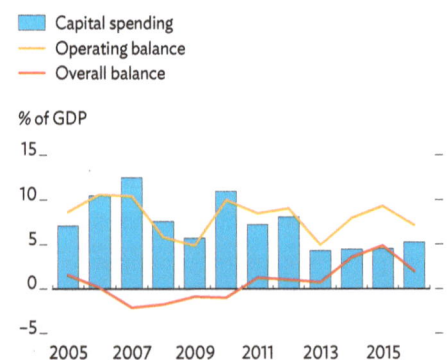

Note: Years are fiscal years ending on 30 September of the same calendar year.
Source: ADB estimates using data from the Republic of Palau FY2015 Economic Review.

South Pacific economies

The South Pacific economies of the Cook Islands, Samoa, and Tonga grew robustly in 2016 on strong agriculture and tourism and, in Samoa and Tonga, the implementation of infrastructure projects financed by development partners. Growth is projected to moderate in all three economies in the near term. A major policy challenge is to maintain prudent macroeconomic management against rising risks from economic and climatic shocks.

Economic performance

The Cook Islands economy grew by 5.5% in FY2016 (ended 30 June 2016) (Figure 3.38.1), supported by public investment and an 11.0% increase in visitor arrivals (Figure 3.38.2). The higher visitor numbers boosted performance in tourism-related retail trade, which grew by 9.8%, and in hotels and restaurants, which expanded by 14.2%. Transport and communications realized growth at 13.4%, helped along by low international fuel prices.

Samoa's economy grew by 6.6% in FY2016, driven by a 41.0% increase in fisheries and a 9.4% increase in visitor arrivals. High growth in the relatively small fishery sector was the result of a new fishing operation that saw a fleet of 22 fishing vessels relocating to Samoa, their catch processed in Apia for export. Hotels and restaurants grew by 36.9% on higher visitor spending despite slower growth in visitor arrivals. Strong tourism and low fuel prices contributed to 21.9% growth in transport during the year. Construction and the manufacturing of food and beverages also grew strongly.

Tonga's economy grew by an estimated 3.1% in FY2016, led by recovery in agriculture and construction, as well as strong private demand. This continues a trend since FY2013 of growth supported by post-disaster reconstruction, improved tourism, and strong recovery in remittances and private sector lending.

In the Cook Islands, prices declined by 0.1% on average, reversing 3.0% inflation in FY2015 as lower international fuel prices cut costs in transport and utilities (Figure 3.38.3). Prices rose in Samoa and Tonga on domestic factors. Electricity tariff adjustments saw annual average inflation at 0.1% in Samoa. Inflation in Tonga reversed from 1.0% deflation in FY2015 to 2.0% in FY2016, accelerating on higher prices for locally produced food following Cyclone Winston in February 2016, higher customs duties on imported food products, and increased construction, primarily on the International Dateline Hotel, which reopened in November 2016, and the St. George Palace office complex.

3.38.1 GDP growth in the South Pacific

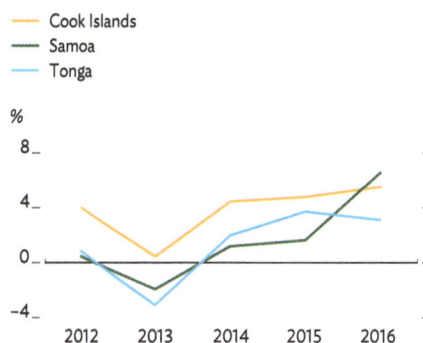

Note: Years are fiscal years ending on 30 June of that year.
Sources: Cook Islands Statistics Office; Samoa Bureau of Statistics; Tonga Department of Statistics; ADB estimates.

3.38.2 Visitor arrivals to the South Pacific

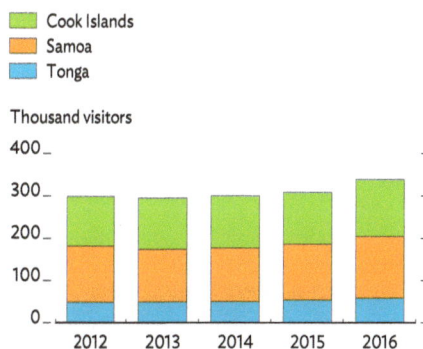

Note: Years are fiscal years ending on 30 June of that year.
Sources: Cook Islands Statistics Office; Samoa Bureau of Statistics; National Reserve Bank of Tonga.

This chapter was written by Shiu Raj Singh of the South Pacific Subregional Office, ADB, Suva; and Cara Tinio and Laisiasa Tora of the Pacific Department, ADB, Manila.

These upward pressures offset declining global food and fuel prices. Inflation remains well below the reference range of 6%–8% set by the National Reserve Bank of Tonga.

The Cook Islands habitually realizes current account surpluses generated by its large tourism services trade surplus, which offsets chronic deficits in merchandise trade and investment income. In FY2016, the current account surplus increased to the equivalent of 20.3% of GDP from 18.8% in FY2015 because of lower service imports and higher fish exports (Figure 3.38.4). In Samoa, the current account deficit widened to 6.6% of GDP from 3.9% in the previous year on higher imports, largely of fuel and lubricants. In Tonga, the current account deficit narrowed to 3.2% of GDP from 11.7% in FY2015 because of lower international food and oil prices. At the end of FY2016, Samoa's gross international reserves provided 4.2 months of cover for merchandise imports, and Tonga's reserves provided 8.8 months.

The Cook Islands realized a fiscal surplus equal to 3.7% of GDP in FY2016, reversing a small deficit in the previous year (Figure 3.38.5). This reflected higher collections of income and value-added taxes, including a one-off collection of withholding taxes, as well as a 43.7% drop in capital expenditure as no new projects were begun during the period. An analysis of debt sustainability undertaken in 2015 as part of a macroeconomic assessment found the Cook Islands at low risk of external debt distress. Net public debt, all of it external, rose from the equivalent of 9.7% of GDP in FY2010 to 26.2% in FY2016 but is still well below the government's ceiling of 35.0%. The government maintains a debt-service reserve equal to 4.6% of GDP.

In Samoa, the fiscal deficit fell in FY2016 to the equivalent of 0.4% of GDP. This was achieved largely through rigorous expenditure control in line with the government's current emphasis on consolidation while sustaining quality spending in priority areas, as well as through higher tax collections, particularly excise and value-added taxes. At the end of the fiscal year, net external debt equaled 52.6% of GDP, down from 57.8% at the end of FY2015.

Tonga incurred a fiscal deficit equal to 3.1% of GDP in FY2016, up from 1.1% in FY2015 despite a strong increase in public revenue thanks to higher tax collection and customs revenue. The reasons for the increase were higher current spending, led by wages, and a 60.3% drop in budget support grants, which were replaced by concessional loans. Net external debt was estimated to equal 43.1% of GDP at the end of FY2016.

Economic prospects

Growth is seen to moderate in all three South Pacific economies during the forecast period. The Cook Islands is projected to decelerate to 5.0% growth in FY2017 and FY2018. The main constraint on growth is tourist accommodation capacity that is inadequate for the peak holiday season. The prospects for expanding capacity are limited because of issues pertaining to landownership and arrangements for leasing.

3.38.3 Inflation

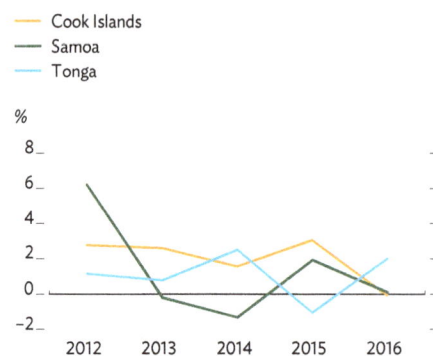

Note: Years are fiscal years ending on 30 June of that year.
Sources: Cook Islands Statistics Office; Samoa Bureau of Statistics; Tonga Department of Statistics; ADB estimates.

3.38.4 Current account balance

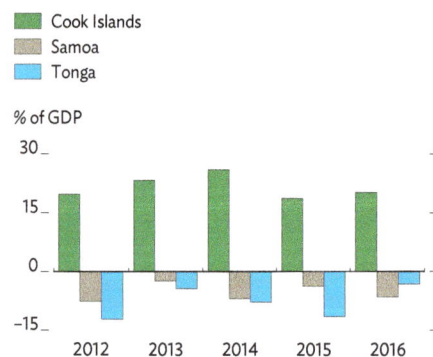

Note: Years are fiscal years ending on 30 June of that year.
Sources: Cook Islands Ministry of Finance and Economic Management; Central Bank of Samoa; Tonga Ministry of Finance.

In Samoa, fishery output is expected to level off, while public sector activity and agriculture look poised to decline. The forecast is for significantly lower growth at 2.0% in FY2017 and, with the closure in August 2017 of a plant manufacturing automotive wire harnesses, further deceleration to 1.5% in FY2018.

The outlook for Tonga remains positive. The economy is forecast to grow by 2.6% in both FY2017 and FY2018, supported by construction, tourism, and wholesale and retail trade in the run-up to the 2019 South Pacific Games.

Inflation is expected to accelerate across all three economies during the forecast period in line with international price movements. In particular, higher international oil prices are seen to support inflation at 0.5% in FY2017 and 1.2% in FY2018 in the Cook Islands and, in both fiscal years, at 2.0% in Samoa and 2.5% in Tonga.

The Government of the Cook Islands will likely return to incurring fiscal deficits in the near term. A deficit equal to 3.9% of GDP is expected for FY2017 with the scheduled commencement of a number of public investment projects in water supply, renewable energy, and roads. These projects will double capital expenditure. The deficit projection further takes into account an estimated 6.5% decline in tax collections. In FY2018, the fiscal deficit is expected to narrow slightly to 3.1% of GDP with lower capital spending and improved tax collection. Despite the projected fiscal deficits, strong economic growth should push net public debt lower to the equivalent of 24.8% of GDP in FY2017 and 22.0% in FY2018.

Samoa's fiscal deficit is expected to equal 3.5% of GDP in FY2017. Following stringent expenditure control and increased focus on revenue collection, this is considerably higher than the deficit in FY2016, the difference largely coming down to the construction of the airport terminal buildings. A deficit equal to 3.0% of GDP is projected for FY2018.

In Tonga, the fiscal deficit is forecast to narrow to the equivalent of 1.6% of GDP in FY2017. A budget surplus of 0.4% on a cash basis is projected for FY2018, narrowed mainly by strong revenue performance, restraint on wages, and a decline in personal emoluments in real terms. Primarily as a result of a government policy to avoid any new borrowing that is not concessional, Tonga's external debt is expected to stay within the target ceiling of 50% of GDP, about 44% in FY2017 and 42% in FY2018.

The Cook Islands is forecast to realize current account surpluses equal to 24.5% of GDP in FY2017 and 21.0% in FY2018. Tourism earnings will likely offset higher imports of goods and services for public investment projects. Samoa's current account deficit is projected to narrow to the equivalent of 4.9% of GDP in FY2017 and 2.8% in FY2018 with contributions from rising remittances and a declining merchandise trade deficit. In Tonga, the current account deficit is expected to increase to the equivalent of 7.7% of GDP in FY2017 and further to 11.9% in FY2018, the gap widened by imports needed to prepare for the South Pacific Games and higher international prices.

3.38.5 Fiscal balance

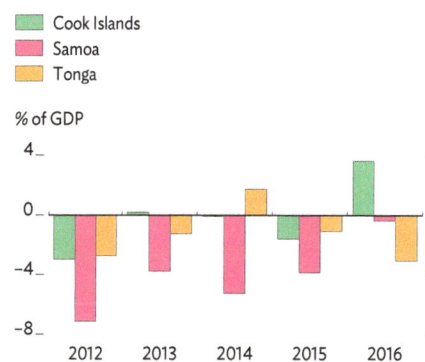

Note: Years are fiscal years ending on 30 June of that year.
Sources: Cook Islands Ministry of Finance and Economic Management; Samoa Ministry of Finance; Tonga Ministry of Finance.

3.38.1 Selected economic indicators (%)

Cook Islands	2017	2018
GDP growth	5.0	5.0
Inflation	0.5	1.2
Current account balance (share of GDP)	24.5	21.0
Samoa		
GDP growth	2.0	1.5
Inflation	2.0	2.0
Current account balance (share of GDP)	−4.9	−2.8
Tonga		
GDP growth	2.6	2.6
Inflation	2.5	2.5
Current account balance (share of GDP)	−7.7	−11.9

Note: Years are fiscal years ending on 30 June of that year.
Source: ADB estimates.

Policy challenge—prudent macroeconomic management for economic resilience

Staying the course on prudent macroeconomic management is vital to the economic outlook for all three South Pacific economies. Across the Pacific, progress is fragile and easily reversible in small states that lack livelihood diversity or economies of scale and are vulnerable to climate shocks.

The Cook Islands has taken steps to mitigate the risks that disasters pose to its tourism sector, but further efforts are needed to ensure sustainable economic growth over the long term. The government needs to address structural impediments to private sector development such as restrictions on foreign investment. The exclusion of foreign investors from most sectors and uncertainty over how applications are processed prevent the economy from fully enjoying the benefits that foreign capital, technology, and know-how can offer. A strategic review of foreign investment policy and more rules-based consideration of proposals could facilitate investment inflows and reduce costs for both investors and the government. Meanwhile, any intervention needs to strike a balance between spurring growth and upholding local cultural values.

Samoa's main challenge is to maintain macroeconomic stability while responding to disasters and fluctuations in the global economic environment. Declining foreign exchange reserves pose a real risk to economic stability and may necessitate an appropriate policy response such as making recurrent spending more efficient toward achieving fiscal consolidation and rebuilding buffers over the medium term. As Samoa is vulnerable to disasters, it requires sufficient fiscal and foreign exchange buffers to finance disaster response and recovery. Because a disaster can erode both these buffers, the authorities are contemplating contingent facilities with multilateral development partners to cover the risk.

Tonga is faced with a growing need to restrain public wage growth to decrease wages' share of current spending, which was 45% in FY2016. The public sector wage bill gradually increased from the equivalent of 11.4% of GDP in FY2012 to 13.8% in FY2016, crowding out capital outlays and spending on operations and maintenance, as well as undermining the implementation of policy priorities under the national development plan. A new formula for the cost-of-living allowance now under development could become a useful annual target starting from FY2017. Broader civil service reform informed by the results of the recent remuneration review should be undertaken in parallel to ensure that employment in government is rationalized and that pay scales adequately reflect responsibilities, while maintaining the quality of public services.

Small island economies

The economies of Kiribati, Nauru, and Tuvalu all grew in 2016. The major contributor to growth was public sector activity, particularly externally funded infrastructure projects. Inflation was stable. Current account deficits in Kiribati and Tuvalu are expected to persist or widen with the waning of El Niño and its transitory boost to fishing revenues. Prudent macroeconomic management is needed to rebuild fiscal buffers and stimulate growth.

Economic performance

From 2011 to 2015, growth averaged 3.5% in Kiribati. It was driven by public expenditure supported by revenues from fishing license fees and investment in transport, water supply, and sanitation infrastructure funded by development partners. Growth moderated to 1.8% in 2016 with the completion of these major projects and a falloff in fisheries as a fading El Niño and cooler waters drew fewer fish to the central Pacific, and as fewer fishing days were allocated to US ships (Figure 3.39.1).

Nauru, by contrast, saw growth accelerate in FY2016 (ended 30 June 2016) to an estimated 7.2% from 2.8% in FY2015. The recovery reflected progress in restoring phosphate exports, growth in services, and the gradual absorption of the refugee community into the local workforce. Government spending continued to increase, but the rate of increase slowed considerably from the previous year. Revised national account estimates suggest that growth in recent years has been much higher than previously estimated. The rebased GDP estimates effectively place a higher weight on service sectors, which have been booming, and less weight on mining and industry, which have been depressed by problems hitting phosphate exports.

Growth in Tuvalu accelerated to 3.0% in 2016 from 2.6% the previous year on spending to expand accommodation capacity ahead of the Pacific Islands Leaders Meeting in September 2019 and large government-funded infrastructure projects, including waterfront reclamation and the building of public schools.

Kiribati's fiscal balance improved markedly from 2012 to 2015, largely thanks to higher revenue from fishing license fees. However, revenue from the sale of fishing licenses peaked in 2015 and fell by almost half to about A$116 million, equivalent to 53% of GDP in 2016 (Figure 3.39.2). This has reversed the government's fiscal position, turning a surplus in 2015 equal to 45.7% of GDP into an 11.8% deficit last year.

In Nauru, the fiscal surplus in FY2016 is estimated at the equivalent of 11.1% of GDP, slightly lower than the 12.5% surplus seen in FY2015. While government spending continued to increase, the 13.5% pace of growth was much slower than in previous years, notably the 72.2%

3.39.1 GDP growth

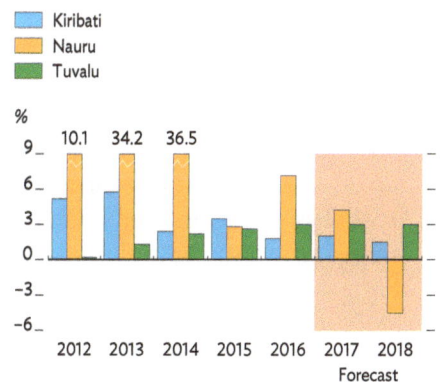

Note: Years are fiscal years ending on 30 June of that year for Nauru and coinciding with the calendar year for Kiribati and Tuvalu.
Sources: Kiribati National Statistics Office; Nauru budget documents; Tuvalu Central Statistics Division; ADB estimates.

3.39.2 Fishing license revenues

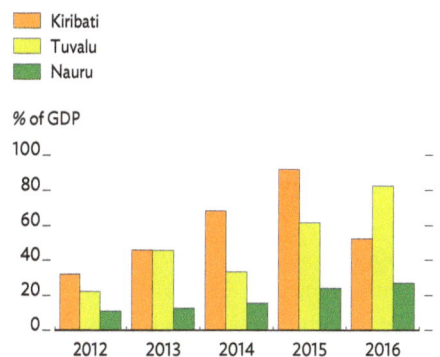

Sources: Kiribati Ministry of Finance and Ministry of Fisheries and Marine Resources Development; Nauru Department of Finance; Tuvalu budget documents; ADB estimates.

This chapter was written by Roland Rajah of the Pacific Liaison and Coordination Office, ADB, Sydney; and Laisiasa Tora of the South Pacific Subregional Office, ADB, Suva.

surge in 2015, when government spending rose in response to large revenue windfalls.

In Tuvalu, revenue from fishing licenses reached a record high estimated at A$37.3 million in 2016, or the equivalent of 82.6% of GDP, up from A$26.5 million in 2015, or 61.6% of GDP. The resulting fiscal surplus was the equivalent of 34.3% of GDP in 2016. With higher fishing revenues, the government has been able to strengthen fiscal buffers through greater investment in the Tuvalu Trust Fund. It also invested A$5 million in the Tuvalu Survival Fund. This new fund, established following Tropical Cyclone Pam in 2015, sets aside resources for disaster response and projects that mitigate and adapt to climate change.

Inflation in 2016 remained steady at 0.7% in Kiribati and moderated in Tuvalu to 2.0% from 3.2% in 2015 (Figure 3.39.3). In Nauru, inflation relented from 11.4% in FY2015 to an estimated 7.2% in FY2016 as growth in domestic demand slowed but damage to the port mooring system continued to hinder supply. All three countries use the Australian dollar as their currency, which helps to keep prices stable.

The current account position of Kiribati switched from a large surplus equal to 44.7% of GDP in 2015 to a 7.0% deficit in 2016 because of the sharp decline in income from fishing licenses and higher imports, which were driven by large inflows of capital equipment for projects both ongoing and about to commence. Tuvalu's current account surplus almost halved from the equivalent of 10.0% of GDP in 2015 to 5.6% in 2016 as deficits in goods and services trade widened, more than offsetting record high collections of fishing license revenue.

Economic prospects

In Kiribati, economic growth is likely to pick up to 2.0% in 2017 as large capital works get under way, mostly with funding from development partners. Especially notable is a project to repair and upgrade Bonriki International Airport, the main gateway. Growth is likely to moderate to 1.5% in 2018 as fishing license revenues continue to fall, weighing on public spending and economic output. The government is in a better position than in the past to withstand a downturn, however, having saved much of the surplus revenue generated from fisheries in the good years to replenish fiscal buffers in its Revenue Equalization Reserve Fund.

For Nauru, the forecast is for growth to moderate to 4.3% in FY2017 because of only gradual recovery in phosphate exports and the plateauing of government spending and activities connected with the Regional Processing Centre (RPC) for asylum seekers and refugees. The outlook for FY2018 is clouded by uncertainty surrounding a potential winding down of the RPC program in connection with a deal announced by Australia that could see many of the refugees currently in Nauru resettled in the United States. Unknown at this stage are the pace, scale, and timing of any change at the RPC, which has become a major source of government revenue since FY2013 (Figure 3.39.4). The assumed scenario has the RPC start to wind down in FY2018, exerting considerable downward pressure on the economy. This should be partly offset by continued recovery in phosphate exports and the

3.39.3 Inflation

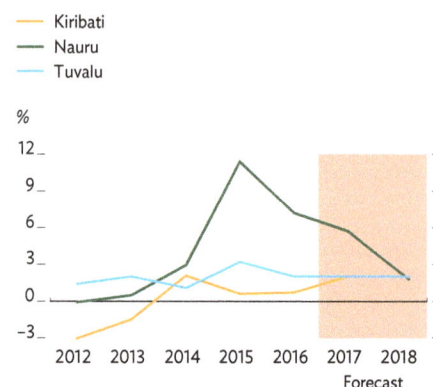

Note: Years are fiscal years ending on 30 June of that year for Nauru and coinciding with the calendar year for Kiribati and Tuvalu.
Sources: Kiribati National Statistics Office; Nauru budget documents; Tuvalu Central Statistics Division; ADB estimates.

3.39.4 Revenues from Regional Processing Centre in Nauru

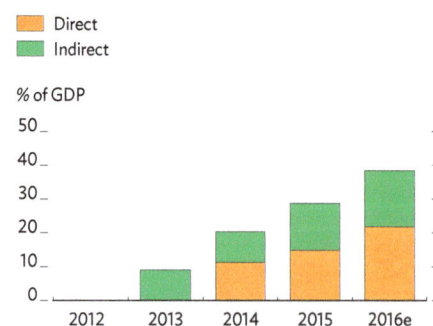

Note: Years are fiscal years ending on 30 June of that year.
Source: ADB estimates based on data from Nauru Department of Finance.

start of construction on a new seaport facility. Nevertheless, output would likely contract by 4.5%.

The macroeconomic outlook for Tuvalu remains upbeat. Growth is expected to hold steady at 3% in 2017 and 2018, supported by stimulus from the implementation of projects funded by development partners, notably one to upgrade maritime infrastructure on outer islands.

Inflation in Kiribati is expected to accelerate to 2.0% in 2017 and 2018 on mildly rising prices for imported food and fuel. It is expected to moderate in Nauru to 5.7% in 2017 and 1.8% in 2018 as supply constraints ease and domestic demand continues to slow. In Tuvalu, inflation is forecast stable at 2.0% in 2017 and 2018 in line with steady growth.

The current account deficit in Kiribati is projected to narrow to the equivalent of 2.4% of GDP in 2017 and further to 1.5% in 2018 as imports fall from last year's peak. Tuvalu is expected to return to current account deficits, equal to 20.8% of GDP in 2017 and 25.4% in 2018, because fishing license revenues are likely to have peaked and the import bill is set to rise to meet continuing demand for imported capital inputs for ongoing projects.

Policy challenge—prudent macroeconomic management

Volatile external revenue flows into small island economies have impacts that require prudent macroeconomic management and especially reform to facilitate private sector growth. In Kiribati, the steep decline in fishery revenue sharply constrains state finances. Prospects for growth therefore depend on sustaining a program of reform to address problems posed by inefficient state-owned enterprises, weak tax compliance, and low collections of corporate tax.

Nauru is challenged to manage public infrastructure assets sustainably. Recent years have seen significant public capital investment related to the RPC, as well as investments by development partners. More investment is planned. However, with the future of the RPC uncertain, its winding down or eventual closure threatens economic and fiscal sustainability, putting into jeopardy the sustainability of the significantly expanded infrastructure stock. Moreover, some new assets may not be needed in the absence of the RPC, forcing Nauru to face difficult challenges adjusting the quantity and mix of its infrastructure assets to its shifting requirements. The government needs to develop and adopt a sustainable infrastructure strategy for financing and implementing effective asset maintenance, as well as for directing any additional investment toward projects that are economically viable.

Tuvalu's heavy reliance on externally sourced income and susceptibility to climate change makes it important for the government to continue pursuing fiscal and structural reforms that boost investment and improve economic performance. The establishment of the Tuvalu Survival Fund enhances the government's ability to respond to disasters.

Further strengthening of fiscal buffers in these small island economies would mitigate fiscal volatility and support sustained growth (Figure 3.39.5).

3.39.1 Selected economic indicators (%)

Kiribati	2017	2018
GDP growth	2.0	1.5
Inflation	2.0	2.0
Current account balance (share of GDP)	–2.4	–1.5
Nauru		
GDP growth	4.3	–4.5
Inflation	5.7	1.8
Current account balance (share of GDP)	...	...
Tuvalu		
GDP growth	3.0	3.0
Inflation	2.0	2.0
Current account balance (share of GDP)	–20.8	–25.4

... = data not available.
Note: Years are fiscal years ending on 30 June of that year for Nauru and coinciding with the calendar year for Kiribati and Tuvalu.
Source: ADB estimates.

3.39.5 Fiscal buffers as of 2016

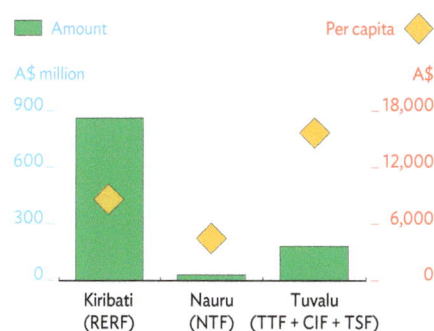

CIF = Consolidated Investment Fund, NTF = Nauru Trust Fund, RERF = Revenue Equalization Reserve Fund, TSF = Tuvalu Survival Fund, TTF = Tuvalu Trust Fund.
Sources: International Monetary Fund; ADB estimates.

STATISTICAL APPENDIX

Statistical notes and tables

The statistical appendix presents selected economic indicators for the 45 developing member economies of the Asian Development Bank (ADB) in 18 tables. The economies are grouped into five subregions: Central Asia, East Asia, South Asia, Southeast Asia, and the Pacific. Most of the tables contain historical data from 2012 to 2016; some have forecasts for 2017 and 2018.

The data were standardized to the degree possible to allow comparability over time and across economies, but differences in statistical methodology, definitions, coverage, and practices make full comparability impossible. The national income accounts section is based on the United Nations System of National Accounts, while the data on balance of payments are based on International Monetary Fund (IMF) accounting standards. Historical data were obtained from official sources, statistical publications and databases, and documents of ADB, the IMF, and the World Bank. For some economies, data for 2016 are estimated from the latest available information. Projections for 2017 and 2018 are generally ADB estimates made on the bases of available quarterly or monthly data, though some projections are from governments.

Most economies report by calendar year. The following record their government finance data by fiscal year: Armenia; Azerbaijan; Brunei Darussalam; Fiji; Hong Kong, China; Kazakhstan; the Kyrgyz Republic; the Lao People's Democratic Republic (Lao PDR); Singapore; Taipei,China; Tajikistan; Thailand; and Uzbekistan. South Asian countries (except for the Maldives and Sri Lanka), the Cook Islands, the Federated States of Micronesia, the Republic of Marshall Islands, Nauru, Myanmar, Palau, Samoa, and Tonga report all variables by fiscal year.

Regional and subregional averages or totals are provided for seven tables (A1, A2, A6, A11, A12, A13, and A14). For tables A1, A2, A6, and A14, the averages are computed using weights derived from gross national income (GNI) in current US dollars following the World Bank Atlas method. The GNI data for 2012–2015 were obtained from the World Bank's World Development Indicators online. Weights for 2015 were carried over through 2018. The GNI data for the Cook Islands and Taipei,China were estimated using the Atlas conversion factor. For tables A11 and A12, the regional and subregional averages were computed on the basis of a consistent sum, which means that if there are missing country data for a given year, the sum of the prior year used for computing the growth rate excludes the corresponding country data.

Tables A1, A2, A3, A4, and A5. These tables show related data on output growth, production, and demand. Changes to the national income accounts series for some countries have been made to accommodate a change in source, methodology, and/or base year. The series for Afghanistan, Bhutan, India, Myanmar, and Pakistan reflect fiscal year data, rather than calendar year data, while those for Timor-Leste reflect GDP excluding the offshore petroleum sector.

Table A1: Growth rate of GDP (% per year). The table shows annual growth rates of GDP valued at constant market prices, factor costs, or basic prices. GDP at market prices is the aggregation of the value added of all resident producers at producers' prices including taxes less subsidies on imports plus all nondeductible value-added or similar taxes. Constant factor cost measures differ from market price measures in that they exclude taxes on production and include subsidies. Basic price valuation is the factor cost plus some taxes on production, such as property and payroll taxes, and less some subsidies, such as labor-related subsidies but not product-related subsidies. Most economies use constant market price valuation. Pakistan uses constant factor costs, while Fiji, the Maldives, and Nepal use basic prices.

Table A2: Growth rate of per capita GDP (% per year). The table provides the growth rates of real per capita GDP, which is defined as GDP at constant prices divided by the population. Data on per capita gross national income in US dollar terms (Atlas method) for 2015 are also shown, sourced from the World Bank's World Development Indicators online. The data for the Cook Islands and Taipei,China were estimated using the Atlas conversion factor.

Table A3: Growth rate of value added in agriculture (% per year). The table shows the growth rates of value added in agriculture at constant prices and its corresponding share in 2015 at current prices. The agriculture sector comprises agricultural crops, livestock, poultry, fisheries, and forestry.

Table A4: Growth rate of value added in industry (% per year). The table provides the growth rates of value added in industry at constant prices and its corresponding share in 2015 at current prices. This sector comprises manufacturing, mining and quarrying, construction, and utilities.

Table A5: Growth rate of value added in services (% per year). The table gives the growth rates of value added in services at constant prices and its corresponding share in 2015 at current prices. Subsectors generally include trade, banking, finance, real estate, public administration, and other services. For Malaysia, electricity, gas, water, and waste management are included under services.

Table A6: Inflation (% per year). Data on inflation rates are period averages. The inflation rates presented are based on consumer price indexes. The consumer price indexes of the following economies are for a given city or group of consumers only: Afghanistan is for Kabul until 2011, Cambodia is for Phnom Penh, the Marshall Islands is for Majuro, Solomon Islands is for Honiara, and Nepal is for urban consumers.

Table A7: Change in money supply (% per year). This table tracks the annual percentage change in the end-of-period supply of broad money as represented by M2 for most countries. M2 is defined as the sum of M1 and quasi-money, where M1 denotes currency in circulation plus demand deposits, and quasi-money consists of time and savings deposits including foreign currency deposits.

Tables A8, A9, and A10: Government finance. These tables give the revenue and expenditure transactions and the fiscal balance of the central government expressed as a percentage of GDP in nominal terms. For Cambodia since 2006, the People's Republic of China, India, Kazakhstan, the Kyrgyz Republic, Mongolia, and Tajikistan, transactions are those reported by the general government.

Table A8: Central government revenues (% of GDP). Central government revenues comprise all nonrepayable receipts, both current and capital, plus grants. These amounts are computed as a percentage of GDP at current prices. For the Republic of Korea, revenues exclude social security contributions. For Singapore, revenues include the net investment returns contribution. For Kazakhstan, revenues include transfers from the national fund. Grants are excluded in Cambodia, the Lao PDR, Malaysia, Singapore, and Thailand; revenues from disinvestment are included for India; and only current revenues are included for Bangladesh.

Table A9: Central government expenditures (% of GDP). Central government expenditures comprise all nonrepayable payments to both current and capital expenses, plus net lending. These amounts are computed as a share of GDP at current prices. For Thailand, expenditures refer to budgetary expenditures excluding externally financed expenditures and corresponding borrowing. Those for Tajikistan include externally financed public investment programs. One-time expenditures are excluded for Pakistan.

Table A10: Fiscal balance of central government (% of GDP). Fiscal balance is the difference between central government revenues and expenditures. The difference is computed as a share of GDP at current prices. Data variations may arise from statistical discrepancies when, for example, balancing items for both central and local governments, and from differences in the concept used in the individual computations of revenues and expenditures as compared with the calculation of the fiscal balance. For Fiji, the fiscal balance excludes total loan repayments. For Thailand, the fiscal balance is a cash balance composed of the budgetary and nonbudgetary balances. Some off-budget accounts are included in the computation of the fiscal balance for Turkmenistan.

Tables A11, A12, A13, and A14: Balance of payments. These tables show selected international economic transactions of countries as recorded in the balance of payments. These items cover annual flows.

Tables A11 and A12: Growth rates of merchandise exports and imports (% per year). These tables show the annual growth rates of exports and imports of goods. Data are in million US dollars, primarily obtained from the balance-of-payments accounts of each economy. Exports are reported free on board. Import data are reported free on board, except for the following economies, which value them on the basis of cost, insurance, and freight: Afghanistan; Bhutan; Cambodia;

Hong Kong, China; India; the Lao PDR; Myanmar; Samoa; Singapore; and Thailand.

Table A13: Trade balance ($ million). The trade balance is the difference between merchandise exports and merchandise imports. Figures in this table are based on the export and import amounts used to generate tables A11 and A12.

Table A14: Current account balance (% of GDP). The current account balance is the sum of the balance of trade for merchandise, net trade in services and factor income, and net transfers. The values reported are divided by GDP at current prices in US dollars. In the case of Cambodia, the Lao PDR, and Viet Nam, official transfers are excluded from the current account balance.

Table A15: Exchange rates to the US dollar (annual average). Annual average exchange rates are quoted as the local currencies per US dollar.

Table A16: Gross international reserves ($ million). Gross international reserves are defined as the US dollar value of holdings of foreign exchange, special drawing rights, reserve position in the IMF, and gold at the end of a given period. For Taipei,China, this heading refers to foreign exchange reserves only. In some economies, the rubric is foreign assets and reserves of national monetary authorities and national oil funds, i.e., foreign assets of the Maldives Monetary Authority, net foreign reserves of the State Bank of Pakistan, and assets of the National Oil Fund of Azerbaijan. The data for India are as of 10 March 2017.

Table A17: External debt outstanding ($ million). For most economies, external debt outstanding, public and private, includes medium- and long-term debt, short-term debt, and IMF credit. For Cambodia and the Lao PDR, only public external debt is reported. For Kazakhstan, the Kyrgyz Republic, Singapore, Sri Lanka, and Thailand, the figures for 2016 are as of the end of September.

Table A18: Debt service ratio (% of exports of goods and services). This table generally presents the total debt service payments of each economy, which comprise principal repayments (excluding on short-term debt) and interest payments on outstanding external debt, as a percentage of exports of goods and services. For Cambodia and the Lao PDR, debt service refers to external public debt only. For Viet Nam, exports of goods are used as the denominator in the calculation of the ratio; for the Philippines, exports of goods, services, and income are used as the denominator. For Bangladesh, the ratio represents debt service payments on medium- and long-term loans as a percentage of exports of goods, nonfactor services, and workers' remittances. For Azerbaijan, the ratio represents public and publicly guaranteed external debt service payments as a percentage of exports of goods and nonfactor services.

Table A1 Growth rate of GDP (% per year)

	2012	2013	2014	2015	2016	2017	2018
Central Asia	5.5	6.6	5.2	3.1	2.1	3.1	3.5
Armenia	7.2	3.3	3.6	3.0	0.2	2.2	2.5
Azerbaijan	2.2	5.8	2.8	1.1	–3.8	–1.1	1.2
Georgia	6.4	3.4	4.6	2.9	2.7	3.8	4.5
Kazakhstan	4.8	6.0	4.2	1.2	1.0	2.4	2.2
Kyrgyz Republic	–0.1	10.9	4.0	3.9	3.8	3.0	3.5
Tajikistan	7.5	7.4	6.7	6.0	6.9	4.8	5.5
Turkmenistan	11.1	10.2	10.3	6.5	6.2	6.5	7.0
Uzbekistan	8.2	8.0	8.1	8.0	7.8	7.0	7.3
East Asia	6.7	6.8	6.6	6.1	6.0	5.8	5.6
China, People's Rep. of	7.9	7.8	7.3	6.9	6.7	6.5	6.2
Hong Kong, China	1.7	3.1	2.8	2.4	1.9	2.0	2.1
Korea, Rep. of	2.3	2.9	3.3	2.6	2.7	2.5	2.7
Mongolia	12.3	11.6	7.9	2.4	1.0	2.5	2.0
Taipei,China	2.1	2.2	4.0	0.7	1.5	1.8	2.2
South Asia	5.5	6.1	6.7	7.2	6.7	7.0	7.2
Afghanistan	11.4	3.9	1.3	0.8	2.0	2.5	3.0
Bangladesh	6.5	6.0	6.1	6.6	7.1	6.9	6.9
Bhutan	6.4	3.6	4.0	6.1	6.4	8.2	9.9
India	5.5	6.5	7.2	7.9	7.1	7.4	7.6
Maldives	2.5	4.7	6.0	2.8	3.4	3.8	4.1
Nepal	4.6	3.8	5.7	2.3	0.8	5.6	5.4
Pakistan	3.8	3.7	4.1	4.0	4.7	5.2	5.5
Sri Lanka	9.1	3.4	5.0	4.8	4.4	5.0	5.0
Southeast Asia	5.9	5.2	4.6	4.6	4.7	4.8	5.0
Brunei Darussalam	0.9	–2.1	–2.5	–0.4	–2.5	1.0	2.5
Cambodia	7.3	7.4	7.1	7.0	7.0	7.1	7.1
Indonesia	6.0	5.6	5.0	4.9	5.0	5.1	5.3
Lao People's Dem. Rep.	7.9	7.8	7.5	6.7	6.8	6.9	7.0
Malaysia	5.5	4.7	6.0	5.0	4.2	4.4	4.6
Myanmar	7.3	8.4	8.0	7.3	6.4	7.7	8.0
Philippines	6.7	7.1	6.2	5.9	6.8	6.4	6.6
Singapore	3.9	5.0	3.6	1.9	2.0	2.2	2.3
Thailand	7.2	2.7	0.9	2.9	3.2	3.5	3.6
Viet Nam	5.2	5.4	6.0	6.7	6.2	6.5	6.7
The Pacific	5.7	4.1	9.6	8.3	2.6	2.9	3.3
Cook Islands	4.0	0.5	4.5	4.8	5.5	5.0	5.0
Fiji	1.4	4.7	5.6	3.6	2.0	3.5	4.0
Kiribati	5.2	5.8	2.4	3.5	1.8	2.0	1.5
Marshall Islands	3.7	2.4	–0.9	0.6	1.5	4.0	2.5
Micronesia, Fed. States of	–1.7	–3.0	–2.4	3.7	3.0	2.5	2.5
Nauru	10.1	34.2	36.5	2.8	7.2	4.3	–4.5
Palau	3.9	–2.1	4.8	11.6	2.2	3.0	5.5
Papua New Guinea	8.1	5.0	13.3	12.0	2.0	2.5	2.8
Samoa	0.4	–1.9	1.2	1.6	6.6	2.0	1.5
Solomon Islands	2.3	2.8	2.0	2.9	3.2	3.0	2.8
Timor-Leste	5.8	2.9	5.9	3.5	5.4	4.0	6.0
Tonga	0.8	–3.1	2.0	3.7	3.1	2.6	2.6
Tuvalu	0.2	1.3	2.2	2.6	3.0	3.0	3.0
Vanuatu	1.8	2.0	2.3	–1.0	3.8	4.3	3.8
Developing Asia	6.4	6.5	6.3	6.0	5.8	5.7	5.7
Developing Asia excluding the NIEs	7.1	7.0	6.8	6.6	6.3	6.3	6.2

Note: The newly industrialized economies (NIEs) are the Republic of Korea, Singapore, Taipei,China, and Hong Kong, China.

Table A2 Growth rate of per capita GDP (% per year)

	2012	2013	2014	2015	2016	2017	2018	Per capita GNI, $, 2015
Central Asia	4.1	5.1	3.7	1.7	0.9	1.7	2.1	
Armenia	7.6	3.1	3.9	3.2	0.6	2.2	2.5	3,880
Azerbaijan	0.9	4.5	1.5	−0.1	−5.0	−2.2	0.1	6,560
Georgia	5.7	3.7	4.4	2.6	2.7	3.8	4.5	4,160
Kazakhstan	3.3	4.5	2.7	−0.3	−0.2	0.9	0.7	11,390
Kyrgyz Republic	−1.4	8.7	2.0	1.8	1.7	1.5	1.0	1,170
Tajikistan	8.2	3.6	2.8	4.2	5.2	1.5	3.3	1,280
Turkmenistan	9.8	8.9	8.9	5.1	4.8	5.1	5.6	7,380
Uzbekistan	5.6	6.3	6.3	6.1	5.9	5.1	5.4	2,160
East Asia	6.2	6.3	6.1	5.6	5.5	5.3	5.1	
China, People's Rep. of	7.3	7.2	6.8	6.4	6.2	6.0	5.7	7,930
Hong Kong, China	0.6	2.7	2.0	1.5	1.3	1.0	1.4	41,000
Korea, Rep. of	1.8	2.4	2.7	2.1	2.3	2.1	2.3	27,450
Mongolia	10.2	9.4	5.6	0.2	−2.1	0.5	0.0	3,870
Taipei,China	1.7	2.0	3.8	0.5	1.3	1.9	2.0	22,452
South Asia	4.3	4.6	5.3	5.8	5.3	5.9	5.8	
Afghanistan	9.2	1.9	−0.6	−1.1	0.0	−0.8	1.0	610
Bangladesh	5.2	4.6	4.6	5.1	5.7	5.5	5.5	1,190
Bhutan	4.6	1.8	2.3	3.4	5.9	6.7	8.4	2,380
India	4.2	5.2	5.9	6.6	5.8	6.5	6.2	1,600
Maldives	0.4	2.6	3.6	0.6	1.1	1.6	1.8	6,950
Nepal	3.1	2.3	4.2	0.9	−0.6	4.2	3.9	730
Pakistan	1.8	1.6	2.0	2.0	2.7	3.2	3.5	1,440
Sri Lanka	11.5	2.6	4.0	3.9	3.2	4.7	4.7	3,800
Southeast Asia	4.5	3.7	3.3	3.3	3.3	3.3	3.8	
Brunei Darussalam	−0.7	−3.7	−3.9	−1.7	−5.1	−5.4	2.2	38,010
Cambodia	5.6	6.1	5.9	5.7	5.7	5.5	5.7	1,070
Indonesia	4.5	4.1	3.6	3.5	3.7	3.2	4.2	3,440
Lao People's Dem. Rep.	6.5	5.7	5.4	2.5	3.8	5.4	5.5	1,740
Malaysia	4.1	2.7	3.6	3.0	2.7	2.6	2.6	10,570
Myanmar	6.5	7.5	10.1	6.4	6.1	7.5	7.9	1,160
Philippines	4.8	5.2	4.4	4.8	4.5	4.7	4.9	3,550
Singapore	1.4	3.3	2.2	0.7	0.8	0.9	1.0	52,090
Thailand	6.6	2.2	0.4	2.0	2.7	3.0	3.1	5,720
Viet Nam	4.1	4.3	4.9	5.5	5.1	5.5	5.7	1,990
The Pacific	3.4	1.8	7.1	5.9	0.3	0.6	1.0	
Cook Islands	2.9	5.3	4.5	4.2	1.2	5.0	5.0	24,071
Fiji	0.6	4.0	5.1	3.0	1.5	2.9	3.5	4,830
Kiribati	3.0	3.6	0.3	1.4	−0.3	−0.1	−0.5	3,390
Marshall Islands	3.3	2.0	−1.3	0.3	−0.7	3.6	2.1	4,770
Micronesia, Fed. States of	−2.2	−3.0	−2.4	3.8	3.1	2.7	2.8	3,560
Nauru	7.0	30.4	34.8	−0.1	4.2	1.4	−7.2	15,420
Palau	5.8	−1.6	3.8	10.5	1.2	2.0	4.5	12,180
Papua New Guinea	4.8	1.8	9.9	8.6	−1.1	−0.6	−0.3	2,199
Samoa	−0.3	−2.7	0.5	0.9	5.8	1.3	0.8	3,930
Solomon Islands	0.0	0.5	−0.3	1.4	0.7	0.5	0.3	1,920
Timor-Leste	3.9	1.0	4.0	1.6	3.5	2.1	4.1	2,180
Tonga	0.7	−3.2	2.0	3.7	3.2	2.7	2.7	4,280
Tuvalu	−1.0	0.0	−0.2	0.8	1.2	1.1	1.3	6,230
Vanuatu	−0.8	−0.5	−0.1	−3.3	1.5	2.0	1.5	3,282
Developing Asia	5.6	5.7	5.5	5.2	5.1	5.0	4.9	
Developing Asia excluding the NIEs	6.3	6.2	5.9	5.8	5.6	5.5	5.4	

Note: The newly industrialized economies (NIEs) are the Republic of Korea, Singapore, Taipei,China, and Hong Kong, China.

Table A3 Growth rate of value added in agriculture (% per year)

	2012	2013	2014	2015	2016	Sector share, 2015, %
Central Asia						
Armenia	9.5	7.6	6.1	13.2	−5.8	19.0
Azerbaijan	5.8	4.9	−2.6	6.6	2.6	6.8
Georgia	−3.8	11.3	1.6	1.6	0.0	9.1
Kazakhstan	−17.4	11.2	1.3	3.5	5.5	5.0
Kyrgyz Republic	1.2	2.6	−0.5	6.2	3.0	15.9
Tajikistan	10.4	7.6	4.5	3.2	5.2	24.7
Turkmenistan	8.1	10.0	4.2	7.9	12.0	9.3
Uzbekistan	7.0	6.8	6.9	6.8	6.6	18.3
East Asia						
China, People's Rep. of	4.5	3.8	4.1	3.9	3.3	8.8
Hong Kong, China	−3.3	4.9	−6.0	−6.8	−3.2	0.1
Korea, Rep. of	−0.9	3.1	3.6	−1.5	−2.8	2.3
Mongolia	21.1	19.2	13.7	10.7	4.8	14.6
Taipei,China	−3.2	1.3	0.5	−7.3	−6.9	1.7
South Asia						
Afghanistan	30.2	0.0	−0.1	−5.0	2.0	21.7
Bangladesh	3.0	2.5	4.4	3.3	2.8	15.5
Bhutan	2.3	2.3	2.4	3.5	4.0	17.6
India	1.5	5.6	−0.3	0.8	4.4	17.5
Maldives	0.0	5.1	0.2	−0.5	7.2	3.3
Nepal	4.6	1.1	4.5	0.8	1.3	31.8
Pakistan	3.6	2.7	2.5	2.5	−0.2	25.1
Sri Lanka	3.9	3.2	4.6	4.8	−4.2	8.8
Southeast Asia						
Brunei Darussalam	8.1	−1.2	4.7	6.4	−3.6	1.1
Cambodia	4.3	1.6	0.3	0.2	1.8	28.2
Indonesia	4.6	4.2	4.2	3.8	3.3	13.9
Lao People's Dem. Rep.	2.5	3.5	2.9	2.0	2.5	27.4
Malaysia	1.0	2.0	2.1	1.2	−5.1	8.6
Myanmar	1.7	3.6	2.8	3.4	...	26.7
Philippines	2.8	1.1	1.7	0.1	−1.3	10.3
Singapore	3.7	4.5	13.4	−3.6	−1.4	0.0
Thailand	2.7	0.7	−0.6	−5.7	0.6	8.7
Viet Nam	2.9	2.6	3.4	2.4	1.4	18.2
The Pacific						
Cook Islands	16.3	−2.8	17.3	−4.4	5.5	8.3
Fiji	−1.9	6.7	1.9	6.3	...	11.3
Kiribati	2.9	−0.2	3.7	...	...	...
Marshall Islands	10.5	0.7	−1.1	−0.2	...	14.3
Micronesia, Fed. States of	−0.2	−3.0	5.0	6.2	...	27.8
Nauru	2.2	5.3	9.5	5.2	...	4.0
Palau	0.7	−9.2	−5.3	−4.6	...	3.4
Papua New Guinea	−1.6	1.8	3.3	2.4	3.1	23.3
Samoa	−7.2	−2.4	9.6	−0.3	6.5	9.4
Solomon Islands	−0.5	−0.8	7.1	...	...	27.5
Timor-Leste	26.6	0.0	−2.5	...	...	...
Tonga	0.5	3.7	3.1	...	...	...
Tuvalu	...	...	...	...	...	...
Vanuatu	2.2	4.8	4.2	...	...	...

... = data not available.

Table A4 Growth rate of value added in industry (% per year)

	2012	2013	2014	2015	2016	Sector share, 2015, %
Central Asia						
Armenia	5.7	0.5	−2.3	3.7	−0.9	28.2
Azerbaijan	−0.6	4.9	0.5	−1.9	−7.1	49.3
Georgia	9.6	2.4	4.6	4.1	5.5	24.7
Kazakhstan	1.8	3.1	1.5	−0.3	0.6	32.5
Kyrgyz Republic	−11.7	30.5	5.7	2.9	5.9	28.4
Tajikistan	10.4	3.9	13.3	11.2	16.0	27.5
Turkmenistan	8.6	7.3	11.4	3.1	1.2	56.9
Uzbekistan	8.0	9.0	8.6	8.0	6.6	34.6
East Asia						
China, People's Rep. of	8.4	8.0	7.4	6.2	6.1	40.9
Hong Kong, China	4.7	1.6	7.6	2.4	1.5	7.4
Korea, Rep. of	1.9	3.3	3.1	1.7	2.9	38.0
Mongolia	14.8	14.6	12.7	9.7	−1.2	33.8
Taipei,China	3.3	1.7	7.0	−0.7	1.9	36.2
South Asia						
Afghanistan	7.2	3.1	2.4	4.1	3.1	23.3
Bangladesh	9.4	9.6	8.2	9.7	11.1	28.1
Bhutan	5.4	5.3	3.8	6.0	7.3	43.1
India	3.4	4.2	6.9	8.2	5.8	29.6
Maldives	0.8	−7.6	12.9	18.3	9.7	23.0
Nepal	3.0	2.7	7.1	1.5	−6.3	14.9
Pakistan	2.5	0.8	4.5	4.8	6.8	20.0
Sri Lanka	9.0	4.1	4.7	2.1	6.7	29.5
Southeast Asia						
Brunei Darussalam	−1.4	−5.6	−4.4	0.0	−2.9	60.2
Cambodia	9.3	10.7	10.1	11.7	10.5	29.4
Indonesia	5.3	4.3	4.2	3.0	3.9	41.3
Lao People's Dem. Rep.	13.7	9.7	8.5	8.0	8.0	30.9
Malaysia	4.9	3.6	6.1	5.2	4.3	36.9
Myanmar	8.0	11.4	12.1	8.7	...	34.5
Philippines	7.3	9.2	7.8	6.0	8.0	30.8
Singapore	2.3	2.0	3.4	−3.1	2.8	26.1
Thailand	7.3	1.6	0.0	2.8	2.0	36.4
Viet Nam	7.4	5.1	6.4	9.6	7.6	38.6
The Pacific						
Cook Islands	19.3	−3.7	−6.8	6.3	−24.0	9.4
Fiji	−2.2	4.4	1.2	2.2	...	18.1
Kiribati	30.1	37.3	−1.4	...	...	...
Marshall Islands	2.9	7.9	−16.7	−1.6	...	10.6
Micronesia, Fed. States of	−1.3	−19.5	−28.5	−7.5	...	6.5
Nauru	1.2	−28.5	−3.6	−17.1	...	6.1
Palau	−5.4	−15.6	1.6	26.4	...	8.7
Papua New Guinea	14.6	9.3	28.6	24.0	1.0	53.0
Samoa	0.2	−3.2	3.8	−6.2	6.1	24.0
Solomon Islands	−1.4	−2.0	−13.2	...	...	15.0
Timor-Leste	−4.0	−9.7	15.8	...	...	...
Tonga	1.2	−14.3	1.3	...	...	...
Tuvalu	...	...	...	...	...	...
Vanuatu	−22.2	9.8	3.2	...	...	...

... = data not available.

Table A5 Growth rate of value added in services (% per year)

	2012	2013	2014	2015	2016	Sector share, 2015, %
Central Asia						
Armenia	6.9	2.8	6.7	0.0	4.0	52.8
Azerbaijan	6.9	7.2	7.4	4.5	−0.7	43.9
Georgia	6.2	3.5	4.6	3.1	2.5	66.2
Kazakhstan	10.4	6.9	5.7	3.1	0.8	62.5
Kyrgyz Republic	6.5	4.7	4.6	3.7	3.0	55.6
Tajikistan	14.5	19.3	1.0	−7.1	−0.3	47.8
Turkmenistan	14.7	12.7	10.6	10.0	11.0	33.8
Uzbekistan	10.4	8.8	9.4	9.8	10.7	47.1
East Asia						
China, People's Rep. of	8.0	8.3	7.8	8.2	7.8	50.2
Hong Kong, China	1.8	2.7	2.5	1.7	2.3	92.6
Korea, Rep. of	2.8	2.9	3.3	2.8	2.5	59.7
Mongolia	10.3	7.8	7.8	1.0	1.7	51.6
Taipei,China	1.5	2.1	2.8	1.6	1.3	62.1
South Asia						
Afghanistan	6.8	5.3	2.2	1.6	1.4	55.0
Bangladesh	6.6	5.5	5.6	5.8	6.2	56.3
Bhutan	6.6	1.1	5.0	8.3	7.1	39.4
India	8.3	7.7	9.5	9.8	7.9	53.0
Maldives	1.5	6.4	4.6	1.6	−1.1	73.7
Nepal	5.0	5.7	6.2	3.6	2.7	53.3
Pakistan	4.4	5.1	4.5	4.3	5.7	54.9
Sri Lanka	11.2	3.8	4.8	5.7	4.2	61.7
Southeast Asia						
Brunei Darussalam	5.5	4.7	0.6	−1.2	−1.6	38.7
Cambodia	8.1	8.7	8.7	7.1	6.7	42.3
Indonesia	6.8	6.4	6.0	5.5	5.6	44.7
Lao People's Dem. Rep.	8.0	9.7	9.0	8.5	9.0	41.7
Malaysia	6.5	5.9	6.6	5.1	5.6	54.5
Myanmar	12.0	10.3	9.1	9.1	...	38.7
Philippines	7.1	7.0	6.2	6.8	7.5	59.0
Singapore	4.6	2.0	3.9	3.2	1.0	73.8
Thailand	8.4	4.1	1.9	4.8	4.7	54.9
Viet Nam	6.7	6.7	6.2	6.3	7.0	43.3
The Pacific						
Cook Islands	1.8	0.0	4.8	5.3	8.8	82.4
Fiji	3.0	4.5	7.4	3.6	...	70.7
Kiribati	2.0	2.6	0.4	...	...	...
Marshall Islands	1.8	1.4	2.5	2.3	...	75.1
Micronesia, Fed. States of	−1.7	−0.8	−1.2	2.7	...	65.8
Nauru	8.7	60.7	41.9	11.6	...	89.9
Palau	3.7	−0.6	6.1	10.7	...	87.9
Papua New Guinea	11.2	4.7	4.2	56.4	6.2	23.6
Samoa	1.6	−1.1	−1.1	5.1	6.7	66.6
Solomon Islands	5.3	7.2	3.6	...	...	57.4
Timor-Leste	9.7	−0.9	...	...	...	...
Tonga	0.5	−0.5	1.6	...	...	...
Tuvalu	...	...	...	...	...	...
Vanuatu	4.4	0.1	2.4	...	...	...

... = data not available.

Table A6 Inflation (% per year)

	2012	2013	2014	2015	2016	2017	2018
Central Asia	5.1	5.9	5.9	6.3	11.1	7.8	7.3
Armenia	2.6	5.8	3.0	3.7	–1.4	1.2	1.8
Azerbaijan	1.1	2.4	1.4	4.0	12.4	9.0	8.0
Georgia	–0.9	–0.5	3.1	4.0	2.1	4.2	4.5
Kazakhstan	5.1	5.8	6.7	6.6	14.6	8.0	7.0
Kyrgyz Republic	2.8	6.6	7.5	6.5	0.4	5.0	4.0
Tajikistan	6.4	3.7	6.1	5.1	6.1	8.0	7.0
Turkmenistan	5.3	6.8	6.0	6.4	6.0	6.0	6.0
Uzbekistan	11.9	11.7	9.1	8.5	8.4	9.5	10.0
East Asia	2.6	2.4	1.9	1.3	1.9	2.3	2.6
China, People's Rep. of	2.6	2.6	2.0	1.4	2.0	2.4	2.8
Hong Kong, China	4.1	4.3	4.4	3.0	2.4	2.0	2.1
Korea, Rep. of	2.2	1.3	1.3	0.7	1.0	1.7	1.8
Mongolia	14.3	9.9	12.8	6.6	1.1	3.5	3.9
Taipei,China	1.9	0.8	1.2	–0.3	1.4	1.3	1.2
South Asia	9.8	8.9	6.3	4.9	4.6	5.2	5.4
Afghanistan	6.4	7.4	4.7	–1.5	4.5	5.5	5.8
Bangladesh	8.7	6.8	7.3	6.4	5.9	6.1	6.3
Bhutan	10.2	8.8	9.6	6.6	3.3	4.9	5.4
India	9.9	9.4	6.0	4.9	4.7	5.2	5.4
Maldives	10.9	3.8	2.1	1.0	0.5	2.1	2.3
Nepal	8.2	9.9	9.1	7.2	9.9	6.0	6.5
Pakistan	11.0	7.3	8.6	4.5	2.9	4.0	4.8
Sri Lanka	7.5	6.9	3.3	3.8	4.0	6.0	6.0
Southeast Asia	3.7	4.2	4.1	2.8	2.1	3.3	3.5
Brunei Darussalam	0.1	0.4	–0.2	–0.4	–0.7	0.1	0.1
Cambodia	2.9	3.0	3.9	1.2	3.0	3.4	3.5
Indonesia	4.0	6.4	6.4	6.4	3.5	4.3	4.5
Lao People's Dem. Rep.	4.3	6.4	4.2	1.3	1.6	2.5	3.0
Malaysia	1.7	2.1	3.1	2.1	2.1	3.3	2.7
Myanmar	2.8	5.7	5.9	11.4	6.5	7.0	7.5
Philippines	3.2	2.9	4.1	1.4	1.8	3.5	3.7
Singapore	4.6	2.4	1.0	–0.5	–0.5	1.0	1.5
Thailand	3.0	2.2	1.9	–0.9	0.2	1.8	2.0
Viet Nam	9.1	6.6	4.1	0.6	2.7	4.0	5.0
The Pacific	5.4	4.9	3.5	4.0	4.6	5.2	5.4
Cook Islands	2.8	2.6	1.6	3.0	–0.1	0.5	1.2
Fiji	3.4	2.9	0.6	1.4	3.9	2.5	2.5
Kiribati	–3.0	–1.5	2.1	0.6	0.7	2.0	2.0
Marshall Islands	4.3	1.9	1.1	–2.2	–1.3	1.5	1.5
Micronesia, Fed. States of	6.3	2.2	0.7	–0.2	–0.3	1.5	2.0
Nauru	–0.1	0.5	3.0	11.4	7.2	5.7	1.8
Palau	5.4	2.8	4.0	2.2	–1.3	1.5	2.0
Papua New Guinea	4.6	5.0	5.2	6.0	7.0	7.5	7.5
Samoa	6.2	–0.2	–1.3	1.9	0.1	2.0	2.0
Solomon Islands	5.9	5.4	5.2	–0.5	1.1	1.8	2.2
Timor-Leste	10.9	9.4	0.7	0.6	–1.4	1.2	3.0
Tonga	1.1	0.8	2.5	–1.0	2.0	2.5	2.5
Tuvalu	1.4	2.0	1.1	3.2	2.0	2.0	2.0
Vanuatu	1.4	1.4	1.0	2.5	0.9	2.4	2.6
Developing Asia	4.0	3.8	3.0	2.2	2.5	3.0	3.2
Developing Asia excluding the NIEs	4.2	4.1	3.2	2.4	2.7	3.2	3.5

Note: The newly industrialized economies (NIEs) are the Republic of Korea, Singapore, Taipei,China, and Hong Kong, China.

Table A7 Change in money supply (% per year)

	2012	2013	2014	2015	2016
Central Asia					
Armenia	19.5	14.8	8.3	10.8	17.5
Azerbaijan	20.7	15.0	11.8	−1.1	−4.9
Georgia	11.4	24.5	13.8	19.3	20.2
Kazakhstan	7.9	10.2	10.5	34.3	15.7
Kyrgyz Republic	23.8	4.4	21.1	14.9	14.6
Tajikistan	19.6	19.7	7.1	18.7	27.9
Turkmenistan	35.6	31.2	11.4	16.1	7.2
Uzbekistan	27.5	22.4	18.0	20.7	14.9
East Asia					
China, People's Rep. of	14.4	13.6	11.0	13.3	11.3
Hong Kong, China	11.1	12.4	9.5	5.5	7.7
Korea, Rep. of	4.8	4.6	8.1	8.2	7.1
Mongolia	20.4	19.3	24.7	−1.3	10.4
Taipei,China	3.5	5.8	6.1	5.8	3.6
South Asia					
Afghanistan	8.8	9.4	8.3	3.3	7.5
Bangladesh	17.4	16.7	16.1	12.4	16.3
Bhutan	5.9	3.3	26.0	3.8	18.6
India	13.6	13.4	10.9	10.1	8.4
Maldives	4.9	18.4	14.7	12.3	0.1
Nepal	22.6	16.4	19.1	19.9	19.5
Pakistan	14.1	15.9	12.5	13.2	13.7
Sri Lanka	17.6	16.7	13.4	17.8	18.4
Southeast Asia					
Brunei Darussalam	0.9	1.5	3.2	−1.8	1.5
Cambodia	20.9	14.7	29.9	14.7	17.9
Indonesia	15.0	12.8	11.9	9.0	10.0
Lao People's Dem. Rep.	31.0	18.6	23.5	14.7	11.0
Malaysia	9.0	7.3	7.0	2.6	3.0
Myanmar	46.6	31.7	17.6	26.3	24.2
Philippines	9.4	31.8	11.2	9.4	12.7
Singapore	7.2	4.3	3.3	1.5	8.0
Thailand	10.4	7.3	4.7	4.4	4.2
Viet Nam	18.5	18.8	17.7	16.2	18.0
The Pacific					
Cook Islands	19.2	−25.6	3.0	9.6	−2.7
Fiji	6.3	23.2	10.6	14.3	6.3
Kiribati	...	...	...	...	...
Marshall Islands	...	...	...	...	...
Micronesia, Fed. States of	24.1	−4.9	5.1	−5.1	−3.8
Nauru	...	...	...	...	...
Palau	22.7	4.5	24.7	2.6	...
Papua New Guinea	11.0	6.7	3.4	8.1	3.8
Samoa	−4.0	−0.8	18.7	0.6	7.1
Solomon Islands	17.4	12.5	5.5	15.0	...
Timor-Leste	26.2	22.9	19.9	7.1	2.6
Tonga	−1.6	7.0	7.9	2.4	12.6
Tuvalu	...	...	...	...	...
Vanuatu	−0.6	−5.5	8.6	...	...

... = data not available.

Table A8 Central government revenues (% of GDP)

	2012	2013	2014	2015	2016
Central Asia					
Armenia	22.2	23.5	23.7	23.2	22.8
Azerbaijan	31.6	33.5	31.2	31.5	29.2
Georgia	28.9	27.7	27.9	28.2	28.5
Kazakhstan	18.7	17.7	18.5	18.7	20.4
Kyrgyz Republic	28.8	26.9	23.4	29.8	28.5
Tajikistan	25.2	26.9	28.4	30.1	32.1
Turkmenistan	21.0	17.1	16.9	16.6	15.1
Uzbekistan	32.8	32.8	33.1	33.3	32.9
East Asia					
China, People's Rep. of	21.7	21.7	21.8	22.1	21.4
Hong Kong, China	21.7	21.3	21.2	18.8	22.5
Korea, Rep. of	18.1	20.0	17.1	17.3	18.9
Mongolia	29.7	31.2	28.4	25.8	24.5
Taipei,China	11.4	11.4	10.7	11.3	11.1
South Asia					
Afghanistan	25.4	24.3	24.0	25.0	29.3
Bangladesh	10.9	10.7	10.4	9.6	9.9
Bhutan	35.8	30.2	33.6	28.8	31.2
India	20.1	21.2	21.3	20.3	21.3
Maldives	26.2	27.7	31.9	32.8	31.3
Nepal	18.6	19.5	20.6	20.9	24.5
Pakistan	12.8	13.3	14.5	14.3	15.0
Sri Lanka	12.2	12.0	11.6	13.3	14.0
Southeast Asia					
Brunei Darussalam	49.4	41.8	34.4	21.7	14.7
Cambodia	14.4	13.5	17.2	16.8	17.6
Indonesia	15.5	15.1	14.7	13.1	12.5
Lao People's Dem. Rep.	17.7	18.1	17.2	20.0	18.5
Malaysia	21.4	20.9	19.9	18.9	17.3
Myanmar	19.0	20.1	21.9	18.8	17.2
Philippines	14.5	14.9	15.1	15.8	15.2
Singapore	15.4	15.1	15.6	15.9	16.7
Thailand	16.0	16.7	15.7	16.1	16.8
Viet Nam	22.7	23.1	22.3	22.1	23.1
The Pacific					
Cook Islands	34.3	34.3	39.8	40.5	38.8
Fiji	27.2	27.2	27.4	25.8	28.2
Kiribati	84.1	91.0	137.1	164.2	135.9
Marshall Islands	51.2	53.4	53.2	58.6	60.6
Micronesia, Fed. States of	65.9	62.0	64.8	66.0	64.4
Nauru	64.8	87.2	106.3	...	...
Palau	45.2	41.0	43.3	40.5	...
Papua New Guinea	21.3	20.9	27.4	23.3	25.9
Samoa	28.1	29.7	32.5	29.9	34.2
Solomon Islands	54.4	54.3	46.2	...	...
Timor-Leste	337.0	328.9	196.1	92.5	85.3
Tonga	27.5	25.3	27.5	28.2	27.3
Tuvalu	86.0	110.7	131.8	151.5	160.3
Vanuatu	21.8	21.4	23.5	31.4	28.2

... = data not available.

Table A9 Central government expenditures (% of GDP)

	2012	2013	2014	2015	2016
Central Asia					
Armenia	23.6	25.1	25.6	28.0	28.2
Azerbaijan	31.8	32.8	31.7	32.7	29.6
Georgia	31.7	30.3	30.7	32.0	33.0
Kazakhstan	21.6	19.7	21.2	20.9	22.0
Kyrgyz Republic	34.1	32.2	22.6	31.3	33.1
Tajikistan	25.1	28.2	29.0	32.4	33.8
Turkmenistan	14.7	15.9	16.0	17.3	15.9
Uzbekistan	32.3	32.8	32.6	34.2	33.9
East Asia					
China, People's Rep. of	23.3	23.6	23.6	25.5	25.2
Hong Kong, China	18.5	20.3	18.0	18.2	18.7
Korea, Rep. of	19.4	16.5	19.1	19.8	21.3
Mongolia	35.9	32.2	32.1	30.9	39.9
Taipei,China	12.9	12.2	11.5	11.4	11.4
South Asia					
Afghanistan	24.3	25.0	25.7	26.4	27.7
Bangladesh	14.4	14.5	14.0	13.5	13.0
Bhutan	36.9	34.4	29.8	27.3	34.2
India	27.0	28.3	28.5	27.6	27.9
Maldives	33.9	31.5	34.5	40.4	38.6
Nepal	20.9	18.8	20.0	21.9	23.1
Pakistan	21.6	21.5	20.0	19.6	19.6
Sri Lanka	17.8	17.4	17.3	20.9	19.7
Southeast Asia					
Brunei Darussalam	31.4	34.1	35.4	37.1	35.7
Cambodia	21.0	20.4	20.7	19.5	17.8
Indonesia	17.3	17.3	16.8	15.7	15.0
Lao People's Dem. Rep.	24.6	29.4	27.6	27.9	24.4
Malaysia	25.7	24.7	23.3	22.1	20.4
Myanmar	18.1	21.4	22.9	22.9	21.8
Philippines	16.8	16.3	15.7	16.8	17.6
Singapore	13.6	13.7	14.5	16.5	17.4
Thailand	17.9	18.4	18.2	18.4	19.1
Viet Nam	28.2	28.8	26.4	26.1	27.5
The Pacific					
Cook Islands	37.3	34.0	39.9	42.1	35.1
Fiji	28.3	27.7	31.6	28.9	29.7
Kiribati	80.7	81.9	113.7	118.6	147.7
Marshall Islands	52.0	53.7	50.0	55.8	60.9
Micronesia, Fed. States of	65.0	59.1	53.6	55.5	53.4
Nauru	65.6	86.9	106.2	...	...
Palau	44.2	40.3	39.8	34.5	...
Papua New Guinea	22.4	27.8	35.7	32.0	30.0
Samoa	35.3	33.5	37.8	33.7	34.5
Solomon Islands	50.6	49.9	44.2	...	...
Timor-Leste	112.4	102.2	116.1	106.6	120.5
Tonga	30.2	26.5	25.7	29.3	30.4
Tuvalu	85.4	87.3	102.0	140.9	126.0
Vanuatu	23.3	21.6	22.5	25.0	38.8

... = data not available.

Table A10 Fiscal balance of central government (% of GDP)

	2012	2013	2014	2015	2016
Central Asia					
Armenia	–1.4	–1.6	–1.9	–4.8	–5.4
Azerbaijan	–0.2	0.7	–0.5	–1.2	–0.4
Georgia	–2.8	–2.6	–2.9	–3.8	–4.5
Kazakhstan	–2.9	–1.9	–2.7	–2.2	–1.6
Kyrgyz Republic	–5.5	–5.3	0.8	–1.5	–4.6
Tajikistan	0.1	–1.3	–0.6	–2.3	–1.7
Turkmenistan	6.3	1.2	0.8	–0.7	–0.8
Uzbekistan	1.3	0.7	0.4	–0.9	–1.0
East Asia					
China, People's Rep. of	–1.6	–1.8	–1.8	–3.4	–3.8
Hong Kong, China	3.2	1.0	3.2	0.6	3.7
Korea, Rep. of	–1.3	3.5	–2.0	–2.4	–2.4
Mongolia	–6.2	–0.9	–3.2	–3.1	–3.1
Taipei,China	–1.6	–0.9	–0.8	–0.1	–0.3
South Asia					
Afghanistan	1.1	–0.6	–1.7	–1.4	1.6
Bangladesh	–3.6	–3.8	–3.6	–3.9	–3.1
Bhutan	–1.1	–4.2	3.8	1.5	–3.0
India	–6.6	–6.9	–4.1	–3.9	–3.5
Maldives	–7.7	–3.8	–2.6	–7.6	–7.4
Nepal	–2.2	0.7	0.6	–1.0	1.4
Pakistan	–8.8	–8.2	–5.5	–5.3	–4.6
Sri Lanka	–5.6	–5.4	–5.7	–7.6	–5.6
Southeast Asia					
Brunei Darussalam	18.0	7.7	–1.0	–15.4	–21.0
Cambodia	–6.8	–7.2	–3.8	–2.6	–0.3
Indonesia	–1.8	–2.2	–2.1	–2.6	–2.5
Lao People's Dem. Rep.	–6.9	–5.6	–4.2	–4.7	–5.9
Malaysia	–4.3	–3.8	–3.4	–3.2	–3.1
Myanmar	0.9	–1.3	–0.9	–4.1	–4.6
Philippines	–2.3	–1.4	–0.6	–0.9	–2.4
Singapore	1.6	1.3	0.1	–1.0	1.3
Thailand	–2.3	–1.6	–2.5	–2.5	–2.7
Viet Nam	–5.5	–5.7	–4.1	–4.0	–4.4
The Pacific					
Cook Islands	–3.0	0.2	–0.1	–1.6	3.7
Fiji	–1.1	–0.5	–4.2	–3.1	–1.5
Kiribati	3.5	9.2	23.5	45.7	–11.8
Marshall Islands	–0.7	–0.2	3.2	2.8	–2.0
Micronesia, Fed. States of	0.9	2.9	11.2	10.5	11.0
Nauru	–0.9	0.3	0.0	–5.7	–0.1
Palau	1.0	0.7	3.5	5.9	2.0
Papua New Guinea	–1.2	–6.9	–8.3	–8.7	–4.1
Samoa	–7.2	–3.8	–5.3	–3.9	–0.4
Solomon Islands	3.8	4.4	2.0	–2.2	–5.9
Timor-Leste	224.6	226.7	80.0	–14.1	–35.2
Tonga	–2.8	–1.3	1.7	–1.1	–3.1
Tuvalu	0.6	23.3	29.8	10.6	34.3
Vanuatu	–1.5	–0.2	1.0	6.4	–10.6

Table A11 Growth rate of merchandise exports (% per year)

	2012	2013	2014	2015	2016	2017	2018
Central Asia	1.1	0.8	–7.5	–34.6	–13.7	12.9	7.1
Armenia	5.9	7.9	3.8	–4.4	14.0	6.5	5.0
Azerbaijan	–5.4	–2.6	–11.1	–44.8	–15.8	22.6	15.0
Georgia	7.6	21.3	–4.1	–23.9	–3.6	8.2	10.5
Kazakhstan	2.0	–1.5	–6.2	–42.1	–20.0	15.2	4.8
Kyrgyz Republic	–13.1	43.6	–12.4	–35.3	5.1	6.0	5.5
Tajikistan	8.2	–14.4	–16.0	–8.9	0.9	5.0	10.0
Turkmenistan	18.9	–4.7	2.0	–38.5	–15.4	12.0	12.0
Uzbekistan	–7.6	6.5	–14.8	–12.3	–3.6	2.0	3.0
East Asia	8.8	7.6	3.6	–5.5	–6.8	4.3	2.5
China, People's Rep. of	9.2	8.9	4.4	–4.5	–7.2	4.5	2.5
Hong Kong, China	7.0	8.0	1.6	–2.4	0.2	1.8	2.4
Korea, Rep. of	2.8	2.4	–0.8	–11.4	–5.7	4.0	3.0
Mongolia	–6.2	–0.3	44.3	–18.7	7.8	9.0	–1.0
Taipei,China	19.2	–1.6	–0.8	–11.1	–7.3	2.3	2.4
South Asia	–1.6	4.1	0.7	–12.9	0.4	5.5	8.1
Afghanistan	–77.3	18.1	8.9	–14.8	3.0	11.9	15.5
Bangladesh	6.2	10.7	12.1	3.1	8.9	6.0	7.0
Bhutan	–7.3	–11.5	–2.0	8.4	–15.0	2.0	7.0
India	–1.1	3.9	–0.6	–15.9	1.1	6.0	9.0
Maldives	–9.2	5.3	–9.1	–20.3	–14.8	–3.6	–1.4
Nepal	5.7	–2.9	5.1	–3.9	–28.8	15.0	12.5
Pakistan	–2.5	0.3	1.1	–3.9	–8.8	1.0	2.5
Sri Lanka	–7.4	6.3	7.1	–5.6	0.1	4.0	5.0
Southeast Asia	3.2	–0.5	1.7	–11.4	–1.7	4.4	6.2
Brunei Darussalam	4.1	–8.1	–6.1	–44.9	–20.4	27.0	8.0
Cambodia	11.9	15.9	13.4	14.1	9.2	11.0	9.5
Indonesia	–2.0	–2.8	–3.7	–14.9	–3.1	7.0	9.9
Lao People's Dem. Rep.	6.1	9.5	10.0	7.1	6.5	7.0	9.5
Malaysia	–3.0	–3.1	2.5	–15.4	–5.8	1.5	4.5
Myanmar	1.1	8.9	11.2	–11.1	2.0	7.0	7.0
Philippines	21.2	–4.0	11.9	–13.3	0.6	6.2	6.4
Singapore	0.4	2.3	–1.1	–14.2	–4.7	–3.5	–3.0
Thailand	2.9	–0.1	–0.3	–5.6	0.0	2.0	4.0
Viet Nam	18.2	15.3	13.8	7.9	8.5	7.0	9.0
The Pacific	3.3	–13.3	28.4	–2.2	–2.5	5.2	2.6
Cook Islands	10.6	21.0	26.4	–50.3	–0.1	47.7	–45.8
Fiji	12.6	–5.5	5.9	–22.5	–1.5	6.4	5.8
Kiribati	–11.4	1.1	8.0	–13.1	–9.3	7.6	–11.3
Marshall Islands	20.1	–2.5	–16.2	–13.0	...	...	...
Micronesia, Fed. States of	42.8	–13.2	–23.9	4.4	...	...	...
Nauru	80.8	–13.7	–12.8	...	...	...	...
Palau	17.2	–3.0	35.0	–15.3	...	...	...
Papua New Guinea	–8.3	–6.0	47.2	1.6	–6.4	3.0	2.0
Samoa	25.8	–6.3	–9.5	11.6	33.2	–23.0	4.9
Solomon Islands	19.9	–10.3	1.6	–7.5	...	...	...
Timor-Leste	16.0	–46.9	–12.4	16.6	11.1	19.7	8.3
Tonga	22.8	–10.2	19.3	0.0	–8.9	–0.6	2.5
Tuvalu	95.1	–11.0	–5.2	–14.4	1.3	3.3	–7.3
Vanuatu	–13.9	–31.2	66.7	–13.5	...	...	...
Developing Asia	6.1	5.7	2.7	–8.0	–5.3	4.7	3.9
Developing Asia excluding the NIEs	6.0	6.3	3.2	–7.6	–5.3	5.0	4.2

... = data not available.

Note: The newly industrialized economies (NIEs) are the Republic of Korea, Singapore, Taipei,China, and Hong Kong, China.

Table A12 Growth rate of merchandise imports (% per year)

	2012	2013	2014	2015	2016	2017	2018
Central Asia	15.7	6.2	–7.1	–17.4	–11.6	2.9	5.3
Armenia	2.4	5.6	–2.0	–25.1	–1.0	2.5	2.5
Azerbaijan	2.5	7.1	–16.3	4.7	–12.7	–6.2	12.5
Georgia	14.3	0.3	8.0	–10.8	25.9	–3.7	5.5
Kazakhstan	20.9	4.1	–13.3	–23.2	–17.6	5.0	3.0
Kyrgyz Republic	26.2	13.0	–5.8	–28.5	–3.7	10.0	5.5
Tajikistan	18.6	9.1	5.3	–20.8	–11.8	–5.0	0.0
Turkmenistan	27.9	11.7	1.8	–31.5	–16.7	10.3	10.3
Uzbekistan	8.2	9.0	11.0	–11.0	–1.2	3.0	4.0
East Asia	5.3	6.0	0.6	–13.6	–4.9	5.0	4.9
China, People's Rep. of	5.2	7.7	1.1	–12.9	–4.6	5.1	5.1
Hong Kong, China	9.5	9.6	2.4	–4.0	–0.9	2.5	2.0
Korea, Rep. of	–0.7	–3.4	–2.1	–19.8	–7.0	6.0	5.0
Mongolia	1.6	–6.2	–16.9	–27.1	–10.7	11.0	10.0
Taipei,China	18.4	–3.3	–2.7	–17.2	–8.0	2.9	2.9
South Asia	–0.1	–5.8	0.5	–11.0	–4.4	7.9	9.2
Afghanistan	–198.9	–9.3	–5.0	–9.7	1.5	3.5	3.7
Bangladesh	2.4	0.8	8.9	3.0	5.5	9.0	10.0
Bhutan	–10.0	–8.8	0.5	8.8	2.4	6.0	2.9
India	0.5	–7.2	–1.0	–14.1	–5.8	7.5	9.0
Maldives	–8.2	8.1	15.1	–3.4	6.5	9.3	10.4
Nepal	4.7	10.9	13.9	8.0	–7.1	39.5	13.5
Pakistan	12.5	–0.5	3.8	–0.9	–2.3	9.0	11.0
Sri Lanka	–5.3	–6.2	7.9	–2.5	–0.6	5.0	6.0
Southeast Asia	9.5	0.7	–0.9	–11.7	–0.6	4.6	6.1
Brunei Darussalam	9.6	19.3	–25.3	–12.3	–17.0	46.0	10.0
Cambodia	13.4	19.8	8.9	12.3	6.1	9.0	8.5
Indonesia	13.6	–1.3	–4.5	–19.7	–4.5	6.4	8.9
Lao People's Dem. Rep.	34.5	17.4	5.0	11.0	5.8	13.0	10.0
Malaysia	1.7	–0.3	0.6	–14.7	–4.4	1.6	4.1
Myanmar	20.2	14.5	16.2	–0.3	12.0	18.0	18.0
Philippines	11.3	–4.8	8.0	–1.0	16.6	7.0	6.7
Singapore	0.8	1.5	–3.1	–17.8	–6.0	–5.6	–4.0
Thailand	8.8	–0.1	–7.9	–10.6	–4.7	4.0	6.0
Viet Nam	8.7	16.5	12.0	12.0	4.6	5.0	6.0
The Pacific	25.9	–4.9	–19.3	–22.8	5.2	5.8	7.7
Cook Islands	15.6	2.3	0.1	–5.0	–4.6	6.7	4.4
Fiji	2.5	16.8	–3.2	–14.5	0.7	3.3	2.4
Kiribati	14.9	–7.5	26.4	–17.5	12.3	–21.1	–11.8
Marshall Islands	4.5	13.0	–7.5	–11.3	...	...	...
Micronesia, Fed. States of	5.0	–2.3	–13.0	7.8	...	...	...
Nauru	17.5	59.3	59.1	...	...	...	...
Palau	11.3	5.4	21.1	–11.5	...	...	...
Papua New Guinea	22.7	–16.1	–36.4	–33.1	10.2	7.9	6.1
Samoa	19.0	–8.1	8.1	–3.8	–4.4	–1.4	–1.8
Solomon Islands	3.0	7.0	–1.0	–4.7	...	...	...
Timor-Leste	67.1	3.7	10.9	–15.4	–14.4	2.4	31.5
Tonga	0.0	–7.9	0.1	15.4	0.3	9.6	11.8
Tuvalu	21.6	41.7	–15.6	–4.3	14.0	4.1	–10.3
Vanuatu	2.8	3.8	–6.3	23.7	...	...	...
Developing Asia	5.4	3.4	0.1	–13.1	–4.4	5.3	5.7
Developing Asia excluding the NIEs	5.5	4.2	0.4	–12.4	–4.1	5.6	6.1

... = data not available.

Note: The newly industrialized economies (NIEs) are the Republic of Korea, Singapore, Taipei,China, and Hong Kong, China.

Table A13 Trade balance ($ million)

	2012	2013	2014	2015	2016	2017	2018
Central Asia	56,713	49,418	45,017	7,971	2,273	10,522	12,839
Armenia	–2,112	–2,196	–2,055	–1,186	–931	–880	–853
Azerbaijan	22,217	20,621	18,928	5,812	4,586	8,078	9,483
Georgia	–4,214	–3,493	–4,280	–4,356	–6,395	–5,801	–5,956
Kazakhstan	38,145	34,792	36,245	12,679	9,444	13,715	14,899
Kyrgyz Republic	–2,993	–2,780	–2,808	–2,176	–1,722	–1,935	–2,041
Tajikistan	–2,419	–2,958	–3,361	–2,544	–2,132	–2,239	–2,463
Turkmenistan	6,527	4,032	4,143	1,485	1,386	1,700	2,066
Uzbekistan	1,561	1,400	–1,795	–1,742	–1,964	–2,116	–2,296
East Asia	388,439	465,798	551,922	739,798	658,864	548,760	522,393
China, People's Rep. of	311,570	358,981	435,042	566,998	485,200	499,308	471,343
Hong Kong, China	–18,918	–27,913	–32,359	–22,871	–17,522	–21,477	–19,861
Korea, Rep. of	49,406	82,781	88,885	122,269	120,446	117,437	112,664
Mongolia	–3,031	–2,619	146	566	1,330	1,380	942
Taipei,China	49,412	54,567	60,209	72,835	69,410	69,549	69,969
South Asia	–245,822	–193,043	–192,670	–178,638	–153,186	–173,690	–192,445
Afghanistan	–9,499	–8,449	–7,928	–7,200	–7,299	–7,493	–7,678
Bangladesh	–9,320	–7,009	–6,794	–6,965	–6,274	–7,842	–9,690
Bhutan	–395	–377	–393	–430	–540	–592	–589
India	–195,656	–147,609	–144,940	–130,079	–104,155	–116,006	–126,447
Maldives	–1,261	–1,372	–1,660	–1,655	–1,814	–2,010	–2,241
Nepal	–4,623	–5,263	–6,079	–6,689	–6,427	–9,139	–10,381
Pakistan	–15,652	–15,355	–16,590	–17,191	–18,370	–21,781	–26,064
Sri Lanka	–9,416	–7,609	–8,287	–8,430	–8,306	–8,826	–9,356
Southeast Asia	107,099	99,958	132,240	126,877	126,083	122,159	124,483
Brunei Darussalam	8,766	6,924	7,443	2,910	2,206	2,294	2,399
Cambodia	–2,506	–3,219	–3,206	–3,467	–3,415	–3,538	–3,736
Indonesia	8,680	5,833	6,983	14,049	15,390	17,242	20,322
Lao People's Dem. Rep.	–2,567	–3,299	–3,265	–3,002	–3,982	–4,800	–5,307
Malaysia	36,593	30,642	34,626	28,050	24,393	24,618	26,298
Myanmar	–2,167	–3,053	–4,109	–5,441	–7,208	–9,755	–12,847
Philippines	–18,926	–17,662	–17,330	–23,309	–34,079	–36,813	–39,418
Singapore	70,404	75,024	81,709	82,850	82,789	85,882	85,936
Thailand	109	55	17,263	26,841	35,752	28,618	26,053
Viet Nam	8,714	8,713	12,126	7,396	14,116	18,341	25,089
The Pacific	–3,847	–3,552	1,643	3,276	3,102	3,102	2,884
Cook Islands	–80	–78	–72	–82	–78	–77	–91
Fiji	–770	–1,168	–1,027	–975	–1,003	–1,007	–997
Kiribati	–89	–82	–105	–86	–99	–75	–66
Marshall Islands	–44	–61	–63	–56	...	...	...
Micronesia, Fed. States of	–125	–129	–117	–128	...	...	...
Nauru	26	4	–27	...	...	...	...
Palau	–125	–133	–160	–142	...	...	...
Papua New Guinea	–1,373	–517	4,646	6,151	5,305	5,320	5,294
Samoa	–307	–281	–309	–294	–270	–275	–268
Solomon Islands	66	–16	–5	–18	...	...	...
Timor-Leste	–638	–679	–756	–635	–539	–548	–726
Tonga	–187	–172	–170	–199	–201	–222	–250
Tuvalu	–2	–13	–9	–10	–14	–15	–13
Vanuatu	–198	–225	–184	–251	...	...	...
Developing Asia	302,582	418,579	538,152	699,284	637,014	628,220	583,123
Developing Asia excluding the NIEs	152,278	234,119	339,708	444,201	381,891	376,829	334,415

... = data not available.

Note: The newly industrialized economies (NIEs) are the Republic of Korea, Singapore, Taipei,China, and Hong Kong, China.

Table A14 Current account balance (% of GDP)

	2012	2013	2014	2015	2016	2017	2018
Central Asia	2.9	1.9	2.0	–3.3	–5.9	–3.0	–1.7
Armenia	–10.0	–7.3	–7.6	–2.7	–2.6	–2.3	–2.0
Azerbaijan	21.4	16.6	13.9	–0.4	–2.1	5.9	11.4
Georgia	–11.4	–5.7	–10.6	–11.9	–13.1	–12.0	–11.5
Kazakhstan	0.5	0.5	2.7	–3.0	–6.1	–3.4	–3.0
Kyrgyz Republic	–15.8	–14.1	–17.2	–15.2	–10.0	–13.0	–13.5
Tajikistan	–2.5	–2.9	–9.1	–5.9	–4.8	–5.5	–6.0
Turkmenistan	0.0	–7.2	–7.5	–10.3	–18.5	–15.0	–13.0
Uzbekistan	1.2	1.6	1.4	0.3	0.1	0.2	0.4
East Asia	3.0	2.4	3.3	3.9	3.0	2.5	2.3
China, People's Rep. of	2.5	1.5	2.6	3.0	1.9	1.8	1.7
Hong Kong, China	1.6	1.5	1.4	3.3	4.5	3.1	3.1
Korea, Rep. of	4.2	6.2	6.0	7.7	7.1	5.8	5.3
Mongolia	–43.8	–37.6	–15.8	–8.1	–4.0	–2.1	–6.3
Taipei,China	8.9	10.0	11.7	14.3	13.4	6.8	6.5
South Asia	–4.1	–1.4	–1.1	–0.9	–0.8	–1.4	–1.6
Afghanistan	5.9	8.7	2.4	4.7	4.4	1.4	–0.2
Bangladesh	–0.3	1.6	0.8	1.5	1.7	–1.0	–0.7
Bhutan	–21.5	–25.4	–26.4	–28.3	–29.4	–27.4	–22.8
India	–4.8	–1.7	–1.3	–1.1	–1.0	–1.3	–1.5
Maldives	–7.4	–4.6	–3.8	–9.5	–17.7	–18.9	–19.1
Nepal	5.0	3.4	4.6	5.1	6.2	–1.6	–3.2
Pakistan	–2.1	–1.1	–1.3	–1.0	–1.2	–2.1	–2.5
Sri Lanka	–5.8	–3.4	–2.5	–2.5	–2.1	–2.2	–2.2
Southeast Asia	2.3	1.7	3.1	3.2	3.6	3.1	3.0
Brunei Darussalam	29.8	20.9	30.7	16.0	11.0	5.3	5.5
Cambodia	–10.2	–14.9	–11.7	–11.1	–10.1	–9.4	–9.0
Indonesia	–2.7	–3.2	–3.1	–2.0	–1.8	–1.7	–1.6
Lao People's Dem. Rep.	–28.5	–30.6	–25.0	–20.3	–18.0	–19.0	–20.0
Malaysia	5.2	3.5	4.4	3.0	2.0	1.8	2.0
Myanmar	–4.0	–4.9	–3.3	–5.2	–7.0	–8.0	–8.0
Philippines	2.8	4.2	3.8	2.5	0.2	0.2	0.5
Singapore	17.9	16.9	19.7	18.1	19.0	19.5	19.8
Thailand	–0.4	–1.2	3.7	8.1	11.4	9.0	7.0
Viet Nam	5.9	4.5	4.9	0.5	3.3	2.0	2.5
The Pacific	20.8	11.7	10.2	8.9	0.6	3.0	–0.5
Cook Islands	19.8	23.4	26.1	18.8	20.3	24.5	21.0
Fiji	–1.3	–9.8	–6.9	–5.6	3.4	3.5	3.0
Kiribati	0.5	15.1	24.1	44.7	–7.0	–2.4	–1.5
Marshall Islands	0.1	–7.7	0.0	17.9	16.0	4.0	4.5
Micronesia, Fed. States of	–13.4	–10.1	1.2	4.2	6.0	4.5	4.5
Nauru	29.0	16.5	–8.2	...	...	...	...
Palau	–11.2	–11.8	–14.5	–3.4	–12.0	–12.5	–15.0
Papua New Guinea	–36.1	–31.4	3.7	13.4	9.4	7.7	6.7
Samoa	–7.7	–2.5	–7.0	–3.9	–6.6	–4.9	–2.8
Solomon Islands	1.5	–4.3	–5.4	–3.7	–7.3	–8.3	–10.7
Timor-Leste	211.9	182.1	76.0	16.4	–49.9	–12.2	–40.2
Tonga	–12.4	–4.5	–7.9	–11.7	–3.2	–7.7	–11.9
Tuvalu	14.7	1.5	13.0	10.0	5.6	–20.8	–25.4
Vanuatu	–6.1	–1.1	0.2	–9.2	–13.8	–17.7	–15.0
Developing Asia	1.8	1.7	2.6	3.0	2.3	1.9	1.7
Developing Asia excluding the NIEs	0.9	0.7	1.7	1.9	1.2	1.1	0.9

... = data not available.

Note: The newly industrialized economies (NIEs) are the Republic of Korea, Singapore, Taipei,China, and Hong Kong, China.

Table A15 Exchange rates to the United States dollar (annual average)

	Currency	Symbol	2012	2013	2014	2015	2016
Central Asia							
Armenia	dram	AMD	401.8	409.6	415.9	477.9	480.5
Azerbaijan	Azerbaijan new manat	AZN	0.8	0.8	0.8	1.0	1.6
Georgia	lari	GEL	1.7	1.7	1.8	2.3	2.4
Kazakhstan	tenge	T	149.1	152.1	179.2	221.7	342.2
Kyrgyz Republic	som	Som	47.0	48.4	53.7	64.5	69.9
Tajikistan	somoni	TJS	4.8	4.8	5.0	6.2	8.0
Turkmenistan	Turkmen manat	TMM	2.9	2.9	2.9	3.5	3.5
Uzbekistan	sum	SUM	1,885.4	2,095.0	2,311.2	2,573.5	2,968.9
East Asia							
China, People's Rep. of	yuan	CNY	6.3	6.2	6.1	6.2	6.7
Hong Kong, China	Hong Kong dollar	HK$	7.8	7.8	7.8	7.8	7.8
Korea, Rep. of	won	W	1,124.5	1,095.4	1,052.2	1,133.1	1,163.3
Mongolia	togrog	MNT	1,359.2	1,523.9	1,817.9	1,970.3	2,145.5
Taipei,China	NT dollar	NT$	29.6	29.8	30.4	31.9	32.3
South Asia							
Afghanistan	afghani	AF	50.9	55.4	57.4	61.1	67.8
Bangladesh	taka	Tk	79.1	79.9	77.7	77.7	78.3
Bhutan	ngultrum	Nu	50.3	54.9	61.5	62.1	66.3
India	Indian rupee/s	Re/Rs	54.4	60.5	61.0	64.2	67.2
Maldives	rufiyaa	Rf	15.4	15.4	15.4	15.4	15.4
Nepal	Nepalese rupee/s	NRe/NRs	80.7	87.7	98.0	99.2	106.1
Pakistan	Pakistan rupee/s	PRe/PRs	89.2	96.7	102.9	101.5	104.4
Sri Lanka	Sri Lanka rupee/s	SLRe/SLRs	127.6	129.1	130.6	135.9	146.0
Southeast Asia							
Brunei Darussalam	Brunei dollar	B$	1.2	1.3	1.3	1.4	1.4
Cambodia	riel	KR	4,033.0	4,027.0	4,030.0	4,025.0	4,030.0
Indonesia	rupiah	Rp	9,386.6	10,461.2	11,865.2	13,389.4	13,307.4
Lao People's Dem. Rep.	kip	KN	7,994.0	7,818.0	8,150.0	8,147.9	8,400.0
Malaysia	ringgit	RM	3.1	3.2	3.3	3.9	4.1
Myanmar	kyat	MK	856.9	964.4	995.0	1,223.0	1,259.1
Philippines	peso	P	42.2	42.4	44.4	45.5	47.5
Singapore	Singapore dollar	S$	1.2	1.3	1.3	1.4	1.4
Thailand	baht	B	31.1	30.7	32.5	34.3	35.3
Viet Nam	dong	D	20,828.0	20,934.6	21,148.8	21,675.6	21,931.0
The Pacific							
Cook Islands	New Zealand dollar	NZ$	1.2	1.2	1.2	1.3	1.5
Fiji	Fiji dollar	F$	1.8	1.8	1.9	2.1	2.1
Kiribati	Australian dollar	A$	1.0	1.0	1.1	1.3	1.3
Marshall Islands	US dollar	US$	1.0	1.0	1.0	1.0	1.0
Micronesia, Fed. States of	US dollar	US$	1.0	1.0	1.0	1.0	1.0
Nauru	Australian dollar	A$	1.0	1.0	1.1	1.3	1.3
Palau	US dollar	US$	1.0	1.0	1.0	1.0	1.0
Papua New Guinea	kina	K	2.1	2.2	2.4	2.8	3.1
Samoa	tala	ST	2.3	2.3	2.3	2.4	2.6
Solomon Islands	Solomon Islands dollar	SI$	7.4	7.3	7.4	7.9	8.1
Timor-Leste	US dollar	US$	1.0	1.0	1.0	1.0	1.0
Tonga	pa'anga	T$	1.7	1.7	1.8	1.9	2.2
Tuvalu	Australian dollar	A$	1.0	1.0	1.1	1.3	1.3
Vanuatu	vatu	Vt	92.6	96.9	102.4	111.0	109.2

Table A16 Gross international reserves ($ million)

	2012	2013	2014	2015	2016
Central Asia					
Armenia	1,799	2,252	1,489	1,775	2,200
Azerbaijan	11,277	15,014	15,549	7,910	7,142
Georgia	2,873	2,800	2,695	2,500	2,756
Kazakhstan	28,269	24,715	29,209	27,871	29,530
Kyrgyz Republic	2,067	2,238	1,958	1,778	1,969
Tajikistan	649	636	511	494	745
Turkmenistan	26,400	29,300	32,400	...	...
Uzbekistan	22,133	22,515	24,140	24,400	24,650
East Asia					
China, People's Rep. of	3,387,863	3,880,383	3,899,285	3,406,100	3,097,845
Hong Kong, China	317,362	311,209	328,516	358,823	386,241
Korea, Rep. of	326,968	346,460	363,593	367,962	371,102
Mongolia	3,630	1,193	1,627	1,300	1,300
Taipei,China	403,169	416,811	418,980	426,031	434,204
South Asia					
Afghanistan	6,867	6,873	7,230	7,000	7,500
Bangladesh	10,364	15,315	21,508	25,025	30,168
Bhutan	674	917	998	958	1,119
India	292,046	304,223	330,213	346,788	364,109
Maldives	305	368	615	564	467
Nepal	4,960	5,614	6,939	8,148	9,737
Pakistan	10,803	6,008	9,098	13,525	18,143
Sri Lanka	6,877	7,495	8,208	7,304	6,019
Southeast Asia					
Brunei Darussalam	3,291	3,406	3,479	3,218	3,329
Cambodia	3,463	3,642	4,391	5,093	6,731
Indonesia	112,781	99,387	111,862	105,931	116,362
Lao People's Dem. Rep.	740	666	816	987	814
Malaysia	139,724	134,911	115,937	95,290	94,525
Myanmar	3,156	4,419	4,803	4,511	4,436
Philippines	83,831	83,187	79,541	80,667	80,692
Singapore	259,307	273,065	256,860	247,747	246,575
Thailand	181,608	167,289	157,108	156,514	171,853
Viet Nam	25,399	25,955	34,330	28,298	41,000
The Pacific					
Cook Islands	...	...	...	...	...
Fiji	915	755	750	926	915
Kiribati	...	...	...	...	...
Marshall Islands	...	...	...	...	...
Micronesia, Fed. States of	...	...	...	...	...
Nauru	...	...	...	...	...
Palau	...	...	...	...	...
Papua New Guinea	4,001	2,826	2,305	2,105	2,219
Samoa	157	137	155	167	178
Solomon Islands	499	532	507	527	...
Timor-Leste	...	...	...	...	...
Tonga	145	148	159	143	159
Tuvalu	...	...	...	...	...
Vanuatu	180	180	185	268	...

... = data not available.

Table A17 External debt outstanding ($ million)

	2012	2013	2014	2015	2016
Central Asia					
Armenia	3,739	3,899	3,785	4,316	4,806
Azerbaijan	5,470	6,059	6,478	6,894	6,913
Georgia	10,057	10,542	10,718	11,983	12,927
Kazakhstan	136,918	150,033	157,428	153,697	165,364
Kyrgyz Republic	5,229	5,930	6,371	6,670	6,874
Tajikistan	2,171	2,152	2,098	2,183	2,276
Turkmenistan	6,365	8,653	8,043	8,354	...
Uzbekistan	6,660	7,500	8,399	10,521	11,413
East Asia					
China, People's Rep. of	736,986	863,167	1,779,900	1,416,200	...
Hong Kong, China	1,029,853	1,160,364	1,301,216	1,300,314	1,329,266
Korea, Rep. of	408,928	423,505	424,325	396,058	393,736
Mongolia	13,112	18,280	20,951	21,590	23,785
Taipei,China	130,821	170,134	177,945	158,954	172,238
South Asia					
Afghanistan	1,320	1,400	1,330	1,380	1,270
Bangladesh	22,095	22,381	24,388	23,901	25,963
Bhutan	1,334	1,607	1,759	1,855	2,316
India	409,374	446,178	475,045	485,614	512,300
Maldives	814	720	744	696	753
Nepal	3,491	3,510	3,617	3,391	3,584
Pakistan	60,268	59,592	65,544	64,609	65,449
Sri Lanka	37,098	39,905	42,914	44,797	47,302
Southeast Asia					
Brunei Darussalam	...	...	...	...	...
Cambodia	4,274	4,828	5,279	5,648	6,200
Indonesia	252,364	266,109	293,328	310,730	316,968
Lao People's Dem. Rep.	4,262	5,489	6,061	6,495	7,422
Malaysia	196,861	212,279	213,951	194,272	202,564
Myanmar	13,700	10,200	8,800	9,600	9,900
Philippines	79,949	78,489	77,674	77,474	74,763
Singapore	1,521,944	1,683,822	1,771,416	1,778,228	1,743,584
Thailand	130,747	141,933	141,715	131,427	131,362
Viet Nam	42,158	45,243	...	...	...
The Pacific					
Cook Islands	38	59	61	73	77
Fiji	523	595	664	593	632
Kiribati	14	14	14	36	45
Marshall Islands	96	98	95	90	91
Micronesia, Fed. States of	88	88	90	81	...
Nauru	...	...	...	...	...
Palau	69	65	71	64	...
Papua New Guinea	1,128	1,357	1,150	1,180	1,691
Samoa	383	415	415	462	413
Solomon Islands	110	102	89	88	75
Timor-Leste	0	6	22	46	153
Tonga	197	204	186	195	171
Tuvalu	8	20	22	18	17
Vanuatu	369	132	149	242	400

... = data not available.

Table A18 Debt service ratio (% of exports of goods and services)

	2012	2013	2014	2015	2016
Central Asia					
Armenia	8.2	27.3	6.8	4.4	4.9
Azerbaijan	...	...	...	...	...
Georgia	22.5	18.1	13.5	15.4	12.9
Kazakhstan	34.8	35.1	36.6	71.5	70.7
Kyrgyz Republic	16.9	20.5	26.9	42.2	32.0
Tajikistan	...	...	...	...	...
Turkmenistan	1.8	2.3	...	...	...
Uzbekistan	6.4	3.5	5.1	5.9	5.6
East Asia					
China, People's Rep. of	1.6	1.6	2.6	5.0	...
Hong Kong, China	49.1	49.0	60.0	65.8	68.9
Korea, Rep. of	7.0	7.2	7.9	8.9	9.0
Mongolia	39.8	50.6	39.8	41.6	88.6
Taipei,China	0.9	1.7	1.4	1.6	2.1
South Asia					
Afghanistan	1.0	6.8	...	...	...
Bangladesh	2.4	2.5	2.7	2.2	2.0
Bhutan	12.9	17.5	27.1	19.9	14.5
India	5.9	5.9	7.6	8.8	7.8
Maldives	2.9	2.1	2.3	2.3	2.7
Nepal	10.6	9.5	8.9	8.1	8.8
Pakistan	15.2	20.6	23.0	18.1	21.5
Sri Lanka	19.7	26.8	20.8	27.7	...
Southeast Asia					
Brunei Darussalam	...	...	...	...	...
Cambodia	1.0	1.1	1.2	1.1	1.4
Indonesia	17.3	18.4	24.0	20.7	20.5
Lao People's Dem. Rep.	4.2	5.1	5.6	5.2	7.1
Malaysia	10.8	10.7	11.4	15.6	16.2
Myanmar	2.2	4.9	5.0	4.7	4.7
Philippines	7.3	8.2	6.3	5.6	6.9
Singapore	...	...	...	...	...
Thailand	4.2	4.0	4.9	6.4	6.4
Viet Nam	4.3	...	...	...	...
The Pacific					
Cook Islands	7.6	6.7	5.9	6.5	6.1
Fiji	1.5	1.6	1.7	1.9	...
Kiribati	32.8	12.8	36.0	2.5	4.6
Marshall Islands	7.7	6.4	6.5	10.0	...
Micronesia, Fed. States of	5.8	6.8	10.6	10.0	...
Nauru	...	...	...	...	...
Palau	4.6	4.4	4.4	4.5	...
Papua New Guinea	1.5	1.4	1.1	0.7	1.4
Samoa	0.0	0.0	0.0	0.0	0.0
Solomon Islands	3.5	6.8	3.3	3.3	...
Timor-Leste	0.0	0.0	0.0	0.0	0.0
Tonga	4.9	7.5	9.2	9.8	9.4
Tuvalu	2.0	2.9	2.9	12.2	12.0
Vanuatu	1.0	1.0	1.0	1.8	...

... = data not available.

www.ingramcontent.com/pod-product-compliance
Lightning Source LLC
Chambersburg PA
CBHW061234270326
41929CB00031B/3481